Brazil 2001

A Revisionary History of Brazilian Literature and Culture

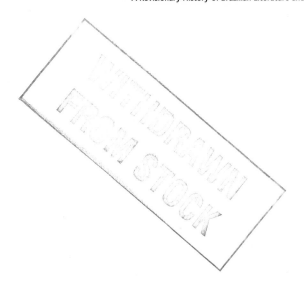

Portuguese Literary & Cultural Studies 4/5

Brazil 2000

A Revisionary History of Brazilian Literature and Culture

Spring/Fall 2000

University of
Massachusetts
Dartmouth

UERJ 50 anos 2000
Universidade do Estado do Rio de Janeiro

Portuguese Literary & Cultural Studies is a multilingual interdisciplinary peer-reviewed journal published semi-annually by the Center for Portuguese Studies and Culture at the University of Massachusetts Dartmouth. The journal addresses the literatures and cultures of the diverse communities of the Portuguese-speaking world in terms of critical and theoretical approaches.

Manuscript Policy

Portuguese Literary & Cultural Studies welcomes submission of original and unpublished manuscripts in English, Portuguese, or Spanish appropriate to the goals of the journal. The first page of the submission must include the following: (*i*), name, mailing address, e-mail address, and appropriate phone and fax numbers; (*ii*), a brief biography, not exceeding a quarter of a page, with reference to institutional affiliation, no more than three publications, and current research; (*iii*), a half-page abstract of the content of the article or review. The article itself may not exceed 20 pages and should be submitted along with the above information in a single digital file. All of the information must be in the same language. PLCS encourages electronic submission in the form of an attached document addressed to greis@umassd.edu. Submission in hard copy and 3.5" diskette (in a protected envelope) may also be sent by regular mail to *Portuguese Literary & Cultural Studies*, Center for Portuguese Studies and Culture, University of Massachusetts Dartmouth, Dartmouth, MA 02747 USA.

Manuscripts should be in accordance with the *MLA Style Manual and Guide to Scholarly Publishing* (latest version) with parenthetical documentation and list of works cited. The author is responsible for the accuracy of all quotations, titles, names, and dates. Notes must be manually typed out at the end of the article (before the list of works cited), regardless of whether they were entered as footnotes or endnotes into the word processor.

The preferred digital format for submissions is, in order, (*i*) the latest version of MS Word (Windows), (*ii*) the latest version of MS Word (Macintosh), or (*iii*) any previous version of MS Word (Windows or Macintosh). The first page mentioned above should have a reference to the format and version in which the article was saved. Font and sizes as close as possible to the style of the previous issue of PLCS should be used throughout the text.

Subscription Information

The annual subscription (2 issues) for institutions is $80.00 and $40.00 for individuals. Single issues may also be purchased for $25.00. From outside the United States add $12.00 for shipping and handling.

Inquiries should be sent to *Portuguese Literary & Cultural Studies* Subscription, Center for Portuguese Studies and Culture, University of Massachusetts Dartmouth, Dartmouth, MA 02747 USA, or by e-mail to: greis@umassd.edu.

Advertising

Portuguese Literary & Cultural Studies accepts advertising that is of interest to scholars in the field of Portuguese, Brazilian, and Luso-African Studies and Critical Theory. Further information is available by contacting the Center for Portuguese Studies and Culture, University of Massachusetts Dartmouth.

Cover

Design: Spencer Ladd

ISSN 1521-804X
© 2001 University of Massachusetts Dartmouth

Printed by RPI Press, Fall River, MA

Table of Contents

Literature

Culture

Cultural Intermediaries

Introduction—"There is no Brazil": A Poet's Writing of Cultural History[1]

João Cezar de Castro Rocha

A paradox that should not be resolved

In one of his most intriguing poems, Carlos Drummond de Andrade provides inspiration for this current volume of *Portuguese Literary & Cultural Studies—Brazil 2001: A Revisionary History of Brazilian Literature and Culture.* The poem, called "Hino Nacional," is a paradoxical reconstruction of variegated efforts aimed at the building of the nation. In the final lines of the poem, however, it is "Brazil"—as an impossible Kantian *thing-in-itself*—that emerges and refuses all attempts to grasp its essence:

> Brazil does not want us! It is sick and tired of us!
> Our Brazil is in the afterworld. This is not Brazil.
> There is no Brazil. By any chance, are there Brazilians?[2]

The paradox cannot be ignored.[3] "Brazil" does not exist, yet it is the same "Brazil" that resists the attempts of some ghostlike Brazilians to render it translatable into, let us suppose, substantial volumes of literary and cultural history—such as, for instance, *Brazil 2001.* The poem belongs to the collection *No Brejo das Almas,* published in 1934. Fours years earlier, the so-called "Revolução de 1930" began a process of modernization that, beyond the predictable transformation of economic and social structures, included an active cultural program whose aim was to make Brazilians "proud" of the country through the acknowledgement and promotion of its neglected potentialities. For that purpose, in 1936 the National Radio of Rio de Janeiro was founded and soon became a main tool for assuring Getúlio Vargas's popularity. Seemingly, Brazil was there to be finally deciphered by Brazilians as well as properly propagated through radio waves, newsreel propaganda films, newspaper reports and books—novels, poems, histories, chronicles: every single genre was welcomed as long as it stressed the mainstream.

In a first reading, Drummond's poem would evidence that the naturalness of the official Brazil was but a cultural by-product carefully orchestrated by the revolutionaries who took power in 1930 with the project of modernizing the political and social life of the country. At least from this perspective, the paradox resolves itself into a critical statement: the official "Brazil" would not coincide with *Brazil*. Perhaps that is why, at the same time, there is no Brazil and yet it is Brazil that reveals its own non-existence. In other words, there is a Brazil that precedes the State and hence cannot naturally be reduced to the official image of the country. Brazil reveals itself as a sign overdetermined by meaning, and it is this abundance of meaning that prevents its being seized by any hermeneutic operation. The long-lived cliché seems to have the upper hand in this reading: as exuberant as its tropical nature, *Brazil-in-itself* can only be heartily felt, not merely interpreted.

This reading, nonetheless, does not meet the complexity of Drummond's insight. If it were adequate, how could the final question of the poem doubt the very existence of Brazilians? If *Brazil-in-itself* unsurprisingly exceeds its official fiction, wouldn't it have inscribed itself into the folk—the last resource of genuine resistance, as any competent Romantic narrative would have it? Even more disturbing than doubting the existence of Brazil is the questioning of the reality of Brazilians. If the folk is as fictional as the Nation-State's narrative of the country, then where are we? According to Miguel Tamen we are in a ghostlike configuration. In the introduction to *A Revisonary History of Portuguese Literature*—whose title we have adapted to our own purposes—Tamen shows how etymologically linked are the notions of *theoria* and *revisio* to the idea of *phantasia* and *phantasma* (Tamen xii-xiii). Let me unfold the consequences of this possibility for our endeavor.

In its Greek roots, a theoretical statement was a pronouncement that implied a complex act of re-vision, for it involved "a set of professional witnesses, perform[ing] ... the function of certifying that a certain event has taken place" and could thus become a subject of consideration within the city (Tamen xii). The listeners to the pronouncement, by definition, could not have seen the event referred to by the *theoroi*; it was the credibility attached to this position that performed the supplemental act of conferring truth on the account. Wlad Godzich clarifies that such an authority was provided in order to discipline the effects of speech in the organization of the city through a clear-cut distinction between "claims" and "theoretical statements." The former could be made by anyone while the latter was an attribute only attainable by officials designated to the public function of *theoros*.[4] This particular context creates a complex scene that might be relevant to a reflection on the writing of cultural and literary histories. In sum, the *theoros* has to convey an event witnessed by him to an audience that was not present at the circumstance of which they will be told. Let me stress that this scene indeed produces two acts of re-vision, and distinguishing them allows us to achieve a better understanding of the paradox intuited by Carlos Drummond de Andrade. The first, performed by the *theoros*, is properly speaking a ghostly statement, for "ghosts are always second to something" (Tamen xiv). In this case, the telling is second to the witnessing of an actual event, not to mention that the process of seeing-telling itself cannot entirely coincide with the event in all its multiple aspects. The second act of re-vision is far more complex, and bears a particular interest for my contention. In the case of the listeners, their re-vised ghosts are "second to nothing" and, at the same time, simultaneous to the speech act of the *theoros*. The listener does not have the memory of seeing an actual event but has to project into the telling of the *theoros* the credibility endowed by the public character of this function. Thus, the memory of the listener is socially engendered and becomes a fact insofar as it is imagined as being a faithful representation of a previous reality. In a nutshell, the performance of telling a story originally supposed the prior act of witnessing an event.

I may now suggest that projects such as *Brazil 2001* are special cases of this second mode of re-vision—cases in which the complexity of the relation between seeing and telling is brought to its utmost. As far as cultural and literary histories are concerned, there is no original event to which the narrative refers and according to which it is organized. In Greek terms, neither the *theoros* nor the listeners have actually witnessed any event—it is worth recalling that the Greek verb *theorein* means "to look at," "to contemplate," "to survey" (Godzich 164). Transposing that problem to the nineteenth-century building of the Nation-State, it becomes clear that, in spite of themselves, literary historians and their patriotic readers were indeed engaged in a playful activity of sharing a belief in an origin that could not be established, for the telling of a nation's history cannot count on a prior vision of its own origins. Rather, the classic relationship has to be literally inverted, for it is the telling that has to prove successful in order to create a retrospective seeing: once an originary event is chosen, the historical gaze organizes accordingly the sequence of events, which in turn attests to the truth of the account. The tautology is insurmountable.[5] Therefore, this account as well as its reception are substantially substanceless; they are inexorably second to nothing; they are ghostly ghosts, so to speak. As such they cannot ground attempts at unveiling the "national character" of a nation—and, once again, the redundancy is unavoidable. Leo Spitzer has given to this problem a definitive formula in his review of Dámaso Alonso's *Poesía Española*. According to Spitzer, this redundancy creates a "national tautology," grounded on "the implied assertion that a Spanish work of art is great because it is genuinely Spanish and it is genuinely Spanish when it is great"[6] (Spitzer 354). This is why Drummond's paradox cannot (and should not) be resolved; otherwise we will be enmeshed in just such a tautology. Indeed, Drummond seems to suggest that, instead of a sign full of self-reinforcing meaning, a nation is much closer to an empty signifier that is given a semantic charge in accordance with different needs shaped by the contingency of historical circumstances.

Homi Bhabha has already keenly remarked that a nation is above all a matter of narration: "the ambivalent figure of the nation is a problem of its transitional history, its conceptual indeterminacy, its wavering between vocabularies" (Bhabha 2). Narrating the nation always produces discourses that, while they promise an all-encompassing inclusion, are mainly determined by exclusions. Therefore, "the 'locality' of national culture is neither unified nor unitary in relation to itself" (Bhabha 4); it continuously engenders the "other" within the supposed discourse of sameness. As any narrative has to rely on an initial selection of elements, it cannot claim to be a representation of a totality and, at the same time, reveals its arbitrariness as well as the interests underlying it. As Ernst Renan already had recognized in his well-known lecture "*Qu'est-ce qu'une Nation?*": "No French citizen knows whether he is a Burgundian, an Alan, a Taifale, or a Visigoth, yet every French citizen has to have forgotten the massacre of Saint Bartholomew, or the massacres that took place in the Midi in the thirteenth century."[7] Therefore it is not only the origin that cannot be known; there is also a great amount of information that a citizen has to remember to forget in order to become "genuinely" French. Here the acuteness of Drummond's insight comes to the fore: such narration is but a *mise en abîme*: the more national histories are written, the less their readers will be able to seize the totality of the nation. By any chance, is there such a totality?

In short, we do not produce collective volumes of cultural and literary history such as *Brazil 2001* because we do not yet know what Brazilians are and because we hope finally to unveil their essence through the very collection of essays. Most likely we organize them because we will surely never know what Brazilians might be—nor, for that matter, Chinese, Uruguayans, Portuguese, South Africans, etc., for, as Homi Bhabha has helped us to understand, this is not a *Brazilian* problem but a theoretical question related to the constitution of modern society. The production of such volumes is inevitably then a fictive enterprise for, as Wolfgang Iser has reminded us, fictionality is a tool through which we try to contact realities far beyond our reach, despite our awareness of the impossibility of actually seizing them.[8] If *Brazil 2001* offers something besides the usual collection of essays it is that it tries to acknowledge the fictionality involved in its endeavor.

Let me conclude these introductory remarks by stressing that this acknowledgement does not imply that literary and cultural histories should not be written. On the contrary, I am suggesting that they should be conceived of in the same vein in which Jean-François Lyotard defined a philosophical question;[9] namely, literary and cultural histories should not be written to provide answers—as the obsession with national identity would have it—but to envision new approaches and therefore give rise to new questions. After all, it does not suffice to remember that cultural differences, understood as "national identities," are culturally "invented," if that also means overlooking actual differences among nations. In the case of *Brazil 2001: A Revisionary History of Brazilian Literature and Culture*, the challenge is to write cultural and literary history while avoiding the tautology of searching for national identity.

The issue

This challenge was met through the reconstruction of different and sometimes opposing views of national identity.[10] The illustrations distributed throughout the volume already evidence this diversity, which, due to its plurality, should discourage an essentialist approach to the question of national character. In other words, instead of embracing a predetermined conception, the collaborators were asked to develop reflections upon texts and contexts that helped to shape portraits of Brazil. If a prior act of seeing is not available in the writing of cultural history, its reconstruction has to begin accordingly with the tradition of telling the nation—after all, traditional cultural history has been but its narration. It is, however, worth calling the reader's attention to the essayistic nature of those reflections, which are intended less to provide a final word on the subject than to entice the readers' imagination in order to prompt them to acquaint themselves with the work presented by our collaborators.

The first section of *Brazil 2001* pays homage to the work of Gilberto Freyre. His masterpiece *Casa-Grande & Senzala* appeared in 1933 at a time when Brazilian intellectuals were obsessed with the so-called negative effects of *mestiçagem*. Freyre's great achievement was related not only to a substantially new approach to the question of miscegenation—seen by Freyre as a culturally productive phenomenon instead of an insoluble racial problem—but also to a unique style that grants *Casa-Grande & Senzala* an interest that exceeds the value of some of its interpretations. Moreover, since its translation, undertaken by Samuel Putnam,[11] Freyre's voice has been highly determinant in the way Brazilian culture is perceived abroad.[12] Therefore, a critical reappraisal of Freyre's work should always be welcomed.

In the sections entitled "Literature" and "Culture," readers have at their disposal an array of textual inventions of Brazil—once again, the sheer plurality of perspectives is an emphatic sign of the fictionality of such endeavors. These textual inventions played an important role given the long absence of universities in Brazilian intellectual history, since universities became solidly established only after the third decade of the twentieth century. Until then, literary works and interpretative essays provided tools for framing the Brazilian historical process into narratives of the country's formation.[13] Moreover, in these sections, the reader will encounter the very beginning of the creation of such images as well as their contemporary models and countermodels.

The following section, "Cultural Intermediaries," is inherently related to the conception of *Brazil 2001* as a paradoxical project. This section was inspired by a thought-provoking suggestion. In the introduction to *Formação da Literatura Brasileira*, Antonio Candido argues that a literature such as that of Brazil demands permanent contact with foreign literatures, since otherwise it runs the risk of losing itself in inevitable provincialism. He distinguishes literatures that do not depend on other literary experiences for their readers to apprehend a particular worldview—such as Russian, English and French literatures—and those literatures that, in contrast, demand permanent contact with foreign texts, as in the case of Brazilian literature. According to Candido: "Those who fed from our literature alone may be identified at first sight because they display provincial taste and lack of proportion, even when they are erudite and intelligent. We are doomed, therefore, to depend on our experience of other literatures" (Candido, *Formação* 9-10).

It is worth acknowledging that this suggestion has given rise to a series of polemical remarks, which I will not be able to contemplate in this introduction.[14] However, I want to call attention to the underlying potential of Candido's approach. It stresses the comparatist nature of Brazilian culture, indeed of post-colonial cultures. Since its very beginnings, the invention of Brazil has been linked inextricably to the contributions of so-called cultural intermediaries, and to such an extent that it may not be paradoxical to conceive of Brazilian culture at least in part as a creation of foreign perspectives.[15] In the section, "Cultural Intermediaries," the reader will find several examples of the presence of such perspectives at different moments of Brazilian history.

The next group of essays provides a panoramic view of "Literary History and Literary Criticism," from its first attempts up to the contemporary scene. Its reach should give the reader a sense of the issues and problems faced by the institution of literary studies in Brazil, which have mainly been concerned with the search for national identity. Therefore, this section offers a strategic location for addressing the project of *Brazil 2001*, namely, the writing of an alternative history—alternative precisely because it aims at detaching itself from any concern with such identity. The careful reader will notice this underlying tension among the essays of "Literary History and Literary Criticism."

The final section, "Audiovisual," represents a necessary although sometimes overlooked acknowledgement, namely, that the inventions of Brazil depended (and still depend) on means other than the representatives of a bookish culture. Due also to high levels of illiteracy, orality has preserved its importance in the transmission of culture—but this should not be understood as a merely negative phenomenon.[16] In the 1960s, films were seen as tools for revolutionary changes. Popular music, for instance, plays a significant role in the definition of Brazilian identities, as do television networks, which are the strongest bonding element in contemporary

Brazilian society. Therefore, an account of Brazilian cultural history would be incomplete without including the audiovisual dimension. This volume aims at advancing in this direction.

In a lucid review, Paulo de Medeiros commented upon the impressive collective work *Portugal heute. Politik. Wirtschaft. Kultur* edited by Dietrich Briesemeister and Axel Schönberger. In spite of the fact that Medeiros raised some pertinent questions concerning the organization of the volume, he envisioned the main achievement of the publication as having made "explicit how much Portuguese Studies needs a serious consideration of its goals, methods and practices" (Medeiros 229). I willingly acknowledge the shortcomings of *Brazil 2001* but would hope that it will represent an important tool for such a reconsideration of Brazilian Studies. Given that this is the first time that such a comprehensive presentation of Brazilian literature and culture is offered to an English-speaking audience, such shortcomings are unavoidable. Shortcomings: by now it should be clear that one can only ever come up short, that despite our best efforts we will always fail to arrive at a Brazil that is not there. Ghostly efforts for a ghostly Brazil, so to speak. Therefore, only those who still believe in achieving totality—that is, still conceive of grasping the essence of the nation—might see in the gaps something other than a stimulus to propose alternative writings and collections. Let us welcome them, for, if ghosts are ultimately what we get closer to, we seem to have no option but to try continuously to conjure them up through the cultural histories that we write.

Acknowledgements

Obviously, an enterprise such as this could never be achieved without extensive collaboration. First of all, let me risk redundancy by thanking Frank F. Sousa and Victor J. Mendes. Without their enthusiasm and unfailing belief this issue (like Drummond's Brazilians) would simply not exist. Gina Reis has provided constant support throughout the difficulties inherent in this project. Memory Holloway always had perfect solutions for difficult problems and still found time to contribute a remarkable piece. In other words, the Center for Portuguese Studies and Culture at the University of Massachusetts Dartmouth has proven to be much more than a friendly place for Brazilian Studies—it has become the main architect of *Brazil 2001*.

Maria Aparecida Salgueiro and André Lázaro represented what Universidade do Estado do Rio de Janeiro (UERJ) is at its best: unconditional support for intellectual projects that make academic everyday life surprisingly pleasant. UERJ's Cultural Department sponsored *Brazil 2001* within the "Comissão UERJ: Brasil 500 Anos," which has proven instrumental for organizing this special issue. Valdei Lopes has contributed from the beginning to the completion of the project. Peonia Viana Guedes and Roberto Acízelo de Souza also have offered the support of the Graduate Program of Literature at UERJ regarding the translation. I also want to thank Muriel Lydia for helping in the editing process. As in many other projects, José Mario Pereira has given me the benefit of intellectual exchange.

Finally, I would like to thank both the translators—whose work made it possible to present *Brazil 2001* completely in English—and our assistant to the editors, Mark Streeter, whose commitment and intelligence were most appreciated. Because of their combined efforts, the essays here published will hopefully acquire a wider readership.

Notes

[1] I want to thank Hans Ulrich Gumbrecht, Luiz Costa Lima, Eduardo Neiva, Victor Mendes and José Mario Pereira for their suggestions and above all criticism regarding this introduction. I want especially to thank Mark Streeter for a thorough revision of this introduction as well as for his perceptive comments.

[2] This is only a literal rendering of the original: "O Brasil não nos quer! Está farto de nós! / Nosso Brasil é no outro mundo. Este não é o Brasil. / Nenhum Brasil existe. E acaso existirão os brasileiros?"

John Gledson has proposed for the last line of the poem the following translation: "No Brazil exists. And who's to say Brazilians do?" (Gledson 6).

[3] The relevance of the notion of paradox in order to approach Brazilian culture was also remarked by John Gledson: "Brazil is a country of paradoxes, and not the least of them is that it seems easy to get to know, and yet the more one gets close, the more complex, the more contradictory it becomes" (Gledson 1).

[4] "The city needed a more official and more ascertainable form of knowledge if it was not to lose itself in endless claims and counterclaims. . . . Only the theoretical attested event could be treated as a fact" (Godzich 165).

[5] In a perfect formulation, Wolfgang Iser synthesizes the impasse created by such a tautology: "Whenever beginnings and ends are postulated, history turns into a testimony for preconceived notions, which are supposed to reveal themselves through history but cannot be identical to it. Moreover, understanding facts would be of minor importance if history were considered as a process of unfolding something existing prior to itself or a march to a goal that by definition would be outside itself" (Iser, *The Range of Interpretation* 58).

Regarding the obsession with "national identity," its tautological understanding turns the very writing of literary histories curiously unnecessary or, at best, an exercise of antiquarians whose sole obligation is to assemble facts concerning a truth that is always already known. In that context, acts of interpretation are obviously unwelcome.

[6] Further in the same review, Spitzer complements his criticism of the "national tautology" with an insightful remark on "the North-American usage of *this country*: it is as if the North-American understands his own country as one among other possible countries, as if he had just arrived in the United States! This relativistic attitude—naturally impossible in Europe—constitutes a healthy lesson towards a national self-criticism" (Spitzer 371 [endnote 2]).

[7] Renan 11. The lecture was held at the Sorbonne, 11 March 1882. Obviously, Renan pronounced it under the effect of the defeat of France by Prussia in the 1871 Franco-Prussian war. Indeed, there was a more recent and troubling massacre to which Renan could have referred: that of the Paris Commune. Thus, in 1882, to be a French citizen required above all forgetting the 1871 massacre of the communards.

[8] See, especially, Iser, *The Fictive and the Imaginary*.

[9] "You philosophers ask questions without answers, questions that have to remain unanswered to deserve being called philosophical. According to you answered questions are only technical matters" (Lyotard 8).

[10] In a recent book, Marilena Chauí has proposed an interesting distinction: "whereas the ideology of 'national character' presents the nation as an achieved totality . . . the ideology of 'national identity' conceives the nation as an incomplete and lacunar totality" (Chauí 27). Nonetheless, in this introduction, I will stress the similarities of both ideologies insofar as they evolve around the obsession with the "national."

[11] Randal Johnson remarked properly that "Putnam's contribution to the study of Brazilian literature has yet to be fully appreciated. In addition to publishing one of the histories of the subject [*Marvelous Journey*, 1948], he has also initiated the Brazilian literature section of the Library of Congress' *Handbook of Latin American Studies*" (Johnson 3).

In 1944 Putnam had already translated Euclides da Cunha's masterpiece *Os Sertões*. It was given the English title, *Rebellion in the Backlands*. Chicago: University of Chicago Press, 1944, with introduction and notes by Samuel Putnam.

[12] Indeed, the main works of Gilberto Freyre are already available in English. For instance, in 1945 there appeared published by Knopf, *Brazil, an Interpretation*. In 1946, also by Knopf, *Casa-Grande & Senzala. Formação da Família Brasileira sob o Regime de Economia Patriarchal* (1933) received the English title *The Masters and the Slaves: A Study of the Development of Brazilian Civilization*. In 1986, a paperback edition, with an introduction by David H. P. Maybury-Lewis, was published by The University of California Press. *Sobrados e Mucambos. Decadência do Patriarcado Rural no Brasil* (1936), translated by Harriet de Onis and published by Knopf in 1963 with an introduction by Frank Tannenbaum, received the English title *The Mansions and the Shanties: The Making of Modern Brazil*. In 1986, a paperback edition, edited by E. Bradford Burns, appeared from The University of California Press. Finally, *Ordem e Progresso; Processo de Desintegração das Sociedades Patriarcal e Semipatriarcal no Brasil sob o Regime de Trabalho Livre: Aspectos de um Quase Meio Século de Transição do Trabalho Escravo para o Trabalho Livre; e da Monarquia para a República* (1959) was translated by Rod W. Horton and published by Knopf in 1970, receiving the English title *Order and Progress; Brazil from Monarchy to Republic*. A paperback edition, with an introduction by Ludwig Lauerhass, Jr., was published by The University of California Press in 1986.

[13] Regarding this issue, Antonio Candido had already remarked: "Differently from what happens in some other countries, in Brazil literature has been, more than philosophy or human sciences, the central phenomenon of the life of the spirit. . . . An Alencar and a Domingos Olímpio were, at the same time, the Gilberto Freyre and the José Lins do Rego of their time; their fiction acquired the meaning of an initiation in the knowledge of the reality of the country" (Candido, "Literatura e Cultura" 130, 136).

[14] Nevertheless, let me mention some of the most important criticisms regarding Antonio Candido's ideas. Afrânio Coutinho replied immediately after the publication of Candido's *Formação da Literatura Brasileira* in *Conceito de Literatura Brasileira*. See also Eduardo Portela,

"Circunstância e Problema da História Literária"; Haroldo de Campos, *O Seqüestro do Barroco na* Formação da Literatura Brasileira: *O Caso Gregório de Mattos*; and Luiz Costa Lima, "Concepção de História Literária na *Formação*."

Ligia Chiappini has considered these criticisms in "Os Equívocos da Crítica à *Formação*." I have already attempted an alternative reading of Candido's suggestion in "*A Formação da Leitura no Brasil*—Esboço de Releitura de Antonio Candido."

15 In a recent groundbreaking book, Luiz Felipe de Alencastro has given an unprecedented historical consistency to this hypothesis: "'Formation of Brazil in the South Atlantic:' the reader who has looked at the cover of the book might be intrigued by its subtitle. Does it mean that Brazil was formed outside Brazil? That is exactly the point: this is the historical paradox that I am aiming at showing in the following pages" (Alencastro 9).

In a nutshell, Alencastro argues that Brazilian colonial history cannot be seen as either an extension of the colonial territory or as a progression towards independence from Portugal, for it was mainly determined through its relationship with the zone of reproduction of slaves sustained by the Portuguese in Angola. Thus, more than a "Brazilian" history, the colonial period witnessed the emergence of a "space without territory, a Lusophone archipelago composed by the enclaves of Portuguese America and of the trade posts of Angola" (9). Alencastro concludes the book with an epigrammatic statement: "The history of the Brazilian market dominated by pillage and commerce is long, but the history of the Brazilian nation dominated by violence and consent is short" (Alencastro 355).

16 In an interview to *L'Express*, Caetano Veloso touched upon this subject: "I believe that, in general, from the 1920s or the 1930s onwards, Brazilian popular music has become an expression which is considered reliable. It is a force that is respected because it says the truth of Brazilian society. (...) There is a very simple reason for that: the poverty of the country, the simplicity of the formation and of the education. The popular songs are a form of expression that is accessible to all" (Faure 10). Indeed, Arto Lindsay had remarked perceptively in his presentation of the CD *Beleza Tropical*: "Brazilian popular music plays a larger role in the cultural life of Brazil than popular music seems to elsewhere. It wasn't until the second half of the twentieth century that a majority of the population was literate. And a large majority of Brazilians still live below the poverty line. Perhaps these facts contributed to the importance of oral traditions in Brazil" (Lindsay, "Presentation").

Works Cited

Alencastro, Luiz Felipe de. *O Trato dos Viventes. Formação do Brasil no Atlântico Sul.* São Paulo: Companhia das Letras, 2000.

Bhabha, Homi. "Introduction: Narrating the Nation." *Nation and Narration.* Ed. Homi Bhabha. London and New York: Routledge, 1990. 1-7.

Briesemeister, Dietrich and Schönberger, Axel, eds. *Portugal heute. Politik. Wirtschaft. Kultur.* Bibliotheca Ibero-Americana, Vol. 64, Frankfurt: Vervuert Verlag, 1997.

Candido, Antonio. *Formação da Literatura Brasileira (Momentos Decisivos).* 1959. Belo Horizonte: Itatiaia, 1981.

———. "Literatura e Cultura de 1900 a 1945." *Literatura e Sociedade: Estudos de Teoria e História Literária.* 7ª ed. São Paulo: Editora Nacional, 1985. 109-138.

Campos, Haroldo de. *O Seqüestro do Barroco na* Formação da Literatura Brasileira: *O Caso Gregório de Mattos.* Salvador: Fundação Casa de Jorge Amado, 1989.

Chauí, Marilena. *Brasil. Mito Fundador e Sociedade Autoritária.* São Paulo: Editora Fundação Perseu Abramo, 2000.

Chiappini, Lígia. "Os Equívocos da Crítica à *Formação.*" *Dentro do Texto, Dentro da Vida. Ensaios sobre Antonio Candido.* Ed. Maria Angela D'Incao and Eloísa Faria Scarabôtolo. São Paulo: Companhia das Letras & Instituto Moreira Salles, 1992. 170-180.

Coutinho, Afrânio. *Conceito de Literatura Brasileira.* Rio de Janeiro: Livraria Acadêmica, 1960.

Faure, Michel. "Caetano Veloso. L'Entretien—'La Musique dit les Vérités de la Société Brésilienne'." *L'Express,* 17/2/2000: 10-13.

Freyre, Gilberto. *Brazil, An Interpretation.* Trans. Samuel Putnam. New York: Knopf, 1945.

———. *The Masters and the Slaves: A Study of the Development of Brazilian Civilization.* Trans. Samuel Putnam. New York: Knopf, 1946.

———. *The Mansions and the Shanties: The Making of Modern Brazil.* Trans. Harriet de Onis. New York: Knopf, 1963.

———. *Order and Progress. Brazil from Monarchy to Republic.* Trans. Rod W. Horton. New York: Knopf, 1970.

Gledson, John. *Brazil: Culture and Identity.* Liverpool: University of Liverpool, Institute of Latin American Studies, Working Paper 14, 1994.

Godzich, Wlad. "The Tiger on the Paper Mat." *The Culture of Literacy.* Cambridge: Harvard UP, 1994. 159-170.

Iser, Wolfgang. *The Fictive and the Imaginary. Charting Literary Anthropology.* Baltimore: The Johns Hopkins UP, 1993.

———. *The Range of Interpretation.* New York: Columbia UP, 2000.

Johnson, Randal. "Introduction." *Tropical Paths. Essays on Modern Brazilian Literature.* Ed. Johnson. New York and London: Garland, 1993. 3-10.

Lima, Luiz Costa. "Concepção de História Literária na *Formação.*" *Pensando nos Trópicos. (Dispersa Demanda II).* Rio de Janeiro: Rocco, 1991. 149-166.

Lindsay, Arto. "Presentation". *Beleza Tropical.* Vol. 1. Compiled by David Byrne. Luaka Bop / Warner Bros. Records, 1989.

Lyotard, Jean-François. "Can Thought Go Without a Body?" *The Inhuman: Reflections on Time.* Stanford: Stanford UP, 1991. 8-23.

Medeiros, Paulo de. Review. "*Portugal heute. Politik. Wirtschaft. Kultur.*" *Portuguese Literary & Cultural Studies* 2 (Spring, 1999): 225-229.

Portela, Eduardo. "Circunstância e Problema da História Literária." *Literatura e Realidade Nacional.* Rio de Janeiro: Edições Tempo Brasileiro, 1975. 21-39.

Renan, Ernst. "What is a Nation?" *Nation and Narration.* Ed. Homi Bhabha. London and New York: Routledge, 1990. 8-22.

Rocha, João Cezar de Castro. "*A Formação da Leitura no Brasil*—Esboço de Releitura de Antonio Candido." *Literatura e Identidades.* Ed. José Luís Jobim. Rio de Janeiro: UERJ, 1999. 57-70.

Spitzer, Leo. "*La Poesía Española* de Dámaso Alonso." *Teoria da Literatura em suas Fontes.* Ed. Luiz Costa Lima. Volume I. Rio de Janeiro: Francisco Alves, 1983. 352-384.

Tamen, Miguel. "Ghosts Revised: An Essay on Literary History." *A Revisionary History of Portuguese Literature.* Ed. Miguel Tamen and Helena C. Buescu. New York and London: Garland Publishing, 1999. xi-xxi.

Gilberto Freyre: 100 Years

A Sea Full of Waves: Ambiguity and Modernity in Brazilian Culture

Ricardo Benzaquen de Araujo
Translated by Paulo Henriques Britto

The present text is a discussion of some aspects of Gilberto Freyre's work, concentrating in particular on his first book, *Casa-Grande & Senzala*, published in 1933 [English translation: *The Masters and the Slaves*, 1946, henceforward abbreviated *MS*], which even today raises issues of major relevance for an understanding of Brazilian history.

From the outset, it should be observed that Freyre's book came out at a time when intellectual debate on Brazil's destiny greatly emphasized the issue of *mestiçagem*—miscegenation. But sex across ethnic boundaries was always seen as a problem, one that either implied biological and cultural sterility, thus hindering development, or delayed the complete domination of the white race, in this way making it more difficult for Brazil to have access to the values of Western civilization. The past was thus seen as above all a burden; because of it, Brazil could attain (to) its destiny, if at all, only in the future.

The tremendous impact of *MS* helped bring about a dramatic change in this view: there was not only a positive reevaluation of Native Brazilian and African influences but also an affirmation of the dignity of the hybrid, malleable melding of traditions that was seen as characteristic of Portuguese colonization. This argument, which gave Brazil a chance to overcome the handicap of the temporary or definitive "incompleteness" that characterized it, would not have been possible—according to Freyre himself, who got his master's degree from Columbia University in 1922—if he had not had contact with US anthropology and Franz Boas' relativistic orientation, which allowed him to separate the notion of culture from that of race and to attribute to the category of culture absolute primacy in the analysis of social life.

So it was that Freyre, swimming against the stream, redefined miscegenation and, in a way, reinvented Brazil.

This redefinition, indeed, begins with the fact that the first group to be classified as racially mixed in *MS* is the Portuguese people. Emphasizing the position of the Iberian Peninsula as a crossroads between Africa and Europe, a locus of ethnic and particularly of cultural exchange, Freyre treats the Portuguese people as a hybrid, as the product of a combination of Arabs, Romans, Gauls, and Jews, among others, a process of miscegenation that began long before they came to America.

But why is the notion of miscegenation used to account for the Portuguese people? It is one, I believe, that implies a process wherein the unique traits of each people are never entirely dissolved, so that the memory of the differences present at the process of miscegenation is indelibly preserved.

Syncretic but never synthetic, this notion allows Freyre to define the Portuguese—and, later, Brazilians—as a "wealth of contradictions" (*MS* 7) that, though balanced and brought closer together, stubbornly refuse to blend into a new, separate identity, indivisible and original. It is precisely this refusal that causes colonial Brazilian society to be seen in *MS* from the angle of polyphony and ambiguity, as

> . . . existing indeterminately between Europe and Africa and belonging uncompromisingly to neither one nor the other of the two continents; with the African influence seething beneath the European and giving a sharp relish to sexual life, to alimentation, and to religion; with Moorish or Negro blood running throughout a great light-skinned mulatto population, when it is not the predominant strain, in regions that to this day are inhabited by a dark-skinned people; and with the hot and oleous air of Africa mitigating the Germanic harshness of institutions and cultural forms, corrupting the doctrinal and moral rigidity of the medieval Church, drawing the bones from Christianity, feudalism, Gothic architecture, canonic discipline, Visigoth law, the Latin tongue, and the very character of the people. (4-5)

This "bi-continentalism," which "in a population so vague and ill-defined corresponds to bisexuality in the individual" (7), deeply affected the spiritual make up of the Portuguese, who became a people whose

> . . . character gives us, above all, the impression of being 'vague, unprecise'… and it is this lack of preciseness that permits the Portuguese to unite within himself so

many contrasts that are impossible of adjustment in the hard and angular Castilian, whose aspect is more definitely Gothic and European. (8)

This indefiniteness has the effect of making the Portuguese eminently porous, permeable, capable of adapting malleably to the most diverse cultural experiences. It is precisely for this reason that, in contrast with, say, the English, "who with gloved hand, so to speak, and preserved from more intimate contact with the natives by [rubber prophylactics],[1] direct[ed] the commercial and political affairs of India" (19), the Portuguese were able to conquer an empire not by imposing a single rule, but by adapting to all sorts of local traditions.

The Portuguese colonial tradition was therefore based on a quite specific view of the racially mixed person: not the necessary and mechanical result of a series of natural determinations, he was rather an essentially ambiguous, indefinite and ultimately unpredictable being. This unpredictability, however, was not at all to be seen as a fault: it was precisely what allowed Brazilian culture—at least since the publication of *MS*—to be perceived as endowed with a creativity all its own and to surprise the post-sixteenth-century world with the originality of the solutions it was able to devise. Because it could accommodate the most contradictory influences, this cultural experience might develop a tendency toward anarchy, but a benignant sort of anarchy, in which the concern with identity tolerated a degree of differentiation, contingency and disorder in the very matrix of social life.

Indeed, the emphasis on what Freyre calls "balancing antagonisms"— antagonisms that were, of course, intensified by the divisions and the despotism typical of colonial slaveholding—is so strong that the question arises whether there was any value or institution capable of at least alleviating them, so that the balance was maintained.

Consideration of this issue will also allow us to examine the second trait that defines Brazilian society in *MS*: the enormous importance of the role played by passions, particularly those of a sexual nature, in the creation of an atmosphere of intimacy and warmth that, while it did not resolve the antagonisms, at least made their coexistence possible.

But it must not be thought that Freyre does no more than extol the passions; indeed, he points out a number of excesses that took place inside the Big House (*casa-grande*) and condemns them in no uncertain terms. Thus, for instance, he writes that "the advantage of miscegenation in Brazil ran parallel to the tremendous disadvantage of syphilis" (70-71), "which was, *par excellence*, the disease of the Big Houses and the *senzalas* [slave quarters]" (70). He sees the introduction of syphilis in Brazil as fundamentally a consequence of the European conquerors' obsession with "physical love."

Moreover, Portuguese sexual voracity, associated with disease, as we have seen, used slavery as an outlet, since

> . . . sexual intercourse between the European conqueror and the Native woman... took place—as later would occur in relations between masters and their female Negro slaves—under circumstances[2] unfavorable to women. [Thus t]he furious passions of the Portuguese must have been vented upon victims who did not always share his sexual tastes. (74-75)

But if this is true, then how could "patriarchal eroticism" give rise to what Freyre calls "zones of fraternization," which brought together the cultural heritages of the different—even antagonistic—groups that made up colonial society?

To answer this question, a short digression is in order. If we turn our attention to the body or—more exactly, to excrements—we may find a relevant clue. Consider the following passage, in which Freyre discusses the preoccupation with obscenity that he finds in the Luso-Brazilian tradition:

> Only in Portugal could such drawing-room foolery take place as that which a distinguished friend described for me. [He was in one of the noblest houses in Lisbon, in extremely fashionable mixed company.][3] At the supper hour it was announced that there was a surprise in store for the guests. This surprise was nothing other than the substitution of toilet paper for plates at table, and upon each bit of paper there lay a slender dark-brown sweet, cut up into small portions. Imagine such a thing among English or North American guests! They would have died of shame. But in Portugal and in Brazil it is common to jest about this and similar subjects, for we are endowed with a crude naturalness that contrasts with the excessive reticence characteristic of Anglo-Saxons. (261)

This prank, it should be said, seems to have the purpose of reminding us that everything that is degrading can also be regenerating. After all, the allusion to feces in this case may well have been intended to bring the guests together, reminding them, in a way that is quite compatible with Christian tradition, that all are made of the same clay and subject to the same contingencies and needs.[4]

Like this curious lesson in humility, all the violence and excess associated with the sexual practices of the Big House also seem to be imbued with an essential ambiguity, pointing both to the vulgar and the sublime, death and resurrection. With its double meaning, stressing the differences even to the point of perversity, but also encouraging some fecundity and fraternization, the rule of passion necessarily allows these antagonisms to coexist in amazing closeness. This endows the experience of the Big House with an ethos of its own.

This experience, however, seems to have become a thing of the past with the reforms that, since the mid-nineteenth century, have attempted to force Brazil to catch up with the civilizing process typical of the modern West. As Freyre observes in another book of the 1930s, *Sobrados e Mucambos* (1936), there was a sort of re-Europeanization of Brazil. It happened through the fast and massive introduction of an all-encompassing, systematic frame of reference that extended its domain over all spheres of social life and proved completely incapable of coexisting with the differences, the passions, the colorful diversity typical of the colonial tradition.

Indeed, this aversion to colorfulness should be taken quite literally. According to Freyre in *Sobrados e Mucambos*,

> . . . the re-Europeanization of Brazil began by removing from our life the Asian, African or Native element that had become most conspicuous in the landscape, clothing and customs in general: all the excesses of color. The color of the houses. The color of the *sobrados* [mansions], nearly always red like cow's blood, or purple, or yellow, many of them covered with *azulejos* [glazed tiles]... The color of women's shawls and men's ponchos;... of the ribbons men wore in their hats, of the vests they sported; of the flowers girls pinned to their hair. The color of church interiors—purple, gold, bright scarlet (in Minas Gerais there were even churches— one church, anyway—with frankly Oriental ornamentation). (260-61)

Thus the variety and excess of the Big House were also manifested in an impressive array of bright, vivid colors, a profusion that

> . . . began to pale in contact with the new Europe, gradually grayed and took on a mark of exceptionalness—the colorfulness of holidays and feast days, of processions and carnival [. . . because] the black frock coat, the black boots, the

RICARDO BENZAQUEN DE ARAUJO

black top hats, the black carriages blackened our lives almost of a sudden; in the cities of the Empire clothes expressed deep mourning [... a perpetual mourning,] as that of a father or mother. (262-63)

What seems to me most striking about the passage just quoted is not the austere, rigorous atmosphere that began to prevail, but the notion of mourning as "deep" and "perpetual," which stresses the obsessively consistent and all-embracing character of this European influence.

This is apparently the reason why Freyre's evaluation of this Westernizing process is often marked by irony and disapproval. Surely he would not be critical of this European reconquest simply because it was foreign, for openness to external influences was precisely one of the basic traits of the porous, flexible and tolerant environment analyzed in *MS*.

What Freyre dislikes is the fact that European values are no longer just one element among others: now they are presented as a uniform, inflexible and exclusionary model, aiming to impose a thoroughgoing order that, displacing the ambiguous and excessive colonial traditions, is reproduced, tautologically, in every sphere of Brazilian society.[5]

If this was the course taken by the civilizing process in Brazil, it seems clear—from the vantage point of a time when, save for the problem of miscegenation, the civilizing process has achieved total victory—that Freyre was, in a way, writing against the prevailing trend of his day. He clearly did not reject modernity wholesale, for he admired both the aesthetic achievements of international modernism and the advances of medicine and engineering; he was simply questioning the narrow, linear, aestheticizing form modernity had assumed in Brazil.

In fact, I believe that it is in this way that we can explain Freyre's attitude toward history, which he takes great pains to dissociate from what he again and again refers to, with marked scorn, as "mere necrophilia." Necrophilia here clearly means the study of the past for its own sake, the adoption of an antiquarian stance, the delight in dwelling among the dead while neglecting the urgent intellectual responsibilities of the day.[6]

How to knock a few holes in this consistent and linear pattern that had pervaded the entire country, so that at least some of the spirit of the past could be revived in order to coexist with modernity and temper it? To tackle this problem, Freyre engaged in a long series of activities from 1922, when he arrived from the US—he was 22 then—to 1933, when *MS* was published:

he lectured, organized congresses and was active both in journalism and in the political life of his native state, Pernambuco.

What should be stressed, however, is that Freyre's effort to revive some values of the past leaves its mark on the very way he presents his case in *MS*, his first sociological work. Freyre rejects the rhetorical conventions imposed on academic writing by the Westernizing regulation of customs and produces a markedly oral text, characterized by an irregularity, a carelessness, an imprecision even, that make it sound much more like an informal conversation than a scientific work.

One of the various characteristics of oral language in *MS* is precisely the unfinished nature of the text, Freyre's complete disregard for the need to arrive at a conclusion, to bring his argument to anything like an adequate ending. The book is made up of five chapters, taking up 517 pages in the original edition, in which the relations between the different groups that settled the country are discussed ceaselessly, and arrives at no conclusion whatsoever: it simply stops, breaks off, with no narrative sequence or even the establishment of a chronological limit for the period under study.

This point becomes even more relevant when one observes that the book's lack of an ending is in counterpoint with the enormous importance of its beginning. The first chapter is a sort of summary of the general argument of the work; the passages quoted above, about balancing antagonisms as the most prominent value in the colonial tradition, are all taken from the first few pages of the opening chapter.

These values, spelled out in the beginning of the book, are naturally reiterated throughout the other chapters; and not only this repetitiveness is much more than a mere reproduction of the issues raised in the book's opening, but above all the points established are never entirely contradicted. From this derives what seems to be the most important consequence of the use of a markedly oral tone in *MS*: since the main values of the colonial period are repeated throughout the book until the end, which contains no real conclusion, they seem to gain a sort of afterlife. In other words, it is as if they take on a certain aura of infinitude, of immortality, so that the reader is left with a suggestion that they perhaps maintained at least part of their influence and vitality well into the 1930s.

This possibility seems even more plausible if we consider the question of the work's oral nature from a different viewpoint: this is not only among the most distinctive aspects of *MS* but also one of the most stimulating objects of study in it. Examined in a number of ways, the oral language of the text, when it assumes the careless, enthralling conversational tone mentioned earlier, directly evokes the influence exerted by slaves and the African element on Brazilian culture. After all, "[t]he Negro nurse did very often with words what she did with food: she mashed them, removed the bones, took away their hardness, and left them as soft and pleasing syllables in the mouth of the white child" (343).

Thus, writing as if he were talking, and adopting an easy, leisurely, irregular tone, Freyre wants to make clear that the popular aspects of Brazilian speech and society remain present in his own text. But his reflection could hardly be reduced to this, since he always lays claim—with much greater emphasis and virtually throughout the entire work—to aristocratic origins.

This claim, present as it is in all of Freyre's writings, is visible in *MS* particularly in a passage of the preface in which the author reproduces the following observation by the Modernist architect Lúcio Costa concerning the old Big Houses of the state of Minas Gerais: "'How one meets oneself here… And one remembers things one never knew but which were there inside one all the while; I do not know how to put it—it would take a Proust to explain it.'" Freyre takes up Costa's argument and reinforces it, adding: "In studying the domestic life of our ancestors we feel that we are completing ourselves: it is another method of searching for the '*temps perdu*,' another means of finding ourselves in others, in those who lived before us and whose life anticipates our own" (xxxvii-xxxviii).

Writing in a style that evokes the way slaves spoke even as he celebrates his ancestors, who belonged to the sugar-mill gentry—balancing antagonisms, once again—Freyre seems to assert the possibility of the survival of colonial values by presenting himself as an intellectual half-breed: a man defined by that ineluctable coexistence of different cultural traditions in his own person, in his own thought.

Freyre's links with Boas and US anthropology clearly remain quite strong. In addition, however, he also seems to imply that his analysis relies fundamentally on memory, being as it is largely founded on an intense, intimate, authentic relation with the objects he discusses.

In this way, Freyre turns into a sort of herald, or rather oracle, of national tradition, and he gives the impression that the values he analyzes are kept alive and influential through his own text—that is, to the extent that they influenced the writing of his text. *The Masters and the Slaves* is thus not just a scholarly work but a sort of miniature Big House, a voice both remote and genuine, a legitimate representative of the experience discussed in its pages; and the author, of course, turns himself into a character in his own book.

Thus author and book are in perfect harmony and authenticate each other's validity. This is precisely the reason why Freyre's stance in *MS*, always on the verge of adopting a tone of celebration or nostalgic, even sentimental, wistfulness, ultimately comes close to what we might call a second innocence.

It is as though Freyre, in the very act of writing, experienced the very same sensations his colonial forebears did, or at least sensations that had been prefigured by them, that need not necessarily be preserved in a continuous, uninterrupted tradition, but that are preserved as a cultural alternative, as "things one never knew but which were there inside one all the while"— things "it would take a Proust to explain."

Notes

[1] I have corrected the text of the English translation. (Translator's note)

[2] I have corrected the text of the English translation. (Translator's note)

[3] This sentence does not appear in the English translation. (Translator's note)

[4] This paragraph was suggested by Bakhtin's (1987) comments on Rabelais.

[5] The tautological and aestheticizing dimension of modernity is discussed by De Man (1984). Observations by Goldman (chap. 5) and Berman (chaps. 5 and 7) are also extremely stimulating.

[6] Nietzsche's classic "On the Uses & Disadvantages of History for Life" is the basic reference for Freyre's reflection.

Works Cited

Araujo, Ricardo Benzaquen de. *Guerra e Paz:* Casa-Grande & Senzala *e a Obra de Gilberto Freyre nos Anos 30.* Rio de Janeiro: Editora 34, 1994.

Bakhtin, Mikhail. *A Cultura Popular na Idade Média e no Renascimento: O Contexto de François Rabelais.* São Paulo/Brasília: Hucitec/UnB, 1987.

Berman, Russel. *Modern Culture and Critical Theory.* Madison: U of Wisconsin P, 1989.

De Man, Paul. "Aesthetic Formalization: Kleist's *Über das Marionettentheater.*" *The Rhetoric of Romanticism.* New York: Columbia UP, 1984. 263-290.

Freyre, Gilberto. *The Masters and the Slaves: A Study in the Development of Brazilian Civilization.* Trans. Samuel Putnam. New York: Knopf, 1946.

———. *Sobrados e Mucambos.* São Paulo: Companhia Editora Nacional, 1936.

———. *The Mansions and the Shanties. The Making of Modern Brazil.* Trans. Harriet de Onis. New York: Knopf, 1963.

Goldman, Harvey. *Max Weber and Thomas Mann—Calling and the Shaping of the Self.* Berkeley: U of California P, 1988.

Nietzsche, Friedrich. "On the Uses & Disadvantages of History for Life." *Untimely Meditations.* Cambridge: Cambridge UP, 1985. 57-123.

The Road to *Casa-Grande*.
Itineraries by Gilberto Freyre

Enrique Rodríguez Larreta
Translated by Nöel de Sousa
and Mark Streeter

Two portraits hang in Gilberto Freyre's library in Apipucos. The first represents Manuel Oliveira Lima (1853-1928), the historian and diplomat from Pernambuco; the other, Franz Boas (1858-1943), a German anthropologist and teacher at the University of Columbia, founder of American Cultural Anthropology. These two authors are constantly referred to in his books and are highlighted in *Casa-Grande & Senzala*. Gilberto Freyre maintained a constant dialogue with them throughout his life.

Recife, 1917

With Oliveira Lima the relationship began early. One of the first texts read by Gilberto Freyre around 1913 was Oliveira Lima's brief lecture "Vida Diplomática" ["Diplomatic Life"].[1] Freyre's first article was devoted to him, and it appeared in "O Lábaro," at the American Baptist College. Freyre was seventeen years-old and already displayed a surprisingly mature critical assessment. The observations on Oliveira Lima as a historian, his style, the use of travel books and documents are already an indication of his own approach to history.

Freyre especially values Lima's qualities as a great narrator as well as the visuality of his prose:

> Oliveira Lima doesn't look, he sees; he has the sensitivity of a photoplate. His diplomatic pilgrimage was not the mere flitting of an Epicurean. He made a beeline up from secretary at the diplomatic mission to the post of minister. He landed in the United States and instead of looking through the narrow prism of

an absent-minded *bon vivant*, with a cigarette in his mouth and a monocle in the corner of his eye, he looked at the great land with a sociologist's sagacity, giving us subsequently a book that Garcia Merou described as the most complete study of Lincoln's Republic.

Oliveira Lima goes about his historical excavations just like a tourist who climbs the snow-clad Swiss mountains with a Kodak. With it he gets some candid shots of types and features. Everybody moves—old chief justices get into their jalopies, amusing and prudish ladies cross the street in palanquins, carried by liveried black men, Alexandre de Gusmão speaks to the Friar King D. João V, and the latter's apparitors gallop through the streets of Lisbon, upon contact with that magic wand which is Oliveira Lima's evocative power.[2]

The strength of the historian lies in his evocative ability. In those lines, written at the age of seventeen years, we already have the central intuition of Freyre's work. And one of the themes is empathy, a notion that he believed he himself was the first to use in studies conducted in the Portuguese language.

His first essay on cultural criticism (1922) was on Oliveira Lima's work. It was an analysis of his *History of Civilization*, a project that took him many hours of reading in New York and that he published in the *Revista do Brasil*. Monteiro Lobato, the director of the publication, didn't overlook the novelty and the brilliance of his style. In the article, Freyre acknowledges the importance of Lima's work but at the same time preserves his own intellectual independence. Moreover, in it there already appear other aspects. The readings of economic history with Seligman, the author of the *Economic Interpretation of History*, and with Charles Beard, one of the creators of the so-called "New History" and an analyst of the economic foundations of the American Constitution, both of whom Freyre studied at Columbia, led him to question the overly political and cultural character of Oliveira Lima's historical perspective. On the other hand, Freyre's vision of the progress of the "carboniferous civilization," as he describes the European modernity in gestation, is more pessimistic than Oliveira Lima's liberal evolutionism. He criticizes the ideology of progress and women's right to vote, a hasty judgment for which he quickly apologized in a private letter.

Oliveira Lima was his mentor for many years, sending him books on urban sociology from Washington and making available to him his major *Brasiliana* [*Brazilian Collection*], as well as his personal ties in America and

Europe, namely, his access to Columbia, and his diplomatic contacts in Lisbon and Paris. Relatively aloof from his father for a good part of his life, the mother is the central family figure for Freyre. Therefore, Oliveira Lima became an all-important father figure, imbued with the entire aura, in the eyes of an imaginative adolescent, of a universal *Pernambucano*, a writer and a character of the epoch towards the end of the Empire.

New York, 1921

It was in connection with Oliveira Lima that Gilberto Freyre met Franz Boas and decided to study at Columbia. In 1921, Franz Boas was an important public intellectual, known for his radical political positions in the racial debate. He enjoyed great prestige in the American academic and cultural world. The relationship between Boas and Gilberto Freyre has been discussed on many occasions, even to the point of doubting his status as Boas' pupil. However, both his correspondence and other sources of the time show that Franz Boas was an emblematic figure for Gilberto Freyre as a student in Texas even before he went on to do his master's in New York.[3] Freyre attended Boas' courses at Columbia and in 1921 carefully read Boas' main work, *The Mind of Primitive Man*. One of his main friends from his student days, Rudiger Bilden, with whom he shared his intellectual concerns and bohemian pastimes at his apartment in the Village, is the one who kept alive the ties with Columbia and Boas during the twenties. It is no mere accident then that the news of Boas' death in 1943, accompanied by the obituary from the *New York Times*, reached him through a letter from Bilden. Rudiger Bilden traveled to Brazil with a scholarship from Columbia in 1926, where he stayed for a year to finish his research on race. Freyre highlights the importance of Bilden's ideas in *Casa-Grande* in several references.[4] For his part, Franz Boas, in *Anthropology and Modern Life*,[5] writes that:

> The race perception between whites, blacks and the native Indians in Brazil seems to be completely different according to how we look at it. Along the coastal area there is a huge black population. The mixing with native Indians is also very striking. The discrimination between those three races is much less present than in our country, and the social obstacles to miscegenation or to social progress are not great. (67)

Freyre attributes that opinion to a report by Rudiger Bilden. In this regard, it may be said that paradoxically Gilberto Freyre did influence Franz Boas. Both in this paragraph and in all of Boas' discussion of race, culture and cultural processes, the position Boas wanted to undermine was that of physical, biological and deterministic anthropology. At the same time, Boas' central idea was the relativization of racial differences based on a cultural point of view. As for Boas, his scientific agnosticism and his aversion to abstract theorization, a *destructive* method, to use a concept from his pupil Edward Sapir, is also present in Gilberto Freyre and in his predilection for the description of social circumstances instead of a theoretical approach, since Freyre disliked generalizations. But just as Boas redefined the theme of race from the point of view of a rich and complex vision of the role of culture— and this was a radical assumption in the 1920s and 1930s—, a similar operation was conducted through the writing in the early thirties of *Casa-Grande* with regard to the interpretation of national culture. In the main, Freyre considered racial miscegenation as being beneficial for civilizing efforts and no longer saw it as a deficiency or an insurmountable barrier, as it had been until then by most Latin American and Brazilian thinkers—for instance, Oliveira Vianna, José Ingenieros and Alcides Arguedas. On the contrary, Freyre saw in the mixed-race culture a positive component, indicative of superiority. In that regard, he was inspired partly by the theme of one of his readings of the time, Randolph Bourne, who in his famous article "Transnational America"[6] highlighted the superiority of America over Europe due to its cultural mixing, as opposed to the provincialisms of European national cultures.

The influence of essayists such as Walter Pater, Lafcadio Hearn and the *fin de siècle* aestheticism in, for example, George Moore and J. K. Huysmans inspired a vivid sense of an erotic and affective dimension of culture, highlighting its sensorial and aesthetic aspects and laying greater store by subjectivity. Nietzsche and Simmel were early readings present in the elegiac and visual tone of *Casa-Grande*, stressing the importance of the erotic both in a sensual and more strictly sexual sense. *Casa-Grande* is an erotica of the Brazilian culture in the sense presented by Susan Sontag in *Against Interpretation*: "Instead of a hermeneutics we need an erotics of art."[7] Gilberto Freyre's own sexual experiences, of which his personal diaries, partially published in *Tempo Morto e Outros Tempos*, have talked at length, undoubtedly contributed to underline his own singular perspective absent from other works of social interpretation of the time.[8] That is certainly why Freyre's was noted by Roland Barthes, who stressed Freyre's freedom in referring to the dimensions of pleasure and sensuality. On the other hand, Barthes himself wrote at the end of his life a personal diary, *Incidents* (1979), with a remarkable likeness to Freyre's taste for the singularity of the intimate biographical detail.

Recife in the 1920s

In the 1920s *Casa-Grande* appears foreshadowed in texts such as Freyre's master's thesis *Social Life in Brazil in the Middle of the Nineteenth Century*,[9] which is already a search for the *temps perdu* of a Brazilian family. In this work, Freyre advances opinions on slavery and family life that will be fully developed in *Casa-Grande & Senzala* and *Sobrados e Mucambos*. In 1925, in *Livro do Nordeste*, he published two articles (one of them, "Aspects of a Century of Transition in the Northeast of Brazil"), both of which were incorporated later on in *Região e Tradição*. In those essays a substantial number of the themes of *Casa-Grande* are already there: slavery, the mixing of races, the socialization of women and men in the patriarchal family, as well as a considerable part of the documental sources. The vivid and evocative style of writing is also already present, as is the taste for the transcription of documents and the visuality of language. But the representation of the system of slavery is less incisive than in *Casa-Grande* and the text sometimes gives the impression of being written from the point of view of the slavocracy, such as when, for example, he describes the slaves' rebellions as "collective insolence."

The 1926 visit of Rudiger Bilden and the preparations for the installation in Recife of the first Sociology Chair prompted Gilberto Freyre to update his readings in social sciences, which were to provide the basis of *Casa-Grande & Senzala*. However, up until 1930 the plan of the work was not defined. Since 1926, Freyre had been thinking of writing a history of Brazilian childhood, a project that he conceived of in New York in 1921 and that he continued to work upon during his visit to Nuremberg, the "city of toys," in 1922. In Lisbon, archive researches are still being carried out in connection with this project.

Stanford, 1931

Everything changes in 1930: the exile, the fleeting passage through Salvador and the coasts of Africa on his way to Lisbon, access to new libraries in Lisbon and, especially, his stay at Stanford. The handwritten notebooks from

Gilberto Freyre's courses at Stanford show the thematic and bibliographical importance of that stay for the plan of *Casa-Grande & Senzala*, especially the readings on the history of Portuguese colonization. Some citations and references in *Casa-Grande* are direct transcriptions of course notes. But perhaps every book requires an event that crystallizes its conception. And in the case of *Casa-Grande* this was, in my opinion, a letter sent by H. L. Mencken. It was, in fact, during his stay in California that he renewed contact with H. L. Mencken, the famous American cultural critic. Freyre offered Mencken his master's thesis. Mencken praised it and suggested to him that he expand it into book form. All the feverish readings, archive research, the many projects and the partial works coalesced at that moment. The unwritten "History of Brazilian Childhood" is replaced with a new book: *Casa-Grande & Senzala*, which only later came to be called by that name. In November 1932, when two chapters had already been completed, the book carried the title of *Vida Sexual e de Família no Brasil Escravocrata*. It was a name, moreover, quite similar to that of his master's thesis, which reveals how close was the source of inspiration for both texts.

Not only the themes but also the focus of the Stanford course was a preparation for *Casa-Grande & Senzala*.[10] As Austregésilo de Athaide recounts in a report written in New York,[11] Freyre defined his course in California as "a type of Loyola's spiritual exercises applied to the study of the past. I try to give my foreign students a realistic vision of the Brazilian past—like the vision Loyola tried to transmit of hell and heaven… It's just that in our case it is about our country and people." In addition, he quickly highlighted the importance of reviving the past in all of its colors and flavors, showing his impatience for political and diplomatic history: "what I'm interested in is the intimate, social details" (Athaide, *Diário de Pernambuco*, 1931, 9).

The context of the time also needs to be illuminated. 1930 is a crucial moment in the modern history of Brazil, when the spaces for thinking the national in a renewed way were created. The reflections undertaken by the modernists and the intellectuals of the 1920s are deepened and the agenda is extensively renewed. The proto-globalization of the thirties and the emergence of new peripheral nations will provide the context for the great essays of national interpretation written by Sergio Buarque de Holanda and Caio Prado Jr. Is *Casa-Grande & Senzala* an expression of the ideology of the "national character"? Yes, insofar as the convergence of those diverse productions is the result both of a culture and of reflection on the past as the laying of the foundations for progress. No, simply insofar as a work such as *Casa-Grande & Senzala* possesses other dimensions; it is more than merely a study of the national character as in Ruth Benedict's understanding of the notion, developed in her *The Chrysanthemum and the Sword*.[12] Freyre's work has yet another historical dimension—it uses economic and social materials that together lead to new researches on the historical formation of Brazil—daily life, food, family, sexuality—, besides reformulating the topic of race. The combination of social history with anthropology substantially enriches the contribution of Gilberto Freyre's work.

The mixing of seemingly diverse materials that acquire new meaning when combined in a new manner characterizes to a high extent the operation of the sociological imagination, which is an effort to represent a civilizing process whose both light and dark sides are projected onto Brazil's centuries to come.

It is, in short, a classic. But the supreme litmus test of all classics is the degree of affliction its reading causes to future readers. From the number of yawns and the feeling of the book dropping from our hands, our distance vis-à-vis the enshrined text is registered. It is that discomfort caused to the body that reminds us that great books, just like empires, nations and human beings are children of time that is to say, mortal. At certain moments, some classics reveal themselves as an unredeemable part of the past: they are boring because they mean nothing to us any more. Is *Casa-Grande & Senzala* readable today? It's a question that we need to ask ourselves. I indeed do think it is, partly due to its original approach to the complex theme of interrelations between race and culture, a subject that is still moot in post-modernity. Gilberto Freyre's interpretations still hold their interest independently of the validity attributed to them. Its reading resuscitates specters of the past we cannot definitively live down. And Freyre accomplishes this with a literary mastery that ensures *Casa-Grande & Senzala* a place among the great works of the modern historical imagination.

Notes

[1] It is worth transcribing a fragment: "How many diplomats, like the Baron of Penedo, in the midst of the splendors of the more sumptuous courts and the refinements of the earliest civilizations would remember with insistent and more than literary longing their native village, modest in itself but guarding the mouth of one of the great rivers of the world, would elevate that longing to the point of coming, after almost five-hundred years, to spend the last days amongst their countrymen? These are the strong and after all happy ones, not those that forget

their horizons, alienate their hearts and renounce their origins. Diplomatic life can always be enviable: the death of the diplomat is so only in similar cases" (32).

[2] "O Lábaro," 26 November 1917.

[3] Freyre 1922.

[4] Bilden n.d.

[5] Boas 67.
Among the vast bibliography on Franz Boas, see A. L. Kroeber, Ruth Benedict, Murray B. Emenau, Melville J. Herskovitz, Gladys A. Reichard and J. Alden Mason; Richard Handler, "Franz Boas 1858-1942," *American Anthropologist New Seriates* 45.3, Part 2 July-Sept. (1943); Richard Handler, "Boasian Anthropology and the Critique of *American Culture*," American Quarterly 42.2 (June 1990), 252-273; Arnold Krupat, "Irony in Anthropology: The Work of Franz Boas," *Modernist Anthropology*, ed. Marc Manganaro (Indiana: Indiana UP, 1995) 133-145; George W. Stocking, Jr., *Race, Culture and Evolution: Essays in the History of Anthropology* (Chicago: U of Chicago P, 1982) and *The Ethnographer's Magic and other Essays in the History of Anthropology* (Madison: U of Wisconsin P, 1995). Boas' theoretical corpus was far from forming a coherent body, built upon an opposition between race and culture, as the exchange between Luiz Costa Lima and Ricardo Benzaquen de Araujo seems to suggest. See Araujo 1994.

[6] Bourne 37.

[7] Sontag 21.

[8] Freyre *Tempo Morto.*

[9] See note 3.

[10] See Needell 1995.

[11] Athaide 9.

[12] Ruth Benedict *The Chrysanthemum and the Sword* (Boston: Houghon Mifflin, 1946).

Works Cited

Araujo, Ricardo Benzaquen de. *Guerra e Paz. Casa-Grande & Senzala e a Obra de Gilberto Freyre nos Anos 30.* Rio de Janeiro: Editora 34, 1994.

Athaide, Austregésilo de. "Na Mesa dum Grande Demônio." *Diário de Pernambuco* 31 July 1931.

Bilden, Rudiger. *Race Relations in Latin America with Special Reference to the Development of Indigenous Culture* (New York City in Institute of Public Affairs, University of Virginia [paper mimeo]).

Boas, Franz. *Anthropology and Modern Life.*1928. New York: Dover, 1986.

Bourne, Randolph. *The History of A Literary Radical & Other Papers.* New York: S. A. Russell, 1956.

Freyre, Gilberto. *Social Life in Brazil in the Middle of the Nineteenth Century. The Hispanic American Historical Review.* Volume 5 (1922): 597-630.

———. *The Masters and the Slaves: A Study in the Development of Brazilian Civilization.* Trans. Samuel Putnam. New York: A. A. Knopf, 1946.

———. *Tempo Morto e Outros Tempos. 1915-1930.* Rio de Janeiro: José Olympio Editora, 1975.

Lima, Manuel de Oliveira. "Vida Diplomática." Second Lecture held at the Instituto Arqueológico do Recife. Recife: Editora do Jornal do Recife, 1904.

Needell, Jeffrey D. "Identity, Race, Gender and Modernity in the Origins of Gilberto Freyre's Œuvre," *American Historical Review* (February 1995): 51-77.

Sontag, Susan. *Against Interpretation.* New York: Anchor Books, 1990.

The UNESCO Project: Social Sciences and Race Studies in Brazil in the 1950s[1]

Marcos Chor Maio

Translated by José Augusto Drummond

During 1951 and 1952, the United Nations Educational, Scientific and Cultural Organization (UNESCO) sponsored a series of studies about race relations in Brazil.[2] This research, conducted simultaneously in regions marked by traditional economic relations such as the Brazilian Northeast and in industrialized areas of the country's Southeast, aimed at presenting to the world the details of an experience in racial interaction which at that time was considered unique and successful, both inside and outside Brazil.

This article will focus on the relationship between race studies and the social sciences in Brazil, taking the "UNESCO Project" on Brazilian race relations as a point of departure. My thesis is that the "UNESCO Project" amounted to the successful implementation of the agenda for the social sciences as proposed by the Brazilian anthropologist Arthur Ramos in the last years of the 1940s.

This agenda followed the pragmatic tradition of social sciences in Brazil, which was systematically concerned with placing Brazil within the circle of modern nations. It included a series of topics that ultimately sought to shed light upon obstacles to progress, modernization and development of Brazilian society. However, in the years immediately following the Holocaust, the success of a particular enterprise, such as the "UNESCO Project" in Brazil, demanded an international connection that would place it in the larger context of the scientific quest for a reasonable explanation for the tragic events of World War II. In other words, there was a confluence of the pragmatic tradition in Brazilian social sciences with UNESCO's goal to understand the tragedy of the Holocaust. In this sense, I try to show that both Brazilian and non-Brazilian social scientists offered UNESCO a special "portrait of Brazil," that is, an account of an original and positive experience in racial matters, in exchange for the acceptance of Brazil into the modern world. These social scientists who studied Brazil were aware of certain goals included in UNESCO's own agenda—such as industrialization, access to education and science—that emerged through pressures exerted by underdeveloped countries. The "UNESCO Project" on Brazilian race relations was based on the belief in a positive Brazilian socialization concerning race matters and on the urge to bring certain social segments of Brazil, including African-Brazilians, into modernity.

In order to better sustain my argument, I will first present a brief description of the origins of the "UNESCO Project." I will then focus on how the research project was put together, and will also discuss its findings. Finally, I will consider the Project's impact.

The Choice of Brazil

The choice of Brazil as the site for such a study was closely related to the international context. After World War II, one of UNESCO's major missions was to understand the conflict itself and its most perverse consequence, that is, the Holocaust. With the persistence of racism in the United States and South Africa, the emergence of the Cold War, and the decolonization of Africa and Asia, the issue of race continued to attract the attention of international agencies. UNESCO stimulated the development of scientific knowledge about racism, looking at the motivations, consequences, and possible ways of overcoming it.

In the late 1940s, two events highlighted the agency's efforts against race intolerance. First, at a meeting of experts on the social and natural sciences, which took place in Paris in 1949, participants discussed the scientific standing of the concept of race. The resulting "Statement on Race," made public in May 1950 at UNESCO's Fifth General Conference in Florence, was the first document published with the support of an international agency that denied any deterministic association between physical characteristics, social behavior and moral attributes—beliefs that were still fashionable during the 1930s and 1940s. Second, at the same conference, Brazil was selected as the object of a comprehensive investigation of economic, social, political, cultural, and psychological aspects that did or did not influence the emergence of cooperative relations between races and ethnic groups. The purpose of choosing Brazil and focusing on its allegedly positive experience was to offer the world a new political awareness about race relations based on the possibility of harmony among the groups.

Since the nineteenth century, travelers, scientists, journalists and politicians from Europe and the United States had recorded with surprise the apparently peaceful coexistence among races and ethnic groups in Brazil. This image of a "racial paradise," in contrast with the persistently turbulent North American experience, was also connected with the fears of the Brazilian elites. Especially after the belated abolition of slavery and the adoption of a republican form of government, Brazil's elites saw the large proportion of African-Brazilians in the population and the frequency of miscegenation as obstacles to the country's march towards modernity. However, during the first decades of the twentieth century, particularly between the 1920s and 1940s, this view started changing. Due to Brazil's economic, social, and political transformations, and also because of the importance given in intellectual circles to the precise identification of the country's national identity, the pessimistic view about the contributions of the founding races was preempted by a positive perspective. In this view, Brazil's racial mix was seen as an indicator of tolerance and harmony, and as a positive and unique feature of the country's national identity.

The most sophisticated elaboration of the controversial belief in Brazilian racial democracy was achieved by Brazilian sociologist Gilberto Freyre. In 1933, Gilberto Freyre published *Casa-Grande & Senzala*, in which he argued that "miscegenation" and the mixing of cultures was not Brazil's damnation but rather its salvation. Freyre created a positive concept of national identity, emphasizing African, Amerindian and Portuguese contributions to the emergence of Brazilian culture. Moreover, according to Freyre, this "portrait of Brazil" produced a social perception of race through a *continuum* of colors and categories used to designate variations of physical appearance.

Freyre described Brazil as a society founded on a series of what he called cultural and economic antagonisms, based on "profound traditional realities," between "sadists and masochists, the learned and the illiterate, individuals of predominantly European culture and other of principally African or Amerindian culture."[3] Although in several passages of his masterpiece Freyre recalls the extreme violence present in black-white relations under slavery, the prevailing idea in *Casa-Grande & Senzala* is that the antagonisms were "balanced" by:

conditions of fraternization and social mobility specific to Brazil: miscegenation, the dispersion of inheritances, easy and frequent changes of employment and residence, the easy and frequent access of mulattos and natural children to elevated social and political positions, the lyrical Portuguese Catholicism, moral tolerance, hospitality to foreigners and intercommunication between the different parts of the country. (89)

Freyre believes that fraternization, the harmonious ideal of races, creeds and cultures would be the hallmark of Brazilian uniqueness, its specificity in relation to other countries, in particular the United States. This belief became one of the major ideological components of Brazilian nationalism, and was substantial enough to gain an international audience.

Arthur Ramos and the Agenda of the Social Sciences

In mid-October of 1949, two months after becoming the Director of the UNESCO's Department of Social Sciences, Brazilian anthropologist Arthur Ramos finished drafting a plan that predicted the development of sociological and anthropological studies in Brazil.[4] In tune with the agency's concern about racism and the socioeconomic difficulties experienced by underdeveloped countries, Ramos believed that it would be necessary to pay special attention to the issue of integrating African and Indigenous people into the modern world. This goal should be supplemented simultaneously with the literacy program being implemented by UNESCO, in cooperation with the Brazilian government.[5]

In June of 1950, the Fifth General Conference of UNESCO approved the research project on race relations in Brazil, but Arthur Ramos, who had been responsible for the idea, had died eight months earlier. He had not defined the details of the study he had in mind. It is remarkable, however, that even without his input the final design and the results of several investigations carried the same concerns that could be found in Ramos' reflections about Brazil.

In one of his last articles,[6] Ramos insisted that Brazil was a "laboratory of civilization," an expression he took from the North American historian Rudiger Bilden.[7] He had already expressed his conviction that Brazil had presented the most scientific and most humane solution to the mixing of races and cultures which was such a serious problem for other peoples.[8] However, years later, Ramos observed that only recently had Brazilian social sciences initiated a process of professional qualification that would allow them to be ready to study this "laboratory."[9]

Ramos believed that the institutionalization of the social sciences would provide a unique opportunity for going beyond the "armchair, bookworm" phase of studies about Indigenous and African peoples.[10] He thought that the appropriate path would be the investigation of the heritage of slavery and its implications for understanding the Brazilian race situation, with special attention to the psycho-sociological influence of the dominant discourse and practice, the relationship among races, the stereotypes of opinions and attitudes, and the sociological factors of caste and class.[11]

As the author himself says, "only after an entire series of investigations of this type have been completed will we be able to propose 'interpretations' of Brazil, that is, comprehensive essays or normative plans for intervention, different from the impressionistic studies produced until now, which although perhaps quite interesting, have led to hasty and dangerous generalizations."[12] According to Ramos, there was no homogeneous Brazilian cultural perspective. There were many cultures that only then were beginning to be studied and understood. Therefore, the existence of a national identity should be based on historical or social criteria. The social sciences agenda, then, as presented by Ramos, prevailed in the design of the "UNESCO Project." The scope of the research project in Brazil was defined between June and December of 1950.

Building the UNESCO Project

In April, 1950, the Swiss-North American anthropologist Alfred Métraux, experienced in ethnological investigations (of indigenous and black groups) both in South and in Central America, became Director of the recently created UNESCO Division for Race Relations. In the first semester of that year, the Brazilian anthropologist Ruy Coelho, who had studied with Roger Bastide at the University of São Paulo and with Melville Herskovits at Northwestern University, became Métraux's major assistant. Métraux and Coelho became UNESCO's representatives heading the research project to be developed in Brazil.

Initially, the "UNESCO Project" was supposed to focus only on the state of Bahia. Since the late nineteenth century there had been a tradition of studies about African-Brazilians in the city of Salvador. These studies used to give special attention to the strong influence of African cultures on that community. Bahia seemed to be the appropriate scenery for UNESCO's purposes. Salvador, with a large number of African-Brazilian residents, always attracted the attention of travelers, writers and researchers and was seen as a privileged place in terms of racial interactions.

However, exchanges between the UNESCO staff and Brazilian and non-Brazilian researchers introduced changes in the original proposal. The social psychologist Otto Klineberg (a Columbia professor, trained by Franz Boas, who had great influence over UNESCO's Department of Social Sciences), Roger Bastide (a French sociologist who taught at the Universidade de São Paulo), Luiz de Aguiar Costa Pinto (a sociologist at the Universidade do Brasil, in Rio de Janeiro) and Charles Wagley (an anthropologist at Columbia University) convinced UNESCO that there were distinct patterns of race relations in Brazil and that it was necessary to study the contrasts, especially between traditional regions and those undergoing urbanization and industrialization. For this purpose, the best counterpoint for Bahia was São Paulo, in which African-Brazilians were a minority and racism was supposedly more visible.

Meanwhile, the UNESCO staff had updated information not only on the state of race studies in Brazil, but also on the degree of professionalization of the Brazilian social sciences, and compiled a list of the Brazilian social scientists who could be engaged in the research project. Despite that, Alfred Métraux spent two months in Brazil before deciding about the final research design. He changed his mind about focusing the project only on Bahia. In a letter to the anthropologist Melville Herskovits, one month after returning from his "rediscovery" trip to Brazil, Métraux wrote:

> Contrary to my previous plans, Bahia will no longer be the focus of our project. We shall study race relations as they appear in four communities and concentrate on the problem of social mobility in the city of Salvador. On the other hand, we shall concentrate on the rapidly deteriorating racial situation of São Paulo. Dr. Costa Pinto will undertake a similar study, but on a lesser scale, in Rio de Janeiro. I expect to get a picture of the racial situation in Brazil, at the end of the year, which will be close to reality and cover both the bright and dark sides.[13]

Nevertheless, the final design of the "UNESCO Project" was reached only a year later, when, visiting Brazil again, Métraux decided to include Recife as part of the research. Contacts between UNESCO and the Joaquim Nabuco

Institute, created by Gilberto Freyre in 1949, started in the first semester of 1951. Freyre was interested in setting up a calendar of activities to be developed in conjunction with the international agency, wishing to strengthen his recently created regional research center. The suggestion was immediately accepted, given the prestige enjoyed by Freyre at that juncture.

These first steps in the assembly of the UNESCO research project indicate the existence of a widely open scenery constructed on the basis of knowledge previously gathered by the social scientists on the staff, enlarged later by contacts and suggestions forwarded by Brazilian and non-Brazilian researchers with experience in teaching and/or doing research in Brazil.

Summing up, the "UNESCO Project" was the result of a concerted action that turns Brazil's image as a country with lessons to offer humanity into an object of negotiation involving individual and collective actors. That is, a group of prestigious social scientists such as Arthur Ramos, Otto Klineberg, Charles Wagley, Louis Wirth, Franklin Frazier, and Lévi-Strauss, pulled together by an international agency (UNESCO); Alfred Métraux, a humanist ethnologist, specifically involved with the study of indigenous communities and African cults, who becomes a political-academic activist at UNESCO; Paulo Estevão Berredo Carneiro, a representative of the Brazilian positivist, anti-racist and integrationist tradition, and Brazil's representative to UNESCO and member of its Executive Council; and, lastly, a community of social scientists (Brazilian and non-Brazilian) dedicated to the institutional consolidation of the social sciences in Brazil and bent on deciphering the society with new parameters (Donald Pierson, Roger Bastide, Florestan Fernandes, Oracy Nogueira, Thales de Azevedo, René Ribeiro, Luiz de Aguiar Costa Pinto and others). This was the transatlantic network assembled to take Arthur Ramos' original project to its ultimate consequences.

It was no longer a matter of looking at Brazil as a mere locus of experiences to be learned. This had already taken place in the 1930s, when Franz Boas had summoned Charles Wagley and Ruth Landes to study African-Brazilians and Indigenous peoples in Brazil, and Robert Park had suggested that Donald Pierson investigate race relations in Bahia. In the 1950s, the stakes were higher: the portrait of Brazil to be given to UNESCO, the assertion of national uniqueness, of the country's cultural specificity translated by positive racial interactions, would serve as the best way to assimilate Brazil into the modern world. This meant that there would be a *quid pro quo*—access for Brazilians to education, to science, to development.

This two-lane road, namely the combination of tradition and modernity, was the basis for the "UNESCO Project." Thus, the demands of a Third World country were negotiated in the "heroic" and "generous" phase of UNESCO, which at that time sought to extract lessons from particular and successful experiences in the realm of relations among peoples in order to enrich the harmony of the nations of the world.

In order to reach these aims, the community of social scientists, both at UNESCO and in Brazil, should use the rhetoric of the country's diversity, showing that Brazil was not just Bahia. Indeed, if a single, encompassing image of Brazilian society could be suggested, the social scientists engaged in the project since its inception were convinced that it would be Brazil as a "land of contrasts."

Research conducted in the Northeast—that is, in economically backward regions—had an enormous ethnographic richness: multiple forms of racial classification, the importance of the cultural dimension as a component of social hierarchy and the detailed description of the forms of prejudice and discrimination against non-whites. In these communities, where large numbers of African-Brazilians lived, studies revealed not only the enormous social distance between whites and them but also the limited social mobility of non-whites. Racial prejudice had more subtle manners of manifesting itself.

The historical-sociological analysis conducted in the Southeast looked at race relations in Brazil's two major developmental centers, Rio de Janeiro and São Paulo. This region was going through an intense process of social and economic change. Local African-Brazilians and mulattoes had to face the arrival of large numbers of European immigrants, especially after the elimination of slavery. Racism was more visible.

Between Science and Politics

The sociologists and anthropologists engaged in the actual research projects clearly perceived the articulation between science and politics so noticeably expressed in UNESCO's decision to initiate the "Brazilian Research Project." Even more, they associated scientific work with commitment. In other words, the social sciences were seen as the best instrument to understand reality, and social research was a privileged form of political commitment to and intervention in needed social change.

What follows is a more detailed exposition of this argument, based on the reflections of Florestan Fernandes, one of the sociologists who achieved the highest visibility in Brazil after the "UNESCO Project." When drafting the research project to be conducted in São Paulo, Fernandes stated that:

> the investigation must be planned on a scientific basis, but its origin and goal are correspondingly *extra-scientific*: it will be used by an institution, UNESCO, that contracted it with the intention of using its results in the social reeducation of adults and in its policy of bringing together the races.[14]

The "UNESCO Project" was conducted at a moment when the social sciences were going through a transition in Brazil. Having gained a foothold in the academic world in the 1930s, the social sciences tried to consolidate their institutionalization through the expansion of the number of departments and institutes during the next decades. They were also experimenting with new theoretical-methodological models capable of yielding a more solid training for this new character, the social scientist.

This process advanced during the democratic period that started in 1945. In the 1950s, when the "UNESCO Project" was being conducted, the question of which pattern of social and economic development should prevail in the country became a mandatory matter of debate. This debate followed several paths, but all of them involved the issue of the role of social scientists in times of social change. Despite the fact that the "UNESCO Project" focused on the specific subject of race relations, it became a "pretext" for several analyses of the transition from archaic to modern society, that is, the analysis of social stratification, social mobility, the obstacles to social changes, the role of intellectuals in public life and the incorporation of certain social strata into the modern society under construction in Brazil.

Therefore, the mere publication of data concerning a particular experience in race matters was seen by most of the social scientists involved in the "UNESCO Project" as quite a limited goal. After all, the opportunity presented by the sponsorship of an internationally known institution should be used to decipher Brazilian reality under new parameters. Even more, all these social scientists believed, in different degrees, that Brazil was a "laboratory of civilization." To deal carefully with this matter, we should consider more closely the conviction of these researchers that Brazilian society was endowed with a uniqueness that required study.

In December of 1959, Florestan Fernandes wrote the preface to the book *Cor e Mobilidade Social em Florianópolis* [*Color and Social Mobility in Florianópolis*], written by his students, the sociologists Fernando Henrique Cardoso, the current president of Brazil, and Octávio Ianni. This book was the result of a project sponsored by two Brazilian government agencies. The book made public the results of a research effort that amounted to an extension of the "UNESCO Project" to the Southern part of the country, a region which until then had not been properly studied.[15] This was the clearest example of the influence of the "UNESCO Project" on the process of the institutionalization of the social sciences in Brazil. This investigation was the first substantial result of the activities under the discipline of Sociology I of the Department of Social Sciences of the Universidade de São Paulo, coordinated by Florestan Fernandes.

In his preface, Fernandes considered that the studies of race relations were a precise indicator of the maturation of the social sciences in Brazil. Besides the importance of theoretical and empirical concerns that were mobilizing Brazilian social scientists, the study of patterns of race relations revealed an interest in answering questions of an immediate nature and with a political content. In Fernandes' own words:

> Nobody ignores how much cultural heterogeneity affected, affects and will continue to affect the possibility for the development of 'Western society' in Brazil. In this respect, the issues pertinent to this subject have the dimension of a *national problem*, and this gives past and current investigations about the subject an unmistakable practical interest.[16]

However, Fernandes observed with sadness that society in general was not paying attention to the significance of such research projects. He attributed this lack of attention to the generalized belief that Brazil lived under the aegis of a "racial democracy." Thus, the ideology of a Brazilian "racial democracy" is an obstacle to the emergence of a new type of mentality capable of channeling efforts in the direction of an industrial society, democratic both in political and in social terms.[17]

Social scientists, according to Fernandes, should discover the foundations of social structure and thus indicate the mechanisms by which racism is reproduced. In this manner, the "*obstacles* to social change" would be identified.[18] Fernandes is unequivocal about this matter:

> There is not an effective racial democracy [in Brazil], because the exchanges between individuals belonging to distinct 'races' begin and end in the realm of a

conventional tolerance. This tolerance may obey the requirements of 'good manners,' of a debatable 'Christian spirit' or of the necessity of 'keeping each one in his proper place.' However, it does not bring men together except on the basis of merely coexisting in the same social space. Where this manages to materialize, it is a restrictive coexistence, regulated by a code that defends inequality, disguising it as one of the principles of the democratic social order.[19]

However, in Fernandes' view, the development of Western civilization in Brazil—amounting to industrialization, democratization of wealth and power, and social improvement—should be aware of "our sociocultural heritage," so that it would be able to cultivate whatever is compatible "with the democratic conception of life and with the creation of democracy in Brazil." He affirmed that this was so because, in his own words, "a people that stimulates swift programs of cultural change, without caring about intelligent and constructive criteria, pays exorbitant prices for social progress."[20]

Fernandes stated, moreover, that "Western civilization is sufficiently rich and plastic to allow for ample differences between national cultural systems, organized on the basis of their basic ideal values;" on this basis it would be necessary to increase the consciousness of citizenship and the more effective practice of democracy without canceling what he called "the tolerance woven into race relations and a minimum of detachment, which characterizes the expression of individualism and the autonomy of each person, both in the 'cultivated man' and in what is called the '*coarse man*'."[21]

Fernandes no doubt startles us when he considers "conventional tolerance in race relations" the factor that at once condemns and redeems Brazilian civilization. In the face of the sweeping process of economic development, urbanization and social mobility that attained new heights during Juscelino Kubitschek's government in the second half of the 1950s, and on account of his conviction that race inequalities are a "national problem," Fernandes warns us about the possible perverse effects of the absence of sociocultural parameters regulating the expansion of capitalism in Brazil. This would be an obstacle to "social reform in the Brazilian manner." In this sense, Fernandes recognizes the positive aspects of the type of sociability extant in Brazil. Florestan Fernandes, in his apparent paradox, spelled out the "Brazilian dilemma."

In the context of the "UNESCO Project," it seems that Brazilian and foreign social scientists did not believe that investigating and publishing information about the prejudice and discrimination present in Brazilian race relations would preclude the acknowledgment of the uniquely congenial treatment given by Brazilian society to race relations.

Finally, research on race relations under UNESCO's auspices in the 1950s brought, first, a reinforcement of the Brazilian sociological tradition of investigating relations between whites and blacks, which had gained earlier prominence in the 1930s with the writings of sociologists Gilberto Freyre and Donald Pierson. Second, the social sciences in Brazil, which were in the process of being institutionalized, expanded their scope and have since then systematically studied the issue of race relations. The "UNESCO Project" itself produced a vast documentation about the existence of prejudice and discrimination against African-Brazilians. Focusing on these issues, the "UNESCO Project" prompted new questions about Brazil and helped identify difficulties, impasses, and conflicts in a society undergoing urbanization and industrialization. However, the recognition that there was a "Brazilian style of racism" did not prevent the participating social scientists from noticing the existence of a set of social relations that could contribute to an authentic racial democracy in Brazil.

Notes

[1] See Maio 1997.

[2] On the series of studies in the UNESCO Race Relations Project, see: Thales de Azevedo, *As Elites de Cor: Um Estudo de Ascensão Social* (São Paulo: Companhia Editora Nacional, 1955); Oracy Nogueira, "Relações Raciais em Itapetininga," *Brancos e Negros em São Paulo*, by Roger Bastide & Florestan Fernandes (São Paulo: Editora Anhembi, 1955); Luiz de Aguiar Costa Pinto, *O Negro no Rio de Janeiro* (São Paulo: Companhia Editora Nacional, 1953); René Ribeiro, *Religião e Classes Sociais* (Rio de Janeiro: Ministério da Educação e Cultura, 1956); Charles Wagley et al., *Race and Class in Rural Brazil* (Paris: UNESCO, 1952). On some aspects of the UNESCO Race Relations Project, see also: Marcos Chor Maio: "A Questão Racial no Pensamento de Guerreiro Ramos," *Raça, ciência e sociedade*, eds. M.C. Maio e R.V. Santos (Rio de Janeiro: Editora da Fiocruz/Centro Cultural Banco do Brasil, 1996) 179-93; "Uma Polêmica Esquecida: Costa Pinto, Guerreiro Ramos e o Tema das Relações Raciais," *Dados* 40.1 (1997): 127-62; "Costa Pinto e a Crítica ao Negro como Espetáculo" (Apresentação), *O Negro no Rio de Janeiro: Relações de Raças numa Sociedade em Mudança*, by Luiz de Aguiar Costa Pinto, 2nd ed. (1953; Rio de Janeiro: Editora da UFRJ, 1998) 17-50; "O Brasil no Concerto das Nações: a Luta Contra o Racismo nos Primórdios da UNESCO," *História, Ciências, Saúde – Manguinhos*, v. 2 (1998): 375-413; "O Diálogo entre Arthur Ramos e Costa Pinto: Dos Estudos Afro-Brasileiros à 'Sociologização' da Antropologia," *Ideais de Modernidade e Sociologia no Brasil: Ensaios sobre Luiz de Aguiar Costa Pinto*, M.C. Maio e G.Villas-Bôas (Porto Alegre: Editora da UFRGS, 1999) 203-21; "Tempo Controverso: Gilberto Freyre e o Projeto UNESCO," *Tempo Social* 11. 1 (1999): 111-36; "UNESCO Race Relations Project in Brazil," *Encarta Africana: Comprehensive Encyclopedia of Black History and Culture*, eds. Anthony Appiah Kwame and

Henry Louis Gates, Jr., CD-ROM. (Microsoft 1999); "O Projeto UNESCO e a Agenda das Ciências Sociais no Brasil dos Anos 40 e 50," *Revista Brasileira de Ciências Sociais* 14. 41 (October 1999): 141-58.

[3] Freyre 87.

[4] Letter from Arthur Ramos to Alceu Maynard de Araújo (10/27/1949), see Azeredo 215.

[5] Letter from Arthur Ramos to Clemente Mariani (10/14/1949). Correspondência Familiar, Seção de Manuscritos, Biblioteca Nacional.

[6] Arthur Ramos, "Os Grandes Problemas da Antropologia Brasileira," *Sociologia* X.4, 213-26.

[7] Bilden 1929.

[8] Ramos 179.

[9] Ramos 213.

[10] Ramos 214-15.

[11] Ramos 219.

[12] Ramos 219.

[13] Letter from Alfred Métraux to Melville Herskovits, 29/1/1951, p. 1. *Statement on Race.* REG file 323.12 A 102. Part II (Box REG 147), UNESCO Archives.

[14] Roger Bastide & Florestan Fernandes 324.

[15] Fernando Henrique Cardoso & Octávio Ianni xxxix-xi.

[16] Florestan Fernandes xi (author's emphasis).

[17] Fernandes xi-xii.

[18] Fernandes xii-xiii (author's emphasis).

[19] Fernandes xiv.

[20] Fernandes xvi.

[21] Fernandes xvi (author's emphasis).

Works Cited

Azeredo, Paulo Roberto. *Antropólogos e Pioneiros: A História da Sociedade Brasileira de Antropologia e Etnologia.* São Paulo: FFLCH/USP 1986.

Bastide Roger & Fernandes, Florestan. "O Preconceito Racial em São Paulo (Projeto de Estudo)." *Brancos e Negros em São Paulo.* 1951. São Paulo: Editora Anhembi, 1955.

Bilden, Rudiger. "Brazil, Laboratory of Civilization." *The Nation* CXXVIII 1/16/1929: 71-74.

Cardoso, Fernando Henrique & Octávio Ianni. *Cor e Mobilidade Social em Florianópolis.* São Paulo; Companhia Editora Nacional, 1960.

Fernandes, Florestan. "Prefácio." *Cor e Mobilidade Social em Florianópolis.* Fernando Henrique Cardoso & Octávio Ianni. São Paulo: Companhia Editora Nacional, 1960. xi-xxiii.

Freyre, Gilberto. *Casa-Grande & Senzala.* 1933. 20th ed. Rio de Janeiro: José Olympio Editora, 1980.

Maio, Marcos Chor. *A História do Projeto UNESCO: Estudos Raciais e Ciências Sociais no Brasil.* Ph. D. Dissertation. Rio de Janeiro: Instituto Universitário de Pesquisas do Rio de Janeiro, 1997.

Ramos, Arthur. *Guerra e Relações de Raça.* Rio de Janeiro: Departamento Editorial da União Nacional dos Estudantes, 1943.

The Mansions and the Shanties: "The Flesh and the Stone" in Nineteenth-Century Brazil*

Mary Del Priore
Translated by David Shepherd
and Tania Shepherd

Let us imagine that the reader of this article has never had the privilege of being immersed in *Sobrados e Mucambos* [*The Mansions and the Shanties*], Gilberto Freyre's *magnum opus*, first published in 1936. The title of the book refers to the buildings that characterized Brazilian urban settlements in the nineteenth century. It depicts both the façades of certain architectural models under whose roofs both rich and poor lived, and it also contains vast amounts of information on the Brazilian people of that period. A formidable lens that inspects walls, as well as customs, habits and traditions, Freyre's work nourishes, changes and questions the notions that we might have entertained of an ecstatic eighteenth-century Brazil.

Summarizing *Sobrados e Mucambos*, as well as introducing its author would be what the French have termed a *"vaste programme."* Both book and author are indeed vast, complex as well as compound. In order to reconcile the historian's need for objectivity with the need to reinterpret the past, I have opted to discuss two themes which permeate the whole of the work, namely, the house[1] and the human body,[2] or the "city" and the "body." After all, they are observatories of the social. Regarding the human body as a social body implies the various forms undertaken by the process of urbanization, and which took place in areas that were, until that time, agricultural and rural. The presence of these themes in Freyre provides evidence of his outstanding modernity, of his capacity to be ahead of his time and to further new approaches and new objectives. Haven't the "flesh" and the "stone" been a recent topic of investigation among American scholars?[3]

However, the reader might ask against what backdrop the relationships between the body and the city may be understood. This is the relationship between patriarchs and female owners of *sobrados*,[4] viscounts and barons, the educated and artisans, merchants, sailors, peddlers, fruit and vegetable store owners, pastry makers, salespeople, mulattoes and free blacks, on the one hand, and the mansions, the clay and thatched houses, shanties, squares, streets, churches, markets and quays, on the other. According to the author's preface to the third edition, published in 1961, his setting is the slow and relentless transformation from rural patriarchy, along with urban development with its myriad of repercussions, "constant elements of existence, as well as norms for co-existence." Such a process, made up of both stable elements and compromises, is that of the "rural patriarchy in decline, as well as its extension in terms of a less inflexible patriarchy of landlords of urban and semi-urban mansions; the development of the cities, the setting up of the Empire, which is, in fact, the formation of Brazilian society."[5] Alencastro summarizes Freyre's work successfully when he claims that

> *The Mansions and the Shanties* surmounts the barriers of patriarchal intimacy and captures the everyday life of the society at the time of the Brazilian Empire. More than *The Masters and the Slaves* (1933), Freyre's classic work, which stretches out in time and in space, *The Mansions and the Shanties* is closer in its approach to that of an outstanding historical study. It has a well-defined theme based on the knowledge of a specific context; it is also restricted to a specific period in terms of this theme; it contains sources which are compatible with the research topic and the era, i.e., diaries, correspondence, travelers' narratives, newspapers and nineteenth-century university theses. Furthermore, as an unexpected bonus, Freyre resorts to oral history to convey the reported memories of witnesses from the days of the Empire. People of highly varied backgrounds, from former slaves to Joaquim Nabuco's widow, were interviewed in the years between 1920-1930, when the majority of Brazilians still had strong rural links, or when, in his own words, living in apartments was limited to either Rio de Janeiro and to São Paulo, while the rest of the country lived in houses which had been planted in semi-rural urban settlements.[6]

Freyre defines the focus of his study as that of the habitual as opposed to the exceptional. It is on this terrain that Freyre unearths a multidimensional view of historical and social reality. He seeks to articulate its various levels in order to capture its entire flow. He is constantly at pains to describe its customs, habits, manners, to analyze the economic and social forces that underlie political confrontation, and to rebuild the logical systems of a racially mixed society. He demonstrates a continued interest in what is hidden or is being neglected, the barely visible representations, the objects of everyday life and the path by which those products that modified both biological and social life were exchanged. However, he also studies the way in which urbanization and resulting human behaviors incorporated both tastes and gestures, those phenomena signified rather than signifying, that is, phenomena that have been absorbed and internalized by society. In this way, Freyre studies the history of physical, mental and religious practices.

Let us take as an example his initial chapters, focusing on those cities that had started to gain shape by eliminating single-story buildings, covered with straw and tiles, interspersed here and there with church towers and narrow streets that meandered over hills. Horizontality was substituted for verticality. Wide-windowed houses were built, opening out to bourgeois streets. Planned squares took the place of crossroads where, in earlier days, slaves would get together to chat. Spaces for the slaughter of domestic animals and for the washing of clothes, that is, the drinking troughs, as well as the plots for the grazing of animals and for cutting wood, were reduced or transferred from the city centers to their outskirts. Domestic architecture flourished, thus turning the public thoroughfare into a "slave of the home." However, authorities tended to develop a new attitude towards these streets, now regarded as public, and which, as a result, had to be kept clean. In Recife, for example, urban transport was implemented thanks to the Baron of Mauá. Public services such as street lighting, sidewalks and sewage appeared as part of the urban scenery. The street had become aristocratic, whereas before it was a space for mules, peddlers, slaves and urchins. Over the recently laid stones, coaches, and carriages now transported the characters of this youthful society.

Portuguese economic policy, as Freyre understood it, placed value on both cities and businessmen. Colonial land aristocracy withered when faced with bourgeois and capitalist demands. According to the author, this bourgeoisie consisted of city aristocrats, described as "wearing gold chains around their necks, English top hats, riding expensive transport, eating raisins, figs, plums, drinking Port, their daughters wearing French fashions to attend concerts at the theaters."[7] The prototype of the slave master's wife, the Donas Brites,

Donas Franciscas, Donas Genebras, the heavy women of wide hips, responsible for culinary knowledge, for the maintenance of the house and the care for the sick, was now outdated. Those women had been the *Iaiás*[8] in charge of the stability of European civilization in Brazil. The society based on shared food, typical of the dining table of sugar plantations, where guests, travelers and peddlers, plantation overseers and priests, whole families from other sugar plantations sat together, was being abandoned. Freyre, however, goes beyond a mere description of those changes imposed by the decline of a rural world, a faded portrait of the demise of the sugarcane, of sugar itself and of slavery in Brazil, at a time when the country was attempting to keep pace with European capitalism. With the precision of an anatomist, Freyre examines the first signs of this change within a body of data which, today, we would call representations. These representations, it must be said, would be capable of taking on board regional, social and racial features, "often responsible for changing other aspects of the status of the same representations," as the author claimed.[9]

From seemingly fragmented elements, namely physical or psychological behavior, value or symbolic systems, conscious or unconscious motivations, Freyre seeks to reconstitute the historical realities of a recently urbanized country in its totality. His magnifying glass was the human body.

He focused, for example, on the inhabitant of Bahia, who would only move in a slovenly fashion on sedan chairs carried by slaves. He focused on the *gaúcho*, agile and muscular while riding his country horse, as well as on the moving body of the southern ranch owner dancing to *fandango* and on the sway of the Rio mulatto, a freed slave, dancing to the chords of the first *samba*. He described the body of the rich city dweller, who was a regular consumer of goods from abroad, including *petits-pois*, raisins, cod, tea, beer and of "civilized" medicines, such as the *Guilhie* anti-cholera potion or *Le Roy* pills. In contrast, he described the body of the poor, of the country yokel, of the inhabitant of the outskirts of the big city, who sought cures by means of herbs and prayers, regular eaters of pumpkin and *bagres*, a type of fish which was regarded as inferior, popularly known as "old mulatto." Freyre depicted the differences between those who slept on beds, a signal of social refinement, and those who rocked to sleep in hammocks. Social value was linked to those items imported from bourgeois Europe, which gave origin to new life-styles opposed to those which were "rural or even patriarchal." Going to the theater replaced the church service; the sword and the whip were replaced by the walking stick; the urban mansions and the shanties slowly took the place of the masters' houses and slave compounds. Western society, encapsulated in the upsurge of machines, British assets and French fashions were now, in the nineteenth century, shaping Brazilian image, thus squeezing out habits such as the head massage known as *cafuné*, the hot bath, women's long black hair styles, all leftovers of the Moorish domination over the Iberian Peninsula.

Freyre criticized superficial interpretations which tended to attribute cultural tensions to "class struggles." He was, in fact, a keen observer of what Roger Chartier (1990) later termed "representation struggle."[10] Freyre's analysis of the appropriation that both African-Brazilians and whites made of the image of Saint George, for example, is a fine sample of the use of an interdisciplinary approach to both history and anthropology. In other words, while the white masters made the image of Saint George on horseback an icon of social conservatism, because it pointed towards the domination of elites who rode horses over the inferior layers of society, the "blacks, in contrast, who were less peaceful and did not conform to their condition of oppressed race," interpreted Saint George as a representation of *Ogum*, the African divinity of war and revenge, a warrior saint who, in the same manner as the catholic saint, carried a sword.[11] Freyre deals as brilliantly with the outcome of these representational tensions, namely, the emergence of the educated African-Brazilian, "well-dressed, behaving like gentle folk, turning white for all social matters."[12] This is a kind of snapshot—at the time of the introduction of the daguerreotype in Brazil—of miscegenation, which left the constrained space of the slave compound to settle in the big city.

In *The Mansions and the Shanties*, Freyre transforms public thoroughfares, dwellings and the human body into historical objects, by highlighting the infinite number of combinations involving individuals and the space surrounding them. He does more. In a pioneering manner, he makes an inventory of the mechanisms used by various groups of society in order to appropriate the changing coastal cities. He casts light on places and means of communication as he investigates the exchanges undertaken between the home and the street, and between Brazil and Europe.

As he turns these topics into historical objects, Freyre in no way wishes to reduce them to a single specific and definitive image. His work avoids imposing a watertight and conclusive discourse, thus showing that he is also a pioneer in this respect. In contrast, Freyre teaches us to creep into the crevices of urban buildings with the help of varying documents. It is these crevices, no more than chinks, which allow us to observe the spasms and paradoxes of historical scholars, to hear either their silent confessions or their wordy discourses. By using varied historical sources, Freyre allows us to visit a coherent object, a live being, that is, the urban space for the practice of activities that are both a system of invention and systems of implicit defense. Such activities, in turn, give rise to aesthetic and emotional practices. Hair styles, clothes, the use of objects, all mirror different sexual behaviors, masculine and feminine ways of appropriation. They also respond both to the frailties and to the economic power of the black, white and mulatto, without ever erasing their differences and harshness. We know that a good historian is the one who exposes the forms and structures of social situations by studying their temporal evolution and underlining their continuities and ruptures. Freyre goes beyond that, as he resuscitates the rhythm of lives long gone and the history of their destinies, their gestures, their uncertainties and their hopes.

Notes

* While writing this essay I counted on the support granted by FAPERJ, which allowed me to teach a graduate course at the History Departament at Pontifícia Universidade Católica in Rio de Janeiro.

[1] On this topic, see Freyre, *A Casa Brasileira*, and *Oh! de Casa*.

[2] This idea was borrowed from Miranda, "Casa, Corpo, Mundo Brasileiro." I would like to thank José Mario Pereira for making me aware of this study.

[3] See Sennet, *Flesh and Stone*.

[4] The word *sobrado* has been correctly translated as "mansion," in the title of Freyre's work, *The Mansions and the Shanties*. However, *sobrado* can also be interpreted as a two-story townhouse, including, as hinted at by the author, its use as a brothel. (Translator's note).

[5] Freyre, *Sobrados*, vol. 1 xxxiii.

[6] Alencastro 7.

[7] Freyre, *Sobrados*, vol. 1 22.

[8] *Iaiá* was the form of address used by the slaves to refer to the wife of the sugar plantation owner. (Translator's note)

[9] Freyre, *Sobrados*, vol. 2 369.

[10] See his classic *A História*.

[11] Freyre, *Sobrados*, vol. 2 504.

[12] Freyre, *Sobrados*, vol. 2 602.

Works Cited

Alencastro, Luís Felipe. Ed. *História da Vida Privada no Brasil: Império: A Corte e a Modernidade Nacional.* São Paulo: Companhia das Letras, 1997.

Chartier, Roger. *A História Cultural entre Práticas e Representações.* Lisboa: Difel, 1990.

Freyre, Gilberto. *Sobrados e Mucambos. Decadência do Patriarcado Rural e Desenvolvimento do Urbano.* 1936. 6th ed., 2 vols. Rio de Janeiro: José Olympio Editora, 1981.

———. *The Mansions and the Shanties. The Making of Modern Brazil.* Trans. Harriet de Onis. New York: Knopf, 1963.

———. *A Casa Brasileira.* Rio de Janeiro: Grifo, 1971.

———. *Oh! de Casa.* Rio de Janeiro: Artenova; Recife: Instituto Joaquim Nabuco de Estudos Sociais, 1979

Miranda, Maria do Carmo Tavares. "Casa, Corpo, Mundo Brasileiro." *Sobrados e Mucambos, Entendimento e Interpretação.* Ed. Edson Nery da Fonseca. Recife: Fundação Joaquim Nabuco Editora Massangana, 1996. 19-32.

Sennet, Richard. *Flesh and Stone—The Body and the City in Western Civilization.* London: Faber & Faber, 1996.

MARY DEL PRIORE

The Origins and Errors of Brazilian Cordiality[1]

João Cezar de Castro Rocha

Translated by Shoshanna Lurie

In 1936 two fundamental books on the history of Brazilian culture were issued. On the one hand, Sérgio Buarque de Holanda published *Raízes do Brasil* [*Roots of Brazil*], a work Antonio Candido considered an instant classic from the moment of its appearance.[2] On the other, Gilberto Freyre continued the study of the formation and decadence of the patriarchal family with *Sobrados e Mucambos* [*The Mansions and the Shanties*]. The coincidence of the dates of publication encourages a parallel study of the two texts. However, Brazilian critics tend to compare *Raízes do Brasil* and Gilberto Freyre's masterpiece *Casa-Grande & Senzala* [*The Masters and the Slaves*], which also received instant recognition. In this essay, I will call this consecrated reading into question. I believe that a richer comparison can be made between *Raízes do Brasil* and *Sobrados e Mucambos*. Since this is not the most common approach, I need to justify my proposal. First, it is worth recalling that *Raízes do Brasil* was the first volume in an important collection coordinated by Gilberto Freyre for the publisher José Olympio, "Coleção Documentos Brasileiros." Freyre also wrote the book's forward, though it concentrated primarily on outlining the aims of the collection. In fact, in the five pages of the Forward, duly titled "Documentos Brasileiros," only one paragraph is dedicated to Sérgio Buarque de Holanda, and instead of an analysis of the content of the book, Freyre stresses the intellectual qualities of its author.

Raízes do Brasil and *Sobrados e Mucambos* share a thematic affinity that is often overlooked. Gilberto Freyre's book contains the revealing subtitle: "Decadence of the Rural Patriarchy in Brazil." Thus, unlike (in) *Casa-Grande*

& Senzala, in which Freyre described the process of "formation of the Brazilian family under the regime of patriarchal economy" (as the subtitle informs), in *Sobrados e Mucambos* he narrated the progressive replacement of the codes of the rural world with the laws of the urban universe. In the author's own expression, with the development of conditions of urbanization, especially during the course of the nineteenth century, the street began to assert its interests before the abuses of the *casa-grande.* The street progressively imposes its rights on the house, instead of simply accepting its will and whims. At the same time, the development of urbanization occurs parallel to the social ascension of the mulatto to such an extent that it seems fair to say that *Sobrados e Mucambos* is a book composed of two intimately related axes: the historical victory of the street over the house and the social success of *mestiçagem* (miscegenation). In other words, if in *Casa-Grande & Senzala* Freyre offered a vast panorama of the formation of Brazilian society under the influence of the rural patriarchy, in *Sobrados e Mucambos* the author studied the social accommodation that took place with the decay of that patriarchy.

Similarly, in *Raízes do Brasil,* Holanda studied the formation of Brazilian society and, above all, the disappearance of the patriarchal family. If the first chapters of his essay are dedicated to identifying the historical roots of that formation, the last two chapters seek to investigate the arrival of a new society, whose principal novelty was precisely overcoming the patriarchal family. This family was the result of Portuguese heritage and contained a pair of characteristics that became fundamental to the establishment of Brazilian society. The most important consisted of the patriarchal family members' resistance to the laws of universal nature characteristic of the modern State. As this is the crucial point of Holanda's argument, it is worth illustrating through the analysis of a key concept.

In Chapter V of *Raízes do Brasil,* entitled "The Cordial Man," Holanda described the essay's best-known concept—cordiality as a type of sociability developed within Brazilian historical conditions. In my proposed reading of *Raízes do Brasil* and *Sobrados e Mucambos,* the discussion of this concept is fundamental. I will attempt to demonstrate that in the last sixty years a curious hermeneutic was produced in Brazilian critical tradition: while critics attribute the concept to the work of Holanda, they tend to interpret it according to Freyre's orientation. However, first I will briefly present the theory propounded by Holanda.

The patriarchal family views itself as self-sufficient. Its members limit the final destiny of deeds and intentions to the domestic circle. A vast network of friendships guarantees the broadening of the circle, given that it reinforces its power as well as affirms its functionality. Characteristic of the rural environment, this is a family whose relatives and immediate circle comprise their own universe, with their own rules and codes. Summing up, the patriarchal family often finds itself in historical conditions in which the defining features of modernity did not take root. For this reason, "it was not easy for those in charge of professional positions of responsibility, educated in this environment, to understand the distinction between the private and the public spheres."[3] As a consequence, the modern ideal of abstraction—implied in the universal character of the rules of the public sphere, an extension of the necessarily impersonal principles that should govern the State, whose limited number of resources has ideally to serve the entire population—meets an almost insurmountable obstacle in the patriarchal order. In its extreme, this order can represent a serious impediment to the "modernization" of society, according to an European viewpoint.

The cordial man is the legitimate son of the patriarchal family and the study of the etymology of the concept is very useful for this discussion. "Cordial" is derived from *cor, cordis*: "heart" in Latin. Under the control of his feelings, the cordial man refuses the characteristics of the modernization of social life, since, living by impulse, he always takes into account the function of private interests. Among these are the affection devoted to his friends and the hate bestowed upon his enemies. Through the saying that is still commonly used to this day, Brazilians show themselves to be within this logic: "*For friends, everything; for enemies, the law.*" In a cordial society, universal principles cease to be a right and become an authentic punishment for those who don't occupy the superior ranks of the multiple hierarchies that organize social exchanges, or for those who don't have contacts in the centers of power.[4]

For this reason, the cordial man is unfamiliar with the moderation of general rules and nothing bothers him more than the search for the middle ground, since he bases his behavior on the interpretation of a complex series of hierarchies. A man of extremes, he hates *and* loves with the same intensity; he desires *and* refuses at the same time; he is greedy *and* generous in the same action—above all, when he operates with public funds that, after all, he understands as also being legitimately his. In addition, as the abstraction of

JOÃO CEZAR DE CASTRO ROCHA

laws imposed by a distant State seems an unnecessary fiction to him, the cordial man can work as the Argentine of Jorge Luis Borges' essay: "The State is impersonal: the Argentine only conceives of personal relations. For this reason, stealing public funds is not a crime to him. I verify a fact; I neither justify nor excuse it."[5]

This is only one aspect of Holanda's analysis. Brasílio Sallum's keen remark should not be forgotten: in *Raízes do Brasil,* "one wishes to identify which past was then being overcome and which embryonic future was contained in that historical present."[6] After establishing the formative elements of Brazilian society, Holanda concentrated his efforts on the radical change that urbanization would bring with its development. On the occasion of a debate with Cassiano Ricardo,[7] the underlying assumption of the essay was clarified: "the cordial man is probably destined to disappear, if he hasn't already completely disappeared."[8] Holanda was less interested in the concept of the "cordial man" than in understanding that cordial relations had no future in the absence of the defining conditions of the rural world. Thus, the growth of cities and the progressive displacement of the rural population to urban centers would lead to the virtual disappearance of cordiality, since it would lose the glue holding it in place: the patriarchal family. It is as if in *Raízes do Brasil,* with an extraordinary power to synthesize, Holanda simultaneously approached the formation of the patriarchal family—the topic of *Casa-Grande & Senzala*—and its disappearance, the topic of *Sobrados e Mucambos.* However, Holanda's imagination seems much more fascinated with the "new times" promised by the phenomenon of urbanization than with investigating the "rural heritage."[9] In Antonio Candido's formulation, "Holanda not only clarified our history, but he foresaw the immediate future."[10] I find the first justification for the approach I propose in this elective affinity.

The concept of the cordial man provides the second justification. In the two books published in 1936, the concept of cordiality performs an important function. Curiously, it has been generally neglected that the two books proposed very distinct meanings for the same concept—although Gilberto Freyre seemed to believe that his assimilation of the concept was faithful to the author of *Raízes do Brasil.* Later critical studies only consider the presence of the concept in Holanda's work. However, as I have already pointed out, their hermeneutic produces a very particular miscegenation, attributing the concept to Holanda, but interpreting it according to Gilberto

JOÃO CEZAR DE CASTRO ROCHA

Freyre's conception. In order to achieve a more adequate understanding of what I suggest here, I must sketch an archeology of the concept.

In a letter to Alfonso Reyes in 1931, Ribeiro Couto called "cordial civilization the attitude of emotional tendencies born of the fusion of Iberian man with the new land and primitive races."[11] Of course, the baptism of the "cordial civilization" belongs to the poet. However, the idea according to which the originality of the Brazilian historical process should be sought in the productive encounter between the Portuguese, the Indigenous, and the African in the lands of the New World was formulated in a nineteenth-century text. In 1840, the "Brazilian Historical and Geographical Institute," under the immediate protection of the emperor Pedro II, organized an international competition, offering an award for the scholar who would present the best plan to narrate national history.[12] Karl Friedrich von Martius won the prize with his monograph "How the History of Brazil Should Be Written."[13] Of what did his project consist? He who wished to guarantee a place for Brazil among Western nations should point out the true novelty represented by the history of this immense tropical country. According to Martius, an epic adventure occurred in Brazilian territory during the centuries of colonization, and the historian must explain the nature of that epic. Generous with the future researcher, the German scholar didn't refrain from revealing its nature. "For this reason, a crucial point for the reflexive historian to demonstrate is how the conditions for the perfection of the three human races that are located side by side in this country in a way unknown in Ancient History are established in the successive development of Brazil, and that they should reciprocally serve as a means and as an end."[14] The races can play a complementary role, but the direction of the process is reserved for the European race—for the Portuguese: "We will never be allowed to doubt that Providence's will destined this mixture to Brazil. Portuguese blood, in a powerful river, should absorb the small tributaries of the Native and African races."[15] In reality, the importance of Martius' essay for the constitution of Brazilian social thought still merits more in-depth research—and at this time it will suffice to point out the possibility.[16] For example, in his classic *Retrato do Brasil*, above all in the *post-scriptum*, Paulo Prado not only celebrated *mestiçagem*, but also mentioned the German's text on various occasions: "This was the brilliant vision that Martius had of our history, while he suggested the study of the three races for its full understanding."[17]

With some prudence, it is not difficult to recognize that this idea is closer to Freyre's vision than to Holanda's conception. Basically, it attempts to identify the origin of Brazilian sociability in the phenomenon of *mestiçagem*. Isn't it true that Freyre structured the text of *Casa-Grande & Senzala* in a way that reminds one of Martius' suggestions? In individual chapters of his masterpiece, the Portuguese, the Native, and the African contributions to the constitution of Brazilian society are studied. In addition, the function of guiding thread in the process is attributed to the Portuguese. Ronaldo Vainfas has recently remarked the link between Martius' essay and Freyre's masterpiece, rereading the German's contribution as the first moment in which the cultural consequences of *mestiçagem* were explicitly acknowledged. Moreover, in Martius' project the "question of ethnic and cultural *mestiçagem* was already at stake."[18] Nonetheless, it is important to recognize that in the 1970s José Honório Rodrigues had clearly stressed the role of Martius' essay in the tradition of Brazilian thought, and even its repercussion in *Casa-Grande & Senzala*, with due emphasis.[19] However, it is equally important and indispensable to highlight the fundamental difference between Martius and Freyre. The German understood the process as the historical and (above all) *racial* synthesis that defines *mestiçagem* as the Brazilian contribution to civilization. Conversely, the Brazilian was interested in studying the historical and (above all) *social* complex of the formation of the patriarchal family that is also based on *mestiçagem*, but understood mainly as a technique of shared living (*"convivência"*). In Martius' text, *mestiçagem* is above all a racial phenomenon, whereas in Freyre's it is mostly a cultural trait.

In *Sobrados e Mucambos, mestiçagem* and cordiality are clearly associated with one another: "congeniality à la *brasileira...*; the 'cordiality,' to which Ribeiro Couto and Holanda refer,[20] that congeniality and cordiality emerge mostly from the mulatto... The Comte de Gobineau himself, who always felt so uncomfortable among Pedro II's subjects, seeing them all as decadent as a result of *mestiçagem*, recognized the supreme cordial being in the Brazilian: *très poli, très accueillant, très aimable.*"[21] Explicit in this paragraph is that Freyre considered cordiality from a dual perspective: on the one hand, as the result of the process of the formation of the society itself, that is, of *mestiçagem*; on the other, as an index of a specific practice of social relationships. In other words, cordiality was a "technique of courteousness" (*"técnica de bondade"*),[22] and as such constituted a typically Brazilian trait. This is what Cassiano Ricardo asserted in his polemic with Holanda about

JOÃO CEZAR DE CASTRO ROCHA

the meaning of the concept. For the poet, "everything in Brazil was created this way, through mediation (…). When that balance between antagonisms Freyre spoke of is upset, mediation has its turn. In the balance of antagonisms, one antagonism feeds the other. In the mediation, antagonisms peacefully destroy each other."[23] Because of this, the characterization of the cordial man as someone who lives between extremes seemed unacceptable to him. Thus, and in a straightforward way, cordiality is related to *mestiçagem*, since in both cases we would be faced with a form of balancing opposing poles until their conversion into a new median point. In the end, cordiality becomes a synonym of Brazilianness as soon as the originality of the Brazilian historical process is defined as the ability to develop a means of harmonious shared living in the cradle of differences. *Mestiçagem* would have done this in relation to the birth of the Brazilian people, while cordiality would have in regards to the establishment of Brazilian sociability.

The same concept in *Raízes do Brasil* has a very different intonation. First, it is worth recalling that, unlike Freyre's position, Holanda opposed cordiality to politeness and included both love as well as hate among typically cordial reactions, as we saw earlier.[24] In other words, the Comte de Gobineau's quotation, employed by Freyre as a confirmation of his understanding of Brazilian cordiality, would be considered an interpretive error by Holanda. Understanding the nature of the misunderstanding is the best way to clarify his conception. Though the expression has its origin in Ribeiro Couto, the theoretical inspiration came from another German author, Carl Schmitt. Holanda illustrated this in a note in the second edition of the book.[25] In Chapter 3 of *The Concept of the Political*, also in a note, Schmitt established the meaning of the defining terms in his understanding of the political,[26] in other words, the difference between friend and enemy, based on the separation between the public and private spheres. Holanda appropriated the concept faithfully: "Hatred can be as cordial as friendship, since both emerge from the *heart*, originate in the intimate, domestic, private, sphere… Hatred, being public and political, and not *cordial*, would more precisely be called hostility."[27]

Holanda never associated the social phenomenon of cordiality with the historical process of *mestiçagem*. On the contrary, he identified its origin in the patriarchal family, in the "rural heritage," whose patterns of sociability suppose the transposition of the private sphere onto the public. The cordial man must also be understood as a Weberian ideal type: he would be formed within a social formation characterized by the hypertrophy of the private sphere and by the predominance of personal relations. That is, cordiality should not be understood as an exclusively *Brazilian* characteristic, but rather as a structural trait that develops in societies whose public space faces serious difficulties asserting its autonomy from the private sphere. The concept of cordiality can become an important analytical instrument for the analysis of any social group endowed with a high degree of self-centeredness and therefore somewhat resistant to external pressure.

I am suggesting that criticism has considered Holanda's notable sociological intuition only as an interpretation of the Brazilian social formation, without realizing its relevance for the theoretical debate.[28] Of course, the author of *Raízes do Brasil* sought to offer an interpretation of the country, as the title of the book itself suggests. However, have we sufficiently understood the breadth of his ideas? Let us read his words: "The idea of a type of immaterial and impersonal entity, floating above individuals and controlling their destinies is difficult for the people of Latin America to imagine. It is common to imagine that we have an appreciation of democratic and liberal principles when, in truth, we fight for one personalism against another."[29] Neither have we been able to identify the affinity between Holanda and Jorge Luis Borges: "The Argentine, unlike North Americans and almost all Europeans, doesn't identify with the State. This can be attributed to the circumstance that in this country governments tend to be terrible or to the general fact that the State is an inconceivable abstraction; that the Argentine is an individual, not a citizen, is certain."[30] And what can we say of the Peruvian sociologist Joaquín Capelo's perception in 1902, anticipating Holanda's observation? While he sought to justify the absence of political parties with a coherent political project in his country, he concluded: "In Perú… every party is personal; their only objective is the elevation of a determined person to power: the *caudillo* to profit and make a living based on each one of his allies."[31] Passages with similar content demonstrate the main divergence between Holanda's and Gilberto Freyre's uses of the concept of cordiality while they help to clarify the reason that the curious hermeneutic miscegenation mentioned earlier was produced in Brazil.

In *Sobrados e Mucambos*, most clearly in the last chapter of the book, cordiality appears as a homology for *mestiçagem* at the social level. In this sense, it is worth pointing out that the structural transformations described by Freyre, which had implications for the decay of the rural patriarchy, did not threaten the permanence of cordial relations. On the contrary, the nineteenth century, according to Freyre, was also the moment of the ascension of the mulatto, the cordial man *par excellence*. In other words, in Freyre's interpretive framework, cordiality is confused with nationality: *the cordial man is the Brazilian himself.*

In *Raízes do Brasil* everything occurs in a very different way. Growing urbanization doesn't only threaten the survival of cordial relations, but condemns them to an inexorable disappearance. Thus, Holanda has no special appreciation of the figure of the cordial man, preferring to concentrate on the changes due to the phenomenon of urbanization. In other words, in Holanda's interpretive framework, cordiality isn't confused with nationality but emerges as a valuable tool for describing the historical constellation dominated by the patriarchal family: *the cordial man is but the symptom of rural heritage.*[32]

In spite of such discrepancies, a particular reading has managed to dominate the tradition of Brazilian intellectual thought. Usually, the concept of cordiality is solely attributed to Holanda's work, as if in the same 1936 Freyre had not proposed an alternative conception that in truth agreed much more with Ribeiro Couto's definition. In this sense, Cassiano Ricardo's quotation in which he mentioned Gilberto Freyre and his idea of "balancing antagonisms"—used by Freyre to define the social dynamic of the pair composed of *casa-grande* and *senzala*—is symptomatic.[33] This citation reveals that Freyre's conception has much more affinity with a certain image of Brazilian culture, whose vocation would be to mediate conflict and not to face it head on.[34]

Nevertheless, although the concept of cordiality is only attributed to Holanda, the more common understanding of the concept is psychological and associates cordiality with friendliness, congeniality, and emotional availability. In other words, the concept is attributed to Holanda, but the interpretation that triumphed was Freyre's understanding! How has this reading been possible, and how is it still common today? Another reading will illustrate this. Some critics have the habit of criticizing Holanda's concept as ideological because the cordial man is *also* violent, as if in the text of *Raízes do Brasil* there were some incompatibility between cordiality and violence. As we saw earlier, the opposite is true. The cordial man *also* has to be violent, since he lives at the mercy of feelings imposed on him by his heart. However, to accept this reasoning would be to abandon a fantasy: "Now, the cordial enemy does not define the Brazilian. It is not having the capacity to be an enemy, cordial or otherwise. This absence of hate, of prejudice."[35] With a very cordial irony (according to Ribeiro Couto, Gilberto Freyre and Cassiano Ricardo's definition), the uncomfortable gaze that Holanda directed toward Brazilian history was not so much faced as mediated through the *topos* of our fundamental congeniality. Noble savages or cordial men, we will probably continue reading *Raízes do Brasil* with the concept of cordiality found in *Sobrados e Mucambos*, since this concept is more in tune with the tradition of Brazilian culture. And like the Argentine in Borges' essay, we probably won't see anything condemnable in this gesture.

Perhaps the authors' different perspectives and above all, the interpretive mixture that emerged in relation to the concept of cordiality, help to illuminate the course of the editions of *Raízes do Brasil*. Holanda introduced a series of changes between the first and second editions, continuing to present them in the third edition.[36] These changes have two basic orientations. On the one hand, the author added some notes, with the objective of substantiating his arguments with new data. This was the historian who, upon rereading the essay from his youth, decided to provide it with a more academic tone. On the other hand, Holanda altered or simply eliminated passages in which he had highly praised Gilberto Freyre's work.[37] This was the thinker who hoped to assert the originality of his ideas. To conclude this essay, I will limit myself to one example. In the first edition, the reader finds the following evaluation of *Casa-Grande & Senzala*: "a work that represents the most serious and complete study of the social formation of Brazil . . ."[38] In the second edition, published in 1947, the comment disappears—the long passage haling Freyre is completely eliminated, as is the forward he wrote for the first edition of *Raízes do Brasil*. Doubtless, Holanda's reaction was drastic. However, isn't more than a generation of readers' obstinate hermeneutic *mestiçagem* even more scandalous?

Notes

[1] I would like to thank Enrique Rodríguez Larreta, Guillermo Giucci, José Mario Pereira and Moema Vergara for their suggestions and especially for their criticism.

[2] Candido, "O Significado" XL. In this famous essay, Candido enumerated the three works that played a decisive role in his generation's formation: *Casa-Grande & Senzala* (1933), by

Gilberto Freyre, *Raízes do Brasil* (1936), by Sérgio Buarque de Holanda and *Formação do Brasil Contemporâneo* (1942), by Caio Prado Jr.

[3] Holanda 105.

[4] For an analysis of sayings and underlying social hierarchies, see Roberto DaMatta, *Carnavais, Malandros e Heróis. Para uma Sociologia do Dilema Brasileiro* (Rio de Janeiro: Editora Guanabara, 1979).

[5] Borges 36.

[6] Sallum 238.

[7] With delectable irony, Dante Moreira Leite observed: "The concept of the cordial man provoked a curious, and cordial, debate between Sérgio Buarque de Holanda and the poet and essayist Cassiano Ricardo." Leite 290.

[8] Holanda 146

[9] Titles from the definitive edition of *Raízes do Brasil*. The opposition was even clearer in the first edition, since two chapters were titled "The Agrarian Past."

[10] Candido, "A Visão Política" 88.

[11] Couto 1987.

[12] The award was announced as follows: "A gold medal in the value of 200,000 réis to the person who presents the most correct Plan for how to write the ancient and modern History of Brazil, organized with a system in which its political, civil, ecclesiastical, and literary parts are included." *Revista do Instituto Histórico e Geográfico Brasileiro* vol. II (1840): 628.

[13] The monograph was published in 1845 in the *Revista do Instituto Histórico e Geográfico Brasileiro*. A more recent edition is Martius 1982.

[14] Martius 89.

[15] Martius 88.

[16] See Martius' novel, *Frey Apollonio. Um Romance do Brasil* (written in 1831, first published in 1992), in which he fictionally anticipated some of the ideas about the (im)possibility of a Brazilian civilization.

[17] Prado 195. On another occasion, Paulo Prado defined Martius' text as a "masterful thesis" (186).

[18] Vainfas 8.

[19] Rodrigues 130-142. "Martius was the first to stress the importance of the contribution of the three races in Brazilian history. He was the first to say that it would be a mistake (...) to reject the contribution and the efforts of the Indigenous population and of imported Africans" (130). "Varnhagen's work method was almost exclusively carrying out material research of the facts Martius pointed out to be important and meaningful" (132). "And for the first time, Martius' old plan... was fully carried out. If Varnhagen followed the plan, he only did so in collecting material, but it was Freyre who brought together and related the facts with a general characterization of Brazilian society and the Brazilian family, demonstrating a great interpretive ability" (142).

Vainfas stresses the discontinuity between Martius' suggestion and the tradition of Brazilian historiography. According to Vainfas, Freyre is the first to unfold the consequences of Martius' essay.

[20] Freyre again mentioned Holanda as the necessary reference when employing the concept of cordiality: "The 'desire to establish intimacy,' which Sérgio Buarque de Holanda considers so characteristic of the Brazilian and with which he associates the characteristic of using diminutives which is so much ours—that serves, he says, to 'create familiarity with objects.'" Freyre 358.

[21] Freyre 356-57.

[22] Cassiano Ricardo employed this expression in his debate with Holanda. "That the Brazilian (when more polished) knows to take advantage of courteousness, and that technique can be called the 'technique of courteousness.'" Ricardo 22.

[23] Ricardo 31, 33.

[24] Faoro notes that "cordial doesn't mean agreeable, dull, but it also encompasses hatred" (62).

[25] Note 157, 106-107 of the edition used here.

[26] Schmitt 55, n. 5. There is an English edition: *The Concept of the Political.* Trans., introd., and notes by George Schwab; with comments on Schmitt's essay by Leo Strauss. New Brunswick: Rutgers UP, 1976.

[27] Holanda 107.

[28] I have partly proposed this hypothesis in "Brasil" 17.

[29] Holanda 138.

[30] Borges 36.

[31] See Kristal 41.

[32] "Finally, I want to point out again that cordiality itself does not seem to me a definitive and exact virtue that must prevail without taking into account the changeable circumstances of our existence. I believe that, at least in the second edition of my book, I have clarified this. In truth, I associate cordiality with the particular conditions of our rural, colonial life that we are rapidly overcoming." Holanda 145.

[33] On the notion of "balancing antagonisms" in Gilberto Freyre's writing, see Araujo, *Guerra e Paz.*

[34] See Ricardo: "All Brazilian revolutions are ended in agreements, and the strictest punishment for our political crimes has never surpassed exile" (41). This was not the case of the dictatorship of Getúlio Vargas' "Estado Novo" (1937-1945) and of the military dictatorship begun in 1964, sadly renowned for their violent repression of political adversaries.

[35] Ricardo 43.

[36] See Rocha, *Literatura* 164-66, in which the changes that refer to the relationship between Holanda and Freyre are stressed.

[37] Though he introduced important changes, Freyre maintained the references to Holanda's work in later editions of *Sobrados e Mucambos.*

[38] Holanda 105, 1st ed.

Works Cited

Araujo, Ricardo Benzaquen de. *Guerra e Paz:* Casa-Grande & Senzala *e a Obra de Gilberto Freyre nos Anos 30.* São Paulo: 34 Letras, 1994.

Borges, Jorge Luis. "Nuestro Pobre Individualismo." *Otras Inquisiciones. Obras Completas,* vol. II. 1952. Buenos Aires: Emecé, 1989. 36-37.

Candido, Antonio. "O Significado de *Raízes do Brasil.*" *Raízes do Brasil.* Sérgio Buarque de Holanda. 1967; Rio de Janeiro: José Olympio, 1989. xxxi-xl.

———. "A Visão Política de Sérgio Buarque de Holanda," *Sérgio Buarque de Holanda e o Brasil.* Ed. Antonio Candido. São Paulo: Editora Fundação Perseu Abramo, 1998. 81-88.

Couto, Ribeiro. "Carta a Alfonso Reyes."1931. *Revista do Brasil* 3.6 (1987): 30-31.

DaMatta, Roberto. *Carnavais, Malandros e Heróis. Para uma Sociologia do Dilema Brasileiro*. Rio de Janeiro: Editora Guanabara, 1979.

Faoro, Raymundo. "Sérgio Buarque de Holanda: Analista das Instituições Brasileiras." *Sérgio Buarque de Holanda e o Brasil*. Ed. Antonio Candido. São Paulo: Editora Fundação Perseu Abramo, 1998. 59-70.

Freyre, Giberto. *Sobrados e Mucambos. Decadência do Patriarcado Rural no Brasil*. São Paulo: Companhia Editora Nacional, 1936.

Holanda, Sérgio Buarque de, *Raízes do Brasil*.1936. Rio de Janeiro: José Olympio, 1987.

Kristal, Efraín. *Una Visión Urbana de los Andes. Génesis y Desarrollo del Indigenismo en el Perú*. 1988. Lima: Instituto de Apoyo Agrario, 1991.

Leite, Dante Moreira. *O Caráter Nacional Brasileiro. História de uma Ideologia*. 1954. São Paulo: Livraria Pioneira Editora, 1969.

Martius, Karl Friedrich von. "Como se Deve Escrever a História do Brasil," *O Estado de Direito entre os Autóctones do Brasil*.1845. São Paulo / Belo Horizonte: Editora da USP / Livraria Editora Itatiaia, 1982. 85-107.

———. *Frey Apollonio. Um Romance do Brasil*. 1831. São Paulo: Brasiliense, 1992.

Prado, Paulo. *Retrato do Brasil. Ensaio sobre a Tristeza Brasileira*. 1928. Ed. Carlos Augusto Calil. São Paulo: Companhia das Letras, 1998.

Ricardo, Cassiano. "O Homem Cordial." *O Homem Cordial e outros Pequenos Estudos Brasileiros*. Rio de Janeiro: Ministério da Educação e Cultura, 1948. 5-46.

Rocha, João Cezar de Castro. *Literatura e Cordialidade. O Público e o Privado na Cultura Brasileira*. Rio de Janeiro: EdUERJ, 1998.

———. "Brasil Nenhum Existe," *Caderno Mais!, Folha de São Paulo*, 9 January 1999.

Rodrigues, José Honório. *Teoria da História do Brasil. Introdução Metodológica*. São Paulo: Companhia Editora Nacional, 1978.

Sallum, Brasílio. "*Raízes do* Brasil." *Introdução ao Brasil. Um Banquete no Trópico*. Ed. Lourenço Dantas Mota. São Paulo: Editora Senac, 1999. 237-256.

Schmitt, Carl. *O Conceito do Político*. 1932. Rio de Janeiro: Vozes, 1992. *The Concept of the Political*. Trans., introd., and notes by George Schwab; with comments on Schmitt's essay by Leo Strauss. New Brunswick: Rutgers UP, 1976.

Vainfas, Ronaldo. "Colonização, Miscigenação e Questão Racial: Notas sobre Equívocos e Tabus da Historiografia Brasileira." *Tempo* 8 (December 1999): 7-22.

JOÃO CEZAR DE CASTRO ROCHA

Literature

Theater of the Impressed:
The Brazilian Stage in the Nineteenth Century

Ross G. Forman

Brazilian theater scholarship has traditionally regarded the nineteenth century as a dead zone, a period in which the theater was dominated by visiting foreign productions or slavish imitations of foreign methods and styles. This essay, however, seeks to challenge this assumption and to suggest how theater entered into the project of nation-building by providing a forum for discussion—among the elites—of topics such as slavery, the corruption of politics, the tension between the metropolitan and the rural, and resistance to the economic imperialism and gunboat diplomacy of European nations such as Britain. Whatever the aesthetic merits of the products of Brazilian theater at this time, and however twentieth-century Brazilian theater has been seen as disembodied from a historical corpus, the role theater played in the field of cultural production during the nineteenth century merits recuperation. The prominence of plays with abolitionist themes, such as João Julião Federado Gonnett's *O Marajó Virtuoso, ou os Horrores do Tráfico da Escravatura*, an historical drama exploring the horrors of the Middle Passage and partly extolling the virtues of the Portuguese, Brazilians, and British in fighting the cruel Spaniards who promote the slave trade, suggests how invested Brazilian theater of the period was in the issues of the day, as well as its implication in the liberal traditions of the urban elites, whose interests often conflicted with those of the landowners supporting the slavocracy.

The nineteenth-century Brazilian stage remains relatively unknown to modern audiences, and critical appraisal of it as debased and dated has helped obscure its revival. From Brazilian scholarship—such as Manuel Bandeira's *A Brief History of Brazilian Literature* (1958), which argues that there was no dramatic tradition at all in the country, and J. Galante Sousa's canonical *O Teatro no Brasil* (1960)—to scholarship published in North America and Europe—such as *The Cambridge History of Latin American Literature* (1996)—Brazilian theater consistently plays second fiddle to other literary forms and nearly always suffers under the labels of "derivative" and "imitative."[1] Nineteenth-century Brazilian theater, in fact, is the example that has come to serve as the epitome of Sílvio Romero's statement that

> we Brazilians are a highly mediocre people; and I do not know whether the anathema of the British historian exaggerates things a bit in saying, when describing our great natural resources, 'much is the flow and abundance of life by which Brazil is marked from all other countries of the earth. But amid all the pomp and splendour of Nature, no place is left for Man.'[2]

Or as Machado de Assis elegantly puts it, writing in 1873, "There is no Brazilian theater today, no national plays are being written, and it is even more rare for a national play to be performed... Today when public taste has reached the ultimate level of decadence and perversion, there is no hope for anyone who feels they have the vocation to compose serious works of art."[3]

More recently, scholars have looked to the Brazilian stage in an effort to construct a history of the flourishing scene of the late-twentieth century and to insert Brazilian theater into a more general literary teleology of nationalism and development. Edwaldo Cafezeiro and Carmem Gadelha, for instance, in their suggestively titled *História do Teatro Brasileiro: Um Percurso de Anchieta a Nelson Rodrigues* (1996), open their work with the statement, "We are studying, from the point of view of dramaturgy, the political realities that Brazilian society produced in its fight for liberation. In this respect, the story of Brazilian theater traveled a parallel path to that of Brazilian history."[4] This Brazilian theater was inherently national and nationalistic in that, whatever its form and wherever the actors performing hailed from, the staging of dramatic spectacles evolved along with the nation and began at the moment of decolonization. As Chichorro da Gama explains in *Através do Teatro Brasileiro* (1907), "Up to the time of Independence, Brazil did not have what could be called a theater of its own."[5] Although this teleology may not be as straight-forward as Cafezeiro, Gadelha, Chichorro da Gama, and others imply, here I want to isolate the mid to late nineteenth-century as a crucial moment for Brazilian dramatics because of its absorption into, or implication in, related projects of nationalism. These projects may lack historical continuity both with the past and the future of the Brazilian stage, but they suggest that the importance of theater in nineteenth-century Brazil has been downplayed unnecessarily. These projects embrace the literary, in the development of Romanticism and Naturalism (José de Alencar, for instance, was both a novelist and playwright); the political, in the royal patronage of certain kinds of theatricals; the economic, in the expansion of venues and forms both within the capital of Rio de Janeiro and in such regional centers as Salvador da Bahia, Recife, and, later, São Paulo; and even the architectural, in the construction of theaters as part of the overall remodeling of Rio as a national capital and in conjunction with the flourishing era of the "tropical *belle époque*." Moreover, while not denying that much Brazilian theater of this period was derivative or performed by foreign actors and amateurs (even including visiting officers of the British Royal Navy, who in the 1860s gave a performance attended by the emperor and his family), I follow Homi Bhabha and others in suggesting that mimicry itself can be a powerful mode of resistance and reconstitution, an enabling mechanism for the staging of uniquely Brazilian concepts of subjectivity.[6]

In his seminal work *Lições Dramáticas*, João Caetano, the most famous dramaturge of the nineteenth century, explains the importance of theater to a nation that is developing both its resources and its sense of identity. He argues for a state-supported theater, performing in Portuguese, that will serve as an outlet for local talent and as a corrective to the standard imported European product performed in Italian or French or translated into (the lesser language of) Portuguese.[7] Caetano's first and foremost "lesson" is the premise that one can tell the state of a nation by its theater. Like Augusto Boal, Caetano credits theater with radical powers to instruct audiences in particular ways, and thus to construct citizenship; however, unlike Boal, he conceives of this citizenship in normative bourgeois terms: "Theater, when well-organized and well-directed, ought to be a real model for education, capable of inspiring youth to patriotism, morality, and good manners; and, either for this or other reasons, cultivated nations have done their best to perfect it…"[8] Caetano therefore calls for the government to provide funding for a school, where actors can be trained to fulfill this educational role—a school which is to do for Brazilian theater what the Brazilian government ostensibly is doing in other realms: to effect "rapid progress, as is its due," and to achieve the autonomy and the "certain level of perfection" that other artistic forms have attained under the Empire. It is an appeal, of course, for financial support—and one which ultimately failed. Yet it is also an appeal to a notion of positivism and a theory of development under an enlightened monarch under which Brazil stands to overcome its inferiority complex with respect to Europe and take its rightful place among the world's great nations. Caetano concludes his work with a "Minute about the Necessity of a Dramatic School to Train People Who Dedicate Themselves to a Theatrical Career, Also Proving the Utility of a National Theater As Well As the Defects and Decay of the Current Situation," which implicitly ties the fate of the theater to the fate of the nation, suggesting that a country which does not publicly support theater is in danger of the decline and decadence that forms the binary opposite to the state's motto and vaunted goal of "order and progress."[9]

Historians often have followed Caetano by conceiving of him as the key force behind the emergence of indigenous theater in nineteenth-century Brazil: as the first director to create a fully Brazilian troupe, to encourage and stage works by Brazilian intellectuals, and to interpret in a truly original way the works of foreign writers such as Shakespeare.[10] His company made its debut in Niterói, a suburb of Rio de Janeiro, in the 1830s with the now-lost *O Príncipe Amante da Liberdade ou Independência da Escócia* (Cafezeiro and Gadelha 116). Caetano also owes his place in history to his successful promotion of the playwright José Carlos Martins Pena, the "Brazilian Molière"[11] heralded as the most important national playwright of the period. Martins Pena's works are credited with being the first to open a space for Brazilian drama on stage, an opening on which subsequent authors were then able to capitalize. Critics have also conceived of the failure of Caetano's bid to open a school and provide a permanent venue for national theater as a signal of Brazil's continued concession of cultural authority to the West and of the ultimate triumph of imitation over innovation.[12] According to this line of reasoning, Caetano was, in fact, the exceptional genius who proved the pervasive influence of mediocrity. As the periodical *O Espectador*, an "organ consecrated to the dramatic arts," noted while commemorating the twentieth anniversary of the great dramaturge's death on August 26, 1883, "His name is that of the respected and popular artistic genius who disappeared after so many triumphs into the obscure arms of the tomb."[13]

The real picture, of course, is somewhat more complicated, suggesting that to a certain degree the image of Brazilian drama as culturally and aesthetically inferior stems as much from a desire on the part of more recent critics to assert their own anxieties about inferiority as it does from the actual inferiority of the work itself. A comparison with nineteenth-century British theater may be apt here, since its primary forms, such as melodrama, were also considered to be debased and inferior. The notion of what constitutes "good theater," i.e. European theater, is thus always located in a more remote historical past—a historical past that Brazil, which only became a nation during the nineteenth century, can never lay claim to. A similar dialectic has functioned in the twentieth century and continues to function in the twenty-first; through Beckett, Brecht, and others, Europe as center continues to assert its influence over theater as a "high cultural" form in Brazil.[14] Moreover, as Harold Bloom suggests in *The Anxiety of Influence* (1973), the creative itself evolves out of patterns of misprision and misrepresentation. Conceived accordingly, Martins Pena's imitation of the European "comedy of manners" produces new theatrical forms precisely in its failure to successfully replicate the European—a point made abundantly clear by a late, unfinished play about a rake written while the author was in Britain; the play is set in Britain, and entirely about British characters, among them the Duke, Sir Tockley, and Davidson Max-Irton, whose names and situations appear comical when juxtaposed with the lived experience of nineteenth-century Brazilians.

Thus the analysis of nineteenth-century Brazilian theater as purely derivative occludes a real richness in the context of the period and in the context of dominant forms of theater in Europe. Brazil enjoyed a more varied and older theatrical tradition than most other Latin American nations. Although theaters catered mainly to the elites, there were more theaters in Brazil than in many other places in the continent, as well as a greater dispersal of theaters or theatrical productions across the Empire.[15]

The first theaters flourished after the removal of the royal court to Rio de Janeiro in 1808, following Napoleon's invasion of Portugal, when Rio became the capital of the Portuguese Empire. Given the small population of the educated elite, a successful play in Rio might be performed only ten or twelve times, with additional performances in later months.[16] For much of the nineteenth century, Brazilian theater did survive, in financial terms, on visiting foreign troupes and slavish imitations and translations of popular European works, mainly French or Italian, or, by the 1880s, even Shakespeare plays translated from the French. A good example of this type of work is the

Barão de Cosenza's *Os Doidos Fingidos* (1869), a "European" comedy, performed by an Italian company, and set abroad.

Yet parallel to this international tradition were national writers whose works signaled the ultimate failure of the imported to dominate the stage and dictate taste, as well as the need for local theater to respond to local conditions. These writers' works may not have been able to claim the same number of performances in theaters across the country, or may have been considered minor because of their interest in burlesque and farce ("lower" forms of theater that were also an important part of the repertoire in European centers). However, in retrospect, they belie the notions that Brazilians chose to express themselves solely through other media, especially the novel. Several major authors now considered canonical for their novels also wrote for the stage. Joaquim Manuel de Macedo, best known for *A Moreninha* (1844), also advanced his abolitionist program through dramas such as *Cobé* (1849).

Perhaps the most noteworthy feature of Brazilian theater during this period is that it alone had the ability to respond quickly and publicly to political and cultural events in the country. For example, Manoel de Araújo Porto-Alegre's *A Estátua Amazônica: Comédia Arqueológica* topically lampoons the Count of Castlenau's "discovery" of an Amazonian figurine which he believed proved the existence of an ancient, great civilization in Brazil. A. de Castro Lopes' *Meu Marido Está Ministro*, presented at the Teatro Ginásio and published in 1864, comments particularly on the instability of governments at this particular moment and the cronyism and corruption that dominated Imperial politics. Similarly, Joaquim José da França Júnior's *Caiu o Ministério*, which appeared in late 1882, narrates events of a cabinet that controlled the government from January to July of that same year.[17] Earlier in the century, a number of plays—among them the 1850 *Os Ingleses no Brasil* by a writer who called himself Lopes de la Vega—hit the stage in response to Britain's passage of the "Aberdeen Act" in 1845, which gave the British Navy wide powers of search and seizure over Brazilian ships suspected of involvement in slave trading. The war between Brazil and Paraguay provoked compositions such as Francisco Corrêa Vasques' *O Brasil e o Paraguai: Cena Patriótica o.d.c. aos Defensores da Pátria pelo Artista Francisco Corrêa Vasques* (1865), a monologue delivered by "Sr. Brasil" in defense of his country and ending with a recitation of the national anthem. The rapidity with which plays could be penned and produced thus allowed theater to follow the press in discussing the immediate affairs of the state, which for a variety of reasons (including publishing constraints) could not easily appear in other literary genres like the novel.

The political, economic, or social influence of foreigners also formed an important theme for the nineteenth-century stage, providing as it did a perfect backdrop for scapegoating non-Brazilians and thus asserting the legitimacy of a Brazilian identity.[18] Oftentimes, images of foreigners (particularly the British) centered on their false promises of industrialization. Martins Pena's *Os Dois, ou o Inglês Maquinista* (1845), for example, revolves around a British entrepreneur aptly named Gainer, who tries to promote his marvelous invention of a process that turns bones into sugar—in one of the world's largest sugar producing economies. Macedo's *A Torre em Concurso* (1863) similarly pokes fun at the Brazilian middle classes's love affair with all things or persons European. In this play, a Brazilian town without any foreign residents holds a competition open only to Englishmen to select a builder for a public project, prompting much farce when a slew of Brazilians pretend to be Englishmen in order to gain the commission. França Júnior's *Caiu o Ministério* itself centers around the figure of Mr. James, who proposes to build a railway line up Corcovado to be run by teams of dogs on treadwheels. (When the play was written, the government had just authorized two Brazilian engineers to build a railway up the mountain in what was to be the country's first railroad for the purposes of tourism.)[19] The rejection of this sort of plan by França Júnior and his audiences—along with the rejection of Mr. James's planned act of miscegenation with the character of Beatriz—is a plea for Brazil to overcome its acritical acceptance of European or American superiority in technical or cultural realms. Thus, although ideologically more conservative, França Júnior shares with the late 1920s *anthropophagy* modernist movement the notion that Brazil needs to ingest and regurgitate what it had taken from the Old World to develop its own voice.

Stereotyping foreigners as a method of establishing a hegemonic Brazilian subjectivity appears in a variety of other sources, where it is advanced principally (though not exclusively) through language. In these works, linguistic incompetence marks other, more fundamental forms of incompetence and permits the assertion of the Brazilian voice as the voice of mastery. The comedy and farce engendered by linguistic and cultural misunderstandings proves not just an organizing principle for such plays, but also a means of imposing mimicry as a technique or problem of the (loosely defined) colonizer, rather than the colonized. At the same time, it upholds Bloom's image of misprision as a creative force, in that this misprision generates the plots and comic situations of these plays, but it transfers real creative power to the Brazilians who are not themselves engaged in acts of misprision. *O Holandês, ou Pagar o Mal que não Fez* (1856) features a Dutchman named Kolk whose comic inability to understand Portuguese is taken advantage of by characters at the inn where he is staying as they successfully extort money out of him by calling into question his sexual propriety. Turning on its head traditional Brazilian notions of hospitality, the play suggests that those who cannot and will not work to understand Brazilian customs and language are fair game; it is the revenge of the Brazilian (importantly figured as lower-class in this example) in the economic dialectic between colonizer and colonized.

These plays are particularly interesting in the way in which they circumvent marriage between the Brazilian and foreign characters (and consequently assimilation). Macedo's *Luxo e Vaidade* (first performed in 1860) satirizes the French servant Petit and the English servant Fanny, who constantly complain in their comical Portuguese about Brazil—Fanny's refrain is "este não se úse n'Ingliterre" ("This no way is it in England")—and who only stay in the employ of their Europe-obsessed Brazilian family because of their affection for each other. The natural destiny of the foreigner is for other foreigners, thus maintaining the integrity of Brazilian society by closing its bloodlines to outside influences in acts of cultural endogamy. Even França Júnior's later play *O Defeito de Família*, performed at the Fênix Dramática in 1870, scorns assimilation through the portrayal of the servant Ruprecht Somernachtstraumenberg, whose dramatic bungling of the Portuguese language is reminiscent of the comic effect produced by the character Dogberry in Shakespeare's *Much Ado About Nothing*. Ruprecht represents an articulation of population shifts within Brazil that saw increasing immigration from Germany, Italy, and Switzerland, calling into question notions of essential Brazilian identity through birth and Portuguese heritage, but the play comes down on the side of maintaining cultural integrity. In the topsy-turvy world that these playwrights evoke, the European and not the Brazilian gets marked as inferior, inept, and impoverished through mimicry. The audience, meanwhile, is both within and outside of Bhabha's spectacle of hybridity through the final insistence on resistance to that which is most fundamental for producing hybridity—sexual union.

Ultimately, these plays and their essentializing of both Brazilians and foreigners point to some of the limitations of nineteenth-century Brazilian theater which are, in historical terms, almost as important as its achievements. First, the limited number of venues in which plays could be performed and their attendance by upper middle-class Brazilians primarily of Portuguese origin meant that audiences generally were confined to members of various elites. As a result, writers tailored their social and political critiques to issues pertinent to an educated, influential milieu, effectively preventing the popularization of theater that occurred in some European countries, such as Britain, with the growth of the music hall. This notion of audience also points to the (often direct) implication of these authors in the governing of the country: Martins Pena earned his living as a diplomat, while Alencar served as a senator. Thus, on a fundamental level, theater succeeded in fulfilling Caetano's vision of government sponsorship by effectively functioning as an extension of the bureaucratic apparatus. Second, because theater as an institution was located primarily in cities, dramatists produced specifically metropolitan products, oftentimes restricting the settings of their plays to the Rio environs familiar to their spectators. The metropolitan focus may help explain the relative absence of the rural plantation or jungle settings so popular in other forms of Brazilian literature—not to mention the conspicuous absence of the "Indian" in drama in comparison to his notable presence in such forms as the novel.[20] Third and finally, the very speed and ease with which the topical and the political could be staged meant that Brazilian theater dated quickly and allowed it to fall into obscurity, and hence justify aesthetic notions of inferiority based on the premise that good art is unbounded by the parameters of time and cultural context.

Nevertheless, reappraising nineteenth-century Brazilian theater on its own terms and through its historical and cultural context, rather than an aesthetic one, leads to the following conclusion: whatever its limitations, the Brazilian stage lived and lives on. "History lies," Antonio José Domingues proclaims in the sonnet he wrote in homage of João Caetano. Caetano and the boards he paced "did not die" and have not been sealed in the tombs of time. Instead, readers and critics are left, like Domingues, to listen for the reverberation of their echo in the auditorium: "Can you not hear that powerful voice on the stage, / Carrying its conviction deep into your soul?"[21]

Notes

1 See Bandeira, *Brief History of Brazilian Literature*, trans. Ralph Edward Dimmick (Washington, DC: Pan American Union, 1958); J. Galante de Sousa, *O Teatro no Brasil*, 2 vols. (Rio: Insituto Nacional do Livro, 1960); Severino João Albuquerque, "The Brazilian Theater up to 1900," *Cambridge History of Latin American Literature* (Cambridge: Cambridge UP, 1996). 240-260. See also Adam Versényi's *Theater in Latin America* (Cambridge: Cambridge UP, 1993), which ignores Brazil entirely, and Clovis Bevilaqua's "O Teatro Brasileiro e as Condições de sua Existência," *Épocas e Individualidades: Estudos Literários* (Recife: Livraria Quintas, 1889) 87-115. All translations of works in Portuguese are my own.

2 Romero 157. Romero's quotation comes from Henry Thomas Buckle, *History of Civilization in England*, vol. 2. (London: John W. Parker, 1857) 95.

3 Assis 24.

4 Cafezeiro and Gadelha 10. Cafezeiro and Gadelha follow Melo Morais Filho and Sílvio Romero in positing seventeenth-century Jesuit *autos* and Anchieta's medieval mystery plays as the origin of Brazilian theater, despite the 250-year hiatus that followed.

5 Gama 5.

6 See Helen Gilbert and Joanne Tompkins, *Post-colonial Drama: Theory, Practice, Politics* (London: Routledge, 1996) and their discussion of the specific markers of post-colonial drama, located in notions of performativity.

7 For background on Caetano's position as the most important figure in Brazilian theater, see Macedo: "João Caetano shined like a genius, and [was] the meteorite of the Brazilian drama scene" (512).

8 Caetano, "Duas Palavras ao Respeitável Público" np.

9 Writes Caetano, "Under such conditions, national theater will never be able to equal that of foreign theaters, and will continue to vegetate, pulling it down to the indifference into which it has fallen and finds itself reduced; it calls out therefore for a prompt and decisive reform" (75).

10 Responding to criticism in Caetano's own period and subsequently that his work was derivative and showed an interest mainly in Italian, French, and British forms of theater, Roberto Seidl comments, "And if in fact he did little for a truly Brazilian theater, we must remember that this 'little' was 'everything' that it was in his power to do" (n.p.).

11 Caetano himself coined the sobriquet "Brazilian Molière" to refer to Martins Pena (Lições 73).

12 Veríssimo colludes in the notion of the inferiority of the Brazilian product, calling Martins Pena's work "vulgar" and concluding that Martins Pena "helped Magalhães and others to start a Brazilian theater and to initiate a national comedy. Certainly he initiated it as an inferior form" (64).

13 See also Moraes Filho: João Caetano was "Brazil's greatest actor"; "incomparable to this date, without model and masters, João Caetano achieved everything by the force of his talent, [and] sought to accomplish everything through the miracle of his genius" (12).

14 Street theater and the project of people like Boal and his *Teatro do Oprimido* group form an obvious "low culture" alternative in this explicitly bourgeois system of categorization.

15 A quick glance at regional newspapers confirms this view. During the Christie Affair, a diplomatic debacle between Brazil and Britain in the mid-1860s, the periodical *O Jequitinhonha* reported on the production of and printed the script of a short play entitled *John Bull*, suggesting that Brazilian theater had the potential to reach citizens outside major urban centers. See *O Jequitinhonha* 3.104 (7 February 1863) and 3.105 (14 February 1863) for reports of the production and the script of the play.

[16] See Faria 106.

[17] See Barman 252.

[18] See Cafezeiro and Gadelha: "Brazilian comedy, laughing at the oppressors, marks and signals the path of independence, which entails both a critique [of oppression] and the capacity to formulate new alternatives" (211).

[19] See Semenovitch 17-19.

[20] Agrário Menezes' *Calabar* (1859) is a poignant exception to this rule of Indian absence, as is Brazil's most famous theatrical export, Carlos Gomes' *Il Guarany* (1870), an opera based on Alencar's novel *O Guarani* and dealing specifically with originary constructions of identity interpolated through the indigene. See Doris Sommer, "*O Guarani* and *Iracema*: A National Romance (Con)Founded," *Foundational Fictions: The National Romances of Latin America* (Berkeley: U of California P, 1991) 138-171.

[21] Domingues 3.

Works Cited

Assis, Machado de. "Instinto de Nacionalidade." published in *O Novo Mundo* (1873) reprinted in *Crítica por Machado de Assis*, ed. Mário de Alencar. Rio de Janeiro: Livraria Garnier, 1924. 7-28.

Barman, Roderick J. "Politics on the Stage: The Late Brazilian Empire as Dramatized by França Júnior," *Luso-Brazilian Review* 13.2 (Winter 1976): 240-260.

Bloom, Harold. *The Anxiety of Influence*. New York: Oxford UP, 1973.

Caetano, João. *Lições Dramáticas*. Rio de Janeiro: Typ. Imp. e Const. de J. Villeneuve & C., 1862.

Cafezeiro, Edwaldo and Carmem Gadelha. *História do Teatro Brasileiro: Um Percurso de Anchieta a Nelson Rodrigues*. Rio de Janeiro: Editora UFRJ/ EDUERJ/ FUNARTE, 1996).

Cosenza, Barão de. *Os Doidos Fingidos: Comédia em Dois Actos*. Rio de Janeiro: Tipografia Imp. e Const. de J. Villeneuve & C., 1869.

Domingues, Antonio José. "João Caetano de Santos." *A Época: Periódico Literário, Crítico e Poético*, 1.5, 4 July 1863.

Faria, João Roberto. *O Teatro Realista no Brasil: 1855-1865*. São Paulo: Editora da Universidade de São Paulo, 1993.

França Júnior, Joaquim José da. Teatro de França Júnior. Ed. Edwaldo Cafezeiro. 2 Vols. Rio de Janeiro: Serviço Nacional de Teatro/Fundação Nacional de Arte, 1980.

Gama, A. C. Chichorro da. *Através do Teatro Brasileiro*. Rio de Janeiro: Livraria Luso-Brasileira, 1907.

Gomes, A. Carlos. *Il Guarany*. Milan: n.p., 1870.

Gonnet, João Julião Federado. *O Marajó Virtuoso, ou os Horrores do Tráfico da Escravatura*. Rio de Janeiro: Np, nd.

———. *O Holandês ou Pagar o Mal que Não Fez*. Rio de Janeiro: Tipografia Dois de Dezembro de Paula Brito, 1856.

Lopes, A. de Castro. *Meu Marido Está Ministro*. Teatro do Doutor A. de Castro Lopes. Vol. 1. Rio de Janeiro: Tipografia do Imperial Instituto Artístico, 1864.

Macedo, Joaquim Manoel de. *Ano Biográfico Brasileiro*, (1876): 509-515.

————. *Teatro Completo*. 2 Vol. Rio de Janeiro: Ministério da Educação e Cultura, Fundação Nacional de Arte, Servico Nacional de Teatro, 1979.

Menezes, Agrario de Souza. *Calabar.* Drama em Verso, e em 5 Actos. Bahia: Tipografia e Livraria de E. Pedroza, 1859.

Moraes Filho, Melo. *João Caetano* (*Estudo de Individualidade*). Rio de Janeiro: Laemmert & C., 1903.

Pena, Luís Carlos Martins. *Teatro de Martins Pena.* 2 Vols. Ed. Darcy Damasceno, 1956.

Porto-Alegre, Manoel de Araújo. *A Estátua Amazônica.* Comédia Arqueológica Dedicada ao Illm. Sr. Manoel Ferreira Lagos. Rio de Janeiro: Tipografia de Francisco de Paula Brito, 1851.

Romero, Silvio. *A Literatura Brasileira e a Crítica Moderna* (Rio: Imprensa Industrial, 1880.

Seidl, Roberto. *João Caetano 1808-1863* (*Apontamentos Biográficos*). Rio de Janeiro: n.p., 1934.

Semenovitch, Jorge Scévola de. *Corcovado: A Conquista da Montanha de Deus.* Rio de Janeiro: Editora Lutécia, 1997.

Vasques, Francisco Corrêa. *O Brasil e o Paraguay.* Cena Patriótica O.D.C aos Defensores da Pátria pelo Artista Francisco Corrêa Vasques. Rio de Janeiro: Tipografia Popular de Azeredo Leite, 1865.

Veríssimo, José. "Martins Pena e o Teatro Brasileiro." *Revista Brasileira* 4.15 (July 1898): 47-64.

Gonçalves Dias

José Luís Jobim

The Brazilian postcolonial period began in 1822, and an entire generation of writers was responsible for creating a national literature. Gonçalves Dias (1823-1864) belongs to this generation, together with some other important writers, including Joaquim Manuel de Macedo (1820-1882), Bernardo Guimarães (1825-1884) and José de Alencar (1829-1877). Their primary aim was to evidence the difference between the old metropolis and the emerging nation. Thus, they chose to focus on Brazilian themes—nature, the Natives, the way of doing things, etc.—and highlighted the differences between Portuguese and Brazilian ways of writing and speaking Portuguese.

Born in a small town in northeastern Brazil, Gonçalves Dias was the son of a Portuguese shopkeeper and a mestizo woman. During his childhood he worked in his father's shop, but later he was sent to study Law at Coimbra University, then the most prestigious higher education institution in Portugal. After graduating in 1844, he returned to Brazil and, after a short stay in Maranhão, settled down in Rio de Janeiro, then Brazil's most important city. There, he made a career as a public servant, first as a teacher, later as an expert in ethnography and education, appointed to scientific missions in his own country and abroad.

Primeiros Cantos (1847), his first book, brought him early recognition, and he was praised as an example of what the literature of the new nation should be. Even the well-known Portuguese writer Alexandre Herculano said: "*Primeiros Cantos* is a beautiful book, it is the inspiration of a great poet" (Dias, *Poesia* 99). It is little wonder that Gonçalves Dias would in later editions publish Herculano's review as a preface to his *Primeiros Cantos*.

His subsequent publications further confirmed his reputation and made him one of the most distinguished Brazilian poets of his time. Nevertheless, although he had a successful career, his personal life was chaotic. He fell in love with the cousin of his best friend, Ana Amélia Ferreira do Vale and wanted to marry her, but her mother would not accept him. He then married another woman, Olímpia Coriolana da Costa, but they were not happy together; as a result, he made himself available for traveling all over the country and abroad on scientific missions, which kept him away from home for long periods at a time. In 1864, while he was returning from one of these missions in Europe, there was a shipwreck. Everyone survived, except for Gonçalves Dias.

Gonçalves Dias' Poetry

Although Gonçalves Dias was the author of a number of ethnographic essays, literary criticism and plays, he is mostly known today for his poetry. As a poet, he managed to achieve a special blend of nationalism and personal inflection. Very early in his career, he claims in the introduction to *Primeiros Cantos* that he had written the poems for himself, not for other people. If his work happened to please others, it would please him, but if not, he would be satisfied with just having written them.

Because he did not want to follow conventional rules, he also said it was his personal preference to have no symmetrical stanzas in his poems. Instead of following the traditional norms, he decided to take advantage of whatever rhythmical resources seemed to suit his objectives (*Poesia* 103). In fact, he had a deep knowledge of Portuguese poetic conventions and a talent to explore new ways of writing. He was thus able to produce some of the most original poems in Brazilian literature in terms of rhythmic and musical texture. This is also why his poems are so difficult to translate without losing this original quality. Therefore, I will only provide literal translations of the lines that I specifically will analyze; otherwise I will quote the poems in Portuguese.

Perhaps his most famous poem is "Canção do exílio," a perfect example of this blend of nationalism and personal inflection, and also of the poet's musical skills:

Canção do Exílio

Kennst du das Land, wo die Citronen blühen,
Im dunkeln Laub die Gold-Orangen glühen,

Kennst du es wohl?—Dahin, dahin!
Möcht' ich...ziehn.
Goethe[1]

Minha terra tem palmeiras,
Onde canta o Sabiá;
As aves, que aqui gorjeiam,
Não gorjeiam como lá.

Nosso céu tem mais estrelas,
Nossas várzeas têm mais flores,
Nossos bosques têm mais vida,
Nossa vida mais amores.

Em cismar, sozinho à noite,
Mais prazer encontro eu lá;
Minha terra tem palmeiras,
Onde canta o Sabiá.

Minha terra tem primores,
Que tais não encontro eu cá;
Em cismar—sozinho, à noite—
Mais prazer encontro eu lá;
Minha terra tem palmeiras,
Onde canta o Sabiá.

Não permita Deus que eu morra,
Sem que eu volte para lá;
Sem que desfrute os primores
Que não encontro por cá;
Sem qu'inda aviste as palmeiras,
Onde canta o sabiá. (*Poesia* 105)

Coimbra - Julho 1843

This poem is one of the single most influential pieces of writing in Brazilian literature and has been repeated, quoted or re-written by many important authors since then. Let me provide a selection of these instances.

Casimiro de Abreu

Se eu tenho de morrer na flor dos anos,
Meu Deus! Não seja já;
Eu quero ouvir na laranjeira, à tarde,
Cantar o sabiá! (Abreu 51)

Oswald de Andrade

Minha terra tem palmares
onde gorjeia o mar
os passarinhos daqui
não cantam como os de lá. (Andrade 82)

Murilo Mendes

Minha terra tem macieiras da Califórnia
onde cantam gaturamos de Veneza. (Mendes 31)

Carlos Drummond de Andrade

Meus olhos brasileiros se fecham saudosos,
Minha boca procura a "Canção do exílio",
Como era mesmo a "Canção do exílio"?
Eu tão esquecido de minha terra...
Ai terra que tem palmeiras
onde canta o sabiá! (Andrade 6)

Um sabiá
na palmeira, longe.
Estas aves cantam
um outro canto. (Andrade 94-5)

Although the title "Canção do Exílio" may suggest a period of imposed exile, Gonçalves Dias had not been banished from his own country when he wrote it. In fact, he was in Portugal of his own free will, studying at Coimbra University. When he uses the words "*aqui*" / "*cá*" ("here") he is, of course, referring to Portugal, while "*lá*" ("there") refers to Brazil. So, the word *exile* in the title expresses the feelings of separation from one's country, and the desire to return there someday: "Não permita Deus que eu morra, / Sem que eu volte para lá" ("Oh God, don't let me die / without going back there").

The epigraph is taken from the first stanza of Goethe's "Mignon" and refers to a paradisiacal place where lemon and orange trees grow abundantly offering their fruits. Of course, in Dias' poem, this idyllic place shares many qualities with his homeland.

The poem is structured on a comparison between what can be found *here* (in Portugal) and *there* (in Brazil). But the result of this comparison is the obvious valorization of the qualities of Dias' own country. Notice the use of the word "mais" ("more"): "Nosso céu tem mais estrelas, ("Our sky has more stars") / Nossas várzeas têm mais flores ("Our meadows have more flowers") / Nossos bosques têm mais vida, ("Our forests have more vitality") / Nossa vida mais amores ("Our life more affection"). In short, Dias' country has a perfection that he cannot find in Portugal.

It is also interesting to note the use of first person pronouns either in the singular ("*eu*", "*minha*") or in the plural "*nossa*" ("our"). The singular forms "*eu*" ("I") and "*minha*" ("my") highlight the subjectivity of the assertions and their relation to the individual who declares that he feels better at night in his homeland and does not want to die in Portugal. But the plural form "*nossa*" ("our") emphasizes a national "imagined community," as described in Benedict Anderson well-known book *Imagined Communities*, which also encompasses the virtual addressee of the poem. Perhaps we could say that this plural form is addressed to an intended unitary subject that is to be recognized as the Brazilian people, which is perhaps why the poem became a sort of national anthem.

Nevertheless, whenever one speaks of nationalism in Gonçalves Dias' work, one of the first things to be mentioned are his poems inspired by the Native Brazilians. It is necessary, therefore, to say something about Dias' participation in the literary movement known as *Indianismo* that sought to make the Native Brazilian the prototype of a national hero.

Gonçalves Dias' *Indianismo*[2]

The first Portuguese document describing their arrival in Brazil is a letter from Pero Vaz de Caminha to his king, in which he reports that the Natives were "colored naked men, without anything to cover their genitals."[3] But he also said they meant no evil in walking around naked, because they showed their bodies as naturally as their face. He credited this to their innocence.[4]

Caminha's expedition sent two Native Brazilians to Europe, and Gonçalves Dias interpreted this as a sign of what the Portuguese conquest would be. He said the vessel assigned to inform the king about the New World had taken those Natives to Portugal against their will; ever since then, taking possession of Brazilian territory would imply a continuous attack on the Natives, performed by "colonos degredados." In other words, criminals recruited in Portuguese prisons to board the vessels and to settle down in the conquered land, or by men of vicious character who came to Brazil only to unfold their perverted nature.[5]

In fact, Gonçalves Dias became part of a group of writers (Gonçalves de Magalhães, José de Alencar and others) who decided to adopt the Native as a national hero. These writers generally try to represent the Native as the authentic offspring of Brazil—that is, as the one who has always lived on the land and fought heroically against the Portuguese.

Of course, the first thing these writers had to do was to react against an inherited tradition of Portuguese and European documents that represent the Native as inferior. Gonçalves de Magalhães (1860) had claimed that when a study of the history of a conquered people is restricted to documents expressing the point of view of the conqueror, who is always interested in justifying his course of action, the true story of the victims can never be adequately known.[6] Magalhães thus argues that "the documents written about Native Brazilians must not be accepted as they are, but must be critically read."[7]

Gonçalves Dias' most well-known poem about the Portuguese conquest, written from the point of view of the Natives, is probably *O Canto do Piaga*. Piaga is the word that designates a priest whose function, among other things, is to give advice to the tribe concerning the course of future actions to be taken. He is supposed to have magic powers to speak in the name of gods. He is also supposed to receive messages from the gods in his dreams and to interpret the signs of nature.

In the poem, a ghost comes to the the *Piaga's* cavern and tells him that *Anhangá*, the evil spirit, will not allow him to see the signs of nature anymore and will also obstruct his dreams:

Tu não viste nos céus um negrume
Toda a face do sol ofuscar;
Não ouviste a coruja, de dia,
Sons estrídulos torva soltar?

Tu não viste dos bosque a coma
Sem aragem—vergar-se e gemer,
Nem a lua de fogo entre nuvens,
Qual em vestes de sangue, nascer?

E tu dormes, ó Piaga divino!
E Anhangá te proíbe sonhar!
E tu dormes, ó Piaga, e não sabes,
E não podes augúrios cantar?! (*Poesia* 109-110)

If the *Piaga* had not been under the influence of *Anhangá* he would certainly have paid attention to the darkness on a sunny day, the shrill of an owl in broad daylight and the trees bending when there was no wind. But the evil spirit did not even allow him to dream. *Anhangá* is a devil associated with the Portuguese. In *Piaga*'s dreams, the conqueror is shown as coming from the sea to kill the Native warriors and take away their wives and daughters.[8] He will bring slavery to the tribe, and even the *Piaga* will become their slave:

Vem trazer-vos algemas pesadas,
Com que a tribo Tupi vai gemer;
Hão de os velhos servirem de escravos,
Mesmo o Piaga inda escravo há de ser! (*Poesia* 111)

In the nineteenth century, Europeans justified the annihilation of Native groups in the name of "progress," rather than in the name of religious salvation, as they had previously done. Dias seems to predict the destiny of the Natives in their encounter with European civilization. In his unfinished poem *Os Timbiras*, he claims to be the voice of an extinct people, whose grave encompasses all of South America, from the Andes Mountains to the Prata and the Amazon Rivers:

. . . —Chame-lhe progresso
Quem do extermínio secular se ufana;
Eu modesto cantor do povo extinto
Chorarei nos vastíssimos sepulcros,
Que vão do mar ao Andes, e do Prata
Ao largo e doce mar das Amazonas (Dias, *Os Timbiras* 5).

In his opinion, the continent was better off before the sea and the wind brought the chains and the evil men from Europe:

> América infeliz, já tão ditosa
> Antes que o mar e os ventos não trouxessem
> A nós o ferro e os cascavéis da Europa?! (*Poesia* 530)

Of course, in Dias' time, mostly owing to the movement of Independence from Portugal (1822), there seems to have been a renewed interest not only in the identity of Brazil, but also in rethinking the colonial past through new approaches that differentiate it from the former metropolis. Gonçalves Dias' poetry could not escape from being influenced by the issues of his time. Indeed it is exactly this fascinating aspect that he represents, namely, that of the indisputably great *national* poet who tries to articulate the experiences, feelings and aspirations of his people.

Notes

[1] Ramos has provided the following translation of Goethe's poem: "Conheces a região onde florescem os limoeiros? / Laranjas de ouro ardem no verde-escuro da folhagem? / ... Conheces bem? Lá, lá / Eu quisera estar." (Ramos 64)

[2] Since the Native Brazilian is called in Portuguese "*índio*," the romantic movement grounded on the celebration of the Indigenous heritage was given the name "*Indianismo*."

[3] "... homens pardos todos nus sem nenhuma coisa que lhes cobrisse suas vergonhas" (Caminha 87).

[4] "Andam nus sem nenhuma cobertura, nem estimam nenhuma coisa cobrir nem mostrar suas vergonhas, e estão acerca disso com tanta inocência como têm em mostrar o rosto" (Caminha 88).

[5] "O primeiro navio destacado da conserva para levar a Portugal a notícia do descobrimento do Brasil, e com instâncias ao rei de Portugal para que por amor da religião se apoderasse d'esta descoberta, cometera a violência de arrancar de suas terras, e sem que a sua vontade fosse consultada, a dois índios, ato contra o qual se tinham pronunciado os capitães da frota de Pedro Álvares. Fizera-se o índice primeiro do que a história da colônia: era a cobiça disfarçada com pretextos da religião, era o ataque aos senhores da terra, à liberdade dos índios; eram colonos degradados, condenados à morte, ou espíritos baixos e viciados que procuravam as florestas para darem largas às depravações do instinto bruto" (Dias, "Brasil e Oceania" 274).

[6] "Quando no estudo da história, religião, usos e costumes de um povo vencido e subjugado outros documentos não temos além das crônicas e relações dos conquistadores, sempre empenhados em todos os tempos a glorificar seus atos com aparências de justiça, e a denegrir as suas vítimas com imputações de todos os gêneros; engano fora se cuidássemos achar a verdade e os fatos expostos com sincera imparcialidade, e devidamente interpretados" (Magalhães 3).

[7] "Os documentos escritos sobre os indígenas do Brasil devem ser julgados pela crítica, e não aceitos cegamente" (Magalhães 3).

JOSÉ LUÍS JOBIM

[8] O colonizador aparece nos sonhos do piaga—o feiticeiro da tribo—saindo das "entranhas das águas" num "marinho arcabouço" (a caravela), e vem "matar vossos bravos guerreiros, / Vem roubar-vos a filha, a mulher!" (Dias, *Poesia* 110)

Works Cited

Abreu, Casimiro de. *Poesias Completas*. São Paulo: Saraiva, 1961.

Anderson, Benedict. *Imagined Communities*. London: Verso, 1991.

Andrade, Carlos Drummond de. *Reunião*. Rio de Janeiro: José Olympio, 1973.

Andrade, Oswald de. *Poesias Reunidas*. Rio de Janeiro: Civilização Brasileira, 1972.

Caminha, Pero Vaz de. *A Carta de Pero Vaz de Caminha*. 1500. 4th ed. Rio de Janeiro: Agir, 1990.

Cesar, Guilhermino. *A Contribuição Européia: Crítica e História Literária*. Vol. 1 in *Historiadores e Críticos do Romantismo*. Rio de Janeiro/São Paulo: LTC/EDUSP, 1978.

Dias, Antonio Gonçalves. "Brasil e Oceania; Memória Apresentada ao Instituto Histórico e Geográfico Brasileiro e lida na Augusta Presença de Sua Majestade Imperial." *Revista Trimestral do IHGB* (Rio de Janeiro) 3rd trim. (1867): 5-192.

———. "Brasil e Oceania; Memória Apresentada ao Instituto Histórico e Geográfico Brasileiro e lida na Augusta Presença de Sua Majestade Imperial." *Revista Trimestral do IHGB* 4th trim. (1867): 257-396.

———. *Os Timbiras: Poema Americano*. Salvador: Livraria Progresso Editora, 1956.

———. *Poesia e Prosa Completas*. Rio de Janeiro: Nova Aguilar, 1998.

Herculano, Alexandre. "Futuro Literário de Portugal e do Brasil." 1847. Antonio Gonçalves Dias. *Poesia e Prosa Completas*. Rio de Janeiro: Nova Aguilar, 1998. 97-100.

Magalhães, G. de. "Os Indígenas do Brasil Perante a História." *Revista Trimestrial do IHGB* 23 (1860): 3-66.

Ramos, Péricles Eugênio da Silva. Ed. *Poesia Romântica; Antologia*. São Paulo: Melhoramentos, 1965.

Memoirs of a Militia Sergeant: A Singular Novel

Marcus Vinicius Nogueira Soares

Translated by Ross G. Forman

Memórias de um Sargento de Milícias, by the doctor and journalist Manuel Antônio de Almeida, was first published anonymously in the Rio-based newspaper *Correio Mercantil*. The novel was serialized in the Sunday supplement "Pacotilha" from June 27, 1852, to July 31, 1853, and tells the story of young Leonardo's exploits during the reign of D. João VI (1808-1821) in the former capital of the colony, Rio de Janeiro. The next two years saw the novel's first publication in book form. *Mémorias* appeared in two volumes, both of which were printed by Maximiniano Gomes Ribeiro's Tipografia Brasiliana and signed with the pseudonym "A Brazilian."

Born in modest circumstances in Rio de Janeiro on November 17, 1831, Almeida studied medicine but never practiced as a physician. Even before his graduation in 1856, he had dabbled in journalism, a profession that he described in the following terms: "It is my pleasure to confess that I have not had one day of remorse, and that only the force of circumstance could take me away from the career on which I have embarked."[1] In addition to editing the *Correio Mercantil*, Almeida also held another position associated with journalism, that of administrator at the "Tipografia Nacional." Nevertheless, "by force of circumstance"—the illness of one of his sisters—the writer was forced to abandon journalism while exiled in Nova Friburgo, a city in the Serra dos Órgãos, in the countryside of what is now the state of Rio de Janeiro. This life change increased his financial burdens considerably and led him to accept an invitation to run for congress. In order to begin his political campaign, Almeida returned to Rio de Janeiro, where he boarded the steamship *Hermes* bound for Campos, on the northern coastline of the state. He died, at the age of 30, when the *Hermes* shipwrecked on November 31, 1861.

It is unclear what importance the author himself gave to his novel during his short and troubled life. However, what is clear is that from 1855, the year in which the second volume of *Memórias* appeared, until the year of his death, Almeida never produced another novel. The rest of his work was confined to journalism and to writing reviews, chronicles, and even the libretto for an operetta called *Dois Amores*. Only in 1862 did the efforts of Quintino Bocaiúva result in a new, posthumous edition of the novel; this edition still appeared under the pseudonym "A Brazilian," even though the book's authorship was no longer a secret. Since then, new editions have appeared regularly, and Almeida's novel has become one of the most celebrated and most frequently read Brazilian novels.

Memórias and Its Contemporaries

What have always bothered twentieth-century Brazilian critics of *Memórias* is how little attention men of letters paid to it when it was published in the 1850s. If the work's success in the public sphere remains a matter of debate, its initial critical reception is not so complicated: the novel was not well-received. No critique or review of *Memórias* was published prior to the author's death in 1861. The first evaluation of the author and his work appeared the same year as his death and was obviously motivated by the tragic event. Yet, curiously, such attention was not sufficient to create more awareness of *Memórias*. The comments published by Francisco Otaviano, Almeida's friend and former boss at the *Correio Mercantil,* only concern the journalist's "ardent imagination" and his "rapid and concise style, the kind that made his articles admirable for their sober phrasing, their wealth of ideas, and their beauty of form."[2] In a biographical sketch published in the *Diário do Rio de Janeiro* in 1862, Augusto Emílio Zaluar, another friend of Almeida's, focused primarily on his role as a friend and journalist; Zaluar only mentions *Memórias* as a work showing Almeida's great potential as a novelist. In the preface to the 1862 edition of the novel, Bocaiúva explains why he decided to inaugurate the publication of Almeida's collected works with *Memórias*: "The novel, which we begin printing today, first appeared anonymously. That edition disappeared, or at least there are few today who own a copy of it."[3]

Without a doubt, the novel suffered a certain marginalization before the author's death. Even after being republished in a new edition in 1862, and despite its increasing popularity, it continued to be poorly received in literary circles. In his *Ano Biográfico Brasileiro*, Joaquim Manoel de Macedo—one of the most prolific and widely read novelists in nineteenth-century Brazil and author of the classic *A Moreninha*—wrote a short profile of the author, considering the novel as "a mild and precise study of the country's old manners" that "shined as the new dawn of a bright day."[4] Meanwhile, in his foreword to an 1876 edition, Almeida's childhood friend Bethencourt da Silva proclaimed that the author's talent "was only lightly stamped" on this novel, since it did not qualify as "one of those sublime works that show the pride of a people or the glory of humanity."[5]

Reassessing *Memórias*

Only in the twentieth century has the novel received a favorable critical reception. The question that arises, therefore, is why did Almeida's work not get the good press normally accorded a great novel? In other words, what was it about the novel that was so distasteful to nineteenth-century critics? This question, of course, might seem rather naive, since it concerns the specific prejudices that affect the evaluation of any single work. However, twentieth-century critics have not sought merely to question the literary values of the nineteenth century, but to demonstrate the degree to which Almeida's work proves unrepresentative of these values.

In this sense, the text of *Memórias* has been reconsidered along two different lines, both of which treat the novel anachronistically. On the one hand, the novel is said to represent a return to a literary precedent, since it recovers long forgotten traditions of writing. On the other, it is said to anticipate forms of Brazilian Realism/Naturalism and of 1920s Modernism. In the first case, the novel is placed alongside the works of Mário de Andrade and Josué Montello; in the second, it joins the works of José Veríssimo, Marques Rebelo and Bernardo de Mendonça.

In the introduction to a 1941 edition of *Memórias*, Mário de Andrade for the first time associated the novel with the tradition of the picaresque. Yet his association is rather tangential: it links the story of a young rake during the "time of the king" with the Spanish picaresque novels, given that the picaresque and Almeida's novel shared a "psychological method of vital non-conformity."[6] This method, Andrade claims, already existed in Herondas and Petronius before making an appearance in the Spanish picaresque. This "vital non-conformity" is characterized by:

MARCUS VINICIUS NOGUEIRA SOARES

a temperamental reactionarism that sets them [the authors] against the rhetoric of their time and above all against life as it is lived, that they then delight in praising, purposely exaggerating the shape of events and of men, by comedy, by humor, by sarcasm, by grotesqueness and caricature. And by folly.[7]

Some years later Josué Montello raised this idea once again, directly linking *Memórias* to such texts as *La Vida de Lazarillo de Tormes* and *Vida y Hechos de Estebanilho González*.[8]

During the last decade of the nineteenth century, José Veríssimo disseminated the idea that Almeida's novel was ahead of its time, in this case predicting the *fin de siècle* movement of Realism and Naturalism.[9] Novelist Marques Rebelo took this idea even further. In his *Vida e Obra de Manuel Antônio de Almeida*, Rebelo recalled the novel's lack of success when published in book form: "not a single literary magazine wrote about it. It just wasn't literature, they agreed."[10] This assessment, for Rebelo, came from the novel's avant-garde quality, even according to the terms of literary conventions in Europe, "where only a few years later... naturalism appeared."[11] He added:

> But Manuel Antônio de Almeida... was for Brazil not only the *pioneer of naturalism*, more importantly he was *the pioneer of the modern novel*, and it is in him that we find the true forefather of one Antônio de Alcântara Machado, who also died before he was 30.[12]

Rebelo thus seeks to establish a genealogy for national literature, whose origin lies in Manuel Antônio de Almeida. In the emphasized passages above, this genealogy manifests itself in the use of definite articles that assure the exclusive nature of Almeida's prescience. It also presents a lineage for literature according to which the birth of Brazilian Romanticism is attributed to an unlucky accident of fate. (In this sense, it is important to remember that, for Rebelo, *Memórias* was not a romantic work, even though it had been written under the aegis of Brazilian Romanticism).

Although acknowledging the merit of the nationalistic impulses of romantic authors—from Gonçalves de Magalhães to José de Alencar, by way of Gonçalves Dias—Rebelo insists on the derivative character of these authors' work, compared to that of their European counterparts, and, consequently, on the absence of an original "Brazilianism." *Memórias de um*

MARCUS VINÍCIUS NOGUEIRA SOARES

Sargento de Milícias, therefore, offers not just an example of literary precocity; instead, it occupies a crucial position in the real lineage leading to the foundation of a national literature. Almeida had accomplished that for which the Romantics only professed an interest: a genuinely national literature. Yet, according to Rebelo, only Naturalism and the work of Machado de Assis developed this realization—that is, only literature produced from the 1870s forward. Recalling Mário de Andrade's observation in his introduction to the 1941 edition of *Memórias*, Rebelo reiterates the stylistic similarity between the two novelists, recognizing Almeida's ghost in Machado de Assis, and by extension, in the Modernist movement of 1922, as his mention of Antônio de Alcântara Machado suggests.

Bernardo de Mendonça takes this position to its extreme. Mendonça sees, in the nineteenth-century's critical disregard of *Memórias*, a symptom of the prolonged delay in the modernization of Brazilian society, given that Almeida was a "pioneer of the modern spirit" and not solely of a literary style or styles.[13]

The Third Way

Although both of these perspectives have circulated widely, they are by no means the only ones possible. There is also a third way, characterized by the rejection of an assumption underlying the other two: the anachronistic feature attributed to *Memórias*.

Writing of Almeida's novel in his seminal *Formação da Literatura Brasileira*, Antonio Candido describes the eccentric quality that characterizes certain texts: "There are in Romanticism some works of fiction that could be called eccentric with respect to the trend started by other works."[14] *Memórias'* eccentricity comes less from its thematization of non-Romantic areas—pre- or post-Romantic ones—as from its valorization of certain characteristics of Romanticism itself, although these characteristics were not considered hegemonic at the time of publication. He writes:

> As to his contemporaries, although they esteemed Manuel Antônio as a man and a journalist, they do not seem to have appreciated his novel quite as much, half out of tune as it was with the patterns and tone of the era.[15]

Neither ahead of its time nor behind it in the literary canon, *Memórias de um Sargento de Milícias* is not marked by anachronism, since Almeida's novel describes elements that, although not dominant at the time of its publication, were potentially available. For Candido, the novel's eccentricity manifests itself in the valorization, on the part of its author, of the novel of manners, instead of the "sentimental exaltation and rhetorical vocation" characteristic of the period.[16] Nevertheless, this valorization implies the perspective of someone well-versed in the sociocultural context of the period. Faced with some typical difficulties with respect to historical circumstances—the country's lack of social complexity, the limits of the literary field, the strictness of the psychological perspective, etc.—, "Manuel Antônio [was] a novelist who was not only aware of his own intentions, but also (within his literary form) of the necessary means to accomplish them."[17] This awareness involves the adaptation of elements of the novel of manners to the discursive conditions for literary production during Almeida's age.

In a later essay Candido once more seeks to explain *Memórias* by trying to refute the notion of anachronism; instead, he attempts to "characterize a rather peculiar morality that manifests itself in Manuel Antônio de Almeida's book," which he calls the "rogue's novel."[18] This neither predicts later developments nor harkens to an earlier tradition, but founds a new one, derived from a specific mode of thematizing the cultural and social conditions of the moment in which *Memórias* was published, and which, according to Candido, also corresponds to "a certain comic and popularesque atmosphere of his era."[19] This atmosphere had already seeped into journalism, especially in leaflet-chronicles, and also into political debates. (One of the principal characteristics of works published in "Pacotilha" was their absorption of this atmosphere.)

Candido's essay surely offers a richer analysis than can be discussed here. What I have attempted to do is merely emphasize his contribution to the discussion of anachronism, which in general has been a focal point of critical attitudes towards *Memórias*. However, the most important aspect to remember is that Almeida's novel has survived despite its innumerable classifications, despite various attempts to assign it a literary affiliation, and, above all, despite the total oblivion which initially greeted it. Today, after myriad editions—including translations into French, Spanish, Italian, and English—the novel still raises new and stimulating questions.[20] Moreover, it remains one of the most popular nineteenth-century novels outside of academic circles—a fact that certainly would have pleased Manuel Antônio de Almeida.

Notes

[1] Rebelo 26.

[2] Otaviano 115-6.

[3] Bocaiúva 177.

[4] Macedo 413.

[5] Silva 253.

[6] Andrade 313.

[7] Andrade 313.

[8] See Josué Montello, "Um Precursor: Manuel Antônio de Almeida," *A Literatura no Brasil.* vol. 2. Ed. Afrânio Coutinho. Rio de Janeiro: Editora Sul Americana, 1968. 37-45.

[9] See José Veríssimo, *Estudos Brasileiros*, 2nd ed. Rio de Janeiro: Laemmert, 1894. 107-124.

[10] Rebelo 38.

[11] Rebelo 38.

[12] Rebelo 38, emphasis mine.

[13] Mendonça xii.

[14] Candido, *Formação* 215.

[15] Candido, *Formação* 215.

[16] Candido, *Formação* 215.

[17] Candido, *Formação* 217.

[18] Candido, "Dialética da Malandragem" 318.

[19] Candido, "Dialética da Malandragem" 322.

[20] French edition: *Mémoires d'un Sergent de la Milice*, trans. Paulo Rónai (Rio de Janeiro: Atlantica, 1944); Spanish edition: *Memorias de un Sargento de Milicias,* trans. Francisco Ayala (Buenos Aires: Argos, 1947); Italian edition: *Il sergente delle milizie*, trad. Cesare Rivelli (Milan; Rome: Fratelli Bocca Editori, 1954); English edition: *Memoirs of a Militia Sergeant,* trans. Linton L. Barrett (Washington, D.C.: Organization of American States, 1959). Recently, a new English translation was published: *Memoirs of a Militia Sergeant,* trans. Ronald W. Sousa, with a Foreword by Thomas H. Holloway and an Afterword by Flora Süssekind. Oxford: Oxford UP, 1999.

Works Cited

Almeida, Manuel Antônio de. *Memórias de um Sargento de Milícias.* Ed. Cecília Lara. Rio de Janeiro: Livraria Técnicos e Científicos, 1978.

Andrade, Mário de. "Introdução." 1941. *Memórias de um Sargento de Milícias.* Manuel Antônio de Almeida. Ed. Cecília Lara. Rio de Janeiro: Livraria Técnicos e Científicos, 1978. 303-315.

Bocaiúva, Quintino. "Advertência," *Memórias de um Sargento de Milícias.* Manuel Antônio de Almeida. Rio de Janeiro: Tipografia do Diário do Rio de Janeiro, 1862-3.

Candido, Antonio. *Formação da Literatura Brasileira* (Momentos Decisivos). Belo Horizonte: Itatiaia, 1959.

———. "Dialética de Malandragem (Caracterização das *Memórias de um sargento de milícias*)." 1970. *Memórias de um Sargento de Milícias,* Ed. Cecília Lara. Rio de Janeiro: Livraria Técnicos e Científicos, 1978. 317-342.

MARCUS VINICIUS NOGUEIRA SOARES

Macedo, Joaquim Manuel de. *Ano Biográfico Brasileiro.* Rio de Janeiro: Tipografia e Litografia do Imperial Instituto Artístico, 1876.

Mendonça, Bernardo de. "D'Almeida, Almeida, Almeidinha, A., Maneco, Um Brasileiro: Mais um Romance de Costume." *Obra Dispersa.* Manuel Antônio de Almeida. Rio de Janeiro: Grafia, 1991. VI-XXXVIII.

Otaviano, Francisco. "Notícias Diversas," Correio Mercantil, 5 December 1861; reprinted in Manuel Antônio de Almeida, *Obra Dispersa* (Rio de Janeiro: Grafica, 1991). 115-6.

Rebelo, Marquelo. *Vida e Obra de Manuel Antônio de Almeida.* Rio de Janeiro: Instituto Nacional do Livro, 1943.

Silva, Bethencourt da. *Dispersas e Bosquejos Artísticos.* Rio de Janeiro: Papelaria Ribeira, 1901.

Iracema: The Tupinization of Portuguese

Ivo Barbieri

Translated by

Dana Stevens

> The mixture of races of the Old with the ones of the New World did not take place only in the blood; it is also in the intelligence, morality, language, religion, entertainment and everyday food.
>
> Couto de Magalhães (152)

When José de Alencar published *Iracema* in 1865, forty-three years had already passed since Brazil liberated itself from Portugal's long colonial rule, and in the literature that was being written, it had been nearly three decades since the formal rupture with the neoclassical canon. Given that for more than three hundred previous years the linguistic and aesthetic norms had been determined mainly by the colonizing metropolis, political emancipation and literary rupture were closely related. But despite the fact that they were motivated by the project of constructing an independent nation, the romantics faced much resistance, conflict and trauma as they tried to create a new literary canon, which was linked with the political moment from its very birth. Brazilian Romanticism undertook the task of establishing a language standard that would speak the soul of the nascent country, a language bursting with exalted rhetoric through which the young nation sought to define the features of its own physiognomy, to recognize and identify itself. Tepid at first, the movement grew quickly in both size and vigor, soon becoming the locus for the conception and dissemination of the national imaginary. Thus, following the well-intentioned but conventionally anachronistic early manifestations in the 1830s, came two decades of abundant production of innovative poems and novels, a creative burst stimulated by voices of support and encouragement from the Old World. More polemical reactions, however, some of which Alencar was personally involved in, temper the effervescence of those years in interesting ways.

Joining in this same nationalist sentiment, poets and prose writers were committed to the formation of a literature that would openly distinguish itself from the Portuguese tradition that had bound it throughout the colonial period. For this, it sought inspiration in local themes, such as the exuberant nature of the tropics, the tribal, nomadic and independent life of the land's first inhabitants, and the culture shock provoked by the first indigenous contact with foreign invaders. The movement defined itself by a conscious return to origins, to the regeneration of the primary source responsible for the formation of the body and soul of the nation. With these goals in mind, the romantics rummaged through ancient documents and wills and passionately reread the chronicles of European historians and visitors to Brazil from the sixteenth, seventeenth and eighteenth centuries, especially valorizing the records of the first contacts of the white man with the Native Brazilian. It was in this initial contact that they situated the inaugural moment, the day of creation of the New World to which they sought to give poetic form. And, in the interest of an even more radical originality, they went back further still, idealizing a mythic pre-history in which the native, free and independent, in permanent contact with a nature uncontaminated by any foreign substance, represented the privileged subject. According to the sentiment of the epoch, this was the genesis of the new civilization. As a result, the indigenous legends and traditions, the contact of the Native with the Portuguese, the struggles between them, and the assimilation of one by the other, were all considered an original source of inspiration, since they represented the initial formation of a national identity, as José Aderaldo Castello observes in *Polemic on the Confederation of the Tamoios and Romantic Indianism* (Castello xxvii). Alongside the attempt to elaborate a language that would apprehend and give form to this literarily unknown world, we also find attempts to construct a theoretical-ideological paradigm that would encourage and sustain the emergence of works committed to the program described above. In "Outline of the History of Brazilian Poetry" (1840) and "General Considerations on Brazilian Literature" (1844), the writer Joaquim Norberto Sousa Silva, from Rio de Janeiro, attempted to recuperate links with a pre-Cabraline poetic tradition. The mission of these essays is clearly the affirmation of the autochthonous origin of the poetic impulse. The author identifies, in the native songs of the *nheengaçaras* (indigenous bards), the "ardent imagination and spontaneity of improvisation with which the indigenous peoples manifested their poetic tendencies, which would reflect their ways, their customs and their myths, as do the songs of all peoples given over to nature who live in the most complete independence" (Silva 1859, 1860). In counterpoint to the Portuguese literary tradition which, at the apogee of its golden age, shone with the brilliance of Camões, Sá de Miranda, Antônio Ferreira, Gil Vicente, João de Barros and many others—a brilliance so extraordinary that it could have extinguished the desire to create a native poetry—Sousa Silva joined his voice to those of European authors like Alexandre Herculano and Ferdinand Denis, who stimulated the new poets to work with American themes and timbres. Antônio Gonçalves Dias, a poet from Maranhão who was of mixed Native and Portuguese blood, was the first to respond competently to these challenges. Under the label "American Poetry," which appeared in his book *Primeiros Cantos* in 1846, the poet began inventing the rules of a new discourse, synthesized with the nationalist anxieties of the moment. Taking up the eighteenth-century Indianist theme once again, Gonçalves Dias was able to fashion it to the contemporary climate, and his contribution was decisive in making Indianism the emblem of a literature engaged in the project of national formation.[1] The Native of the "American Poems," in rhythms punctuated like martial cadences, highlights the heroic figure of the valiant warrior, even as he laments in a minor key the solitude of the *mestiço*, abandoned and discriminated against within his own tribe. The most lasting poetic feat of Gonçalves Dias was that, as a poet of native blood, he knew the language, customs and tradition of the Tupi-Guarani tribes; he was thus able to inaugurate a standard of poetic language whose melodies and idealizing projections would become a model of the proper diction for Brazilian poetry. If we add to this accomplishment, extraordinary in itself, the serialized novels of Joaquim Manuel de Macedo and Manuel Antônio de Almeida, and the hilarious comedies of manners of the playwright Martins Pena, we will have laid the scene for the entrance of José de Alencar onto the stage of Brazilian letters.

In the middle of the nineteenth century, as it is well-known, the city of Rio de Janeiro was the only South American metropolis whose demographic density and cultural apparatus was sufficient to support a vigorous burst in fictional production marked with its own unique characteristics. It is in this context that, in 1857, *O Guarani* explodes onto the scene, a novel adapted to the tropical heat, seasoned with local color, and with a lively plot that moves through space and time in a fantastical manner, narrating the romantic passions and chivalrous adventures of a Native hero. Alongside the placement of a patriarchal family in a noble and solemn framework, Alencar presents a paradisiacal scenery for the emergence of the heroic figure of Peri, the model of the "good savage," patterned after the types provided by Montaigne, Rousseau, Chateaubriand and Cooper. And just as Gonçalves Dias had refined his poetic diction through the diapason of a musical composition, cadenced by the pulse of fiery epics and lyrical confessions, so José de Alencar gave his prose the easy fluency of a melodic prosody. Thanks to these resources, it is as if the rudenesses of agrarian life and the cruel shocks between nomadic primitivism and a patriarchy walled up in its conventional self-sufficiency are dissolved in a froth of gentle language. Tempered in the arduous polemic against Gonçalves Magalhães—an academic poet favored by the court of Emperor Dom Pedro II—and trained in the art of spinning novelistic plots and weaving involving fables, Alencar prepares for the great leap forward in quality that would come with the publication of *Iracema*. He is fascinated by the "vigor of the language" and the "colorful images unique to the children of nature," as he writes in the seventh letter of *The Confederation of Tamoios* (50-58). With *Iracema*, Alencar perfects the art of the word, becoming the founder of a fictional prose with Brazilian accent, so to speak. While *O Guarani* was the first sign of this new movement, *Iracema* epitomizes its diction. A mixture of poetry and prose, song and declamation, exhausting every resource of poetic efficacy and compactness of language, the text brings together an historical plot with the legend of a primitive imaginary full of epic-lyrical fantasy, complete with details from nature and documentary notes. *Iracema*'s prose is the offspring of the marriage between Brazilian Portuguese spoken with Lusitanian erudition and elements of the Tupi-Guarani language.

The Tupinization of the Portuguese language, attested to by the appearance in the text of numerous words of Indigenous origin, is an indication of the general process of miscegenation. This is the great theme that cuts across the work at every level: historical plot, fable, mythical projections, ideological implication, discourse and narrative. In fact, the meeting and crossing of two cultures is the axis of articulation for the entire work, a center of gravity that is the site of convergence for a variety of fictional components. The episode with the white warrior from far-off who lands (Martim) in order to dominate his milieu and overcome those hostile to his colonizing intentions, and who must combat adverse forces and ally himself with those favorable to him, represents, on the one hand, the schema of domination of the strongest, of the white man with all the tricks on his side. On the other hand, the facility with which this adventurer falls prey to the charm, grace and seduction of nature and of the Native woman of this new welcoming land attests to his vulnerability to local emblematic values. Thus, he lets himself be impregnated with Indigenous ways, customs and traditions. The generic portrait of the conqueror takes on the specific face of a peculiar cultural hero, the initiator of the foundation of a new civilization. The Native woman, for her part, proves extremely receptive and permeable to the alien settler. At first hostile and aggressive, Iracema, the guardian of the sacred traditions of the Tabajara tribe, hesitates for only a few minutes before approaching the foreigner; she immediately falls madly in love with the white warrior, who has no sooner arrived than finds himself the target of the most generous hospitality of the "great Tabajara nation." Only a little time passes and the Native woman is wholly committed to the foreigner; she will not hesitate to enter into conflict with the emerging leader of her tribe and the sacred duty that ties her to them in votive dedication. Iracema gives herself to Martim and is immediately abandoned by the *jandaia*, the bird symbolizing the ethnic purity of the Tabajaras, for having violated the tribal commandments. Solely her passion, weakness or courage cannot explain the heroine's transgression. It can be seen in her behavior from the very beginning, like a plan conceived beyond the main characters' actions. Like some inexorable command, instinct or destiny seems to impel these heroes forward so that, apparently casually, one collides with the other, and both suddenly find themselves imprisoned in indissoluble chains. Circumstances seem to conspire in favor of some destiny that operates above the level of the individual. Nothing can stand in its way—neither cultural distance, nor a war among rival Native peoples, nor the precepts of Tupã. Even the old witch doctor (*"pajé"*) becomes an accomplice in this betrayal, as, in the sacred name of hospitality, he protects the foreigner from the brutal fury of Irapuã, the warrior's rival, who has been chosen to be Iracema's companion. In Alencar's fable-making, in which history, myth and legend interlace, Martim and Iracema play the role of protagonists in the first miscegenation, that of the meeting of white man and the Native woman. Their embrace thus assumes all the implications of the founding myth of miscegenation as the ethnic and cultural prototype of nationality. The conversion of the Indigenous Poti to the Christian religion in the last chapter of the book, when Martim's friend and ally is baptized with the name of Antônio Felipe Camarão, stands in symmetrical counterpoint to the Indigenous ritual of Chapter XXIV, when Martim's body is painted with the colors of the Potiguara nation and the "young warrior of strange race, from far-off lands" becomes "a red warrior, son of Tupã," taking on the name of Coatiabo ("painted warrior") (53). Despite the observation of Silviano Santiago that "[t]he ceremony is purely epidermic and superficial, as there is no basic change in either the gestures or the customs of Martim, nor even in his way of thinking" (46), the symbolism of this scene is very powerful, and deserves to be compared with that of the baptism of Poti. The parallel correspondences signaled between the two scenes create a chiasmatic crossing of two cultural currents: on the one side, the traditions rooted in the atavistic memory of "savage" tribes; on the other, the beliefs inherited from an expansionist civilization. The mediation, operated through language, which is itself the chessboard on which the contradictions and dissonances of this interethnic dialogue play themselves out, makes the transfusions and transformations that result from this crossing all the more transparent. The best analysts of *Iracema* develop this topic at considerable length, assisted by Alencar himself, who, despite the thirty-three philological notes he adds to the text, nonetheless entered into linguistic controversies with famous philologists. Responding to the critiques of Antônio Henriques Leal, who had denounced "the monomania of creating a Brazilian idiom" (217), Alencar shows himself superior to the philologist in both linguistic knowledge and aesthetic sensibility. Contrasting the freedom of the writer with the inertia of routine and the rigidity of dogma, Alencar reaffirms the differences between American Portuguese and that of Europe, an opinion he bases on the analogous situations of English and Spanish in the New World, whose difference from their mother tongues in Europe "becomes more salient with each passing day" (239). And, rejecting the imitation of metropolitan models, he concludes that, "the truly national writer finds in the civilization of his country, and in the history already created by its people, the elements not only of his idea, but of the language that should express it" (240).

Iracema is a harmonious marriage of subject and expression, incorporating the fluency of a melodious Portuguese with the singsong sonorities of a Tupi-Guarani aesthetically adjusted to the rhythms of orality. Departing from

Alencar's ingenious notes, M. Cavalcanti Proença has exhaustively studied the poetics of the text, giving special attention to the recurrent figures of simile and apposition as rhetorical procedures that place in relief the appearance of Tupi terms. The agglutinative nature of the Tupi-Guarani language, attested to by Tupi scholars, is evident in the very title *Iracema*, a name composed from two roots—*ira* ("honey") + *tembe* ("lips"), altered to *ceme* in the formation of the composite—translated by the author in the expression *the virgin with lips of honey*. By incorporating his translation into the text, rather than explaining it in a footnote, Alencar sets up a standard of literary language that is notable for its straddling of heteroclite elements, its simultaneous undoing of two culturally differentiated semantic fields. It would be easy to suppose that both the form of Indigenous phonemes and their division into semantic units undergo violent transformations in the process of transposition into the fictional text, whether through contagion from the phonic and semantic spectrum of the Portuguese language or through the necessity of making them conform to the author's aesthetic project. When the exacting scruples of modern linguists attempted to "correct" the novelist, upbraiding him for his "simple and ingenuous technique" or his "etymological fantasy," they opened up what Haroldo de Campos rightly called "an abyss of incomprehension between the prudence of Tupinological research, necessary and respectable in the scientific realm where it belongs, and the freely inventive poetics of the amateur Tupinologist Alencar" (69). The novelist, who neither made claims to being a philologist nor aspired to scientific rigor, worked on his poetic project with a clear consciousness of the differences and virtualities that emerge in the contact and friction between two languages, of which the translator must make the best. The justification he presents as to the choice of a Portuguese term most suited to the Tupi word *piguara* gives a good measure of his aesthetic sense and of the semantic nuances he pursued.

> A guide, the Indigenous peoples called the lord of the way, *piguara*. The beauty of this savage expression in its literal and etymological translation seems quite salient to me. They do not say 'knowledgeable one,' although that term exists, *couab*, because that phrase would not express the energy of their thought. The 'road' does not exist in the savage state; it is not an object of knowledge; this expression is used on the occasion of a walk through the forest or the field in a certain direction; he who has or gives the way at that time, is truly the lord of the way. (142)

Antonio Machado's verses—*Caminante no hay camino / se hace camino al andar*—might be evoked to confirm Alencar's poetic intuition here. But intuition aside, this note reveals the novelist's preoccupation with the faithful translation of "savage" thought into "educated" language. Alencar's prose is more than a simple and superficial lexical contamination operated through the assimilation of words referring to geographical features, Brazilian flora and fauna, and Indigenous tools, garments, acts and rituals. The novelist also succeeds in transfusing modes of perception and expression that are foreign to the linguistic habits of educated speakers. This effect of estrangement, produced everywhere in his work, is largely based on the agglutinative nature of Tupi-Guarani. By combining semes that, separately, have their own use and meaning, agglutinative word formation makes the sign both semantically transparent and systematically motivated. "Each name," attests Couto de Magalhães, "gives the description of the object it represents." This affirmation can be duly proven by the ethnographer with examples like that of the well-known fruit, the *acaju* or *caju*, which can be broken down thus: *a*, "fruit;" *ju*, "yellow;" *aca*, "with horns;" or "the yellow fruit with horns;" and there, he concludes, is the description of the *caju*. (Magalhães 154). Long before the researcher/linguist/indigenist Magalhães, Alencar had already studied a vast repertory of cases that brilliantly illustrates the same thesis, as can be seen in his documentary notes reproduced in the centennial critical edition (145-160). Alencar translates practically all of the anthroponyms and toponyms of Tupi-Guarani origin that appear in his text through the apposition of analytic expressions which translate their respective meanings, thereby constructing a semantic atmosphere that allows heteroclite elements to coexist in harmony. After a few pages, this procedure ceases to seem strange and becomes familiar to the reader. This naturalization of hybridism gives certain fluency to the transit of words from one language to another, as if cultural frontiers had been abolished. Rather than linguistic assimilation, this transcultural dialogue favors a communion of sentiments between the Native and the white man, as can be seen in this conversation between Poti and Martim:

> "Why are you called Mocoripe of the great hill of sands?"
> "The fisherman on the beach, who sails in a *jangada* out where the *ati* bird flies, grows sad, far from land and from his hut, where sleep the sons of his blood. When he looks back and his eyes first see the hill of sands, pleasure returns to his heart. So he says that the hill of sands brings joy."

"The fisherman speaks well; for your brother, like him, grew happy when he saw the mountain of sands." (104)

Here the text functions as a vehicle of mediation between different languages and cultures, annulling the hierarchy between the colonizer and the colonized and eliding cultural distances. In this discursive space, each understands the other as a brother, and they share a common feeling. The translation of the peculiarities of one language into the other becomes a dialogical understanding, and the narrator no longer intrudes so obviously on the scene. Mediating between Tupi and Portuguese, Alencar seeks a moment of equilibrium, a stasis in which alterities can combine harmonically. It is a complex process in which Tupinisms, explained on the surface of the text, indicate the verticality of the dialogic action. M. Cavalcanti Proença, in what is perhaps the most complete study of *Iracema*, analyzes in detail Alencar's position as interpreter and translator of the primitive imagination and of distinct narrative models. I will transcribe here the passage in which Proença introduces synthetically the idea he will develop throughout his essay:

> The Indigenous terms translated by appositives: "*tabajaras*, lords of the villages;" images drawn from flora and fauna: "the cut of the palm tree"; "faster than a wild emu"—are reinforced by the ornate way in which the language is presented: using paraphrase to avoid repetition, to take the place of the reduced vocabulary that the indigenous people must have; the use of simile, in search of precision for a primitive language; the use of the third person, even as the subject is speaking, a trace of the language of children and, by analogy, of the Indigenous people; even the use of classical language, to accentuate the move backwards in time, the age of the legend. (282)

Here again is Alencar, in the letter cited above, describing his own role as he defines the Brazilian poet as a translator:

> Without a doubt, the Brazilian poet must translate into his own language the ideas of the Natives, rough and coarse as they may be; but in this translation lies great difficulty; civilized language must mold itself as best it can to the primitive singularity of the barbarous one; and represent Indigenous images and thoughts only by terms and phrases which will seem natural to the reader in the mouth of a savage. (141)

Here we can clearly see the reach of Haroldo de Campos' essay, where he develops the idea of Alencar as a pioneer who made daring advances in the conception and execution of translation and of the place of the translator in transcultural dialogue. The translator is able to expose himself to "the violent impulse that comes from a foreign language" (Walter Benjamin qtd. by Campos 69). He not only operates "a heteroglossic grafting onto Portuguese, but also, in order to capture the "savage mind," brings together, on the one hand, the need to 'barbarize' (read 'Tupinize') Portuguese in order to submit it to Indigenous 'modes of thought,' and, on the other, 'that sense of rejection of an exhausted form' through the critique of 'classical language'" (Campos 73). The contamination between Tupi and Portuguese, two distinct and distant languages and cultures, happens, as it were, on the negotiating table, in a space of mutual concessions and reciprocal assent. While Portuguese "barbarizes" or Tupinizes itself according to the ways of the "savage," Tupi is "civilized," becoming Lusitanian as it meets up with the melodic phraseology of José de Alencar's literary Portuguese. Couto de Magalhães speaks of a "true crossing, which happens when one language is placed in contact with another." And, considering such a phenomenon both progressive and inevitable, he assures us that Brazilian Portuguese has been irremediably modified by Tupi and that this modification will become ever more noticeable, the heterogeneous elements being apparent only in its first, crude productions. Little by little, however, these elements will blend together; their characteristic signs will disappear, giving way to a homogenous product (Magalhães 89). Like a good evolutionist, the phases that the author of *The Savage* saw as distinct stages in a continuous process, may be found synchronically present in Alencar's text. There, the heteroclite moment provoked by the shock of first contact appears alongside the homogenous result of the moment of synthesis. Taking care to model his discourse after the Natives' speech, the author of *Iracema* forms a chain of images to translate the energy and vivacity of impressions, once more foreseeing the propositions of Magalhães in *The Savage* when he describes some features of the language of primitive peoples: "much more laconic and less analytic than those of educated peoples, the rapid flow of images suppressing and sometimes replacing the use of extended reasoning" (64). This means that, beyond questions of lexicon and of grammatical syntax, the author has "barbarized" (read "Tupinized") the syntax of thought as well by referring to figures of language that not only describe and valorize local color, but also seek ways to make literary discourse adequate to a primitive mentality, presented in a simple and direct but at the same time imaginative style. Cavalcanti Proença develops in his own way this Alencarian impregnation of Tupi syntax.

By fictionalizing "the historic ideal of harmonious fusion of the Portuguese colonizer with the Indigenous people" (Castello xxvii), Alencar took advantage of motifs drawn from historiographic sources going back to the earliest days of national formation, which stressed the plasticity of the colonial dweller, whether in adapting to the adversities of the physical environment or in taking on new cultural habits. The mating of the Portuguese with the Native, resulting in the first Brazilian miscegenation, seems to have been a rather common practice in the first decades of colonization. In *The Territorial Formation of Brazil,* Raposo Tavares affirms: "The colonizer, for whom there was no shortage of tribes into which he could insert himself, freely chose to be Tupinized through polygamy. And not only through polygamy, but also taking on, along with the Tupi language, many other customs and cultural acquisitions" (See Caldeira 31). Capistrano de Abreu, an historian from Ceará who did extensive research into colonial history, writes:

> On the part of the Natives, miscegenation can be explained by the ambition to have children belonging to a superior race [sic], for according to ideas widely held among them, only the paternal lineage counted. Furthermore, it was not easy to resist millionaires who possessed fabulous treasures like fishing poles, combs, knives, coins, and mirrors. On the part of the foreigners, a major influence must have been the scarcity, if not the absence, of women of their own blood. This is a fact that can be observed in all maritime migrations, and which survives even after the invention of the steam engine, with the accompanying change in the speed and safety of ocean crossings. (32-33)

While they may have helped to stimulate the literary genesis of *Iracema,* none of these reasons are explicitly introduced in the union of Martim with the "Tabajara virgin." The novelist's imagination reelaborates historical information according to its sublimation by the sense of nobility with which he endows his poetic invention. And just as he ennobles the love of the Indian for the white warrior, purifying it of any pragmatic interest, so he also purifies the character and lineage of Martim. It is Capistrano who follows the trail of the Portuguese Martim Soares Moreno through the Brazilian Northeast. He informs us that, having arrived from Portugal in 1602, to "learn the language of the land and familiarize himself with its customs," he joins the first Eastward expedition of Pedro Coelho at the age of eighteen. Since he had gotten along so well with the Natives, Jacaúna, the Potiguar chief, attaches himself to Martim with a father's love. After several visits to his friend, Martim has dissipated so many rancors and prejudices that the Native allows him to settle in Ceará territory with two soldiers. Thus, he manages to start a fort on the Ceará river, where he will resist the attacks of Natives not under Jacaúna's rule. With Jacaúna's help, he takes two foreign ships, "bare and painted with the juice of genipapo fruit, in the style of his helpers" (Abreu 69). These historical references to the Portuguese colonizer are enough to provide an historical plot interest for *Iracema*.

Juxtaposed with the fable woven by Alencar, such references reveal the sense of the transformations he puts in place. First, Alencar naturalizes the foreigner, having him be born in Brazilian territory without denying him Latin blood and a Latin name. Second, he replaces the opaque Jacaúna with Poti, an Indigenous hero nationally known for his participation in the struggles that followed in the wake of the expulsion of the Dutch from Brazilian shores. Finally, he magnifies the foundation of a small fortification, transforming it into the founding act of a new civilization. In the meantime, he takes advantage of historical givens like the learning of Native languages and the submission to the ritual of body painting, since these details, like the Brazilianization of the colonizer, serve to eliminate foreign elements and to root his poem in the ground that will make it grow. Affirming that a European would be incapable of writing this book, Araripe Júnior finds in "the love of country," the "sense of the land, which exudes from every page," sufficient reason to call *Iracema* "the most Brazilian of our books" (252). And, ever since Afrânio Peixoto, textbooks on Brazilian literature have been accustomed to read in the title of *Iracema* the anagram of America. Alencar himself once confided to a friend: "This book, then, is an essay, or rather, a sample. You will find actualized in it my ideas about national literature, and you will find there poetry that is entirely Brazilian, drawn from the language of savages" (143). A work of imagination nourished by history, *Iracema* is a poetic synthesis of literary nationalism at its inventive apex in the nineteenth-century Brazilian Romanticism. It has become an enduring work by efficiently consummating the ideas of that time. It is a classic of Brazilian letters that has continued to inspire avant-garde authors of the twentieth century such as Mário de Andrade and Guimarães Rosa.

In a burst of iconoclastic humor typical of his radical poetics, Oswald de Andrade makes a joke out of what he calls an error of the Portuguese: "When the Portuguese arrived / Under a brutal rain / He dressed the Native / What a shame! / If it had been a sunny morning / The Native would have stripped / The Portuguese" (161). In the inspired poetry of *Iracema*, José de Alencar, with historical documentation and in all seriousness, has the Native strip the Portuguese! Historians like Capistrano de Abreu, tracing the advance of the colonizer into Brazilian territory, had already shown that, in certain situations, the Portuguese had allowed themelves to be stripped by the Natives. The body-painting ritual practiced on Martim Soares Moreno proves it. Hypnotized by the inebriating effects of the *jurema* plant, Martim, a fictional character, is literally stripped by Iracema. Meanwhile, on the literary level, Alencar strips his hero of civilized habits, of the stereotypes and conventions of the colonizer, in order to clothe him in legendary ideality, transmuting him into the mythic founder of a civilization based on the principle of miscegenation. The birth of Moacir, the fruit of the union of a foreign man with an Indigenous woman, successfully crowns the heroic acts of the protagonist, who, having violated and tamed ethnic and cultural boundaries, "barbarizes" himself in order to "civilize." The apparent contradiction and conflicts resulting from this culture shock are resolved in the combination of heteroclite terms that come together in the fluency of a melodic and harmonizing discourse. Drenched in lyricism and plasticity, the narrative anchors itself in a regional space that is the cradle of the writer, from which the historical and fictional material proceeds. In this way, *Iracema* metabolizes personal reminiscence into collective memory, operating a synthesis between the local, the regional and the national. The fable that its author subtitled *Legend of Ceará* projects itself, in turn, beyond the limited moment of literary nationalism in which it was written, inscribing itself in the trans-historical time of those masterpieces which, by inquiring into the genesis of the past, provoke the emergence of new beginnings.

Notes

[1] Since the Native Brazilian is called in Portuguese "*índio*," the romantic movement grounded on the celebration of the Indigenous heritage was given the name "*Indianismo*."

Works Cited

Abreu, Capistrano de. *Capítulos de História Colonial (1500-1800).* 3rd ed. Rio de Janeiro: Briguet, 1934.

Alencar, José de. *Iracema—Lenda do Ceará.* Edição do Centenário. Rio de Janeiro: José Olympio, 1965.

———. *Iracema. A Novel.* Trans. Clifford E. Landers; with a Foreword by Naomi Lindstrom; and an Afterword by Alcides Villaça. New York: Oxford UP, 2000.

Andrade, Oswald de. *Poesias Reunidas.* São Paulo: Difusão Européia do Livro, 1966.

Araripe Jr. *Obra Crítica de Araripe Júnior.* Vol. I, 1868-1887. Rio de Janeiro: Casa de Rui Barbosa, 1958.

Caldeira, Jorge. *A Nação Mercantilista: Ensaio sobre o Brasil.* São Paulo: Editora 34, 1999.

Campos, Haroldo de. "Iracema: Uma Arqueologia da Vanguarda." *Revista USP* 5 (mar-abr-mai 1990): 67-74.

Castello, José Aderaldo. *A Polêmica sobre "A Confederação dos Tamoios."* São Paulo: Faculdade de Filosofia, Ciências e Letras da Universidade de São Paulo, 1953.

Leal, Henriques. "*Iracema—Lenda do Ceará* de José de Alencar. Questão Filológica *in Iracema.*" Edição do Centenário. Rio de Janeiro: José Olympio, 1965. 210-17

Magalhães, General Couto de. *O Selvagem.* Belo Horizonte: Itatiaia, 1975.

Proença, M. Cavalcanti. "Transforma-se o Amador na Coisa Amada em *Iracema.*" *Iracema— Lenda do Ceará.* Edição do Centenário. Rio de Janeiro: José Olympio, 1965. 281-328.

Silva, Joaquim Norberto Sousa. "Bosquejo da História da Poesia Brasileira." *Revista Popular* 1.4 (out-dez 1859): 357-64.

———. "Considerações Gerais sobre a Literatura Brasileira." *Revista Popular* 1.7 (jul-set 1860): 153-63.

Santiago, Silviano. *Romances para Estudo: Iracema.* Rio de Janeiro: Francisco Alves, 1975.

Machado de Assis and *The Posthumous Memoirs of Brás Cubas*

Bluma Waddington Vilar

Translated by Shoshanna Lurie

Whether in handbooks of literary history or in critical essays and books, any foreign student interested in Brazilian literature will surely encounter the assertion that Machado de Assis is one of the greatest Portuguese language writers. Grandson of freed slaves on his father's side, son of a Brazilian wall painter and a Portuguese woman from the Azores who was also of humble origins, the mestizo Joaquim Maria Machado de Assis was born in Rio de Janeiro on June 21, 1839. His parents, who were both literate, were servants (*"agregados"*) at the Livramento farm. Its proprietor, the rich widow of an Imperial senator, was the writer's godmother. According to the most accepted biographical tradition between 1856 and 1858 Machado de Assis worked as an apprentice at the "Tipografia Nacional." During this time, he had already begun to collaborate with newspapers and magazines, an activity he would continue for almost his entire life as a poet, critic, chronicler, storyteller, translator, and novelist. He worked as a public servant, joining the Ministry of Agriculture, Commerce and Public Works in 1873 as a scribe. Before this he had worked in other positions related to public administration as a theater censor and as assistant to the director of the *Diário Oficial.* He completed no special schooling, nor a college degree, and he was, above all, self-taught. In 1896, together with other writers, he founded the Brazilian Academy of Letters, and was its president-elect until his death in 1908. Having practiced all literary genres—short story, novel, chronicle, poetry, and drama—he excelled most in the first three, as well as in literary criticism.

Machado began publishing his work in book form during the period immediately following the height of the "indianista"[1] trend in Brazil, or, in other words, during a period in which Romanticism still dominated the

Brazilian literary scene, as it did until Naturalism entered the field in the 1880s. Machado's first volume of short stories is *Contos Fluminenses* (1870), and his first novel *Ressurreição* (1872). In 1880, Machado published *The Posthumous Memoirs of Brás Cubas* as a serial *feuilleton*, and the text was collected into book form the following year (1881). This was the same year that *O Mulato*, by Aluísio Azevedo (1857-1913) was published, a novel that would come to represent the beginning of Brazilian Naturalism, even though another naturalist novel, Inglês de Sousa's *O Coronel Sangrado* (1877) had already been published. In this essay, I will provide an overview of Machadian studies, primarily through a survey of critical analyses of his most acclaimed novel, *The Posthumous Memoirs of Brás Cubas*.

Critics traditionally divide Machado's novelistic production into two phases: the first, of romantic extraction, includes the first four novels— *Ressurreição, A Mão e a Luva* (1874), *Helena* (1876), *Iaiá Garcia* (1878)—and the second, inaugurated with *The Posthumous Memoirs*, includes four other novels—*Quincas Borba* (1891), *Dom Casmurro* (1899), *Esaú e Jacó* (1904), and *Memorial de Aires* (1908). Meanwhile, critics from different periods and traditions have suggested that the differences in form and narrative technique between the two phases—the extraordinary jump in quality, the subtle changes between the two—do not reflect a radical rupture; rather, they are a "dialectical rupture" in which there is no "absolute negation of the previous works" (Astrogildo Pereira), or, in other words, a "progressive maturation" (Afrânio Coutinho).[2]

In a famous critical essay, titled "Notícia da Atual Literatura Brasileira: Instinto de Nacionalidade," (1873) Machado defined what in his opinion constituted the degree of national identity that a writer should demonstrate. With this gesture he not only clarified his position, but also anticipated the incomprehension that many would show for his work, always responding to the allegation that his work was not representative of the country because it lacked an interest in domestic problems and reality. Machado believed that literature, and primarily a young literature such as Brazilian literature, should portray the topics with which its region provides it. This would correspond to a necessary stage in the development of a national literature—being new, it would pass through a period of self-affirmation. And not without irony, Machado made the following comment on the mandatory presence of a "national touch" in the works of Brazilian writers: "The literary youth, above all, make this point into a legitimate question of self-love" (1873, 801). The "general desire to create a more independent literature" (1873, 802) confirmed that an orientation toward the national was justifiable. The author forewarned that this orientation should not become an absolute and tyrannical value. Thus, it should not suggest a narrow or impoverishing nationalism, which would only reduce the thematic and formal breadth of the new literature, removing its possibility for exploration and accomplishment.

The "national instinct" (*"instinto de nacionalidade"*) expected of a writer was, in the frequently cited Machadian formula, an "intimate feeling, that makes him a man of his time and of his country, even when he portrays topics remote in time and space" (1873, 804). It was not dependent, therefore, on landscapes, on characteristic types, on series of elements that might be superficially present or be described according to a foreign gaze, from an only slightly or non-Brazilian perspective. The feeling to which Machado referred could be expressed even when the topic, the language, and the form at first glance reflect very little of the national. Topics and forms of an initially universal character can reveal themselves as extremely Brazilian on another level of articulation, one less superficial and evident. Roberto Schwarz' book, *Um Mestre na Periferia do Capitalismo* (1990), seeks to demonstrate that this is precisely what occurs in *The Posthumous Memoirs*. As Schwarz had already pointed out in a previous essay, Machado "presents a Brazilianism of that internal type which makes local color unnecessary."[3] In reality, the presence and visibility of the national in the work of Machado can be identified on more than one level, as much in a more immediate, concrete, and descriptive sphere as on a more abstract plane:

> ... the country's evident singularities—those in which the fellow countrymen recognize themselves with pride or with laughter—are not absent from Machado's novel, but they do not set the tone of the book. In brief, let us say that instead of *elements* of identification, Machado sought *relations* and *forms*. The national crafting of these is profound, without being obvious.[4]

The complexity of this issue has given rise to three approaches that can be identified in the reception of Machado's work. The first, that of the "localists," already referred to above, accused the writer of disregard or even disdain for the Brazilian—its nature, society, history, customs—, since he often portrayed local color ironically. A second current, that of the "universalists," found what the localists considered an absence to be of high quality, lauding Machado precisely for not conceding primacy to the most visible particularities of the country nor to the most evident and typical elements of national identification—those which, as Schwarz underscores, frequently appear in the author's novels, though in a brief, casual, discrete, and deliberately diminished way and almost always as the target of Machadian irony. These critics esteem the de-provincialization in Machado, the focus on universal issues, and the concern with "human nature," that were motivated, for example, by the novelist's recourse to the seventeenth-century French moralists (and not only in terms of psychological analysis and quotes, but also in terms of style, given the sententious form that Machadian prose assumes in numerous passages). Nevertheless, Schwarz, by recovering Antonio Candido's argument, doesn't neglect to point out that these two currents are affiliated with the same movement to valorize Brazil, seeking to create a literature that could serve as an instrument of national affirmation, be it through equating Brazilian intellectual production to cultured European standards or through expressing Brazilian local realities and originality.[5]

A third current, in which Schwarz situates himself, proposes a "dialectic of the local and the universal" (1989, 168). This position claims that Machado was able to take perfect advantage of social material and existing Brazilian fiction without having to resort to the picturesque and the exotic, while at the same time making use of various foreign models. The influence of these models was assimilated into and *declared* in a poetics that is fundamentally marked by the *rereading of tradition*. Machado incorporated the production of earlier Brazilian authors, especially that of Joaquim Manuel de Macedo (1820-1882), Manuel Antônio de Almeida (1831-1861) and José de Alencar (1829-1877),[6] as well as what the Western literary tradition put at the disposal of such an astute reader.[7] Antonio Candido's observation on the independence of mature Machadian fiction in relation to the literary fashion of the time is important in this regard:

> At a moment when Flaubert was systematizing the theory of the 'novel that narrates itself,' erasing the narrator behind narrative objectivity; at a moment in which Zola advocated the exhaustive inventory of reality, observed in the smallest details, he freely cultivated the elliptical, the incomplete, the fragmentary, intervening in the narrative with delectable scheming, reminding the reader that his conventional voice was behind it. It was a way of maintaining, in the second

half of the nineteenth century, Sterne's whimsical tone… It was also an echo of the *'conte philosophique,'* in the style of Voltaire…[8]

As Enylton de Sá Rego demonstrated in the indispensable *O Calundu e a Panacéia: Machado de Assis, a Sátira Menipéia e a Tradição Luciânica* (1989), in order to compose the texts of the so-called second phase of his work, the author chose models in Western literature that included authors belonging to the long-lived tradition of Menippean satire, begun in the second century BC. Upon publication, *The Posthumous Memoirs*, with its discontinuous format and digressive narrative, was subject to inquiry regarding the genre to which it would belong. Meanwhile, as the narrator himself indicated in the "prologue" of the book, the memoirs served as a prime example of the Menippean tradition. The narrator Brás Cubas claims to have adopted in his autobiography "the free form of a Sterne or a Xavier de Maistre" (1881, Prologue) two authors whose works—*Tristram Shandy* (1760-7), *A Sentimental Journey* (1768) and *Voyage Autour de ma Chambre* (1795)—are representative of the Menippean genre. The mere mention of antecedents in the Menippean lineage is one of the constants of this tradition. (In addition to the two authors mentioned in the prologue, later in the novel Seneca and Erasmus are mentioned directly, and Lucian indirectly.) The narrator also claims to have written "with the quill of jest and the ink of melancholy" (1881, 16, 1), and the hybrid, serious-comic nature is a typical mixture of the satiric tradition linked to Menippus of Gadara.

Although they reflect entirely distinct critical perspectives, it is important to highlight that the insightful study by Sá Rego[9] of the relationships between some of the texts from Machado's second phase and this satiric tradition does not generally contradict Schwarz' sociological reading of *The Posthumous Memoirs* in the now classic *Um Mestre na Periferia do Capitalismo*. Adequately situating them in the context of literary tradition, Sá Rego's book contributes by identifying, specifying, and re-dimensioning the techniques, processes, and topics employed by Machado. Included in these are those described by Schwarz as aspects of the formal principle that structures the narrative of *The Posthumous Memoirs*, as we will see later. *O Calundu e a Panacéia* allows for a greater understanding of the writer's poetics.

Returning to the reading that Schwarz proposes of later Machadian fiction, both the localist and the universalist critical currents fall into the same mistake: that of viewing local representation in Machado's novel as

BLUMA WADDINGTON VILAR

unimportant, as a result of the diminutive position that this representation occupies. This position, not the absence or scarcity of local elements, becomes the "delicate overcoat in Machado's mocking contrast with so-called universal values that he uses a material for his fiction."[10] Schwarz points exactly to the absurdity of the association, the laughable disproportion between the local fact and the general reflection evoked by it as one of the keys to Machadian narrative and its national character as well as its *social* (and not merely psychological) realism, which are offered to the interpretation of the careful reader.[11] *Um Mestre na Periferia do Capitalismo* attempts to demonstrate how this social realism manifests itself in *The Posthumous Memoirs* through specific processes or mechanisms, among which is the "mismatched" and comic conjuncture between the local and the universal that lacks the necessary mediation between one plane and the other.

"To the Worm Who Gnawed the Cold Flesh of My Corpse I Dedicate these Posthumous Memoirs as a Nostalgic Remembrance."[12] Upon reading this dedication, the reader becomes aware of the paradox and the jest of the title: it is not an autobiography published posthumously, but one written *post mortem* by a "deceased author," as Brás defines himself in the first chapter. In this chapter, titled "The Author's Demise," he explains his decision to begin his story at the end, that is, with the death and burial of the very narrator that describes them. The alleged motives—that for the posthumous author "the grave was a second cradle" and that "the writing would be more distinctive and novel this way"—are summed up by a sacrilegious comparison of his book with the *Pentateuch*; though Moses "who also wrote about his own death" did not have the originality of doing it at the beginning (1881, chap.1). This beginning chapter provides a good sense of the meddlesome tone of the narrator-author, characterized by an irreverence, jest, or irony that are not deterred by any topic, person, or situation.

In the Prologue, the reader is immediately insulted and prepared for an entire litany of aggressions, jokes, and ironies that the narrator reserves for him during the course of the book. Therefore, the constant "dialogue" with the reader is not always friendly. Metanarrative comments also become frequent and the narrator often considers the composition, style, organization, and progress of his narrative. In addition, he engages in countless philosophical digressions that depart from a trivial episode, a local and simple circumstance, or a personal and selfish interest, in order to comically reach a universally valid conclusion.

Brás Cubas' story, which is thus systematically interrupted, begins with the "author" narrating his death and burial: discussing the *causa mortis*; digressing to trace his genealogy; returning to the *causa mortis*, the fixed idea of the invention of a universal panacea, a poultice capable of "alleviating our melancholy humanity;"[13] returning to the period of his illness, when he received a visit from an old secret lover and experiences his famous delirium. After Chapter 10, Brás' life as a wealthy and idle member of Rio's elite is related in chronological order, the "narrative part" continuously being interrupted by "reflection"[14] in a *drunken* style, as the narrator himself describes in Chapter 71, "The Defect of this Book":

> ... the main defect of this book is you, reader. You're in a hurry to grow old and the book moves slowly. You love direct and continuous narration, a regular and fluid style, and this book and my style are like drunkards, they stagger left and right, they walk and stop, mumble, yell, cackle, shake their fists at the sky, stumble, and fall....

In the famous final passage of Chapter 27, titled "Virgília?," the narrator defines human existence as a succession of editions in which each new version reviews and corrects the previous one:

> Let Pascal say that man is a thinking reed. No. He's a thinking erratum, that's what he is. Every season of life is an edition that corrects the one before and which will also be corrected until the definitive edition, which the publisher gives to the worms gratis.

Thus, a clear homology is established between life and composition—the writing of his autobiography—, since the narrative of *The Posthumous Memoirs* also develops through a series of shifts in direction, digressions, contemplations, exceptions, and corrections. In other words, it is organized and proceeds according to what can be appropriately labeled a *principle of erratum* (*"princípio da errata"*),[15] which is responsible for its interrupted and irregular pace. The "theory of human editions," of man as a "thinking erratum," therefore has a textual equivalent in this principle.

Though there is not enough space to address them in this article, points of contact clearly exist between the perspective outlined through the principle of erratum and Roberto Schwarz' exhaustively developed hypothesis in *Um Mestre na Periferia do Capitalismo*.[16] In Schwarz' words, what occurs is a "correspondence between Machadian style and the particularities of a simultaneously slave-holding and bourgeois Brazilian society." A link is also established between the structure and function of nineteenth-century Brazilian society and the literary form, "Machado's narrative formula," in which there is a "systematic alternation of perspectives" by the narrator. This narrator constantly changes perspective in an arbitrary way, continuously disidentifying himself with the position assumed in the preceding sentence, paragraph, chapter, or episode and establishing this *volubility* as a "rule of writing." This capricious and voluble movement that the narrator imposes on *The Posthumous Memoirs* should be understood as both a "rule of the narrative composition" and as a "stylization of the conduct of the Brazilian dominant class." As Schwarz underscores, "in the course of his affirmation, the narrator's versatility scorns all the forms and contents that appear in the *Memoirs* and subordinates them… In this sense the volubility is… the formal principle of the book."[17] According to this perspective, the point of interest is the link between the literary and the extra-literary, or in Schwarz's terms, between "literary form and social process;" between narrative structure and the "structure of the country;" between "Machadian style" and "social relations"[18] that were characteristic of Brazilian reality of the time. Thus, in this approach intertextual relationships are of less importance.

The proposed principle of erratum also foregrounds the relationship between the literary and the extra-literary, since this famous editorial metaphor brings life and the human condition themselves into the book's universe. In this regard, there are few relevant passages. In his delirium, Brás Cubas felt himself "transformed into Aquinas' *Summa Theologica*, printed in one volume and morocco-bound, with silver clasps and illustrations. This was an idea that gave my body a most complete immobility…" (Chap. 7, "Delirium"). Later the narrator defines himself in the following manner: "we're not an *in-folio* public but an *in-*12 one, not much text, wide margins, elegant type, gold trim, and ornamental designs… designs above all" (Chap. 22, "Return to Rio"). Another approach can yet be conceived of through the analysis of an intriguing procedure evidenced in Chapter 55— "The Old Dialogue of Adam and Eve"—and Chapter 139—"How I Didn't Get to Be Minister of State"—which evoke numerous passages in Sterne's *Tristram Shandy* and do without words altogether, limiting themselves to the use of punctuation marks, such as the line of dots that entitles Chapter 53.

The dedication, Chapters 26 ("The Author Hesitates"), 125 ("Epitaph") and 142 ("The Secret Request") explore the possibilities of diagramming and reproducing the book.

It is worthwhile, therefore, to analyze the implications this emphasis has for the literary and, ultimately, for everything in the realm of writing and printed books, making the peculiarities of this media salient: its materiality, its typographical and editorial aspects, and its reproducibility. Within this line of inquiry, it would also be necessary to study the relationship between publication in newspapers and journals and fiction writing. The "decisive role" of the "continuous dialogue with the press, with printing,"[19] in Machadian fictional craftsmanship is the subject of Flora Süssekind's valuable article "Machado de Assis e a Musa Mecânica," included in *Papéis Colados* (1993). The author asserts:

> If Machado de Assis is one of the Brazilian writers who was best able to articulate local literary production's ties to newspaper publication and give shape to the tension between writing and printing,… something in his work, beyond this relationship and within the literary form itself, in the tensions between composition and medium of transmission, seems to repeatedly suggest them.[20]

As elements that suggest such tensions—either through the assimilation of certain characteristics of publication in newspapers or magazines, of mechanical reproduction, or through resistance to other aspects of publication—Süssekind indicates the great fragmentation of the chapters; the "display of the graphic materiality of the printed text;" the very strong presence of the narrator, who is thus unfit for typical narration of news and *faits divers*, and, due to his repeated principle of erratum, is also incompatible with "neat pagination, control of letters and lines, and of the apparently definitive aspect of the printed page." According to Süssekind, these elements are compounded with the "powerful image of the book," "the bookish form of the quotidian," "of love, life, and people"[21] in Machado's fiction.

Another contribution to be examined is Juracy Saraiva's study, "*Memórias Póstumas de Brás Cubas*: Edição e Errata," in the book *O Circuito das Memórias em Machado de Assis* (1993), given its clear proximity to my suggested reading in at least one fundamental aspect. A *correspondence* becomes apparent in the author's interpretation, between the ambivalent discourse of the *Memoirs*' narrator and human life, whose course is permeated with contradictions. Thus, Saraiva writes towards the end of her study:

BLUMA WADDINGTON VILAR

The contradictory, inherent to life, is represented by the narrator through an ambivalent discourse that excludes not only semantic univocality, but also structural uni-textuality. When the I-enunciator conceives biography itself as a reading of life and books, he unites two semantic universes and institutes a process of refraction, whose reciprocal effects allow life to be glanced in texts and the configuration of texts, in the process of life.[22]

For Saraiva, there are two "formal principles of the story" told by the narrator: "*discontinuity*" and "*multiplicity.*" These principles are related, as perceivable in the chapter that, according to her, illustrates both of them— Chapter 4, "The *Idée Fixe.*" Saraiva observes that diegetic progression is interrupted in this chapter, as it is repeatedly in the rest of the narrative, according to the whims of the narrator's eccentric imagination. In addition to avoiding thematic uniformity, diverse perspectives are invoked through the meeting of "historical truth and the fantastic, the dogmatic and its deconstruction through humor, philosophical reflection and banalities." Thus, the narrator emphasizes the discontinuous and the multiple, which are converted into a "systematic process," and "expose the *formal orientation of the text.*"[23]

After reading Juracy Saraiva's comments, it is clear that the formal principles that she refers to as *discontinuity* and *multiplicity* are not so distant from what Schwarz had already labeled *volubility*. Nevertheless, to Saraiva, a relationship between the narrator's characteristic style and class behavior typical of the nineteenth-century land-holding elite is not established. Volubility betrayed arbitrariness; excess; smug superiority; the tendency toward an exhibitionist and mocking domination of almost all Western cultural tradition; a confrontational and arrogant triumphal attitude; an "ideological ambivalence of the Brazilian elite," (Schwarz, 1990, 41) imposed or granted them by the historical circumstances of Post-Independence Brazil. In other words, this reflected the accommodation promoted by the Brazilian dominant class between liberal bourgeois ideology adopted by the civilized nations and concepts and practices contradictory to this ideology, such as slavery and patronage, which were characteristic of a society still tied to the colonial productive system.

In this essay, I have attempted to synthesize some interpretations of *The Posthumous Memoirs.* Although I gave particular attention to Roberto Schwarz' sociological reading, I would like to stress the importance of exploring different angles when approaching the Machadian text. It is important to integrate these perspectives, when possible, in an analysis that takes into account and articulates the various levels of reading that this text can sustain. If *The Posthumous Memoirs* consists of a rereading both of the old Menippean tradition and of contemporary Brazilian fiction, this re-elaboration of forms and content was done in a way that brings the perverse operation of the ambivalent and unjust Brazilian social structure of the second half of the nineteenth century to the sphere of textual organization. This transposition remains current, given the persistence of the same mechanisms in contemporary Brazilian society. The incorporation of other thematic axes and other links between theme and form into the analysis, some of which have been discussed and others in need of more diligent study, will only lead to a more complex and richer critical understanding of *The Memoirs* and of Machado's work.

Notes

[1] Since the Native Brazilian is called in Portuguese "*índio,*" the romantic movement grounded on the celebration of the Indigenous heritage was given the name "*Indianismo.*" (Translator's note.)

[2] See Astrogildo Pereira, "Antes e Depois do 'Brás Cubas,'" *Machado de Assis: Ensaios e Apontamentos Avulsos* (Rio de Janeiro: Livraria São José, 1959) 183-9; Afrânio Coutinho, "Machado de Assis na Literatura Brasileira," *Obra Completa,* by J. M. Machado de Assis, 4th ed., vol. 1 (1959; Rio de Janeiro: Nova Aguilar, 1979) 23-65, especially 25-28; and, above all, Roberto Schwarz, "A novidade das *Memórias Póstumas de Brás Cubas,*" *Machado de Assis, uma Revisão,* eds. Antonio Carlos Secchin et al. (Rio de Janeiro: In-Fólio, 1998) 47-64.

[3] Schwarz, "Duas Notas" 166.

[4] Schwarz, "Duas Notas" 166.

[5] Schwarz, "Duas Notas" 167, 169-70; Candido, *Formação* 9-22, especially 9-11.

[6] On the relationship between Machado's fiction and that of these three authors, see, among others, Antonio Candido, "Um Instrumento de Descoberta e Interpretação," *Formação da Literatura Brasileira.* Vol. II. 109-118, especially 117-8; Temístocles Linhares, "Macedo e o Romance Brasileiro," *Revista do Livro* (Rio de Janeiro) 4.14 (junho 1959): 97-105; Roberto Schwarz, "A Importação do Romance e suas Contradições em Alencar," *Ao Vencedor as Batatas: Forma Literária e Processo Social nos Inícios do Romance Brasileiro* (São Paulo: Duas Cidades, 1977) 29-60; Schwarz, "A Novidade" 63-4; Flora Süssekind, *O Brasil Não é Longe Daqui: O Narrador, a Viagem* (São Paulo: Companhia das Letras, 1990) especially 152-55, 260-76; and *O Sobrinho pelo Tio* (Rio de Janeiro: Fundação Casa de Rui Barbosa, 1995) especially 9, 10, 15, 16, 21-29.

[7] On the relationship of Machado's work to Western literary tradition, see, among others, Eugênio Gomes, *Machado de Assis: Influências Inglesas* (Rio de Janeiro: Pallas; Brasília: INL, 1976); Helen Caldwell, *The Brazilian Othello of Machado de Assis: A Study of Dom Casmurro* (Berkeley: U of California P, 1960); Luiz Costa Lima, "A Recepção do *Tristram Shandy* no

BLUMA WADDINGTON VILAR

Romance Machadiano," *Dispersa Demanda: Ensaios Sobre Literatura e Teoria* (Rio de Janeiro: Francisco Alves, 1980) 59-64; Antonio Candido, "À Roda do Quarto e da Vida," *Revista USP* 2 (June/July/August 1989): 101-4; Gilberto Pinheiro Passos, *Poética do Legado: Presença Francesa em* Memórias Póstumas de Brás Cubas (São Paulo: Annablume, 1996); Marta de Senna, *O Olhar Oblíquo do Bruxo: Ensaios em Torno de Machado de Assis* (Rio de Janeiro: Nova Fronteira, 1998); Regina Zilberman, "*Memórias Póstumas de Brás Cubas*: Diálogos com a Tradição Literária," *Revista Tempo Brasileiro* 133/134 (1998): 155-170.

[8] Antonio Candido, "Esquema de Machado de Assis," *Vários Escritos*, 2nd ed. (São Paulo: Duas Cidades, 1977) 22.

[9] See Enylton de Sá Rego, *O Calundu e a Panacéia.*

[10] Schwarz, "Duas Notas" 168.

[11] See John Gledson, *Machado de Assis: Ficção e História*, and *Machado de Assis: Impostura e Realismo. Uma Reinterpretação de* Dom Casmurro.

[12] All quoted passages are taken from Gregory Rabassa's translation: J. M. Machado de Assis, *The Posthumous Memoirs of Brás Cubas* (New York; Oxford: Oxford UP, 1997). (Translator's note)

[13] Assis, *The Posthumous* 9.

[14] Assis, *The Posthumous* 11.

[15] On the denomination, suggested by the novel itself, see Süssekind, "Brás Cubas e a Literatura como Errata."

[16] Schwarz had already developed the same hypothesis on various occasions. See, for example, Alfredo Bosi et al., "Mesa-redonda," *Machado de Assis* (São Paulo: Ática, Coleção "Escritores Brasileiros: Antologia e Estudos," 1982) 316-21, 329-30, 334-5, 339; Schwarz, "Complexo, Moderno, Nacional, e Negativo," *Que Horas São?* 115-25; Schwarz, "A Novidade." He discusses this hypothesis again in "Um Mestre na Periferia do Capitalismo (Entrevista)," *Seqüências Brasileiras: Ensaios* (São Paulo: Companhia das Letras, 1999) 220-6.

[17] Schwarz, *Um Mestre* 11, 12, 17 and 31.

[18] Schwarz, *Um Mestre* 11-12. "Forma Literária e Processo Social nos Inícios do Romance Brasileiro" was the subtitle of the book *Ao Vencedor as Batatas* (1977).

[19] Süssekind, "Machado de Assis e a Musa Mecânica" 184.

[20] Süssekind, "Machado" 188.

[21] Süssekind, "Machado" 188-9. Regarding this issue, the most important recent contribution to the interpretation of Machado's fiction is the work of Abel Barros Baptista, *Autobibliografias*, which discusses Machado's fiction in its relation to the "question of the book."

[22] Saraiva 88.

[23] Saraiva 88.

Works Cited

Assis, J.M. Machado de. 1881. *Memórias Póstumas de Brás Cubas.* São Paulo: Ática, 1998. 24° ed.

———. *The Posthumous Memoirs of Brás Cubas.* Trans. Gregory Rabassa; with a Foreword by Enylton de Sá Rego; and an Afterword by Gilberto Pinheiro Passos. New York; Oxford: Oxford UP, 1997.

Baptista, Abel Barros. *Autobibliografias. Solicitação do Livro na Ficção e na Ficção de Machado de Assis.* Lisboa: Relógio D'Água, 1998.

Bosi, Alfredo et al. "Mesa-redonda." *Machado de Assis*. São Paulo: Ática, Coleção "Escritores Brasileiros: Antologia e Estudos" , 1982. 310-343.

Candido, Antonio. *Formação da Literatura Brasileira: Momentos Decisivos* (1959). Belo Horizonte: Itatiaia, 1981, 6a ed., vol. 2.

————. "Esquema de Machado de Assis" (1968). *Vários Escritos*. 2a ed. São Paulo: Duas Cidades, 1977. 15-32.

————. "À Roda do Quarto e da Vida." *Revista USP* 2 (June/July/August 1989): 101-104.

Coutinho, Afrânio. "Machado de Assis na Literatura Brasileira." Assis, J. M. Machado de. *Obra Completa* (1959). Rio de Janeiro: Nova Aguilar, 1979. 25-65.

Gledson, John. *Machado de Assis: Ficção e História*. Tradução de Sônia Coutinho, Rio de Janeiro: Paz e Terra, 1986.

————. *Machado de Assis: Impostura e Realismo. Uma Reinterpretação de* Dom Casmurro. Tradução de Fernando Py, São Paulo: Companhia das Letras, 1991.

Rego, Enylton de Sá. *O Calundu e a Panacéia: Machado de Assis, a Sátira Menipéia e a Tradição Luciânica*. Rio de Janeiro: Forense Universitária, 1989.

Saraiva, Juracy Assmann. "*Memórias Póstumas de Brás Cubas*: Edição e Errata." *O Circuito das Memórias em Machado de Assis*. São Paulo: EdUSP, 1993. 43-92.

Schwarz, Roberto. "A Importação do Romance e suas Contradições em Alencar." *Ao Vencedor as Batatas. Forma Literária e Processo Social nos Inícios do Romance Brasileiro*. São Paulo: Duas Cidades, 1977. 29-60.

————. "Complexo, Moderno, Nacional, e Negativo." *Que Horas São?* 1987. São Paulo: Companhia das Letras, 1989. 115-125.

————. "Duas Notas sobre Machado de Assis." *Que Horas São?* Op. cit. 165-178.

————. *Um Mestre na Periferia do Capitalismo: Machado de Assis*. São Paulo: Duas Cidades, 1990.

————. "A Novidade das *Memórias Póstumas de Brás Cubas*." Secchin, Antonio Carlos et al.(org.). *Machado de Assis: Uma Revisão*. Rio de Janeiro: In-Fólio, 1998. 47-64.

————. "*Um Mestre na Periferia do Capitalismo* (entrevista)." *Seqüências Brasileiras: Ensaios*. São Paulo: Companhia das Letras, 1999. 220-226.

Süssekind, Flora. "Brás Cubas e a Literatura como Errata." *Revista Tempo Brasileiro*, 81 (April/June 1985): 13-21.

————. "Machado de Assis e a Musa Mecânica." *Papéis Colados*. Rio de Janeiro: Editora UFRJ, 1993. 183-191.

Rebellion in the Backlands: Landscape with Figures

Walnice Nogueira Galvão
Translated by Paulo Henriques Britto

Brazil's historical situation in the period immediately preceding the writing of *Os Sertões*[1] informs the very conception of the book. The Republic was proclaimed in 1889, one year after the abolition of slavery, and the early years of the republican period were marked by a number of more or less serious and protracted insurrections, as well as small local uprisings. It took some time for the new regime to consolidate and begin to function properly. The Canudos War, which took place in the hinterland of Bahia in 1896-1897, is just one among the various revolts that punctuated the period of transition. *Os Sertões* is a chronicle of this historical event, to which the author was an eyewitness.

*

Euclides da Cunha first came into contact with his subject matter when he was sent to Bahia by the daily *O Estado de São Paulo* as a special correspondent to cover the Canudos War. The series of reports he sent from the battlefield made him famous. But his journalistic writings now interest us mostly because they can be read as the origins of *Os Sertões*.

The tremendous impact of the war made it a turning point in the history of the Brazilian press: for the first time ever in the country, a large number of newspapers sent reporters to the scene of the events themselves. Throughout the duration of the war, the major dailies of Rio, São Paulo and Bahia kept a special column—simply titled "Canudos" in most of them—that was exclusively dedicated to the topic. Everything and anything related to Canudos was published: outright fabrications, dogmatic statements by party stalwarts, forged documents, faked letters. All these publications had the purpose of reinforcing the idea of an imminent restoration of monarchy. The importance of the press in this context cannot be underestimated: at a time when audiovisual resources had not yet been invented, the newspaper was the mass medium *par excellence.*

*

Returning from the war, Euclides da Cunha dedicated himself to the task of amassing a broad range of knowledge in order to work on his book, which was published only five years later, in 1902. It was met with overwhelming praise. Like a majestic portico, the opening section of *Os Sertões,* entitled "The Land," provides a splendid description of the spatial context of the war.

The author describes the region of Canudos from three points of view— the topographic, the geological and the meteorological—in a passionate language that creates imposing natural vistas. Rivers rush onward, waterfalls cascade; the land itself appears to mimic the flow of the rivers in the contortions of its features and the clashes between the different geological layers that underlie it. It is an extraordinary landscape, which seems to be man-made on a monumental scale, reminding one of colossal *menhirs* or the ruins of a cyclopean colosseum.

All of this, however, is seen from a great distance, providing a sort of God's-eye view of an immemorial desert, parched by an unforgiving sun. The cosmic forces themselves can only be referred to by means of antitheses.

To convey to the reader a sense of the unfamiliarity of the *sertão,* the author relies on shock tactics: he presents a soldier who seems to be asleep, only to disclose that in fact he has been dead for months, his intact body having been naturally mummified by the dry air.

The scourge of chronic droughts is analyzed at length; a number of explanations are proposed for their occurrence, ranging from the influence of sunspots to the region's peculiar wind patterns. Later on, the author will move on from hypotheses to actual proposals for solutions.

The vegetation of the *caatinga* must face two unfavorable conditions: the aridity of the land and the heat of the sun. Thus, its adaptive mutations all involve protection against death caused by a lack of water or by overexposure to the sun. The defensive strategies are varied: some plants turn into dwarfs in order to expose as little surface as possible to the harshness of the elements; other species bury themselves so that only a small portion of them appears above ground; yet others join together to form social plants, developing common roots that retain a maximum of water and topsoil, in addition to reinforcing mutual security.

Euclides da Cunha concludes that the *sertão* environment of Canudos is unique, since its characteristics do not coincide exactly with any pre-existing category, emphasizing that "nature here rejoices in a play of antitheses" (Chap. V).

*

Having examined the physical environment, the author proceeds to analyze the ethnic groups of the region. He believes that the fundamental and most complex question in the study of Brazil's population is the issue of miscegenation, a thorny issue that engaged the attention of all the nation's intellectuals of the time. The mixture of races had given rise to the *sertanejo*, a racial type with unique physical and spiritual characteristics inherited from the three ethnic groups from which it originated. These characteristics, Euclides da Cunha believed, had advantages as well as disadvantages. Their positive qualities were adaptability to a hostile environment, resistance and a stoic attitude. The handicaps were religious fanaticism, superstitiousness, a precarious psychological balance and a marked backwardness in relation to the progress of civilization.

The deterministic reasoning applied to the analyses of the physical environment and ethnic components is also applied to the examination of the personality of Antonio Vicente Mendes Maciel, the Pilgrim, also known as Antonio Conselheiro. Euclides da Cunha sees him as a synthesis of the historical process that resulted from the different populations that settled the land, shaped by miscegenation and isolation.

The author's diagnosis of Antonio Conselheiro is contradictory: the reader realizes that Cunha hesitates between admiring his greatness and branding him "a very sick man" suffering from paranoia. This leader of men, who concentrates in his person "the obscurantism of three separate races," "grew in stature until he was projected into History" (Chap. IV).

Antonio Conselheiro, a mystical Catholic leader, wandered through the *sertão* accompanied by his followers, leading a life of penitence, preaching and presiding over the building and rebuilding of churches, cemeteries and dams. He lived this way for thirty years with his following growing continuously.

In an attempt to elucidate the origins of the Canudos War, Cunha shows how the advent of the Republic brought about changes that disturbed the *conselheiristas*: new taxes, the separation of church and state, religious freedom and civil marriage, which was felt to be a flagrant rejection of a Catholic sacrament.

WALNICE NOGUEIRA GALVÃO

Shunned by all, around 1893 the pilgrims finally found refuge in the ruins of an abandoned farm known as Canudos, deep in the hinterland of Bahia. Gradually they erected the wattle houses that were constituted by what Cunha referred to as the oxymoronic "mud-walled Troy" (Chap. II).

There is no wood in the *sertão*, where the typical vegetation, the *caatinga*, is a stunted growth of gnarled brush, twigs and cacti. The people of Canudos had, therefore, bought a certain amount of planks for the New Church they were building. The purchase was made, and paid for in advance, in the city of Juazeiro. But the goods were not delivered, and Conselheiro's followers marched unarmed toward Juazeiro, singing religious hymns. They were met by an ambush of state troopers whom the local authorities in Uauá had summoned. The soldiers decimated them but were then forced to retreat.

In January 1897, a new offensive was mounted with more and better equipped soldiers. Once again, the government forces were defeated.

The third expedition was to be commanded by Colonel Moreira César, who had recently crushed another insurrection in the South. His method of repression there had been so violent that he had earned the nickname "Cutthroat." After the two earlier losses, Canudos was now perceived as a national threat that was too serious to be left to the responsibility of state troops. A major attack was prepared, with federal troops convoked from all over the country and with modern weaponry that included cannon, accompanied by a nationwide campaign to win over public opinion. Excitement was in the air, the buzz of patriotic demagoguery; some began to suggest that the events in the remote *sertão* indicated an attempt to restore the monarchy.

The whole nation was watching when the third expedition gathered in Salvador and departed for Canudos. The government forces attacked the settlement; however, a few hours later, having suffered heavy losses, including that of their commander, they fled in retreat. In order to run faster, soldiers abandoned their weapons and ammunition—collected and treasured by the rebels—and even parts of their uniforms, such as jackets and boots.

Euclides describes in vivid imagery the uproar that followed the third defeat. In Rio and São Paulo, the country's largest cities, there were demonstrations in the streets that culminated in riots; the crowd's fury turned against the most obvious targets—the few remaining monarchist newspapers. Four newspaper offices were destroyed, and the owner of one of them was lynched. There was a general demand that the threat to the newborn

Republic be quashed. Students signed a petition calling for the extermination of the followers of the "degenerate." Congress spoke of nothing else. The press described the defeat as a national disaster, disseminating a sense of insecurity and alarm throughout the country, publishing false information and forged letters, and speaking of domestic and even international conspiracies.

A fourth expedition was planned, this headed by an even higher-ranking officer than the previous one: the commander was to be General Artur Oscar de Andrade Guimarães, assisted by four other generals. The expedition even included a marshal, for the Minister of War, Marshal Machado Bittencourt, went to Canudos with his entire general staff, effectively moving his ministry to the theater of operations. Troops were mobilized around the country. It was as a member of this expedition, in the double position of reporter and aide to the Minister's general staff, that Euclides da Cunha became an eyewitness of the war.

The fourth expedition headed for Canudos in June 1897. The rebel town was entirely surrounded so that no reinforcements or support parties could reach it. Most of all, the siege deprived the town of water, a precious commodity in the drought-ridden *caatinga*, laboriously fetched by the townspeople from water holes dug in the dry bed of the Vaza-Barris, a seasonal stream.

Meanwhile, the people of Canudos, who previously had possessed no more than a few ancient muzzle-loading firearms such as harquebuses and blunderbusses, now owned some of the most advanced weapons of the time—including highly valued repeating rifles like the Austrian Mannlicher and the Belgian Comblains—which had been discarded during the rout of the third expedition.

As the siege began to have an effect and some sectors of Canudos fell into government hands, the obstinate resistance of the rebels began to defy understanding and to be seen as something of an enigma. A few days before the end, a surrender was negotiated. However, to the chagrin of the army, the only insurrectionists who actually surrendered were about three hundred women, who had been reduced to walking skeletons by extreme hunger, accompanied by their children and a few old men; freed of this dead weight, the resistance became even more intense. Finally, after several days of heavy bombing, including the unprecedented use of a sort of improvised napalm (gasoline was poured on houses that were still occupied and ignited with thrown sticks of dynamite), Canudos was silenced on October 5, 1897,

WALNICE NOGUEIRA GALVÃO

without having surrendered. Of the final four resisters, whose burned bodies were found in a pit on the central square surrounded by churches, one was an old man and the other a young boy.

According to the army's official report, there were 5,200 houses in the settlement. If we estimate conservatively that there were five people living in each house—in the *sertão* the figure was usually higher—the population of the rebel town was 26,000. This would have meant that Canudos was the second largest city in Bahia. (At the time, São Paulo had no more than 200,000 inhabitants.) Antonio Conselheiro had died a few days before the final collapse of the resistance; his body was exhumed and beheaded, and the head was taken to the Bahia Faculty of Medicine for an autopsy. The purpose was to discover what had been wrong with him. According to Cesare Lombroso's theories, widely accepted at the time, measurements of the skull and dissection of the brain might provide an answer. Unfortunately, however, the results of the studies proved inconclusive.

This, in short, is the tragic plot of *Os Sertões*.

*

After a war that turned out to have been an inglorious massacre of destitute wretches, it became clear that there had been no conspiracy; the desperately poor peasants had had no connection whatsoever with real monarchists—white, upper-class urbanites, who were horrified at the very thought of associating with such a "riffraff" of "fanatics"—and had enjoyed no logistical support from anyone in Brazil or abroad.

Public opinion then underwent a striking about-face; the war began to be seen as a regrettable massacre of brave Brazilians engaged in a fratricidal struggle. In addition, it was no longer a secret that the army's conduct had been far from irreproachable. A few war correspondents had already disclosed that it had been common practice—approved by the commanders—to tie up prisoners and behead them in public.

Another important consequence of the Canudos War, the importance of which should not be underestimated, is the fact that it completed the solidification of the republican regime and finally exorcised the specter of monarchical restoration. On the basis of contemporary witnesses, it seems clear now that public opinion had been manipulated and that the "rebels" in Canudos were the scapegoats of this process. They were forced into the role of an internal enemy of the nation, an enemy that had to be faced in a common effort that promoted national unity.

*

The transformation of the newspaper stories into book form required five years of work and intense ambition. The body of information contained in the reports was unified by a naturalist style, the dominant trend in Brazilian literature at the time, with additional Parnassian touches in the evocation of the landscape. The typically Naturalist combination of impersonal description and genetic concern—in the widest sense of "genetic"—is here put to use to chronicle a war in which the dramatic genre is necessarily concentrated.

However, as if by means of a process of contamination, the first and second sections, concerning the land and the people, are also treated dramatically. In the first, the components of nature are anthropomorphized and endowed with feelings and even purpose. In the second, the central theme is the fierce clash between three races in a struggle for hegemony. But, as often occurs in Naturalist works, at each moment ideas and theories are advanced and acquire individual voices of their own. Determinism, scientism, evolutionism, the notion of the ineluctable linearity of progress, heredity, all play major roles in the narrative. The polyphonic character of the book as a whole is the first element of its composition that should be underscored.

The second element is intertextuality. Throughout *Os Sertões*, a variety of texts and authors are quoted and discussed and provide the book with an encyclopedic texture. In the section titled "The Rebellion," the author relies not only on his own dispatches and notebooks but also on news stories by other correspondents, the army's orders of the day, and government reports. The opening section, "The Land," draws on geology, meteorology, botany, zoology, physics and chemistry. In "Man," the most polemic part of the book and rife with conjectures of all kinds, Euclides da Cunha reviews works on ethnology, the history of Brazilian colonization, folklore, psychiatry, neurology and sociology.

The coexistence of polyphony with intertextuality, complementing each other without coming into conflict, poses the obvious problem of having to deal with an excessive body of knowledge and results in a succession of discordant paraphrases. Unable to reach a synthesis, or even a number of partial syntheses, the text advances through all kinds of antitheses, which often amount to oxymorons—thus Canudos is a "mud-walled Troy," and the *sertanejo*, the inhabitant of the *sertão*, is a "Hercules-Quasimodo"—and a series of contradictions.

These are, in general terms, the complex issues surrounding the composition of *Os Sertões*. The complexity of the subject matter is dealt with in the text by means such as polyphony and intertextuality that are in no way simplistic or linear. To confer unity on his material, the author relies on an eschatological view borrowed from the millenialists and messianists who gathered in Canudos, their Promised Land; they were waiting, praying constantly for the salvation of their souls and the Final Judgment that the end of the century heralded. By so doing, Cunha shows how it is possible, by a demonic inversion of the Biblical imagery of a salvationist myth, to get a glimpse of the insurrectionists' own viewpoint. Their world had become disenchanted. "Belo Monte"—"Mount Beautiful," as they had renamed the town, their New Jerusalem—had been changed into its opposite: Hell. The river of the City of God, the river of eternal life, was embodied in the dry bed of the Vaza-Barris. The gold walls promised to the just are made of mud and twigs. The luxuriant vegetation of the Garden of Delights they long for decays into the dry and bare *caatinga*. And so on.

In this way, through mimesis of the great syntagmatic narrative of the Bible, which begins with Genesis and ends with the Apocalypse, *Os Sertões* covers the full span of the story of Canudos, from the foundation of the town to its destruction by fire, in accordance with Biblical prophecy.

Notes

[1] Are quotes are taken from Samuel Putnam's translation *Rebellion in the Backlands.* (Translator's note)

Works Cited

Cunha, Euclides da. *Rebellion in the Backlands.* 1902. Trans. Samuel Putnam. New York: Knopf, 1952.

The Patriot: The Exclusion of the Hero Full of Character

Beatriz Resende

Translated by Shoshanna Lurie

Lima Barreto was born in Rio de Janeiro on May 13, 1881, the day that in 1888 slavery would be abolished in Brazil. He was a *pardo*, as mulattoes were registered at the time, and was given the name of a Portuguese king: Afonso Henriques. He died at the end of 1922, the same year as the Week of Modern Art, while quarreling with the São Paulo modernists whom he considered to be futurists and followers of "the charlatanisms of Marinetti," a poet who irritated him primarily for praising war.[1] Upon receiving from Mário de Andrade the recently released magazine *Klaxon*, it seemed to Lima Barreto that the Fascism of the young Italian writer had been compounded with an absolutely unforgivable taste for Americanism in these intellectuals. Politically, he was opposed to Modernism, and Lima Barreto was answered with an unforgiving attack from the strongest movement in Brazilian literature. Thus, he died excluded from a Modernism that he himself had anticipated. Literary history, for lack of a better label, has called him "pre-modernist." He remains betwixt and between, an *almost*, which is a function of his peripheral biography.

As a mulatto, he was sufficiently white to enroll in a racist and prejudiced university. Although he almost received his undergraduate degree, he was expelled before graduating. He was too black to enter the Brazilian Academy of Letters on either of his two justified attempts. White enough to practice journalism, he was too black to challenge the owner of the newspaper where he began his career. After the publication of his first novel, *Recordações do Escrivão Isaías Caminha*, which strongly criticizes the powerful men of the press, the then powerful *Correio da Manhã* declared a complete boycott of his work. His status as a poor mulatto, a resident of the suburbs of the capital of the First Republic (1889-1930), clinched his definite preference for *Marginália*, as he entitled one of his volumes of short stories and chronicles.[2]

The conflict that arose during this period of the First Republic between Lima Barreto and the pillars of Literature—the proprietors of cultural power—had two faces. On the one hand, it isolated his novelistic production from the moment of publication, and on the other, made it very peculiar. The elitist and Parnassian-oriented criticism denied him a legitimating discourse, while his peripheral status preserved it. Lima Barreto emerged as an independent intellectual at a moment when the coopting of intellectuals by the dominant military power structure was common.[3] Free from any ties that would have linked his production to the State or to any other legitimating political forces, he would relentlessly criticize the very foundations of the First Republic—patriotism and the prevailing warlike conception of the nation, scientism, racism supported by a dangerous form of Darwinism, and finally, the nationalism which in Latin America gave rise to populism.

In 1909, Lima Barreto personally financed the publication of *Recordações do Escrivão Isaías Caminha*, having it edited in Portugal. According to Lima Barreto himself, the book was written to assert his opposition to the Parnassian formal and pedantic literature. In a letter to the art critic and novelist Gonzaga Duque, Lima Barreto asserts that the book was "intentionally poorly written, at times brutal, but always sincere. I very much hope it will scandalize and displease" (*Correspondência* 169). The third and most important of his novels, *Triste Fim de Policarpo Quaresma* (*The Patriot*, 1911), was initially published in serial installments in the *Jornal do Comércio*. Neither his novels nor the magazine *Floreal*, which he edited during its four editions, brought him recognition, though *Policarpo* received some positive reviews. The First World War and the Russian Revolution defined his political positions: in favor of anarchism, sympathetic to bolshevism, and in strict defense of the universal right to full citizenship.

Triste Fim de Policarpo Quaresma was published as a book in 1916, also at the expense of the author himself. The character Policarpo Quaresma is a bureaucrat from Rio de Janeiro, then the national capital, who is determined to know and value Brazil's true national identity, to save the immense but abandoned interior of the country, to defend the Brazilian flag, to assert national values, and to fight for the Republic.

In the first part of the novel, Policarpo attempts to assert the legitimacy of Tupi-Guarani as the authentic Brazilian language by writing a document in the

Indigenous language. He is consequently considered insane, and committed to the National Asylum. The narrative highlights the system of favor that runs the country, the ornamental nature of culture, and the "bovarism" of the character.

> "Quaresma is crazy."…
>
> "Nothing else could be expected," doctor Florencio said. "Those books, that mania for reading…"
>
> "I'd go so far as to say that having books should be forbidden to those who don't have an academic degree," Genelício said. "That way these disasters could be avoided… That Quaresma might have been okay, but he went and got involved with books… That's it! Me, I haven't picked up a book in forty years (...)." (*Triste Fim* 77,78)

After leaving the insane asylum, he decides that the salvation of Brazil can be found in the countryside. Belief in the land where "through planting all is provided," as Pero Vaz de Caminha said in the letter relating the discovery of the new land to the King of Portugal, is in accordance with a belief in the certainty of scientific methods. But ants and *coronelismo* (the dictatorship of large landholders) defeat him. Still, he designs a land reform project that he delivers to the president. The response that the president gives him concludes the second part of the book: "You, Quaresma, are a visionary."

Soon afterwards, the nation appears to be in danger. Facing the "Revolt of the Armada"—sailors subjected to sub-human conditions serve as a pretext for the republican conflict—it is necessary for Policarpo to leave the countryside to fight alongside the "Marechal de Ferro," Floriano Peixoto, the fool who was made president through authoritarian measures. The *pátria* ("fatherland"), with all the dangerous connotations that this concept can assume, emerges for Quaresma as the great utopia for which he should struggle. Yet again this common man addresses the authorities. At the end of the book, when the humble rebels are condemned to death, the point of view of the main character contaminates that of the narrator:

> He couldn't contain himself. That lot of ill-fated poor fellows leaving that way, at such an unreasonable time, for a distant carnage. He had expressed all of his feelings, placed his moral principles before their eyes; he had challenged their moral courage and their human solidarity; and he had written the letter with vehemence, passion, and indignation. (*Triste Fim* 284)

Lima Barreto struggled against the ultra-nationalist trend of the intellectuals of the First Republic—born out of a military coup d'état—, which he viewed as "the regime of corruption. All opinions must, for whatever type of compensation, be established by the powerful of the moment," (*Marginália* 78) critiquing patriotism in a manner uncommon for the beginning of the century.

The novel ends with the disenchantment of the defeated patriot Policarpo Quaresma, who perceives everything too late, already en route to his own death:

> The fatherland I sought was a myth; it was an apparition created inside his cabinet. There was neither the physical, nor the intellectual, nor the political that I thought existed. (*Triste Fim* 285)

The theme continues in an absolutely novel way for an era in which no one had even begun to think that the nation could be an "imagined community" or that the defense of territories and borders could draw the entire world into generalized fratricidal wars with other inhabitants of the same territories, even within the Europe thought to be the core of civility and the bastion of the practice of citizenship.

In a chronicle published in the magazine *Careta*, later collected with others from the same period in *Coisas do Reino do Jambom*, Lima Barreto astutely linked the dangers of nationalism to those of racism:

> … the State's charlatans, in the name of the Fatherland and of the stupid theory of races, instilled aggressive warlike feelings in the ignorant masses… The fatherland is a religious idea belonging to a religion that died a long time ago… In regards to race, the reproducers of the stupid German racial theories are completely lacking the most elementary notions of science, if not, they would clearly know that race is an abstraction. (*Coisas do Reino* 75)

It was 1914, and the world was entering into its first great war. In a 1919 chronicle, Lima Barreto would continue with the same conviction:

> Not being a patriot, and actually desiring the weakening of the sense of fatherland, an exclusive and even aggressive feeling, in order to permit the strengthening of a larger unit that would encompass, with the land, the entire human species… (*Marginália* 78)

After 1917, difficulties with the publication of his novels led him to intensify his activities as a journalist, as a collaborator on not very sophisticated illustrated magazines, and as an episodic chronicler in newspapers and magazines such as *O País* and *Diário de Notícias*. He also worked as an editor of critical publications such as *Careta,* progressive ones such as *ABC,* and anarchist ones including *A Voz do Trabalhador* and *O Debate.* These smaller and more radical publications were always short-lived, being shut down rapidly by the police in that fragile democracy. Given the context of the time, the author opted for satire and published *Crônicas sobre a República das Bruzundangas* and *Coisas do Reino do Jambom.*

It was as if the defeat of the visionary Major Quaresma, who is shot dead by the dictator at the end of the book, had brought the author to abandon the more formal standards of a seriously critical literature. He was left with satire, as traditional criticism generally classifies these writings. I prefer to see them as parody, in an intertextual context in which his work contests texts such as *Contos Pátrios* by authors of high Parnassian literature like Coelho Neto and Olavo Bilac, or *Por que me Ufano do meu País,* by the deservedly forgotten Conde Afonso Celso. Lima Barreto created parodies of official history, of the heroic tales of republican memory.

The author attained the greatest visibility in his newspaper chronicles, making this a permanent activity until the end of his life and the vehicle through which he would seek to play a role in city life. But the chronicle, as we know, was for a long time considered a "lesser genre." The chronicler is an artist who is pursued by *chronos,* always driven by the need to continue forward, with no time to look back. The circumstances of speed and professional obligation characteristic of the modern chronicle lead to the choice of a pleasant colloquiality that makes the reader an accomplice. These conditions of production and the chronicle's direct link to the vehicle in which it circulates, the newspaper—which can be read today and used to wrap fish tomorrow, as they said during the time when fish were still wrapped in newspaper—bring imperfections, eventual errors (like those caused by the fact that chroniclers always cite from memory), and the presence of contradictions. Being contradictory and polemical is often a characteristic of the chronicle itself. However, its fragmentary aspect is the most interesting, linking it to other less *noble* and consecrated literary genres such as memoirs, testimonies, and diaries. There is a little of all of these genres in the literary chronicle, including the possibility to publicly assume the defense of the downtrodden and offended. The chronicler in Brazil does exactly this in real campaigns such as the defense of women assassinated by their husbands or lovers: "Let women love as they wish. Don't kill them, for the love of God;" of striking laborers: "The workers that are about to protest to their bosses and the government about the living conditions imposed on them have acted prudently and with saints' patience until now;" or of anarchist militants, Spaniards and Italians threatened with deportation: "the anarchists talk about humanity to humanity, about humankind to humankind, and not in the name of the small abilities of political figures."[4]

The writer who had allied himself with peripheral genres rejected by defenders of "high literature" was, at that time, himself one of those excluded from Rio society. In 1917, Lima Barreto wrote in his personal diary: "I was going downtown, when I began to feel ill, I had been drinking all month, mostly *parati*.[5] Drink after drink, admitted or not. Eating little and sleeping God knows how. I was disgusting, filthy" (*Diário* 193). Alcohol, the poverty reflected in his clothing, living far from downtown—all these factors led to his construction of that *exile in the city*, obsessively adopted as a theme in all of his work.

The image of this man, who crossed the city daily and at the end of the day wrote his chronicle, was strangely opposed to that of his professional colleagues: "I'm not that type of model and I know I irritate the elevated spirits of intellectual puppets." Occasionally, however, the writer assumed this role with a kind of arrogance, as in the chronicle in which he wrote: "and don't be offended by my worn out attire, because this is my elegance and my charm" (*Bagatelas* 138). Rejection from contemporary legitimating literary sources could only have produced rebelliousness such as that beautifully and painfully expressed in a chronicle from the early part of his career: "I want to be a writer because I wish to and I am ready to assume the life and the place toward which I am headed. I burned my ships, I left everything, everything, for the stuff of letters."[6]

Alcoholism would lead Lima Barreto into the strongest of all exclusions: the exclusion of insanity. Life imitates art. Before writing *Triste Fim de Policarpo Quaresma*, his contact with insanity was through accompanying the mental illness that also affected his father. Lima Barreto was committed to an asylum for the first time in 1914. Since *Policarpo Quaresma* was not published until 1916, many critics see traces of Lima's biography in the insanity of the character. This was not true, or at least it wasn't yet. A fear of mental illness was present—the dread that, according to the deterministic principles prevalent at the time, he would be guaranteed the same fate as his father. The fact is that the description of Policarpo's stay at the asylum is as moving as the one he would write about his own stay at the "Praia de Saudade"[7] in his unfinished novel *Cemitério dos Vivos*:

> Other visitors came on the streetcar and none of them delayed in getting off at the door of the asylum. As at all the doors of our social hells, there were all types of people, of many conditions, origins, and fortunes. It is not only death that levels; insanity, crime, and disease all raze the distinctions we invent. (*Triste Fim* 99)

On Christmas Eve 1919, Lima Barreto was taken a second time to the "National Asylum for the Alienated," a difficult stay from which he would never have time to recover. On his intake form, the psychiatrist of the Pinel Section of the Hospital wrote a curious history of his disease, transcribed in Francisco de Assis Barbosa's important biography of Lima Barreto:

> Perfectly oriented in time, place and medium, he immediately confesses to excessively using *parati*, which he understood to be a very damaging addiction; however, regardless of great efforts, he cannot manage to give the drink up... An individual of intellectual culture, *he calls himself a writer*, having published four novels, and he is currently a collaborator on *Careta*. (Barbosa 356-357, my emphases)

In order to make his internment coherent, and despite his cultured traits place him in the ward with the most wretched patients for three months, it was necessary to put into question the work of that citizen gone crazy—as if his declaration of being a writer were part of his delusion. In the situation in which he found himself then, he was left with the only radical reaction to the accusation of insanity: the assertion of his own words. Lima Barreto began to make notes in which he sought to salvage his own individuality, looking to save the humiliated man. He wrote one of the strongest and most moving documents in defense of the citizenship of the most excluded citizens: the mentally ill. He wrote the *Diário do Hospício* [*Asylum Diary*], his chronicle of insanity. At this time, he felt close to the great writers of the Western canon. At the beginning of the *Diário* he wrote:

> ... he made me wash the patio, clean the bathroom, where he gave me an excellent shower with a whip. We were all naked, with the doors open, and I was

very timid. I remembered Dostoyevski's steam baths in *House of the Dead.* When I washed, I cried; but I remembered Cervantes, Dostoyevski himself, who probably suffered more. (*O Cemitério* 24)

Lima Barreto's last novel, *Clara dos Anjos,* finished in January of 1922, was a lifelong project that was very difficult for him to finish. It ends with a comment from its main character, a young, poor, mulatta, suburban woman, who was deflowered by a young white man: "We aren't anything in this life" (*Clara dos Anjos* 196).

Mikhail Bakhtin says that, "an author is a prisoner of his time, of his contemporaneity. Later eras free him from this prison and literary scholars should aid in this liberation" (Bakhtin 350). However, in order for Bakhtin's assertion to help us, we need to understand that for him literature is an inalienable facet of culture and cannot be understood outside the context of all culture. The most intense and productive cultural life emerges from the interstices between its different zones and not when these zones close around their individual specificities, as Bakhtin asserted in a 1970 interview with the magazine *Novy Mir.*

When he died, Lima Barreto left a large portion of his work unpublished, in the form of a book. He left it carefully prepared for publishing, with the chronicles in volumes, almost all with titles. It remained for the historian and literary critic Francisco de Assis Barbosa to publish the almost complete set of work—twenty-seven volumes—in 1956. On this occasion, the diaries, correspondence, and chronicles were made accessible to the reading public. However, twenty more years were still necessary for the academy to become interested in the author in a more positive way, and it was only after the 1980s that Lima Barreto began to be considered an important figure in the Brazilian literary arena.

It is interesting to observe that what occurred in this short time was a transformation of the theoretical understanding of what comprises literature, introducing a critical pluralism necessary for a new literary history.

Lima Barreto's literature was always condemned to its era by the same pretext: the lack of literary refinement, for being *careless* writing, for too *lazy* a syntax, for, in other words, not meeting the norms of high literature. Today, as a result of the critical attention it receives and, above all, because it is frequently adapted for the theater and film, his work is achieving the objectives of its author: to reach large masses of users, newspaper readers,

readers of chronicles or satiric texts. This desire to speak to and for the subaltern sectors of society is what made him the "itinerant libertarian who was extinguished by fate under the barbarism of the tropics," as Antônio Arnoni Prado calls him (13).

We return to the title of the novel. In the anticipatory "*triste fim*" that inverts the narrative's order, the very impossibility of Policarpo Quaresma's heroism full of character is recognized from the beginning—a thesis definitively confirmed when Mário de Andrade created the anthropophagic character Macunaíma, the "characterless hero."

Notes

[1] In 1922, Mário de Andrade, through Sérgio Buarque de Holanda, sent an issue of *Klaxon* to Lima Barreto. However, Lima immediately disliked the title of the magazine, writing in the Rio de Janeiro-based magazine *Careta*: "those young men really believe that we do not know what futurism is? For more than twenty years it is a widespread subject, and it is not possible to read the cheapest French or Italian journal without being informed of the latest boast of 'Il Marinetti'." (*Careta*, July 22, 1922).

[2] The Portuguese term *crônica* refers to a type of short composition related to current events or social reality that is usually published in a newspaper or magazine. (Translator's note)

[3] For more details, see Resende, "Lima Barreto."

[4] Estas crônicas estão estudadas em Resende, *Lima Barreto*.

[5] *Parati* is a type of *cachaça*, Brazilian sugarcane liquor.

[6] A moving statement, written in a chronicle when he was 30 years old, and published in the newspaper *Gazeta da Tarde*, June 28, 1911. He repeated this statement throughout his life.

[7] This is a name given to *Praia Vermelha* in that era, an area in the South Zone of Rio de Janeiro where the National Asylum was located.

Works Cited

Bakhtin, M. M. "Respuesta a la Pregunta hecha por la Revista *Novy Mir*". *Estética de la Creación Verbal*. Madrid: Siglo Veintiuno, 1982. 346-347.

Barbosa, Francisco de Assis. *A Vida de Lima Barreto*. 5th ed. Rio de Janeiro: José Olympio, 1975.

Barreto, Afonso Henrique de Lima. *Triste Fim de Policarpo Quaresma. Obras de Lima Barreto*. Vol. II. Ed. Francisco de Assis Barbosa. São Paulo: Brasiliense, 1956.

———. *The Patriot*. Trans. Robert Scott-Buccleuch. London: Callings, 1978.

———. *Clara dos Anjos. Obras de Lima Barreto*. Vol. V. Ed. Francisco de Assis Barbosa. São Paulo: Brasiliense, 1956.

———. *Coisas do Reino do Jambom. Obras de Lima Barreto*. Vol. VIII. Ed. Francisco de Assis Barbosa. São Paulo: Brasiliense, 1956.

———. *Bagatelas. Obras de Lima Barreto*. Vol. IX. Ed. Francisco de Assis Barbosa. São Paulo: Brasiliense, 1956.

————. *Marginália. Obras de Lima Barreto.* Vol. XII. Ed. Francisco de Assis Barbosa. São Paulo: Brasiliense, 1956.

————. *Diário Íntimo. Obras de Lima Barreto.* Vol. XIV. Ed. Francisco de Assis Barbosa. São Paulo: Brasiliense, 1956.

————. *O Cemitério dos Vivos. Obras de Lima Barreto.* Vol. XV. Ed. Francisco de Assis Barbosa. São Paulo: Brasiliense, 1956.

Prado, Antonio Arnoni. "Prefácio." *Lima Barreto e o Rio de Janeiro em Fragmentos.* Beatriz Resende. Rio de Janeiro: Editora da UFRJ / Campinas: Editora UNICAMP, 1993. 13-15.

Resende, Beatriz. "Lima Barreto, a Opção pela Marginália," *Os Pobres na Literatura Brasileira.* Ed. Roberto Schwarz. São Paulo: Brasiliense, 1983. 73-78.

————. *Lima Barreto e o Rio de Janeiro em Fragmentos.* Editora UFRJ/UNICAMP, 1993.

Plantation Boy: The Memory of Loss

Heloisa Toller Gomes
Translated by David Shepherd and
Tania Shepherd

"My uncle explained to me the way that black clay made sugar white."
José Lins do Rego (1932)

In the decade between 1922, the year of the "Week of Modern Art" in São Paulo, and 1932, when *Menino de Engenho* (*Plantation Boy*) was published, Brazilian literature was driven by strong winds of renewal. This was due to reasons that transcend the literary scene—as is almost always the case. These were the turbulent years in Brazil, which saw the end of the "Old Republic" (*"República Velha"*, 1889-1930). They witnessed the mutiny of young officers at the Copacabana Forte, they accompanied the crisis provoked by the slump in world coffee prices, the overthrow of President Washington Luís, the Revolution of 1930 and Getúlio Vargas' rise to power. These were also years of liberal modernization and widespread intellectual ferment.

It was during this time that the most progressive Brazilian intellectuals began their search, within the domestic scene, for parameters within which to debate important national issues. These included the need for new guidelines for aesthetic creativity in an effort to rid themselves of external or Europeanized standards. It was a decade of polemic and provocative Prefaces and modernist Manifestos, among which may be cited, "Arte Moderna" by Menotti del Picchi, and "Prefácio Interessantíssimo" by Mário de Andrade (1922); "O Espírito Moderno" by Graça Aranha, and "Manifesto da Poesia Pau-Brasil" by Oswald de Andrade (1924); "Manifesto Regionalista" of 1926,[1] the Manifestos published in the *Festa* and *Verde* magazines (1927), "Manifesto Antropófago" by Oswald de Andrade (1928), and the "Manifesto do Verde-Amarelismo, ou da Escola da Anta" (1929).

During those years the two main currents of Brazilian literary modernism were outlined. One of these came from the South of the country, with its irreverent nationalism and its iconoclastic writing, the generator of and heir to the "Week of Modern Art." The second was the regional modernism of the Northeast, more sullen and introspective, distrusting the flamboyant humor of the new Paulista literature, and less explicitly daring in formal terms. This second stream of modernism despised "the sidewalks of inaccessible cities"[2] and opted for settings such as the large sugarcane plantations, or for the desolate drought-stricken regions of the Northeast, the *caatinga*. The insistence on this physical and anthropo-social setting, with its swamp and semi-desert, reflected Northeastern modernism's independent search for sounds, tastes and smells as a platform from which to mold space, personalities and events that were uniquely Brazilian. Thus the so-called "novels of the 30s" emerged, of which José Lins do Rego's *Menino de Engenho* is one of the most celebrated. For many, the initial starting point of this era was the year 1928, marked by the publication of *A Bagaceira* (*Trash: A Novel*) by José Américo de Almeida.

The feeling of Brazilianess in the literary production of the Northeast, although very different from that exhibited by the modernists in São Paulo and Rio de Janeiro, was no less ambitious in terms of its aesthetic aims. It went far beyond the rich national repertoire of images and themes, which had been exhaustively exploited since Romanticism, and which were now colorfully re-inaugurated in the novelty of the diverse modernistic nuances. The truth is that these two perspectives, from the South and from the Northeast, complemented each other in relation to the new Brazil. For the country was taking uncertain steps towards a controversial and overpowering modernity, which, of necessity, dramatized and confronted, within the literary scene of that time and in the subsequent decades, both the sophistication and the misery which extended from the metropoles to the huge arid backlands and the decadent mansions (*"casas-grandes"*) with their "slave compounds from the times of captivity."[3]

For the authors from the Northeast, their raw material, pregnant with Brazilianess, became an inseparable part of existential experience, which was utilized from the inside-out, as it were, to authenticate and validate their product as national literature and as creative fiction. From this Brazilian kernel, this "inside-out" succeeded, at certain key moments, in transcending the limited environment of a "regional literature" that was defined, primarily, by its geographical location. In this sense, whether from the perspective of a fictional memoir and an autobiographical standpoint—the case of *Menino de Engenho*—, or whether from the adoption of a more impersonal, or detached, narrative posture—as in *Fogo Morto* or in *Vidas Secas*—, the narrative voice invariably works from the *sertão*[4] to the outside world, rather than from the outside world to the *sertão*. This contrasts with the urban, cosmopolitan references which frequently mark Paulista modernism, in its attempts to "discover" Brazil from the outside-in.[5]

In common with what often occurred in writing from the South, which also explored the rich seam of fictional memoirs,[6] the novel with an autobiographical stamp also served the aims of Northeast modernism. "There is an intellectual narrator who speaks of himself, and of others, taking stock of the past. The individual's memoir becomes a record of the experiences of many, revealing the general characteristics of his era," wrote Adriana Oliveira, emphasizing the supremacy of the discourse of the dominant class within this literary production.[7]

The appeal of a retrospective vision of childhood nestled in nature, and the consequent memoir posture, is not restricted to fictional prose. It is equally well expressed in the poetry of the Northeast. Thus in his own poetry, Jorge de Lima writes that,

I jumped over so many sugarcane juice boilers,
I swam through so many streams,
I knew so many deep water holes![8]

Similarly, the historical documentary facts are intertwined in *Menino de Engenho* with the fictional as both are woven into the individual experience of the author, the latter being relatively concealed (and liberated) by fictitious names.

The 75th edition of José Lins do Rego's first novel was published in 1999. Its acclaim is well justified. The novel conveys the fluency of the popular tale and the "contours of the fable," which so enchanted Carlos Drummond de Andrade. It recalls childhood memories of the home where the narrator-protagonist lived on his grandfather's sugarcane plantation. From these introspective details of domestic life, the text paints a subjective physical anthropo-social mural of pre-industrial agrarian life, which was sustained through a rigid and paternalistic hierarchy of classes.

The plot is straightforward. The text opens by describing the traumatic effect a mother's assassination has on a four-year-old child. The initial chapters paint a picture of family tragedy by following the fragments of childhood experience. The little boy goes to live on the sugarcane plantation and the reader shares with him his experiences and impressions of life in the mansion, with the poor working in the fields and among the animals left to pasture. Finally, when twelve years old, he takes a train in the opposite direction when he leaves the plantation to enroll in a high school in Recife. His stay in the Catholic boarding school is the theme of Rego's second novel, *Doidinho* (1933). But the protagonist's existential course is doomed to failure. "The character-narrator of the trilogy *Menino de Engenho—Doidinho—Bangüê*, Carlos de Melo, or Carlinhos, narrates his own trajectory towards nothingness."[9]

The character's structural fragility, confirmed in these later novels, is not only restricted to himself, but encompasses an infirm social order destined to crumble. In common with William Faulkner's relationship with the American Deep South, Rego strove to record in his fiction the decadence of the former dominant class and the repercussions of this process on their descendants and on those who depended upon them. Rego's world of the Northeast describes, first and foremost, the decadent sugarcane plantations, their dramatic transitional phase from a mercantilism inherited from colonial times to an emergent capitalist economy, and the no more than nominal liberation of the slaves.[10] The text of *Menino de Engenho* is incisive in this respect: "The Santa Rosa slave quarters did not disappear with abolition. They continued glued to the mansion, with the black women giving birth, the good breastfeeders and the good workers of the settlement" (41). It is an endearing novel, with its orality and spontaneous patterning. In Blaise Cendrars' words, "Brazil in its entirety can be found in this transparent book."[11] This "transparency" is, however, illusory; it is an integrated part of the captivating character of the text itself. It is not only by chance that so many elements of fantasy are inserted into the text, which are much more than an homage to Northeastern imagination.

These fantastical elements include the stories told by old Totonha of "king and queen," of "hangings and fortune-tellings," of strange jungle creatures, the childhood terrors of the supernatural, "a world inhabited entirely of goblins, in flesh and blood lived for my sake" (34), states the narrator. This retelling of fantasy, at times in the form of text within text, is contrasted with the factual, concrete retelling, represented (always through the eyes of the narrator) by the grandfather's voice. "My grandfather's stories captured my attention in a very different way to those told by old Totonha. Grandfather's stories never appealed to my imagination, to fantasy. There were no miraculous solutions, as in the others… They were the work of a storyteller stirred by reality" (62).

One of the pleasures of working with *Menino de Engenho* is that the novel is endowed with a vitality often lacking in several of its characters. It flows in a way that suggests the "transparency" so highly praised by Cendrars, and yet harbors in its core a powerful tension. This tension is inherent in the (utopic) attempt, on the part of the text, to frame itself as a continuous, seamless woven cloth, devoid of ruptures and obstacles. And this despite the fact that the text depicts the difficulties of life and the social injustices, which are *presented* and *exhibited* but never *questioned*. A textual reading reveals this desire to create continuity and a magical piece of writing—similar to old Totonha's stories, with "miraculous solutions"—whose narrative flow neutralizes the thorns. The craving for smoothness and for continuity unfolds as metonymy, and the narrative voice takes momentary pleasure in the uninterrupted size of "Grandfather José Paulino's lands." It is indicative that at this very moment the narrator resorts to a fairy-tale vocabulary, mixing it with a description of the large estates of the Brazilian Northeast.

> The lands of Santa Rosa stretched for leagues and leagues from north to south. Old José Paulino took pleasure in looking out over his dominions as far as the eye could see. He liked to rest his eyes on his own horizons. All he wanted was to buy land and more land. He inherited a small Santa Rosa, and *turned it into a kingdom*, bursting its boundaries by buying neighboring properties. (51, my emphasis).

Menino de Engenho suffers, paradoxically, from the tension caused by refusing to address these tensions that are derived not only from the nature of the literary text itself, but also its immersion in the harsh theme of the Northeast and its people. This tension interrupts the seductive fluency and the melancholic reminiscences upon which the novel is built. Within the narrative posture that directs the text, however, there is nothing that is intentionally destabilizing; everything appears to adhere to a higher order. It is considered a true fact that nature always returns to normal after calamities, like the flooding of the River Paraíba. On the human level, this can be seen in the charismatic figure of the elderly patriarch, who corrects mistakes, reprimands, takes care of the ill and the needy: "on the estate, my grandfather gave balm to the wounded" (58).

Menino de Engenho circumvents any tensions to such an extent that several of its active characters, as well as those simply named (e.g. the urchin Ricardo, Vitorino "Papa-Rabo," the saddler José Amaro, Colonel Lula de Holanda, and even Carlos de Melo), have no depth, and, in some cases, lack the tragic qualities that they will acquire in later novels. Thus the grandfather José Paulino is here portrayed as the "saint who planted sugar" (62). Colonel Lula, a pathetic figure in *Fogo Morto*, is here described as "that pleasant elderly gentleman… with his Santa Fé estate falling to pieces" (52). The poor, for their part, stoically accept their lot and the adversities that befall them.

> And my Aunt Maria distributed all the dried meat and rice which we had bought for those people. They appeared happy, no matter what, very submissive and very content with their fate. The flood had washed away their clearing of cassava, taking with it the little, almost nothing, they had. But they did not raise their arms to curse their ill luck, they were not indignant. They were gentle folk. (21)

The tension thus emerges from the text obliquely. It is not by chance that Carlinhos is "a sad little lad" because his life is made up of a series of losses: his mother and his small cousin, Lili, are taken away by murder and disease, respectively. The father-assassin, placed in a mental institution, is never seen again, nor is Maria Clara, his first sweetheart ("I'd lost my companion of the cashew trees," 66) his second mother, "Aunt Mary," was lost because of her marriage to the Gameleira's cousin; his own innocence, lost in the brutality of premature sexual encounters with a series of prostitutes and barnyard animals; and, finally, the loss of the sugarcane plantation itself, with his departure for the boarding school.

The text, however, is more artful than it appears and warns the reader, in the simplicity of its title, that it is not focusing primarily on the *engenho* (the sugarcane plantation), but rather on the *menino* (the little boy) who lives there. The boy is the novel's narrative filter but does not possess the *engenho*. On the contrary, *he is possessed by it*: "Lost little boy, little boy from the sugarcane plantation," are the final words of the novel. In spite of childhood fantasies and the ever-glorified reality of a still-powerful grandfather, this sugar plantation and its universe escape the protagonist's grasp. Similarly, the rural world of the Northeast, so raw and painfully poignant, spills over and frustrates the powers of the novelist's writing, inserting itself into its gaps, colliding with the well-accomplished narrative flow.

As already mentioned, the view of the dominant class prevails in *Menino de Engenho*. Thus, the important point of reference, the axis of narrative balance, will always be the authority of the grandfather. (According to the narrative voice, José Paulino does not talk "with," but talks "to" others—e.g., "Every evening, after supper, my grandfather used to talk to all who sat silently at the dinner table" [60]). Each and every demonstration of independence or rebellion is neutralized when faced with the greater power.

The following example is odd, because here it seems that two voices oppose each other.

> João Rouco came to the clearing with his three sons. His wife and the smaller boys stayed at home, near the fields. He was more than seventy years old, but managed to handle the tough work, just like his youngest son. His mouth was wrinkled, toothless, his arms muscled, his legs strong. Nothing was difficult for this old backwoodsman that worked for my grandfather. He was never subservient like the others. He answered Colonel Paulino's shouts with shouts. Perhaps it is because they were the same age and had played together as children. (59)

However, immediately afterwards, the narrator's voice relents and concludes the episode: "And when [grandfather] needed a reliable person for a heavy job there was always a message for João Rouco."

The presence of living nature is also found in Carlinhos' reminiscences, always restrained by a stronger force, namely the social class to which he belonged. This is evident in the following: "All this was a delight for me: the cattle, foamy warm milk, the chill of five o' clock in the morning, the tall, solemn figure of my grandfather." And it is this social class standing which initiates the little boy in the mysteries of the sugar plantation: "Uncle Juca took me to bathe in the river. With a towel around his neck and a big cup in his hand he called me to bathe. 'You have to learn what it means to survive as a country lad.'" The episode assumes a truly ritual character: "On the way back Uncle Juca said, smiling: 'Now you have been baptized'" (8).

The anxiety of the text lies in the inevitable clash between the dominant social class, however absolute, and the documentary inclination that also inhabits the novel. The account of the prosperity of this class, which is carried out in retrospect, contains, of necessity, elements that foretell its decadence. The utopia of the harmonious discourse, of appeasement, is occasionally diverted by an escape towards magic, whether by nostalgic memories, found in the references to old Totonha, or by secrets of terror: "Werewolves had been spotted at Rolo forest" or "Zombies were also found on the sugarcane plantation" (32-33). A different textual posture, or, rather, an intertwining of the documentary material (seen critically, in its social sense) and the aesthetic organization, would be the same as admitting the tensions that *Menino de Engenho* had opted to negate. In this way, the text appears to gain strength and leave the task (of criticism) for later.

Only in José Lins do Rego's entire oeuvre (or singly in *Fogo Morto*) would existential and socio-economic issues of the decadent patriarchal Northeast society—formerly well embedded in mono-culture and slavery—be questioned with greater dramatic intensity. In this latter novel, his masterpiece, the greater complexity of points of view, the emphasis on characters from various socio-economic strata, and the ruptured chronology, confer both strength and dynamism to the composition. This composition is based precisely on the recognition of the gaps denied by his first novel.

José Lins do Rego's oeuvre is a *post facto* dramatization of the decadence of the large estates, the extinguishing of the old sugarcane plantations and the development of the sugar mills: the "dead furnace" of that semi-feudal world which is a "kingdom" in the eyes of the narrator of *Menino de Engenho*. This kingdom is persuasive because the narrator is able to evoke, without sentimentality, the poetry of childhood. Even though the night is close, sheep turn into stallions: "Below the hog plum, the dark cold of night grew nearer. The sheep ran. And the fear of the silence at the end of the day, those heavy shadows, made me run faster with my stallion" (51). However, even when giving up space to magic, the text is persecuted by the surrounding reality. In the same passage: "Workers with hoes on their shoulders came home from work. They talked boisterously, as if the twelve hours of work did not weigh heavily on their backs" (51).

According to Antonio Carlos Villaça, *Menino de Engenho* witnesses a victory of the novelist over the author of memoirs.[12] Further, this first novel by José Lins do Rego achieves a poetic balance between an honest documentation of the real, its illusory negation, and the complex "as if" in the building up of the difficult remembrance of loss.

Notes

HELOISA TOLLER GOMES

[1] The influence of the "Regional Manifesto," and of Gilberto Freyre, its great spokesman, was decisive on the works of José Lins do Rego in general, and especially on *Menino de Engenho*. While acknowledging this well-known fact, the present essay uses an alternative interpretive approach.

[2] Andrade 126.

[3] *Menino de Engenho* 38. This and the remaining quotations from the novel by José Lins do Rego are taken from the 75th edition (Rio de Janeiro: José Olympio, 1999). (Translator's note: The translations of all quotations from *Menino de Engenho* are our own.)

[4] The *sertão* is an arid, semi-desert backland region found in the Northeast of Brazil. (Translator's note)

[5] See Paulo Prado's 1924 testimony about his friend, Oswald de Andrade: "In Paris, at the top of a studio in Place Clichy, the navel of the world, Oswald de Andrade was dazzled by the discovery of his own country. Returning to his homeland he confirmed—in the enchantment of the Portuguese medieval architecture—the surprising revelation that Brazil did exist. This fact, which others had doubted, opened his eyes to an ecstatic vision of a new world, unexplored and mysterious. The poetry '*pau-brasil*' (brazil-wood) was created." Prado 5.

[6] Related to this, Silviano Santiago wrote that, "Oswald de Andrade and Lins do Rego…, after publishing novels of memoirs at the beginning of their careers, including *Memórias Sentimentais de João Miramar* and *Menino de Engenho*, respectively, felt the need, in their old age, to rewrite the *same* novel. However, their writing now stemmed from memory, without the conniving framework of the 'novel,' namely, *Um Homem sem Profissão* and *Meus Verdes Anos*. This coincidence is very significant because it demonstrates how fragile the distinctions of the literary schools are… and how fluid and of what little worth there is in the frontiers between the discourse of fictional memoirs and autobiographical discourse are in terms of the Brazilian definition." Santiago 33.

[7] Oliveira 32.

[8] Lima, "Flor Sanctorum" 32.

[9] Milton Marques Jr. and Elizabeth Marinheiro 20.

[10] Gomes 38.

[11] Blaise Cendrars, qtd. in Villaça, xv.

[12] Villaça xx.

Works Cited

Andrade, Oswald de. "Dote." *Cântico dos Cânticos para Flauta e Violão, Oswald de Andrade— Poesias Reunidas: Obras Completas*. Vol. 7. Rio de Janeiro: MEC/Civilização Brasileira, 1972.

Gomes, Heloisa Toller. *O Poder Rural na Ficção*. São Paulo: Ática, 1981.

Lima, Jorge de. "Flor Sanctorum." *Novos Poemas: Poemas Escolhidos/Poemas Negros*. Rio de Janeiro: Lacerda Editores, 1997.

Marques Jr., Milton and Elizabeth Marinheiro. *O Ser e o Fazer na Obra Ficcional de Lins do Rego*. Paraíba: Edições FUNESC, 1990.

Oliveira, Adriana A. de. *Memorialismo e Autobiografia—Na Reconstrução da Infância na Literatura Brasileira*. Master's Thesis Pontifícia Universidade Católica / Rio de Janeiro, 1991.

Prado, Paulo. 1924. "Poesia Pau-Brasil." *Oswald de Andrade. Poesias Reunidas: Obras Completas.* Vol. 7 (Rio de Janeiro: MEC/Civilização Brasileira, 1972.

Rego, José Lins do. *Menino de Engenho.* 1932. 75th edition. Rio de Janeiro: José Olympio, 1999.

———. *Plantation Boy.* Trans. Emmi Baum. New York: Knopf, 1966.

Santiago, Silviano. "Vale Quanto Pesa (A Ficção Brasileira Modernista)." *Vale Quanto Pesa: Ensaios sobre Questões Político-Culturais.* São Paulo: Paz e Terra, 1982. 25-40.

Villaça, Antonio Carlos. "*Menino de Engenho.*" José Lins do Rego. *Menino de Engenho.* 75th edition. Rio de Janeiro: José Olympio, 1999. xv-xxi.

Monteiro Lobato Today—Semicolon[1]

Silviano Santiago
Translated by Nöel de Souza
and Mark Streeter

I'm anxious to find out for myself whether death is a comma, a semicolon or a period.
Monteiro Lobato (1948), qtd. by Edgard Cavalheiro

Describing the last days of Monteiro Lobato's life, Edgard Cavalheiro, his admirer and first biographer, recalls that the writer faced his imminent end with humor and courage. On April 21, 1948, he suffered an aneurysm. The authors of the most recent biography of Lobato, entitled *Furacão da Botocúndia*, suggest that Lobato's brain was affected in the two abilities most highly developed in him: reading and writing. The writer suddenly turned agraphic, asked his close friends: "How is it possible for me not to know what's written in that book?" Fifty years ago, facing his imminent death, the writer's lively and restless eyes, framed by thick, black brows, stared out and danced in the air, replacing the silence of his sick body with the abundance of an unsettled spiritual life.

Lobato, let us recall, was not the kind to fear death. This attitude of his is already quite clear in the short story "Bocatorta," which, according to *Furacão na Botocúndia*, was the first written by the author. Subsequently included in *Urupês*, "Bocatorta" is a homegrown version of the North American classic *King Kong* and the French film *Beauty and the Beast*, written and directed by Jean Cocteau. A wretched black man, deformed and ghastly, a freed Quasimodo, falls in love with the farmer's beautiful and distant daughter. Unable either to demonstrate his sublime love or to satisfy his vile desires, the monstrous figure watches over the girl by day and at night steps into her dreams. The virgin dies from a strange and incomprehensible disease and is buried by her parents and fiancé. In the first hours of the day, the black man desecrates the grave and embraces the white girl, kissing her. The narrator describes the macabre scene: "a white body lay outside the tomb— embraced by a live, black man squirming like an octopus." Life, love and death are woven together in conflict, like a decadent sculpture.

Thanks to his uncontrollable interest in others' lives, Lobato as a youth already knew a great deal about human death. His motto as a writer is expressed in one of his short narratives: "Stories walk around on tiptoes, driven from one end to the other, the question is how to catch them." The writer's predisposition drove him to conquer Brazilian literature, spinning funny, scary, painful and loving yarns, narrated firsthand by the kind of ordinary country folk with whom he socialized. In the anecdotes he "catches" in order to narrate, trivial intrigues are given special emphasis; life and love are woven into the fatal encounter of characters with death itself. Early on, Lobato became familiar with the bitter taste of death without having truly tasted it. He tried it, keeping his ear to the ground and jotting down those extraordinary stories "that pull like a magnet," as he affirmed.

Had it not been for the inappropriate advice of the physician and hygienist from Bahia, Artur Neiva, *Urupês*, his first and most famous collection of short stories would have been called *Doze Mortes Trágicas*, a more suggestive and adequate title. Thanks to the friend's unfortunate suggestion, Lobato abandoned "tragic death" as the thread for the initial reading of the twelve stories to accept the metaphoric name of the *caboclo*'s ethos—the tree parasite known as *urupê*. "Somber *urupê* of rotten wood, lying silently in the recess of the grottos"—this is how his future character-type, Jeca Tatu, was already described at that time. Lobato is obsessive and, therefore, recidivistic.

In his next book, Lobato abandons his friend's clumsy advice and ventures into the labyrinths of the ghost cities in the interior of São Paulo. The author does not hesitate this time. He gives the new book a fair and appropriate title: *Cidades Mortas*. Communities that used to be rich, lively and prosperous came crumbling down like termite-eaten wood during the transition from the Monarchy to the Republic. The narrator's seemingly objective gaze is caustically enchanted by decadence and progress and dwells at length on the detailed description of big houses in ruin, "which recall brontosaurus bones from which the meat, blood and life had fled forever."

The writer's pen, wielding an abundant, extravagant and multicolored vocabulary, walks through the death of the mansions as if he were chatting with a companion of adventurers. In the short story "Os Negros" ("The Blacks"), the description of the decrepitude of the mansion is passionate: "A web of cracks spreading through the walls, stained by leaks, with vague vestiges of paper. Odd furniture—two Louis XV chairs, with the inside torn, and a center table of the same style, with the marble dirtied by bat guano." And the character adds: "I'll be damned if this is not the headquarters of all the winged rats of this world and the next!"

Obsessive and recidivist, already touched by the morbid pleasure provided by the repeated experience of death, Lobato devotes himself to painting the majestic funereal scenery where the ghost cities rest and where farmers and *caboclos* move. Fire took over the country's forests, covering them with "black crepe." Just a strike of a match and nature, thirsty for rain, erupts into flames and begins to lead the funereal cortege of flora and fauna into extinction. Borrowing the war images that were suggested to him from Europe by the incendiary feats of the German "*vons*" (the text is written right at the outset of the First World War), Lobato denounces the annual burnings that spread furiously with impunity through the mountain of Mantiqueira. It burns just like the villages in Europe.

The burning of forests, the demise of nature. Mantiqueira, he denounces, is "today an immense ashtray." The patriot remarks: "The old layers of humus destroyed; the precious salts that the floods will shortly be carrying downriver into the ocean; the forest's rejuvenation of the soil paralyzed and retreating; the destruction of wild birds and the possible coming of insect plagues...." It's not hard to imagine. The half-a-dozen or so rustic Neros that Lobato describes at the beginning of the century have mushroomed at the end of this millennium, burning down what at the time was still the remote region of Roraima.

It is no wonder that the writer from São Paulo, who since his very early days had become familiar with death, should be well disposed towards the end of his own life, employing black humor and indulging in jokes about the disease and the state in which it had left him. The time had come. He will have to move on—he reckons, retiring to his bedroom—, to other experiences, to learn new things. In the short story "Os Pequeninos," included in *Negrinha*, the character feels that he is becoming acquainted with the painfully bloody life of wild animals by having silenced his inner voice, which reminded him of foolish memories from the past, and by having sharpened his hearing, which made him extremely curious about the twists and turns of an original story told by a stranger.

The story, told by another and heard secretly on the docks, seems much more interesting to the character than the subjective intrigues to which the writer's imagination usually surrenders. The character says: "One of the interruptions [in my remembrances] seemed to me to be more interesting than evoking the past, because the outer life is more lively than the inner…" Internalized in the writer's addicted memory, the anecdote told by another gains a pure and stylish language and is widely circulated through the press. At the same time, it loses its original authenticity and naturalness. The other's story, from the moment it is molded by the novelist's creative spirit and is transformed into a short story, enters a zero-sum game. In short: Lobato's literary text is less interesting than the circumstances that generated it and made it possible.

For Guimarães Rosa—let us remember the forewords to *Tutaméia*—, the anecdote is like a match: once struck, once burnt, it's useless. But be careful!, adds Rosa, it acquires another, harsher usefulness. In the fictional universe of *Tutaméia*, the anecdote, even burnt, serves as a support to Guimarães Rosa "in the matters of poetry and transcendence" (3). Lobato agrees only with the first part of Rosa's reasoning. A story is taken and a manner of storytelling is overridden. Once it has been burned, Lobato takes hold of the oral narrative, stylizes it, because if he does not he neither writes stories nor publishes books. But this author is decidedly against stylizing. The narrator of the short story "Mata-pau" clarifies: "A friend told me the story that was transposed here in a possibly faithful way. The best of it has vanished, the freshness, the flow, the ingenuity of a tale narrated by someone who never learned to place pronouns properly and who, for that very reason, narrates better than all those who have assimilated literary works and grammar, anxious to acquire style." And he concludes: "Great *feuilleton* writers walk through life in God's world lost among the country folk, who have no sense of grammar, but can tell a story in a more picturesque fashion than anyone else." Lobato also clarified in another story: "I don't reproduce his words in the way [the anonymous *feuilleton* writer] has uttered them. It would be impossible, even too harmful to the understanding of the reader."

Lobato depreciates literary stylization to such a point that the editor of his works insists on transmitting to future generations of readers a recurring sentence out of the mouth of the storyteller. He is believed to have said and repeated: "My best book would be the one in which I recounted how and why I wrote my stories, one by one; the source of the stories is better than what they become."

According to Lobato, creative subjectivity matters little; what actually matters is the gesture of "catching" the story of another, a stance typical of a writer who is simultaneously a traveler, a detective and, lastly, a believer in the civilizing process. The author minimizes the complex process of internalization of an oral narrative and its expression through literary language in an attempt to enlarge the external circumstances of its delivery. Boiled down to the artistic product as such, Lobato was barely interested in the process of writing fiction, or the problems concerning the psychology of literary composition. His ramblings, somewhat poetic, closely follow the lessons of the 1870s generation of Sílvio Romero and José Veríssimo and are reduced to a critique of the nationalist idealizations produced by Brazilian Romantic literature.

In a well-known statement on the literary expression of nationality, included in *Cidades Mortas*, Lobato replaced the Native Brazilian with the post-slavery *caboclo*. The simplicity in evolutionary reasoning is so great that it would seem that we are facing a hardly thoughtful misprint. Lobato writes: "The macaw's crest of feathers turned into a straw hat, pulled down over the forehead; the open space in the forest into a thatched hut; the Native Brazilian club tapering off, growing a trigger, placing its ear to the ground, is now a rifle…"—and so continues the enumeration. In "A Criação do Estilo" he returns to his hobbyhorse. He proposes that fauns, satyrs and bacchantes, fruits of the European imaginary, be replaced with "Iaras" (queens of the waters) and "Marabás" (beautiful women, offspring of a Native Brazilian woman and a white man). Once again he lashes out at romantic novelists in *Cidades Mortas*. This time he chooses the famous novelist Bernardo Guimarães as scapegoat: "To read him is like going to the brushwood, to the bush—but to a bush as described by a Catholic girl in high school, where the grasslands are *pleasant*, the orchards *in blossom*, the rivers *torrential*, the forests *verdant*…"—and so on and so forth.

Having questioned the literary value of his own short story, what interests Lobato more is the eventual consumer of the good. He is interested in another *external and unexpected* circumstance—the dialogue between the book and the reader. Books are there to be read. This is Lobato's small but fundamental discovery in a country of illiterate people. The story "Facada Imortal," a real masterpiece, was written for sentimental reasons. It would have been more appropriate to write the circumstances that prompted it instead of the story itself. His friend Raul is the main character, and "Facada

Imortal" was also written for him. When the writer comes across his friend, whose body is suffering from a terminal disease, he seeks to alleviate his pain. How? By inventing a story in which the sick man himself would be the character. The reading of the short story ended by serving, as the editor's note reveals, "as the best morphine injection he had ever been given." Lobato believed that stories help friends to bear the sufferings of death.

Perhaps for these and similar reasons, Lobato as both an editor and publisher of books—so very much present in the series of substantive articles collected under the title "Opinions"—matters more than Lobato the writer and the incurable gossiper. But the reasons for writing and reading the short story are not always those dictated by Christian charity and good brotherly sentiments. Edgard Cavalheiro boldly draws one's attention to the fact that the brilliant creation of Jeca Tatu can be taken as "the unsuccessful farmer's revenge" (20). Stories help us to take vengeance on small and wretched betrayals, believed Lobato.

Sérgio Milliet probes the wound with greater precision. He affirms that "Jeca Tatu is almost a personal vengeance; he is the miserable *caboclo* as seen through the harsh eyes of the frustrated farmer" (267). Jeca Tatu was written by a farmer for the servants, to be read by those who regard themselves as the "Jeca Tatus" of life. It is no mere chance that, up to 1982, the editions of the booklet *Jeca Tatuzinho*, funded by the Fontoura Medical Laboratory, should have sold more than one hundred million copies. It should be at the top of the Brazilian bestsellers list. Because of this, Milliet detects less humor and more sarcasm in Lobato's satirical short stories. The critic explains: "humor, a connoisseur once said, springs from the tenderness and sense of modesty of those who are shy. It is a kind of compensation, while sarcasm is a transfer of the spirit of revolt. It is with sarcasm that the intellectual avenges himself on others; it is through humor that he punishes himself" (267).

Monteiro Lobato was very much aware of his own value and the value of his legacy. At the time when an aneurysm brought him close to death, between a joke or two, the kind that serve to restrain memories of the past, Lobato uttered a sentence which his biographer and admirer was quick to copy. He said that he was anxious "to find out for himself if death was a comma, a semicolon or a period" (Cavalheiro 59).

Appearing to be a mere joke cracked by a gossipy and grumpy old man, the sentence mentioned above takes up afresh the obsessive idea that I have been highlighting in this reading of Monteiro Lobato's literary works for grownups. A pragmatic man, he wanted to know immediately the value and the relevance of life and work. Death is the only yardstick and therefore the real instrument by which to measure and assess life, be it the life of a man, of an animal, or of a vegetable. Death is also the yardstick that can be used to measure and assess man's works. During his life of trials and tribulations, Lobato became well versed in death thanks to countless characters and situations, which abound in his stories and fictional impressions. That was not enough though.

Affected temporarily by agraphia, he seeks to listen to the voice beyond the grave. He wants to meet death *personally*. He wants to find a new scale, new weights and measures. Is it not in the game behind a death/life antithesis, the antithesis that is always mediated by love, that one discovers the truth about a life and an artistic work? In the already mentioned and famous tale "Facada Imortal," the narrator asks: "what is a story if not a stylized antithesis"? In the story in *Urupês* dedicated to Maupassant, Lobato, while clarifying the principles of the French writer's fictional art, declares with the same words the orienting principle of his own fictional art: "Because life is love and death, and Maupassant's art is nine times out of ten an ingenious setting of love and death." Let us recall once again that the original title of *Urupês* focused on tragic deaths, *Doze Mortes Trágicas*.

The yardstick Lobato chose to measure life and work he borrowed from the grammatical model, which he learned in order to build his Baroque, metaphoric, affirmative and booming sentences. A stop in life may be of little importance—the sentence is prolonged to become incisive after a *comma*. A stop can be a fleeting stumble, which allows the sentence to breathe, to attain balance and to expand—the sentence continues to be robust after a *semicolon*. A full stop in life can occur—here lies the fate of a single *period*. It is through the sentences he listened to as a prying eavesdropper and jotted down as an anthropologist, it is through the sentences he wrote and which defined him as a fiction writer, it is through the sentences he chiseled and published in print form that he became a writer, it is through the worked and rebellious sentence, sheer dynamite, that Lobato wants to be judged by the citizens and the critics.

Would the life and work of Monteiro Lobato disappear definitively, as did "Bocatorta," the ghost cities and the mountain of Mantiqueira? Or would they find refuge for some years in a few generous, critical words? Or would they win fame and be enshrined *post mortem* by many a repeated word of praise, uttered at fiftieth anniversaries or centenary celebrations?

SILVIANO SANTIAGO

One of his most lucid and merciless critics, Sérgio Milliet, formulated the question of Monteiro Lobato's legacy quite early on and answered it four years prior to the author's death on September 30, 1944. In the second volume of his *Diário Crítico*, we read that Lobato "will be put through the strainer of merciless revisions, and will still find mind-boggling enthusiasm. In the end, a dozen model stories will enter into anthologies. Also, the better part of his children's literature, which only finds its match in the great international children's literature" (269).

Lobato not only opposed tropical indolence, but was also openly in favor of both work—which lends soul to man and builds charismatic leaders—and the evolution of science—which brings progress to the nation—as well as the evolution of techniques which foster the well-being of citizens. In spite of these notions, Lobato began his professional life at a time when the country was given over to total moral and civic abandonment. The literature of the time is clearly pessimistic and bitter, given the works of Afonso Arinos (*Pelo Sertão*), Euclides da Cunha (*Os Sertões*) and Lima Barreto (*Triste Fim de Policarpo Quaresma*). In the Old Republic, these are the "ingenious framers of love and death." In his early discovery of the movement that gives rise to these conflicts of "stylized antithesis" there is perhaps to be found one of the reasons for why Lobato has always been so sensitive to and impatient before any stop—any kind of abandonment, any paralysis, or any "cachexia" ("emaciation"), to use his own precious vocabulary, so out of fashion in the minimalist aesthetics dominant today.

"Our Progress," he wrote in *Cidades Mortas*, "is nomadic and subject to sudden paralysis." And he goes on: "The gypsy's progress survives in tents. It migrates, leaving behind it a train of ugly shanties." In a subsequent book, *Mr. Slang e o Brasil,* he will add: "Everything in our midst is an emergency, that is to say, a personal, occasional, momentary and temporary solution." Lobato looks for and has always looked for the precise meaning of any stop, of any abandonment or of any paralysis in order to better criticize them. For that, the yardstick of life was worthwhile. Worthwhile too was the desire to point out the reasons for the country's backwardness. He was a fighter who, through the easy and disabused use of the harsh and unexpected word, projected a rebellious attitude, who disliked the powers of the Old Republic, of the New Republic and of the dictatorial state proclaimed by Getúlio Vargas' New State ("Estado Novo").

Master of a sophisticated style as well as remarkably erudite, how could Monteiro Lobato have arrived at such simplistic and all-encompassing diagnoses of Brazilian cultural, social and economic reality? The background for the answer to this question lies in the aristocratic pessimism, full of good intentions, that Monteiro Lobato, like Paulo Prado, the author of *Retrato do Brasil,* cultivated in the scenery of Brazil's ethnic formation. The definitive coloring of that aristocratic scenery lies in the almost proverbial saying found in *Mr. Slang e o Brasil*: "Chickpea, lazybones and gumbo banana and the black man with gumbo have given unto our land the fruits they could." Foreshadowing the "tropicalist" movement led by Caetano Veloso and Glauber Rocha, Monteiro Lobato settles into being a writer, doubling as a doctor, a hygienist, a biologist, a bible preacher and an economist.

He stands up to the "technical experts" of this or that specific discipline with the common sense of the people, taking his cue from Henry Ford. Combining the encyclopedic knowledge of a generalist, imbued with patriotic pessimism, naive but driven by the ideology of individual progress through work, Lobato succeeds in diagnosing with *imprecise details* the true dilemmas of the nation. With the spirit of a generalist mixed with that of the common people, he diagnoses the simple causes of the diseases of Brazilian tropical civilization (causes described as complex by a stupid and corrupt State and the deceitful elite, see the short story "Um Suplício Moderno") and attempts to save them with the proselytizing typical of an evangelical preacher.

The generalist takes the prescription book out of his pocket and hands over a prescription for the cashier to prepare. The former is likely to prescribe for each illness diagnosed, the perfect and efficacious medicine, and the latter is likely to give the miraculous injections, laying down new guidelines for the development and progress that would deliver country and citizens from the asphyxiating paralysis. The simplicity of the analysis, we might repeat, is favorable to an all-encompassing vision and also to miraculous cures.

Latent in both Lobatos was a "Fordism" that became obvious and explicit after his trip to the United States at the end of the 1920s. In *Mr. Slang e o Brasil,* he writes: "After Henry Ford demonstrated how you can employ even the blind and the crippled, nobody's got the right to allege he's of no use. Everyone has some value. Even a blind man, even a mutilated man is of some use. The whole question then lies in *providing them with the conditions necessary to be of some use.*"

Lobato's long-standing and definitive battle, which brought him early fame, was the desire to provide the conditions necessary for the parasite Jeca

Tatu to be of some use. To arrive at the diagnosis of Jeca Tatu's backwardness, the "doctor" neutralized the harmful effects caused by him and his peers in constituting their miserable object of study. And that is why Lobato posed as the liberator of the people and, notwithstanding, was unfair and merciless towards the same people. Lobato forgot that he—and other landholding friends—were the true parasites of the ancestors of the current servants, as they had been of the former slaves as well. It was in this parasitical condition that it fell to him to diagnose the illness of the *caboclo*-parasite. The guilt of the one who exploits other people's work (the landowner) is hidden in order that the indolence of the exploited (the *caboclo*) may be highlighted.

The *caboclo* lived—if it can be called living—like a parasite of the earth, affirms Lobato the farmer. The *caboclo* seemed to him the "louse of the earth," in every manner akin to *Argas*—which attacks chickens—and *Sarcoptes mutans*—which attacks the legs of domestic birds. He was a predator, loose in social space, like one of the monsters in the most recent Hollywood science fiction films. He is against life. Just like the *mata-pau* (the "parasite"), the *caboclo* is a parasite that destroys life. "The tree dies and leaves within itself [the "*mata-pau*"] rotten wood." It destroys the good seed. The *caboclo* is a *native of the tropics*, he is as wild as the nature that formed him, which is why one is a copy of the other. There is not a single history that recounts the fight of those "parasited" against tropical nature and the powerful elite, which only later found them to be parasites. All the *caboclos* are spongers and thugs. It is thus necessary to exterminate the race of internal villains. "Hygiene is the secret key to victory," repeats Lobato. A task for hygienists, Lobato turns to them. A beneficial and patriotic task, without a doubt, but what then?

Countless are the literary versions that Lobato gives us of the ills of the miserable Brazilian parasitism, sophisticated versions always backed up by the encyclopedic knowledge of a generalist, who quotes examples from biology and zoology. The classic example, the theme of a short story in *Urupês*, is the parasitic tree the *mata-pau*, which kills another (the drawing of the *mata-pau* skillfully sketched by the writer circulates in beautiful reproductions in his books (*Furacão na Botocúndia* 85). In the face of the *mata-pau*, the narrator's imagination does not merely think about it, it thinks of literature. In literature he discovers classical references: "the serpents of Laocoon, the warm viper in the breast of the man of the fable, King Lear's daughters, all the classic figures of ingratitude."

There is another example of parasitism in the constant references to the bird known as the shiny cowbird (*chupim*). The most disturbing of the parasitic figures undoubtedly appears in the short story "Os Pequeninos." The small bird known as the *periperi* discovers and mercilessly attacks the weak point of a great ostrich. The *periperi* settles under a wing, where it cannot be removed by the ostrich. The ostrich spins like a lunatic ennobled by pain, without ever succeeding in freeing itself from the bloodsucker. The parasite has a Darwinian moral: it will be strong by killing the ostrich. Let's set aside the good intentions in reading this apologue. Who is the ostrich? Who is the parasite? Why are the demonic "little ones" (*pequeninhos*) diabolical, and the ostrich noble?

Transferring the theme of the *caboclo* stories to the urban world, Lobato once again lends biological images to parasitism and creates new characters. In "O Fisco," included in the collection *Negrinha*, the narrator establishes successive comparisons between certain functions of the human body and life in the city. The street is the artery, those in transit are the blood. The troublemaker, the drunk and the thief are the harmful microbes, disturbing the circulatory rhythm determined by the work of, in particular, the Italian immigrants. The policeman is the leucocyte—the Metchenikoff's *phagocyte*. And so goes the short story: "No sooner is the traffic congested by the antisocial action of the troublemaker than the phagocyte gets cracking, it walks, runs, it pounces on the bad element and drags it down to the slammer." The fight against urban parasitism devises a repressive city—São Paulo—whose attitude, powerful and orderly, is disturbed only by the State's harmful restrictions to free initiative, which themselves appear in the form of the "corrupt tax authority" (see "Da Camisola de Força," *Mr. Slang e o Brasil*).

Roberto Ventura, in a remarkable chapter of *Estilo Tropical*, showed how Manuel Bonfim (*A América Latina*, 1905) conceived of society as an organism, but he also tried to investigate the non-biological laws proper to social facts. Instead of establishing simple homologies between biological and social knowledge (as did Monteiro Lobato), he mapped the differences between the fields. Manuel Bonfim borrowed concepts from biology and zoology, but he also clearly and precisely defined the validity of the transfer of scientific concepts to the analysis of the social field. Therefore, a comparative study of the concept of *parasitism* in Manuel Bonfim and Monteiro Lobato calls for careful consideration.

SILVIANO SANTIAGO

In the shift from Bonfim to Lobato there is a bourgeoisification, a theoretical impoverishment in the fecundity of the homological patterns likely to serve as tools to explain the social reality of the country and of the Western world. In Bonfim, the pattern of the parasite and the parasited in nature would help to explain the dominant and the dominated in society, masters and slaves, capital and work, metropolis and colony, imperialism and nationalism. The most important step Bonfim has taken is in refusing the homology between biology and society. Thus, Roberto Ventura writes, the essayist has to establish "the differences between *organic* parasitism, which would bring about irreversible modifications in the organisms, and *social parasitism*, which could be extirpated by those parasited—the slave, the worker, the proletarian, the nation—by means of struggling against the various forms of exploitation" (157). That is how, Ventura continues, Bonfim escapes the pessimism and determinism of the theories of milieu, race and Brazilian national character.

Antonio Candido, in a brief and definitive article on Manuel Bonfim, complements the words of Roberto Ventura, signaling that parasitism, described in *A América Latina* as "the original sin," shows how the parasite, living off the total exploitation of the parasited, ends up unable to survive without it, and so deteriorates and drops, allowing for the emergence of important new elements. Candido concludes: "This is how the continuity of the structure is preserved through the change of the agents; thus the conditions are never truly created for really free work, which would make for well-being and social balance" (138).

Notes

[1] This essay was originally published in the Supplement "Mais!" in *Folha de S. Paulo*, July 1998.

Works Cited

Azevedo, Carmen Lúcia de, Maria Mascarenhas de Rezende Camargos, and Vladimir Sacchetta. *Monteiro Lobato: Furacão na Botacúndia.* São Paulo: SENAC, 1997.

Candido, Antonio. "Os Brasileiros e a Nossa América." *Recortes.* São Paulo: Companhia das Letras, 1993. 130-139.

Cavalheiro, Edgar. "Vida e Obra de Monteiro Lobato." *Urupês.* By Monteiro Lobato. São Paulo, Brasiliense, Monteiro Lobato. *Obras Completas.* Primeira Série, Literatura Geral. 9th ed. São Paulo: Brasiliense, 1959. 3-79.

Milliet, Sérgio. *Diário Crítico de Sérgio Milliet.* 2nd ed. São Paulo: EdUSP, 1981.

Rosa, João Guimarães. "Aletria e Hermenêutica." *Tutaméia.* Rio de Janeiro: José Olympio, 1967. 3-12.

Ventura, Roberto. *Estilo Tropical: História Cultural e Polêmicas Literárias no Brasil. 1870-1914.* São Paulo: Companhia das Letras, 1991.

Contemporary Brazilian Women's Autobiography and the Forgotten Case of Adalgisa Nery

Sabrina Karpa-Wilson

Since the early decades of the twentieth century autobiography has enjoyed increasing popularity in Brazil.[1] Prior to 1933, a year Antonio Candido identifies as a major watershed due to the success of Humberto de Campos' *Memórias,* autobiographical publications were relatively rare ("Literatura" 12). An impulse towards self-revelation may be found in some eighteenth-century poetry and a handful of nineteenth-century literary-political memoirs, but such self-display was the exception rather than the rule (Candido, "Poesia" 51-2). Beginning in the 1930s, this situation was drastically reversed as Modernism threw the autobiographical floodgates wide open. Since then, different decades have seen differing emphases on the political or the psychological, on the seemingly trivial details of childhood or the experience of prison and torture, but cultivation of openly personal literature has not significantly waned.[2]

Curiously, autobiography in twentieth-century Brazil seems to have been largely a male affair, or so it would appear from a perusal of the few bibliographies on the subject.[3] With only a few exceptions, the most famous probably being Helena Morley and Carolina Maria de Jesus, women have either opted out of writing their autobiographies or perhaps have not been able to interest publishers in them.[4] This is not to say that they have not written self-referentially, but they have tended to favor other prose or poetic vehicles over explicit, book-length autobiography. The *crônica,* "a short form of commentary principally based upon life experiences that has developed into a literary genre unique to Brazil" (Vieira 354), has been one way in which many women writers have cultivated self-writing. Another popular vehicle has been the autobiographical novel.

A potential explanation for such preferences may be found in Rachel de Queiroz' recent auto/biography, *Tantos Anos* (1998). Including a composite of passages written by Rachel, reproductions of conversations between her and her sister Maria Luíza, and various "interventions" by the latter (10), the book is both an autobiography and a biography. The reason for its hybrid composition, according to Maria Luíza, was Rachel's reluctance to write her own memoirs (9-10). In the opening pages, Rachel spells out her reservations about the autobiographical act:

> You know I don't like memoirs… It is a literary genre—and is it really literary?—in which the author places himself openly as protagonist and, whether saying good things about himself or confessing evil deeds, he is in reality indulging the pretensions of his ego… The most dubious aspect of memoirs is confession, a genre I have always abhorred, for there are some things in one's life that are not to be told. (11)[5]

According to this, what most perturbs the writer, aside from the genre's dubious literary status,[6] is its impropriety: its emphasis on self-aggrandizement and the airing of dirty laundry. Whether or not this was indeed the main factor in keeping her from writing her memoirs, it is suggestive that Rachel should invoke such notions as modesty, self-effacement and discretion, all attributes of "proper" female behavior expected of earlier generations, including her own.[7] Here such attributes are generalized, through the use of the "universalizing" male noun *"o autor"* in the quote above, as desired characteristics for all "literary" writers.

If a writer should not "place [her]self openly as protagonist," however, it would seem she can forge her protagonists in her own image. In several novels Rachel de Queiroz explored personal concerns through female characters which appear as more or less transparent alter egos. Such is the case in *O Quinze* (1930) and *As Três Marias* (1939), for example, in which tensions between "emancipated" femininity vs. traditional female roles are ambivalently probed (*Três* 446). In these and other novels, Rachel makes use of the fictional medium to play out conflicting positions and to give shape to desires and fears without the uncomfortable exposure of "confession." Of course, the same could be said of all writers of fiction—that their fictional edifices and personal memories and experiences are inevitably and deeply implicated in each other. Graciliano Ramos, a contemporary of Rachel, speaks

SABRINA KARPA-WILSON

of his novelistic production as such: "I was never able to leave myself... And if my characters behave in different ways, it is because I am not one" (Senna 55).[8] Yet, unlike Rachel, Graciliano eventually turns to explicit autobiography, publicly discarding the character masks in favor of the naked, "irritating little [first-person] pronoun" (Ramos 1: 37).

For Graciliano, as for other Brazilian male writers, autobiography seems to provide something fiction does not: a stronger authoritative position from which to bear witness. The opening pages of Graciliano's prison memoirs are revealing in this regard: while the writer eschews any naive notion of absolute truth in autobiography, his urgent "duty" to bear witness to historical atrocities cannot be met through fictional "deforma[tion]," but only through the assumption of full personal responsibility performed by autobiography's self-exposure (Ramos 1: 35, 33). In his view, this assumption, rather than any claim to a more exact truth, lends a special authority to the autobiographical act.

This idea of autobiography's peculiar value may shed further light on Brazilian women writers' choices. If many women have favored the novel's "autobiography by intermediary" over outright autobiography, it is perhaps not only out of questions of propriety, but out of the related and fundamental issue of authority. For in order to lay claim to the special authority of autobiography, a writer must already possess a certain measure of authority. That is, he or she must believe that autobiography's founding affirmation of personal responsibility will carry significant social weight and command readers' respect. Such a belief has historically been more problematic for women writers than for men.

The problem of autobiography and authority is perhaps most cogently formulated by Adalgisa Nery, who develops an incisive theory and practice of female autobiographics. Well-known during her lifetime as a poet, novelist, journalist and politician, Adalgisa Nery (1905-1980) has since been all but forgotten by literary scholars. She is now remembered mostly for her journalistic and political activities, a selective focus demonstrated in a recent biography.[9] And yet her first novel, A Imaginária (1959), was acclaimed by critics and well-received by the general public, running through three subsequent editions (Callado 100). Most readers seem to have immediately recognized the novel as a thinly veiled autobiography (Callado 33), and the appeal of an intimate confession by the widow of renowned painter Ismael Nery may have contributed to the book's success. While the general and critical public alike were quick to be seduced by the prospect of juicy gossip, they seem to have remained largely unattuned to the more subtle literary, social and psychological aspects of Nery's narrative. In one of the few published critical readings of *A Imaginária*, Affonso Romano de Sant'Anna argues that it is "a fundamental text for studying the constitution of the female narrator in modern Brazilian fiction" (91). I would go further, and add that it is fundamental for studying the female *autobiographical* narrator in Brazilian letters.

Although noting that the novel lies "between biography and fiction," Sant'Anna does not present this as a critical problem (92). However, in the last two decades, feminist scholarship has highlighted the urgency of attending to the specificities of women's autobiographical practice, particularly to the ways in which gender ideologies, notions of subjectivity and self-writing necessarily inform each other. In the case of *A Imaginária*, this urgency is underscored by the novel itself, which calls repeated attention to the disparities between female reality and the requirements of traditional autobiography. In his model of autobiography, Philippe Lejeune grounds the distinctiveness of the genre in a "pact," in which, through use of his "proper name" the writer enters into an implied contract with his reader (8-14). The contract is one Graciliano Ramos would probably recognize, for it involves an assumption of personal responsibility, the promise that the writer will "honor" his declaration of identity (14). Lejeune's contractual/legal model of autobiography poses significant problems for the reading of women's texts, however, because it rests on a masculine notion of the proper name's authority. A woman's name, on the other hand, has historically carried little authority, signaling most often not her entrance into an authoritative subjectivity, but rather her subjection as property (Gilmore 81). As site of a problematic identity, marked by limitations rather than confirmations of agency, the female signature has therefore frequently been evaded, through use of a pseudonym, "Anon" or fictional disguise (Gilmore 81).

Adalgisa Nery seems to be acutely aware of these tensions, which become major structuring elements in her text. How can a woman lay claim to the powerful authority of autobiography in order to bear witness to female experience? This question itself drives *A Imaginária*, which proposes a solution through irony, among other novelistic strategies. The text's first move is to call itself a novel while making no effort to disguise its autobiographical provenance. This would seem to simply collapse fiction into autobiography, erasing all significant distinctions. However, a framing device reintroduces generic difference, foregrounding the text's packaging as a deliberate—and ironic—choice. In the opening pages of the narrative, Berenice, the female narrator-protagonist, denies that she intends to write her "autobiography": "I could not describe my entire life... because then I would be trying to write autobiography... I want precisely to avoid this idea, for... I feel I am at the juncture of... an experience and not an event. Experience does not carry the sense of the definite" (7). Autobiography pertains to definitive event, whereas what she has to tell falls under "muta[ble]" experience (7). This denial is repeated more forcefully in the book's final pages, where it acquires a distinctly self-denigrating cast: "Were I less high-strung, if I did not live continuously under the caustic eye of disbelief and analysis, were I not certain of my life's lack of importance, I would try to begin my biography" (208). After a sleepless night, Berenice feels she has fruitlessly brooded over her unimportant life, but we, of course, have just finished reading her autobiography. This framework of a double denial opens up two distinctions—between fiction and autobiography, and between fictional protagonist and authorial structuring will—and destabilizes the idea of autobiographical authority.

Berenice tells us that autobiography demands both a particular content and a particular attitude of the autobiographer. Autobiographers must be self-confident in the importance of their lives, which is based on the perception of life as "event." Elsewhere, however, she herself questions the hierarchical dichotomy between event and experience. In a scene in which she watches an unnamed "revolutionary movement" march by her front door, event is equated with history, and promptly unmasked as anything but definitive. When she asks one of the protesting men what he means by shouting "Down with oppression," his words are revealed to be "puerile," mere slogans he repeats without any personal knowledge of their meaning (123). The "revolution"—probably a reference to the Revolution of 1930 and a major event in national history—is rooted in empty words. Meanwhile, Berenice realizes she has a much more solid understanding of "oppression," founded on intimate female experience: "My oppression was within the home" (123). The values of experience and event are inverted, and autobiography's importance and authority, as Berenice understands them, suddenly appear to be based on far less solid ground.

The narrative frame and Berenice's reading of the "revolution," along with various other scenes in the text, achieve their particular meanings through an ironic gap between the character's perceptions and the views of the implied author or what I have called the authorial structuring will. Berenice voices conventional wisdom on generic and gender categories, but her narrative undermines that wisdom. If by the novel's end the protagonist still feels she cannot write her "biography," the implied author has redefined what constitutes legitimate autobiographical material: not event, which historically has been a male domain, but female experience. Despite *A Imaginária*'s early success, it would seem that the significance of this message was not understood, judging from the subsequent critical silence. We would do well to look again, for Nery's narrative offers a strategic model for female self-writing, in which fictional tools are used not as guardians of propriety but, on the contrary, as invaluable instruments of genre and gender critique.

Notes

[1] Philippe Lejeune's now famous definition of autobiography limits it to "a retrospective prose narrative written by a real person . . . where the focus is his individual life" (4). I, however, follow Antonio Candido's broader use of the term, to include both narratives focused primarily on an individual and family/community memoirs. See "Poesia" and "Literatura."

[2] See Zagury on Brazilian childhood autobiography, Santiago on modernist autobiography and more recent trends, and Süssekind on post-1964 political memoirs.

[3] See Sodré and, more recently, Vieira.

[4] Morley's *Minha Vida de Menina* (1942) and Jesus' *Quarto de Despejo* (1960) were both bestsellers and have been translated into English, among other languages. It is unclear how many other women may have written autobiographies that await recovery, but since the wave of political memoirs in the 1970s and 1980s there has been a visible increase in the publication of female autobiographies.

[5] This and other translations of literary passages are mine.

[6] See Molloy on the unstable status of autobiography in Spanish America. The general lines of her argument speak to Brazil as well.

[7] Another potential explanation for her resistance to writing memoirs may lie in a desire for "discretion" concerning her support of the 1964 military coup and subsequent dictatorship.

[8] Or, as Georges Gusdorf observes, "[e]very novel is an autobiography by intermediary" (46).

[9] See Callado.

Works Cited

Callado, Ana Arruda. *Adalgisa Nery. Muito Amada e Muito Só*. Rio de Janeiro: Relume-Dumará, 1999.

Candido, Antonio. "A Literatura Brasileira em 1972." *Revista Iberoamericana* 43 (1977): 5-16.

———. "Poesia e Ficção na Autobiografia." *A Educação pela Noite*. São Paulo: Ática, 1987. 51-69.

Gilmore, Leigh. *Autobiographics: A Feminist Theory of Women's Self-Representation.* Ithaca: Cornell UP, 1994.

Gusdorf, Georges. "Conditions and Limits of Autobiography." *Autobiography: Essays Theoretical and Critical.* Ed. James Olney. Princeton: Princeton UP, 1980. 28-48.

Lejeune, Philippe. *On Autobiography.* 1975. Ed. Paul John Eakin. Trans. Katherine Leary. Minneapolis: U of Minnesota P, 1989.

Molloy, Sylvia. *At Face Value: Autobiographical Writing in Spanish America.* Cambridge: Cambridge UP, 1991.

Nery, Adalgisa. *A Imaginária.* 3rd ed. Rio de Janeiro: José Olympio, 1970.

Queiroz, Rachel and Maria Luíza de. *Tantos Anos.* São Paulo: Siciliano, 1998.

Queiroz, Rachel de. *As Três Marias. Quatro Romances de Rachel de Queiroz.* Rio de Janeiro: José Olympio, 1960.

Ramos, Graciliano. *Memórias do Cárcere.* 28th ed. 2 vols. Rio de Janeiro: Record, 1994.

Sant'Anna, Affonso Romano de. "Masculine Vampirism or the Denunciation of Pygmalion: A Reading of Adalgisa Nery's *A Imaginária.*" *Tropical Paths: Essays on Modern Brazilian Literature.* Ed. Randal Johnson. New York: Garland, 1993. 91-99.

Santiago, Silviano. "Prosa Literária Atual no Brasil." *Nas Malhas da Letra.* São Paulo: Companhia da Letras, 1989. 24-37.

———. "Vale Quanto Pesa." *Vale Quanto Pesa.* Rio de Janeiro: Paz e Terra, 1982. 25-40.

Senna, Homero. "Revisão do Modernismo." *Graciliano Ramos.* Ed. Sônia Brayner. Rio de Janeiro: Civilização Brasileira, 1977. 46-59.

Sodré, Nelson Werneck. "Memórias e Correspondência." *O Que Se Deve Ler para Conhecer o Brasil.* Rio de Janeiro: Civilização Brasileira, 1967. 357-364.

Süssekind, Flora. "Polêmicas, Retratos & Diários (Reflexos Parciais sobre a Literatura e a Vida Cultural no Brasil Pós-64)." *Fascismo y Experiencia Literaria: Reflexiones para una Recanonización.* Ed. Hernan Vidal. Minneapolis: Institute for the Study of Ideologies and Literature, 1985. 255-295.

Vieira, Nelson H. "A Brazilian Biographical Bibliography." *Biography* 5.4 (1982): 351-364.

Zagury, Eliane. *A Escrita do Eu.* Rio de Janeiro: Civilização Brasileira, 1982.

SABRINA KARPA-WILSON

Devil to Pay in the Backlands and João Guimarães Rosa's Quest for Universality

Kathrin H. Rosenfield

Almost thirty years after the death of João Guimarães Rosa, his major novel, *Grande Sertão: Veredas* (*GSV*),[1] is still considered to be an incomparable masterpiece. "Incomparable" in two ways: in the metaphorical sense of an unparalleled work of art, and as an effort for both a literary and intellectual elaboration of a Brazilian problem that has not been equaled since. This problem goes back to the end of the nineteenth century's effort to consolidate Brazil's identity as independent from European models, though not ignorant of universal intellectual and cultural frameworks. Euclides da Cunha's *Os Sertões*[2] is one of the most important achievements in terms of addressing these issues. He describes and analyzes the material and spiritual conditions which led to the dreadful extermination, by the troops of the federal government, of a sect of *sertanejos*—inhabitants of the semi-arid highlands—who gathered around Antonio Conselheiro, driven by misery, social injustice and millennialist hopes. Euclides da Cunha's essay was a real "revelation" to the Brazilian intelligentsia. It's immediate, widespread success suddenly unveiled a region and a way of life that was previously almost completely unknown, namely that of the ethnic "minority" of the so-called *sertanejo*, i.e. the descendants of a typically Brazilian ethnic mixture of Europeans, Africans and Natives who herded cattle in the vast backlands, totally isolated from the culture of the coastal regions. This revelation of a surprising, shocking and admirable "otherness" was meant to be the starting point for a new way of conceiving of Brazil and Brazilianess.

It was understood thus by Guimarães Rosa, whose œuvre is a rare (if not unique) successor to Euclides da Cunha's integration of Brazilian particularity into a set of universally shared concepts and thoughts.[3] Written for the cultured public in the urban centers—for a reader who is paradigmatically present as the erudite (but ever silent) *Senhor* with whom the *sertanejo*-hero of the novel, Riobaldo,[4] mono-dialogues—*GSV* very successfully bridges the imaginary gap between the educated, intellectual world of Brazilian cities and the universe of the still remote, rural backlands.

Like Euclides' essay, *GSV* rapidly achieved wide admiration and a very select status within literary criticism, due to the extraordinarily subtle conciliation of modern and traditional artistic claims (modernist phono-semantic techniques within a well-constructed epic frame). All this has not sufficed, however, to ensure a large popularity for the novel among the wider Brazilian public. Abroad as well, the German, North American and French translations have not had the response one might expect for this extraordinary novel. To a large extent this is due to the difficulty of Rosa's rather "Joycean" artistic language, based, on the one hand, on the musicality of popular dialects, and, on the other hand, upon clusters and incrustations of foreign idioms, scholarly elaborated charades, and philosophical puns. This well-balanced mixture of "native" and foreign languages, of the naive and the erudite, of extreme simplicity and utter subtlety, of common sense and philosophical rigor, locates this novel about an almost medieval "quest" in a rather hybrid literary position: somewhere between lyrics and epics, or between traditional folk tales and the modern novels of Joyce and Proust. *GSV* thus represents a quite unusual artifact which merges different Brazilian and universal imaginaries into a harmonious epic structure constituted by the most heterogeneous of elements: local everyday language, tales and myths, reminiscences of Brazilian nineteenth-century essays, fragments of romantic and popular poetry, Platonic dialogues, Freudian free association and Heideggerian reflections on pre-Socratic thought.

Riobaldo's Quest for "Nothing" and "All"

Nonada—"nothing," "it's not worthwhile," "trifle"—is the first word which opens the unending mono-dialogue of the hero, Riobaldo, who, as an old man, looks back on his life as a *jagunço*, one of the warrior-herdsmen who take care of their landlord's cattle and transform themselves into faithful gunmen in times of electoral conflicts between the proprietors of the vast regions of the *sertão*—the semi-arid highlands extending between the North of Minas Gerais, Goiás, Bahia, Pernambuco up to Piauí. Riobaldo retired to his *padrinho*'s properties that he inherited after the death of Selorico Mendes, who revealed his fatherhood only by leaving all of his *fazendas* to his son. This now wealthy *sertanejo* keeps talking to an invisible and mute *senhor*,[5] explaining the inexplicable, i.e., the ever-changing qualities of the *jagunço*'s life and the disconcerting experience of the mutability of things. His first words: "No, it's nothing, what you thought of importance means nothing at all"— are deliberately presented as a fragment of the conversation-monologue which constitutes the novel. Within the overall context of the neverending mono-dialogue, the trifling and unimportant word *nonada* will assume other meanings: it can also mean "within nothing," "lost in non-being," recognizing the contradictions of equivocal experience. Riobaldo talks about this kind of experience through words and sentences that are equally ambiguous and dense, images evoking clusters of multiple significance. The name of Riobaldo's adversary, Hermógenes, for example, brings up the difficult question of natural language in Plato's *Cratylus*, apart from the connotations concerning the ambiguous beings engendered by the god Hermes (hermo-geneos) and their unlawful way of life. A weasel-like animal, the *irara*, associated with the names of Hermógenes and of Diadorim (Riobaldo's beloved companion of arms), is, in Brazilian myths, an emblem of burning desire, whereas the *tamanduá* ("anteater") refers not only to a common animal of the *sertão*, but means in popular language "a hard-to-tackle moral problem." What seemed to be, at first sight, a simple description of local colors or particularities, turns out to be a philosophical reflection on good and evil and on the essence of human existence.

These subliminal layers of signification are very difficult to translate and require not only a careful, sensitive reading, but also scholarly introductions and commentaries,[6] which have been rare, particularly abroad. At a first reading, Rosa's language seems to be extremely modern and experimental, combining free associative techniques with melopaic, phono-semantic and pictographical devices—evidence of his familiarity with the modern poetry of Ezra Pound and T. S. Eliot. However, Rosa is also an admirer of Homer and Dante, Goethe, Mann and Musil, and that means that he appreciates thoroughly epic construction.[7] Like Eliot's *The Waste Land*, *Grande Sertão: Veredas* is not a mere "fragment," but "rhythmical grumbling."[8] It is an anguished reflection that de-constructs—systematically and in a logically coherent manner—the elements of novelistic and lyric traditions, rearranging them in a new, harmonious constellation. The essentially lyrical form of this

KATHRIN H. ROSENFIELD

novel, which is particularly noticeable when read aloud, is like a poem that evokes the intense beauty and the poetic "volume" of popular oral discourse. It does not exclude a well-elaborated plot, which emerges gradually, after some fifty pages of deliberately "free" associative roaming.

The Evil and the "Mutative Matter"

The initial, almost musical theme of the novel is a rather solipsistic conversation on evil. The old *fazendeiro* Riobaldo talks incessantly about his former life as a *jagunço*, trying to extract the secret meaning from his chaotic and multifarious reminiscences. In the Brazilian context, the traditional European imagery of devilish evil has been enriched by African and Native beliefs, thus creating hybridity between disparate traditions—Native and African, Indo-European and Greek, Roman and Christian. Rosa exploits this heterogeneousness in brilliant ways, questioning, through the clashes of different imagery and irreconcilable modes of being or behavior, the consistency of what we call "good" and "evil." After introducing an avalanche of chaotic—that Rosa calls "magmaic"—thoughts and images, the protagonist's ruminations conjure the faint outlines of an epic plot: the reminiscences of the childhood and of the adventures of the young man who seeks shelter in several *jagunço* clans; his intense friendship with the enigmatic and beautiful Diadorim makes him endure more of the violence and bloodshed than he normally would be inclined to experience, transforming the passive follower into the chief leader of war for the allied clans. The overall setting is the (very faint) horizon of rather traditional Brazilian conflicts: the local landowner's lack of conformance to the laws of the federal government and the almost fratricidal clashes between rival clans of landowners.[9]

With the wonderful narrative concision of a popular storyteller (*contador de casos*), Rosa outlines the features of his hero. Riobaldo was born as the son of "Bigri," a name suggesting the mestizo condition of his mother who lives and works as an *agregada* for different landlords after having had this only child from a father who is unknown to the son. After Bigri's death, the boy is received like a son by rich Selorico Mendes, who, as he finds out later, is his real father. This origin, revealed accidentally by a third person, does not act as a revelation to Riobaldo of his "real" status; rather, it perpetuates his status as a *jagunço*: a being who is eternally precarious and "improvised," undefined and undefinable, always in-between the insider and the outsider, rich and poor, the cultured and the illiterate, civilized and savage. Rosa presents this ambiguity, characteristic of the social reality of a *jagunço*, as the essence of the human condition, giving it metaphysical significance and depth. Every second word becomes a pun or a Freudian slip, sentences conceal charades, images are of anamorphic consistency, names and concepts turn out to be anagrams. The father-figure Zé Bebelo becomes a demonic *trickster* (anagram of *Belzebub*), the angelic-motherlike *Diadorim* slips into diabolic *Diá* ("devil"), whereas the devilish *Hermógenes* assumes the role of a mother-like, sheltering protector. This kind of slipperiness is the essence of the *sertão*, of life within quicksilvery "mutative matter" (*matéria vertente, azougue maligno,* "quicksilver"). Rosa's artistic language spreads out this theme on different metalevels: in subliminal discussions about the essence of storytelling and writing or of philosophical thinking within aesthetic concreteness. "The evil dog possesses me again," he once wrote to Eduardo Bizzarri, "the limitlessness of [artistic] invention is an ever-present demon!"[10]

In order to keep "pure" poetry and aesthetic invention within formal limits, Rosa inscribes his fragmentary language experiments into an epic structure and a social practice of capital imaginary weight. Contrary to the tendencies of Brazilian modernism, he chooses for his novel the frame of popular storytelling ("*casos,*" "*causos*") anchored in the powerful Brazilian modes of informal, conversational intercourse that tend to blur the limits between public and private life, between purely subjective intimacy and factual objectivity. A series of formal characteristics indicate that Rosa intended to prolong and re-elaborate in a novelistic form Euclides da Cunha's half-dramatic, half-essayistic analysis of the geographical and anthropological specificity of the Brazilian highlands, thus adding to Euclides' essay the dimensions of contemplative poetic thought.

Euro-Brazilian Transpositions

The well-read author who spoke seven idioms fluently and another half-dozen fairly well, loved to play language games by transposing lexical, syntactic and imaginary structures from one context to another. This may be a normal modern practice, but in Rosa's case this art achieves an extraordinarily high level of integration with the specific Brazilian local colors; a naive reader may not even perceive that the system of proper names is almost always over-determined with foreign or erudite significations. Names and titles often seem to be thoroughly authentic, popular creations,

KATHRIN H. ROSENFIELD

even though they carry intentionally foreign significations. An example is the title "Cara de Bronze," alluding to the idiomatic English expression of "brazenfaced," boldness, or the name of a love-song, "canção de Siruiz," which, at first sight, seems to be one of the frequent reminiscences of medieval sagas, while "siruiz" is in fact the way a Romanian man addresses his woman-lover as "my well-beloved."

The same thing happens with narrative structures, as exemplified in one of the most strikingly enchanting scenes of the novel: the encounter of the fourteen-year-old Riobaldo with a miraculously beautiful and courageous boy of his age, with whom he crosses the river São Francisco in a canoe. It inscribes the opening structure of a medieval epic—the crossing of the frontier between familiar, civilized life and adventure, the Percival theme— into the mold of Brazilian popular narrative. Rosa's incomparable art lies in his way of making the reader absorb intertextual references without even noting their depth and their complexities. Their semantic tissue is developed within local narrative practices, like the *casos*—small stories about practical problems with moral or spiritual implications, like the medieval *exemplum*. Rearranging these miniature narratives like musical variations on a theme, Rosa achieves constellations of images and thoughts with a highly philosophical potential. Apparently naive questions about the devil, about deliberate or unconscious violence and gratuitous evil, start to crystallize alongside coherent conceptual axes, such as the theological and philosophical questions surrounding radical or relative evil. The insidious presentation of apparently naive and unconscious forms of sadism evoke in an absolutely indirect and secret way the recent contemporary experience of the banality of evil,[11] of the infinite slips and nuances which cause originally "good" intentions to slide into inexplicable malignity.

When Riobaldo tries to abandon the terrible violence he observes while living as a teacher in Zé Bebelo's clan, he re-encounters the marvelous boy of his childhood, Reinaldo-Diadorim, who introduces him to the clan leaders Joca Ramiro, Medeiro Vaz and Hermógenes. Fleeing their war, he subsequently becomes actively involved in the *jagunços'* warfare. Diadorim's fascinating aura makes Riobaldo remain, adopting the habits of violence and abjection that he would normally have rejected. At the same time, however, the narrative investigation of the past shows that these customs, apparently against his free will and moral convictions, are based on the logic of subliminal needs and desires, which subvert and usurp the structures of

KATHRIN H. ROSENFIELD

intentional thought, of communicative language and of action. At this level of deep structures, seemingly opposed figures such as beautiful Diadorim and ugly, disgusting Hermógenes—the traitor and assassin of Joca Ramiro—become chiasmic "doublets." Under the spell of Diadorim's inexplicable charm, Riobaldo becomes more and more deeply enmeshed with the *jagunço's* habits and, although the aggravating reproduction of hostilities becomes progressively senseless and abhorred by him, he is unable to separate himself from his friend. By and by, he adopts—against his own will—Diadorim's request to assume the leadership position in the fight against the traitor Hermógenes. This campaign is marked by almost carnavalesque, intuitive gestures and ideas, extravagant and almost mad behaviors, eccentric and seemingly unrealizable projects. These entirely unreasonable, deviant and strangely instinctive steps finally lead to the long-desired confrontation with the enemy. The two final battles repeat the reversive structure of the novel (and of life): the first one ends in heroic victory. During the second one, however, Riobaldo experiences again—and in a most awful and tragic way—his passive dependence on infinite, half-concealed mechanisms whose lawful interlocking become perceptible only *ex post facto*, after the tragic occurrences. Waiting for the second battle, invincible Riobaldo-Urutu Branco ("White Snake") is possessed by a desire for rest and refreshment. Giving way to a tendency concealed in the etymology of his first name—Riobaldo is linked to Dante's *baldanza*, lazy, passive enjoyment—, he is surprised by the enemy's attack, loses control of the battle and watches, in a state of feverish alienation, the mortal single combat Diadorim forces on Hermógenes. Wailing over his friend's corpse, he discovers a woman's body, and Hermógenes' wife reveals to him that this girl-warrior was Joca Ramiro's daughter Deodorina.

Riobaldo's grumbling is provoked by these enigmatic reversals of the purely apparant and "mutative" value of all things or experiences. They manifest themselves through surprising changes that reveal that things are entirely different from what we thought them to be; nevertheless, their reversal makes us perceive that we might have recognized their real significance had we been able to interlock the diverse "insignificant" details involving their appearance.

The gap between finite and infinite comprehension is what provokes the narrator's grumbling: telling the story of the *Grande Sertão* is an effort to re-articulate "quicksilvery" reality, shaping and giving form to the "devilish" ambiguities of experience. Like Plato's *Cratylus*, Riobaldo tries to reconstruct possible links which may (or may not) give us the idea that even utter contingency may rest on firm universal laws. He sums up the precarious results of his grumbling in a paradoxical formula, saying that the devil—just like the *sertão*—does not exist… even though both always tend to reappear.

Notes

[1] First published in 1959-60; translation published as *The Devil to Pay in the Backlands*.

[2] First published in 1902.

[3] Lourenço 19-24. The critic stresses the importance of Rosa's avoiding certain modernistic tendencies and his successful integration of modern realism into universal thought and metaphysical claims.

[4] The novel's setting is based on a rather speculative (or mystic or metaphysical) concept of dialogue—such as Blanchot's *L'Entretien Infini*—for whom "distance, interval and recognition of otherness" are the fundamental characteristics of dialogue. Within this framework, there is no problem for the "dialogue" taking place between the two terms of the subject's own otherness (present, in the novel, as Riobaldo-*jagunço* and as Riobaldo-storyteller). In Freudian terms, one could say that otherness is "introjected."

[5] This *Senhor* may be his own cultured, educated self or *the Senhor*—"God," the ideal of metaphysical Order.

[6] Brazilian secondary literature has mainly studied the socio-economic and political context of the novel and the importance of "oral discourse" in Rosa's art, as it can be seen in well-known essays by Antonio Candido, Luiz Costa Lima, Walnice Nogueira Galvão, Bento Prado Jr., David Arrigucci Jr.. The role of Brazilian folklore in Rosa's work has been analyzed, for instance, by Leonardo Arroio. For the metaphysical dimension and the philosophical contexts privileged by the author, see Rosenfield, *Os Descaminhos do Demo*. Other approaches mix Rosa's "metaphysics" with hermeticism and esotericism.

[7] We are currently preparing a detailed study of the Brazilian and universal intertextuality in Rosa's work for a forthcoming book: *The Work of Guimarães Rosa: An Introduction*.

[8] That was the way in which Eliot defined *The Waste Land*. See Rosenfield, "Poesia em Tempo de Prosa" 144.

[9] For these anthropological aspects, see Euclides da Cunha's *Os Sertões* (1902) and Sérgio Buarque de Holanda's *Raízes do Brasil* (1936).

[10] João Guimarães Rosa, *Correspondência com Edoardo Bizzarri* 67-8.

[11] Rosa, who saved several lives while he worked as a diplomat at the Brazilian Embassy in Hamburg during the Nazi regime, may have transposed Hannah Arendt's idea of "the banality of evil."

Works Cited

Blanchot, Maurice. *L'Entretien Infini*. Paris: Gallimard, 1969.

Cunha, Euclides da. *Os Sertões*. Rio de Janeiro: Laemmert, 1902.

Holanda, Sérgio Buarque de. *Raízes do Brasil*. Rio de Janeiro: José Olympio, 1936.

Lourenço, Eduardo. "G. Rosa ou o Terceiro Sertão," *Terceira Margem* (Porto) 2 (1999): 19-24.

Rosa, João Guimarães. *Grande Sertão: Veredas.* Rio de Janeiro: José Olympio, 1959-1960.

————. *The Devil to Pay in the Backlands.* Trans. James L. Taylor and Harriet de Onis. New York: Knopf, 1963.

————. *Correspondência com Edoardo Bizzarri.* São Paulo: T. A. Queiroz, 1981.

Rosenfield, Kathrin. *Os Descaminhos do Demo.* Rio de Janeiro: Imago, 1992.

————. "Poesia em Tempo de Prosa." *Poesia em Tempo de Prosa.* São Paulo: Iluminuras, 1996. 127-165.

KATHRIN H. ROSENFIELD

Archives and Memories of Pedro Nava

Eneida Maria de Souza
Translated by David Shepherd
and Tania Shepherd

...one of the things that has most impressed me before today, and which has acted as a Proustian madeleine for me, is a watch chain that my father gave me when I was a small boy. My father would take me out, and sometimes dressed in an identical fashion to him. And so he gave me a watch and a chain, which were obviously cheap. But I hadn't seen that watch chain for ages, and I had completely forgotten about it, until one day mother showed it to me. She said, "This watch chain was yours." Then I remembered all these facts entirely. This watch chain held me captive, and linked me to the past in such a way that I would never have imagined.

Pedro Nava ("Entrevista" 107-08)

Pedro Nava (1903-1984) began to write his *Memórias* in 1968, after he had retired from the medical profession, in which he had practiced for over thirty years. His literary experience, begun in the 1920s in the city of Belo Horizonte, included the company of those young writers who were about to play their part in the São Paulo modernist movement. Carlos Drummond de Andrade, Abgar Renault, Emílio Moura, among others, became nationally known poets, in contrast with Nava, who only published *Baú de Ossos*, the first volume of his *Memórias*, in 1972. His later efforts at literature would fulfill an agreement made earlier with colleagues of his generation, because with the exception of a few poems published in the *Revista* in 1925, Nava did not write very regularly. Of his few poetic manifestations, "Mestre Aurélio entre as Rosas" and "O Defunto," reedited by Manuel Bandeira in his *Antologia dos Poetas Bissextos*, in 1946, may be cited as outstanding.

This "getting even" with the past made Nava the most important name in the genre of memoir writing in Brazilian modernist literature. This resulted from three factors, all of which were related to diligent efforts on his part. The first is his encyclopedic knowledge, the second, his painstaking passion for details, and the third, his effort to reconstruct the histories of his family, of his own educational and professional training, and of the intellectual generation to which he belonged. Carlos Drummond de Andrade (*Boitempo, Menino Antigo*) and Murilo Mendes (*A Idade do Serrote*) had already produced works belonging to the memoir genre, evoking childhood reminiscences and thoughts regarding the patriarchal landowning structure of the society of Minas Gerais, but neither of them attempted to create a narrative of the epic, monumental dimensions in the manner of Nava's works.

Six volumes were published within a period of just over ten years (1972-1983), covering thirty years of Nava's life, apart from thirty-six unpublished pages of *Cera das Almas*, the book that continued the series. *Baú de Ossos* (1972), *Balão Cativo* (1973), *Chão de Ferro* (1976), *Beira-Mar* (1978), *Galo das Trevas* (1981) and *O Círio Perfeito* (1983) constitute the author's memoir œuvre. The texts are somewhere between fiction and documentary, a reinvention of the facts as experienced by both the writer and his generation.

The impact caused by publication of the first volume of *Memórias* provided a re-reading of the Brazilian literary canon, as late as the 1970s. The renewal of the Brazilian memoir tradition represented for the critics the need to reflect on concepts that had been suppressed by the literary avant-garde, such as tradition, memory, writing about oneself and autobiography. The publication of Nava's work unveiled a new panorama for Brazilian letters, in which history and fiction, the old and the new were blended, in an effort to extend the concept of memoir genre and to enrich the literary text. A boom in autobiographical writing was soon to take place in contemporary literature, especially with the political liberalization following the military regime, together with the return of former exiles to Brazil. This record of experiences during the period of military dictatorship initiated another form of storytelling.

Nava's memoir text, which included his participation in the 1920 modernist movement, was presented in a different form from the autobiographical accounts of the generation of exiles who returned to the Brazil at the end of the 1970s, such as, for example, that of Fernando

Gabeira. Nava's writing included a narrative of his life from childhood to the beginning of maturity; this is one of the reasons it is considered all-encompassing, in the sense that it fulfilled a narrative project in a highly detailed and grandiose way, combining various stages of the writer's private and public life. The same is not true of the texts written by exiles, because their basic tenet was either to deny or ignore the individual's familial past or his genealogy; theirs was a type of writing that aimed at canonizing neither the individual nor a particular social class. Nava's *Memórias* not only revitalized a literary genre that had been disregarded and undervalued, but also provided an historical, political and cultural reference for Brazilian reality in those first decades of the twentieth century. A further result is that literary critics were forced to revise methodologies and theories by creating space for approaches that were more interdisciplinary and cultural, because they felt the need to enlarge the concept of "literariness," as well as to review the place of the writer in the act of writing, whether fictional, memoir-oriented, or essayist.

Nava made used of a substantial number of metaphors in elaborating the vast material stocked in his memory. As well as being useful for understanding his creative process, these metaphors have been explored by those critics who have focused specifically on Nava's work. Images multiply and reinforce each other as a result of the writer's continuously revealed need to resort to metalanguage and to theorizing while writing. His writing is "Frankensteinian" in nature, elaborated like a puzzle, a kaleidoscope, a palimpsest and a *bricolage*, in which fragments and pieces of text, memories and objects kept in a dusty trunk are collated. Thus, literary critics appropriated these images and elaborated concepts related to Nava's writing process, namely, "a memory mobile" and "a tree-like construction" (Davi Arrigucci Jr.); "sponge-like memory" (Antônio Sérgio Bueno), "Frankenstein-type writing" (Celina Fontenele Garcia), "skeleton memory of many vertebrae" (Joaquim Alves de Aguiar), "a trunkful of madeleines" (Maria do Carmo Savietto), and so forth.

Reading Nava's *Memórias* entails going through various levels of textual analysis, as the memoir-document is an artistic object, a source of knowledge and a cultural fact. The continuous act of dealing with the manuscripts left by the writer is linked to a time in motion, to a direct intervention in the present, as well as to an enunciation that is both intermittent and continuous at various stages during the reading process.

The reader establishes contact with the text, but also develops an awareness of wherein the text results from a biographical act that culminates eventually culminate in a vast cultural panorama.

Among of the most significant sources for the study of Nava's work are Pedro Nava's personal files, housed in the "Fundação Casa de Rui Barbosa." The interlacing between the files, the writing and the memoirs can be in the profusion of photos, postcards and drawings seem used to construct various phases in the elaboration of his text. A surgical dissection of this material involved eliminating substantial amounts of data. An assessment based just the book version itself made it difficult to evaluate the full dimension of what took place before the writing of the definitive text. Inspecting of the files revealed that the preceding work resembles the technique of *bricolage*, which, in this case, collates information and the life experiences of the somewhat fragmented subject of the discourse.

Nava's creative process appears in three phases. First, there are cards and loose sheets of paper filled with the writer's own research, including drawings, photos, newspaper clippings, together with information sent to him by his friends. At a second stage, there is an organization of the "dolls" ("bonecos"), a concept to which I will return below, around which the chapters and their future development are outlined. At a third stage, both the corpse and the "doll" gain life and a voice by means of the typewritten text, almost ready to be sent to the publishers, despite the fact that a blank page among the originals may later include corrections added during revision.

The relationship between the medical and the literary series is materialized by means of the image of the "doll," which acquires a number of meanings in Nava's work, ranging from its original form shown on the drafts to its metaphorical unfoldings. The mark of the physician is observable in the material used in the draft work of *Memórias*, written on either paper or cards stamped with the address of Doctor Pedro Nava. This mark is both the writer's reverse and his mirror, the complementary face of the memoir writer. In this web of textual intercrossings, the "doll," the second stage in the writing process, may refer either to the image of the graphic project of a book or to the idea of a corpse, already dissected and prepared for study. As an outline and simulacrum, the "doll" does not have the status of a finished product, but reveals a constant process of elaboration. This text incorporates the image of a corpse-text, to be manipulated, reworked and collated by his creator. The acts of cutting, sewing, dissecting, and forming the internal configuration of the human body during anatomy lessons associate memoir writing with the practice of the student-doctor and his doll-corpses, or rather the doctor and the monster, the writer and his creature, in a type of Frankensteinian writing.

This latter technique in Pedro Nava's memoir writing may be observed in two scenes from *Beira-Mar*, which especially emphasize the difference between archives and memory. The scenes also focus on the circumstances in which memory may be regarded as a static, fossilized procedure. In the first of these scenes, the maternal grandfather decides to get rid of the things that he has been hoarding by throwing out the documents related to Nava's maternal family. The future guardian of the family's histories collects the papers and the photos of the Halfelds, ties the material in bundles and organizes what was left out. He thus becomes the legitimate proprietor of an heirloom, and thanks to this, writes part of *Baú de Ossos*, specifically that part related to his maternal genealogy.

The second scene concerns the sale of the gold watch inherited from his paternal grandfather, which has no value as an object of memory because it has no functional role. The watch displayed the family initials PSN, referring to Pedro da Silva Nava. The young Nava discards it, however, because he regards it as a dead object, the symbol of a time separated from memory, time as fetish:

> During the day, I had sold an old watch, which had belonged to my paternal grandfather, at the *Joalheria Diamantina*, a watch bought in Switzerland, the glass covered by a precious layer of gold, a double lock also made of gold. The two lids displayed the same initials, PSN, beautifully engraved. It was a wind-up watch, but the key was missing and the watch had thus become a useless object. (*Beira-Mar* 128)

Nava keeps the texts and the documents in the memory trunk. He strips the broken family watch of any meaning as a parasitical memory, or as a corpse that is unable to be touched and brought back to life. He detaches and links his name to the object, which he then sells as a meaningless inheritance, one that has no value as an archival document, because it is a dead document. However, this position differs from that of another object, the doctor's ring that had belonged to his father, received as a deserved gift and as a symbol of professional continuity and conquered inheritance. The watch chain received as a gift from his father later becomes a real Proustian "madeleine," due to its magical power to light up and reactivate the memory of the interpreter of the family histories.

Archive memory, nostalgia and a passion for one's origins, or, in Derrida's words "*mal d'archive*" (142)—these are the principles that guide the endless excavation work of textual genealogy. Being ill, being possessed by the "*mal d'archive*" is to consider this work as a specter and a corpse, a phantom that allows for the continuous dialogue of death and life. It is thus the duty of memoir writing to fulfill the role of both a supplement to, and simulacrum of, this dialogue.

Works Cited

Aguiar, Joaquim Alves de. *Espaços da Memória: Um Estudo sobre Pedro Nava*. São Paulo: EdUSP, Fapesp, 1998.

Arrigucci Jr., Davi. "Móbile da Memória." *Enigma e Comentário*. São Paulo: Companhia das Letras, 1987. 67-111.

Bueno, Antônio Sérgio. *Vísceras da Memória*. Belo Horizonte: Editora UFMG, 1997.

Derrida, Jacques. *Mal d'Archive*. Paris: Galilée, 1995.

Garcia, Celina Fontenele. *A Escrita Frankenstein de Pedro Nava*. Fortaleza: UFC, 1997.

Nava, Pedro. *Baú de Ossos*. Vol. 1. *Memórias*. Rio de Janeiro: Sabiá, 1972.

———. *Balão Cativo*. Vol. 2. *Memórias*. Rio de Janeiro: José Olympio, 1973.

———. *Chão de Ferro*. Vol. 3. *Memórias*. Rio de Janeiro: José Olympio, 1976.

———. *Beira-Mar*. Vol. 4. *Memórias*. Rio de Janeiro: José Olympio, 1978.

———. *Galo das Trevas*. Vol. 5. *Memórias*. Rio de Janeiro: José Olympio, 1981.

———. *O Círio Perfeito*. Vol.6. *Memórias*. Rio de Janeiro: José Olympio, 1983.

———. "Entrevista." Santilli, Maria Aparecida. Ed. Seleção de Textos, Notas, Estudo Biográfico, Histórico e Exercícios. *Pedro Nava. Literatura Comentada*. São Paulo: Abril Educação, 1983. 105-108.

Savieto, Maria do Carmo. *Baú de Madeleines*. Diss. FFLCH—Universidade de São Paulo, 1998.

The Hour of the Star or Clarice Lispector's Trash Hour

Italo Moriconi

Translated by

Paulo Henriques Britto

Written in 1976 and published one month before the author's hospitalization that ended with her death in December 1977, *A Hora da Estrela* (*The Hour of the Star*) is part of a group of texts by Clarice Lispector that not only make up her final body of work but also stage the end, depicting it as dissolution. The end of a life, the end of a career, the end of an œuvre. This was a phase in Lispector's writing that she referred to as "trash time" in her reply to criticism of her collection of short stories *A Via-crúcis do Corpo* (1974).[1] Hour of the star, trash time. *Via-crúcis* had been criticized for the sketchy nature of the narratives and for the author's allegedly blunt approach to sexual themes. Trash time, death time. The death of Macabéa, the very reverse of a movie star, a nontragic character, the protagonist of a non-life that culminates when she is run over by a car at the end, the caricature of a banal apocalypse. Physical death of the author, who may have been aware of her illness by the time she began writing *A Hora da Estrela*.

Lispector's "trash time" covers a relatively short period in her career, and includes her final writings following *Água Viva* (1973). It is no more than a further step in the radicalization of a writer who had from the very beginning been labeled radical or idiosyncratic by all of the canonic tendencies in Brazilian literary criticism. The radical aspect of the texts of the "trash time" phase is closely associated with *Água Viva*. They are all part of the same aesthetic gesture, the development of an interplay between the sublime and desublimation. While *Água Viva* can still be read in terms of the feminine sublime, associated with the valorization of the sublime activities of painting and/or writing, which were already prominent features of the author's first work (*Perto do Coração Selvagem*, 1944), in *A Hora da Estrela* we are confronted with the complete inversion of this dynamics.[2] The female narrator and/or protagonist is replaced by the brutal, sadistic (if vacillating) voice of a male narrator. The narrative act makes few concessions to anything that is not sarcastic or grotesque. The dialectical interchange between the sublime and the desublimed, which is so evident in *Água Viva*, with its frequent references to the merely organic and visceral, is here frozen. Trash time means the refusal of all sublimation. *Água Viva* may then be seen as the moment of *luxo* ("luxury") that precedes the plunge into *lixo* ("trash") as an aesthetic entity.[3]

The labeling of Lispector's work as radical or idiosyncratic may be ascribed initially to the fact that its sense cannot be grasped in terms of the nationalistic, social, historical and referent-based values that were dominant in the Modernist critical canon. Lispector debuted in 1944 with a subjectivist fiction and a nonmimetic rhetoric, full of unusual metaphors, violent metonymic shifts, effects of estrangement produced by a narrative flow characterized by allusive description and based on heightened attention to sensory impressions and details.[4] She brought a sophisticated element into Brazilian fiction, an introspective basis for moral and existential questioning. It is a type of fiction which is to this day mostly unaccounted for by the dominant conceptual models of academic literary history, although individually some of the authors in this current have received some critical attention—Cornélio Pena, Otávio de Faria, Lúcio Cardoso, among others. But Lispector's work, unlike theirs, was seen as surprising because of its unmistakably experimental component associated with a commitment to the darker aspects of existence—evil, sin, crime—as the privileged, though not exclusive topics for literature and art in general.

The experimental nature of Lispector's work continued to increase, undergoing various inflections that pointed both to linear evolution and to an order of "repetition": the repetition, with variations, of the same transgressive gesture, bringing progressive changes to her discourse. Following *A Maçã no Escuro* (1961), this dynamics was intensified; from then on, the self-reflective element was radicalized in the context of an avant-garde textual logic, as in *A Paixão Segundo G. H.* (1964) and *Uma Aprendizagem, ou o Livro dos Prazeres* (1969). The former is a woman's rewriting of Kafka's myth of the man-cockroach, while the latter—a text that begins with a comma—is from the outset presented as a *writerly* text (to use Barthes's term), as has been observed by a number of critics.[5]

In some ways, the texts produced in what I have been calling Lispector's trash time stage the limits, the exhaustion of a project of progressive radicalization of self-reflective writing. From an aesthetic viewpoint, this is the most spectacular ending possible, the one that probably determines all others: the end of modernism. From a descriptive viewpoint, the trash-time texts—and now *Água Viva* is being included in this category as well—are characterized by extreme fragmentation. The books are short, the short stories are sketchy and edgy. What I am referring to as "books" are in fact collages of fragments unified by some sort of thread: *Água Viva, A Hora da Estrela* and the posthumously published *Um Sopro de Vida*. This radical fragmentation interacts with a journalistic aspect. Lispector published portions of her books and the stories as part of her *crônicas* in the Rio de Janeiro daily *Jornal do Brasil,* to which she was a regular contributor from 1967 to 1973. Her *crônicas*, in turn, are frequently "literary" and philosophical in tone, including reflections, meditations, metaphors and ironic games that are typical of her literary work. Thus, communication was established between the two genres, a system of erratic interchange that was part of Lispector's permanent practice of rewriting.

Lispector's trash time is characterized by a duality between the literary and the journalistic, avant-garde erudition and kitsch, good taste and bad taste, high and low, poetry and cliché, irony and sentimentality. In Brazilian literature, the *crônica* is a paraliterary genre, which in the 1950s and 1960s was seen as addressed to readers with a "literary sensibility." On the one hand then, the trash-time texts signal the author's acceptance of her popular side, expressed in the meditative *crônicas*: a taste for Lispector had become a myth in Brazilian culture, amounting to a declaration of "sensitiveness." On the other hand, they also participate in her experimental, avant-garde, literary side, expressed in her books, where the "lowness" of sentimental-existential clichés is intertwined with the estrangement caused by the complexity of the self-referential language characteristic of high modernism.

*

In *Água Viva, A Hora da Estrela* and *Um Sopro de Vida,* the most striking discursive strategy is the narrator's expressed intention to create effects of simultaneity in the text. The writing is intended as the simultaneous actualization of thinking and feeling. To use the iconic expression coined in *Água Viva*: a writing of the *now-moment* ("*instante-já*"). This simultaneity is associated with the way the narrator's subjectivity is presented. While in Lispector's works previous to *Água Viva* this subjectivity is conveyed by means of the classic interplay of narrative enunciation and characters, here narrative viewpoint is placed at the center of the stage. The fictive philosophy of subjectivity in Lispector is now concentrated exclusively on the figure of an ego that is an *ego scriptor*, whether naive, as in the case of the painter who decides to write in *Água Viva*, or an experienced writer—male in *A Hora da Estrela*, male and female in *Um Sopro de Vida*.

The writerly subjectivity is not only engendered but also split, and it traces a trajectory from the dialogic to the diasporic. In *Água Viva* the split takes place by means of a strategy of intersubjectivity. The painter-narrator directs her discourse to a male addressee, which in this way becomes a simulacrum of a letter. Intersubjectivity is defined here as dialogical, its third term being a referent: the reality or truth of pure sensation. The search for simultaneity between writing and happening preserves an *ontological* concept of the experienced, seen as a substance to be attained by representational activity, which, however, obviously fails every time. The narrator of *Água Viva* is unable to go beyond the abyss of *différance*, figured in the text by the use of graphic and thematic spacing.

In *A Hora da Estrela*, the aim is no longer to reach a substantial reality. The triangle of communication is now made up of the male narrator (Rodrigo S. M.), the reader and the character, Macabéa, whose story is reduced to minimal biographical data: an orphan, she works as typist, has a failed loved affair, loses her boyfriend to a fellow worker, goes to a fortuneteller and, in the closing scene, is run over by a car and killed. The effect of simultaneity here is given by the fact that the most important narrative plane of the text is that on which the narrator discusses with the reader the process by means of which he creates a fictional character that is entirely alien to him. The central motif of *A Hora da Estrela* is the sequence of the narrator's conflicting feelings towards the character he wants to create, an effort that never gets much farther than mere caricature. The simultaneity sought here is no longer between writing and sensation, but between writing and reading. Treated as the very axis of the narrative, the self-reflective dimension takes shape as the narrator's self-reflection concerning his *relation* to the character. Among the fascinating effects produced by this discursive operation are the exposure of the reader's own nature as a simulacrum. Radicalizing Machado de Assis' experiment with Bentinho, the narrator of *Dom Casmurro*, Lispector creates a Rodrigo who is S. M. ("sadomasochistic") in relation to both the character and the reader.

*

But Macabéa is not just another character, which is why practically everything that has been written about *A Hora da Estrela* (as well as Suzana Amaral's movie version of the book) centers on her figure. Macabéa is the caricature of a Northeastern woman. And "Northeastern" is by no means a neutral category in Brazilian culture: in Brazilian literature, Northeasterners are always poor, excluded, peripheral, anachronistic remnants of a bygone era in the modernized Brazil that has emerged since the late nineteenth century, culturally and economically dominated by the powerful Southeast. In terms of the ideology imposed by the civilized Southeast, Northeasterners are labeled members of an "underdeveloped" or "inferior race," stigmatized by poverty. Macabéa more or less corresponds to what North American racist discourse might call "white trash," though she is described in terms of a typically Brazilian and quite flexible notion of "white race," for her skin is said to be *parda* (light brown).

On the mimetic or documentary level, one of the marks of the originality of *A Hora da Estrela* is the fact that Rodrigo S. M. depicts an urbanized Northeastern girl: neither a Northeasterner in her native backlands nor one migrating south fleeing destitution, two typically Modernist images. Rodrigo S. M.'s Macabéa is a postmodern migrant, settled in a working-class suburb of a large Southeastern city, a type also portrayed in Brazilian movies of the 1970s such as Nelson Pereira dos Santos' *O Amuleto de Ogum* (1975). In this contemporary post-1970s setting, not even the Northeastern *sertão* region (backlands) can be depicted in the substantialistic language of genuine origin. As in Walter Sales's recent film *Central do Brasil* (*Central Station*) (1999), the *sertão* as location is no longer a wasteland of spiny cactuses and cow skulls, but simply an area in the periphery of a city occupied by a housing development very much like the ones found outside the metropolises of the Southeast. Macabéa, created by Rodrigo S. M. as an emblem of poverty, is not only Northeastern but also a grotesque and stereotyped representation of a subjectivity totally defined by the most obvious forms of consumerism: she lives on Coca-Cola and her sole pastime is listening to "Rádio Relógio," a radio station that tells the time and combines ads with bits of useless "cultural" information.

Lispector has Rodrigo S. M. break all the sentimental and socially utopian rules that have traditionally underpinned the literary myth of the Northeasterner in Modernist literature. In this sense, the relation between the narrator and Macabéa is an allegorical representation of the relation between the Modernist intellectual and the poor, deprived sectors of the population. In the more populist versions of Modernism, writers expiate their own social guilt by writing texts that denounce the status quo in order to "save" the poor. Of the major authors from the generation that arose in the 1920s and 1930s, only Graciliano Ramos, in *Memórias do Cárcere*, and Carlos Drummond de Andrade, in some of his deconstructive so-called "social" poems, dared to allude to what Lispector renders in such harsh colors: the hypocrisy and sadism that underlie the relations between the intelligentsia and the poor in Brazilian cultural tradition.

Rodrigo S. M. tries to do something that seems impossible in Brazil—to speak of social marginalization without being demagogic. Lispector's text, in fact, was published at the very time when a momentous change took place in Brazilian political culture at the turn of the 1970s: for the first time, marginalized groups spoke out for themselves, rather than through middle-class populist parties, politicians and intellectuals.[6] Rodrigo S. M. is aware that his motivation lies entirely outside the drama actually experienced by those who provide the model for his Macabéa. "Why do I write?" he asks in the beginning of this narrative, and answers: "Above all, because I have captured the spirit of the language, so that sometimes it is form that produces content. Therefore I write not because of the Northeastern girl, but by dint of a serious 'act of God,' as they say in official documents, an 'act of law.'" (23) From this point on, the narrator's leitmotif is the conflict of feelings caused in him by his Herculean effort to *identify* with Macabéa. Rodrigo S. M. wavers between repugnance and empathy, between cruel indifference and pity, reviving the interplay of sadism and sentimentality that Gilberto Freyre identified in *Casa-Grande & Senzala* (*The Masters and the Slaves*, 1933) as essential to the social relations between the white or brown ruling class and black slaves in Brazil. To provide minimal illustration for my argument, here is the paragraph in which Rodrigo S. M. presents Macabéa for the first time.

> She came from the worst sort of background and now looked like the child of a what-is--this with an air of apologizing for taking up space. Absently, before the mirror, she closely examined some patches on her face. Up in Alagoas they were known as 'cloths,' people said it was the liver that caused them. She covered them up with a thick layer of rice powder, which made her look whitewashed but

anyhow it was better than being brown. She was a bit dingy, since she hardly ever washed. During the day she wore a blouse and a skirt, and at night she slept in her slip. One of her roommates could never bring herself to tell her she had a musty smell... Nothing about her shimmered, though in between the patches on her face there was a slight opalescence. But that did not matter. No one ever looked at her on the street, she was cold coffee. (34)

Rodrigo S. M. parrots all the clichés of racial and social prejudice against Northeasterners—uncleanliness, disease, ignorance—, carrying them to extreme lengths, to the point of buffoonery, as part of his effort to avoid a demagogic, artificial identification with Macabéa.[7] However, it is impossible to write about someone else without a minimum of empathy, of subjective projection. But even this empathy surfaces in the text as parody. Here is the passage immediately following the one quoted above:

Thus time passed for this girl. She used the hem of her slip to blow her nose in. She had none of that delicate thing known as enchantment. I alone see her as someone enchanting. Only I, her author, love her. And suffer for her. And only I can tell her: 'Whatever you ask me for with a tear, I give to you with a song.'(34)

There is only one aspect in which Rodrigo S. M. is able to establish nonparodic identification with Macabéa, though even this is done on a farcical plane, given the radical heterogeneity between creator and creature: loneliness. This is the single link that makes it possible to construct a discourse across such a yawning abyss of difference. In a completely exterior and artificial way, Rodrigo S. M. also draws a parallel between the inevitable solitude of the *ego scriptor* and Macabéa's dumb anonymity. Solitude confines the writer to a residual sphere in the order of things, and it is as residue, it is by means of the idea of residue, that Rodrigo is able to establish the tenuous thread of identification with the Northeastern girl. But this identification still contains a crucial element of difference, for the writer possesses the priceless gift of the word, of which Macabéa is bereft:

How I wish she would open her mouth and say:
'I'm all alone in the world and I don't believe in anybody, they all lie, sometimes even in the hour of love, I don't believe anyone can ever really talk to someone else, the truth comes to me only when I'm alone.'

Maca, however, has never spoken in sentences, first because she is not much given to talking. And it so happens that she had no self-awareness and did not complain of anything; indeed, she thought she was happy. (. . .) (I see I have tried to attribute to Maca a trait of my own: I need a few hours of solitude every day, or else me muero.) (83)

The final scene, when Macabéa is run over by a Mercedes Benz instead of meeting the blond fiancé the fortuneteller had promised her, underscores the artificiality of social pity as a motive for artistic creation. "Was the ending grand enough for your needs?" (104) is the question asked of the reader by the most cynical narrator ever created by Clarice Lispector. Macabéa's dead body lying in the gutter is not only an allegory of a certain concept of *ego scriptor* but, more importantly, serves as a merciless self-image conceived by Lispector in her final hour, through the mouthpiece of Rodrigo, the author's sadomasochistic transvestite:

I write because there is nothing for me to do in the world: I have been left behind, and there is no room for me in the world of men. I write because I am a desperate man and I am tired, I can't stand any longer the routine of being myself, and if it were not for the ever-new practice of writing I would die symbolically every day. But I am prepared to go out discreetly through the back door. I have tried almost everything, including passion and the despair of passion. And now all I would like to have is what I would have been and never was. (27)

Notes

[1] See, for instance, Gotlib 417; Ferreira 268.

[2] On the feminine sublime in Lispector, see Peixoto 68-72.

[3] In the original text, the author plays with the words *luxo* ("luxury") and *lixo* ("trash"), two opposite and yet complementary aesthetic terms that were used as a kind of minimalistic slogan in one the most popular visual poems written by the avant-garde poet Augusto de Campos at the height of the Concretista movement in the late Fifties. In the original Portuguese there is also a lexical comparison being made between the title of the novel, *A Hora da Estrela*, and the period called the "hora do lixo." (Translator's note)

[4] See Santiago, "A aula" 13-30.

[5] See, for instance, Santos and Helena.

[6] See Santiago, "Democratização" 11-23.

[7] For a very original and interesting reading of the clownish element in *A Hora da Estrela*, see Arêas.

Works Cited

Antelo, Raúl, et al. *Declínio da Arte / Ascensão da Cultura.* Florianópolis: Letras Contemporâneas, 1998.

Arêas, Wilma. "O Sexo dos *Clowns.*" *Revista Tempo Brasileiro* 104 (1991): 145-153.

Ferreira, Tereza Cristina M. *Eu Sou Uma Pergunta: Uma Biografia de Clarice Lispector.* Rio de Janeiro: Rocco, 1999.

Gotlib, Nádia Battella. *Clarice: Uma Vida que se Conta.* São Paulo: Ática, 1995.

Helena, Lucia. *Nem Musa, nem Medusa: Itinerários da Escrita em Clarice Lispector.* Rio de Janeiro: Ed. Universidade Federal Fluminense, 1997.

Lispector, Clarice. *Água Viva.* Rio de Janeiro: Artenova, 1973.

———. *Uma Aprendizagem ou O Livro dos Prazeres.* Rio de Janeiro: José Olympio, 1969.

———. *A Hora da Estrela.* 4a ed. Rio de Janeiro: José Olympio, 1978.

———. *The Hour of the Star.* Trans. Giovanni Pontiero. Manchester: Carcanet, 1986.

———. *A Maçã no Escuro.* Rio de Janeiro: Francisco Alves, 1961.

———. *The Apple in the Dark.* Trans. Gregory Rabassa. New York: Knopf, 1967.

———. *A Paixão Segundo G.H.* Rio de Janeiro: Ed. Autor, 1964.

———. *The Passion According to G.H.* Trans. Ronald W. Souza. Minneapolis: U of Minnesota P, 1988.

———. *Perto do Coração Selvagem.* Rio de Janeiro: A Noite, 1944.

———. *Near to the Wild Heart.* Trans. Giovanni Pontiero. New York: New Directions, 1990.

———. *Um Sopro de Vida.* Rio de Janeiro: Nova Fronteira, 1978.

———. *A Via-crúcis do Corpo.* Rio de Janeiro: Artenova, 1974.

Miranda, Wander Melo. Ed. *Narrativas da Modernidade.* Belo Horizonte: Autêntica, 1999.

Peixoto, Marta. *Passionate Fictions: Gender, Narrative and Violence in Clarice Lispector.* Minneapolis: U of Minnesota P 1994.

Rosenbaum, Yudith. *Metamorfoses do Mal—Uma Leitura de Clarice Lispector.* São Paulo: Edusp/Fapesp, 1999.

Santiago, Silviano. "Democratização no Brasil—1979-1981—Cultura versus Arte." *Declínio da Arte / Ascensão da Cultura.* Eds. Raúl Antelo, et al. Florianópolis: Letras Contemporâneas, 1998. 11-23.

———. "A aula inaugural de Clarice." *Narrativas da Modernidade.* Ed. Wander Melo Miranda. Belo Horizonte: Autêntica, 1999. 13-30.

Santos, Roberto Corrêa dos. *Lendo Clarice.* Rio de Janeiro: Atual, 1986.

The Case of Rubem Fonseca—The Search for Reality

Karl Erik Schøllhammer
Translated by David Shepherd and
Tania Shepherd

Don't say armpit. *Say axilla.*
Fonseca, 1973, 17.

If reality could establish direct contact with our conscious mind, if we could communicate immediately with things and with ourselves, art would probably be useless, or rather, we would all be artists.
Fonseca, 1973, 99.

There are more than enough reasons to highlight the importance of Rubem Fonseca (1925) within contemporary Brazilian literature. Fonseca is central to the trajectory of contemporary prose, with 18 titles ranging from novels to collections of short stories. However, it is not the purpose of this essay to praise the excellence of the writer's œuvre, because national critics have already taken care of this task. It is more important, rather, to understand his innovative contribution to the mainstream trends of Brazilian literature. Among critics, there is a consensus that Fonseca has consolidated in prose the urban tendencies of the last three decades and thus represents the literary emergence of the literature of a modern, metropolitan Brazil. It is also usually agreed that the portrait of a new urban reality, as painted by Fonseca, privileges a marginal dimension of both violence and crime that allegorically represents a form of political resistance against the authoritarian regime that came to power after the "Revolution of 1964."[1]

In the 1970s, there were three tendencies that aligned literary approaches with the sociopolitical situation of the time. First, there was a new prose addressing the theme of struggle against both the military regime and clandestine lives, with titles such as *A Casa de Vidro* by Ivan Angelo (1979), *O Calor das Coisas* by Nélida Piñon (1980) and *Os Carbonários* by Alfredo Sirkis (1981).[2] The second tendency that was becoming popular was documentary realism, inspired by press reports which denounced the repressive violence of the police and which avoided the censorship imposed on newspapers by using literature as the medium. This was exemplified by *Pixote, a Lei do Mais Fraco* and *Lúcio Flávio: Passageiro da Agonia* by José Louzeiro, or *A República dos Assassinos* (1976) by Aguinaldo Silva. The third trend has been called "brutalism" by Alfredo Bosi.[3] It had already exploded in 1963 with Rubem Fonseca's short story collection, *Os Prisioneiros*.

"Brutalism" was characterized thematically by descriptions and re-creations of social violence among outlaws, prostitutes, bouncers, corrupt policemen and tramps. Without making any concessions to a literary commitment, Fonseca created his own style, which was succinct, direct, and communicative. His themes focused on the Rio underworld, by appropriating not only its stories and tragedies, but also its colloquial language, which, in turn, became innovative within Fonseca's "marginal realism." Other writers—such as Ignácio Loyola Brandão, Roberto Drummond and, later, Sérgio Sant'Anna, Caio Fernando Abreu, as well as João Gilberto Noll—followed in the footsteps of both Fonseca and his friend, precursor and twin soul, the Paraná-born writer, Dalton Trevisan, by exposing a "human rawness" hitherto unseen in Brazilian literature.

Besides representing a realist element within an urban literature, it would seem that the exploration of violence also initiated a search for the renewal of national prose. City life, mainly the marginal life of *bas-fond*, had become a new backdrop for revitalizing literary realism. Violence was an element that was extremely difficult to represent, and this was, in turn, a challenge for writers' poetic efforts. The literature of the last decades has been drawing a new image, both of urban reality and of the city, as a symbolic and socio-cultural space, attempting to overcome the limitations of either a memorial or documentary realism which, despite the fact that it has followed socio-cultural changes, has been unable to depict the city as a radically new condition for historical experience. In the prose of the 1960s and 1970s, the complex reality of the large Brazilian metropolis offers a new setting for the narrative of an emergent generation. The city as such no longer represents a universe ruled by justice and rationality, but rather a divided reality; the

KARL ERIK SCHØLLHAMMER

symbolic division, which was formerly placed between "country" and "city," is now placed between "official city" and "marginal city."[4]

For the majority of critics and for certain state censors,[5] the revelation of the violent passions and of the de-humanization of urban life contained an implicit denouncement of the brutal reality under a repressive political regime. Not without reason, they perceived in Fonseca's literature an implicit argument in favor of violence, inciting violent revolts against an illegitimate regime. It was like saying that if social reality is violent and self-destructive, it is only a consequence of a wider violence deriving from the system itself, which, in turn, ends up legitimizing social violence, provided that this same violence is directed against the powerful when guided in a politically correct way.

However, seen from another point of view, this literature represented an attempt to comprehend both an excluding social reality of the time and the urban middle-class reaction against growing social inequalities, or rather armed robberies, kidnappings and murders. In this sense, the fictionalization of the criminal world can be understood in terms of a re-symbolization of the violent reality deriving from social confrontations in the underworld of the big cities. The literary re-creation of a coarse, colloquial language, unknown to the reading public, the large majority of whom were middle class, represented a will to overcome the barriers of social communication; at the same time, it gave literary language itself a new vitality in order to be able to get out of the deadlock of traditional realism vis-à-vis modern urban reality. Fonseca's prose created a successful symbiosis between, on the one hand, a literature with a clear political-social concern, and on the other, an artistic search for an expression which could solve representative impasses which were noticeable in historical and regional realism.

In "Intestino Grosso," the final short story of *Feliz Ano Novo* (1975), the plot is built by means of an interview with a writer who has been accused of being "pornographic," hinting that the character may be the author's own alter ego. Running the risk of being taken in by Fonseca's fictional game, it is relevant to consider some of the character's opinions as keys to an understanding of the author's œuvre. To begin with, the writer reports how, at the beginning of his career, he was harmed by the expectations of the publishers, critics and newspaper's literary supplements, for they all insisted that he "write like Machado de Assis." For someone who "lived in a block of apartments in the center of town," listening to the "noise of motorcar engines," this did not make much sense. Next, the critique of the character-oriented Brazilian literary tradition manifests itself in opposition to both Naturalism and Historical Realism, as well as to folklore-oriented Regionalism. These tendencies are rejected as inadequate vis-à-vis the new urban experience, paving the way for the sordid life stories of the marginal underworlds that are excluded from the large metropolis. Accused of being a pornographic writer, the interviewed author challenges this criticism by admitting positively that his books are "peopled by toothless destitutes" (1994, 461). Thus, the notion of pornography—fiercely defended by the character in order to reject the censors' favorite justification—does not correspond to a traditional definition. Instead of identifying his literature as within the characteristics inherent to the genre, the author-character claims that "pornography" is that literature which seeks a new expressive economy of literary language, by revealing both forbidden and excluded themes. According to him, the problem with the present-day naturalist and realist novel is that it no longer offers a representation of reality that is capable of arousing the reader's emotions. This happens, in the first place, because of a lack of thematic focus in which "typical landscapes," which used to serve as a backdrop for historical narratives, have long moved away from the new urban reality within which the majority of the population lives. Secondly, it means that the conventional representational language of realism, when used as a tool for fictional identification, no longer reflects reality, nor is capable of provoking an affective and sensual effect equal to contemporary passions and emotions.

According to the fictional author, this loss of expressive force has been affecting literature's ability to convey the symbolic vis-à-vis a new reality. Despite the fact that realism is still directed at the historical world and still seeks to maintain an imitative fidelity, it has ceased to extract valuable plots from social themes due to the absence of a literary language that could express living experience. Given this impotence, one option for contemporary authors is to choose those themes and objects that are excluded and banned from their culture. Such themes focus not only on sex—no longer branded with the same cultural stigma today—, but also misery, violence, madness and death.

Confronted with forbidden themes, literary language may recover an important cultural role by confronting, in an indirect way, an exclusionary discursive regime that dominates Brazilian society and which, materially, perpetuates itself through modes of communication, cybernetic structures and other ideological apparatuses. When in search of an expressive innovation, literature confronts the limits of representation; it manages to express, in the defeat of transgression, the most concrete form of its own prohibition. In this way, the struggle takes place within language, swinging between subversive literature and affirmative discourses, whose main objective is to define what deserves to be regarded as real or otherwise. At the core of literary creation, the poetic aims to create, fictionally, certain "effects" of reality through more violent emotions, and not to search for illusive pleasures. For the author-character this means searching for a "real four-letter word," because only the four-letter word can create the right shock. For him the four-letter word is different from the well-behaved word. The latter derives from the expression of human shame as confronted with its own nakedness and animal nature. He claims that "[m]etaphors appeared so that our forefathers did not to have to say 'fuck,'"[6] at the same time highlighting the "word" as the focal point of artistic struggle with society.

It may seem useless to attempt this type of scandalous effect, but it is also part of an old tradition whose origin may have a significant kinship with the modern notion of literature. Michel Foucault claimed, in 1963, that the real precursors of modern literature included the English gothic novel and the work of the Marquis de Sade. The French philosopher argued that the gothic novel, which soon gave rise to fantasy in literature, as well as the intriguing work of de Sade, which was in its own way also a type of gothic literature, constitute the first time that there was a conscious effort by writers to create a sensorial effect beyond the message that the narrative could convey to the reader.[7] Fear, terror, restlessness and excitement are no more than a sampling of the feelings that a text could provoke. Literature thus went beyond a means of representing realities within conventional classic molds by creating its own receptive reality.[8] The "new" in modern literature, as seen in the examples provided by Foucault, meant that the sensory effect here did not necessarily corroborate the content of the message. It did, however, indicate a limit for this content, while it pointed towards a meaning beyond itself, or rather towards non-meaning. Within this limit, the language of modern literature faced its opposite, its unnamable or its ineffable.

Fonseca's first novel, *O Caso Morel* (1973), represents a clear example of the author's literary project as well as a relative exception. In harmony with the textual and discursive criticism of the 1970s, the novel appears exceptional as a formal experiment which mixes various fragments of genres such as the novel, the diary, the police report, apocryphal citations, an autopsy report, and letters, to name a few. Within a pseudo-academic metadiscussion of how to represent reality,[9] the plot develops as a search for the truth about Joan's death (or Heloisa's), the lover of Morel, and Morel himself, who is the main narrator and who is accused of murder. In Fonseca's later novels, this type of intertextual staging is not as common.[10] But here narration retains a double articulation; on the one hand, the narration of a crime, and on the other, the story of the future of narration. Thus, for the narrator and main character, the musician-painter-photographer Paul Morel (or Morais), writing serves as an explicit means of remembering the facts that led to Joana's death, a kind of Freudian *Durcharbeitung* ("working-through"), in which the narrator tries to relive those facts through the artistic process of creation. In this way, the words in the narrator's conscience seek their origin within an enigma which, albeit articulated as the conventional secret of the detective genre—i.e., who's done it—hides a more fundamental enigma about the relationship between writing and events. During the narrator's search, the facts around Joana's death are revealed. However, at the same time, writing appears to be, for the narrator, the means by which reality emerges, an event that embodies that which is real and can be felt. As a narrative, the novel reconstructs events through an immersion in Morel's occulted memory. From the point of view of reading, events emerge between various textual explanations in a growing intertwining of words and things. The real enigma is conveyed as an insurmountable distance that, despite the characters' and the readers' efforts, remains undiluted, like the silence of the victim Joana. The key question about what really happened between Morel and Joana remains unanswered.

In a first version, Morel writes:

> We spent the afternoon drinking, in silence. Afterwards we went out and Joana lay down on the sand. We gazed at the sunset. Afterwards, I kicked Joana, as if she were an empty tin can.
>
> "You see what you've made me do?"
>
> She didn't answer.
>
> "I hate cruelty," I said, almost in tears.
>
> Joana opened her eyes and calmly looked at the sky. Her mouth was stained with blood but she did not appear to be in pain.
>
> "I never want to see you again," I said.

I went home. (1973, 111)

Soon after this, a second version appears:

> I kicked Joana. She laughed. I kept on kicking her while she laughed and I looked
> at the sunset. It was a beautiful thing, indescribable.
> Joana stopped laughing. (1973, 113)

The account comes to an end without easing the doubt about what really happened on that day. Whether Joana died as a consequence of Morel's kicking; whether Francisco, her caring admirer, or the poor couple of caretakers, who had hidden her body, were responsible for her death. Who is guilty of Joana's death if she seemed to search for it and provoke it in sadomasochist rituals?

The novel includes a typical characteristic of Fonseca's detective novels, that of the enigma without resolution, without hermeneutic relief for the reader. In the detective's frustrated search, Fonseca copies a *noir* feature from the *Maltese Falcon*, but also draws attention to the appearance of reality vis-à-vis the meaning of language. With the same impetus as Morel, who searches for an affective communication with an alienated world, a search that culminates in the explicit violence against Joana, the novel tries to penetrate palpable reality by taking the "word" to the verge of an eclipse in the silence of death. The unnamable and incommunicable facts thus transpire in the text like the underside of an expression that is impossible to represent.

In conclusion, the thematic option for violence in Fonseca's prose may be understood as reflecting an expressive search aimed at innovating traditional literary languages. Fonseca has been labeled a "post-modern" author due to the fact that, for example, the presence of media reality can be detected in his characters' conscience. However, Fonseca's literature should not be identified as a skeptical de-stabilization of reality and of the meaning of reality. The main objective of his prose appears to be the search for a language or for a literary expression that is adequate to urban reality vis-à-vis the impotence of historical realism, on one side, and modernist experience on the other. The prose is best described as *neo-realist*, with the safeguard that the labels neo-, hyper- or trans-realism qualify his work in a singular manner within the thematic perspective of violence. Historical realism searched for an "illusion of reality" by means of direct mimesis, which was, in turn, distinct from conventionally common language, or, in Barthes' words, an "effect of reality."[11] Fonseca's *realism* resides in the sensorial concreteness of his language, which appears, in turn, to contain the direct experience of the event—an "affect of reality"—in which the representation of violence becomes the violence of representation.

Notes

[1] The "Revolução de 64" was the name received by a military coup d'état which ousted democratically elected president João Goulart and led to the military control of Brazil which lasted for 20 years. (Translator's note)

[2] This was a literary genre that resembled autobiographical memoirs, along the same lines as *O Que é Isso Companheiro?* (1981), by Fernando Gabeira.

[3] Bosi 18.

[4] The idea of a divided city underpins Brazilian urban sociology, especially in the books by Carvalho (1994) and Ventura (1994).

[5] In 1976, Fonseca's short-story collection *Feliz Ano Novo* was confiscated by state censors for "offending public morals." The writer appealed the decision, but in 1980 the Court of Appeals upheld the sentence, claiming that the book "incited violence." It was only in 1988 that the Courts decided to judge in favor of the writer, thus allowing the reprinting of the book, as well as granting him indemnity for material losses.

[6] "Certain anthropologists attribute these restrictions on the so-called four-letter word to the ancestral taboo of incest. Philosophers claim that what disturbs and alarms are not events themselves, but human beings' own opinions and fantasies about them. This is the case because human beings live in a symbolic universe, which contains language, myth, art, religion as varied threads which weave the close web of human experience." Fonseca, *Contos Reunidos* 463-4.

[7] See Foucault, "Language to Infinity;" essay originally published in 1963 in *Tel Quel*.

[8] This literary function has obviously been acknowledged since Antiquity. For example, in the Aristotelian notion of *catharsis* in Greek tragedy, the ritualistic and symbolic role of drama is emphasized, always in close connection with the universality of plot, or rather, content.

[9] "Thanks for the encouragement. We have, therefore, what can be called the reality of image on one side, and the reality of *l'image*, on the other" (163).

[10] Despite a certain generic experimentation in the short stories "Lúcia McCartney" and "Romance Negro."

[11] Barthes explains the description of apparently insignificant details in the fiction of Balzac as a kind of mimetic redundancy which only significance is that "this is real." See Barthes, "L'Effet de Reel."

Works Cited

Barthes, Roland. "L'Effet de Réel." *Comunications*, 11 (1968): 84-89.

Bosi, Alfredo. "Situação e Formas do Conto Brasileiro Contemporâneo." *O Conto Brasileiro Contemporâneo*. São Paulo: Cultrix, 1975. 7-22.

Carvalho, Maria Alice Rezende de. *Quatro Vezes Cidade*. Rio de Janeiro: Sette Letras, 1994.

Fonseca, Rubem. *O Caso Morel*. Rio de Janeiro: Artenova, 1973.

————. *Contos Reunidos*. São Paulo: Companhia das Letras, 1994.

Foucault, Michel. "Language to Infinity." 1963. *Language, Counter-Memory, Practice: Selected Essays and Interviews*. Transl. and ed. Donald D. Bouchard. Ithaca, New York: Cornell UP, 1977. 53-67.

Ventura, Zuenir. *Cidade Partida*. São Paulo: Companhia das Letras, 1994.

KARL ERIK SCHØLLHAMMER

João Cabral in Perspective

Antonio Carlos Secchin
Translated by Nöel de Souza
Revised by Mark Streeter

This essay begins by considering João Cabral de Melo Neto's place in Brazilian literature. One is always wondering: what is this poet's place, what position does he occupy, what circle does he belong to and what is his standing in the context of Brazilian literature? It would be no exaggeration to say that Brazilian literary critics place him in the same rank as Carlos Drummond de Andrade as one of Brazil's greatest poets of the century. But, although both are exceptional poets, they are not so in the same vein. Great poets are those that add new chapters to the history of literature, and certainly Drummond wrote some fundamental texts for Brazilian poetry. But authors such as João Cabral go beyond adding a chapter; indeed, they devise a new grammar. The difference between a chapter and grammar is that the chapter, however extraordinary it may be, occupies a place in a sequence formed by other preceding and subsequent chapters. Drummond's writings rose out of the poetic fermentation of the Brazilian modernism of 1922, of which it is the most perfect expression. In this regard, Drummond is responsible for new and important chapters in connection with a history that is explained by the literary and cultural context of Brazil of the 1920s and 1930s. On the contrary, the work of João Cabral de Melo Neto stands almost in isolation in our literary panorama, since there is no visible lineage of which it can be made a part, with the possible exception of the writing of Graciliano Ramos. Cabral does not fall in line with the generation of 1945, to which he chronologically belongs, and furthermore does not view himself as a direct continuation of the aesthetic and ideological complex of the poetry of 1922. He is an author who blazed a new trail, just like Machado de Assis and

Guimarães Rosa, who exploded (into) Brazilian literature, bringing to it a deeply personal inflection. The fact that the poet has created a new grammar also implies a certain degree of discomfort for the reader, who will have to deal with this discourse using only the grammars already known. The initial tendency is one of rejection, which leads to paradoxical consequences. João Cabral is a much-appreciated poet, but perhaps insufficiently read in his complexity. He is basically known for *Morte e Vida Severina*,[1] an extraordinary success with the public, and perhaps it is the Brazilian book of poetry with the largest number of editions published in a short span of time. Published in 1956, *Morte e Vida Severina* has already surpassed 50 editions, which is absolutely astonishing for a market that is usually so indifferent to poetry. It is actually a text read aloud, loved, and acted out on the stage, in the movies, on television, but it represents just *one* aspect of João Cabral's work, and not necessarily the most innovative.

In 1956, when the poet launched his first great collection, he significantly entitled it *Duas Águas*, explaining that the title meant two types of utterance, two styles of writing poetry.[2] One of them collects the "to-be-read-aloud," in which the recipient was more a listener than a reader. This "water" would of course include the most communicative texts, such as *Morte e Vida Severina*. The other "water," which I will not describe as first or second so as to avoid establishing a hierarchy, is made up of poems which would call for a reading and a *rereading*, through silent contact with the text. Almost the whole of João Cabral's work, with certain reciprocal influences, could be categorized into poems of one or the other "water," one of immediate communication, the other of meditative reading. João Cabral's true dimension only comes across when both are considered, and not if only the water that "communicates," as in *Morte e Vida Severina*, is valued. Besides the communicative ocean, there is the depleted stream from Northeastern Brazil, a stream, dry and tiny, beckoning a patient reader to slip into its flow. The ocean of communication reaches fifty editions, whereas the vein (or stream) of the most meditative, complex and intellectualized poetry remains in the neglected and poorly fed second or third edition. It is as though there were two poets at the same time, one who reaps the public's grace and the other who earns its disgrace, insofar as the public is unaware of his texts.

The reader, however, may feel attracted by that supposedly complicated poetry as well as by the simpler poetry, upon discovering that in both João Cabral expresses the same loathing for the vague and the formless. The poet's work is clear, plenty of brightness, because it is sunny, meridian, invaded by light. It is also clear, in terms of lucidity, because it does not offer puzzles. It is not about "what does this mean? What is the hidden message?" Everything is there, right on the page, as it stands in the text. But too much clarity obscures. So we are lost vis-à-vis the poem, not because it is abstruse, but because we recoil in the face of its clarity. The game proposed is manifestly visible, and we, seekers of dazzling depths, forego the chance of accepting a treasure that is on the surface, void of any mystery whatsoever. And when I speak of the surface, I immediately think of the notion of syntax. Cabral writes poetry in which beings and objects are woven together, they are intertwined through a very elaborate syntax. The poet opens a sentence in verse 1 and, sometimes, will only conclude it in verse 32. The reader, accustomed to instant poetry (*"poesia-minuto"*), in which the poet's enlightenment lasts for only 3 verses, is stunned upon noticing that he is already in the middle of a long poem and that Cabral is yet to unroll his first thread. The urgency of speed, the cult of the instantaneous and praise for the intuitive outburst are the opposite of Cabral's poetry. His poetry calls for a reading that seeks to gently wander through the many meanderings of an intelligence that unfolds through syntactic intrigues, in a discursiveness opposed to the idea of text as an instantaneous flash. The best correlate of Cabral's art is not photography, but cinema, with its ability to project itself in space and time.

João Cabral published twenty books and it is obviously impossible within the constraints of a single essay to run through the entire range of his works. I will nonetheless attempt to stress Cabral's originality, not by following his texts in a linear fashion, but rather by cutting through to the innovative elements of his works, from the smallest—that is, the phoneme—to the largest—that is, an entire book. Between the phoneme and the book, we will also pass through the word, the verse, the stanza and the poem, in a gradual expansion of the field of reference.

Based upon the classic opposition between consonants and vowels, we used to welcome the sort of poetry associated with the tradition of the melodic-vocalic: suffice it to remember the famous poem by Rimbaud that describes synesthesias and fantasies latent in the vowels. João Cabral, however, is a writer of consonants. He declares war upon melody as numbing, a source of amusement, and instead values the rough acoustics of consonantal encounters, which flee the melodious predictability of the vowel.

In terms of a semantic correlate, such a friction of consonants presents the stone as a sign, not as an obstacle to be avoided, but rather as a supreme horizon to be reached. Somebody is absentmindedly walking along and suddenly stumbles. The stumble is the act of waking up; it implies switching from a position of daydreaming to one of confronting the ground trodden, with the bluntness of the objects that surround us. For João Cabral, that sharpness, albeit uncomfortable, is a necessary prerequisite for poetry. In a poem entitled "Catar Feijão,"[3] he compares poetic creation to the prosaic gesture of sorting beans, because both involve a manual practice, though with clear differences. In sorting beans, the seeker keeps the grain and throws away the stone or the pit, while the poet does quite the opposite. In sorting beans (that is, in sifting words in a poem), the poet should keep the stones and write verse with them, combating melody by means of vocabulary, syntactic and phonetic stones. Let us recall another poet, Vinícius de Moraes, who is usually placed as a counterpoint to João Cabral. Both shared at least two circumstances. Both were diplomats, persecuted and kicked out of the Brazilian Foreign Office, and both developed an unmistakable calling for poetry, albeit in opposing directions. Vinícius is the poet of celebration, of feeling, of mystique, of the night, of metaphysics, of love, of vowels…. João Cabral would have said that Vinícius wrote poetry to lull the reader to sleep, while he wrote it in order to knock the reader down. He felt that Vinícius was the greatest talent wasted in Brazilian poetry, a poet with tremendous potential drained by his connections to popular music, who was very competent but without any greater force or radicalness.

If, from the phoneme, we move on to the next level, we arrive at the word. Cabral's word will chiefly be concrete, linked to a sensory experience, and furthermore, socializable. Cabral argues that when the word "table" or "microphone" is uttered everybody knows what it is. But if somebody utters the words "beauty," "love," or "longing" (*"saudade"*), each individual will understand them in their own way, obstructing, through polysemy, the univocally shared dimension aspired to by the poet. We find in João Cabral's work an undisputed prevalence of concrete substantives over abstract ones. Another interesting point is that he denies the existence of words that are *a priori* "poetic," because that would imply the dismissal of the poet himself, reduced to merely collecting an already defined group of words. João Cabral argues that the poetic is a *syntactic* effect, obtained through the poet's hard work with words, and he introduces vocabulary into poetry that no one had dared to use, such as *cabra* ("goat") *ovo de galinha* ("chicken's egg"), *aranha* ("spider"), *gasolina* ("gasoline"), all prosaic, "pedestrian," signs. And he makes an avowed exception: he never was able to include the word "cigar" (*"charuto"*) in his work, considering it the least useful term in the Portuguese language. As to the hallmark of the poetic tradition, once again Vinícius de Moraes, João Cabral's opposite, may be evoked. When the musical movement of *Bossa Nova* appeared, João Cabral heard Vinícius sing his compositions with Tom Jobim, and he began to get upset because the word "heart" appeared in all the lyrics. However, diplomatically and politely he kept quiet. During the fourth song, the word "heart" appeared again. He couldn't take it any more and begged: "Vinícius, is it so impossible to change organs?" How about a poem with liver, lung, pancreas...

Another important datum: João Cabral holds that in addition to nouns, there are also concrete adjectives: "crooked," "rough" and "square" would be concrete; "beautiful" and "intelligent," abstract. In order to differentiate them, one must check if the adjective is linked or not to a sensory reality: we perceive something to be rough or smooth, but beautiful or intelligent belongs to the same impalpable category of nouns such as beauty and intelligence. Once again it is the stone that symbolizes this universe to perfection. It is no longer the phoneme, but the word, because Cabral's stone, unlike Drummond's (which was in the middle of the road), accompanies him all the way: it is a portable object. In the 1968 edition of *Poesias Completas*, a rather telling fact became manifest: João Cabral's first book was entitled *Pedra do Sono* (1942), and the (at that time) latest one, *A Educação pela Pedra* (1966). A stone planted at the outset and another at the end of the road; the first one, of slumber, comes from a Cabral unlike Cabral himself, in his only nocturnal work, typical of a strong surrealist influence. The latter book welcomes a stone awakened, active and pedagogic, which proposes a pattern of behavior to the human being: to keep in regular contact with the stone in order to learn its resistance to disintegration, its insolubleness. Instead of *projecting* a multitude of ghosts into reality, João Cabral attempts to *draw* ethical models and behaviors from reality. The poet is not a master, but an apprentice of the universe.

By inscribing the word into a larger unit, we arrive at the verse. Upon combating the melodic, he rejects the three standards that represent, *par excellence*, the singing metrics of the Portuguese language: the minor rondel, the major rondel and the decasyllable. Whence a special effect: oftentimes, the syllables seem to be either left over or lacking in his texts. With the melodic verse, the reader can even stop listening to what is being said, in order to remain anesthetized by the background music. In order to combat such passive, automated listening, João Cabral resorts to verses of eight, nine, or eleven syllables, or in the rondel he cleverly shifts the tonic accentuation in the sequence of the verses, since melody becomes foreseeable only when the cadence of the syllables is strictly predetermined.

By placing the verse within a wider structure, we arrive at the stanza. Starting with "O Rio" (1954) the poet begins to work obsessively with a stanza of four lines (*"quadra"*). It is not a matter of detail or a formal arabesque, for such an option easily accedes to a very precise meaning. Cabral abhors odd numbers and chooses the number four because the odd number always leaves a number floating: one connects with three, for example, while two remains isolated. When he opts for four lines, the poet creates more self-centered, stable and solid relationships. He seeks to visualize the figure four in front of him, as a complete structure in itself. In the book *Museu de Tudo*, he succeeds in creating a poem dedicated to the number four.[4] For Cabral, there are very few objects more admirable than a table, for the solidity of its joined legs, for the balance and distribution of its points of support. Even the wheel would be an invention of the figure four: primarily a square, but having been so rotated as to become itself an angular structure. João Cabral wagers on everything that is angular, with sharp ends and edges. He loathes what is softened and attenuated, because such configurations harbor torpor, shade, and slumber, while the edge and the angle are part of a system of watchfulness and a keen eye.

Cabral can sometimes maintain a single long stanza, seemingly unhindered by the number four. But, if we were to reckon the total number of verses, we would arrive at sixteen, thirty-two, sixty-four.... With every number four a sort of insularity of meaning occurs, as if the poet actually needed this number in order to organize his thoughts. Another aspect that is somewhat less pronounced in his work is the profusion of rhymes, without its ever really becoming self-evident. His type of rhyme is not common in Portuguese lyrics. The traditional rhyme is of the resonant type in which there emerges from the tonic vowel a perfect phonic coincidence. João Cabral uses rhyme of the consonant type, as in Spanish, yet which a distracted reader scarcely notices. There is a tonic vowel coincidence, but with no clear connection for the rhyme: *negro* ("black") and *rede* ("hammock"), for

ANTONIO CARLOS SECCHIN

example. João Cabral once explained why he rhymed, especially since he was known for his aversion to melody, and since rhyme is, after all, a melodic resource. He argued that the consonantal rhyme was not melodic, and that, on the contrary, he needed rhyme as a challenge for writing verse. And he resorted to quite an odd comparison by Robert Frost: to do verses without rhyme was like playing tennis without a net....

If we move from the stanza to the next level, we arrive at the poem. For Cabral, the poem is conceived as a language-producing machine, where each element is fashioned with a purpose, and in turn each word or image only acquires meaning via the connection it establishes with those around it and with the poem as a whole. In an interview granted to the widely circulated magazine *Veja*, Cabral observed that the tradition of Portuguese-language poetry consists in valuing the texture at the expense of structure.[5] The artist, rapt with wonder, embellishes the metaphor, changes a word, embroiders another image, everything within the "retail business" of the verse, and not in the "wholesale business" of the poem. The object of that criticism, I think, could be Murilo Mendes, about whose poetry João Cabral expressed at least one reservation: his failure to structure.[6] He was a poet with abundant imagery, true, but perhaps for that very reason, he was unable to find a thread to weave them together. His poems happen by explosion and, therefore, in bits and scraps which do not yield themselves to the notion of a whole. This is important when we think of the role João Cabral grants to syntax as the element responsible for the transformation from chaos into structure. This is the thread that will run through the poem, which will sew it together and ensure the poetic fabric a degree of organicity. Besides the syntax, in the traditional sense of grammar, there is syntax of another kind in Cabral, one of images, in which new metaphors emerge from a parent metaphor upon a pathway opposite to that of a random proliferation of the imaginary. There is an imagistic *continuum*, which is similar to João Cabral's syntactic structure. Furthermore, his poems are also bold enough to redesign poetic forms abandoned by literature since Romanticism. João Cabral affirmed, in a lecture in the 1950s, that the modern poet wrote without taking into consideration the existence of the new means of mass communication.[7] By taking that new audience into account, it is no accident that shortly afterwards he began to publish his "to-be-read-aloud" poems. He also regretted the confusion between poetry and lyricism brought about since the nineteenth century. Until the eighteenth century, poetry was not ashamed to tell a story. Besides being lyrical, it could be didactic, narrative, bucolic.... With the inflation of the "I" in the nineteenth century, the lyric poem swept across the entire realm of verse, relegating to the backyard of literature other forms of poetic expression. Narrative in verses was welcomed as a survivor in scarcely "noble" niches, like *literatura de cordel,* heir to a tradition expelled from the scene by the great poets of the nineteenth and twentieth centuries. João Cabral suggested the recovery of those popular forms; he proposed it in theory and accomplished it in practice. "O Rio" is a narrative poem, in which the Capibaribe river tells its story in the first person, from its birth in the interior to its merging with the Atlantic. *Morte e Vida Severina* is a dramatic poem based on the folklore of Northeastern Brazil and Spain. In both cases, popular poetry works hand in hand with sophisticated literature by revitalizing sources that had formerly been scorned.

Starting with the poem, let us now turn to its inscription within a book, understood both as an instance of organization of the material included in it and as a graphic object. João Cabral served as consul in Barcelona and there bought a press so that he could publish books made by his own hand. This practice fits in well with Cabral's concepts concerning the development of handicrafts—the poet literally got his hands dirty in seeing the work born. As for the internal organization, let us strike a contrast with the book of a Brazilian romantic poet like Casimiro de Abreu. In his work we find a poem dedicated to his mother, since the poet happened to be missing her on a certain day; later he visited the orchard, and composed some verses for the orange tree... The romantic's work was a type of mirror of existential dispersion, a portrait of the diffuse character of the artist's experiences. Cabral, obsessively given to cultivating organization, does not allow the work to merely flow in an arbitrary fashion. Often the organization of his own book is as laboriously crafted as the production of each individual text. It is a macro-structural relationship: just as the romantic creates in tune with the moment and his poem randomly becomes part of a collection, Cabral, combating randomness, will try to integrate the poem functionally into the larger frame of the book. In *Serial* (1961), he worked that mechanism down to a system that is so lucid that it seems to border on madness. The book contains sixteen poems, that is to say, four squared. The number repeats with such consistency that it cannot be a mere coincidence. In terms of rhymes, there are four poems in the pattern a-b-a-b. As for the meter, there are four texts with hexasyllables, four with heptasyllables, four with octosyllables, and

ANTONIO CARLOS SECCHIN

four with different combinations of hexa- and octosyllables. Each poem of *Serial* is split into four parts; four of them have parts consisting of two stanzas, another four of four stanzas, another four of six and the last four, eight. In some texts there are words in italics, which work as a thematic synthesis; there are eight poems with words in italics, and the italics occur in four grammatical categories: verb, common noun, proper noun and adjective. Lastly, the separation between the four parts of each poem is made by the use of four different symbols, each one with its own specific way of functioning in the poem: dash, asterisk, number or paragraph marker.[8] On an increasing scale of difficulty, the poet has concretely laid out the foundations of the book and, based upon them, he has furnished it with sixteen pieces of strict measurement, thereby fashioning a laborious, arduous and beautiful poem, which is the book itself in its architectural entirety.

Following all these considerations of a generic nature, I propose that we finally examine the functioning of João Cabral's poetic engineering in a specific text, "Tecendo a Manhã."[9] It is a fairly well-known poem, even read aloud at union demonstrations, although generally on those occasions they read only its first stanza, which is the simplest. João Cabral recounts that it took eight years to complete the text, which he finalized after more than thirty-two versions. The poem is presented here in its entirety:

1

One rooster does not weave a morning:
he will always need the other roosters.
One to pick up the shout that he
and toss it to another; another rooster
to pick up the shout that rooster before
and toss it to another; and other roosters
with many other roosters to crisscross
the sun-threads of their rooster shouts,
so that the morning, starting from a frail cobweb,
may go on being woven, among all the roosters.

2

And growing larger, becoming cloth,
Pitching itself a tent, they may all enter,
Inter-unfurling itself for them all, in the tent
(the morning), which soars free of ties and ropes,
The morning, tent of a weave so light
That, woven itself through itself: balloon light.[10]

I would like to propose three levels of reading for this poem. The first
would be almost literal: one can perceive the morning being born, whose
clarity does not emanate from the sun, but from a light coming from the
ground, kept safe in the beak of the rooster. In this paraphrastic reading, the
roosters do not shout, but release threads that become intertwined and
thicken, creating the morning as a gift for all. A second level, also very visible,
consists in reappropriating and stylizing the saying "one swallow does not
make a summer"—"one rooster does not weave a morning." Such a
politicized line in the text implies praise for the work of solidarity. But João
Cabral toys with common expectations for the setting, by introducing
politics where it is least expected: amidst the roosters, and not in the
dichotomy of boss, worker, slave and master, which configure an already
diluted rhetoric representing good and evil in domesticated spaces and
languages. In order to access the third reading, let us assume that verses 1 and
2 refer to an unproductive rooster: alone, he does not weave the morning.
Such a solitary rooster would be syntactically trapped in the initial verses
through a period. Here, form and content belong together: Cabral speaks
about an isolated rooster and the syntax of the text reinforces the isolation in
the "prison" of the couplet. In the third verse, the solitude is broken. The
syntax of the poem once again expresses solidarity, because it does not isolate
or enclose: a rooster crisscrosses its thread with that of another, while a
sentence links up with the previous sentence and tosses it over to the
following before going quiet. The verb, which would make us perceive the
sentence as conclusive, is omitted. Thus, the verse is halted halfway by the
poet as the thread of the rooster that had been caught in the air by another
rooster. All of this occurs in a process of convergence between the event that
is being expressed, the dawn of day, and the form of the poem, replicating
what is being narrated. There are two threads that meet, one of light and
another of syntax, in the discourse of a poet who builds the morning and the

text at the same time. Therefore, at that third level, a subtle metalinguistic exercise occurs; as with the rooster, one word alone does not weave a poem. It will always need another one to pick up that thread, which it tosses to another, until that text, beginning from a tenuous sentence, keeps weaving its way through all the words. To make material the idea of something very light, a fine gauze, taking shape, João Cabral fosters a thickening around the phoneme /t/: *tela* ("screen") is thicker than *teia* ("web"), and *tenda* ("tent"), more than *tela* ("screen"). Then, with *todos* ("everybody") and *toldo* ("tent"), the solidarity of meaning is once again reflected in the phonic stratum, through the paronomasian game of words that reciprocally "support each other." The whole text unfolds in solidarity with webs of meaning, syntax and phonetics, in an irrepressible flow towards the morning. And the poem draws an object that is symmetrically inverted at the end: in the beginning, two verses with an imprisoned rooster; in the epilogue, two verses with the morning set free, in a shining metaphor of freedom.

Notes

[1] *Morte e Vida Severina.* 1956. Melo Neto. *Obra Completa,* 169-202.

[2] *Duas Águas.* Rio de Janeiro: José Olympio, 1956.

[3] "Catar Feijão." *Educação pela Pedra.* 1966. Melo Neto. *Obra Completa,* 346-347.

[4] "O Número 4." Museu *de Tudo.* 1975. Melo Neto. *Obra Completa,* 396.

[5] "Entrevista." *Revista Veja* 199 (June 28 1972): 4.

[6] Regarding the criticism on Murilo Mendes' poetry see "Entrevista de João Cabral de Melo Neto." *João Cabral: A Poesia do Menos,* 1999, 327. The interview was given on November 1980.

[7] The lecture, "The Modern Function of Poetry," was presented in the "Congresso de Poesia," held in São Paulo in 1954, and was published in the same year. Melo Neto. *Obra Completa,* 769.

[8] In my book *João Cabral: A Poesia do Menos,* I analyze in detail all those configurations, see especially 230-232.

[9] The poem is in *Educação pela Pedra*:

1

Um galo sozinho não tece uma manhã:
ele precisará sempre de outros galos.
De um que apanhe esse grito que ele
e o lance a outro; de um outro galo
que apanhe o grito que um galo antes
e o lance a outro; e de outros galos
que com muitos outros galos se cruzem
os fios de sol de seus gritos de galo,

para que a manhã, desde uma teia tênue,
se vá tecendo, entre todos os galos.

2

E se encorpando em tela, entre todos,
se erguendo tenda, onde entrem todos,
se entretendendo para todos, no toldo
(a manhã) que plana livre de armação.
A manhã, toldo de um tecido tão aéreo
que, tecido, se eleva por si: luz balão.

Melo Neto. *Obra Completa*, 345.

[10] João Cabral de Melo Neto. *Selected Poetry, 1937—1990*. Djelal Kadir. Ed. Translations by Elizabeth Bishop et al. Hanover: University Press of New England [for] Wesleyan University Press, 1994, 137. The poem "Tecendo a Manhã," was translated by Galway Kinnel.

Works Cited

Barbieri, Ivo. *Geometria da Composição*. Rio de Janeiro: Sette Letras, 1997.

Barbosa, João Alexandre. *A Imitação da Forma*. São Paulo: Duas Cidades, 1975.

Cadernos de Literatura Brasileira 1—João Cabral de Melo Neto. São Paulo: Instituto Moreira Salles, 1996.

Lima, Luiz Costa. "A Traição Conseqüente ou a Poesia de Cabral." *Lira & Antilira. Mário, Drummond, Cabral.* 1968. 2 ed. Rio de Janeiro: Topbooks, 1995. 177-331.

Melo Neto, João Cabral de. *Obra Completa*. Rio de Janeiro: Nova Aguilar, 1994.

———. "Entrevista de João Cabral de Melo Neto." Antonio Carlos Secchin. *João Cabral: A Poesia do Menos.* 2 ed. Rio de Janeiro: Topbooks, 1999. 325-333.

———. "Da Função Moderna da Poesia." *Obra Completa.* 765-770.

———. "Entrevista." *Revista Veja* 1972 (28 June 1972): 4.

Merquior, José Guilherme. "Nuvem Civil Sonhada." *A Astúcia da Mímese.* Rio de Janeiro: José Olympio, 1972. 69-172.

Nunes, Benedito. *João Cabral de Melo Neto*. Petrópolis: Vozes, 1971.

Secchin, Antonio Carlos. *João Cabral: A Poesia do Menos.* 2 ed. Rio de Janeiro: Topbooks, 1999.

Two Poetics, Two Moments

Heloísa Buarque de Hollanda
Translated by Shoshanna Lurie

This essay will examine the emerging poetry of the Brazilian cultural and political scene at two specific moments, both identified as moments of collapse, or at least decline, in the freedom and quality of artistic production. This is the case of *marginal poetry*—produced in the 1970s during the toughest period of the military dictatorship—and of a *new aesthetics of rigor*, as the new poetry of the 1990s has been called. The latter is produced under the most recent form of dictatorship imposed by the logic of consumption and the processes of globalization. I will begin by discussing the so-called marginal poetry that, taking into account the negative reception of this generation of poets at their own time, paradoxically entered into the canon as the expression *par excellence* of 1970s poetics in Brazil.

What we now call marginal poetry was a kind of cultural event or, better yet, a poetic "outbreak" (to avoid the word *movement*, which implies a homogeneous and programmatic project) around 1972-73 that had a significant impact on the cultural environment dominated by silence, which had been dictated by censorship and by the violence of military repression in Brazil. This poetry was characterized by structural informality, not only in terms of a textual production marked by colloquial and witty expression, but also in terms of the manner in which these authors conceived an artisan's production and the independent distribution of new and creative books of poetry.

The name marginal—ambiguous from the start—oscillated between an inexhaustible series of meanings: marginal to the canon, marginal to the editorial market, marginal to the political life of the country. A first sign of the novelty of this production was the unexpected way that it succeeded in mobilizing a large young audience around poetry. This group, until then more linked to music, film, concerts, and cartoons, represented an audience very different from the traditional consumer of literature. This phenomenon of intense mobilization around poetry, as well as being quantitatively significant, introduced some innovations of style and *performance* to the Republic of Letters.

Marginal poetry showed signs of its ambivalence from the very beginning. It emerged as a "light" and unpretentious poetry, but one that brought a serious and relevant issue to the fore: the *ethos* of a generation traumatized by the limitations imposed upon its social experience and by the restriction of its access to information and freedom of expression by the violent pressure of censorship and the repressive mechanisms developed during the period of military dictatorship. This is certainly one of the most salient aspects of this poetry that became one of the most striking records of the testimony of the generation known as the AI5.[1]

The telling of the story and of the experience of this generation, whose distinctive feature was precisely that of being restricted from narrating their own stories, emerges in each "poem-joke" (*"poema-piada"*), in each improvisation, in each rhyme contained in these texts. In this way, marginal poems reveal a sharp sensitivity in making reference to—with varying clarity and literary skill—the day-to-day of the political moment that these poets lived. These poems frequently experimented with the use of allegory as a tool to enable reference to the *status quo*, as Antônio Carlos de Brito does in "Aquarela" ("Watercolor"):

The body on the rack
is an agonizing bird
exhausted from its own shrieking.
Ransacked entrails
initiate the
countdown.
Blood on the floor
dilutes into shades
that the breeze kisses and shakes:
the green—of our forests
the yellow—of our gold
the blue—of our sky

the white the black the black.

Or poems that convey the dry and unusual traits of Francisco Alvim, as in "Aquela Tarde" ("That Afternoon"):

> They told me he had died the evening before.
> That he had been taken prisoner, tortured.
> That he had died in the Military Hospital. The
> burial would be that afternoon.
> (a priest chose the place for the tribune.
> It seemed he was going to speak. He didn't.
> Mother and sister cried.)

Among the youngest group, the most common approach was the description or account of apparently insignificant facts that denounced the feeling of paranoia permeating Brazilian daily life after 1968. Chacal describes this in a fragment of the "epic poem" *Orlando Takapau*:

> Sitting and student-like, Orlando contemplated the
> absurd and the teacher's ass. All of a sudden—
> footsteps in the hall behind the closed door.
> "were they police or late students?"
> Taka passed the woman with chalk and opened the door.
> The informer, ears glued to the door
> took off. His swastika fell to
> the floor. Orlando understood the incident and thought nothing
> walked down the staircase and never went back.
> For what?

Another expression of the "poetics of suffocation" (*"poética do sufoco"*)— as marginal poetry was also called—can be found in aggressive and performative poems such as those by Wally Salomão. He wrote a book of hybrid style—part poetry, part prose, part drama, part music—suggestively named *Me Segura que eu Vou Dar um Troço (Control Me, I'm Going to Freak Out)*, which became a hit at the time.

These poets, determined not to allow "silence" to reign, defined a poetry with strong "anti-literary" characteristics that clashed with the erudite experimentalism of the avant-garde of the moment. A poetic style that, above all, seemed determined to "play" with the prevailing norms of literary quality, the hermeneutic depth of the poetic text, as well as that of a reader qualified to fully appreciate the poem and its subtexts.

In this way, with only one gesture, the marginal poets questioned literary criticism and literary institutions by offering a colloquial, disposable, and biodegradable poetry that didn't seem concerned with the permanence of its production nor with the recognition of a criticism informed by the canonical standards of literary historiography. Conversely, they defined their position by not expressing any literary or political project and by presenting themselves as clearly non-programmatic, contradicting formal schools and approaches. Through the irreverent and ironic use of poetic language, the artifice created for its dissemination, and the assertion of a practice outside of the system, in reality, marginal poets seemed to be searching for a radical fusion of art and life. This behavior, along with the general climate of transgression that set the tone of this poetry, inevitably resulted in the questioning of the very notion of literary value. As a consequence, new frontiers opened into not only the experimentation with a variety of styles and new fields of expression unthinkable until then, but also into the no less significant plurality of projects as well as political and cultural perspectives in the understanding of poetry.

Without a doubt, along with the resistance that it offered to the cultural void generated by censorship and repression, the rupture of paradigms that happened at this time is the greatest literary contribution of marginal poetry, decisively reflecting upon poetry of the 1990s. The development of this new poetry—a poetry known for bearing the marks of a no less radical dictatorship, the dictatorship of the market—is very indebted to marginal poetry. If in the 1970s young poets confronted the limits imposed by censorship, today poets find themselves in a situation dominated by the logic of an extremely competitive cultural market guided by an accelerated process of massification, transnationalization, and specialization in the production and commercialization of its products. In other words, a new game of power has arisen that requires new strategies of production.

Nevertheless, the poet of the 1990s seeks to face the new challenges. His or her profile is one of a lettered poet that invests, above all, in the recovery of formal and technical expertise in literary work, clearly differentiating him or herself from the antiestablishment convictions of the generation of marginal poets. However, like every dictatorship, the dictatorship of consumption has its own gaps. If, from a distance, contemporary poetic production seems fairly unoriginal, a little amorphous, with few apparent innovations, at the same time a surprising plurality of voices impresses the reader. This is the first significant difference of this poetry.

The presence of women on the literary scene, which had been one of the *pièces de resistance* of the last decade, now reflects definitive growth that translates into near equivalence between men and women on the poetry market. Black poetry can also be noticed more clearly in the current context. A new trait common to both groups, introduced decisively by the production of the 1990s, is a previously unprecedented experimental freedom that differs substantially from the previous generation's production. In this earlier poetry, the presence of a lyricism committed to and engaged with the affirmation of identity was the thematic and formal *leitmotif* of poetry written by women and black Brazilians. Recent examples, including the poets Cláudia Roquette-Pinto, Lu Menezes, Joseli Vianna, Vivian Kogut, and many others attest to the current work in women's poetry and the different and creative outcomes resulting from the broadening of movements attained through the political and poetic struggle of feminists during the previous period.

Most significantly, the pluralistic panorama of 1990s opened spaces definitively for some voices that had not found much possibility for expression in previous decades. Here I call attention to the emergence of an erudite and self-ironic sensitivity assumed as Jewish (a cultural assertion curiously rare in Brazil) and, very particularly, to the aggressive and original presence of "gay outing" in the poetry of the 1990s. In this case, these are some of our best and most representative new poets, including Nelson Ascher, Antonio Cicero, and Valdo Mota, among others.

However, in reality the greatest surprise in the Brazilian poetic panorama of the end of the millenium is the growing literary presence of poets emerging from peripheral and suburban low-income neighborhoods and the intensification of editorial activity in *favelas* and poorer residential communities. In other words, for the first time, the poor poet is somewhat attaining a chance and a voice. During the last decade, numerous collections were published in Rio de Janeiro, including the *Antologia de Poetas da Baixada Fluminense (Anthology of Poets from the Baixada Fluminense)* (RioArte), *Tem Poeta no Morro (There are Poets in the Favela),* (Federação das Associações de Favelas do Estado do Rio de Janeiro), *Poetas do Vidigal (Poets from Vidigal)* and the book *Fora de Perigo (Out of Danger),* by José Alberto

Moreira da Silva, which features multimedia poetry. In 1992, the anthology *Poetas do Araguaia* [*Poets from Araguaia*] and *Ausência em Falso* [*Mistaken Absence*] introduced alternatives for rethinking the Brazil of the landless ("*sem-terra*").

The strategies of production chosen by the poetry of the 1990s also merit attention. Poetry has benefited from the establishment of small publishing houses using the tools offered by new technologies of digital reproduction, allowing the printing of editions with a small number of copies at reasonable prices. It has also taken advantage of the unexpected popularity of collections of poetry on CD, like the series *Poesia Falada (Spoken Poetry)* by the producer Paulinho Lima, *A Voz do Poeta (The Poet's Voice)* by the Drum label, and the production of poetry CDs by the larger recording companies including Som Livre and Leblon Records. Accompanying this success, live poetry readings also became common. For example, those by Maria Bethânia and Chico Buarque often fill theatres and cultural arenas. Interesting and odd cases remain, such as the Elisa Lucinda phenomenon, mixing poetry, theater, and "pocket-show"[2] in a format until recently unthinkable for literature, that of poetry as mass consumption, or poetry as show business.

It could be said that poetry is beginning to lean in the direction of a culturalization or an unprecedented amplification of its breadth of consumption—and even of its very social function—through the opening of non-formal cultural spaces and the emergence of new social and behavioral habits.

The decisive effect of the process of eroding borders between high (or elite) culture and low (or mass or popular) culture on the textuality of 1990s literature is also very important to and characteristic of this moment. These divisions were, *par excellence*, a sign of culture during the rise of modernity. In the case of 1990s poetry, the view of this process often becomes crystal clear. In fact, the formation of a hybrid texture can be seen in this poetic production in which it is no longer possible to distinguish a real imbalance between elite and mass forms of artistic expression or between cultures of different media. The poem-clip, tri-dimensional video-poetry, or other experiments such as the "photonouvellevague," a genre created by Filipe Nepomuceno, are eloquent evidence of this development. The "photonouvellevague," in addition to continuously slipping between Spanish and Portuguese, presents a mixed form of the comic strip, the printed photographic soap opera, the fragmentation of contact prints, written words, and a soundtrack with instrumental sound and poetry reading.

It is also important to emphasize that this new experimental texture of 1990s poetry presents very unique characteristics of structural hybridization that can be confused with neither the avant-garde's programmatic procedures of rejecting the "purity" of literary language through the use of themes and techniques made available by new media nor the creativity of the graphic improvisations of the alternative poetry of the 1970s.

However, this is still not the most polemic point of this new poetry. The incontestable presence of a total heterogeneity in experimentation and an uncommitted and almost cynical adherence to any given style, ideology, or school, provokes a disconcerting reaction from traditional criticism, which is used to approaching poetic movements in search of a coherent aesthetic or political project. Meanwhile, the new poets diagnose this phenomenon with the utmost ease as the practice of a "literature of invention." They understand literature of invention as a "literature that seeks language in certain materials."[3] *Material*, in this case, would be a repertoire that indiscriminately includes long verse and short verse, metaphor and metonymy, surrealistic language and realistic language; all are equivalent, available, and equally employable as a function of the poet's greater or lesser skill.

Instead of defining paths, the 1990s poet displays only two commitments: first, the expansion of his or her informational inventory and, second, the acquisition of a secure command of meter, prosody, and new technologies, or, in other words, of his or her expressional resources, making these commitments the stamp and the advance of the literature of the 1990s. The new is identified with the assertion of a competent performance, with originality in articulation, and with experimental and creative reinvention of literary tradition. Substantially different from previous logics, in this one it becomes difficult to identify a political or ideological trend, or at least a project that might serve as a parameter for establishing the values that inform the production.

In addition, the criteria for gauging the quality of a poem change axis: they slip from the consideration of the presence of a varying critical or innovative value towards the presence of the ability to articulate opposing processes and to expand the repertoire of references to be re-deployed or even "cloned" by the new poet. The logic of influences in an author's work becomes chaotic, and often, almost museological, revealing clear symptoms of the emergence of new forms of recodification of the past in the present as an axis of a post-modern temporality. This recodification, in the case of 1990s poetry, is not limited to taking inventory of or even experimenting with the new links between literary schools and styles. Above all, it comprises a critical exercise of re-semanticization and of aesthetic creation. Gaps open for the new poets' invention and intervention precisely within this interstice.

In the midst of growing political and aesthetic neo-conservatism, today a literary production emerges, largely in the field of poetry, seeking to question, more than to explore, cultural codes, and to explore, more than to disguise, political and social affiliations. This poetry is less concerned with aesthetic rigor in itself and more invested in the search for strategies to enable critical and innovative positions in the face of the challenges of the new *Zeitgeist*. It is a poetry that begins to stake out its position in the small space that is available today for artistic creation and for the exercise of a conceivable political imagination.

Notes

[1] AI5: abbreviation for the Institutional Act 5 implemented in Brazil on December 13, 1968, eliminating freedom of speech and institutionalizing censorship.

[2] A sort of performance that has contributed to the dissemination of 1990s poetry, which includes presentations, and poetry readings in small theaters or halls. (Translator's note)

[3] A definition proposed by Carlito Azevedo in a debate held at Universidade Federal Fluminense, Rio de Janeiro. He is one of the most important poets of the 1990s. Currently, he is editor of the journal *Inimigo Rumor* (Sette Letras).

Works Cited

Alvim. Francisco. *Sol dos Cegos.* Rio de Janeiro: José Olympio, 1967.

———. *Passa Tempo.* Rio de Janeiro: n.p., 1974.

———. *Lago Montanha.* Rio de Janeiro: n.p., 1978

———. *Elefante.* São Paulo: Companhia das Letras, 2000.

Azevedo, Carlito. *Collapsus Linguae.* Rio de Janeiro: Lynx, 1991

———. *As Banhistas.* Rio de Janeiro: Imago, 1993.

———. *Sob a Noite Física.* Rio de Janeiro: Sette Letras, 1996.

Batista, Josely Vianna. *Ar.* São Paulo: Iluminuras, 1991.

———. *Corpografia—Autópsia—Poética das Passagens.* São Paulo: Iluminuras, 1992.

Brito, Antonio Carlos de: *Palavra Cerzida.* Rio de Janeiro: José Olympio, 1967.

———. *Grupo Escolar.* Rio de Janeiro: n.p., 1975

———. *Segunda Classe.* Rio de Janeiro: n.p., 1975.

————. *Beijo na Boca*. Rio de Janeiro: n.p., 1976.

————. *Mar de Mineiro*. Rio de Janeiro: n.p., 1982.

Hollanda, Heloísa Buarque de. Ed. *26 Poetas Hoje*. 1976. Rio de Janeiro: Aeroplano, 1999.

————. Ed. *Esses Poetas: Uma Antologia dos Anos 90*. Rio de Janeiro: Aeroplano, 1999.

Kogut, Vivian. *Água Rara*. Rio de Janeiro: Sette Letras, 1996.

Martins, Alberto: *Poemas*. Coleção Claro Enigma. São Paulo: Duas Cidades, 1990.

Menezes, Lu. *Abre-te Rosebud!* Rio de Janeiro: Sette Letras, 1996.

Nepomuceno, Filipe. *O Marciano*. Rio de Janeiro: Sette Letras 1997.

Roquette-Pinto, Cláudia. *Os Dias Gagos*. Rio de Janeiro: Rio de Janeiro: n.p., 1991.

————. *Saxífraga*. Rio de Janeiro: Salamandra, 1993.

————. *Zona de Sombra*. Rio de Janeiro: Sette Letras, 1997.

————. *Corola*. São Paulo: Ateliê Editorial, 2000.

Brazilian Fiction Today: A Point of Departure

Therezinha Barbieri

Translated by Ross G. Forman

This essay seeks to understand the Brazilian literary production of the 1980s and 1990s through a contextual dialogue between languages that make the visual image their axis of articulation and development. However, although I concentrate on the moment when image and text come together, it is important not to lose sight of the context of simultaneity in which this encounter occurs. For this reason, my attention returns at the end of this study to a more general perspective that places these works on an open plain, leaving a reading of them as fictional texts for another time.

The synthesis with which I am working comes from statements made by Hans Ulrich Gumbrecht in an interview with the *Jornal do Brasil* on September 3, 1988. Gumbrecht took the intellectual, political and moral pulse of Brazil at that moment and rendered it in acutely comprehensible terms. During this particular visit to Brazil, Gumbrecht saw a country assaulted by the despair, disillusionment, and disintegration that seemed to characterize culture at the end of the millennium. In this so-called lost decade, we relived our illusions. The keen eyes of a well-read, well-traveled foreigner perceived this situation at once, and Gumbrecht immediately entered the debate. Quoting Habermas, he reinforced the idea of an opaque state of affairs, dense and dark. He commented, "we are approaching something akin to paralysis, since the post-modern is the era of the end of great myths, of great cosmological models to explain the world."[1] Perhaps it was a time of crisis for ideology, a time of crisis for utopian visions of the future, and a time of crisis for the avant-garde. Along the same lines, Silviano Santiago noted that "the social fabric is composed of passionate differences, and thus the negation of difference is itself the massacre of individual liberties, the repression of more authentic means of being human."2 These two quotations contradict and complete each other. Gumbrecht inscribes the image of a particular moment into the overall picture of ideas in motion; Santiago sees in the unified text divergent signs that call attention to the potential risks. At the same time, all means of communication are limited to registering this crisis without being able to provide instruments to see through the fog. And it is in this context that the intervention of literary texts should be conjured up, here and there, like an unnerving voice calling out from the chorus of perplexities and general paralysis that constitute this fog.

In a world without values, assaulted by the general breakdown of patterns and paradigms, every gesture is measured by its effect. More than ever, it remains difficult to identify criteria for evaluation that allow us to line up, side by side, arranged in an understandable way, lines of divergence and contrast, contradictions and multiple incongruities. Assuming the volatility of the situation, shifts in taste place art on the horizon of the probable, and the idea of an enduring work disappears. Even the classics are constantly revised, and consecrated patterns assume the precariousness of the fleeting. Is it possible that literature or poetry still have a place in this extremely mutable world? What sense is there in so many apparent breakdowns? These and other questions haunt me when I interrogate the recent prose fiction produced in Brazil. Is the immediately obvious sense of formal anarchy a symptom of agony or a symbol of regeneration? With the exhaustion of the experimentation of the avant-garde, the desecration of the inspirational sources of the sublime and of Romantic idealism, the anachronism of patterns of mimetic reproduction, what angles remain for literary narrative to pursue? Yet, despite all this, we can still see signs of life in this altered body. I believe, like Octavio Paz, that poetry and literature—although compelled to bury themselves in tombs impervious to the ceremony and pomp of the world at large—live on, unmistakable in accent and tone, as *the other voice*.3

I now want to return to the map laid out by Gumbrecht, whose components of despair, disillusionment, and disintegration turn up quite startlingly in a narrative typical of the mood in Brazil during the 1980s—João Gilberto Noll's *Hotel Atlântico*. In this text, the novelist attempts to perform the impossible task of fixing in words the mutability of a world without values, disinherited of utopias and weighed down by ideologies in crisis.

Hotel Atlântico is the story of a journey without end—and, apparently, without direction—by an outcast from the world of the money, of work, and of fashion. The plot is dull and prosaic: an unemployed actor, quitting Rio de Janeiro, takes a bus along the paved roads of the South-Southeast and gets off at a hotel along the southern coast. Without knowing the reason for this trip, the protagonist finds himself in extravagant settings and becomes involved in strange scenes. The persecuted and the persecutor fuse into a single figure in this half dreamy, half sleepless journey in which anxiety and pleasure, distraction and tension, sex and death, are juxtaposed. Surveying the alienated conscience of all this, in this trip full of banalities and hallucinations, there is a sharp eye that follows him like the eye of a camera compelled to record, microscopically, his every motion. Behind the camera lies a narrator-director who is busy choosing images, developing snapshots and splicing fragments. Readers find themselves faced with a fictional game of whose rules they are ignorant. If they wish to capture the spirit of this new dynamic, they must redevelop their pact with the text, since this text, without ceasing to be literary, is no longer exclusively literary.

I want to connect my intuition with regard to this type of narrative to Umberto Eco's *Six Walks in the Fictional Woods*:

> ... the reader must tacitly accept a fictional agreement... The reader has to know that what is being narrated is an imaginary story, but he must not therefore believe that the writer is telling lies. According to John Searle, the author simply *pretends* to be telling the truth. We accept the fictional agreement and we *pretend* that what is narrated has really taken place.[4]

Accepting this fictional agreement, sustained by Noll's concrete imaginary, readers appropriate for themselves an agile gaze that focuses on the character and that allows them to dislocate themselves pleasurably in this movable scene. It is a game of representation in crisis, played equally by both the reader and the writer. Yet multiple meanings collide in the twists of this text of apparent nonsense. The drifting ex-actor inhabits a liminal space. Amidst hotels, dead bodies, lovers, haphazard routes, the reader witnesses the gradual immobilization of this I-in-motion, forced to use crutches and a wheelchair, forced into silence and into the simultaneous interruption of a geographical and verbal flux of images that we read/see forming and decomposing in unstable motion. At this semiotic junction, Noll's narrative methods suddenly seem similar to the

THEREZINHA BARBIERI

cinematic narrative scheme of Wim Wenders. In *The Logic of Images*, Wenders states, "A lot of my films start off with roadmaps instead of scripts. Sometimes it feels like flying blind without instruments. You fly all night and in the morning you arrive somewhere."[5] In *Paris, Texas* and *Hotel Atlântico* the image and the word fly all night, without instruments. In both, we see the construction of characters devoid of human attributes, removed from fixed links with time and space. A blind, unguided flight marks the trajectory of Noll's character in transit and in trouble: "I started walking with my stick again. Along the same path as before, as one who could not be scattered like an earthly object, as one who puts up with a blindness that puts him in contact with the powers that be. Stopping would have been an insult."[6]

To the paradox of blindness, which—instead of sealing off—opens up possibilities of contact, Noll adds the fatality of wandering, a sort of blessed curse for the victim, who finds in it the reason for his existence. Bare, dry, and terse language accentuates the psychological and physical destruction of the protagonist-narrator. Such is Noll's prose: unpoetic ground. The creator of images that create him, as an author Noll perceives the modern world in visual terms; it is a compact and concentrated world.

To better situate the idea of thinking through images that is so central to Noll's style, I now want to consider literature that places itself at the border with other forms of artistic expression. *Notas de Manfredo Rangel, Repórter (A Respeito de Kramer)* by Sérgio Sant'Anna (1973), is a key title in this respect not only because it signals the rise of a new writer, but above all because Sant'Anna's work of fiction is born out of a highly successful intersemiotic mélange of languages. Running through the twenty-one narrative strands that make up the text gives a sense of the significance of this type of writing. The discontinuity of the narrative discourse is revealed through the repetition of multiple fractures, through reminiscences, repeated clichés, rhetorical emphases, bits of news footage, films, plays, and television. It is impossible not to invoke the notion of the simulacrum here to prove that Sant'Anna operates in an area once removed from the field of representation. The representation of representations, his fiction makes no attempt to conquer virgin territory. From the very first story, entitled "Pela Janela," the narrator calls attention to such repetition:

> The old woman kept talking. She acted as if the man already knew exactly what she was going to say. As if it were a book he had already read many times before.

The man had the impression that he and the old woman weren't real. They were just characters in some morbid and grotesque story, which was repeated day after day without any possibility of changing the tiniest phrase or element of their destiny.[7]

In this doubling of the text back onto itself, the crisis of representation centers around discourses that have become boring, atrophied, and emptied of signification. "O Espetáculo Não Pode Parar," the last story of the book, closes the circle with a paragraph that offers a key to the reading of the text I have proposed:

The spectacle is horrible: grotesque, vulgar, and even obvious, at times practically trash. The spectacle is, above all, pathological. But the public loves it. It takes place every day, except Mondays.[8]

In this fragment of a monologue, the actor-narrator joins, within the transparency of the simulacrum, clichés of critical jargon with an account of a theatrical display that, in turn, presupposes a confidential chat about a particular experience, incorporating into his discussion elements of other discussions, anonymous and impersonal expressions. It is exactly what the eponymous reporter-narrator Manfredo Rangel says in the title story: "I began to understand that anything that is said or written, even real personal details, always becomes mythical, exaggerated, and arbitrary."[9] The stakes of this declaration are clarified in the narrative's "Supplementary Notes," a sort of an Afterword. After juxtaposing hypotheses, extracts of testimony, interviews, proclamations, intimate confessions, public acclamations, scenes from television, rumors and the grapevine, news and notices—all jumbled together in the manner of an unfinished news documentary—the narrative approaches, in its notes in the margins, the double nature of rehearsal that characterizes this type of prose. It is a rehearsal in the theatrical sense of preparatory exercises for a spectacle and in the metalinguistic sense of self-reflexive discourse. From this perspective Sant'Anna's work opens itself up to a combination of influences: the site of various confluences, his fiction reveals itself as invaded and developed by the media of film, newspapers, radio, and television. Instead of rejecting these influences in the name of an untenable literary specificity, the writer draws strength from hybridity and goes on to fix the text at the junction of a multisemiotic grammar. Open to the iconic-audio-scenic signs of forms of mass communication, the literary text establishes an ironic and critical dialogue with them, thereby adding to the value of the simulacrum:

> A Psychological Analysis of Kramer: when Fio jumped above Brito in the goalbox and headed the ball to make the winning goal in the match between Flamengo and Botafogo, Kramer's happiness, embracing everyone in the Maracanã stadium, seemed totally spontaneous. A politician is an actor. And a good politician is an excellent actor along Stanislavski's model. In other words, he identifies himself with the character, fully assuming his role, to such an extent that he actually comes to feel and act exactly how he wants—and needs—to feel and act. Kramer's happiness when Flamengo scored was almost real.[10]

All this opportunism and mystification of Kramer, the character-object of Rangel's notes—and all these ambiguities, additions, and omissions of the reporter, the character-subject of the narration—are crucial attributes of a discourse that, by exposing the reader to the method of composition, offers a critique as much of the character being depicted as of the character doing the depicting. The writer mystifies / demystifies images following a course devoid of subtext, in conformity with the reporter's other postscript: "These abbreviated notes are really like a film script. It's as if I was trying to find Kramer's most photogenic angles. Of course I imagined a really powerful final scene: Kramer whipped and crucified on a polling post in Recife-Pernambuco."[11]

"No Último Minuto," the second text of the anthology, presents a forceful and economic image-synthesis of modes of expression synchronized with the moment under focus. The timeframe for the scene, which is never directly staged, is less than a minute: a goal shot in the last minute of a soccer match. The moment of the kick itself is filmed by three television stations, and is played and replayed from various angles, in normal time and in slow motion, from the perspective of the goalie. The obsessive and tormenting image of the goal is multiplied and fixed forever by television. It is clear that this story is not a sadomasochistic digression. The story simulates the practices of mass communication, which—obsessed as they are with audience ratings—lower themselves to the point at which they transform healthy social outlets into pathology. Thus Sérgio Sant'Anna stamps a pop feature on the literary output of a decade ruled by mass media. A great deal of *Manfredo*

THEREZINHA BARBIERI

Rangel's originality and inventiveness stems from the recurrent appropriation of resources from a wide range of discursive practices.

In the list of literary innovators influenced by film, Rubem Fonseca is undoubtedly a critical figure. The influence of film stems not only from his work with the medium as a scriptwriter, but also from the cinematographic syntax he employs in his short stories and novels. His familiarity with the language of film led him to present his 1994 novel, *O Selvagem da Ópera*, in the form of a script waiting to be filmed. The author explains this decision towards the beginning of the book:

> This is a film, or better yet, the text of a film that takes opera as its subject matter. The main character is a musician once praised and beloved by all, who has been forgotten and abandoned. It is a film which asks whether someone can become something they aren't. It is a film that talks about the strength needed to do something and the fear of failure.[12]

As early as his first collection of stories, *Os Prisoneiros* (1963), we can see the hallmarks of his narrative style. This style reveals an obsession with adapting visual images to literature. His style also involves the frequent use of cuts and montage. The juxtaposition of fragments for the purposes of analogy or contrast and the insertion of abrupt ellipses that punctuate the discontinuity of action are common techniques of the author's narrative economy. Readers familiar with his works can identify, in these forms of expression, traces of a brutal language appropriate to the raw material that the author collects from the criminal underworld, as well as from the highest social circles, where violent perversions lay hidden. This refreshing form of expression—one that he constantly reinterprets—first crops up in the fifteen short stories that make up *Feliz Ano Novo* (1975), each one in itself a good example of Fonseca's cutting sense of humor. There are traces of this technique even in his earliest efforts, but over time Fonseca perfects this process, gaining the clear control over the means of expression that his mature work evinces. "Duzentas e Vinte Cinco Gramas" illustrates this point. The story depicts the cruel coldness of a lawyer who, after repeatedly turning over the body of a young girl who has been murdered, starts to tear apart her body. Suddenly, like a butcher, he throws some of the organs he has wrenched out on a scale to illustrate, in a metonymic fashion, the work of the narrator, who is always immersed in bits of shocking material, which he pulls from a shattered corpse and rudely exposes to the reader. An affinity with film is even more evident in the title story "Lúcia McCartney" (1970), in which bits of different discussions, of telephone conversations, of love letters, and flashes of encounters and misencounters occupy the narrative space as literary alternatives to the cinematic techniques of cut and montage. Referring to the plurality of voices "that melt together, alternate, and confuse" in the work of Fonseca, Boris Schnaiderman places particular emphasis on "A Opção," which appears in the book *A Coleira do Cão*:

> In addition to the speeches of each character, an interior voice in confrontation with the voices of the culture arises, warped in one place or another by quotation. The voice of the narrator is abruptly cut off at the end of the story, as if to demand the reader's collaboration in interpreting the outcome. And the entire narrative unfolds in short cuts, marked by the voices of different characters.[13]

Allow me to add, from the vantage point in which I am situating my reading of these texts, that in addition to working with the notion of polyphony, Fonseca employs *poliedolia*, that is, phonic images that come coupled with visual ones. There is perhaps no better work in which the author refines this mixing of sound and image than his story "Olhar," which appears in the collection *Romance Negro* (1992). Littering the text with allusions to writers and composers, to musical and literary works, the narrator parades a train of visual images in front of the reader, each one accompanied by classical music, offering clues to the complex movement of the plot. Narrated in the first person, the story's point of view neatly shifts from subjective considerations to a detailed description of the world of objects. Representing himself as a classical writer interested in bibliographic rarities, the character-narrator builds a literary-musical wall around himself that protects him from crude contact with the world at large. Having discovered an "interesting synergy between music and literature," he spends his days at home writing or "listening to music and rereading Petrarch, or Bach and Dante, or Brahms and Saint Thomas Aquinas, or Chopin and Camões."[14] He thinks of film as a lesser art—a "cultural manifestation incapable of producing a true classic" (62). Yet the great project of his life is to break the cycle of educated alienation, which he describes as "sublime fruition," and enter into communion with his animal side. This shift from contemplative passivity to instinctive activity, or this descent from culture to barbarism (in Schnaiderman's terms) takes place through the gaze. "Art is hunger" (65), Dr. Goldblum has told him pointedly, just before inviting him to dine at the city's best fish restaurant. It is not the restaurant itself, but rather "an enormous aquarium filled with blue trout" (65) that becomes the node for redirecting the arc of this polite character's trajectory, for transforming this lover of the classics. Suddenly, at the precise moment in which his gaze crosses that of a fish that "swam more elegantly than any of the others," he is touched by a sense of novelty. From that moment on, his life is split between the ritual of the classics and the pleasures of the table. Yet the only dishes that whet his appetite are those prepared with the flesh of animals that, before being killed, engage in a moment of profound communion, eye-to-eye, with their devourer. Pleasure, formerly found in "sublime fruition," is now located in the satiating of impulsive appetites. And it is the visual senses that are compromised by this change. The gaze thus falls from the ethereal level at which it has hovered to the solid ground of instinctive acts. As the narrative progresses, the gaze turns patently perverse and, at its climax, it freezes on a blood ritual—the slaughter, skinning, and evisceration of a rabbit. This scene, in all its sadomasochistic glory, takes place in the bathroom to the tune of Beethoven's Ninth Symphony. The synergy between music and literature is here transformed into a transgressive celebration, into the cacophonous collision of the sublime and the cruel. The scene's elements—the setting in a bathroom, the cruel sacrifice of the rabbit, and the musical score of Beethoven's Ninth—result in a shocking montage of dramatic impact. In this expressive synthesis of aesthetics and dissonance, this piling up of misplaced objects, "Olhar" denounces the cultural conditions that, in the West, destroyed harmonious human development by privileging only the conceptual senses (vision and hearing). At the same time, it signals the sense of modernity contained within Fonseca's prose, which, through an aesthetics of shock, aims to arouse the numbed sensibility of our time. In fact, I would go so far as to say that in this story the novelist offers a devastating critique of Western culture, historically implicated in the mythification of the civilized gaze through a pattern of behavior that stretches from the ancient classics to the present day. Between a gaze fetishized by the shadows at the back of Plato's cave and a gaze hypnotized by shadows dancing around the rectangular box of the television lie fifteen centuries of theory and praxis around images. Nothing better could be found to denounce the erosion of values implicit in the intellectual perversion of our time than the banalization of Mozart's celebrated *Symphony 41*, "Jupiter," used as table music ("Tafelmusik") while the educated man seasons and heartily eats the rabbit that he has sacrificed and stewed.

Saturated by films and videos, photos and TVs, cartoons and animation, billboards and neon signs, "posters and graffiti," culture in the age of techniques of mechanical reproduction has given rise to the expression "the age of the image." This label, forced and sustained acritically by mass forms of communication, requires some explanation. In seeking to discuss literary fiction as it has been contaminated by cinematic language, I have sought to point out the captive presence of the visual image in literature of this period. However, I do not mean to suggest that this aspect by itself explains the complexity of prose fiction, nor that it serves as the exclusive index for all texts produced during this time. Certainly, the ubiquity of the image has provoked critical and theoretical reflections for a long time, given the primacy of the visual to the twentieth century's various means of communication. What most interests me about this topic, however, is the way in which film has influenced changes in the mode through which texts are accessed and in the means through which they disseminate and interact with readers. In his seminal essay "The Work of Art in the Age of Mechanical Reproduction," Walter Benjamin pinpoints film's role in changing an audience's relation to a text. Establishing a parallel to Freud's works, Benjamin notes, "For the entire spectrum of optical, and now also acoustical, perception the film has brought about a similar deepening of appreciation."[15]

If, Benjamin suggests, the techniques of reproduction as applied to the work of art as art "chang[e] the reaction of the masses towards art" (688), it can easily be imagined how much this affects an author's imagination. Edgar Telles Ribeiro's *O Criado-mudo* (1991) provides a good example of this interaction of different languages. Through an emphasis on detail, the narrative's four characters capture the reader's gaze, as if a camera were pointed right at them. Statements and commentaries by writers about the influence of film on contemporary fiction are relatively clear. Italo Calvino, for instance, under the title of "Visibility," dedicates the fourth of his five *Lezioni Americane (Six Memos for the Next Millennium)* to the fundamental role of the visual image in the process of literary invention.[16] Confessing himself to be enthralled by film, he refers to the productive activity of the imagination that he calls "mental cinema" as the human mind's trans-historical mode of perception. He cites verse 25, canto XVII of Dante's

Purgatory, "Poi piovve dentro a l'alta fantasia" ("Then rained down into the high fantasy") and questions the signification of images that, in the context of Dante, form themselves directly in the author's mind.[17]

This digression to Calvino offers a scheme under which the production of images described by an author, bombarded by images on all sides, can be visualized not only from an historical perspective, but also from the context of the possibilities present. The idea of a mental cinema that predates the invention of film brings the visual image back to its real source: the imagination. Greek philosophy's distinction between "phantasm" and "fantasy"—one being the image and the other the faculty that produces it— brings the most diverse manifestations of the imaginary back to a common source, in accordance with the theories of Jean Starobinski.[18] According to this perspective, intersemiotic exchange is the agent that revitalizes the literary, in that it diversifies and enriches the languages of our era. The works discussed above provide a clear demonstration of this process.

I would now like to return to João Gilberto Noll. He seems to write while glancing over his shoulder at film, rearticulating word and image through the creative imagination. The language of the stories that make up *O Cego e a Dançarina* (1980) imprints on the written text the presence of neon signs, films, striptease shows, TV and radio programs, video games, and the like. "Marilyn no Inferno" is one of the stories in which word and image are intertwined. Here, the author works with characters without depth; he imagines a protagonist drawn from the first Western filmed in Brazil— indeed, the main character of this short story is an extra (*"figurante"*) of the movie. The Baixada Fluminense simulates the prairies of Arizona, and, in the same tableau, mixes together stars from Hollywood, Eisenstein, and Kung Fu: "The guy casually raised the shotgun and wounded the blue sky of the Baixada Fluminense" (36). The director recalled Eisenstein and wanted to make it an homage to the Soviet moviemaker. Daydreams become coupled with childhood memories, with what the child loved to hear:

> ... the uncle also loved to tell stories about Hollywood stars, like do you know how film directors there treat stars? Shit, Bette Davis got slapped in the face, she left the shoot all red when she forgot her lines or couldn't get the gesture or the walk right. When they were filming *The Seven Year Itch*, Billy Wilder whipped Marilyn. They say that he tied her to a post and gave her 37 lashes, and she was a real mess, but that's how she learned and made such a beautiful film. (37)

The narrative—a kind of cinematic take without the camera—blends together flashbacks, the brief involvement of the figure from the Western of the Baixada Fluminense, daydreams, and two-dimensional images drawn from posters and magazines, all of which the character wants to use to transform himself. And transformation arrives in the form of a huge billboard at a movie theater in Caxias announcing Kung Fu, the obstacle that strikes the extra, the static image that breaks the boy's body in motion: "Kung Fu against the sword swipes of Damascus, Kung Fu! repeated the little boy, who could not bear so much glory, and he hurled a big gob of spit at the poster, which tore and sent a big jet of blood into Kung Fu's eye" (39).

Imitating the movement of the camera, the speed of the narrative shocks with its static image of a paper Kung Fu felling the toy soldier. The moving body of this extra, provoking an explosion in space, at the same time ends the daydream. In this way, he puts into practice the recycling of used images, one of the alternatives proposed by Calvino. It is not by chance that the scenario for this pastiche is the Baixada Fluminense. For it is there, on the edge of the big city, that tons of images of the poorest quality manufactured for acritical consumption by the masses (deprived of access to liberatory sources of emancipatory energy) get thrown away every day. Indirectly and hyperbolically, Noll's story denounces this situation, creating a simulacrum of alienated deformity out of a cinematic parable. During an interview with the *Jornal de Brasília* on October 31, 1990, Noll responded to a question about film's role in his life and work as follows:

> Film was the great utopian breath blowing against the limitations of day-to-day life for the middle class of my day... At Sunday matinées, you could see there were other worlds out there, other ways to escape from the apathy of the stupid schools we had to attend. It was an escape from our families, too. I immersed myself not only in foreign films, but also in the films of Atlântida.

Autobiographical reminisces help the author to revisit his adolescence, as if these memories were the best way to explain his deepest motives for writing. The passion for film that grabbed hold of the teenager lives on in the referential nature of his fictional œuvre. The reader's interest in following the journey of protagonists who are always in transit conjures memories of scenes of flight and persecution. The writer signals the opportune nature of this type of approach in his final comment in the interview above:

I write wishing I were doing something else: making a movie. There's definitely a cinematic simulacrum in my prose. I am really more interested in making films than in writing literature. The only reason I did not go into film is that it's much easier to write fiction, and anyway I was very shy. But between Antonioni and Thomas Mann, I'll stick with Antonioni. In spite of the fact that Thomas Mann moves me to tears. The poetic charge of the word is just as emancipatory as that of film.

I could probably find no better quotation to end this essay, for in it we find the three keywords that I have made my focus: simulacrum, film, and literature.

Notes

[1] Gumbrecht 10-11.
[2] Santiago 35.
[3] Paz 133-148.
[4] Eco 75.
[5] Wenders, *The Logic of Images.*
[6] Noll, *Hotel Atlântico* 66.
[7] Sant'Anna 9.
[8] Sant'Anna 212.
[9] Sant'Anna 205.
[10] Sant'Anna 187.
[11] Sant'Anna 205.
[12] Fonseca, *O Selvagem da Ópera* 10-11.
[13] Schnaiderman 777.
[14] Fonseca, *Romance Negro* 10-11.
[15] Benjamin 689.
[16] Calvino, *Six Memos for the Next Millennium.*
[17] Calvino 81.
[18] Starobinski, "L'Empire de l'Imaginaire."

Works Cited

Benjamin, Walter. "The Work of Art in the Age of Mechanical Reproduction." *Film Theory and Criticism: Introductory Readings.* Gerald Mast and Marshall Cohen. Eds. 3rd ed. New York: Oxford UP, 1985.

Calvino, Italo. *Six Memos for the Next Millennium.* Trans. Patrick Creagh. London: Jonathan Cape, 1988.

Eco, Umberto. *Six Walks in the Fictional Woods*. Cambridge: Harvard UP, 1994.

Fonseca, Rubem. *O Selvagem da Ópera*. São Paulo: Companhia das Letras, 1994.

———. *Romance Negro*. São Paulo: Companhia de Letras, 1994.

Gumbrecht, Hans Ulrich. "Entrevista." José Castelo, "Caderno Idéias," *Jornal do Brasil*, September 3, 1988: 10-11.

Noll, João Gilberto. *O Cego e a Dançarina*. Rio de Janeiro: Civilização Brasileira, 1980.

———. *Hotel Atlântico*. Rio de Janeiro: Fransciso Alves, 1995.

Paz, Octavio. *A Outra Voz*. Trans. Waldir Dupont. São Paulo: Siciliano, 1993.

Sant'Anna, Sérgio. *Notas de Manfredo Rangel, Repórter (A Respeito de Kramer)*, 2nd ed. Rio de Janeiro: Civilização Brasileira, 1977.

Santiago, Silviano. *Nas Malhas das Letras*. São Paulo: Companhia das Letras, 1989.

Schnaiderman, Boris. "Vozes de Barbárie, Vozes de Cultura. Uma Leitura dos Contos de Rubem Fonseca." Rubem Fonseca. *Contos Reunidos*. São Paulo: Companhia das Letras, 1994. 773-777.

Starobinski, Jean. "L'Empire de L'Imaginaire." *La Relation Critique*. Paris: Gallimard, 1970. 177-181.

Wenders, Wim: *The Logic of Images: Essays and Conversations*. Trans. Michael Hofmann. London: Faber and Faber, 1991.

A Brief Introduction to Contemporary Afro-Brazilian Women's Literature

Maria Aparecida Ferreira de Andrade Salgueiro
Translated by Shoshanna Lurie

Introduction

Afro-Brazilian women have been writing and publishing in an organized fashion for some years and, like African-American women in the United States, have become a group with specific features of their own. However, due to national cultural traits, and in spite of the fact that a large portion of their work has been translated and become the subject of debate for scholars abroad, recognition of their production and literary value has yet to arrive in Brazil.

In poems, short stories, novels, and essays these writers demonstrate a rare sensibility at mastering the written word. In many ways, this literature reflects a generation in search of lost identity, a central theme in modern and contemporary works. This is a group of women who identify themselves as having African descent, not only for ethnic, but primarily for historical and political reasons (Davies 1995).

Taking the similarities and contrasts into consideration as based on historical specificities, many parallels can be drawn between Afro-Brazilian and African-American writers today. In terms of the United States, literary critics unanimously assert that one of the most influential factors in the recognition of African-American literature was the feminist movement. Since the 1970s, African-American women writers have become a powerful force, producing a large number of texts and reaching an ever-growing number of readers. This group includes authors such as Toni Morrison, winner of the Nobel Prize for Literature in 1993, Alice Walker, an important activist during the Civil Rights Movement, and Maya Angelou.

We know, however, that this production is not recent. Literary studies centered on gender theory and familiar with the female literary text have cast light on authors such as Phyllis Wheatley, in the eighteenth century, and Zora Neale Hurston and Nella Larson of the Harlem Renaissance who, in Alice Walker's words, were forgotten due to "contrary instincts." This focus has also been influential in defining a cultural profile of the nation that allows for new paths to be cleared within ethnic studies. In Brazil, this search for earlier voices has lead to Afro-Brazilian authors such as Josephina Alvares de Azevedo, a nineteenth-century playwright. Or, recalling the ever present Simone de Beauvoir: "In this century, women can recover their destiny for freedom through literature" (Gennari). In Brazil, many Afro-Brazilian women writers are engaged in this battle. As representatives of a women's movement with literary expression, they seek to rescue names forgotten by literary history and to prompt the appearance of others, as well as to express emotions squelched, silenced, and oppressed for many centuries.

Writing from the perspective of both a "woman" and a "black," these writers of African descent examine individuality and personal relations as a way of interrogating complex social issues. By analyzing principles such as racism and sexism that are institutionalized not only in society but also within the family and intimate relationships, these authors bring into focus dilemmas that affect everyone, regardless of race or gender. Nevertheless, passing through anger and pain, these writers place the most value on difference, often expressed through a constructive optimism. Difference appears then as an element of construction and growth.

Beyond presenting a voice that has been ignored or little heard, these groups seek to re-evaluate the concept of a literary canon. Groups (re)organize themselves in society, and this panorama is obviously reflected by cultural production. Literature positions itself under the aegis of a new profile. Groups who had until now been considered lacking in literary production begin to come forward, and raise awareness of a previously unknown text, or one that was considered lost. In a 1974 interview, Toni Morrison stated that one of her greatest goals was to contribute to the creation of a canon of African-American works. Always producing literature and emancipatory polemics that seek to make up for lost time, Morrison discusses these topics in her text *Playing in the Dark: Whiteness and the Literary Imagination* (1992).

This concept is strongly framed by politico-cultural issues. At a historical moment when "globalization" is being debated, when the number of nationalist rebellions and struggles is rising, and when the very notion of *nation* according to traditional parameters is being severely questioned, it is not surprising that the notion of canon is also being challenged. In the United States and Brazil, for various intrinsic and specific reasons, but with a similar backdrop, we are witnessing a great turning point that sheds light on and values literatures of an "Afro" origin.

In Brazil, in addition to Afro-Brazilian women who are publishing more and more of their writing in an organized fashion, we have the systematic publication of the annual journal *Cadernos Negros*. Since its founding, the journal has alternated between editions of poetry and prose; it has survived and progressed, and has contributed significantly to the dissemination and expression of both male and female Afro-Brazilian writers. Today, *Cadernos Negros* is a basic reference for the analysis of this literature and mandatory reading for any researcher in the field.

Within this panorama of re-vision, though fairly different from the North American case due to differences in our colonization processes and the nationalities involved, one should note that in a masked or latent, implicit or explicit form, the question of race is still only apparently resolved in today's Brazil. In reality, it is an issue loaded with emotion and prejudice.

Names that have entered into "official" literature are often studied without reference to the ethnic origin of the author. When some reference is made there is usually no analysis of the subject from a contextual, cultural, or historical point of view, as if no difference existed that could lead to cultural enrichment. Specific examples can be found in Castro Alves, Olavo Bilac, Aluísio Azevedo, Machado de Assis, Cruz e Souza, and Lima Barreto. And it should be well noted that no women are included in this list. In truth, the presence of blacks in Brazilian Literature does not escape this marginalizing treatment, and when they are mentioned, as Proença explains, it is either in "literature *about* blacks, on the one hand, and (more recently visible), *black* literature, on the other" (159).

Following the international trend of extensive discussions on ethnicity, Brazil today is discussing the concept of "racial democracy" and its myths. After the broad debate that preceded the 1995 tricentennial of Zumbi—the leader of "Palmares," the largest fugitive slave village (*"quilombo"*) in colonial Brazil—it has become clearer that racial democracy is possible only with social democracy. African-American and Afro-Brazilian women have paid close attention to these issues since the 1970s, in conjunction with the Black Movement efforts in Brazil and in the United States.

These activities begin with the apparently most "simple" things, such as the terms used to designate ethnic issues. In contemporary Brazil, the word *negro* is frequently used to place value on color and race. The term *afro-brasileiro* has also begun to appear. Darcy Ribeiro, a contemporary Brazilian writer, anthropologist, and politician, even used this term in his work *O Povo Brasileiro*, written shortly before his death in 1997.[1]

The current historical moment in Brazil is similar to the experiences of blacks in the United States. Government gestures, affirmative action, black media, and celebrities seek change through their own initiatives. Groups are organized around different topics related to black culture, many events revolving around discussions related to the black population occur within and outside of universities, and the question of formal education for blacks is widely discussed. Currently, the polemical discussion of quotas for black students in public universities is occurring in the National Congress in Brazil. This is complemented by different cultural manifestations in music, record production, art, theater, and the press with the monthly publication of *Raça Brasil: A Revista dos Negros Brasileiros*—this last being strongly influenced, even in its title, by North American models. All these elements together are slowly creating a new environment that attempts to be specifically Afro-Brazilian.

Afro-Brazilian Women Writers

Authors including Conceição Evaristo, Miriam Alves, Esmeralda Ribeiro and Lia Vieira have been translated and published in works such as the one organized by Carol Boyce Davies, *Black Women, Writing and Identity* (1994). Sonia Fátima da Conceição and Geni Guimarães are also part of this group, which is being increasingly solicited to present their work and to have their texts translated abroad. Elisa Lucinda, who has begun to do public shows in Rio de Janeiro, is slowly gaining popularity in Brazil and in the rest of the world. Actually, this phenomenon is typical of Afro-Brazilian literary production. These are writers who, because of the attention they receive abroad—being frequently invited to give talks outside their country and to sign contracts for translations of their work— feel much more recognized abroad than in Brazil. It is only slowly that their production achieves a Brazilian audience.

Some common traits of the authors mentioned are their professional/political activities; their consistent presence in *Cadernos Negros* since the 1980s, not only in publishing and collaborating in the editing process, but also helping in its distribution, which has earned some of them very good reviews abroad; the invitations they receive to participate in and talk at meetings and seminars on women and literature inside and outside of Brazil. Moreover, while remaining completely unknown in Brazil, their works are frequently translated. Finally, these authors develop their own reflections on the issue of black or Afro-Brazilian literature.[2]

Maria da Conceição Evaristo de Brito, one of the most important representatives of this group, was born in 1946 in Belo Horizonte, the capital of the state of Minas Gerais. She is a teacher in the city public schools, and has worked for some years at the José Bonifácio Cultural Center—a public city agency for the rescue and dissemination of African-Brazilian culture, particularly that specific to Rio de Janeiro. The center is also a cradle for the activities of the Black Movement. At the cultural center, she is responsible for writing statements, pamphlets, and for disseminating material regarding information on African-Brazilian culture chosen for exhibition and other public events.

Conceição Evaristo is noteworthy for having consistently published in *Cadernos Negros* since 1989. Her literary work, now beginning to be recognized, is divided into published poems and short stories, as well as an unpublished novel. She narrates black women's day-to-day problems with a distinctively feminine perspective. She writes fully utilizing poetic and cultural references, seeking strong historical moments for a culture that is in the process of reconstructing itself.

Miriam Alves is known for her poetry and also for her excellent work in editing and distributing the beautiful bilingual anthology of poetry entitled *Enfim Nós/Finally Us: Contemporary Black Brazilian Women Writers.* According to Caroline Durham, a North American scholar who wrote the introduction, the work "is an important step on the path to present a collective literary vision to the reading public of the Americas" (23). In several texts, Alves challenges the stereotype of the black woman's passivity.

Esmeralda Ribeiro asserts that Afro-Brazilian women can reveal their true selves through literature, and stresses that writing can also challenge negative, stereotypical, and distorted images presented by both past and current male writers, such as that of the "sensual *mulata*."

MARIA APARECIDA FERREIRA DE ANDRADE SALGUEIRO

In *Marcas, Sonhos e Raízes,* Sonia Fátima da Conceição stresses the idea that literature is an instrument in which critical liberating strategies for spreading the voice of black people can be taken advantage of. In this work, Sonia seeks to recreate the atmosphere in black organizations, dealing with the difficulties and conflicts that arise from the struggle for a world without violence and discrimination. The author follows the development of situations through the gaze of a male character, who finds himself trapped by the habits of sexist behavior.

Geni Guimarães stands out for her production of two powerful books of short stories, *Leite do Peito* and *A Cor da Ternura.* In addition, the author has written beautiful poems and children's stories, and some of her work has been translated into German.

Conclusions

Authors of short stories, a few novels, many poems, and essays—this is undoubtedly a production of great value, originality and literary innovation, in search of Brazilian traits and roots. There is no doubt that the study of an emerging literature with African features will significantly aid in the understanding of culture within a contemporary perspective that includes ethnicity.

The themes of motherhood, tradition and identity are only three of the topics approached by these contemporary Afro-Brazilian women writers. The effects of race, gender, and class become evident in the interpretation of these topics. Creative, affirmative, and subversive elements expressed in their works are forms of resistance directed against racism and sexism.

By creating their own history in their struggle, Afro-Brazilian women writers retrace black Brazilian women's minds and hearts, and over time establish themselves as mandatory references in the panorama of their country's contemporary literature. Always combating discrimination, African-American and Afro-Brazilian women writers adopt specific and distinct strategies in their struggle. Nevertheless, there are recurring commonalities, solid and effective personal trajectories that unite them and have an impact on the literary scene. For example, utilizing the art of the written word, they have forced a re-discussion of the canon, a definitive contribution to universal literature for the feminist movement and for the struggle for human rights, whether in Brazil or in the United States.

Notes

[1] Darcy Ribeiro. *O Povo Brasileiro: A Formação e o Sentido do Brasil.* São Paulo: Companhia das Letras, 1995.

[2] For instance, Conceição Evaristo Brito discusses the use of the adjectives *negro* and *afro-brasileiro* in her master's thesis *Literatura Negra.*

Works Cited and Suggestions for Further Reading

Alves, M., ed. *Enfim ... Nós / Finally ... Us: Escritoras Negras Brasileiras Contemporâneas / Contemporary Black Brazilian Women Writers: Dual Brazilian-English Poetry Anthology.* Trans. C. R. Durham. Colorado Springs: Three Continents Press, 1995.

Bhabha, H. K. *Nation and Narration.* London: Routledge, 1993.

———. *The Location of Culture.* London: Routledge, 1994.

Brito, M. C. E. *Literatura Negra: Uma Poética de Nossa Afro-Brasilidade.* Master's Thesis. Pontifícia Universidade Católica do Rio de Janeiro, 1996.

Butler-Evans, E. *Race, Gender, and Desire.* Philadelphia: Temple UP, 1989.

Cadernos Negros 12: Contos. São Paulo: Quilombhoje, 1989.

———. 13: Poemas. São Paulo: Quilombhoje, 1990.

———. 14: Contos. São Paulo: Quilombhoje: Edição dos Autores, 1991.

———. 15: Poemas. São Paulo: Quilombhoje, 1992.

———. 16: Contos. São Paulo: Quilombhoje, 1993.

———. 17: Poemas. São Paulo: Quilombhoje/ Editora Anita, 1994.

———. 18: Contos Afro-Brasileiros. São Paulo: Quilombhoje/ Editora Anita, 1995.

———. 19: Poemas Afro-Brasileiros. São Paulo: Quilombhoje/ Editora Anita, 1996.

Callaloo 18.4. (1995).

Carrol, P.N., and D. W. Noble. *The Free and the Unfree: A New History of the United States.* New York: Penguin Books, 1984.

Conceição, S. F. *Marcas, Sonhos e Raízes: Novel.* São Paulo: Quilombhoje, 1991.

Davies, C. B. *Black Women, Writing and Identity: Migrations of the Subject.* London: Routledge, 1994.

———. Ed. and intro. *Black Women's Diasporas.* Vol. II of *Moving Beyond Boundaries.* London: Pluto Press, 1995.

———. and M. Ogundipe-Leslie. Eds. and intro. *International Dimensions of Black Women's Writing.* Vol I of *Moving Beyond Boundaries.* London: Pluto Press, 1995.

Durham, C. R. "The Beat of a Different Drum: Resistance in Contemporary Poetry by African-Brazilian Women." *Afro-Hispanic Review* (Fall 1995): 21-26.

Fanon, F. *Les Damnés de la Terre.* Paris: Éditions La Découverte, 1968.

———. *Peau Noire, Masques Blancs.* Paris: Éditions du Seuil, 1975.

Gates Jr., H. L. *Figures in Black: Words, Signs, and the "Racial" Self.* New York: Oxford UP, 1989.

———. *Loose Canons: Notes on the Culture Wars.* New York: Oxford UP, 1993.

Gazola, A. L. A. Ed. *A Mulher na Literatura.* 3 vols. Belo Horizonte: UFMG, 1990.

Gennari, G. *Simone de Beauvoir.* Nouvelle Édition Revue et Completée. Paris: Classiques du XXᵉ Siècle, 1958.

Groden, M. and M. Kreiswirth. Eds. *The Johns Hopkins Guide to Literary Theory and Criticism.* Baltimore: The Johns Hopkins UP, 1994.

Guimarães, G. *Leite do Peito.* São Paulo: Fundação Nestlé de Cultura, 1988.

———. *A Cor da Ternura.* São Paulo: FTD, 1989.

Morrison, T. *Beloved.* 1987. New York: Plume, 1988.

———. *Playing in the Dark: Whiteness and the Literary Imagination.* 1992. New York: Vintage Books, 1993.

———. *The Bluest Eye.* 1970. New York: Plume, 1994.

Novais, F. A., coord., and L. K. M. Schwarz. Ed. *Contrastes da Intimidade Contemporânea.* Vol. IV of História da Vida Privada no Brasil. São Paulo: Companhia das Letras, 1998.

Proença Filho, D. "A Trajetória do Negro na Literatura Brasileira." *Negro Brasileiro Negro: Revista do Patrimônio Histórico e Artístico Nacional* (IPHAN) 25 (1997): 159-177.

Ruthven, K. K. *Feminist Literary Studies: An Introduction.* Cambridge: Cambridge UP, 1990.

Tindall, G. B. and D. E. Shi. *America.* 2nd ed. New York: W. W. Norton, 1989.

Walker, A. *In Love & Trouble: Stories of Black Women.* San Diego: Harcourt Brace & Company, n.p., 1973.

———. *The Color Purple.* 1982. New York: Pocket Books, 1985.

———. *Meridian.* 1976. New York: Pocket Books, 1986.

Down with Tordesillas!

Jorge Schwartz
Translated by Nöel de Souza
Revised by Mark Streeter

… children from the same continent, almost of the same land, hailing from the same peoples, in short from the same race, or at least from the same cultural background. We, Latin Americans, share great common interests and live, slightly more than others do, but indifferent to each other, ignoring one another almost totally.

Words of welcome addressed by José Veríssimo to Rubén Darío, on the occasion of his visit to the Academia Brasileira de Letras, in 1912.

Continentalist rhetoric has increasingly utilized the term "Latin America." But does Brazil, the "sleeping giant," continue to be ignored by the critics that seek to look at the literary works of the continent in an open-minded fashion? Are Mário de Andrade's words from April 1928 still relevant? He said that "in the huge corner of South America, Brazil stands immense and alien."[1] Perhaps, if we extend the statement and interrogate Brazil's position in the *corpus* of Latin America's literary critical discourse. It is worth recalling César Vallejo's words from 1926:

> Latin America. Two words, which in Europe have been and are exploited in all manners imaginable of ruthless ambition: Latin America. It is a name that you can put up and take down, from one boulevard to another in Paris, from one museum to another, from one magazine to another, be it merely literary or in-between. In the name of Latin America they gain wealth, fame and prestige. Latin America lends itself to speeches, verses, tales, film festivals with music, food and beverages and Sunday entertainment. In the name of Latin America plundering is on the

rise by European officials who exploit the humilities of an America they can boast about while propagating a senseless folklore and archeology and offering decorative aphorisms of a cheap sociology. In the name of Latin America the perilous diplomatic role of oratory is practiced, rife with flattery at banquets and anniversaries, for the benefit of the dazzling lions of European politics. These two words lend themselves to all of this. They are greatly used by all those who cannot do a thing on their own, except hang on to their country of origin, to events gone by and to family ties.[2]

Obviously, Vallejo here was very far from thinking of Brazil's problematic integration into Latin America. But he did capture the timely use of the term, and it is possible that he was a witness to its use in Paris during the 1920s, when he wrote this piece. I am prompted yet to wonder how far Brazil finds itself today from the conditions described decades ago by Mário de Andrade and César Vallejo.

Without dwelling on the historical issues, which explain the existing cultural chasm between Spain and Portugal,[3] I would like to mention at the outset the classic language problem that makes Spanish more accessible to the Brazilian reader than Portuguese to the Hispano-American reader. This is one of the barriers that has kept the Hispano-Americans away from reading works written in Portuguese. Save a few exceptional cases, the literary critics of Brazil have shown much greater interest in their neighbors' literature than have the latter shown for Brazilian literature. It has only been since the middle of the twentieth century that you find any Hispanic intellectual who showed the same all-encompassing and systematic interest that José Veríssimo, Mário de Andrade or Manuel Bandeira devoted to the literatures of the continent.

Mindful of this problem, Emir Rodríguez Monegal, who always swam in both waters, stated that "cultivated Brazilians are far more familiar with Hispano-American literature and read more of it than do their Hispanic colleagues of Brazilian literature, due to their laziness (or their inability) to find out if indeed Portuguese is truly hard to read."[4]

Alfonso Reyes is a case in point. He scarcely benefited from his experience as a diplomat in Brazil in terms of a closer exchange with Brazilian literature. During the four years he was in Rio de Janeiro as the head of the Monterrey *Correo Literario de Alfonso Reyes* (an erudite periodical published entirely in Spanish), he devoted an extremely small space to

Brazil. His experiences were nothing more than anecdotal or personal, and Brazil hardly exerted any influence on his thinking. Even so, there were some exceptions, such as the implicit dialogue between Sor Juana and Padre Vieira, for instance, bringing to light one of the keenest and most controversial aspects of the Mexican poetess; the obvious influence of Góngora and Quevedo in Gregório de Matos' work, the greatest Brazilian Baroque poet; or the presence of Latin America in *O Guesa Errante* by Sousândrade. These writers nonetheless did not bother with creating a literary system. (As Antonio Candido points out, this is a process that was not to take place until the nineteenth century.) At the present moment it is not of any particular interest to examine these rare examples of literary intertextuality between the literatures of the Spanish and Portuguese languages. What I am seeking is to provide a critical reflection on the place Brazil occupies in Latin America.

We also need to remember that as of 1850, when attempts were being made to distinguish a Latin American culture from an Anglo-American one, Brazil was a monarchy surrounded by republics. In contrast, most of the Spanish-speaking countries had begun their independence process in the early decades of the nineteenth century accompanied, almost without exception, by movements affirming a national language. Thus, besides the linguistic and cultural differences, there was a huge political rift.

As a concept applied to political and literary matters alike, the term "Latin America" emerges for the very first time in 1836, in an article by Michel Chevalier, and was vigorously taken up by the Colombian writer and diplomat José María Torres Caicedo (1827-1889). Torres Caicedo was a staunch champion and the greatest disseminator of the term in the second half of the nineteenth century, in particular through his book *Unión Latinoamericana* (1865). His work was exhumed from oblivion by the Venezuelan Arturo Ardao who defends Caicedo's ideas in the seminal *Génesis de la Idea y el Nombre de América Latina* (1980), and commits himself, *inter alia*, to correct the error—today almost a myth—of the term "Latin America" as having been coined and spread by the ideologues of Napoleon III as a justification for the invasion of Mexico.[5] Further, in the extraordinary *América Latina en su Literatura* (1972), the organizer César Fernández Moreno encountered difficulties in forming an opinion about the term: "Latin America, although an undefined entity, is one that presents at first glance the consistency of the real."[6]

From an Hispanic point of view, I can mention the works of Arturo Torres-Ríoseco (*Nueva Historia de la Gran Literatura Iberoamericana,* 1945) and Pedro Henríquez-Ureña (*Historia de la Cultura en la América Hispánica,* 1947). These two works, without a shadow of a doubt, are forerunners. In both of them one notes an approach in which the totalizing intention prevails in its special emphasis on the diachronic. Torres-Ríoseco's work devotes a separate chapter to Brazilian literature, but at least does not ignore it. The Dominican critic Pedro Henríquez-Ureña makes a stupendous effort at integration, drawing our attention to the definition with which he opens his work: "Hispanic America, which is currently known by the name of Latin America, today covers nineteen nations. The one that speaks Portuguese, i.e. Brazil, is the largest in terms of surface area. Eighteen speak Spanish."[7] Pedro Henríquez-Ureña's words may give the impression that he was opposed to the Pan-Americanist or Latin-Americanist set of political and social ideas, since Brazil was the last country in the region to become part of the continental panorama and has remained under the heading of Hispanicism. In fact, he is making use of the most traditional sense of the Roman concept of Hispania, equivalent today to Iberoamerica.[8]

These initiatives continued into the following decades in the works of Emir Rodríguez Monegal and Ángel Rama, who put together a project likely to integrate Brazil into the continental parameters. The two major Uruguayan critics first had the advantage of living in a bordering country. Given the extraordinary differences that stood between them, it is surprising that they became the contemporary Hispano-American critics who took so much interest in Brazilian literature. Monegal spent a better part of his youth in Brazil, which made it easier for him to understand the language. The integrating qualities of the author's critique stands out in almost all of his work; this is clear to see in the list of contributors to the famous *Mundo Nuevo,* published in the 1960s and, especially, in the *Borzoi Anthology of Latin American Literature.* As for Ángel Rama, the original intention of his extraordinary editorial project—the "Ayacucho Library Collection"—was to incorporate literary works of Brazil. Although Rama came to know Brazilian literature after Monegal, in 1954 he had already published an article on the "Nueva Poesía Brasileña."[9] Ángel Rama is also regarded as one of the first, if not the first, to make a comparative study of the Argentine avant-garde movement—"Martinfierrismo"—with the Brazilian modernism of 1922, in an article with the encouraging title "Las Dos Vanguardias Latinoamericanas."[10]

The most important thing today is to shed light on those critics who, as Lezama Lima said, constructed "a bridge, a huge bridge you can't see" ("*un puente, un gran puente que no se le ve*").

*

In the early decades of the twentieth century, José Veríssimo was the most informed Brazilian intellectual about the social, historical and literary issues in Latin America. Albeit a contemporary of Manoel Bomfim and Sílvio Romero—who fueled the fierce debate in their books with the same title, *A América Latina*, published in 1905 and 1906 respectively—, Veríssimo's approach is completely different from theirs. His historical knowledge of the political development of countries such as Argentina, Mexico, Venezuela and Paraguay, as well as his keen political understanding, always helped him to strike out against the Monroe Doctrine. And he maintained an engaged and vehement position, without in any way sliding towards the impressionism of the time. Veríssimo also distinguished himself from his predecessors by jettisoning the racist or evolutionist theories, which Bomfim and Romero were still applying. Of all of the intellectuals at the beginning of the twentieth century, he was undoubtedly the one who was following the literature of the Hispanic countries the most closely. There was already a conception of a "*Latin American literature*" with a continentalist vision, which openly assumed the rhetoric of "We, Latin Americans," and which drew early attention to the processes of mutual exclusion existing between Brazil and its neighbors:

> I've already had the opportunity to confess my ignorance of Hispano-American
> literatures. I believe that in all fairness it is true of all my companions, albeit men
> of letters. I've also said that this ignorance is reciprocal; that is to say, the other
> Hispano-Americans (I say the others because we too are Hispano-Americans,...)
> are also ignorant of our literatures.[11]

Of Veríssimo's seven articles on literature collected by João Alexandre Barbosa in *Cultura, Literatura e Política na América Latina*, three refer to Argentine literature. Whether due to geographical proximity, or to the intellectual quality of its works, Argentina was the country that aroused the most interest amongst Brazilians. In this regard, Veríssimo did not limit his praise for Bartolomé Mitre and Paul Groussac, the latter being director of the National Library in Buenos Aires and editor of the *Anales de la Biblioteca*. He was an equally avid reader of José Ingenieros, one of the most important Argentine thinkers and writers of the nineteenth century. It was José Veríssimo's task to record the translations into Spanish of *Inocência* by Taunay, *Canaã* by Graça Aranha, and *Esaú e Jacó* by Machado de Assis that were made by Roberto Payró at the beginning of the twentieth century. Veríssimo's level of information and his ability to keep up-to-date is indeed striking. Only Mário de Andrade, Brito Broca and Manuel Bandeira were able to achieve a similar vision in the decades to come.

*

A voracious writer, tireless bibliophile and keen correspondent, Mário de Andrade always insisted on keeping abreast of what was happening in the literature and arts of the neighboring countries of Brazil, in particular Argentina. Perhaps full of anarchistic ideals and global confraternization, Mário de Andrade rejected any defense of nationalism in the name of universal values. This is why he also rebelled against the idea of Latin America: "But any and all spread of the concept of motherland, which does not include all of humankind, appears obnoxious to me. I 'loathe' this much talkabout *Latin America* today."[12] In spite of this statement, Mário de Andrade was one of the pioneering scholars of this integrative vision. His amazing essays on Argentine literature, published in 1927 and 1928 in the *Diário Nacional* of São Paulo, provide a fair understanding of his grasp of the entire Argentine literature of the time. It is indeed he who, to a certain extent, lends continuity to José Veríssimo's integrationist thought, and he who also was able to express early and correct opinions, such as "Borges appears to me to be the most outstanding personality of Argentina's modern generation."[13] Nothing, however, attracted him more than the comparison Brazil/Argentina, São Paulo/Buenos Aires. Mário was interested in a comparative work of cultures, almost a thesis in social anthropology. He insisted on a difference based on the *social psychology* of the Brazilian, as opposed to that of the Argentine, Peruvian or Mexican. He did not neglect the geographical diversities, showing the profound differences between the impact on the cultural imagination of sterile regions like Patagonia and of the lush Amazon region that was a source of inspiration for *Macunaíma*. Furthermore, Mário de Andrade looked at the different qualities that define the Brazilian and Argentine ways of speaking. His literary considerations are suggestive of a writer who was well-informed about the intellectual pulse of the bordering country.

*

An avid reader and literary critic, with the chronicle as his preferred genre, Brito Broca published seven essays under the title *Americanos* (first series, 1944) with the publishing house Guaíba of Curitiba. Currently, the Brito Broca collection of the University of Campinas—at the "Alexandre Eulalio Cultural Documentation Center" (CEDAE)—has a second series, also composed of seven articles.[14] (It is not known if they were organized by Brito Broca himself or by Alexandre Eulalio.) Besides these, there are approximately a dozen other articles of a similar theme published in Rio de Janeiro in the 1940s under the heading *Latin American Literature* and, subsequently, *Pan-American Literature*, in the newspapers *Cultura e Política* and *A Manhã*. It is important to know that Brito Broca's continental vision is extensive, including authors such as Walt Whitman, James Fenimore Cooper and Mark Twain. Although the emphasis is on the Hispano-Americans, Brito Broca's literary excursion is a true exercise in comparative literature. While the tone is impressionist, descriptive and anecdotal, his intuition enables him to draw accurate literary parallels. What is stunning is the number of readings the critic offers; after José Veríssimo, it is Brito Broca who most explicitly claims an integrationist cultural policy in the continent.

In his readings of various authors, Brito Broca gave special importance to geographic space over language as a differentiating form of expression. This explains his fascination for the Argentine pampas in the texts of W. H. Hudson, Ricardo Güiraldes and Benito Lynch, for the Colombian wilderness in *La Vorágine* by José Eustasio Rivera, and for the Colombian hinterland in *María* by Jorge Isaacs. This very predilection for geography prompted him to describe Latin American literary works from Paris ("A Sedução de Paris"), highlighting the Guatemalan Enrique Gómez Carrillo's chronicle and placing him as a counterpoint to the Brazilian writer João do Rio: Broca found more color and vibration in João do Rio's style, according to him, unquestionably more artistic than Gómez Carrillo's.

By tracking the interest Brazilian intellectuals showed for Hispano-American literature, Brito Broca highlighted the role played by the modernists, in particular Ronald de Carvalho, in the poems of *Toda América*. As the critic suggests, the first Argentine novel translated into Portuguese was *O Mal Metafísico* by Manuel Gálvez. He also stressed the importance of Monteiro Lobato in spreading Hispano-American literature through the *Revista do Brasil* and the "South American Library," in which were published

JORGE SCHWARTZ

Facundo by Sarmiento and *Nacha Regules* by Gálvez. Moreover, in 1947, under the pseudonym Miguel P. García, Monteiro Lobato is said to have published in Buenos Aires the didactic and political novel designed to promote Perón's five-year plan, *La Nueva Argentina*. Brito Broca also kept records of the visits made to Brazil by Miguel Ángel Asturias and Horacio Quiroga. The latter, author of *Cuentos de la Selva* and *Anaconda*, was the target of a funny greeting by Lobato, during the tribute paid to him in São Paulo by various writers; Brito Broca recalled that

> [Lobato] called him a friend of snakes, the greatest *cobraphile* until then known. Living with them in the land of *Misiones*, raising them with love, as soon as [Quiroga] got to São Paulo, his first question was: 'Where is Butantã?,' i.e. the 'Instituto Butantã de São Paulo' for snakes, ophidia, etc. 'Those of us who knew of this craze of his,' said Lobato, 'would try to throw a snake party.' Tables wrapped in anacondas, viper waiters, rattlesnake broth, rat snake sausage, omelet made of jararaca eggs and various bottles of antidote.

The most important journey undertaken by Brito Broca was to Buenos Aires and La Plata in 1947. It led to lively interviews with Roberto Giusti, Eduardo Mallea and Benito Lynch. Although the critic's readings indicate a tendency for settling literary scores, his appreciation of Jorge Luis Borges appears watered down and indirect. Thus, as with most Argentines, he too became aware of Borges' work only through the French:

> There is at the present moment in Argentina a very original writer of great merit, whose work has been much appreciated in France: Jorge Luis Borges… In Brazil, who knows him? Who reads him? Except for my friend Alexandre Eulalio, more and more in love with the spiritual refinement and poetic humor of books such as *Historia de la Infamia*, I reckon only two or three extravagant persons know his work, since it still happens to be more or less exceptional for one of us to get interested in a Hispano-American writer. [15]

It does seem odd that, twenty years after Mário de Andrade introduced Borges to the Brazilians through articles in the *Diário Nacional*, Brito Broca should exclude Mário from his panorama of Latin-Americanists and rediscover Borges via Europe. In a creative reading of the relations between Brito Broca/Alexandre Eulalio/Borges, Davi Arrigucci Jr. highlights the "[inability] of an appropriate critical recognition of the great writer and his true position vis-à-vis the tradition from which he arose," and describes this dialogue as "ghost talk."[16] In fact, when Brito Broca visited Buenos Aires, Borges had already published not only *Ficciones* but also various books of poetry and essays.

*

The path that was opened by José Veríssimo, followed ten years later by Mário de Andrade, and productively tracked by Brito Broca, comes to a moment of extraordinary expressiveness in Manuel Bandeira. Bandeira distinguishes himself in various ways from his predecessors, in particular by the professional character of his studies. Bandeira taught Hispano-American literature at the Federal University of Rio de Janeiro from 1943 to 1956, and he was the first to disseminate Hispano-American literature in Brazil *in a systematic fashion*. Among these works, the two editions of *Literatura Hispano-Americana* (1949 and 1960), and the *Três Conferências sobre Cultura Hispano-Americana* (1959) are worth mentioning. Bandeira also succeeded in crossing a huge publishing bridge with his *Panorama de la Poesía Brasileña* (1951), published by the Mexican publisher Fondo de Cultura Económica.

Although called *Literatura Hispano-Americana*, the book is far more than that. It includes a broad reading of the culture of Latin America from the pre-Colombian manifestations up to Bandeira's contemporary poets and essayists. It is quite astonishing to think that, in spite of the 27 chapters chronologically organized, this chronology is subject to a very individual taste. The book is likely to hold our attention on even the most diverse subjects such as "Os Primeiros Colégios e Universidades: A Introdução da Imprensa," or on the chapters fully devoted to his favorite chroniclers, poets, playwrights and essayists (such as Garcilaso de la Vega, Sor Juana Inés de la Cruz, Juan Ruiz de Alarcón, Andrés Bello or Rodó). In this regard, Bandeira dwells on the many different types of literary genre that constitute Hispano-American literature— from the narratives of the discovery, baroque and modernist poetry, to contemporary criticism. If Bandeira's work is erudite, startling with its number of readings and amount of information, it is not cumulative, sterile or tiring, and almost seems like an encyclopedia. His criticism is extremely opinionated, yet he scarcely makes qualitative mistakes in his assessment. For example, when dealing with the baroque poets, he exalts the poetry of Sor Juana. On the other hand, Bandeira asserts that "the terrible quality of the Mexican Gongorists is abundantly documented in the *Triunfo Parténico* by Carlos de

Sigüenza y Góngora… Their poetry is worthless."[17] His taste for comparative work and desire for a Latin American literary policy is evident in the opening of the chapter, "Literatura do Descobrimento e da Conquista": "just as the *Carta* of Pero Vaz de Caminha begins the Portuguese-language literature in Brazil, the *Cartas-Relaciones* of Columbus initiate the Spanish-language literature in Hispano-America."[18] Similarly, he compares the Peruvian poet Caviedes to Gregório de Matos: "Caviedes was the incarnation of Lima's spirit; he became the shaker of many a hornet's nest in the Society of Lima through his disabused and mordant satires."[19] Yet another of his moments of critical daring was to consider Herrera y Reissig to be of better quality than Rubén Darío: "he was Uruguay's greatest poet, one of the most original voices of Hispano-American poetry, considered by some to be substantially stronger and more genuine than that of Darío himself."[20]

Bandeira also informs the reader that the important Argentine novelist of the nineteenth century, José Mármol, author of *Amalia*, lived in Rio de Janeiro for two years, between 1843 and 1844: "Here he wrote the major part of his long poem *El Peregrino*, a kind of American *Childe Harold's Pilgrimage*, with a song entirely devoted to Brazil."[21] Another surprising presence in Rio de Janeiro during the nineteenth century is that of the Argentine poet and journalist Carlos Guido y Spano:

> At the age of thirteen [in 1842], he came to Rio de Janeiro, where his father served as a diplomat. Guido y Spano succeeded in mastering the Portuguese language, into which he translated Lamartine's *Raphael*. In Rio he took part in the Romantic Movement and his prestige in our literary circles can be judged by the fact that Gonçalves Dias, already famous and four years older than him, should have asked him to write a preface to *Últimos Cantos*.[22]

Unlike earlier critics, Bandeira also includes the most important Hispano-American female voices in his wide-ranging repertoire. He earned the honor of being the first to earnestly divulge the name of Sor Juana de la Cruz, decades before she became fashionable as a feminist. Moreover, he described her as a "feminist nun" in 1949.[23] Perhaps due to his relationship with Gabriela Mistral, who was a personal friend during his official stay in Rio de Janeiro, Bandeira includes the most expressive voices of women's poetry of the early decades of the twentieth century—Mistral herself, Delmira Agustini, María Eugenia Vaz Ferreira, Juana de Ibarbourou and Alfonsina Storni.

The authors Bandeira has commented on are indicative of his awareness of the best avant-garde poetry of the continent. In this regard, major Nicaraguan poets are mentioned, such as Salomón de la Selva, José Coronel Urtecho, Pablo Antonio Cuadra, Vallejo, Huidobro, Neruda and Carrera Andrade. Bandeira also became familiar with Afro-American poetry through the voices of Nicolás Guillén, Emilio Ballagas and Palés Matos.

Bandeira also knew the *Martinfierrista* generation, mentioning the manifestos and magazines, as well as the very important Mexican generation surrounding the magazine *Contemporáneos*. But here he makes two serious errors. First, he did not articulate the relationship between these movements and the Week of 1922, where he played an active role; second, he virtually ignored the presence of Borges, who had already published various books of poetry, essays, *Ficciones* and *El Aleph*. Bandeira was very close to Mário de Andrade and Alfonso Reyes. Both, in turn, knew the Argentine writer. Nevertheless, the only reference to Borges is odd: "A young Argentine poet who then lived in Madrid, Jorge Luis Borges, born in 1900, on returning to Buenos Aires in 1921, began the promotion of 'ultraism' among his fellow countrymen..."[24]

If, on the one hand, it is surprising how little attention he gave to Borges, on the other hand, the special importance given to Mariátegui is pleasing: "America has prematurely lost in José Carlos Marátegui (1891-1930) one of its strongest and noblest personalities."[25]

Unlike José Veríssimo, Mário de Andrade and Brito Broca, Bandeira did not give any special importance to the Argentines. They are nonetheless duly represented and compared in the continental description attempted by the author of *Libertinagem*.

*

Manuel Bandeira's chair at the Universidade Federal do Rio de Janeiro (UFRJ) was succeeded by Bella Jozef, author of *História da Literatura Hispano-Americana*.[26] It has been reissued several times and is an essential textbook for Brazilian students of Hispano-American literature today.

Raúl Antelo belongs to the new generation of critics committed, as I am, to eliminating the line of Tordesillas. An Argentine residing in Brazil, bilingual and bicultural, his work, *Na Ilha de Marapatá: Mário de Andrade lê os Hispano-Americanos* (1986), is dedicated to the readings that Mário de Andrade made of the Hispano-Americans. It's a kind of ideological snapshot of the time, based on readings, marginal annotations, clippings and correspondence by Mário de Andrade with the Hispano-American world. Antelo also demonstrates how the selective process of the São Paulo writer influenced his poetic works. Far from confining himself to the Hispanic material in the work of Mário de Andrade, Antelo shows us the Brazilian presence in Hispanic America. For instance, it includes two rare reviews by Borges of 1933: one of *Versos* by Paulo de Magalhães, and another of *Nordeste e Outros Poemas do Brasil* by Ribeiro Couto, as well as an article by María Rosa Oliver, published in *Sur*, on the occasion of Mário de Andrade's death. This work has some continuity with the essay "*Macunaíma*: Apropriação e Originalidade," which was published in the critical edition of *Macunaíma* in the collection "Archives," and in which Antelo learnedly reveals the Latin American roots of the novel.[27]

Davi Arrigucci Jr.'s work escapes any simple categorization, in particular his brilliant work on Julio Cortázar—*O Escorpião Encalacrado* (1973)—, unfortunately inaccessible to the Hispano-American public not so much because of the enigmatic title but rather because of the fatality of having been written in Portuguese.

Antonio Candido and Haroldo de Campos today represent the two major pillars of the integrative discourse of cultures in Brazil. Both have incorporated into their reflections the literary and critical works of Hispanic America. In his classic essay "Literatura e Subdesenvolvimento" (1972), Antonio Candido weaves together relations that are founded on the ties of mutual cultural dependence, the awareness of underdevelopment and the importance of models in order to finally bolster regionalism and integrate it with a super-regionalism. His criticism, as defined by Davi Arrigucci Jr., clearly

> . . . defends and demonstrates through analytical practices the legitimacy of the historical point of view in the study of literature, without abandoning an aesthetic perspective. The latter cannot be mistaken, in his view, with any reductive formalism, and seeks to address the work as reality itself, without however losing sight of human, psychic and social reality, to which the former relates, without being confined to it.[28]

Besides his critical work, Antonio Candido has distinguished himself for having favored integrationist cultural policies and projects in the past decades, to which I will return shortly.

Haroldo de Campos already favors *topos* over *chronos*. Inspired by Eliot, Jakobson and Borges, his theoretical construction is based on a synchronic poetics.[29] In "Superação das Linguagens Exclusivas" (1972), expanded and published in Brazil as *Ruptura dos Gêneros na Literatura Latino-Americana* (1977), the founder of Concrete Poetry crosses the frontiers of aesthetic categories: the merging of poetry and prose (Lezama Lima, Clarice Lispector, Guimarães Rosa, Severo Sarduy), metalanguage (Machado de Assis, Macedonio Fernández, Jorge Luis Borges, Julio Cortázar), or a poetic lineage which points to the concreteness of the poem (Huidobro, Paz, Parra; Drummond, João Cabral and the concrete poets themselves). As one who "transcreates," Haroldo de Campos represents one of the most fecund and creative voices in this dialogue: Sor Juana, Vallejo, Cortázar and the marvelous *Transblanco* by Octavio Paz. Incorporated into this *paideuma* are also Huidobro, Girondo, Lezama Lima and Sarduy.

*

I would now like to mention some of the projects that make Latin America a unified cultural *corpus* that actively includes Brazil.

First of all, the collection of "Latin American Literature" by the Casa de las Américas (Cuba), begun in 1963, is an impressive and pioneering attempt at this integrative vision. The first title is appropriately *Memórias Póstumas de Brás Cubas* by Machado de Assis. Of the 134 titles hitherto published, 33 belong to Brazil.[30]

Second, the already mentioned *América Latina en su Literatura*, published in 1972 with UNESCO's sponsorship, is a forerunner to the scholarship on Latin America as a totalizing perspective of cultures. In the form of essays brought together thematically, the twenty-seven contributions include twelve countries. Sérgio Buarque de Holanda and Afonso Arinos de Melo Franco represented Brazil in various preparatory meetings that began in Buenos Aires in 1969. As a result, four first-rate Brazilian intellectuals were included in the volume: Antonio Houaiss, who dealt with the linguistic plurality of the Iberian countries; Haroldo de Campos, with the already mentioned essay "Superação das Linguagens Exclusivas;" Antonio Candido, with his classic "Literatura e Subdesenvolvimento;" and José Guilherme Merquior, who studied the role of the writer in the continent since the colonial times. For the very first time, a project proposed a coherent attempt to pull down the wall of Tordesillas. The objective is stated explicitly in the introduction by César Fernández Moreno:

JORGE SCHWARTZ

This is why we have requested that everyone collaborate on the project, to try to deal with their works based on this concept of unity. To meet such a request naturally presented serious difficulties, given the traditional lack of communication that has existed among the countries of Latin America, in particular with regard to its linguistic regions: Latin America includes a large area, almost a continent in itself, that speaks Portuguese, and which does not always have a complete vision of what is happening in the Spanish-speaking areas, and vice versa.[31]

As a result of this unifying and interactive proposal, the four Brazilians cast an all-embracing glance over American literatures and languages. But with only a few exceptions, the same cannot be said of their Hispano-American colleagues vis-à-vis Brazilian literature and language.

Third, the "Ayacucho Library" is a project that was designed by Ángel Rama and begun in 1976. With the assistance of Antonio Candido, this collection, which perhaps drew inspiration from the model of Casa de las Américas, significantly incorporates Brazilian literary works. The works translated into Spanish provide those interested with a bridge to Brazilian literature and culture, as do the introductory texts to Brazilian literary criticism.

A fourth and quite different editorial project is the collection "Archives," organized by Amos Segala and also sponsored by UNESCO. Eight signatory countries support the project. It publishes critical editions in original languages and thus with a profile totally different from that of Casa de las Américas or the "Ayacucho Library". Besides looking for the definitive edition of the text, with all its variants, the works are published with a plethora of critical material. Twenty-two countries, including Dominica, Jamaica, Guyana and Haiti, participate in the project. Two facts deserve special attention. First, the collection "Archives," as well as the Casa de las Américas, includes the French- and English-speaking countries of the Caribbean in their concept of Latin America. Second, Brazil is represented by the same number of volumes as Argentina and Mexico, twelve in all. Some volumes have already been released: *Macunaíma* by Mário de Andrade, *A Paixão Segundo G. H.* by Clarice Lispector and *Crônica da Casa Assassinada* by Lúcio Cardoso, for instance. Of all the projects already accomplished, the collection "Archives" has the largest number of collaborators and is the most ambitious and comprehensive.

Equally worth mentioning are two additional projects. The first, conceived years ago by Ángel Rama and Antonio Candido, has three volumes scheduled for the collection *Latin America: Culture, Language and Literature.* It was originally conceived of as a three-volume history of literature with one-third of the compiled essays in Portuguese. Currently, those responsible for the project are Ana Pizarro for the Hispanic part and Antonio Candido, Alfredo Bosi and Roberto Schwarz for each of the parts devoted to Brazil.

The last project is "DELAL": *Diccionario de las Letras de América Latina,* organized by Nelson Osório Tejada, a true encyclopedia with 2200 entries that were written by specialists from various countries and in which Brazil will be duly represented.

Last but not least, I would like to point out that the work of Torres-Ríoseco, Casa de las Américas, the "Ayacucho Library", the "Borzoi Anthology", the "Collection Archives" and the dictionary "DELAL" all place Brazil *next* to Hispano-America. And by next to is meant the literal sense of Brazil *alongside* Hispanic America. It is perhaps utopian to seek a *unified,* intertwined, representation. Some of the critics mentioned in this text have already done so to an extent. At any rate, it is striking that classics such as *Formação da Literatura Brasileira* by Antonio Candido have not been translated into Spanish nor a single book of essays by Haroldo de Campos. It is as if Brazil, to Hispano-American readers, is of interest only as an entry in reference works. If it is true that the Fifth Centenary of the arrival of the Portuguese in Brazil was commemorated in the year 2000, I sincerely hope that we won't have to wait until the twenty-first century for our neighbors to discover Brazilian literature.

Notes

[1] Andrade, "Literatura Modernista Argentina."

[2] *Favorables París Poemas* 2 (Oct. 1926): 14.

[3] Already in 1914, upon making a rough copy of the book by Oliveira Lima, *América Latina e América Inglesa,* José Veríssimo observed: "There isn't in the Portuguese conquest of America anything comparable to the Spanish conquest of Mexico, Peru or Chile. The civil fights here never—thank goodness—were repeated, lasted or saw the same massacres as the Spanish colonies, prior to or after independence."

[4] Monegal 12.

[5] See Ardao.

[6] Moreno 9.

[7] Henríquez-Ureña 7.

[8] Ardao points out: "In its broad acceptance, based on the former application of the Roman name Hispania to all of the Iberian peninsula, Hispano-America—with its variants Hispano America and especially Hispanic America—covers both the Spanish and Portuguese Americas: the American countries of Spanish origin and Brazil" (21).

[9] See *El Nacional,* 17 May 1954.

[10] *Maldoror 9* (1973): 58-64.

[11] Veríssimo 74.

[12] Monegal 74.

[13] Monegal 101.

[14] The following quotes from Brito Broca's essays as well as newspapers reports were obtained in the archives of the aforementioned "Centro de Documentação Alexandre Eulálio" (CEDAE) at Universidade de Campinas (UNICAMP).

[15] See note 14.

[16] Arrigucci Jr., "Conversa entre Fantasmas" 71.

[17] Bandeira, *Literatura Hispano-Americana.*

[18] Bandeira, *Literatura* 15.

[19] Bandeira, *Literatura* 65.

[20] Bandeira, *Literatura* 166-67.

[21] Bandeira, *Literatura* 95

[22] Bandeira, *Literatura* 97.

[23] Bandeira, *Literatura* 63.

[24] Bandeira, *Literatura* 198-99.

[25] Bandeira, *Literatura* 207.

[26] Petrópolis: Vozes, 1971.

[27] *Macunaíma. O Herói Sem Nenhum Caráter* by Mário de Andrade, Critical edition, ed. Telê Ancona Lopez (Brasilia: CNPq, 1988) 255-265.

[28] Arrigucci Jr., "Movimentos de um Leitor."

[29] Campos., "Texto e História."

[30] The first ten Brazilian titles, published in Spanish, are as follows: Machado de Assis, *Memorias Póstumas de Brás Cubas,* 1963 (trans. A. Alatorre); Graciliano Ramos, *Vidas Secas,* 1964 (prologue by José Rodríguez Feo); Carolina Maria de Jesus, *La Favela,* 1965 (prologue by Mario Trejo); José Lins do Rego, *Niño de Ingenio,* 1969 (prologue by José Triana); Carlos Drummond de Andrade, *Poemas,* 1970 (prologue by Muñoz Unsain); Machado de Assis, *Varias Historias,* 1972 (prologue by Antonio Benítez Rojo); Euclides da Cunha, *Los Sertones,* 1973 (prologue by Glauber Rocha); Jorge Amado, *Gabriela, Clavo y Canela,* 1975 (prologue by Adolfo Martí Fuentes); João Guimarães Rosa, *Gran Sertón: Veredas,* 1979 (prologue by Trinidad Pérez Valdés). I thank Silvia Gil for this useful information.

[31] Moreno 17.

Works Cited

Andrade, Mário de. "Literatura Modernista Argentina." *Diário Nacional.* São Paulo. April 22, 1928.

———. *Macunaíma. O Herói Sem Nenhum Caráter.* Ed. Telê Ancona Lopez. Brasilia: CNPq, 1988.

Antelo, Raúl. *Na Ilha de Marapatá: Mário de Andrade lê os Hispano-Americanos* São Paulo: HUCITEC, 1986.

Ardao, Arturo. *Génesis de la Idea y el Nombre de América Latina.* Caracas: Centro Rómulo Gallegos, 1980.

Arrigucci Jr, Davi. *O Escorpião Encalacrado.* São Paulo: Perspectiva, 1973.

———. "Conversa entre Fantasmas (Brito Broca e as Américas)," *Remates de Males* 11 (Campinas 1991): 71.

———. "Movimentos de um Leitor. Ensaio e Imaginação Crítica em Antonio Candido," *Folha de São Paulo,* November 23, 1991.

Bandeira, Manuel. *Literatura Hispano-Americana.* 1949. Rio de Janeiro: Fundo de Cultura, 1960.

———. *Panorama de la Poesía Brasileña.* México: Fondo de Cultura Económica: 1951.

Campos, Haroldo de. "Texto e História." *A Operação do Texto.* São Paulo: Perspectiva, 1976. 13-22.

Candido, Antonio. "Literatura y Subdesarrollo." Ed. César Fernández Moreno. *América Latina en su Literatura.* México: Siglo XXI/Unesco, 1972. 335-353.

Henríquez-Ureña, Pedro. *Historia de la Cultura en la América Hispánica.* México: Fondo de Cultura Económica,1947.

Jozef, Bella. *História da Literatura Hispano-Americana.* Petrópolis: Vozes, 1971.

Monegal, Emir Rodríguez. *Mário de Andrade/Borges. Um Diálogo dos Anos 20.* São Paulo: Perspectiva, 1978. 12.

Moreno, César Fernández. Ed. *América Latina en su Literatura.* México: Siglo XXI/Unesco, 1972.

Rama, Ángel. "Nueva Poesía Brasileña." *El Nacional.* 17 May 1954.

———. "Las Dos Vanguardias Latinoamericanas." *Maldoror 9* (1973): 58-64.

Vallejo, César. *Favorables París Poemas* 2 (Oct. 1926): 14.

Veríssimo, José. *Cultura, Literatura e Política na América Latina.* Ed. João Alexandre Barbosa São Paulo: Brasiliense, 1986.

Victor Meirelles
The First Mass in Brazil
1860
Oil on canvas
268x356cm
Museu Nacional de Belas Artes

Lia Mittarakis
The First Mass in Brazil on April 26, 1500
1980
Acrylic on canvas
1.14x1.44m
Museu Internacional de Arte Naif do Brasil

Nelson Leirner
Land at First Sight (The First Mass)
1983-2000
Mixed media
Museu de Arte Contemporanea da Prefeitura de Niterói

Culture

Politics as History and Literature

Valdei Lopes Araujo
Translated by Marcelo Amorim
Revised by Mark Streeter

The imposing figure of the lawyer, politician and diplomat Joaquim Nabuco almost conceals the writer of the first great synopsis of the Brazilian Empire. When he wrote the biography of Senator Nabuco de Araújo, Joaquim Nabuco simultaneously composed the history of the Empire, of the Emperor Pedro II and of his father.

Born in 1849 to an important family of politicians from Northeastern Brazil, Joaquim Nabuco, similar to most representatives of the imperial political elite, was a landowner's child whose wishes did not find any opposition from slaves or servants.[1] During the first years of his childhood, he was taken care of by his widowed great-aunt. He inherited her estate, which was immediately sold in order to finance his first trip to Europe, between 1873 and 1874. This trip left a deeply impression on him. His European style of dressing, speaking, thinking and writing is definitely established through his activity as an attaché for the Brazilian diplomatic legation, first in Washington and then in London.

Nabuco's European style, partly due to the urban culture influence of Recife,[2] partly due to the impact of his diplomatic life, has not gone unnoticed. He was accused of having his feet in Brazil but his mind in Europe. In the modernist generation of the 1920s, "Nabuco's disease" was a synonym for the Brazilian intellectuals' artificiality and Europeanization.[3] Sérgio Buarque de Holanda, in the opening paragraph of his most influential book, *Raízes do Brasil*, summed up the phenomenon: "even nowadays we are expatriates in our own homeland."

Recent studies, however, have contributed for a better understanding of this polemical issue. Raymundo Faoro has stressed the cosmopolitanism of the author of *Um Estadista do Império*, who was a critical reader of the historiographers of the nineteenth century: Ranke, Mommsen, Curtius, Taine, Burckhardt and Macaulay.[4] In a relevant essay, Evaldo Cabral de Mello stressed that the modernist experience of the 1920s and 1930s, as a cultural phenomenon, has made impossible "our ability to understand the mentality of the average Brazilian of the 'Segundo Reinado' and of the 'República Velha;'"[5] the obsession with national identity would have prevented us from perceiving Nabuco's true cosmopolitanism.

Taking advantage of Mello's powerful insight, we can suggest that the reception of Nabuco's works was decisively conditioned by the cultural discontinuity that occurred between the Monarchy and the Republic. More than a single substitution of political systems, what took place was indeed the questioning of the "place" of Brazil in the "civilized world."[6] If, after decades of a well-thought cultural program, the Monarchy had established a "place" grounded on the continuity with European civilization—a continuity that allowed Nabuco to feel at home in Rio de Janeiro, Paris or London—to the republicans the same "place" had been inexorably lost.

When Nabuco's father died in 1878, his election to the Municipal Legislative Board was already settled among the old senator's political allies. However, in 1879 when Nabuco became a deputy he surprised them by defending the abolishment of slavery. The fight for abolition soon left the Legislative Board, and in 1880 became the "Campanha Abolicionista," the first organized movement of public opinion in the Empire. That movement had men such as José do Patrocínio, André Rebouças and Joaquim Nabuco as leaders.

The 1879 legislative body was dissolved. Therefore, Nabuco had to face election again in 1881, but he could no longer count on his father's allies nor on his party members for support. His defeat then was not a surprise. He became popular with the campaign, but he also neglected the old political mechanisms. Moreover, none of the abolitionists were successful in the election that year.

Whether in his trips to Europe, where he made speeches and took part in international meetings, or in Parliament, to which he was elected in 1885 and 1887, or even as a journalist and writer, Joaquim Nabuco devoted himself, until 1888, almost exclusively to the cause of emancipation.

In 1888, even earlier than Nabuco's most optimistic forecasts, the Legislative Board passed the abolition law. By means of the abolition, another campaign grew stronger: the Republican Campaign. As a defender of Monarchy and parliamentarism and an admirer of the English political model, Nabuco opposed this campaign. He feared that Brazil would become another Latin-American Republic being overwhelmed by civil wars and having its political life ruled by military groups in constant uprising. When the Republic was proclaimed in 1889, Nabuco retired from parliamentary life for ten years, although he kept moderately active working on behalf of the monarchic restoration.

Nabuco returned to public life in 1899, when he promoted the Brazilian cause during the dispute with England over the frontier with British Guyana. In the following year, Nabuco took upon himself the task of leading the Brazilian diplomatic legation in London. The miscarried dispute with England coincided with the opening of the Brazilian Embassy in Washington, for which Nabuco was designated as the first Ambassador in 1905, a position that he held until he died in 1910. In the atmosphere of the Monroe Doctrine, Nabuco's enthusiastic and sometimes naive performance on behalf of Pan-Americanism[7] would initiate the transfer of the Brazilian diplomatic center from London to Washington.

The Emperor died in 1891. One year after that, in a letter, Joaquim Nabuco mentioned the "old" project of writing about his father's life. *Um Estadista do Império* came out in three volumes between 1897 and 1899. The spirit of the book was already visible in its preface, where Nabuco writes: "I was engaged in this preliminary job from 1893 to 1894, mostly during the months of the Revolt when, immersed in the memories of our old peaceful fights, I heard outside the duel between sea and land artilleries in this bay."[8] The book should be not only his father's biography, but also and above all the chronicle of an entire period.

Um Estadista do Império is divided into eight parts. The first six follow chronologically the life of Senator Nabuco de Araújo (1813-1878). The book mainly focuses on the ministerial cabinets, as if political life were the natural measure for organizing the history of the Empire. The seventh part breaks the linearity by introducing three thematic chapters, in which Senator Nabuco's activities as a jurist, lawyer, government adviser and writer of the Civil Code are studied. The general narrative thread is recovered in the eighth, final and privileged part, which deals with the period between Senator Nabuco's death and the end of the Empire in 1889, exceeding the old Senator's lifetime limits, since he died in 1878.

According to Nabuco, the history of the Empire was a picture of the individuals who built the nation. In addition, that account should include the biography of the man who was the center of national life:

> When I write about the life of the Senator Nabuco de Araújo, I provide nothing but a partial view of his time. The main figure of the time is the Emperor himself. Only the one who would write about his life and illustrate it by means of the documents... could bring to a focus, in its convergence point, the *Great Brazilian Era.*[9]

In a letter dated 1894, he lamented not knowing the whereabouts of Pedro II's private archives: "I would like to entirely dedicate myself to the writing of *Dom Pedro II's Life* in the light of the documents he left."[10] Repeatedly Nabuco comments on the privileged position of Pedro II, who, as the center of the political life, had access to all versions of the conflicts between different groups. Moreover, the Emperor had also received letters and documents from different parties and interests. Symbolically and materially, the Emperor stood at the center of the political life. The book, however, offers much more than a traditional political history. When he describes social life, Nabuco resorts to *mechanical* not to *organic* metaphors, as it was common in his time. More than a history book, *Um Estadista do Império* is a work of memory, focusing on an irreversible *temps perdu*.

Senator Nabuco de Araújo's life presents no surprises, for it portrays the imperial political elite: he graduated in Law from the college of Olinda, held public positions in the bureaucratic branches of the Government, became a prosecuting attorney in Recife, Province President, Senator and, at last, Adviser. The life of Nabuco de Araújo followed the standard of the Brazilian political elite, as José Murilo de Carvalho pointed out. According to Carvalho, this homogeneity in education and personal background was one of the main reasons for the political and territorial integrity of the Brazilian Empire, in contrast with the fragmentation that occurred in Spanish America. [11]

It is based on such a background that Nabuco reconstructs the principal events in imperial history, always having in mind the general understanding of Brazil's "Great Era," marked by stability and continuity. Even peaceful ruptures, like the coup d'état that forced the abdication of Pedro I in 1831, are depicted in reconciling tones: "Deep down, the Revolution of April 7 was a friendly divorce between the Emperor and the nation..."[12]

The most troubled period in the imperial history, marked by several political and social uprisings, is thus advantageously changed in favor of the Monarchy. According to Nabuco, such revolts resulted from our first republican experience, namely, the period of the regency dating from Pedro I's abdication, in 1831, to the anticipation of Pedro II's full legal age, in 1840. In his opinion, "if Legal Age did not safeguard the nation… it would have been cast into an abyss."[13]

Nabuco explains that he intended to polish the Empire builders' image: "Maybe I have drawn a picture free of shades, I spoke as highly as I could of everyone, without speaking ill, as others could do."[14] However, that does not prevent the author from having a deep understanding—maybe he was one of the first Brazilian intellectuals to be conscious of this—of the social dimension of some central events in political history. This dimension is perfectly developed in the understanding and analysis of the 1848 "Revolução Praieira," until then regarded as a mere revolt. Nabuco proves to know the social frame of the Revolution. The Praia "Party," after dominating the political setting, Recife, had its attempts to penetrate inward into the Province frustrated by the rural/patrimonial structure, where poor freemen ("*agregados*") gathered around a great landowner by means of personal bonds and favors. The conflicts between the urban world and an inaccessible rural world, together with the retail supply problem in the capital (basically monopolized by Portuguese merchants), are identified as the causes of the popular rebellion: "the 'Revolução Praiera' was composed of these two elements—the foreign and the territorial; more than a political it was a social movement."[15]

However, it is in the description of human types that Nabuco excels. Regarded as a gentleman, Nabuco uses his genius to narrate the successive parliamentarian generations occupying the Legislative Board during the nineteenth century. Elegance and politeness were more than simply social qualities because they demanded discipline and self-knowledge. Moreover they were taken as real social forces, a clear sign of the politician's career and importance. When he describes the arrival of politicians from the Province of Pernambuco at Court in Rio de Janeiro, Nabuco asserts:

> The arrival of the so-called *leões do norte* ("Northern vehement politicians") had always been a social happening. They had a tradition of manners and noble treatment that set them apart from the others in the political world, who generally

> were so careless and neglectful concerning lifestyle and indifferent to gallantry... Politeness and elegance together demand attention at every minute to every gesture, even when they become 'natural.' ... Apathy of manners easily becomes apathy of character and apathy of heart.[16]

The individual is one of the axis of the book. Each personality is part of the secrets of that history and registers, in his speech, his gestures, his clothes, the spirit of every generation, which composes the great panorama of the Empire. Although the figure of Senator Nabuco de Araújo is the one that naturally prevails in the portrayal, some of the most vivid lines are dedicated to other characters, often the Senator's political opponents, as the remarkable description of Ângelo Muniz da Silva Ferraz:

> At the platform, he was a terrible adversary. His words came naturally, easily, abundantly, expressively, steadily, energetically; usually they were common; sometimes, they were fulminating. Because of his style of attacking deeply, exposing himself, he enraptured the spectators. As a passionate, impetuous, sometimes rude and always daring speaker, Ferraz was also of a generous nature and easy to understand.[17]

Nabuco often describes two characters together and outlines contrasts that are either divergent or complementary. Sometimes, using short sentences (which resemble formulas), he deciphers some social structures reflected in his characters. This happens with one of the greatest political leaders from Pernambuco: "Boa Vista was *the* diplomat, the *grand seigneur*, the adorning figure in his provincial Court, which comprised relatives, adherents, hangers-on."[18]

Through his father's eyes, he could revive the dying century that was the conclusion of an era. From the standpoint of the end of the Monarchy, the whole century seemed a progressive disintegration of political generations, although the material progress presumed the opposite:

> The march, the enhancement of the country since 1822 is an unquestionable reality, but who would not feel... that habits present another integrity, life has a different dignity, society has other bonds, character bears another temper insofar as we refer to the past.[19]

Nabuco's nostalgic state of mind has two clearly distinct sources. Nostalgia appears when the liberal regrets the loss of a political system—the parliamentary monarchy—, which he believed to be the only model capable of mediating Brazilian conflicts. Another type of deeper nostalgia appears when he longs for an aristocratic society, whose social relations seemed to be based solidly on tradition. At times, it is almost impossible to dissociate these two types of nostalgia.

Few men are successful in withstanding the passage of time. The continuity between periods, whose generations decayed inversely to the growth of material wealth, is the greatest challenge that Nabuco met in his book. In most cases, the march of time devours the men who remain strongly attached to their own era. That is the case with Antônio Rebouças and Teófilo Ottoni. Regarding Rebouças, Nabuco writes:

Everything in him reminds one of another time, a past and God-forsaken period: spirit, manners, arguments; above all, however, he was a singular nature, that held aristocratic refinement as well as that spirit of equality peculiar to those who possess the same sense of honor and equity.[20]

Regarding Ottoni, Nabuco wrote this well-known comment on the 1860 elections:

If he had not become, as in the words of Disraeli, 'an extinct volcano,' a worn-out man, from other times, who had not renewed his political means since 1831, a novice veteran, looking like a live anachronism in view of the generations educated in a modern way...[21]

In Nabuco's opinion, to think of "political history" was almost a redundant expression, for history and politics become synonyms. Writing the Empire's history was a way to remain politically active, not only through the defense of Monarchy, but mainly by means of the mission of providing the nation with a record of this "Great Exemplary Era." His narrative takes up the task of discovering the truth that survives the passage of time. Only feelings, ideas and lessons remained from that society, of which he was one of the hopes, and which had come to an end. In his autobiography, Nabuco shed light on the mission he took upon himself: "to polish images, feelings, remembrances that I desired to carry in my soul..."[22]

Notes

[1] For the biography of Joaquim Nabuco, refer to Carolina Nabuco, *A Vida de Joaquim Nabuco*.

[2] See Mello, "O Fim das Casas Grandes."

[3] Regarding the usage of this expression by Mário de Andrade, see Neves 278.

[4] Faoro 23.

[5] Mello, "No Centenário de Minha Formação" 13.

[6] Regarding the imperial solution, refer to Mattos 80-101, especially 101.

[7] See Prado, "O Cavaleiro Andante dos Princípios e das Reformas."

[8] Nabuco, *Um Estadista* 31.

[9] Nabuco, *Um Estadista* 32.

[10] Nabuco, *Um Estadista* 1318.

[11] See Carvalho, *A Construção da Ordem*.

[12] Nabuco, *Um Estadista* 66.

[13] Nabuco, *Um Estadista* 67.

[14] Nabuco, *Um Estadista* 1354.

[15] Nabuco, *Um Estadista* 114.

[16] Nabuco, *Um Estadista* 74.

[17] Nabuco, *Um Estadista* 175-76.

[18] Nabuco, *Um Estadista* 403-04.

[19] Nabuco, *Um Estadista* 184.

[20] Nabuco, *Um Estadista* 406.

[21] Nabuco, *Um Estadista* 422.

On the difficult process of modernization of the aesthetic, scientific and moral spheres in Brazil, see Costa Lima, *Terra Ignota*, especially chapters I and V. On the permanence of rhetoric instruction in Brazil, see Acízelo, *O Império da Eloqüência*.

[22] Nabuco, *Minha Formação* 220.

Works Cited

Acízelo, Roberto. *O Império da Eloqüência*. Rio de Janeiro: EdUERJ, 1999.

Carvalho, José Murilo de. *A Construção da Ordem. O Teatro de Sombras*. Rio de Janeiro: Editora da UFRJ; Relume Dumará, 1997.

Costa Lima, Luiz. *Terra Ignota. A Construção de Os Sertões*. Rio de Janeiro: Civilização Brasileira, 1997.

Faoro, Raymundo. "História e Arte." Joaquim Nabuco. *Um Estadista do Império*, 5th ed. Rio de Janeiro: Topbooks, 1997. 21-30.

Mattos, Ilmar Rohloff de. *O Tempo Saquarema: A Formação do Estado Imperial*. São Paulo: Ed. Hucitec, 1990.

Mello, Evaldo Cabral de "O Fim das Casas Grandes." *História da Vida Privada no Brasil: Império*. Ed. Luiz Felipe de Alencastro. São Paulo: Cia das Letras, 1997. 385-437.

———. "No Centenário de Minha Formação." Joaquim Nabuco. *Minha Formação*. Rio de Janeiro: Topbooks, 1999. 9-16.

Nabuco, Carolina. *A Vida de Joaquim Nabuco.* Rio de Janeiro: José Olympio; Brasília: INL, 1979

————. *The Life of Joaquim Nabuco.* Stanford: Stanford UP, 1950.

Nabuco, Joaquim *Um Estadista do Império.* 1897-1899. 5th ed. Rio de Janeiro: Topbooks, 1997.

————. *Minha Formação.* 1900. Rio de Janeiro: Topbooks, 1999.

Neves, Margarida de Souza "Da Maloca do Tietê ao Império do Mato Virgem. Mário de Andrade: Roteiros e Descobrimentos," *A História Contada: Capítulos de História Social da Literatura no Brasil.* Eds. Sidney Chalhoub and Leonardo de Miranda Pereira. Rio de Janeiro: Nova Fronteira, 1998. 265-300.

Prado, Maria Emília. "O Cavaleiro Andante dos Princípios e das Reformas: Joaquim Nabuco e a Política," *O Estado como Vocação.* Ed. Maria Emília Prado. Rio de Janeiro: Access, 1999. 239-66.

Manoel Bomfim: The State and Elites Seen as Parasites of the People-Nation

Roberto Ventura
Translated by David Shepherd
and Tania Shepherd

Manoel Bomfim's *A América Latina*, published in 1905, presents a provocative reflection on the problems of the origins of the countries of South America. Intellectuals at that time chose to blame inferior racial mixtures and the tropical climate for the backwardness of these countries. In contrast, Bomfim discussed the exploitation of the colonies by the metropolis and the exploitation of the slaves and workers by plantation owners by resorting to a concept derived from biology, namely, parasitism. He criticized the Brazilian State as both tyrannical and exploitative and demonstrated the artificiality of an incomplete democracy that merely served to perpetuate the power of the elites. He believed that the lack of democracy would only be overcome by spreading primary education, given that illiterates were not allowed to vote in the elections at that time, i.e., during the Brazilian First Republic (1889-1930).

Manoel Bomfim (1868-1932) was a politician, historian and educator, and one of Brazil's most original thinkers. He was praised by Darcy Ribeiro as one of the founders of Brazilian anthropology for his investigations into the formation of the Brazilian people. He was also considered by Antonio Candido as the most radical thinker at the start of the century, due to his criticism of the elites. Bomfim proposed, together with other radicals, including the abolitionist leader Joaquim Nabuco, a set of ideas and attitudes which provided a counterpoint to the conservative movement which had always held sway. Stemming from the middle classes and enlightened sections of the dominant classes, the radical is, above all, someone who is indignant, who reflects on problems and proposes solutions for the nation as a whole, going beyond class conflicts as Candido exposed in "Radicalismos" (16).

Bomfim was born in Aracaju, the capital of the state of Sergipe. He studied medicine in Salvador, Bahia, and Rio de Janeiro. While studying psychology in Paris, in 1903, he wrote *A América Latina: Males de Origem*. His book was a reaction to the unfavorable view which the Europeans had of South America. Earlier, in 1897, he had manifested an interest in Latin American affairs. He then became Secretary for Public Education in Rio de Janeiro and offered his services as the expert reader in a contest aimed at choosing a book on the history of the Americas to be used in the schools of the Federal District. He wrote a critique of the only work that was presented, the *História da América* (1899) by Rocha Pombo, in which the problems of the Latin American countries were seen as the result of the evil colonial heritage.

In *A América Latina* Bomfim investigated the evils that afflicted the former Iberian colonies of Latin America, explaining them in terms of a parasitism that had been transmitted from the metropoles. He used the book by Rocha Pombo as a source on Hispanic America. He also based his essay on the calamitous vision of Iberian decadence conveyed in the *História de Portugal* (1879), written by the Portuguese historian Oliveira Martins. He was thus among those interpreters of Latin American society who used as a starting point the colonial heritage, adopting a genetic method as a means of explaining the present in the light of the past. .

Bomfim based his description of the relations among the classes and the countries of Latin America on the biological concept of parasitism, taken from botany and zoology. Given his medical training he was able to consult studies by J. D. Vandervelde and J. Massart, who formulated a theory of parasitism in their book *Parasitisme Biologique et Parasitisme Social*. This theory was applied to both biological relations between living species, as well as the social and economic ties among individuals and groups.

For Bomfim, parasitism is the "cause of causes" or the "primary cause," capable of explaining the appearance or the disappearance of nations and civilizations. For him, the eternal struggle between parasite and prey would be, therefore, the principal factor behind historical transformations. He investigated the historical causes of the backwardness of the former colonies of Portugal and Spain in a manner similar to that of a doctor who needs to know the past of a patient in order to diagnose and establish treatment. "The cure depends, in large part, on the importance of this 'historical background'" (Bomfim, *A América Latina*, henceforth *AAL* 22).

Just as in nature there exist parasites which live from other organisms, there are, in society, the dominant and the dominated, masters and slaves, owners and workers, the metropolis and the colony, foreign capital and the nation, the State and the people. Social parasitism would produce the same characteristics as biological parasitism, which leads to the weakening of the organism being attacked, subject to the violence of the parasite, which milks the energy from that organism. But the parasite itself becomes degenerated when its host organisms atrophy, which, in the end, leads to its decadence and extinction.

The "national character," as the sum of the hereditary characteristics, leads to biological inheritance as much as to social education, according to Bomfim. The Iberian parasitism, which derived from the war-like spirit and the plundering tendencies of the peninsular peoples, was one of the features transmitted to the Latin American countries by colonization. This led, in turn, to the brutal process of economic exploitation, resulting in the contempt for the work imposed on the slave, the "victim of victims," who produced the entire wealth absorbed by the metropolis. The idea of hereditary transmission of these psychological traits, however, was contradicted by the proposed pedagogical solution, which advocated a program of popular education, capable of modifying the characteristics of the Brazilian people (Leite 255).

The State was set up as an "oppressive organ" serving the metropolis and had as its function the aim of "taxing, coercing and punishing those who refused to pay the centralized, absolutist and monopolizing government." The State thus became a "reality apart," a "dominating, tyrannical, onerous and almost pointless organization." It was disconnected from the nation and from the interests of the population, organized in order to milk the entire wealth and production of the colony. Alienated from the nation, the State existed solely as a tax collector and organizer of the armed forces, acting as a parasite, feeding on the body it exploited: "it existed solely as an oppressive force to coerce the dominated, the proletarian mass, to produce to the advantage of the dominators" (*AAL* 146).

According to Bomfim, this parasitic role of the State did not change with either the proclamation of Independence, or the introduction of the republican regime. For example, he demonstrated how the 1903 budget included excessive expenses for State institutions and for the armed forces, which had become disproportionate when compared with the miniscule budgets for education and culture. He proposed as a solution the reorganization of the State, which should abandon its "warrior-police function" and assume a protective role in order "to protect individuals against nature, against the natural causes of weakness and misery, against prejudice and against superstition" (213).

In addition, Bomfim attacked the imperialism of the United States. At that moment, US imperialism was extending its influence over Latin American countries in the guise of Pan-Americanism, expressed through the Monroe Doctrine, which prohibited the intervention of European nations in the Americas. This doctrine was viewed sympathetically by politicians and intellectuals, including the Barão do Rio Branco, Rui Barbosa, Joaquim Nabuco, and even rebels such as Sílvio Romero. Bomfim recognized that Pan-Americanism was an instrument used by the United States to expel the European economic presence and establish its own hegemony (Candido, "Radicalimos" 6).

Bomfim ends *A América Latina* with the proposal for a program of popular education, which he saw as capable of achieving political reform by preparing the majority of the population to be active citizens: "We will carry out a campaign against ignorance; there is no other way of saving this America" (400). This educational solution was criticized by Antonio Candido, for whom the book ended with a "disappointing argumentative strangulation," presenting teaching as a panacea, rather than defending the transformation of social and political structures (Candido, "Literatura" 147). Bomfim only rejected this illusion in his final book, *O Brasil Nação*, in which he advocated the need for a popular national insurrection against the ruling classes, the State apparatus and the imperialist nations, in order to bring the excluded groups to power.

Parasites and Prey

Using the notion of parasitism as a starting point, Bomfim created a "biological theory of surplus-value," in which the local elites and the colonial and neo-colonial metropoles are the parasites of the working classes, acquiring for themselves the wealth which the workers produced. By means of this organological conception he attempted to account for the production and appropriation of the value of work, at the internal level of the relations among classes, and in international terms of the links among peripheral countries and imperialist powers. Starting from these biological concepts, Bomfim came to conclusions similar to those formulated by Karl Marx in *Das*

Kapital with regards to the concept of surplus. However, he only came to read the works of the German in the 1920s, while writing *O Brasil Nação*.

The essayist of *A América Latina* destroyed the certainties of the intellectuals of his time by criticizing the use of positivism, evolutionism and racism as models for justifying the dominance of the weak by the powerful. Bomfim also denied progress as a means of giving "definitive guidance" in following predetermined historical stages. He demonstrated how racist theories and the belief in the superiority of the so-called "white races" were linked to the neo-colonial interests of European countries: "science alleged by the philosophers of massacre is science adapted for exploitation." These theories were no more than a "private ethnology for the powerful plundering nations," and the "abject sophism of human egoism, hypocritically masked by cheap science" (*AAL* 278-398).

Before 1910 only a small number of intellectuals, including the literary critic Araripe Júnior and Machado de Assis, attacked the hierarchy among races. Araripe Júnior attributed the racism of European science to the expansionism of the dominant nations, who condemned the non-white and mixed races as a means of "authorizing expansion and justifying the expropriation of poor peoples." For him the racist theories were "packaged sociologies" which "unsuccessfully camouflaged the deeper intentions of the ruling classes and the governments on the opposite side of the Atlantic" (Araripe Júnior, "Sílvio Romero Polemista" 327).

Bomfim also demonstrated the mistakes of the evolutionists who would justify free competition without State interference by means of the idea of natural selection, which the English naturalist Charles Darwin had formulated only for living species. In Bomfim's view, the social Darwinism of Herbert Spencer was no more than an apology for economic liberalism, condemning the benefits of the intervention of the State in the economy. Spencer argued that this intervention would disturb the natural selection and evolution of the human species. In contrast, Bomfim condemned the application to society of biological concepts and Darwinian categories, including the fight for survival and the law of the survival of the fittest: "It is somewhat discredited, within sociology, this tendency to assimilate societies, in every way, and for everything, in terms of biological organisms" (*AAL* 20).

Bomfim attempted to reestablish the original meaning which Darwin himself had attributed to the expression "struggle for existence" in *The Origin of Species*. "I should premise—wrote Darwin—that I use the term struggle for existence in a large and metaphorical sense, including dependence of one being on another" (Darwin 1859, 69). Bomfim therefore concluded that the praise of free competition accredited to evolutionists, in addition to the assertion of innate differences among ethnic groups by the followers of racial theories, were in flagrant contradiction of the naturalist's original ideas: "Darwin never intended that the law of natural selection be applied to the human species, as claimed by the theorists of egoism and plundering" (*AAL* 288).

According to Bomfim, liberal ideology and evolutionary methodology were based on the unacceptable transposition of Darwin's concept of the struggle among species to the social field, which led to the apology for free competition among individuals. In contrast to these arguments of the evolutionists, the struggle between the species would be substituted in society for competition and solidarity between peoples, and could only be applied to society in the figurative sense because of the relations of dependency and cooperation. The author of *A América Latina* thus came close to Karl Marx and Friedrich Engels, who considered the struggle for existence valid solely for other, non-human species. For Marx and Engels, human history is not ruled by Darwin's law, but, rather, by the class struggle, taken as a universal law (Engels, "Discurso" 213).

Although Bomfim conceived of society as an organism, he attempted to investigate non-biological laws, specific to social facts, which he saw as more complex than the biological. He questioned the concept of parasitism by establishing the differences between *organic* parasitism, which brought irreversible modifications in organisms, and *social* parasitism, which could be eliminated by the parasited, e.g., the slaves, the workers, the proletariat, the nation, by means of popular education or rebellion against the various forms of exploitation: "The population could reform their social education, correcting the vices inherent in the parasitic tradition, and thus lead to progress; it is a question of reeducation" (*AAL* 276). By criticizing the identity between nature and society Bomfim avoided the pessimism and the determinism of the environmental, racial and national character theories and pointed to educational or revolutionary solutions to overcome the backwardness in Brazil.

From education to revolution

Manoel Bomfim was the target of a smear campaign following the publication of *A América Latina*. Sílvio Romero attacked him in a series of twenty-five articles in the weekly *Os Anais*, later published in a single volume in 1906 entitled *A América Latina: Análise do Livro de Igual Título do Dr. Manoel Bomfim*. Romero indignantly observed that Bomfim had moved from the field of science into that of personal passions when attacking the racist theories of Gustave Le Bon. Romero believed, in contrast to Bomfim, that the theory of ethnic inequalities was the unbiased result of scientific investigations, and he used this theory in his own literary and folklore studies, found in *História da Literatura Brasileira* (1888) and in *Estudos sobre a Poesia Popular no Brasil* (1888). For Romero, the notion of parasitism was a generic idea, or an unproven metaphor without conceptual rigor that could not serve as the basis for an explanation of political, economic or historical life: "In a certain sense the entire enormous category of existence is no more than an immense chain of parasitism". Romero even called his opponent, Bomfim, "an Iberian-American mestizo," a member of a "band of evildoers of good sense and good taste" (Romero, *A América Latina* 46). This at a time when racial mixture was taken to be synonymous with degeneration.

After the publication of *A América Latina*, Bomfim spent the following two decades teaching, and left aside the historical themes of his pioneering work. He was Secretary of Education for the Federal District, and Director of the Experimental Psychology Institute, in Rio de Janeiro, as well as Editor and Director of the pedagogical journal *Educação e Ensino*. He was elected as a representative of the State of Sergipe. During the second and third decades of the twentieth century he published several works on pedagogy and psychology, including *Lições de Pedagogia* (1915), *Noções de Psicologia* (1916) and *Pensar e Dizer* (1923), in addition to textbooks for primary schools, as for instance *Através do Brasil* (1910), together with the poet Olavo Bilac.

He only returned to writing historical works at the end of the 1920s, when he was already ill. In 1926 he discovered he had prostrate cancer and went through a series of operations until his death in 1932. In a little more than six years he wrote and published three other historical works: *O Brasil na América*, *O Brasil na História* and *O Brasil Nação*. In *O Brasil na América* (1929) he returned to those concepts outlined in *A América Latina*, as a means of characterizing the Brazilian historical process. He used as a starting point those conditions that led to colonialism in Latin America.

In *O Brasil na História* (1930) he dealt with works on Brazilian history, written by both Brazilian and foreign authors. He criticized the depreciation of national traditions made by these historians, including Francisco Adolfo de Varnhagen, author of *História Geral do Brasil* (1855), whose work aimed at describing "a history for the throne," thus defending the dominant interests of the Portuguese court. For Bomfim history was no longer a means of "orienting and stimulating social progress," as this was biased towards the benefit of the elites and the State, ignoring the defeated and excluded (Bomfim, *O Brasil na História* 22). The so-called "universal history" had been developed by the powerful nations aimed at stressing their own greatness to the detriment of the dominated peoples, on whom the same version of history was imposed.

Bomfim ended his historical studies with *O Brasil Nação* (1931), in which he radicalized his proposals to solve the national problems: "It was no longer possible to devise the destinies of this homeland within parameters of normality" (Vol. 1, 7-9). He considered that the Republic (1889) had brought about the "degradation of political habits" and had been converted into a "totally rotten world" by creating "a democracy without people or even citizens," in which no more than a tiny proportion of the population participated in the political and electoral process. He also criticized the 1930 Revolution in which groups from the Southern State of Rio Grande do Sul contested the political hegemony of the States of São Paulo and Minas Gerais. He believed that these incidents failed to change political programs and rulers. Instead of being a revolution, the 1930 movement was no more than a "fermentation of the ruling classes," encouraged by politicians.

In this last work, he abandoned the proposal, presented in *A América Latina*, in which popular education was seen as the salvation of the masses. In *O Brasil Nação*, he wrote: "The remedy for the Brazilian problem is to be found in revolution." Thus distancing himself from his earlier positions, he believed it would be improbable that the ruling classes would lead the popular masses to achieve political sovereignty by means of education. He advocated a socialist revolution by which excluded groups would occupy power, heralding a "holy chaos," capable of transforming Brazil's political structure and redefining its place in the world. According to Bomfim a "true revolution ought to lead to the conquest of power by a class which had never occupied this space, and through this establish a new standard of values" (Vol. 2, 337-71). But his revolutionary program did not move beyond the opposition of people and nation, on the one hand, and the State and the exploiting nations, on the other, and failed to provide concrete proposals for political and economic reorganization.

Bomfim in History

Manoel Bomfim was a precursor of sociologists and historians, including Gilberto Freyre in *Casa-Grande & Senzala* (1933), Sérgio Buarque de Holanda in *Raízes do Brasil* (1936) and Caio Prado Junior in *História Econômica do Brasil* (1945). All these authors emphasized social and cultural rather than racial factors in the interpretation of history and society. Their interpretations were no longer shaped by concepts such as race and nature, but by culture and character (Ventura 66-68). In the preface to *Casa-Grande & Senzala* Freyre observed that his study was based on the difference between culture and race as a means of separating genetic factors from social and cultural influences (Freyre 77-78).

Bomfim's ideas did not have a noticeable impact in his own time, because he disturbed the intellectual and political elites, to whom he attributed the responsibility for Brazil's backwardness, and because of his criticism of the thinking of the then ruling classes regarding racism, evolutionism and positivism. Due to his anger regarding social injustices, his language is full of verve and passion, which he admits in the introduction to *A América Latina*. There he reveals his preference for passion rather than "the varnish of impassiveness." "The passion of the language, which has not been diluted here, reflects the sincerity about which these topics were thought and written" (xii).

This tone of vehemence and passion gave a picturesque quality to his writing, in which Brazil's colonial past and its political independence are seen through an ironic and satirical standpoint. This can be illustrated by his argument that the production system in colonial Brazil can be best described as "a few hundred slaves and a whip." However, his indignation and revolt at social injustices meant that his books, above all, *O Brasil na América, O Brasil na História* and *O Brasil Nação*, written at the end of his life, were emphatic and repetitive. *A América Latina*, his first lengthy work, remained his most outstanding contribution.

Despite the pioneering character of his ideas, Bomfim remained forgotten for many years after his death. His books were not reedited, with the exception of an anthology edited by Carlos Maul in 1935, and a second edition of *A América Latina*. His work was not rediscovered until 1984 through an essay by Darcy Ribeiro, who raised him to the category of the most original thinker of Latin America, and with the anthology edited by Flora Süssekind and myself entitled *História e Dependência: Cultura e*

ROBERTO VENTURA

Sociedade em Manoel Bomfim. Bomfim was read again after 1993 when *A América Latina* was republished, followed by his other books. But the doctor and educator contributed in his own way to the silence towards his work. He had adapted biological notions, including parasitism, which fell into disuse in the human sciences from the 1930s onward, due to the predominance of anthropological, sociological and economic models. Although he pointed out the failure of biological analogies, Bomfim was unable to create a new conceptual system or a new interpretative language capable of moving beyond an organological approach. He based his work, in contrast, on biological categories, including the notion of parasitism, which was used metaphorically. His historic-social stance is thus profoundly ambiguous because of its simultaneous criticism and use of a biological and organological approach as a starting point from which an historical theory of the appropriation of the value of work is proposed.

Works Cited and Suggestions for Further Reading

Aguiar, Ronaldo Conde. *O Rebelde Esquecido: Tempo, Vida e Obra de Manoel Bonfim.* Rio de Janeiro: Topbooks, 2000.

Alves Filho, Aluizio. *Pensamento Político no Brasil: Manoel Bonfim, um Ensaísta Esquecido.* Rio de Janeiro: Achiamé, 1979.

Araripe Júnior, Tristão de Alencar. "Sílvio Romero Polemista." 1898-9. *Obra Crítica.* Vol 3. Ed. Afrânio Coutinho. Rio de Janeiro: Casa de Rui Barbosa, 1963. 271-332.

———. "Clóvis Beviláqua." 1899. *Obra Crítica.* Vol 3. Ed. Afrânio Coutinho. Rio de Janeiro: Casa de Rui Barbosa, 1963. 367- 401.

Bomfim, Manoel. *A América Latina: Males de Origem (O Parasitismo Social e Evolução).* 1905. Rev. ed. Rio de Janeiro: Topbooks, 1993.

———. *Através do Brasil: Leitura para o Curso Médio das Escolas Primárias.* Com Olavo Bilac, 1910. Ed. Marisa Lajolo, São Paulo: Companhia das Letras, 2000.

———. *Lições de Pedagogia: Teoria e Prática da Educação.* Rio de Janeiro: Escolar, 1915.

———. *Noções de Psicologia.* Rio de Janeiro: Escolar, 1916.

———. *Pensar e Dizer: Estudo do Símbolo e do Pensamento na Linguagem.* Rio de Janeiro: Electros, 1923.

———. *O Brasil na América: Caracterização da Formação Brasileira.* 1929. Rev. ed. Rio de Janeiro: Topbooks, 1997.

———. *O Brasil na História: Deturpação das Tradições, Degradação Política.* Rio de Janeiro: Francisco Alves, 1930.

———. *O Brasil Nação: Realidade da Soberania Brasileira.* 1931. Vol. 1-2. Rev. ed. Rio de Janeiro: Topbooks, 1996.

———. *O Brasil.* Ed. Carlos Maul. São Paulo: Nacional, 1935.

Candido, Antonio. "Literatura e Subdesenvolvimento." 1973. *A Educação pela Noite e Outros Ensaios.* São Paulo: Ática, 1987. 140-162.

———. "Radicalismos." *Estudos Avançados* 4/8 (1990): 4-18.

———. "Os brasileiros e a nossa América." *Recortes.* São Paulo: Companhia das Letras, 1993.

Darwin, Charles. *The Origin of Species.* 1859. Cambridge/Mass: Harvard UP, 1964.

Engels, Friedrich. "Discurso Diante da Sepultura de Marx." Karl Marx e Friedrich Engels. *Textos.* Vol. 2. São Paulo: Alfa-Ômega, 1976. 211-14.

———. "Introdução à *Dialética da Natureza.*" Karl Marx e Friedrich Engels. *Textos.* Vol. 2. São Paulo: Alfa-Ômega, 1976. 151-68.

Freyre, Gilberto. *Casa-Grande & Senzala.* 1933. *Obra Escolhida.* Rio de Janeiro: Nova Aguilar, 1977.

Holanda, Sérgio Buarque de. *Raízes do Brasil.* 1936. Rio de Janeiro: José Olympio, 1978.

Leite, Dante Moreira. *O Caráter Nacional Brasileiro: História de uma Ideologia.* 1954. São Paulo: Pioneira, 1976.

Kropf, Simone Petraglia. "Manuel Bonfim e Euclides da Cunha: Vozes Dissonantes nos Horizontes do Progresso." *História, Ciências, Saúde: Manguinhos.* Vol. III, 1 (mar.-jun. 1996): 80-90.

Martins, Oliveira. *História de Portugal.* 1879. Lisboa: Guimarães, 1972.

Marx, Karl. *Das Kapital: Kritik der politischen Ökonomie.* 1867-1962. 4 vols. Berlin: Dietz, 1988.

Prado Júnior, Caio. *História Econômica do Brasil.* 1945. São Paulo: Brasiliense, 1980.

Ribeiro, Darcy. "Manoel Bomfim, Antropólogo." *Revista do Brasil* 2 (1984): 48-59.

Romero, Sílvio. *Estudos sobre a Poesia Popular do Brasil* (1870-1888). Rio de Janeiro: Laemmert, 1888.

———. *História da Literatura Brasileira.* 1888. 2nd. ed. 2 vols. Rio de Janeiro: Garnier, 1902-3.

———. *A América Latina: Análise de Livro de Igual Título do Dr. Manoel Bomfim.* Porto: Lello & Irmão, 1906.

Skidmore, Thomas. *Black into White: Race and Nationality in Brazilian Thought.* New York: Oxford Univ. Press, 1974. Trad. *Preto no branco: Raça e Nacionalidade no Pensamento Brasileiro.* Rio de Janeiro: Paz e Terra, 1976.

Süssekind, Flora, and Roberto Ventura. *História e Dependência: Cultura e Sociedade em Manoel Bomfim.* São Paulo: Moderna, 1984.

Süssekind, Flora. "Introdução." *Manoel Bomfim. A América Latina: Males de origem.* Silviano Santiago (org.). *Intérpretes do Brasil.* Rio de Janeiro: Nova Aguilar, 2000. Vol. 1. 609-25.

Varnhagen, Francisco Adolfo de. *História Geral do Brasil.* 1855. 3 vols. São Paulo: Melhoramentos, 1978.

Ventura, Roberto. *Estilo Tropical: História Cultural e Polêmicas Literárias no Brasil* (1870-1914). São Paulo: Companhia das Letras, 1991.

D. João VI no Brasil

Luiz Costa Lima
Translated by Nöel de Souza
and Mark Streeter

Originally published in 1908, *D. João VI no Brasil* was republished only in 1945. It would be no exaggeration to say that its real merit began to be recognized only after the third edition in 1996. Two factors seem to be responsible for this delay: first, the author's restlessness, his quarrelsome attitude and hot temper. In spite of being a diplomat, Oliveira Lima (1865-1928) was scarcely diplomatic. His temper earned him the animosity of prestigious politicians and of eminent intellectuals at the time of the so-called Brazilian First Republic (1889-1930), namely, Rio Branco and Joaquim Nabuco. This, in a country lacking an established academic and intellectual tradition, could only plunge him into obscurity. Due to intrigues, Oliveira Lima gave up diplomatic service, which had enabled him to conduct research for his works. Having become the subject of satire in the country's capital because of his "corpulent Quixotic body" (Gilberto Freyre), Oliveira Lima preferred to teach at the Catholic University of Washington, to which, in a sort of vengeful act, he donated his library. Finally, he retired to his native city, Recife, in the Northeast, a region that had already lost the economic importance that sugarcane had brought it as well as the political power it had wielded during the reign of Pedro II (1840–1889).

Gilberto Freyre, who claimed to be Lima's "close disciple," was one of the few to defend him, without, however, noting his unique intellectual qualities. As to his foremost work, *D. João VI no Brasil*, Freyre compares what Oliveira Lima had done for the Portuguese King's rehabilitation to "a feat of a Quixote: a Quixote who was ahead of his time in rehabilitating an apparent Sancho Panza" (Freyre 53). In reality, D. João was frequently associated with a caricature figure and a foolish monarch that only the quirks of history could have transformed into the pivotal figure pivotal for the singular manner in which Brazil achieved its political independence. It may be said that for someone interested in defending the historian's work, Freyre could have done more.

There was a second reason for Oliveira Lima's oblivion: between 1950 and 1980, Brazil experienced great political and economic change and at the same time a burst of intellectual activity. The industrialization of the country, which during the Juscelino Kubitschek's administration (1955–1960) made its way through the so-called developmentalist cycle, led to the emergence of populist politics, only to be quashed by the coup d'état of 1964. On the intellectual side, change occurred with the systematic study of Marxism, performed above all by a group of young intellectuals linked to the Universidade de São Paulo. This group, although suppressed (they were expelled from the University and exiled), sharply influenced the national intelligentsia. However, the Marxist approach did not find any affinity with the narrative and political history in which Oliveira Lima excelled. In earlier decades, his greatest book was ignored because of its author's "shortcomings," but later because it offered little aid to economic inquiry, which at the time was highly privileged. Only in the foreword to a recent edition of another of his books, *O Movimento da Independência, 1821— 1822* (1922), did Oliveira Lima receive the long-denied praise for his "narrative history in the best sense" and for his "history based on the similarity of the formation of several colonial centers," which encompass the Deep South of the US, the English and French possessions in the Caribbean and in the Brazilian Northeast, and the highlands of Mexico and Peru, among others (Mello 11, 14).

This praise from the historian Evaldo Cabral de Mello also includes the 1908 book, since its theme, which focuses on the Portuguese king's stay in the Brazilian colony (1808–1821), is developed in a similar comparative fashion. More specifically, it is approached through examination of a large number of intrigues: the fight between Bonaparte and the English interests on the Iberian Peninsula, the new triangulation between England, Brazil and Hispanic America established after his departure, and the role of the Holy Alliance with regards to the slave trade.

Oliveira Lima's comparative approach, however, is not limited to the wide range of fronts on which the author had to operate. It has a more specific outcome: if *D. João VI no Brasil* can be taken as a biography about the central period of the Portuguese king's life, it also has to be seen as a plural biography of not only the prince regent, but an entire epoch, its noblemen and bourgeoisie. The text is a biography and yet also constitutes a heterogeneous and multiple repository of invaluable sources that Oliveira Lima was the first to research systematically: the French consul Colonel Maler's notes, the North American Thomas Sumter's travel diaries, the journals and notes of researchers like Martius, Mawe, Tollenare, Luccock, Koster, Mary Graham, and Luthold, not to mention the data on schemers and gossip mongers such as Filipe Contucci and Luiz Joaquim dos Santos Marrocos. Their reports and letters are considered as precious as the official or unofficial documents written by Portuguese and foreign diplomats about the decisions made either in Brazil or on Brazil and kept in the archives in London, Paris, Washington. The historian, needless to say, did not limit himself to the archives of the Ministry of Foreign Affairs.

And even that extended circle of concerns does not offer the slightest idea of Lima's book. By calling it a multifarious biography we understand that it is so mainly because it proposes to analyze a plurality of subjects. For the sake of brevity, let's confine ourselves to highlighting the following: 1. the situation of Portugal on the eve of the transfer of the royal court; 2. the daily life immigrants faced in Rio; 3. the international situation; 4. the return.

1.

The years that preceded November 29, 1807, the date on which the Anglo-Portuguese fleet departed from Lisbon carrying the Queen Mother, the Prince Regent and his large court, reveal the deplorable situation at which Portugal had arrived. The country had been reduced to the status of "a British trading post," in Oliveira Lima's fine expression, and was threatened by yearning for Iberian unification, which Spain had never abandoned. The meteoric ascension of Bonaparte had left Portugal in a state of calamity. The small and impoverished kingdom had to defend itself against three enemies, two of which, France and England, wished to dominate both Europe and the colonies. Moreover, a series of rather conflicting treaties were signed. The treaty signed in London in September 1793 not only required the Portuguese kingdom to provide ships to reinforce the British armada, but also obliged Portuguese auxiliary divisions to join the Spaniards to confront the French.

LUIZ COSTA LIMA

Besides the "routine" expenses involved in both of these measures, as a result of the agreement the French corsairs caused damage in excess of 200 million francs "to almost everything in the way of cargo coming in from Brazil" (Lima 25). Two years later, in 1795, Spain made peace separately with France. While Portugal attempted to get along with the "Directoire" in France, Spain, a former ally, threatened to punish the little kingdom if it did not declare war on England. In 1797, Portugal succeeded in signing a treaty with France. Nonetheless, alleging the delaying tactics of the Portuguese, the French "Directoire" annulled it, and Portugal was threatened with invasion by Spain. That situation forced Portugal both to turn to the English, accepting the garrison of six thousand British soldiers, and to gather its own squads. Together, they defeated the Spaniards at Cape St. Vincent.

These fluctuating circumstances constituted a blatantly dangerous game, however unavoidable. If, on the one hand, the Napoleonic armies were gaining ground across Europe, on the other it was not new to British policy to undermine rival merchant navies, especially to the detriment of Portugal, which had forged ahead in the conquest of foreign trading posts. No matter which side it might have opted for, Portugal had to face up to a much more powerful enemy. A permanent triangulation was thus formed whereby defeat or loss was only a matter of time. The Portuguese government could do no more than bide its time until the arrival of the conqueror.

In 1806, the situation came to a head. Victorious in the Prussian campaign, scarcely able to bend the English armada, France had decreed the continental blockade. It thus hoped to bring the sea trade of its great rival to a collapse. Not to respect the blockade would, for Portugal, be tantamount to a mere annexation. By the terms of the "Fontainebleau Treaty" of October 1807, the Portuguese kingdom was divided into three parts, with its overseas colonies distributed between France and Spain, and with the Spanish Emperor holding the title of Emperor of the two Americas. However, Spain was no longer a simple pawn in Bonaparte's chess game. In a move that soon would not favor him, Bonaparte invaded Spanish territory, arrested the king and, thus, indirectly triggered the revolt of the Hispano-American colonies. What works to his detriment naturally benefits British commercial interests. No matter how you look at it from the Portuguese point of view, the French invasion of Spain meant that Portugal could no longer afford to waver. The postponement achieved by submission to the English proposal, viz., transferring the kingdom to the American colony, had to be accomplished in the shortest possible period. It is within this critical framework that the court, the Mad Queen and the Prince Regent found themselves rubbing shoulders aboard the Portuguese ships, which, escorted by the British, left for Salvador, and subsequently for Rio de Janeiro. Portugal lost its king in order to keep the sovereignty of the kingdom. In exchange, though of course without the Prince Regent being aware, he arrived in America to lose it. Among the rivals of the moment, France had never been close to conquering it. British trade, on the contrary, seemed to go on comfortably in the midst of the distressed Portuguese noblemen.

2.

First and foremost, *D. João VI no Brasil* is a remarkable diplomatic history. Second, it is a forerunner of what might be described today as an everyday life story. It aims to describe day-to-day living in Rio as experienced by the itinerant court entourage. In both cases, the historian excels as an investigator of archives, a detective out to get reports, official rulings and rare or unpublished papers. The historian uncovers the manner in which court music was organized and how opportunity was given both to musicians brought from Portugal and to local talent, with whom the Prince Regent tried to satisfy his megalomaniacal taste. Considering the human landscape of the streets, Oliveira Lima turns into a verbal Debret, depicting the smells, noises, and shades of nature, and uses travelers' accounts in order to reconstitute the period. Although all of this is valuable (and Gilberto Freyre has been able to explore it better than anyone else), it still lacks the interpretative force of this seminal passage:

> The inordinate distribution of titles was in fact one of the most efficient means used by D. João to involuntarily democratize the royalty, or perhaps to take away its prestige and to weaken it, thus opening that fountainhead and allowing it to run dry in a land where business chiefly hinged upon the favor of the one who called the shots, and where D. João patriarchically ran court society by dragging along within his sphere of influence an entourage of sycophants. (Lima 60)

Although Oliveira Lima sees in D. João an astute and pragmatic character, the historian was unwilling to entertain the notion that making it easy to grant titles was part of some calculated act. Nor was it easy for him to interpret the meaning of D. João's decision. Whence both his description of D. João as "involuntarily" having democratized the royalty and, upon reconsideration, his expression of serious doubts about that same description: "or perhaps took away its prestige and weakened it." D. João's cunning would have consisted of putting an end to the separation of the nobles of the kingdom from the inhabitants of the colony whom, for some contingent reason, he sought to flatter. But with that he would have achieved what he did not foresee, viz., involuntary democratization. With an even less foreseeable result, he took away from the royalty its prestige and weakened it. Thus, in his attempt to get closer to the inhabitants of the colony and, therefore, in a pragmatic fashion, to facilitate his ability to govern under unexpected conditions, he adopted a practice he would already have been familiar with: peddling favors, which resulted in an "entourage of sycophants."

The manner in which the historian grounds his interpretation indicates that the result could not be explained as merely a calculation of the ruler, since the interpreter himself has doubts as to whether the lavish distribution of titles was positive for society. But just as D. João would have to pay a heavy price for his magnanimity (since, without anyone to support him at the moment when he had to return to Europe, he hesitated and lost control of the political situation), so in the same fashion will Oliveira Lima's work come up short, since the historian is not fully aware of where his intuition might have led his interpretation. Is it not this same hesitation that is transformed by Gilberto Freyre into the principle of flexibility, with which the sociologist will interpret the colonial man's behavior vis-à-vis the black man? Is the breaking down of borders not related to the masterful cordiality with which Sérgio Buarque de Holanda saw that a traditional public space in Brazil did not exist? If the term "cordiality" does not appear in Oliveira Lima's work— and this no doubt because the specific sense that the term will assume in Sérgio Buarque depended on a source, Carl Schmitt, non-existent for Oliveira Lima—in him the element that serves as an articulating source is quite explicit: influence peddling. It is influence peddling that underpins the experience of the "cordial man," as described in Holanda's *Raízes do Brasil.*

Regardless of its adequacy, this speculation is based on unquestionable data. Oliveira Lima notices that, through an act of cunning, D. João introduced into the colony a certain confusion as to how people should be treated—inequality coupled with affection, ascending the social ladder without the assistance of a social dynamics. This is something that would become deeply rooted in our social life and something from which, almost two centuries later, we are still not free. Our aim is simply to point out a source that has been overlooked regarding one of the most complicated subjects Brazilian society still faces.

In the same vein, there is another observation. While the historian did not mention the Baroque—which was not a well-understood phenomenon at the time when he wrote his book—it is legitimate to think that, in the religious scene described below, he marked the transformation that the Baroque underwent at the beginning of the nineteenth century in Rio:

> The procession of *Corpus Dei,*... with St. George on horseback, the iron man (*"o homem de ferro"*), riders and horses richly bedecked from the Royal House, black musicians in scarlet vestments, rocket shooters: a palette of opposing colors on skins and fabrics, a gallery of attires of varied styles and materials, an amazing combination of satins and velvets, gold and silver ornaments, rare brocades and garish ribbons. (Lima 597)

What in the seventeenth-century Baroque was a feast for the eyes aimed at both fascinating and disciplining the amazed and stunned subjects, was in Rio at the beginning of the nineteenth century an almost daily theater. What in the Baroque was ostentation and artifice put to the service of absolutism, became in that nineteenth-century society a stimulus to carnival. The rich and spectacular is maintained in sharp contrast with poverty, while also being superimposed upon it. One has the contrast and simultaneous superimposition of wealth and poverty, the overabundance of titles and swarms of slaves. There is no cunning that can explain that outcome.

3.

If, on the home front, D. João's politics surpassed any known form of rationality, there remained the stage of international politics as a means to get him to return to expected attitudes. The fact of being safe from Napoleonic expansionism only made him more desirable for British interests. Thus, if one of his most active collaborators, the count of Palmela, dreamed of taking advantage of D. João's marriage with the Spanish woman Carlota Joaquina and of thereby fostering Iberian unity in America, upon arriving at the signing ceremony for the treaty that recognized the rights of the queen to the throne of Spain (1810), not even England could be blamed for devising such plans. Later Palmela would acknowledge that he had dreamed too loudly: "[The] Lady of the seas... wanted for England to open markets galore"; "the southern continent" was reserved "for the economic expansion of the Anglo-Saxon people" (Lima 188-89). To understand the failed dream as the fantasy of a Portuguese nobleman was no reason, for Oliveira Lima, to be moved by patriotic indignation for his country, although he did explain that, before acceding to independence, Brazil was doomed to future colonization. The same analytical coldness that he assumes in this particular instance does not prevent him from commenting on the Portuguese decision, which would favor the Brazilian merchants. In connection with the opening of the (Brazilian) ports to friendly nations (that is, to British ships), he observes that the decision of the Prince Regent above all favored the Brazilians or those who had settled there. With the decision both the English and the Brazilians would stand to gain, given that "the worst consequence of that measure worked against Portugal since she was not a manufacturing country and consumed relatively few of the colonial goods,… and lived economically off commissions from the freights and the profits from warehousing for other countries" (Lima 137). The objective conditions under which the regent's decisions were made could only harm his own people. This does not in any way mean that they were always favorable to the inhabitants of the colony. On other occasions, the results of such decisions were ambiguous, when not clearly negative for the future of the colony. This is what happened with the public institutions that were transplanted, i.e., "the judiciary, the military, and the schools, which were created with the same drawbacks and problems" that had already been revealed in the metropolis (Lima 136). Likewise, the medical schools did not do well because they were not well staffed and the Military Academy failed to arouse any enthusiasm in a people without a martial past (Lima 163). In a more general manner, the economic initiatives came to nothing. And economic *rationality* did not seem to play a part in the Portuguese court's reckoning. Even the "Banco do Brasil," one of the royal initiatives, was almost ransacked "to help the royal family to return to Portugal" (Lima 245).

4.

Let us reduce the fourth point to a brief reference to D. João VI's return to Portugal. However satisfactory or even pleasant his long stay in Rio may have been, the truth of the matter is that the king was no more than a relatively insignificant pawn on a chessboard commanded by foreign players. So long as Bonaparte was opposed to British interests, D. João would still enjoy certain prerogatives. With the "usurper" defeated, the king more than ever became a subject of England. Thus, when the Congress of Vienna meets, Portugal, just like Spain, will play a very secondary role. The Iberian voice only rants and raves against the idea to abolish the black slave trade. England and her allies emerge as the great champions of human rights. Resorting to the *Correio Brasiliense*, which had always been among his most frequent sources, Oliveira Lima laces his comment with a caustic bite:

> The Congress that led to the Holy Alliance showed keen interest in the natural freedom of the blacks, but failed, in the incisive sentence of Hipólito [da Costa], to show any interest in the natural freedom of the whites of Europe, who were already or were soon to be deprived of the freedom of the press, the freedom to discuss, the freedom of worship and other civil and political freedoms. (Lima 276)

The Iberian reaction was to delay as much as possible the prohibition of the slave trade. As for D. João, he would be pressured to return to Lisbon. Shortly afterwards he would die. The crown prince he had left in his stead soon found it preferable to proclaim the country's independence, rather than bow to the demands of the Portuguese courts that were calling for a return to the old *status quo*. A short time later, he decided to abdicate and fight his brother in order to gain the Portuguese throne. The question of slavery was to continue to live on in Brazil for another sixty-six years (until 1888). The abolition of slavery was to culminate in the decline of the monarchy, which fell the following year, without those freed truly obtaining real freedom. That precarious freedom was to proceed along the same lines as the involuntary democratization and carnivalized Baroque that had been latent since D. João's times. A pawn on the chessboard of international politics, he remained one in the history of the country that would soon become autonomous.

In sum, this is but a brief presentation of an important book, one which our social scientists could, until recently, afford to ignore.

Works Cited

Freyre, Gilberto. *Oliveira Lima, Dom Quixote Gordo.* Recife: Universidade Federal de Pernambuco, 1968.

Lima, Oliveira. *D. João VI no Brasil.* 1908. 3rd ed. Rio de Janeiro: Topbooks, 1996.

Mello, Evaldo Cabral de. "Depois de *D. João VI.*" *O Movimento da Independência. 1821–1822.* 1922. 6th ed. Rio de Janeiro: Topbooks, 1997. 11–16.

Citizenship in Rui Barbosa:
"A Questão Social e Política no Brasil"

Tarcisio Costa

Translated by Paulo Henriques Britto

A few months before the 1919 presidential election, in which he ran against Epitácio Pessoa, Rui Barbosa gave a lecture at Rio de Janeiro's Teatro Lírico titled "The Social and Political Question in Brazil," addressing a working-class audience. In this lecture, a text of major importance in his work, Barbosa proposed innovative approaches to and suggested hitherto unexplored options for political action. He introduced the theme of workers' rights (*"direitos sociais"*) in Brazilian liberal discourse, recommending the establishment of social citizenship together with the modernization of political institutions. My purpose here is to discuss this text as a theoretical essay and a political act as well.

A warning is in order for readers of Rui Barbosa's lecture. There is a startling note in his introduction to the social issues (*"questão social"*) of his day for he presents the defense of workers' rights as an extension of his abolitionist convictions. Barbosa states that there is a continuity between the principles that inspired him in the struggle for the emancipation of slaves and those behind his effort to alleviate the poverty among workers. His defense of abolition emphasized that it was not enough for slave owners to sustain their slaves but that it was just as important to ensure freedmen's social and economic redemption. In this vein, he called for a "second emancipation" that would conclude the task of improving workers' conditions in Brazil (Barbosa, "Questão" 427). It was of utmost importance to respond to the appeals for welfare from the growing number of urban and rural workers. As had been the case with abolition, it was a question of justice that called for a veritable moral crusade, one that should be led by those who made a point of "placing the law before iniquity" (429).

After stating his ambition to be acknowledged as patron of the workers' cause, Rui Barbosa changes his tone. He seems convinced that the honor to which he aspires will naturally be bestowed upon him due to "the consistency of his acts" (430). He no longer points to affinities between abolition and social reform. Instead of emphasizing similarities, he begins to point out differences. True, he reiterates that abolition and the "second emancipation" are subject to "the same moral order of ideas" (430), since both experiences are concerned with the dignification of labor. However, in spite of a common objective, he acknowledges that there are differences between the historical situations, which are "worlds apart" (430) with regards to labor and capital. Capitalists are now less intolerant and more intelligent, and no longer claim "rights against humanity" (*"direitos contra a humanidade"*). Workers, on the other hand, are no longer doomed "to the political and civil death that buried slaves alive" (429).

Although the situation in 1919 was less desperate, Rui Barbosa warned that it nonetheless implied unprecedented requirements. What was at stake now was not simply the attainment of the basic attributes of human rights (*"atributos da pessoa humana"*), but the challenge of promoting workers' economic independence. It was no longer convenient to insist on the defense of a formal contractual freedom (*"liberdade contratual"*) that had characterized liberal discourse during the Monarchy and in the early decades of the Republic. An increase in State participation in social welfare had become necessary. This much was demanded by the "wave of social concern" predominant throughout the world at the time (453), and which had influenced Rui Barbosa as well.

When asked his official opinion about a bill concerning the building of public housing in 1892, Rui Barbosa referred to the social issues as "melancholy, guilty, *ersatz*," and influenced by European historical trends (Barbosa, "Casas para Operários"). The very idea of the State regulating work conditions seemed to him misplaced in Brazil. It might make sense in Europe, he argued, where the disorderly occupation of land already required supervision by the government. But in Brazil, where the population was sparse and natural resources were abundant, quite the opposite was required: unrestrained expansion of private initiative without any State-imposed limits. In a country that had such potential for generating wealth, nothing could be less apropos than controlling the expansion of capital and subjecting it to legal constraints, as socialist doctrine preached.

Those who had been seduced by the language of confrontation between capital and labor, Barbosa believed, should note the evolution in the thought of such socialists as Proudhon, who had undergone a conversion and was now such a believer in the virtue of capitalism that he preached that the right of property should be absolute, even if it implied abuse, for in the long run it would purify itself. Now, if a socialist thinker whose critique of the market was notorious for its virulence had finally accepted the "excellence" of the institution of property, why not expect the same from Brazilian workers, who would have much to gain if free enterprise were left to develop unchecked in the country?

The contrast between such ideas and those Rui Barbosa defended in his Teatro Lírico lecture could not be sharper. The evolution in his thought from 1892 to 1919 was comparable to the change he himself believed had taken place in Proudhon's ideas, only in precisely the opposite direction. Although Barbosa had not become an enemy of property, he now affirmed the "preeminence" of labor over the other factors of production. Quoting Lincoln, he stated that capital was nothing if not the fruit of labor; thus labor deserved "much higher consideration" ("Questão" 426). In addition, such an acknowledgment was taking place in the sphere of the law, for in a number of countries the individualistic view of human rights was increasingly giving way to the assertion of workers' rights:

Society is no longer seen as a mere aggregate, a juxtaposition of individual units. … but rather as a naturally organic entity, in which the sphere of the individual has as its inevitable limit… collectivity. Law is gradually yielding to morality, the individual to the association, egoism to solidarity. (431)

The model Rui Barbosa announces and to which he immediately affirms his allegiance is labeled "social democracy" (431). Based on the social doctrine of the Catholic Church, it allegedly contains features defined on the basis of the socialist experience, or of two antagonistic modes of socialism: "devastating socialism" and "benevolent socialism." The former, reducing as it did social issues to class struggle, was the very opposite of the "ample, serene and sincere" democracy at which it supposedly aimed. Barbosa's model, however, had much in common with "benevolent socialism," in particular a commitment to social equity. Just as relevant to the building of "social democracy" was the socialist experience concerning the regulation of labor:

But [socialism] is also right when... it lays down the foundations of a body of workers' law, in which the absolute freedom of contracts is limited in order to protect the weakness of the needy against the greed of the affluent, restricting the imperatives of capital. (431)

Here, then, is the unambiguous sign of a radical change in Rui Barbosa's thought. The champion of a formal contractual freedom who was instrumental in the 1891 Constitution's prohibition of State regulation of labor relations, now claims that legislators should intervene in order to protect workers from capitalist abuse. He qualifies as "imaginary" the assumption of equality between employers and employees, a principle he has previously affirmed in order to defend contractual freedom and autonomy. He claims that pure contractualism ("contratualismo puro") has had the effect of contributing to the subjection of workers to degrading work conditions, a fact he claims is acknowledged by the League of Nations and advanced countries, including the United States, a nation highly committed to contractual freedom (436). Now, he says, is the time for Brazil to take the necessary steps to conform to "universal juridical conscience" (453). The first of these steps should be constitutional reform, in order to allow Congress to legislate on such social issues without hindrance.

Next, Rui Barbosa enlarges upon a possible social agenda for Congress. He has no pretension of being exhaustive. Rather, he is commenting on "basic points" which seem to him ripe for normative treatment (443). He begins with a discussion of work injury compensation, the object of a bill passed in January of that year (1919) and Congress' first action in the sphere of labor law since the proclamation of the Republic that he considers worthy of note. But Barbosa feels that this law will never be enforced, because it does not specify a deposit or insurance that would ensure compliance. Next, he demands equal pay for both sexes: "equal work, equal pay" (444). The third item has to do with child labor. He proposes that the exploitation of children be outlawed, and that a minimum age and a decent wage scale be established. Also, the number of working hours should be fixed in rural and urban contexts. This should not be left "to the discretion of contracts," which would lead to "the ineluctable preponderance of the stronger party over the weaker" (445). Another proposal is the prohibition or drastic reduction of night work. Barbosa also condemns the practice, common among small factories, of assigning piecework to craftsmen do be done at home, under wretched work conditions and for insufficient pay, because this reduces the worker to "the sad condition of a servant" (445). The next "basic point" has to do with protection of pregnant workers, a subject which, given its social relevance, cannot be consigned to "the whim of interested parties" (446). He concludes his suggestions with a call for control of landowners' practice of forcing workers to buy basic staples from their own stores at prices that ensured indebtedness which he calls a system of "perpetual, slow usury" (446).

Some of Rui Barbosa's proposals show his concern that social legislation should not leave out rural workers, which at the time accounted for more than half of the national work force. It seemed to him unjustifiable that, in an "essentially agricultural country" (439), the law should give preferential treatment to urban workers, particularly when peasants were often submitted to the yoke of "cruel and irresponsible employers" (440).

His defense of workers' rights makes it clear that Rui Barbosa no longer stands for the possessive individualism that characterized his liberal peers. But the text of his lecture also shows that he remained attached to the cause that had until then been his main concern: Brazil's political and institutional modernization. In it, he reiterates the theses on political reform that he had originally presented in his previous presidential campaign (1910), recontextualizing their historical significance and placing them in the service of the affirmation of social citizenship. In this way, he anticipates T. H. Marshall in his study of the evolution of citizenship in England, where social attributes are expected to result from the free and generalized exercise of political rights. Here Rui Barbosa's lecture gains relevance as a political act for its questioning of the authoritarian formula that orthodox Positivism forwarded as a corrective to the institutions of the Old Republic (1889–1930) and as a way to deal with growing social conflict. The general strike of 1917, the outcome of almost two decades of union mobilization, was an unmistakable reminder that the social issues had come to stay. The problem was what to do about it. To Barbosa, the solution was to be found in social legislation, or "legislative guardianship," so long as it was adopted by means of democratic methods, which required reformed representative institutions (453).

At the opening of his lecture, Rui Barbosa vehemently expresses his hope that popular sovereignty will put an end to oligarchy. He calls on the people to combat the stigma of apathy and laziness that the power elite has attributed to them. To him, the "panjandrums" of the Republic assume that they live in a country of "unlimited resignation and docile indifference" whose people are "a riffraff… of born slaves, conceived for the exclusive purpose of obeying orders" (422). Hence the insolence of those who wield political power. Decisions are made with complete disregard for "national opinion" (422). It is high time for the people to become aware of their power and to make it plain that "this is not Brazil" (423), that the country is not to be identified with "ballot riggers" and "fake statesmen" (424). "The people's rediscovery of their own majesty" will not take place by force or civil disobedience, but by vote, in an election that actually reflects the will of voters, quite unlike what has until now characterized political practice in the Republic (424). An example of this was the "electoral swindle" (457) that had led to his defeat in the presidential race against Hermes da Fonseca in 1910. The doctoring of returns and the mechanism of Congressional ratification[1] had robbed him of the presidency. Constitutional reform can no longer be postponed—a theme Barbosa had insisted on in his 1910 presidential campaign, proposing, among other innovations, the prior registration of voters and the secret ballot. He suggested that the possibility of adopting the parliamentary system be discussed, for such a system seemed to him less subject to authoritarian pitfalls than presidential government. In the Teatro Lírico lecture he once again repeats this argument, praising parliamentarism because it allows more space for deliberation and for "moral crusades" such as his present crusade for the regeneration of labor (428).

Rui Barbosa's demands for political reform were squarely aimed at the Positivism that had been espoused by Júlio de Castilhos and his followers. Although in his youth he had been sympathetic to Comte, he had gradually distanced himself from Positivism, particularly from the political current that seemed to have acquired permanent control of Rio Grande do Sul and that was behind Epitácio Pessoa's candidacy. Barbosa referred to *castilhismo* as "the radical offspring of Comtism" (451). What he objected to in particular was the authoritarian tendency of orthodox Positivism, expressed in the State constitution of Rio Grande do Sul by the exacerbation of executive power at the expense of legislative power. Comte's apostles preferred to concentrate normative functions in the hands of the head of government, who was expected to provide the scientific laws that would make Brazil rise to a higher level of civilization—which also implied progress in the social sphere. In the first year of the Republic, the Positivists had suggested—unsuccessfully, as it turned out—that Marshall Deodoro da Fonseca issue a body of social legislation including such items as rights of tenure and limits on work hours. Such measures, it was hoped, would allow the executive branch of government to protect Brazil from any threats to the cohesion between capital and labor that was felt to be indispensable and that was perceived as challenged by the country's transformation into a mass society. Since the 1920s, such authors as Azevedo Amaral and Oliveira Vianna had been busy conferring scientific status on the Positivist platform, publishing works that were to provide the foundations for Getúlio Vargas's labor policy, put into practice after the 1930 Revolution by his Labor Minister, Lindolfo Collor, who had a *castilhista* background. Rui Barbosa would not live long enough to debate with Vianna or clash with Vargas, but he foresaw that Brazilian social policy was not going to be pursued by means of democratic methods, as he desired. He anticipated breaks with the constitutional order: "If I seem to be so concerned with the imminence of disturbances... it is not because I desire such things... but because... I see them looming in the distance, and would like to convince those who promote them that we should all unite against the tremendous danger they contain" (453).

With the victory of authoritarian Positivism, not only were Rui Barbosa's theses shelved but his very image was distorted. He began to be portrayed as an ideologue of the *ancien régime*, an intellectual committed to foreign models—a "utopian idealist," as Vianna wrote (2: 28-29). So much the worse for the history of ideas in Brazil, because an understanding of Barbosa's era was in this way compromised. It became received wisdom that there had been only two forces in the period: oligarchic liberalism and *castilhista* Positivism, with no third way. This led to the conclusion that the hegemony of authoritarian thought was a natural consequence of the exhaustion of belletristic liberalism, or even a historical necessity, dictated by factors cultural (the sheer weight of Iberian statism) or economic (the requirements of the diversification of the productive basis). Historical process was deprived of indeterminacy; the emergence of the "Estado Novo"[2] could no longer be seen as the choice of one political alternative among others.

In a recent work, Bolívar Lamounier (1999) attributes this misreading of Rui Barbosa to the influence of two discourses: orthodox Positivism and authoritarian leftism, both skeptical of the value of liberal institutions. I will not discuss Lamounier's argument here, but would like to add that the historical role of liberals (or self-described liberals) since the "Estado Novo" has been decisive in this respect. In his commitment to public freedoms and his concern for workers' rights, Rui Barbosa was disowned by his peers. The history of Brazilian liberals since 1945 is a succession of coups, compliance with authoritarianism and social insensitivity.

These days there is much talk about the "deconstitutionalization" of workers' rights, in order to promote the autonomy of opposing parties. Has Brazil become so egalitarian that lopsided work contracts are definitely a thing of the past? Rui Barbosa was a lone voice in his time. And, most likely, so he would be again, should he come back to life today.

Notes

[1] After an election, the winning candidates were screened by the Chamber of Deputies for ratification. In actual practice, this meant that only those candidates who were supported by the governors or by the President were allowed to hold office. (Translator's note)

[2] The authoritarian regime ("New State") imposed by Getúlio Vargas from 1937 to 1945. (Translator's note)

Works Cited and Suggestions For Further Reading

Barbosa, Rui. "A Questão Social e Política no Brasil." *Escritos e Discursos Seletos.* Rio de Janeiro: Nova Aguilar, 1995. 420-459.

———. "Casas para Operários." *Obras Completas de Rui Barbosa.* Vol. XIX. II. Rio de Janeiro: Ministério da Educação e Saúde, 1948. 237-260.

———. "Plataforma." *Escritos e Discursos Seletos.* Rio de Janeiro: Nova Aguilar, 1995. 335-388.

———. "Às Classes Conservadoras." *Escritos e Discursos Seletos.* Rio de Janeiro: Nova Aguilar, 1995. 389-419.

Barreto, Vicente, ed. *O Liberalismo e a Constituição de 1988.* Rio de Janeiro: Nova Fronteira, 1991.

Carvalho, José Murilo de. *Desenvolvimiento de la Ciudadanía en Brasil.* Mexico City: Fondo de Cultura Económica, 1995.

Dantas, San Tiago. "Rui Barbosa e a Renovação da Sociedade." *Escritos e Discursos Seletos de Rui Barbosa.* Rio de Janeiro: Nova Aguilar, 1995. 55-70.

Lacombe, Américo Jacobina. *À Sombra de Rui Barbosa.* Brasiliana. Vol. 365. São Paulo: Companhia Editora Nacional, Instituto Nacional do Livro, 1978.

Lamounier, Bolívar. "Rui Barbosa e a Construção Institucional da Democracia Brasileira." *Rui Barbosa.* Rio de Janeiro: Nova Fronteira, 1999. 49-123.

Marshall, T. H. *Citizenship and Social Class.* London: Pluto Perspectives, 1992.

Reali, Miguel. "A Posição de Rui Barbosa no Mundo da Filosofia." *Escritos e Discursos Seletos de Rui Barbosa.* Rio de Janeiro: Nova Aguilar, 1995. 817-836.

Santos, Wanderley Guilherme. *Décadas de Espanto e uma Apologia Democrática.* Rio de Janeiro: Rocco, 1998.

Vianna, Oliveira. *Instituições Políticas Brasileiras.* 2 vols. Belo Horizonte: Itatiaia, 1987.

"A Portrait of Brazil" in the Postmodern Context

Tereza Virginia de Almeida

Retrato do Brasil's title (*A Portrait of Brazil*) clearly presents the book as one of several attempts to represent a culture whose history of colonization has introduced into its intellectual tradition a major concern about questions of origin and national identity. However the reappearance of *Retrato do Brasil* in 1998 is a cultural fact that requires a consideration of the singular history of the book during the seventy years since its first publication in 1928.

Printed four times during its author's lifetime, *Retrato do Brasil* can be considered a publishing phenomenon. There were two editions in 1929 and a revised one in 1931. Ten years later, Paulo Prado refused to authorize the book's translation into Spanish, arguing that it had been written for his country, and that he had already decided not to publish *Retrato do Brasil* again. Only in 1944 did the fifth edition come out, following Prado's death in 1943. Further editions were published in the next decades: 1962, 1971 and 1981.[1]

Although it is possible to explain the intervals between the successive printings of the book by means of the unstable character of the Brazilian economy, I would like to suggest that these intervals concern both the polemical character of the work and the very process of Brazilian modernist canon formation. In other words, my approach to *Retrato do Brasil* aims at presenting the 1998 printing from within the frame of contemporary Brazilian culture in its relation to its own major modernist artifacts.

Paulo Prado utilized material collected from travelers' and Jesuits' accounts, through which he reconstructs a Brazilian history in which both the seductive appeal of sensual pleasure and the land's material resources determine the characteristic features of the racially mixed population that emerged from the encounter of the Portuguese colonizers with the Native and African peoples.

Retrato do Brasil consists of chapters that work as entries through which Paulo Prado constructs his thesis about the country. "Lust," "Greed," "Sadness," and "Romanticism" are the four key themes that allow the narrating of four centuries of Brazilian cultural foundation, from the discovery of the New World in the sixteenth century to the national identification with romantic ideals in the eighteenth and nineteenth centuries.

The first century of colonization is for Paulo Prado determined by the process of degeneration that characterized the Portuguese world in the sixteenth century. During this period, Portugal experienced a political crisis and a weakening of power that culminated in its domination by Spain in 1580. Far from the heroic conquerors of the fifteenth century, the Portuguese colonizers who came to Brazil were single young males predisposed to experience all sorts of pleasures that the tropics could offer. This predisposition led to immediate miscegenation with the Native women: from the contact of this sensuality with the disruption and dissolution of the European colonizer there appeared our mixed primitive population.[2]

This colonizer was also a wretched adventurer who was prone to take on any type of risk and even to commit crimes in order to find material resources such as silver, gold and precious stones. This ambition resonated with the attitude that Portugal sustained in relation to its colony as it received the results of the exploratory expeditions, for which people would abandon the steady cultivation of the land in search of immediate profit.

Sadness was therefore a main outcome of the conjunction of racial miscegenation and the historical constraints of the first centuries: "Popular poetry, legends, music and dances reveal the melancholic obsession that only disappears with the absorption in love or lust" (144). Due to this very melancholic tendency, the country was ready to receive in the eighteenth century the influence of Romanticism, which Paulo Prado describes with reference to a broad trajectory from Rousseau to romantic nationalism and literary expression.

Edited and introduced by Carlos Augusto Calil, the 1998 edition includes paratexts that are crucial for the reader in order to understand the book's original context and its critical reception. In addition to an introduction and chronology, the editor organized an appendix that includes letters, reviews and some portraits of the author from the period. Through these paratexts it is possible to contextualize a work whose subtitle—"Essay on Brazilian Sadness"—promises a representation of the country that seems to contradict that which had been dominant through the centuries, namely, the image of a tropical landscape characterized by vibrant rhythms and colorful festivals.

The contemporary reader of Paulo Prado's text may recognize that the author relies both on biological and geographical determinations as well as on concepts of race that have been problematized by a complex set of debates on cultural issues that have emerged in the humanities and social sciences in the last decades. However, it is the 1998 edition itself, in the relations it establishes between Paulo Prado's text and its paratexts, which allows the reader to take the necessary distance from the book's thesis in order to enjoy the piece as a cultural artifact that is emblematic of the specificity of Brazilian modernism.

In the appendix, the reviews demonstrate the tendency of critics to oscillate between fascination by the book's style and rejection of certain aspects of its thesis. João Ribeiro reacts against the idea of sadness: "The land of holidays, of tomorrow, of the 'be patient,' of rhetoric, and of Carnival cannot be the dwelling place of melancholia" (223-224). Oswald de Andrade reacts against Paulo Prado's interpretation of "Lust" in the meeting of the colonizer with Native and African people: "Notice that *Retrato do Brasil* is in this chapter the repetition of all the monstrous judgments that the Western world has made about the discovered America" (229). In 1928, Oswald de Andrade published his "Manifesto Antropófago" ("Cannibalist Manifest") in which the idea of anthropophagy works as an ironic metaphor that neutralizes the notion of cultural dependency through positing the infinite capacity of incorporation as the main feature of Brazilian culture.

Although it seems clear that *Retrato do Brasil's* thesis was capable of giving rise to a polemical debate on the intellectual scene, it is important to notice that this challenging character of Paulo Prado's book is connected with an intellectual context in which both the identification of the work as an historiographic text and the author's social position are relevant.

On the one hand, *Retrato do Brasil* is a text that is clearly recognizable as an example of the practice defined as "history of mentalities." On the other hand, the book is produced by one of the participants in "The Week of Modern Art" that took place in São Paulo in February 1922, an event that has been represented by literary history as the origin of modernism in Brazil.[3]

Part of a traditional and wealthy family of coffee exporters, Paulo Prado was one of the organizers and sponsors of the "Week of Modern Art," which was planned by a group of artists and intellectuals who were in dialogue with the European avant-garde. Dissatisfied with the Brazilian importation of literary trends, they decided to react through a movement that would update Brazilian art in the modern world and, at the same time, liberate Brazilian artistic expression from its colonized tradition. The result of this challenging enterprise is a set of heterogeneous and contradictory trends that originates in "The Week of 22" and is expressed in various manners throughout this century.

The fact that a director of a trade company produced an important work of historiography makes manifest the traditional relations between intellectual debate and the economically dominant classes in Brazil. Paulo Prado (1869–1943) attended university in Rio de Janeiro, where his father was a deputy at the time, and obtained an undergraduate degree in Law in 1889. Afterwards, he traveled to Paris, where he lived until 1897, when his father asked him to return to Brazil in order to take care of the family's business. Parallel to his main occupation as a businessman, Prado was active as a journalist since 1892, when he had started writing the column "News from Europe" for the *Jornal do Comércio*. In Brazil, he wrote newspaper articles and directed, along with Monteiro Lobato, the *Revista do Brasil*. He also published, in 1925, a volume called *Paulística*, which brought together articles previously published in *O Estado de São Paulo*. Prado's interest in history was influenced by the historian Capistrano de Abreu, who had been Prado's mentor since 1918 and with whom he organized and edited some volumes of Brazilian history.[4]

One of the most characteristic features of Brazilian modernism is reflected in Paulo Prado's decision to write an historical work, for it illustrates an ambivalent relation to the past. Although modernist aesthetics tends to be related to the search for originality and innovation, in the Brazilian case this search is connected with the recovery and rewriting of Brazilian past. For example, the legacies of oral traditions—from Native and African myths, rituals and folklore—are strongly present in the work of Mário de Andrade, especially in *Macunaíma* (1928). Oswald de Andrade also exhibited this trend in his allusions to the primitive world that are present both in the "Manifesto da Poesia Pau-Brasil" (1924) and in the "Manifesto Antropófago" (1928).[5]

In the work of Pablo Picasso, for example, it is clear that such a theme can be associated with avant-garde aesthetics. But it is important to notice that the primitive image is for Picasso something similar to what the Orient is for Ezra Pound's poetry: the allusion to a radically discontinuous idea of time and space which establishes a sense of rupture in history. The Brazilian modernist enterprise therefore seems to incorporate this aesthetic conception but finds as its main challenge the fact that the primitive world is an essential part of the country's own colonized history.

If this problematic ambivalence is resolved aesthetically in the case of Mário de Andrade and Oswald de Andrade, Paulo Prado is confronted with the challenge of constructing an historical narrative that could cover the period between the repressed primitive world and modernity. In his words, the portrait "was made as an impressionist picture... the dates disappear almost entirely. There remain only the aspects, the emotions, and the mental representation of events that result more from speculative deduction than from a coherent sequence of facts" (185-186). Paulo Prado's task is to construct a representation through which Brazilian cultural complexities at the beginning of the century could find their own explanations and causalities in light of modernity's demands and promises, a task that seems to be stimulated by the desire to organize the past in the interest of Brazilian self-legitimization in the twentieth century. *Retrato do Brasil* proved to be a polemical book precisely because of Paulo Prado's decision to present the country as a set of problems that originates in the process of colonization instead of inverting and subverting the history of dependency as does Oswald through the notion of anthropophagy. In the wake of modern revolutions, Brazil lies for Paulo Prado "in a colonial slumber" in which, "despite the appearance of civilization, we live isolated, blind and immobile, within the very mediocrity that pleases both governors and governed" (210-211).

Retrato do Brasil is in the contemporary context a sort of precious appendix to the Brazilian modernist canon. If literary critics have consecrated Oswald's anthropophagy as the explanatory image that was able to embrace an entire cultural formation, *Retrato do Brasil* is one of those texts that challenges criticism to denaturalize its own representational frames. The portrait that its own author tried to erase from history certainly does not offer

TEREZA VIRGINIA DE ALMEIDA

an answer as ready to be appropriated as Oswald's anthropophagy. But in its own problematic thesis appears the expression of a desire for representation whose questions are incredibly vivid at the end of the millennium.

It is important to observe that Paulo Prado's thesis is explicitly presented in 1928 as a claim for "modernity," a word that worked as a magical passport to infinite development and freedom. Seventy years later, globalization and the failure of emancipatory discourses have brought to Western society and to the Brazilian context determinations that have completely transfigured the value and definition of "modernity."

In the last decades, intellectual debate has been utilizing the idea of the postmodern as a key term for the problematization of modernity. In 1985, Jean-François Lyotard presented an analogy between the postmodern and the psychoanalytic process by means of which modern neurosis could be "worked through," in the Freudian sense of *Durcharbeitung*: "the 'post-' of 'postmodern' does not signify a movement of *comeback, flashback*, or *feedback*, that is, not a movement of repetition but a procedure in 'ana': a procedure of analysis, anamnesis, anagogy, and anamorphosis that elaborates an 'initial forgetting.'"[6]

In this sense, it is possible to understand that, if the postmodern debate fails to resolve itself into a new paradigm that could promote a satisfying set of characteristics for defining a postmodern aesthetics, it is exactly because its main assumptions challenge the idea of the coherent whole inherent in periodization.

If one takes Lyotard's proposal as a clue in order to approach a book such as *Retrato do Brasil* in the postmodern context, Paulo Prado's very commitments to modern utopias crystallize into a "modern neurosis" determined by the urge for totalizing frames and representations typical of modern thought. However, the reader can enjoy the book apart from its compromised quest for a stable and coherent representation of the country and can see that through stylistic features and vivid metaphors the book fulfills what its narrative fails to explain, stabilize or resolve. At the end of the millennium, in its failure to offer a major representation of Brazil through the remaking of previous representations, *Retrato do Brasil* makes explicit its discursive nature and challenges the very idea of nation that led to its production seventy years ago.

Notes

[1] The first posthumous edition was authorized by Paulo Prado's son, Paulo Caio Prado, and was published by Editora Brasiliense. José Olympio Editora published the book in 1962 and republished it in 1972 in a volume entitled *Província e Nação*, which contains two books: *Retrato do Brasil* and *Paulística*.

[2] Prado 76.

[3] For information in English about the event, see K. David Jackson, *Literature of the São Paulo Week of Modern Art* (Austin: Institute of Latin American Studies, U of Texas P, 1987).

[4] Capistrano de Abreu (1853-1927) is the author of *Capítulos de História Colonial* (1907) which was translated into English by Arthur Brackel as *Chapters of Colonial History, 1500—1800* (New York: Oxford UP, 1997).

[5] *Macunaíma* was translated into English by E. A. Goodland: Mário de Andrade, *Macunaíma* (New York: Random House, 1984). Both of Oswald de Andrade's "Manifestos" were translated into English and published in the *Latin American Literary Review*. "Manifesto of Pau-Brasil Poetry", translated by Stella M. de Sá Rego, appears in volume 14.27 (1986): 184-187; "Cannibalist Manifesto," translated by Leslie Bary, appears in volume 19.38 (1991): 35-47.

[6] Lyotard 77.

Works Cited

Andrade, Oswald de. "Retoques ao *Retrato do Brasil*." Paulo Prado. *Retrato do Brasil*. 1928. Ed. Carlos Augusto Calil. São Paulo: Companhia das Letras, 1998. 228-232.

Lyotard, Jean-François. "Note on the Meaning of 'Post.'" *The Postmodern Explained*. Minneapolis: U of Minnesota P, 1993. 75-80.

Prado, Paulo. *Retrato do Brasil*. 1928. Ed. Carlos Augusto Calil. São Paulo: Companhia das Letras, 1998.

Ribeiro, João. "Paulo Prado—*Retrato do Brasil*." Paulo Prado. *Retrato do Brasil*. 1928. Ed. Carlos Augusto Calil. São Paulo: Companhia das Letras, 1998. 223-228.

TEREZA VIRGINIA DE ALMEIDA

The USA and Brazil: Capitalism and Pre-Capitalism According to Oliveira Vianna

Ângela de Castro Gomes
Translated by Bonnie Wasserman
Revised by Mark Streeter

The work of Oliveira Vianna appears today, unquestionably, as a classic of Brazilian social thought. The link between his analyses and his proposal for an authoritarian State, highlighted by his political engagement with the *Estado Novo* ("New State") machinery (1937–1945), for a long time hindered the debate regarding his work—branded, simplistically, as racist and reactionary. Today, however, these characteristics are being transformed into an initiative to reevaluate his work. At last, along with Francisco Campos, Cassiano Ricardo, Almir de Andrade and others, he represents the intellectual who proposes to escape the limits of academia, thinking that only through participation in government he could implement his ideas. This renewed interest explains the 1987 reprinting of an unedited text by this historian and sociologist who died in 1951: *História Social da Economia Capitalista no Brasil* (*The Social History of Economic Capitalism in Brazil*).

This two-volume book was never finished—certain chapters remained incomplete, while others were merely outlined. However, this does not matter. In it Vianna effects a re-vision of his entire work, obliging the reader to accompany him. To survey this rereading would necessarily be a difficult task, one that we cannot accomplish fully in these introductory remarks.

Throughout the book, Oliveira Vianna addresses and develops themes that are already central in his earlier works. The principal theme is the "social problem" found in the world and in Brazil, viewed as a sign and product of the development of modern capitalism. To understand and resolve the "social problem," the common approach in the 1930s was to start with the analysis of the social formation of Brazil. The resolution of problems like the representation of modern conflicts between capital and labor appeared to Vianna to be something that would merit an investigation that dealt specifically with the characteristics of a nation and its people. It is not by accident, however, that the book begins with a reference to *Direito do Trabalho e Democracia Social. O Problema da Incorporação do Trabalho* (1951), and often refers as well to Vianna's first book, *Populações Meridionais no Brasil* (1920), which also has a strong historical emphasis.

The initial aim of the book is expressed in its title: it tries to be a social history, not a history of the capitalist economy of Brazil, which would analyze the facts of the country's technological production and evolution. The author himself notes in the preface that it is one thing to acknowledge and accompany the material development of capitalism, and another to analyze the social consequences that unfold from the beginning of these new conditions. This in turn would warrant a study of the uses, the traditions, the mentality and the social types found in the country.

Nevertheless, if this is the aim that organizes the book, the author confesses that he was obliged to alter its framework significantly. This is because his assumption that the "capitalistic economy had dominated all of Brazil" was false. From this new perspective there emerged two Brazils, and capitalist culture was limited in fact to a small fraction of the people. The vast majority of Brazil's regional populations were shielded far away from the influence of supercapitalism, and "maintained themselves close to its primitive structure and pre-capitalist mentality, the same that had been formed from the early days of Brazilian civilization and history" (1: 20). And this would in turn be the central thesis of the two volumes.

In order to ground his analysis, Oliveira Vianna retraces an immense and diversified number of sources. First of all, there are the "modern historians and sociologists of the more recent European and American economies," such as Werner Sombart, Max Weber, Henri Pirenne, Gaetan Pirou, among Europeans; and Lewis Mumford, Edward Ross, Thornstein Veblen, A. Berle and J. F. Normano, among Americans. What is important to point out is that the whole work has, in fact, a remarkable comparative perspective that includes the experience of European countries and, especially, the United States. Secondly, there are sources on Brazil, including accounts of European travelers (such as Johann Baptist von Spix, Karl Friedrich von Martius, Johann Moritz Rugendas and John Luccock); texts of chroniclers and Brazilian historians (such as Antônio Vieira, André João Antonil, Afonso

Taunay, Joaquim Nabuco, Ambrósio Fernandes Brandão, Joaquim Francisco Lisboa and Manuel de Oliveira Lima); the censuses from 1920 and 1940; and even references from the literary works of past and contemporary writers, such as José Lins do Rego and Jorge Amado.

Besides the theoretical orientations that define the work and the conclusions it reaches, there must also be stressed the originality and sensibility with which Oliveira Vianna understood certain cultural characteristics of what can be called "our peoples" and from which he provided a fascinating bibliography for the study of Brazil.

The initial section of the first volume is a general introduction. In it there is a definition of what Sombart calls modern capitalism. In the last decades, this has transformed into supercapitalism. The author's goal is necessary: there has to be a clear understanding of this new capitalism, so that it will enable an evaluation of its presence and duration in Brazil and, more specifically, in order to analyze its social repercussions (in the sense of the sociological school of Frederic Le Pay). Among these questions, one concerns him the most: the effects of supercapitalism on labor conflicts and therefore on the government's orientations towards a new social policy. His reflection on "the social problem" is always determined by what he sees as the singularity of Brazil's historical and geographic formation insofar as it regards both "our sentiments and traditional attitudes" towards workers and the new political directives adopted in Brazil after the 1930 Revolution.

Oliveira Vianna also systematically turns to the work of Mumford and Ross, considered by him as exponents of the modern North American social sciences. Together with Sombart, they allow him to analyze three aspects of capitalism—the technical, the legal and the psychological. These aspects may or may not overlap in time and space, although each has an independent emergence and development.

"Technological capitalism" is marked by technical modernization, especially in the phenomenon of multiple concentrations (capital, motor power, production, work force, industry profits, etc...). "Legal capitalism" is characterized by new techniques of investment and companies with new legal structures. These are the immense societies that the author calls *mamutes*— the cartels and German *konzerns,* the French *ententes,* the North American trusts and holdings.

No other country exemplifies this new type of capitalism and its complex mastery of technical organization better than the United States of America.

ÂNGELA DE CASTRO GOMES

And it is also there that the psychological dimension of supercapitalism most manifests itself. This "psychological capitalism"—coined by Sombart— would be, according to Oliveira Vianna, entirely dominated by the unlimited spirit of profit. It constitutes not only North American businessmen, but also the entire population that works and lives with the expectation to participate in the "economy of profit." In societies in which this "drive" (*"estado de espírito"*) predominates, man is what he has; if he doesn't have anything, he doesn't know anything and is nothing (1: 41). In its psychological aspect, however, modern capitalism corresponds to a society exclusively attached to profit.

For the author, the "primitive elements of this spirit of profit" were transmitted to the North Americans from old Europe through the cycle of the great marine companies and their mercantilism. This cultural inheritance or legacy would have been exacerbated in American lands by what Mumford calls the mineral complex. No other people of the new continent were so affected by a tradition of getting rich quickly and easily. Therefore, they ended up transferring everything to the areas of productive activity. It is this element that distinguishes the economic and social trajectory of the United States from that of Brazil, for instance. Brazilian periods of financial prosperity, as in those of mining and of coffee cultivation, did not have the recurrence or the intensity that occurred in the American experience. For this reason, the spirit of profit did not persist in Brazil, nor did it radiate, having been up to a certain point engulfed by a different cultural tradition.

Meanwhile, to understand the specific *ethos* of a society, it is necessary to analyze its historical trajectory as well as its distinguishing elements, such as the dynamic of different economic factors and the construction of a cultural heritage. However, the domination of a certain social mentality would not be permanent. For Oliveira Vianna, the social history of North American capitalism suggests distinct periodizations. Until the Civil War and the abolition of slavery, the North American agricultural civilization was frankly pre-capitalist. It was only in the short interval between 1890 and 1905 that "the spirit of capitalism" burst in and dominated without retreat. Afterwards, it was felt that an "ethical reaction" to its material excesses was needed, "which culminated in the corporatist and anti-capitalist policies of Roosevelt's New Deal" (1: 41).

Nonetheless, the situation was different in Brazil. The country was still struggling in the pre-capitalist mentality, when there appeared "islands" here and there of capitalistic culture. Indeed, this is the thesis that *História Social* tries to demonstrate. In the first phase, the author analyzes the social history of agriculture and the commercial and industrial economy in order to make evident the characteristics, the force and the permanence of the "pre-capitalist spirit." In the second phase, he examines the development of supercapitalism and the obstacles that it encounters in Brazil, insisting on the predominance of the mentality of the "economy of maintenance" over the "economy of profit."

However, if Brazil's society was still "pre-capitalist," this was not due, for Oliveira Vianna, to social stagnation. Brazilians were and are capable of mercantilist forms of acting and thinking. But among Brazilians these forms return to mix with the pre-capitalist mentality, or are blocked for being judged inadequate. In *História Social* he gives special attention to the Brazilian industrial regime and to the leaders of the industrial class, abandoning the customary emphasis on the territorial aristocracy. He treats this choice, nevertheless, only as a question of emphasis, since the beginning of Brazilian history lay in the cultivation of lands through the plantation system.

A historical survey of the colonial period and the Empire reveals the system of the agrarian nobility, the characteristics of which the author labels the "economy of maintenance," as much in life (subsistence), as in social position (status). All Brazilian economic activity over the centuries had two basic motivations: nobility and abundance.

But this picture is also not static. One identifies this landlord mentality and its persistence throughout time; Oliveira Vianna recognizes a certain permeability in Brazil's rural society to the styles of modern capitalism. He points out the sugar industry and the coffee culture as agrarian experiments that were able to be penetrated by "technical capitalism" as much as by "psychological capitalism." From this, having as a reference the "territorial nobility" (1: 99), Vianna analyzes the evolution and the role of the commercial and industrial middle class in Brazil. Underlying this work is the study of the formation of Brazilian society, which was "grounded on slavery, which disqualifies not only the manual work but also any type of occupation in profitable professions" (1: 180). In relation to commerce, he shows that, on the one hand, the upper middle class only began to develop in southern Brazil, and much later than the "coffee civilization." On the other hand, the commercial activity itself never reached a level to be considered. In relation to the industrial middle class, the picture is not much different, while the craft industry is disqualified even more so since from the beginning it was practiced by Africans.

But, even with these obstacles—especially foreign competition, protected by free capitalists—the evolution of Brazilian industrial capitalism did not cease. Using census statistics, the author argues that a constant though discontinuous increase in the rhythm of Brazil's industrial progress can be observed (1: 211). The important moment in this ascension is the period after World War I, when a nucleus of modern industrial capitalism emerged in a triple aspect in São Paulo—technical, legal and economic.

Thus, after noting the late and localized appearance of the focal points of this supercapitalism, especially in the technical and legal dimensions, Oliveira Vianna shows that a series of economic, social and political contingencies brought harsh resistance to this tendency. This was also the reaction articulated by the very same corporatist "National State." Therefore, the examination of the conditions of the historical development of certain productive activities of the classes that were responsible for them shows that modern capitalism did not fully develop in Brazil.

Vianna then comes to the conclusion that the pre-capitalist economy in Brazil is predominant, and especially so in the permanence of the "spirit of the classes that are not engaged in commercial activities" (1: 52). This path, distinctly anti-Enlightenment, does not appear to be regression or a return to the past, once a "historical as well as a sociological law" is revealed through the dynamics of Brazilian society (1: 92). It is natural that, in opposition to a historical cycle like that of supercapitalism, there will be reactions that express at the same time the boredom, the fatigue, and the repulsion of men to this specific cycle, and that they will then attempt to articulate alternative historical experiences. If the new economic cycle—involving a directed economy, corporatism and socialism—should appear to restore the old pre-capitalistic civilization, it would not be simply a repetition of an earlier already overcome cycle but its recreation. The occurrence of the phenomenon in the very core of supercapitalism, namely the United States, would be an undisputed proof of this "law" (1: 105).

If, in the "material aspect," supercapitalism in Brazil encountered obstacles to its expansion, even greater difficulties would result for its "psychological aspect." While admitting that, in the distant future, the "spirit of supercapitalism" might be able to dominate industrial companies, especially those of São Paulo, Vianna considers that even these companies for a long time continued to be the "basis of living for their owners, directed by the good and traditional pre-capitalist manner—in a spirit of pure economy of maintenance and status" (2: 63).

The diagnosis is made without ambiguity. If, from the point of view of material development, it can be said that in Brazil there is modern capitalism,

> ... nothing of this, however, affects the general conclusion: from the psychological point of view, we still have much of the pre-capitalist phase. Not only are spiritual values very important but also money is not everything in these two capitalist centers; university degrees are here and there [Rio de Janeiro and São Paulo] still the better chance for the communication of individuals in elite positions. Our enriched superindustrials, making themselves papal counts, truly reveal that they do not feel that in itself money is enough; but also Christian virtues are needed. (2: 196)

Happily, concludes the author, the "spirit of capitalism" in Brazil is the exception that confirms the rule of the predominance of the pre-capitalist mentality. Cultural reasons grounded on moral origins—born in the mentality of Brazil's agrarian aristocracies—, and political reasons—expressed in the neo-corporatist directives of the social politics of the National State preserved in the Constitution of 1946—make one believe that for a long time the country was free from the "spirit of greed and violence," protected by the "old pre-capitalist mentality, that so much nobility, justice and dignity were spread in the life and traditions of our people" (2: 197).

In the end, Vianna's book proposes a conservative project—updated and coherent—for a modern and moral economy, in which the technological improvement would coexist with the ethical responsibility of the richest for the poorest. In short, a classic project in which the traditional and the modern would interact in a synthesis both necessary and possible. Moreover, according to Vianna, such a synthesis would be entirely Brazilian.

Work Cited

Vianna, Oliveira. *História Social da Economia Capitalista no Brasil*. Belo Horizonte: Itatiaia/Niterói: Editora da Universidade Federal Fluminense, 1987.

ÂNGELA DE CASTRO GOMES

Raymundo Faoro's Roundabout Voyage in *Os Donos do Poder*

Marcelo Jasmin
Translated by Ross G. Forman

There are two different editions of *Os Donos do Poder: Formação do Patronato Político Brasileiro* by Raymundo Faoro (b. 1925): the original, published in 1958 by Editora Globo in Porto Alegre, and the second edition, revised and expanded, published in 1975 by the same publisher in association with the Editora da Universidade de São Paulo. The two editions are physically different: the first comprises one volume, 271 pages, 14 chapters, and 140 notes. The second consists of two volumes, 750 pages, 1335 notes and many more bibliographic references. The presence of Marx and Engels in the notes of the 1975 edition, for instance, contrasts with their remarkable absence in the original edition. Two new chapters offer a detailed expansion of Faoro's argument into the Republican period, a subject almost ignored in the first edition. These additions, however, neither alter the basic structure of the work nor its principal ideas. True, the second version is more erudite and offers a more extensive grounding for its thesis based on the Weberian sociology of traditional domination, but the thesis itself remains unaltered. The revisions of the second edition have not always been viewed as improvements by academic critics. The alterations place additional weight on a vigorous and persuasive study marked by the simplicity of its interpretation, a weight that some critics find weakens the force of the original's concise style (see, for instance, Iglésias 142).[1]

Nonetheless, the two-volume version enjoyed extraordinary success. It may have taken seventeen years for a second edition to appear in April 1975, but various reprints followed more quickly, one in January 1976 and another a year later. The edition's popularity, however, had little to do with the new form of the text. A cultural atmosphere of resistance to dictatorship welcomed a book whose very title criticized authoritarian power and which proposed new ways to understand the persistence of the military's control over the Brazilian State.

The work's first edition, appearing at the end of the 1950s, situated itself within a cultural and political debate centering around disputed notions of such terms as nationalism and development. This may explain, in part, the book's modest reception by the intellectual community at the time, even though it received an award from the Academia Brasileira de Letras.

A history of the reception of *Os Donos do Poder*'s has yet to be written. It could be argued with some truth that Raymundo Faoro's public activities in defence of the rule of law—either as prosecutor for the State of Guanabara or as a spokesperson for the Brazilian bar association, the "Ordem dos Advogados do Brasil" (a group that, together with the "Associação Brasileira de Imprensa" and the "Conferência Nacional dos Bispos do Brasil," spearheaded civil society's fight against dictatorship)—brought attention first to the author and then to his work. And it is reasonable to suppose that the success of such a large and difficult book, in the form of an expanded second edition, owes much to the prominent position that Faoro occupied in the public eye.

It is also likely that the continuation of military rule and the radicalization of the dictatorship in 1968 stimulated sensitivity to an argument about the continuity of a patrimonial rule and a bureaucratic status group in Brazilian development. It became prudent to imagine once more that this status group (or an element of it, the military) reinforced the main trends of Brazilian history, giving the military coup a new sense of intelligibility through the interpretative frame of *Os Donos do Poder*. If facts seemed to confirm the book's thesis, in the 1970s this made it a tool in the battle against the military, expanding its reception beyond academic circles.

Yet it would be a mistake to attribute the book's status as a "classic" exclusively to the lawyer's renown or to those particular historical circumstances. Instead, its critical acclaim rests in a persuasive argument that offered a historical explanation to make sense of the nation's present, as well as in the alternative view it provided to the local intelligentsia's hegemonic conceptions.

The changes between the first and second editions of the book do not, as I have said, affect Faoro's principal thesis. From his perspective, the course of Brazilian history is marked by patrimonial domination, transplanted from Portugal to Brazil through the process of colonization. It concerns the obstinate continuity of the structures developed during the consolidation of the modern Portuguese State, which—from the fourteenth century onwards—freed itself of feudal vestiges and promoted State centralization and a form of capitalism politically designed to benefit the monarchical State.

Faoro describes Portuguese history using Max Weber's categories of traditional domination. At first, there is a patriarchal system by which kings govern a kingdom "like their own households," directed by the regulations of a "natural economy." Thus "the nation is administered as part of the sovereign's household, limiting market action and almost eliminating the need for currency." A second stage begins at the moment when a monetary economy is implemented: an administrative staff is formed which—although originally "just the meeting of members of court with those they protect"— becomes a "body of domination" (*Os Donos* 11-12).[2] Here, as in Weber's theory, traditional domination goes from being patriarchal to patrimonial and estate-type through the way in which the administrative staff appropriates to itself judicial and military powers (as if it privately owned everything), and the economic potentials those powers imply.[3]

Faoro derives his central ideas from this initial premise. First, he accepts the idea that patrimonial domination, as it evolved in the Portuguese State and was transported to Brazil, involves a form of politically oriented capitalism that prevents the free expansion of a market economy. Controlled by a status group and for its own benefit, mercantile capitalism is dominated by monopolies and by royal intervention that "irrationally limit economic development" (*Os Donos* 11-12). A political capitalism (in which colonization is included) "springs up in the shadow of the royal household, making itself an appendix to the state." By contrast, a "rational economy, run according to its own rules, with a system of accounting for its operations, is strangled at birth" (*Os Donos* 12). The lack of a formally rationalized economy and of "market conditions" hinders the "stability of long-term planning" and, as a consequence, forestalls industrial enterprise that might provide a regular economic base and the rational capacity for planning. "Rational law, the field through which [industrial enterprise] expands, neither exists nor is able to develop" (*Os Donos* 13).

Faoro's explanation for the "reasons why [modern industrial] capitalism is prevented from flourishing" follow that described by Weber's ideal type:

... patrimonialism, be it patriarchal or with a staff, has the power to materially regulate the economy, diverting it from its proper course and redirecting it to meet the goals of the State, [that is] utilitarian, military, socioethical, or cultural goals and values. This, in sum, is the principal, special circumstance; by virtue of it, economic activity is alienated from formal rational organization in order to subordinate it to the needs and the haphazard discretion of the prince. (*Os Donos* 13)

In other words: "Capitalism, prevented from being freely expressed, is diverted and subjugated to the political" (*Os Donos* 12). The bureaucratic status group, according to this scheme, opposes and prevents the development of autonomous social classes. Thus the absence of a "rational economy" corresponds to the lack of groups that can organize their interests according to impersonal and universal market rules and without depending on a privileged relationship with the State. As a result the development of a liberal political thinking, appropriate to the dynamic center of modern capitalism as established in Weber's ideal type, is obstructed. In the context of Brazilian history, the true center of activity can be found exactly where this interpretation of Weber's theory affirms it ought not to be: in the State.

This analysis thus elaborates a structure of domination that divides the State from the nation, making the first the exclusive pole for all social, economic, and political initiatives and making the second an unwilling witness of the deleterious consequences of politically motivated capitalism. Economic anemia is also political anemia, and if the failure of industrial capitalism is the cause of underdevelopment, the lack of autonomous classes explains the authoritarian and exclusionary character of national politics. As a result there is no independent civil society, liberal thought, or rational capitalism (the presumed signs of modernity), only patrimonial, estate-type, and bureaucratic domination.

Thus translated to Brazilian history, the theory of Weberian types of domination paints the picture of an "absence," of an impossibility, a picture that reveals something *other*, perhaps desirable, but that does not now and has never existed in Brazil. It is no accident that Faoro's thesis is better formulated through negation: estate-type and bureaucratic patrimonialism in Brazil made the modern conditions of a rational economy and the legality of a state of law inviable.[4] Significantly, Faoro called this "diversion of capitalism" "the original sin of Portuguese development"—a sin which, like Adam's and Eve's, indelibly marked posterity and "still exerts a vivid and powerful influence over Brazil in the twentieth century" (*Os Donos* 12).[5]

This connection between the absence of the thing coveted and original sin constructs the long *durée* of Faoro's theory of national history as a sort of "non-history" or of "dialectic without synthesis" in Hegelian terminology. In the 1958 edition, Faoro sought, by combining the theories of Leon Trotsky (*The History of the Russian Revolution*) and Arnold Toynbee (*A Study of History*), a philosophy of history that could explain the reasons why the "rise of a genuine Brazilian culture" was frustrated (*Os Donos* 269-71). From Trotsky's "law of combined development," he drew an understanding of cycles of development in the "backward countries" of the global economy. The need to protect their economies from competition regarding world economic powers obliged the governments of backward nations to "leap forward, skipping over the intermediate steps of normal evolution and provoking serious incongruities in economic and cultural spheres" (*Os Donos* 265). In opposition to this supposed pattern of "normal evolution," with its well-defined phases of harmonious economic development, one can see in the context of the inequality of economic rhythms, a "combination of distinct phases, an amalgam of archaic forms with the most modern ones" (Trotsky, cited in *Os Donos* 266). This gives rise, Faoro concludes, to "striking cultural incongruities," combining high technology (machine guns and radios, for example) with "strong cultural residues" ("folk remedies, with strong superstitious connotations, administered to the sound of prayers and blessings") (*Os Donos* 266).

This schizophrenic mixing of the modern and the archaic corresponds to the schism between State and nation as "different realities, alienated and opposed to each other and mutually distrustful of one another." Two societies are juxtaposed: "one, cultivated and educated, the other, primitive, unstratified, lacking in tellurian symbolism." Floating "like phantasms" between a European culture that "informs the intellectual layer of their thinking" and the culture "of the common people, that impresses their unconscious temperament," members of the status group are turned into "men without roots" whose calling is one of "an idealism superior to reality," one of "irrealism disconnected from the sources of imagination." On one side are the legislators and politicians, with their propensity for "jurism," seeking to "construct reality through the force of law"; on the other side are the common people, marked by a "primitivism," which makes no distinction between religious and political systems of value, and who survive "through a

MARCELO JASMIM

confusion of undifferentiated impulses," expressing their anxieties through a sort of "politics of salvation" while waiting for a thaumaturge (Faoro, *Os Donos* 268-69).

This schizophrenia does not resolve itself, but is supported by the patrimonialist State that gains strength from this discord and frustrates the possibility of a "genuine Brazilian culture." Here, the explanation of these phenomena comes not just from Trotsky, but also from Toynbee's theory of the birth of civilizations. At the end of the first volume of *A Study of History*, Toynbee elaborates a pattern for the emergence of what he calls "related civilizations," that is, societies whose historical origins derive from a process of differentiation and internal secession from a previous civilization to which they retain ties of "apparentation" and "affiliation."[6] According to this pattern, a decline in the "creative power" that previously inspired voluntary allegiance from the whole of that civilization causes it to disintegrate into two opposite poles: on one side, a "dominant minority" that, remaining tied to the old society, seeks to preserve itself; on the other side, a "proletariat" (identified as a group by being "negatively privileged in relation to the dominant minority") which, not finding in the dominant minority any real representation for itself, becomes "conscious that it has a soul of its own" and "mak[es] up its mind to save its soul alive." Within this conflict between the preservation of the *status quo* by the minority and the desire to secede inscribed in the soul of the now self-aware proletariat, "we can discern one of those dramatic spiritual encounters which renew the work of creation by carrying the life of the Universe out of the stagnation of autumn through the pains of winter into the ferment of spring" (Toynbee 336; cited in Faoro, *Os Donos* 270).

However, in Brazil's case the "secession" of the proletariat did not occur, and therefore did not bring about a "spring." In Brazil, "the nation, the classes, and the people did not succeed in differentiating themselves," squeezed as they were by the bureaucratic status group. The result was a "frail" civilization, "ailing from birth, as if it had been attacked by infantile paralysis." "Toynbee's lesson," Faoro says, leads to the conclusion that "resistance from anachronistic institutions stymied the expansion of Brazilian society." Such anachronism translated into a backward force, an impediment to historical innovation, preventing the realization of a (desired) modernity. Failing to follow the pattern of differentiation-secession created a civilization of "social monstrosity." Vacillating between the modern and the archaic, between to be or not to be, Brazilian civilization according to Faoro deserves the label of "fancy" (Faoro, *Os Donos* 271; Faoro, *Os Donos* [1977] 748).

Nonetheless, the book's second edition revisited, without being explicitly self-critical, some of the terms of its historical perspective from 1958, which naively upheld a strongly linear notion of universal history. In 1975, criticizing the idea that capitalist society represented the "culmination of history," Faoro affirmed that the "compatibility of modern capitalism with patterns of tradition wrongly identified as pre-capitalism" was "one of the keys to understanding the phenomenon of Brazilian-Portuguese history" (*Os Donos* [1977] 735-37). Yet this revision is made in order to reinforce his principal point about the "frustration" of Brazilian culture and the way in which it was weighed down by "the suffocating embrace of the administrative shell" (*Os Donos* [1977] 748).

The argument itself was maintained. Neither the growth of the national State and the inevitable bureacratization which accompanied it nor the disappearance of the monarchy nor even the establishment of the "Estado Novo" (1937–1945) shook an analytic frame that reaffirmed an empire of bureaucratic order. As explained in the 1958 edition, the principal changes derived from the national economy's inevitable involvement in the global dynamic of capitalism reinforced the structure of domination: "private capital, unable to stay in the race, is absorbed by the State, which controls, regulates, and protects it, strengthening the bureaucratic status group, which now has become the nation's purveyor" (*Os Donos* 43).

Modernization, the principal method for historical change, is also the principal "cause of the continuance" of the "patrimonial and bureaucratic estate-type order" (*Os Donos* 265). Faoro's theory of history expresses itself in this mechanism of self-reproduction: if there are changes over time, these changes reinforce the structure of domination, which remain fully intact, neutralizing all potential innovations. This historical dynamic implies a permanent updating of estate-type power (the manifestation of original sin), which corresponds to an eternal return to the absence of what is desired (unrealized secession, modernity). The final chapter of the 1975 edition, with its suggestive title "The Roundabout Journey: From Patrimonialism to the Status Group"[7] carries with it an expression of the dramatic nature of this secular continuity: "From Dom João I to Getúlio Vargas, over a six-century long trip, a political and social structure resisted all fundamental transformations, all profound challenges and the crossing of the wide ocean"

MARCELO JASMIM

(*Os Donos* [1977] 733).

Notes

[1] Explanations of Faoro's argument can be found in Iglésias (1976), Mendonça (1995) and Mello e Souza (1999). For an overview of Faoro's thinking, especially subsequent to the publication of *Os Donos do Poder*, see Mendonça (1999). An excellent discussion of Faoro in the context of Max Weber's reception in Brazil appears in Werneck Vianna (1999). For a critique of the notion of bureaucratic status group in Brazilian history, see Carvalho (1996) 129-53.

[2] All citations for Faoro's *Os Donos do Poder* refer to the first edition, unless otherwise noted.

[3] "*Patrimonialism* and, in the extreme case, *sultanism* tend to arise whenever traditional domination develops an administration and a military force which are purely personal instruments of the master" (Weber 231). "*Estate-type domination* [*ständische Herrschaft*] is that form of patrimonial authority under which the administrative staff appropriates particular powers and the corresponding economic assets" (Weber 232). In the estate-type domination, "the appropriation of judicial and military powers tends to be treated as a legal basis for a privileged status position of those appropriating them" (Weber 236).

[4] The view according to which the Brazilian nation lacked the positive attributes necessary to the development of modern life has a long tradition. See, for instance, Moraes' work on the "Portraits of Brazil" (60-67).

[5] Patrimonialism, Faoro stated in a 1993 article, "is as deep as Brazilian history, and by that I include its Iberian origins. It extends from the patrimonial monarchy, which during the dynasty of Avis (in the fourteenth century) found its vocation in the maritime, to the fiscal plans of the '80s and '90s of this century" (Faoro, "A Aventura Liberal" 17).

[6] For a summary of this system of classification, see Toynbee 130-31.

[7] In the original, "A Viagem Redonda: do Patrimonialismo ao Estamento." (Translator's note)

Works Cited

Carvalho, José Murilo de. *A Construção da Ordem; Teatro de Sombras.* 2nd ed. Rio de Janeiro: UFRJ/Relume-Dumará, 1996.

Faoro, Raymundo. *Os Donos do Poder: A Formação do Patronato Político Brasileiro.* Rio de Janeiro/Porto Alegre/São Paulo: Globo, 1958.

———. *Os Donos do Poder: A Formação do Patronato Político Brasileiro.* 2 vols. 4th ed. Porto Alegre: Globo, 1977.

———. "A Aventura Liberal numa Ordem Patrimonialista". *Revista USP* 17 (1993): 14-29.

———. *Existe um Pensamento Político Brasileiro?* São Paulo: Ática, 1994.

Iglésias, Francisco. "Revisão de Raymundo Faoro." *Cadernos do Departamento de Ciência Política* 3 (1976): 123-42.

Mello e Souza, Laura de. "Raymundo Faoro: Os Donos do Poder." *Introdução ao Brasil: Um Banquete no Trópico.* Ed. Lourenço Dantas Mota. São Paulo: SENAC, 1999. 335-55.

Mendonça, Kátia M. "Um Projeto Civilizador: Revisitando Faoro." *Lua Nova* 36 (1995): 181-96.

———. "Faoro e o Encontro entre Ética e Política." *Lua Nova* 48 (1999): 94-108.

Moraes, Eduardo Jardim de. *A Constituição da Idéia de Modernidade no Modernismo Brasileiro.*

Diss. Rio de Janeiro: IFCS/UFRJ, 1983.

Souza, Jessé. "A Ética Protestante e a Ideologia do Atraso Brasileiro." *Revista Brasileira de Ciências Sociais* 13. 38 (1998): 97-116.

Toynbee, Arnold J. *A Study of History.* 2nd ed. London: Oxford UP, 1956.

Weber, Max. *Economy and Society.* Eds. Günther Roth and Claus Wittich. New York: Bedminster Press, 1968.

Werneck Vianna, Luiz. "Weber e a Intrepretação do Brasil." *O Malandro e o Protestante.* Ed. Jessé Souza. Brasília: UnB, 1999. 173-95.

MARCELO JASMIM

America, Joy of Man's Desiring:
A Comparison of *Visão do Paraíso* with *Wilderness and Paradise in Christian Thought*

Robert Wegner[1]

Translated by Luiz Augusto da Silveira

In a recent study on millennialism, Jean Delumeau points out that hope for a period of bliss and tranquillity on earth played an important role from the fifteenth to the seventeenth centuries in Europe. The scarcity of studies on this subject consequently means that periods situated between the end of the Middle Ages and the Renaissance remain obscure. Furthermore, these ideas are just as relevant for the American continent; thus, the French historian finds it reasonable for L. I. Sweet to state that "the history of America began with the expectancy for the millennium."[2] About forty years ago, having noticed the importance of ideas on the wish for happiness and fulfillment, Sérgio Buarque de Holanda performed the research on Edenic motifs in the discovery and colonization of Brazil that led to *Visão do Paraíso* (*Vision of Paradise*), published in 1959. The Brazilian historian was fifty-seven years old at the time and, after having published *Raízes do Brasil* (1936), *Monções* (1945), and *Caminhos e Fronteiras* (1957), this was his fourth book, based on the thesis he had written in order to become Chair of History of Brazilian Civilization at the Universidade de São Paulo (USP).

Even if the book of Genesis' Garden of Eden from which our ancestors were expelled existed somewhere on earth, according to Catholic Church doctrine as outlined by St. Augustine (A. D. 354-430), it would still be inaccessible. Furthermore, the millennialist belief in a period of happiness on earth to precede a second coming of Jesus Christ and the Church's definitive redemption had already been rejected.[3] In spite of that, myths related to the existence of an earthly Paradise still held a strong attraction for medieval men, some of whom even believed that it could be reached physically or at least glimpsed, as with Moses before Canaan.[4] At the time of the discovery of America by the Europeans, it was not difficult for the focus of these hopes, normally directed to the East, to be shifted to the new continent, a transferal whose history was researched by Buarque de Holanda in *Visão do Paraíso*.

In his book, Buarque de Holanda presents the descriptions made by Portuguese and Spanish travelers and clergy as marked by Edenic and wonderland motifs that fused Christian and pagan literary traditions. Such motifs worked as a sort of lens deployed to view the new lands, and which despite having been revised or attenuated, continued to thrive for a long time. Buarque de Holanda maps out a number of these recurrent *topoi* both in texts descriptive of American lands and in those that sought to demonstrate that the Biblical garden from which Adam and Eve had been expelled was in fact to be found there. These *topoi* or literary lenses become variegated and, to a greater or lesser degree, are reinvented at the moment of their confrontation with new experiences, as if some sort of compromise existed between literary tradition and historical experience, the consequences of which led to the search for a "middle path" (*"via mediana"*) between practical conclusions emerging from the discovery of unknown lands and the prestige of the sages' authority, be it Christian or pagan.[5]

The belief in the existence of "paradise on earth" in some unknown place was widespread even outside the Iberian peninsula, and it acquired very different contours and overtones depending on where it originated. According to Buarque de Holanda's study, whereas in Spain the belief was painted in strong colors, among the Portuguese it was portrayed in a more discreet and simple manner. Thus, the new experiences supplied by the American world were described by the former in bold and delirious inductions, and by the latter in a way that recalls the "prosaic 'realism' and particularism characteristic of Medieval art, chiefly that which was produced toward the end of the Middle Ages":

> [An] art in which even the angelic figures appear to give up flying, settling for more plausible and reserved gestures (such as walking on small clouds that would serve them as a base, as if they owned tangible bodies), and in which miracles assert themselves through more convincing resources than haloes and nimbuses, so familiar to painters of other times.[6]

This phenomenon, involving a coldness and realism nearly unheard-of for the Portuguese *cinquecento* mentality so alien to a "sense of the impossible," as Lucien Febvre noted,[7] Sérgio Buarque named "plausible attenuation."[8] Yet the historian believes that the contrast between a naive credulous background (*"um fundo singelamente crédulo"*) and realism is not as sharp as it may be surmised on first consideration. For in fact, this realism is rooted in the credulity of the Portuguese, "which in the face of reality tends to constitute a sort of radical passivity and meekness."[9] Satisfied with the description of the self-evident, immediate and usable, the credulity that nurtures Portuguese realism is evidence of "an extremely rich emotional undercurrent that, given its power, can barely achieve the standards of minimal neutrality necessary to objectify oneself in fantastic representations" associated with common fifteenth- and sixteenth-century European paradise-on-earth *topoi*.[10] In that way, the "plausible attenuation" phenomenon refers to the plasticity of the Portuguese as discussed by Buarque de Holanda in his first book, *Raízes do Brasil* (1936). In this work, Portuguese colonizers appear as "sowers" of cities, in that they would adapt their construction plans to environmental circumstances and local geography. In this sense, the Portuguese differed from the Spanish. The latter came through as the greater builders, for by rejecting the former's complacency they were able to overcome geographic accidents and accomplish their town building projects in the desired sites.

Representative of this Portuguese brand of prosaism that contrasts with the wondrous Hispanic descriptions is the fact that, out of the different myths disseminated in the continental conquest, most legends, such as belief in "Amazons," the existence of mountain ridges of silver, of fountains of youth and magical lagoons, were propagated by the Spanish. As soon as such beliefs entered into Brazilian territory they tended to fade, to lose their sharpness; that is, they went through attenuations toward the plausible.[11] Just one myth appears to have a Portuguese-Brazilian origin, that of São Tomé, in which the follower of Jesus appeared in America as the herald of good news from God. But even more meaningful than the dissemination of a single myth out of Portuguese America is the fact that when the myth first appeared it was very close to the prosaic and yet as it spread toward Spanish America it lost its humble character, making the figure of São Tomé appear gradually better dressed. Thus the historian wrote:

If we are to give credit to a number of statements about the saint's wanderings, in Brazil São Tomé walked barefoot, taking along with him one companion at most—someone who could be a follower of Jesus or even his own guardian angel.

... However, judging by the footsteps left in the cluster of rocks near Asunción, as mentioned by Lourenço Mendoza and Antonio Ruiz, the Paraguayan version of the myth has the saint wear sandals. In reaching Peru, the Natives had him wearing three-soled shoes that resembled sandals such as those he left behind near Arequipa's volcano after having crossed smoking lava fields that flowed like torrential rivers. The shoes' internal soles exhibited the imprint of the sweaty feet of a man so huge as to make everyone gape in wonderment.[12]

To conclude the counterpoint established with the humble tableau of a nearly Franciscan disciple of Jesus as portrayed in Portuguese America, it should be noted that according to Buarque de Holanda, "differently from what happened in Brazil, where, stalked by the Native Brazilians, he would try to flee from their treachery and tyranny, the Peruvian São Tomé legend described the saint as intolerant of any offense."[13]

Yet, in spite of the prosaic and humble character acquired by the myths in Brazil, despite the phenomenon of "attenuation toward the plausible," it cannot be said that "during the Middle Ages and in the time of overseas discoveries, the Portuguese were less seduced by the Edenic theme than the other Christian peoples of Europe, or even the Jewish and Muslim peoples."[14] Among the Portuguese descriptions and eulogies of the new lands usually related them to Edenic visions whose nexus—almost an absolute criterion of identification—consisted in a balanced, "neither cold nor hot" climate that had been associated with the Biblical paradise since Isidoro de Sevilla.[15] Thus, a text by Father Simão de Vasconcelos, which was censored immediately after its publication in 1663, may be viewed as an instance of the existence of this *topos* in Brazil. In it, the Catholic priest, following written tradition, analyzes the likelihood of the Earthly Paradise being located in America. He wrote at one point:

> Saint Boaventura... clearly states that God placed Paradise near the Equinox: *Quia secus Equinoctia est ibi magna temperies temporaris*: for near the Equinox the climate is quite tempered... One may add: that place in the Equinox has a mild climate, abundance of water, and frequent winds to purify the air, for experience has shown that the regions under the Torrid Zone, held by the ancients as uninhabitable, are mild and inhabited with great comfort by men.[16]

This is how, based on the medieval religious and pagan traditions associated with narratives about the new worlds, Vasconcelos argues for the idea that the earthly Paradise must have been located in Brazilian soil. There one would find an agreeable place unaffected by the curses issued from the first sin, where, of course, pain, aging and death were inexistent. And there, again, man would be free from having to sweat in order to earn his daily sustenance. Paradise lost was, therefore, in Brazilian lands.

The Edenic vision described by Buarque de Holanda and that prevailed among Iberian settlers—a vision which was even taken to refer to the "land without evil" of the Guarani[17]—was well synthesized by George Williams in his *Wilderness and Paradise in Christian Thought* (1962). There he summarized Buarque de Holanda's work when he wrote that in the Southern parts of the continent "the vision of an Earthly Paradise *merely waiting to be gained*" prevailed.[18]

Moreover, if in *Visão do Paraíso* it is possible to note a counterpoint between the colors and tonalities of Edenic motifs in the Portuguese and Spanish conquests, the reading of *Wilderness and Paradise in Christian Thought*, in which the professor of Ecclesiastical History at Oxford University compiles his studies on the search by Anglo-Saxon settlers for a paradise on earth, may be of help in outlining a more complete sketch of Edenic ideas in the colonization of the Americas as a whole. In this sense, even a rough comparison between Williams' and Buarque de Hollanda's works may help light the way and even suggest engaging solutions towards a comparative approach of the Iberian and Anglo-Saxon processes of colonization.

To conclude this sketch, I believe it is useful to employ one of the most constant paradise-on-earth motifs as noted by Buarque de Holanda: the temperate climate. It is quite possible to find visions similar to those that circulated among the Iberians who sought to discover lost paradise ready and waiting. A good example of the similarity is provided by Thomas Morton, the Puritan who upon arriving in New England in 1622 thought that he had found "new Canaan." What made Morton believe this was again precisely the *locus amoenus* criterion, since for him the new land: "shares heat and cold at the same time, though it is overburdened by neither. In truth, it may be said to be located within the boundaries of an intermediate position, which is very suited for settlement and reproduction, for God Almighty, the Great Creator, placed it in the so-called temperate zone."[19]

However, even with cases such as this one narrated by Delumeau, George Williams' insistence in pursuing a vision that is nearly antagonistic to the one that prevailed among the Iberians seems plausible, for although *there is* an ongoing search for Eden, it does not follow of necessity that the garden of the New World is ready to be inhabited. On the contrary, the image most often used among the Puritans to describe the new land is that of the wilderness. Here the US historian traces a long tradition back to the Old Testament and the exodus of the Jewish people from Egypt when, under the guidance of Moses, Israel wanders for forty years in the desert before reaching the promised land. The double significance of the word "wilderness" survives in this long tradition, exhibiting both the positive meaning of a place of protection and one suitable for Christian missions, and the negative one of a wasteland without redemption. In any case, it signifies the place where Eden is to be built—even though it may be of just a temporary nature, an idea faithful to the millenarian movements. Thus, prepared for the true Church that has been persecuted since the time of Moses, the wilderness becomes a place of refuge and of missionary activity, capable of becoming the Garden of the Lord by means of moral and spiritual temperance rather than through mere physical conquest.[20] Within this context, with the temperate climate no longer being a quality inherent to the new lands, the preaching on the construction of the true church in the desert may transform itself into a metaphor for the transformational action of the pioneers. An example of this is a nineteenth-century case presented by Williams, that of Yale's founder, Timothy Dwight, who, while discoursing on the mission of educational establishments in 1812, preached as follows:

> The Gospel is the rain and sunshine of heaven upon the moral world. Wherever its beams are shed, and its showers fall, the wilderness blossoms as the rose, and the desert as the garden of God: while the world beside is an Arabian waste, where no fountains flow, and no verdure springs, and where life itself fades, languishes and expires.[21]

In that way, it may be said that if the *topos* of the *locus amoenus* was present among North American Puritans, this motif was a metaphor for the purifying action of the Gospel rather than an attribute of the place where the colonizer ought to settle, quite independent in this case of knowing whether this was merely a literary cliché that found a correspondence in the actual climate.

Though in his book Buarque de Holanda refrained from making generalizations and from inferring consequences from his thesis that might have had longer-lasting effects on the history of Brazil, it may be considered, as a conclusion, that although these myths concerning the earthly Paradise began to fade both in the northern and southern regions of the American continent, they continued to exert their power, and thus—like gods who even after having lost their currency in belief continue to wield an influence on the actions of men—remained present in the beliefs of New World inhabitants. These are George Williams' views as Buarque de Holanda transcribed them from the US professor's book. There, Williams says that the widely diverse feelings moving the men of the Old World would lead them to formulate living patterns that were quite distinct from one another, and that the effects of these patterns determine to the present day the distinct behaviors of their descendants in our continent.[22] Nevertheless, one should preserve one's misgivings about stereotypes that simplify internal complexities and that dilute the history of America either into myths of paradise to be gained, or an Eden to be conquered, as if there were no dissonant voices in Portuguese and Spanish as well as in Anglo-Saxon America, voices that crop up even in a short essay such as this, and which here find an example in Thomas Morton, the Puritan who upon laying eyes on the New World describes it as a pleasant place and a land of delights.

Even then, as Williams points out, the search for Edenic motifs among settlers may suggest explanatory keys for the history of the continent that are more complex and fruitful than, for instance, the opposition between a Catholic and a Protestant America.[23] By the same token, one might add that Catholic America becomes more complex when the differences in tone pointed out in *Visão do Paraíso* are explored in the apparently similar myths linked to what Williams characterized as an earthly Paradise merely waiting to be secured, but that can be less colorful and more humble among the Portuguese than amid the Spanish.

Notes

[1] The author is grateful to the "Fundação Casa de Oswaldo Cruz," who sponsored the translation of this article from Portuguese into English through its "Incentive Program for the Publication in a Foreign Language."

[2] Delumeau 87, 200.

[3] Holanda 174; Delumeau chap. 1; Saint Augustine Book XIII, chap. XXI; Book XXII, chap. XXX.

[4] *Deuteronomy* (4:23-29).

[5] Holanda 288.

[6] Holanda 1-2.

[7] Lucien Febvre, see Holanda 5.

[8] Holanda 130.

[9] Holanda 105.

[10] Holanda 148.

[11] Holanda 130.

[12] Holanda 119.

[13] Holanda 119.

[14] Holanda 149.

[15] See Holanda 560-636. On the *locus amoenus* topos, in addition to *Visão do Paraíso*, see Curtius chap. 10.

[16] Qtd. in Holanda 363-64.

[17] Holanda 141-42.

[18] Williams 100. My emphasis. Buarque de Holanda comments on Williams' book, including the synthesis he makes of *Visão do Paraíso*, in the preface to the second edition of his book (xii, xiii). Buarque de Holanda had the opportunity of teaching and researching in the libraries of Indiana and New York universities between 1966 and 1967. It was at this time that he was able to update himself on US publications on themes kindred to his own book's, again, reviewing them in 1968 in "Prefácio à Segunda Edição" of *Visão do Paraíso*.

[19] Qtd. by Delumeau 237. On Thomas Morton, refer to Slotkin, *Regeneration Through Violence*, esp. 58-65.

[20] Williams 5.

[21] Quoted by Williams 124.

[22] Williams 100. Qtd. by Buarque de Holanda in "Prefácio à Segunda Edição" of *Visão do Paraíso*, xiii.

[23] Williams 100. Qtd. by Buarque de Holanda, *Visão* xiii.

Works Cited

Saint Augustine. *Cidade de Deus*. Petrópolis: Vozes, 1990.

Curtius, Ernst Robert. *European Literature and the Latin Middle Ages*. 1948. Tans. Willard R. Trask. Princeton: Princeton UP, 1973.

Delumeau, Jean. *Mil Anos de Felicidade: Uma História do Paraíso*. 1995. Trans. Paulo Neves. São Paulo: Companhia das Letras, 1997.

Holanda, Sérgio Buarque de. *Visão do Paraíso: Os Motivos Edênicos no Descobrimento e Colonização do Brasil*. 1959. 5a ed. São Paulo, Brasiliense, 1992.

Slotkin, Richard. *Regeneration Through Violence: The Mythology of the American Frontier, 1600-1860*. 1973. 2nd ed. New York: Harper Collins, 1996.

Williams, George H. *Wilderness and Paradise in Christian Thought: The Biblical Experience of the Desert in the History of Christianity & The Paradise Theme in the Theological Idea of the University*. New York: Harper and Brothers, 1962.

Florestan Fernandes: Memory and Utopia

Carlos Guilherme Mota
Translated by Nöel de Souza
Revised by Mark Streeter

In 1977, in an Italian tavern next to Tavistock Square in London, during a conversation with Prof. Eric J. Hobsbawm on the obstacles to the consolidation of democracy in Brazil, I was so bold as to comment on certain difficulties in understanding this country's ambiguous current history. This great historian smiled discreetly, pointing out that one of the five greatest social scientists and interpreters of our time was Brazilian, namely, Florestan Fernandes, who, at that moment was living in Canada. I started to wonder who the other three interpreters would be....

Today, as the lights of "the age of extremes" go out, I remember this London meeting, which was indeed so important to me at a time when I was reading through essays on the life and work of Florestan, a great teacher, friend and socialist. Florestan was a simple man just like Hobsbawm, just like the much missed Albert Soboul, Joaquim Barradas de Carvalho and Warren Dean. All are leftist intellectuals, great researchers and exceptionally creative writers who helped us place Brazilian studies on the map of today's world.

Florestan was a multifarious intellectual, whose exemplary and conscious trajectory reflects and, at the same time, eclectically questions the political and cultural history of São Paulo, Brazil and Latin America. The "uprooted" Florestan's personal history has solid roots in São Paulo, in a socio-cultural formation of which the new oligarchies and emerging bourgeois classes are composed and reproduced with method and rigor. I don't believe that any other social scientist or writer has reflected so much and so compulsively on their own institutional and political role and on the significance of their discipline throughout Brazilian history. Indeed, two disciplines, Sociology and History, fascinated the young researcher from the very outset. It may even it may be said that the constellation known as the "Escola Histórico-Sociológica de São Paulo," as it is internationally known, was centered on him.

Student and soon master of a new discipline—Sociology—, he was called upon in the 1940s—along with his steady partner, Antonio Candido, and at the invitation of his teacher Fernando de Azevedo, one of the founders of the Universidade de São Paulo—to develop new approaches for a society which was then discovered to be "backward" and "archaic": Brazilian society. Sociology was gaining ground in Brazilian studies with the innovative works of Gilberto Freyre. Nevertheless, although innovative in the 1930s, Freyre's voice was that of the decadent stately classes; his works were thus, considered groundbreaking only because Brazil was "very much backward"—as Caio Prado Jr. still believed even in the early 1980s.

Florestan quickly performed the role of spokesperson of world visions and values of newly emerging classes, which had only begun to emerge on the national scene. He represented—or rather imagined he was representing based on his own life story—the "dispossessed," those "from below," those excluded by Brazilian society, which he defined as an autocratic bourgeois model. Florestan was an impressive man due to his capacity for hard work, his seriousness, and sharpness. In his classic book *A Cultura Brasileira*,[1] the always demanding and straightforward Fernando de Azevedo wrote that Florestan, besides being the greatest intellectual talent he ever met, had a genuine vocation for the social sciences. Again, it was Florestan who in the 1950s and 1960s, in collaboration with Roger Bastide,[2] the innovative and most combative researcher of an avant-garde institution, created the important Faculty of Philosophy, Sciences and Arts at the Universidade de São Paulo, which, not by chance, was dismembered and devitalized under the military dictatorship established with the 1964 coup d'état.

In the 1970s, with his license withdrawn by the military dictatorship, Florestan deepened his reflection on Brazil and on his condition as a sociologist with socialist leanings. Expelled from the university, he soon discovered the Latin America of Martí and Mariátegui, Pablo González Casanova, Orlando Fals Borda, Moreno Fraginals and Aníbal Quijano, writing two of his most decisive books: *Capitalismo Dependente e Classes Sociais na América Latina* and *Poder e Contrapoder na América Latina*. But he does not distract his attention from Brazilian history. At the same time he also produced *Circuito Fechado*, an important contribution to understanding the influence of the colonial past. In the United States his main interlocutors were Stanley and Barbara Stein, Charles Wagley, Richard Morse and Warren Dean.

In the 1980s, he himself actually engaged himself in a political party, the "Partido dos Trabalhadores" ("The Workers' Party"), becoming an active agent of the ups and downs of national political life along with a wide and emerging sector of Brazilian society, the labor world, linked to radical elements of the middle class.

The 1990s began for Florestan with an homage—he was granted the title of doctor *honoris causa* by the Universidade de Coimbra, then celebrating its 700 years of existence, and recognizing him as one of the most important intellectuals of the Luso-Afro-Brazilian world. Towards the end of his life, the son of the Portuguese immigrant D. Maria returned to Portugal to receive the recognition of Coimbra, thanks to its most progressive sector—a sector lead by intellectuals such as the sociologist Boaventura de Sousa Santos.

The 1990s also found him in a state of serene maturity, busy with the activity of the great socialist public intellectual he turned into, surrounded by friends, his wife Myriam and younger and livelier advisers such as Vladimir Saccheta, Márcia Camargos and Paulo Martinez. Death caught up with him—the verb is fitting—in a phase of total lucidity, aligned with the most significant avant-garde events of Brazil.

The main aim of Florestan's works was to reveal the profound syntony between theory and praxis. After all, due to his poor childhood, Florestan himself knew well what it meant to live in a peripheral condition—geographically politically and socially. Florestan therefore combined biography and intellectual responsibility as an important researcher. Complex intersections: Florestan was neither a manual worker nor held the means of production or property, thus belonging to none of the so-called fundamental classes. He was neither son nor grandson of oligarchs; nor did he benefit from scholarships or support from national or international foundations; nor did he come from a family of liberal professionals; nor from the class of bureaucrats and/or the military, as did most of his colleagues and pupils.

He was very much a self-made intellectual, quite close in this regard to Anatol Rosenfeld or Maurício Tragtemberg, both of whom did not by mere chance adopt a certain critical concept of culture as well as São Paulo as their city. At times, Florestan described himself as having an odd *sans-culotte* behavior and his mindset stood somewhere in this foggy region between the mental horizons of the urban *petite bourgeoisie* and those of the proletariat. But he was neither one nor the other. Moreover, he did just about everything in order to earn his living, from being a tailor's assistant to a waiter. In that situation, as an outsider, he cultivated a strategic angle from where he could observe the life of the stately and bureaucratic classes, as well as the variations of some segments of the middle class of which he finally became part.

Florestan grew up in a world in which (as Karl Marx defined in *The German Ideology*) former classes—from which Caio Prado Jr., Sérgio Buarque, Afonso Arinos, Gilberto Freyre come from—lived on familiar terms with future classes; indeed, former classes were part of the future ones or entered into intense conflict with them. Those were classes from which personalities such as his great friend and the great journalist Hermínio Sacchetta belonged or from which important political figures such as Luiz Inácio Lula da Silva and Luiza Erundina emerged. But his gaze came "from below" and that is why—like Jean-Jacques Rousseau—he was able to detect the foundations upon which the Brazilian autocratic model stands in all of its social dimension. In other words, Florestan could keenly unveil the persistent heritage from the past slavocratic class, both in its network of social relations and in its mentality. A great friend to his friends, filled with a strong sense of genuine *fraternity* (I am thinking of the specific sense in which this term was used in 1793), on more than one occasion I witnessed his rustic and direct style, half *sans-culotte*, half Jacobite and half Rousseauite. On the other hand, he was excellent at imposing the radical combative character he created, apparently unpleasant when he faced his far too conservative, intransigent or reactionary opponents. His logic then would stand up to the immovable and ice-cold Caio Prado Jr., whom he respected over all the other Brazilian intellectuals.

In more recent years, he would get upset when his dense and well-articulated parliamentary speeches as a representative of the "Partido dos Trabalhadores" were not listened to. He would criticize the predominant mediocrity at the National Congress and would even deplore that not even one single conservative, however prepared, like the parliamentarian Roberto Campos, deserved the attention of this audience. "What a waste," he thought. He thought that major national themes were going unnoticed by the political class, the press and universities. Furthermore, Florestan, the Member of Parliament, rendered accounts and heeded the suggestions of his electorate like no one else, for he took responsibility as representative of a group, a project, a utopia.

But how does a Florestan Fernandes emerge in a historical and cultural process like ours? In noteworthy texts, written after his death, such as those by Heloísa Rodrigues Fernandes, his daughter and also a sociologist of merit, or by Boris Schnaiderman, an important writer and literary critic, we gathered information about his daily life as an intellectual, his way of working, reading and how he prepared himself to understand the world. I was able to accompany him during a few periods of his life and witnessed the impact of certain readings, such as *The Unbearable Lightness of Being*, by Milan Kundera, or *Viva o Povo Brasileiro*, by João Ubaldo Ribeiro. Or even, at the end of the 1970s, the serene effect from re-reading Thomas Mann and Proust.

Florestan had a taste for reading, for studying, and for a non-bookish but informed analysis. And intellectually he was bold. He created concepts, combining theories and crossing research from different fields. But one comes to the conclusion that indeed he was a self-made man. He forged himself into a mixed model of an individualist militant and an old-fashioned gentleman, having surely learnt a lot—including "good manners," let's say—with his "brother" Antonio Candido, another socialist who even to this day continues to serve as an important reference for new generations.

In this regard, Antonio Candido, through his statements, clarifies the early times of Florestan, the politician, when he comments on the ups and downs of the obscure democratic left and the emergence of the "Partido Socialista Brasileiro," a party consistent in its ideas but precarious in its actions.[3] Thus, one can understand the orthodoxy and the former controversial "eclecticism" of the São Paulo sociologist, or rather the uniqueness of his concept of socialism. Indeed, the concept of a radical, popular and anti-populist democracy, a concept that makes a world of difference in a country whose political culture is dominated both by the oligarchic interests and populism. It was, so to speak, a São Paulo tailored form of socialism—Florestan was deeply "paulistano," that is, capable of a rude frankness uttered in simple and direct sentences. At the same time he was an open man, urbane and polite, which was the hallmark of our industrial city, formerly famous for its people's hospitality—not populist,

CARLOS GUILHERME MOTA

may I insist—, but lively and democratic. A hospitality which the sociologist cultivated and which today has become rare, though it is terribly needed.

One can, however, never overemphasize the rare ability at self-criticism Florestan had. Various recent studies evidence courageous corrections of his intellectual trajectory—always within a leftist thought, it is worth stressing—as well as his visceral lack of desire for reconciliation of any type. As it is well-known, this is precisely what is happening today in Brazilian society and this desire for reconciliation at any cost might dangerously tear apart the very political basis of the country. That obviously did not stop him from mingling with personalities different from his own leanings, like Júlio de Mesquita Filho, director of *O Estado de São Paulo*—who during a certain period, at the start of the 1960s, kept weekly contacts with Florestan, at least by telephone.

But to mingle or socialize did not mean to reconcile. Likewise, he accepted companions from the orthodox and even dogmatic left. Again, this did not stop him from criticizing the *mores* indigenous to Brazil (on the right as well as on the left, especially when the latter proved to be simplistic or opportunistic), or, on the contrary, supporting already in the 1950s the leaders of the black, gay or women's movements. Perhaps his pessimism vis-à-vis the action of the generation to which he belonged may have been overdone. At a certain point he described it as "the lost generation," a rather pompous, exaggerated title of a remarkable and well-known essay by him— exaggerated in particular if one looks closely at the following generation, which is very conciliatory.

And lastly, his studies still raise major questions about the ambiguities of the so-called Brazilian culture, this gelatinous octopus whose tentacles point time after time towards conciliation and demobilization, a culture in which civil rights and workers' victories are not consolidated. Five years after his death, the vortex of time and things seems to engulf the memory of Florestan's actions, erasing the outline of his trajectory and shrinking the significance of his battles, many of which stemmed from his individualist militancy or his methodology. As the "scandal fixer" in many a decisive situation, he would not spare even his closest interlocutors, friends or associates, compelling them to forge further ahead in their combats.

Florestan finally saw himself as a battering ram preceding the construction of a democratic order and he knew better than anyone else the difficulties that construction entailed. For it was—and still is—very difficult for someone who "comes from below" to break out of his political and cultural class—which helps explain the astonishment of those who perchance have succeeded in landing positions in the hierarchies within the current social model.

In sum, Florestan Fernandes can be situated and understood as the supreme conscience of our time. In the field of Human Sciences, he was a creator who supplied the critical flesh of this society, not sparing himself from profound self-criticism—into which at times were dragged his generation and his university colleagues or party mates—but always conferring meaning upon our experiences and our time, criticizing, building, examining, improving, proposing a counter-move, expressing irony. He had the sense of history and of the intense historicity of daily life, in addition to his solid and programmed historiographic readings. From Gibbon to Mantoux, from Dobb and Baran to Faoro, he had an opinion, a sharp comment, based on his reading. In that regard, I would not hesitate to say that he was without exaggeration, the most important and complete character of our intellectual history. And, in a way, he also was a great historian.

What can be said of Florestan's personal courage? (And mind that this is not an idle issue if one remembers the violence of the military dictatorship established in Brazil in 1964.) I witnessed him in difficult situations, as on that evening of November 1975, shortly after the murder of Wladimir Herzog. At the Dominican Convent, in Rua Caiubi, with Perseu Abramo, José de Souza Martins and others, when we tried to organize the civil society in order to stop the barbarism that was being announced by the increasing violence of the regime, Florestan—the last speaker and certainly the most targeted of us all—laid out a caustic argument, showing how on the crest of the bourgeois revolutions "civil rights" in fact were recognized only in a "minority of equals"... I can't imagine how we got away unscathed (he, in particular) from that night, on to fresh clashes, departing soon after, when things began to heat up, for a short sojourn in Austin, Texas. There I had, along with my family, the displeasure of running once again into Brazilian right thugs—bravely confronted by the historian and friend of mine Richard Graham—and went on to face cold Toronto and the theoretical clashes with the sociologist Amitai Etzioni.

Of those long and depressing months in Texas, I remember how brilliant was the interdisciplinary colloquium on his recently published *A Revolução Burguesa no Brasil*. The colloquium, organized in collaboration with the brave Professor Graham, was held with great difficulty, and counted on the participation of Emília Viotti da Costa, Silviano Santiago, the late Alejandro Losada,[4] K. David Jackson, Graham and others. Something of this thought-provoking meeting was preserved, and was published by Moacyr Félix and by the great publisher and man of culture Enio Silveira in the *Encontros da Civilização Brasileira: De Tudo fica um Pouco*.

Of Florestan much has remained, namely a stimulating and diversified work that constitutes an encompassing theory for understanding Brazil. What also remains is a sense of a warm friendship, a general feeling for things in an era where "our modernity" insists on the predominance of "the non-feeling."

Notes

[1] This important book was translated as *Brazilian Culture: An Introduction to the Study of Culture in Brazil.*

[2] Along with Roger Bastide, Fernandes published *Relações Raciais entre Negros e Brancos em São Paulo.*

[3] This constitutes a topic that deserves a study by historians of ideas as well as by political scientists.

[4] On that occasion, Losada drew an interesting parallel between Mariátegui and Florestan.

Works Cited

Azevedo, Fernando de. *Brazilian Culture: An Introduction to the Study of Culture in Brazil.* 1943. Trans. William Rex Crawford. New York: Macmillan, 1950.

Fernandes, Florestan. *A Integração do Negro na Sociedade de Classes.* 2 vols. São Paulo: Dominus, 1965.

———. *The Negro in Brazilian Society.* Trans. Jacqueline D. Skiles, A. Brunel and Arthur Rothwell. Ed. Phylis B. Eveleth. New York: Atheneum, 1971.

———. *Capitalismo Dependente e Classes Sociais na América Latina.* Rio de Janeiro: Zahar Editores, 1973.

———. *Poder e Contrapoder na América Latina.* Rio de Janeiro: Zahar Editores, 1981.

———. *Reflections on the Brazilian Counter-revolution.* Trans. Michel Vale and Patrick M. Hughes. Ed. with an introduction by Warren Dean. New York: M.E. Sharpe, 1981.

Fernandes, Florestan and Roger Bastide. *Relações Raciais entre Negros e Brancos em São Paulo.* São Paulo: Anhembi, 1955.

Discovering "Brazil's Soul":
A Reading of Luís da Câmara Cascudo

Margarida de Souza Neves
Translated by Shoshanna Lurie

Have you consulted Cascudo? Cascudo's the one who knows. Bring me Cascudo here. Cascudo arrives and finds the solution. Everyone respects 'him' and agrees with 'him.' He's not really a person, but rather, he's a person in two thick volumes, in the form of a dictionary, always worth having within arm's reach. Ready when a doubt arises about our people's customs, celebrations, and arts. He explains every detail of Brazil's soul—its magical heritage, its rituals, its behavior in the face of simple mystery and reality. Instead of saying 'Brazilian Dictionary,' one would save time saying 'Cascudo,' its author. The author, however, is much more than simply a dictionary. His vast bibliography of folkloric and historical studies reflects a wonderful life's work within the concern for experiencing Brazil.
Carlos Drummond de Andrade (1998, 13)

Carlos Drummond de Andrade's brief profile of Luís da Câmara Cascudo is very expressive. Drummond highlights specific characteristics, and the poet's choice of definition for the folklorist and historian is telling both for what it selects and for what it seems to overlook.

A twofold movement guides Drummond's portrait of Câmara Cascudo. On the one hand, it expresses tension between the metonymic value attributed to his most significant work, the monumental *Dicionário do Folclore Brasileiro* (*Dictionary of Brazilian Folklore*), and the recognition that Cascudo had done "much more." On the other, it reflects the recurring association between the author and Brazil, since Cascudo is presented as a person who knows and makes "Brazil's soul" known, and whose intellectual work is guided by the "concern for experiencing Brazil."

The task of presenting a synthesis of Cascudo's work is not a trivial one. He was an intense and galvanizing personality, son of a Northeastern colonel who assumed the conservative identity of his ancestors as his family surname.[1] Cascudo was simultaneously an internationally respected researcher[2] and an habitué of the *zona da Ribeira*;[3] a translator of Walt Whitman's poetry and an enthusiast of the *cordel*[4] of the Brazilian backlands;[5] a passionate husband who, in his later years, liked to contemplate the moon while holding his wife's hand, and also a renowned drinker and bohemian; the catholic to whom the Vatican granted the ecclesiastical benefice of the São Gregório Magno order and a specialist in white magic, superstition and fetish[6] and a mandatory presence at all Natal *terreiros*;[7] coordinator of the Rio Grande do Norte integralist movement in the 1930s and a writer who in the 1960s was admired and respected by leftist intellectuals such as Celso Furtado, Jorge Amado, and Moacyr de Góes; a learned expert in classical and renaissance literature and the captivated interlocutor of the fishermen Chico Preto and Pedro Perna Santo and of Bibi, his parent's old house servant whom he considered a "humble and illiterate Sheherazade;"[8] a great figure in Brazilian ethnography and folklore studies and a writer infrequently read by more recent generations of social scientists.

In the labyrinth that appears before those who dare to approach the life and work of Câmara Cascudo, Drummond's short portrait suggests, through the magic of the poet's words, an Ariadne's thread that allows one to follow the paths that cross the multifaceted body of Luís da Câmara Cascudo's works: the encyclopedic nature of the work and the author's profile as an explorer of Brazil.

A Brazilian Encyclopedia

"*The Cascudo*," thus converted into a noun, signifies to Drummond and to many other Brazilians the *Dicionário do Folclore Brasileiro*, published in 1954 by the Ministry of Education and Culture through the "Instituto Nacional do Livro" ("National Book Institute"). This is why the poet identifies the author with one of his books and asserts that Cascudo "is not really a person, but rather, he's a person in two thick volumes, in the form of a dictionary, always worth having within arm's reach."

In the prologue to the first edition, while explaining the genealogy of the *Dicionário*, Câmara Cascudo provides an important key to its reading. This refers to one of the many attempts to revive the dream of encyclopedists of all times—deconstructing and summarizing the world. The *Dicionário* was Cascudo's response to Augusto Meyer, then president of the "National Book Institute," who had invited a group of Brazilian intellectuals to carry out Mário de Andrade's frustrated 1939 preliminary plan for a *Brazilian Encyclopedia.*[9] Still, the *Enciclopédia* would remain only a project. However, its only effectively realized fragment, Cascudo's *Dicionário*, seemed to accomplish Mário de Andrade's hopes for the great *Enciclopédia*—to provide a synthesis of Brazil both "to the educated man" and "to working-class homes."[10] Still a unique work of its genre to date, Cascudo's *Dicionário do Folclore Brasileiro* is a basic reference for scholarly researchers as well as for participants, popular singers, and carnival directors (*"carnavalescos"*) who prepare samba school themes (*"enredos"*).[11]

The *Dicionário* reflects a synthesis of Cascudo's work, and was updated until the end of his life in various new editions.[12] In it, the author expressed his intellectual credo by asserting:

> Contrary to teachers' lessons, I believe in the dual existence of culture among all peoples. In each of them, there is a sacred, official culture, reserved for formal ceremonies, and a popular culture, open only for oral transmission, made of hunting and fishing stories, of comic and war episodes, the exploits of the heroes most accessible to children's retentive memory. A vast and common repository of anecdotes exists among indigenous Brazilians, alongside the secrets of higher beings, donors of land cultivation techniques and of precious seeds. The secret of Jurupari is inviolable and the discloser is punished with death, but there are stories of Jurupari without the sacred unction and without the rigors of secrecy, known by almost all the men of the tribes. They are positive examples of the two cultures. The second is really folkloric.[13]

The *Dicionário* was also the work of a careful and obstinate collector who, since the publication of *Vaqueiros e Cantadores* in 1939, had begun to "slowly put together a guide for Brazilian folklore."[14] His work shaped the majority of the entries, aided by the collaboration of some of his many correspondents throughout the country, the musicians Villa-Lobos and Guerra Peixe, the folklorists Edison Carneiro and Renato Almeida, and the professors Manuel Diegues Junior and Gonçalves Fernandes.

In the "prologue," Cascudo summarized his method of work as the rigorous completion of what he understood as the protocol of his occupation:

MARGARIDA DE SOUZA NEVES

"The three phases of folkloric study—collection, analysis and comparison of data, and research on origins."[15]

Nevertheless, if the importance and publishing of the *Dicionário* seemed to justify the discursive slippage allowing Drummond to declare that "*The Cascudo*" was the *Dicionário* capable of resolving all doubts about Brazilian popular culture, the poet does not fail to establish that Cascudo the author was "much more."

A prolific writer, Câmara Cascudo authored more than 150 books on the most diverse topics related to Brazilian culture. As an ethnographer and folklorist, he collected, analyzed, and incessantly published legends,[16] proverbs,[17] and stories.[18] He also produced numerous monographs, among which his books on the hammock[19] and the *jangada*[20] stand out, and wrote texts of a more theoretical character.[21] As an historian he produced works that can be considered part of the tradition of positivist history,[22] as well as many others that characterize what he himself called "micro-history."[23] A chronicle-writer for more than fifty years, he published his "Actas Diurnas" ("Daily Report") in the Natal newspaper *A República*, and also wrote for newspapers in Rio de Janeiro, São Paulo, and many other Brazilian cities. He also recorded his memories in four books of memoirs;[24] an untiring researcher, he communicated the results of his investigations in scientific journals in Brazil and abroad. Also a man of letters, he wrote poetry and a novel to which he attributed particular importance. For the author, "no other book possesses emotional totality as does this one."[25] A compulsive correspondent, he exchanged letters with intellectuals of the broadest geographical and academic range.

Drummond was correct when declaring that the author from Rio Grande do Norte was "much more" than his best-known work, the *Dicionário do Folclore Brasileiro*. Each time anyone enters into *Babilônia*, as Cascudo humorously called his chaotic library—now threatened by the neglect of those responsible for preserving cultural memory in Brazil—new manuscripts are discovered.[26]

Discoveries

Drummond was not the only one to associate Cascudo so directly with the search for the "Brazilian soul." He had already been deemed "a man called Brazil" (Oliveira 1999), and the association of his name with the illustrious modern explorers of Brazil, intellectuals who, through different itineraries, dedicated their lives to the always novel and always constant and unchanging task of unmasking the secrets of the Brazilian land and its people.

Câmara Cascudo sought to understand and explain Brazil as did many others, among whom many were his principal correspondents. They included Mário de Andrade, with whom he maintained an extremely important epistolary exchange from 1924 until the death of *Macunaíma*'s author; Monteiro Lobato, to whom Cascudo wrote more than four hundred letters; Edison Carneiro, with whom he held a rich correspondence regarding the folkloric movement in Brazil; Gilberto Freyre, with whom he also maintained a correspondence governed by the mutual respect characteristic of relationships between Northeastern patriarchs; Villa-Lobos, Guimarães Rosa, Josué de Castro and many others. The originality of the itineraries of Cascudo's explorations and his unique profile as an explorer were less obvious.

In Cascudo's case, an important distinguishing element is the fact that he was an explorer who developed a vast symbolic cartography of Brazil without ever lifting anchor from his home harbor.

An eccentric explorer who obstinately refused to be seduced by the large Southeastern urban centers, where the dynamism of intellectual life, the country's most important universities, the direction of the folkloric movement on a national level, the abundant libraries and the offering of public positions summoned him more than once during his eighty-seven years. He repeatedly refused to trade in the Northeastern city of Natal where he was born for other larger cities and he assumed as a proud title the identity of "incurable provincial" given to him by Afrânio Peixoto (Peixoto 6). His countless trips were always work-related, both within Brazil and abroad. But his refuge was always Natal and his private lookout, the large Ladeira house that was then called *Junqueira Aires* and today carries his name.

Nevertheless, this mark of distinction was not exclusively his own. Gilberto Freyre, the master of Apipucos, decided to return to his native Recife after his years of study abroad. Like Freyre, Cascudo investigated the Brazil rooted in the Northeast and was a plural and versatile writer, but his navigational routes were different from those taken by the Pernambucan sociologist.

The peculiarity of Câmara Cascudo's exploration of Brazil resides, in the first place, in the methods he adopted. The key to this method seems to lie in the notion of *convivência* (shared living).

MARGARIDA DE SOUZA NEVES

Cascudo bases his ethnographic authority on his *convivência* with the people and popular traditions, for having been a child from the backlands and for never having abandoned provincial life. For this reason, he considered himself an expert—in an almost intimate way—of popular speech, gestures, mysteries and myths, and, in his later years, a master of an erudition recognized by all. In the "prologue" of *Tradição, Ciência do Povo*, he boasted of the method used for the research collected there in an almost emblematic summary, "not libraries, but *convivência*,"[27] suggesting the valorization of the experience of shared living (*con vivere*) as a form of construction of knowledge.

However, if it is through what he calls *convivência* that Cascudo particularizes his research methodology, he enables the identification of the course of his particular *exploration of Brazil* in the relationship between this fundamental process of shared living and the collection of his work's most relevant empirical data—folklore studies. This constituted one side of his work; the other necessarily was related to the "translation" of the empirical data into interpretive syntheses.

It is possible that both the description of his process of collection of folkloric material and the understanding of his function as a folklorist, mediator and interpreter of that which, though seen by and familiar to all, is only revealed to very few, are most clearly reduced to their most simple expression in *Canto do Muro*. In this book, while describing his observations of the animal world, to which he attributes intelligence and inventiveness, Cascudo claims to have carefully noted everything he had observed of the animals that traversed his yard: "characters defined by the freedom of all the hours of the day and night... they were observed by me without knowing that they were to be the subject of future scholarly investigation."[28]

Such an assertion, made in the context of a work with clear allegorical connotations, allows an adaptive appropriation indicative not only of what *convivência* meant to him as a method, but also of the modality of his observation as an ethnographer.

For Câmara Cascudo, folklore was tradition and tradition was the "science of the people." In one of his definitions of folklore, he synthesized the importance of his study:

> All the countries of the world, races, human groups, families, professional classes, possess a patrimony of traditions that is transmitted orally and defended and

preserved by custom. This patrimony is both ancient and contemporary. It grows daily as long as it is integrated into group and national customs. This patrimony is FOLKLORE. 'Folk': people, nation, family, kinship. 'Lore': instruction, knowledge, in the sense of an individual awareness of knowledge. Knowledge that knows. The here and now, an immediate awareness of knowledge made present.[29]

In later writings, he expands on the same topic and points to elements that identify why the secret of the "Brazilian soul" resides in folklore. In 1973, he claimed:

Memory is the Imagination of the People, communicable through Tradition, putting Cultures into motion, brought together for Use, over Time. ... The People keep and defend their Traditional Science, a secular patrimony which contains elements of all ages and locations in the World.[30]

And in 1986:

No science so much as Folklore possesses a larger space for research and for approaching human life. It is a science of collective psychology, of Mankind's broad culture, of tradition and of the timeless in the Present, of the heroic in the everyday, it is a true Standard History of the People."[31]

Consequently, what "Brazilian" is assumes meaning in folklore, since it is in it that the relationship between each of popular culture's particular manifestations and "the general culture of mankind," between the particular and the universal, and between the momentary and the timeless becomes evident.

Cascudo qualified the "standard man," the common man, as the bearer of Brazilian originality. That which made the Brazilian people both different from all others, and, paradoxically, what founded their myths, traditions, behavior, narratives, and beliefs in the universal could be seen in the daily life of the people and in their imaginary.

For this reason he compared the people to a coelacanth,[32] a prehistoric being that survives unaltered into the present. Citing Cláudio Bastos, he categorically asserted: "The people are a classic that survives."[33]

To Cascudo, the folklorist-explorer seemed to have a mission: that of observing and seeing the world of the people's culture in a way analogous to that which had characterized other explorers, the nineteenth-century naturalists, in their approach to the natural world, because: "The naturalist-traveler's gaze is based on the principle of the insertion of particular beings into a universal order."[34]

Cascudo pertinaciously sought to follow this same route through the territory of popular culture in both endless research in the library, which he considered his laboratory, and in his fieldwork and in all of his writing. In order to know and explain the "Brazilian soul," it was necessary to seek out that which identified it. However, it should not be sought through the definition of a substantive Brazilian identity. According to Cascudo, it was possible to discover the secret of "origins" in a twofold process of insertion. Let us dwell on this process.

First, the *exploration* was made through the identification of the common "origins" of high and popular culture and through the insertion of both into the same cultural universe, in this case, that of Brazilian culture. Thus Cascudo, undertaking a trip through Brazilian oral literature, was able to assert, with a scientist's certainty upon finding the empirical evidence that he sought: "Alongside literature and educated intellectual thought, run the parallel, solitary, and powerful waters of memory and popular imagination."[35] Later he added: "I proved the single roots of these two forests, separate and proud of their exterior independence."[36]

Second, Cascudo attempted to map another insertion that permitted Brazil to be located as a continent in the vast ocean of universal culture. This was possible through the careful classification of popular behavior, myths, legends, and proverbs and the identification of "common origins," understood as a mysterious permanence, among those and many other similar cultural traits belonging to remote times and distant locations.

This constant search compelled him to travel to Africa in search of the waters that depart from that continent and flow into the vast estuary of Brazilian culture. Other trips, representative of this search, led him through classical literature and through the traditions of many lands, in order to find in them a common source of the specific amalgam that, for him, was Brazil.

When he encountered what he sought, he did not shrink from announcing it far and wide, with the pride of explorers of all eras. This is what happened when he was surprised to find in the words of a midwife from the backlands of Rio Grande do Norte in 1920 a long-forgotten tradition recorded in Ovid's *Metamorphoses*. This tradition attests that in the room of a woman in labor no one should cross their legs, since doing so would put the birth of the baby in danger:

The midwife from the backlands of Santa Cruz helped Ilitia, like all Greek and Roman mothers, thousands of years before Christ... —Kids, I witnessed it![37] ... I had seen a sacred rite to protect the life of the child, from the Greek Thebes to the backlands of Rio Grande do Norte. Typical. Real.[38]

To Luís da Câmara Cascudo, the "Brazilian soul" to be discovered was the amalgam of multiple and ancient traditions that, translated by the specific chemistry resulting from the "lucky convergence of the three races,"[39] made up the Brazilian population through indigenous "participation," black "survival," and Portuguese "permanence."[40] The result was a fusion, without confusion, of the Brazilian people with the "human race."[41]

Notes

[1]"Cascudo doesn't really denominate my paternal family name... My grandfather, Antônio Justino de Oliveira (1829-1894)—son of Antônio Marques Leal (1801-1891), received his father's Portuguese name—was, during his later years called 'old Cascudo' because of devotion to the Conservative Party which also had this nickname. Two sons, Francisco (1863-1935) and Manuel (1864-1909), had the idea of attaching Cascudo to the name." Cascudo, *O Tempo e Eu* 32-33.

[2] Câmara Cascudo was a member of the American Folklore Society; of the Mexican, Chilean, Bolivian, Argentine, Uruguayan, Peruvian, Irish, and English Folkloric Societies; of the Sociedade de Geografia de Lisboa; of the Société des Américanistes de Paris; of the Societé Suisse des Américanistes; of the Centro Italiano degli Studi Americani di Roma; of the Instituto Português de Arqueologia, História e Etnologia; of the Associación Española de Etnología y Folk-lore; of the Academia Nacional de Historia y Geografía de México; of the Comission Internationale des Arts et Traditions Populaires de Paris; of the International Society for Folk Narrative Research of Göttingen, in Germany; of the Academia das Ciências in Lisbon; an Honorary Member of the Sociedade Portuguesa de Antropologia e Etnologia of the Universidade do Porto; and received an Honorary Life Membership of the American International Academy.

[3] The neighborhood of *Ribeira* is the city of Natal's red-light district.

[4] The *cordel* is a type of popular Northeastern literature, accompanied by drawings and disseminated in the form of pamphlets, often telling the stories of local personalities and offering moralizing lessons. (Translator's note)

[5] See Cascudo, *Vaqueiros e Cantadores.*

[6] In 1951, he published the study and testimony on white magic titled *Meleagro*; on superstition, *Superstições e Costumes* (1958); *Voz de Nessus* (1966, and republished in 1973 as one of the chapters of the book *Tradição, Ciência do Povo*); and on fetishes, he published *Gorgoneion* in 1949.

[7] Houses of Afro-Brazilian worship. (Translator's note)

MARGARIDA DE SOUZA NEVES

[8] Cascudo, *Trinta "Estórias" Brasileiras* 13. Bibi, frequently cited as a favorite informant in Cascudo's many works, was named Luísa Freire.

[9] See Andrade, *Enciclopédia Brasileira*.

[10] Andrade 6 and 22.

[11] See the interview with João Clemente Jorge Trinta (Joãozinho Trinta), a *carnavalesco* known for his bold innovation while working with the Beija-Flor and Viradouro samba schools. Oliveira 357-59.

[12] Until 1988 there were six editions of the *Dicionário*.

[13] Cascudo, *Dicionário do Folclore Brasileiro* xiii. In the note about Jurupari, the author explains that this is an indigenous myth about the incarnation of the spirit of evil, the knowledge of which is reserved to the initiated. These are men who upon reaching puberty demonstrated an ability to tolerate pain.

[14] Cascudo, *Dicionário* xi.

[15] Cascudo, *Dicionário* xiii.

[16] Luís da Câmara Cascudo, *Lendas Brasileiras. 21 Histórias Criadas pela Imaginação de Nosso Povo*. Rio de Janeiro: Tecnoprint, 1988.

[17] Luís da Câmara Cascudo, *Coisas que o Povo Diz* (Rio de Janeiro: Editora Bloch, 1968).

[18] Luís da Câmara Cascudo, *Cinco Livros do Povo* (Rio de Janeiro: José Olympio, 1953); *Contos Tradicionais do Brasil* (Rio de Janeiro: América Editora, 1946).

[19] Luís da Câmara Cascudo, *Rede de Dormir: Uma Pesquisa Etnográfica* (Rio de Janeiro: MEC, 1959).

[20] Luís da Câmara Cascudo, *Jangada: Uma Pesquisa Etnográfica* (Rio de Janeiro, MEC, 1957). The jangada is a sailing raft used especially on the Northern and Northeastern Brazilian coasts for fishing. (Translator's note)

[21] See, above all, *Civilização e Cultura: Pesquisas e Notas de Etnografia Geral* (Rio de Janeiro/Brasília: José Olympio/MEC-INL, 1973); *Ensaios de Etnografia Brasileira* (Rio de Janeiro: INL, 1971); *Folclore do Brasil* (*Pesquisas e Notas*) (Rio de Janeiro: Fundo de Cultura, 1967) and *Tradição, Ciência do Povo* (São Paulo: Perspectiva, 1973).

[22] Among these works, the following stand out: *O Conde D'Eu* (São Paulo: Companhia Editora Nacional, 1933); *A Intencionalidade no Descobrimento do Brasil* (Funchal, Tipografia d' "O Jornal," 1937) and *História do Rio Grande do Norte* (Rio de Janeiro: MEC, 1955).

[23] Luís da Câmara Cascudo, "O Sorriso da História," *A República* (Natal, 04/01/1940). Included in the group of books that can be considered part of this category, are, for example, *História dos Nossos Gestos: Uma Pesquisa Mímica do Brasil* (São Paulo: Edições Melhoramentos, 1976) and *História da Alimentação no Brasil* (São Paulo: Companhia Editora Nacional, 1967).

[24] Luís da Câmara Cascudo, *O Tempo e Eu. Confidências e Proposições* (Natal: Imprensa Universitária, 1968); *Ontem: Imaginações e Notas de um Professor de Província* (Natal: Imprensa Universitária, 1972); *Pequeno Manual do Doente Aprendiz: Notas e Imaginações* (Natal: UFRN, 1969); and *Na Ronda do Tempo: Diário de 1969* (Natal: Imprensa Universitária, 1971).

[25] Cascudo, *Canto do Muro* 266.

[26] In 1999, the originals of two of his writings from the 1930s were located. One was a history of transatlantic aviation entitled *No Caminho do Avião* and the other, *A Casa de Cunhaú*, the story of the massacre of a group of Catholics in the seventeenth century.

[27] Cascudo, *Tradição, Ciência do Povo* 10.

[28] Cascudo, *Canto do Muro* 2.

[29] Cascudo, *Folclore do Brasil* 9.

[30] Cascudo, *Tradição, Ciência do Povo* 9, 29. The use of capital letters in the middle of sentences in order to indicate the importance of an idea or concept, as in this segment, is common in Câmara Cascudo.

[31] Cascudo, *Contos Tradicionais* 15.

[32] Cascudo, *O Tempo e Eu* 211.

[33] Cascudo, *Folclore do Brasil* 18.

[34] Lorelai Kury and Magali Romero Sá, "Os Três Reinos da Natureza" 29.

[35] Cascudo, *Contos Tradicionais* 15.

[36] Cascudo, *Literatura Oral no Brasil* 16.

[37] An allusion to the poem by Gonçalves Dias, "Y-Juca-Pirama," in which an older warrior recounts his observations ("Meninos, eu vi!") through oral history to the younger generation. By invoking this well-known phrase, Cascudo links oral transmission of observed experience to the type of continuity of tradition he identified between the Greco-Roman period and his observations in Santa Cruz. (Translator's note)

[38] Cascudo, *Tradição, Ciência do Povo* 150.

[39] Cascudo, *Folclore do Brasil* 101.

[40] The topic of fusion between the three races as a particular chemical reaction responsible for Brazilian identity is a constant in Cascudo's work and is extensively dealt with in Chapters 3, 4, and 5 of *Literatura Oral no Brasil* 78-183.

[41] Cascudo, *Canto do Muro* 58.

Works Cited and Bibliography on Luís da Câmara Cascudo

Andrade, Carlos Drummond de. " Imagem de Cascudo." 1968. *Revista Província* 2 (1998). Natal: UFRN / IHRGN.

Andrade, Mário de. *Enciclopédia Brasileira*. São Paulo, Loyola/EDUSP, 1993.

Araújo, Humberto Hermenegildo. *O Modernismo. Anos 20 no Rio Grande do Norte*. Natal: Editora Universitária, 1995.

Batista, Octacílio. *Câmara Cascudo*. Natal: Gráfica União, 1975.

Bregues, Sebastião Geraldo. "A Singularidade e o Papel de Luís da Câmara Cascudo no Estudo do Folclore Brasileiro." *Revista do Conselho Estadual de Cultura de Minas Gerais* 9 (1979): 129-137.

Cascudo, Luís da Câmara. Vaqueiros e Cantadores: *Folclore Poético do Sertão de Pernambuco, Paraíba, Rio Grande do Norte e Ceará*. Porto Alegre, Livraria do Globo, 1939.

———. *Literatura Oral no Brasil*. 1952. 2nd ed. Rio de Janeiro/Brasília: José Olympio/ INL, 1978.

———. *Dicionário do Folclore* Brasileiro. Rio de Janeiro: Instituto Nacional do Livro, 1954.

———. *Trinta "Estórias" Brasileiras*. Lisboa: Portucalense Editora, 1955.

———. *Canto do Muro*. Rio de Janeiro: José Olympio, 1959.

———. *Folclore do Brasil*. Rio de Janeiro. Editora Fundo de Cultura, 1967.

———. *O Tempo e Eu. Confidências e Proposições*. Natal: Imprensa Universitária, 1968.

Costa, Américo de Oliveira. *Viagem ao Universo de Câmara Cascudo. Tentativa de Ensaio Biográfico*. Natal: Fundação José Augusto, 1969.

Gico, Vânia. *Luís da Câmara Cascudo: Bibliografia Comentada* (1968-1995). Natal: EDUFRN, 1996.

Holanda, Aurélio Buarque de, and Peregrino Jr. "Visita do Escritor Câmara Cascudo." *Anais da Academia Brasileira de Letras* 117 (Jan./Jun. 1967).

Kury, Lorelai and Magali Romero Sá. "Os Três Reinos da Natureza," *O Brasil Redescoberto,* ed. Carlos Martins. Rio de Janeiro: Paço Imperial/Minc-SPHAN, 1999.

Lima, Diógenes da Cunha. *Câmara Cascudo. Um Brasileiro Feliz.* 3rd ed. Rio de Janeiro: Lidador, 1998.

Mamede, Zila. *Luís da Câmara Cascudo: 50 Anos de Vida Intelectual, 1918-1968; Bibliografia Anotada.* 3 vols. Natal: Fundação José Augusto, 1970.

Oliveira, Gildson. *Câmara Cascudo. Um Homem Chamado Brasil.* Brasília: Editora Brasília Jurídica, 1999.

Peixoto, Afrânio. "Um Provinciano Incurável." 1968. *Revista Província* 2 (1998). Natal: UFRN / IHRGN.

Silva, Marcos A. da. "Câmara Cascudo e a Erudição Popular." *Projeto História Revista do Programa de Pós-Graduação em História da PUC-SP.* 17 *Trabalhos da Memória* (Nov. 1998): 317-34.

Veríssimo de Melo, Luís. "O Folclore de Cascudo." *Folclore* 12. Guarujá: Associação de Folclore e Artesanato, 1976.

———. Ed. *Cartas de Mario de Andrade a Luís da Câmara Cascudo.* Belo Horizonte: Vila Rica, 1991.

Vilhena, Luís Rodolfo. *Projeto e Missão. O Movimento Folclórico Brasileiro 1947-1964.* Rio de Janeiro: FUNARTE/FGV, 1997.

The Theater of Politics: The King as Character in the Imperial Brazilian State—A Reading of *A Construção da Ordem: A Elite Política Imperial* and *Teatro de Sombras: A Política Imperial*

Lilia K. Moritz Schwarcz
Translated by Ross G. Forman

Originally presented in December 1974 as a doctoral dissertation at Stanford University, *Teatro de Sombras: A Política Imperial* [*Elite and State-Building in Imperial Brazil*] is actually the second part of a more extensive work by José Murilo de Carvalho. In the collective work, which offers a veritable x-ray of the Brazilian Empire, the historian reviews the foundation of local political elites, their relationship with imperial political parties, and their paradoxical ties to the State itself.

In the first part of the study, *A Construção da Ordem: A Elite Política Imperial*, Murilo de Carvalho argues that the choice of a Monarchy for Brazil—a country surrounded on all sides by Republics—, the continued political unity of the former colony, and the construction of a stable civilian government mainly resulted from the type of political elite existing at independence in 1822. The configuration of the Portuguese colony itself generated this elite, which was characterized, above all, by ideological homogeneity and by a type of breeding that involved a form of socialization passed on through education, occupation, and politics.

In this way, Murilo de Carvalho resists limiting himself to more traditional explanations that credited the Monarchy alone with the task of centralizing an Empire of continental proportions. Instead, he focuses on the formation of Brazilian elites, subject to a common and homogenous political training, and traces the character of the State inherited from the absolutist and patrimonial Portuguese tradition. Out of this narrow but ambiguous communication between the State and the elite, there arose some of the more obvious traces of the imperial political system, such as Monarchy, unity, centralization, and low levels of political representation. Implicated in a relationship that, to some degree, fed itself, the State-produced elite was quick to strengthen itself and guarantee its role in social control.

Such is the pattern traced by Murilo de Carvalho in the first part of his work. In an effort to explain the multiple facets of this imperial elite, *A Construção da Ordem* considers bureaucrats, judges, priests, soldiers, and politics: "a veritable island of literates" (74) in this sea of illiteracy.

The goal of *Teatro de Sombras* is similar to that of *A Construção da Ordem*, but the route to it is even more direct. This time, Murilo de Carvalho seeks to analyze the new levels of activity of the elites and of the Empire following the conservatives' return to power in 1837. The year 1837 was a moment when the storms of the Regency period gave way to an attempt to consolidate control—an attempt that was centered in the alliance between the sovereign and the higher levels of the judiciary on the one hand, and big business and larger landholders (above all the Fluminense coffee growers), on the other.

As a result, the Regency rebellions of the 1830s and 1840s offer the starkest examples of the problems in establishing a national system of rule, based on a model of Monarchy. There were two basic cycles of resistance. The first began after the abdication of D. Pedro I and lasted until 1835. The second began shortly after the "Additional Act" was passed and continued into the Second Reign, until the "Revolução Praieira" ("Praieira Revolution") in Pernambuco in 1848. The force and geographical distribution of these movements served to clarify an increasingly defined political course: the slowly growing conviction that the Monarchy served the proprietors, who were preoccupied with a system of order subject to constant disruption, even today.

Murilo de Carvalho thus uses the experiences of the Regency period (which vacillated between greater and lesser political centralization) and of the decade of 1850—which saw the end of the slave trade and the passage of both the "Lei das Terras" ("Land Bill") and the Reform Bill for the National Guard—as a backdrop for a close study of the fluctuations in the relation between the Crown, the political elite, and the landowners. D. Pedro II, who nationalized the monarchy to a much greater extent than his father Pedro I, relied on the political elite to mediate his relationship with the coffee planters, who were completely dependent on slave labor.

Turning the court into a great "baroncy of coffee," the king transformed the distribution of titles into a token of the bonds and closeness between the landowners and their sovereign. In reality, the Court sought to pay in status symbols for that which it recouped in material gains. This is the reason why Murilo de Carvalho rigorously analyzes not only the monetary and distribution policies of the State, but also the evolution of abolition and the land question. These latter issues were close to the hearts of the great landowners and formed the backbone of imperial politics. Yet although they became nobles of the Empire, the great coffee growers still saw their capital fluctuate according to the Monarchy's policies. In the end, as historian Sérgio Buarque de Holanda has noted, "the empire of the landowners only began in Brazil with the fall of the Empire" (4: 87).

It is in this vein that Murilo de Carvalho also invokes the terms of Guerreiro Ramos, who characterized the dynamics of the relations between the imperial bureaucracy and rural landowners as a "dialectic of ambiguity." Such "ambiguity" installed itself between the king and the barons with respect to budgetary policy, but also and especially with respect to the Land Bill and the abolition of slavery. An analysis of the tense relationship between the State and the local elite further breaks down the simplified image of the Empire either as a period of quiet domination by landowners or slaveholders or a period of calm, autocratic bureaucracy. In fact, the existence of a moderating power—a sort of fourth power wielded exclusively by the king—suggests that the function of the Emperor was clearly crucial. Just as the remains of absolutism—in a tropical reading of Benjamin Constant's model—gave the Emperor powers of intervention over the Legislative and Executive branches and influenced the formation of political elites, so did it favor competition between different factions of the dominant groups and their alternation in power.

Murilo de Carvalho also shows that this same line of reasoning leads to the conclusion that the fall of the monarchy began in 1871, shortly after the passage of the "Lei do Ventre Livre"("Law of Free Birth"). The act opened up the first major breach between the Emperor and the barons, who, distressed by this measure, saw it as a kind of "dynastic madness." Then followed the law of 1885 (which freed slaves over the age of sixty) and finally the abolition of slavery in 1888. Through these steps, the Crown undermined its legitimacy with the landowners (who believed their interests were being attacked) and left the Emperor increasingly isolated towards the end of the 1880s.

Yet the disagreements did not stop there. As Murilo de Carvalho shows, the ideas and values—as much as the institutions developed by the same

LILIA K. MORITZ SCHWARCZ

elite—also suggest an "ambiguous" relationship of agreement and disagreement between D. Pedro II and the elite with respect to political and social realities: "a slave-based society governed by liberal institutions; an agrarian and illiterate society run by a cosmopolitan elite according to a European model of civilization" (202).

Between the "constitutional Monarchy" and the discretion of the moderating power, between the stability of the Council of State ("the brain of the Monarchy," according to Joaquim Nabuco) and the tedious changes of government between imperial parties that, despite representing different coalitions, maintained a rather predictable course of action (the Conservative Party represented an alliance of big business and the major export trades, while the Liberal Party represented the alliance of liberal urban professionals and farmers for the internal market and from recently colonized areas), there persisted a monarchy that oscillated between semblance and substance. As a result, the country was governed by a model of "formalism"—or more exactly, by a model of the discrepancy between the norm and the reality. Rather than reflecting an attitude of alienation, the process of adopting ideas and institutions from abroad (articulated as the world of origins or reference) was, according to Carvalho, a strategy for social mobility. The model to be followed was that of "civilized" countries, with constitutional governments and efficiently organized administrations that inspired local "copies," which were at times ill-advised.

Gradually, this formalism made power extremely visible, centered as it was in the figure of the Emperor and in the moderating power, thus also obscuring the process of mutual obligation inherent to the political system. By means of this process, nearly all political weight fell on the Crown, which, through pomp, ritual, and the personal charisma of D. Pedro II reinforced political centralization.

Yet, as Murilo de Carvalho clearly demonstrates, this power was in part illusory: "the State bureaucracy had a big head with short arms" (211). Here was yet another "ambiguity" distorting contemporary political analyses, not to mention innumerable later interpretations. This ambiguity involved the complex mechanism through which fiction became reality and reality fiction, as the theatrical side of the imperial game of politics staged it—in the aspect of representing and of "pretending."

Whether through the cruel and critical picture of Ferreira Vianna—who, in the play *Conferência dos Divinos* (1867), depicted a tyrannical and despotic emperor of Imperial Rome—or whether through the complimentary image of Joaquim Nabuco—who, in the book *O Abolicionismo* (1833), depicted D. Pedro II as having devoted 50 years to trying to govern a free people—the metaphor of a "game of appearances" and of dissimulation imposed itself as one of great theater. Yet this theater was not just any theater, but a "theater of shadows," given that the government was the shadow of slavery, in the same way that politicians had transformed themselves into the shadow of imperial power. Above all, it was a theater in which the different actors confused their roles.

Thus, through the metaphor of the theater, Murilo de Carvalho highlights the (good) side of interdisciplinarity and of the work on disciplinary margins at the exact moment in which he introduces an anthropological perspective and offers an analysis of the ritual and symbolic dimensions of political power. The American anthropologist Clifford Geertz, with his study of the nineteenth-century Balinese State called *Negara: The Theater-State in Nineteenth-Century Bali*, evidenced the close relationship between reality and representation and the importance of political rituals. Ritual and symbolism (along with charisma), he argues, form part of all modern means of exercising power, a notion which Carvalho's metaphor of the theater underscores. Political representation resembles theatrical representation, with their similar rules for action, actors, platforms, scenes lighted to a greater or lesser extent, and their use of fiction. If monarchy seems to make this ritual element more obvious—cropping up even in the body of laws passed and in the iconic status of the king—it must be remembered that representation usually assumes a central role in politics. Carvalho makes this point skillfully—he shows himself to be an excellent stage director, so to speak.

And what better image to conclude the final drama of the Monarchy could there be than the huge ball at the "Ilha Fiscal" to honor the arrival at court of officials from Chile that took place about one month before the fall of the Empire? The ritual seemed to heal—if only momentarily—all the conflicts of the evening. All the principal actors appeared on this richly decorated set: "the Liberal hosts, the Conservative guests; there were the Emperor and his court" (389). As always, the general populace milling outside the ball celebrated the occasion by dancing *lundus* and *fandangos* in a square just in front of the Ilha Fiscal: it was a demonstration, albeit an entertaining one, of how leisure was leagues away from traditional politics.

LILIA K. MORITZ SCHWARCZ

As the sun set on the Empire, as Murilo de Carvalho puts it, all the conflicting parties came together to dance a waltz by Strauss, played in the heat of the tropics.

However, this was to be the last act of the Imperial drama. The fragile and isolated Monarchy was more or less a shadow of its former self. Far from demonstrating the Monarchy's symbolic efficacy, the ritual proved ridiculous and became the subject of spoof. The fall of the Monarchy came from an unexpected source, one which even seemed to surprise the officials of the new republican regime. Yet this is surely another story, albeit one discussed in other books by José Murilo de Carvalho, including *Os Bestializados: O Rio de Janeiro e a República que não foi* (1987) and *A Formação das Almas: O Imaginário da República no Brasil* (1990).

It is now time to finish this brief presentation of *Teatro de Sombras*. In the end, Murilo de Carvalho's works engage in a dialogue with each other, as if each new book were responding to the one before it or asking questions for the following books to answer. At the same time, *Teatro de Sombras* has become a crucial work for Brazilian historiography because of its rescue of the political profile of the Brazilian Monarchy and of the trajectory leading from Empire to Republic, with all its scenes, actors, and dramatic tensions. Murilo de Carvalho sheds light on a period that has been poorly covered by local historiography. Local historiography generally focuses on the exotic nature of colonial Portuguese America, on its baroque richness, as interpreted by the modernists in the 1920s, or even on the ups and downs of the Republican period and the "Estado Novo" (1937–1945). Moreover, it views the Brazilian Empire as a kind of intermission, a temporary moment, a replica of models produced elsewhere. Labeled a "big mistake," the period of the monarchy often gets discounted, as if it had no role in the modern republican legacy or in the analysis of more recent Brazilian traditions.

Teatro de Sombras, by contrast, devotes itself to uncovering the structure of the Brazilian Monarchy, with its contradictions and ambiguities, and also to explaining the force of a model which made the Emperor the principal player on a stage beyond his control. Or more accurately, beyond anyone's control. Indeed it was a time when it was difficult to tell the difference between representation and reality. It was the theater of politics that imposed itself in a different way and imposed itself as fiction.

Works Cited

Carvalho, José Murilo de. *Elite and State-Building in Imperial Brazil.* Stanford, Californa, 1974. Ph.D. Thesis Department of Political Science, Stanford University, 1975.

———. *Os Bestializados: O Rio de Janeiro e a República que não foi.* São Paulo: Companhia das Letras, 1987.

———. *A Formação das Almas: O Imaginário da República no Brasil.* São Paulo: Companhia das Letras, 1990.

———. *A Construção da Ordem: A Elite Política Imperial; Teatro de Sombras: A Política Imperial.* Rio de Janeiro: UFRJ/Relume Dumará, 1996.

Geertz, Clifford. *Negara: The Theater-State in Nineteenth-Century Bali.* Princeton: Princeton UP, 1980.

Holanda, Sérgio Buarque de. *O Brasil Monárquico.* São Paulo: Difel, 1977.

References, Responsibilities and Reading:
A *Época Pombalina*[1]

Marcus Alexandre Motta
Translated by David Shepherd
and Tania Shepherd
Revised by Mark Streeter

Let us open *A Época Pombalina*, by Francisco Calazans Falcon. The book is as long as its importance is vast. [2] It teaches more than its contents express. It points back to the man who developed it. Knowing this book then presupposes accounting for a generation of historians.

Here I am thinking of a certain historical sensibility that is encouraged because of either one's interest or one's capacity for understanding. In this essay, the issue of the authorship of Falcon will be disclosed. I will center my essay on the conclusion of *A Época Pombalina*, quoting some passages from it. I will try to avoid obvious commentaries regarding the transcribed excerpts, for I refuse to reiterate what the author has already said. I wish to maintain the author's passages in their formal dignity, so to speak. In order to achieve this I will not try to uncover what lies beyond the text. Rather, I will set myself the task of reading in an essay style, hoping the reader will accept the path I have chosen.

I read the conclusion imagining a kind of man who is strongly attached to principles and aims, with little possibility of adapting himself to external circumstances. I attempt to write of a moral imperative, the responsibility of understanding, and of synecdochal force in the organization of his discourse. I venture, however, to give necessary attention to excerpts of the author's work, analyzing them with some care. This entails the same sensation of loneliness that we feel in front of images that we watch fixedly, or rather, images that we do not see any more precisely because we stare at them.

My choice of the conclusion of Falcon's book may be justified to begin with by having admitted previously that the conclusion is the textual space in which moral imperative finds its most perfect form. I refer, then, to the synthesized outline of the research. Finally, I will suggest a reading of the "silence of the author," especially important if one remembers the acclaim given to Falcon's work.

> Throughout this study we have used as basic references Mercantilism and Enlightenment, both in theory and in practice, from a general European point of view, as well as from an Iberian point of view, specifically the Portuguese. What is it now possible to conclude, in order to complete the analysis of the Pombaline era vis-à-vis these references? (483)

Falcon builds up cognition of the conceptual entities of "Enlightenment" and "Mercantilism." The empirical formulation demands the possession of language as an attribute in itself. We no longer possess these certainties. We no longer count on the possibilities that once were available. Nonetheless, the duty to reference is compulsory, for between writers and their discourse what is essential is exhaustive research. The naturalness of the meaning of the concepts exempts them from the absence that all discourse suggests.

> Two conclusions appear to stand out in the first place: the mercantilist character that is revealed in both theory and practice, and the enlightened character, somewhat imprecise in theory yet undeniable in practice, even if we consider the limits from which it has developed. A Mercantilism of a classical mold, but adjusted to the Portuguese society that was out-of-phase, adequate for reforming absolutism, for which it served as an instrument to increase changes... Enlightenment in a peripheral country, for many years closed in upon itself, and in which the enlightened movement was, fatally, something from outside, 'foreign.' (483)

The required presence at the ambivalent moment of the conclusion in *A Época Pombalina* and the interpretative movement of knowledge force the discourse to position itself as its own audience and to be conscious of its own ideal reader. As the indeterminacy of the referent was inadmissible, so the pertinence of the question is metaphorically conventionalized to the value of the synecdoche. The text therefore concocts a synecdochical representation of the moral sensation that resides beside the text, i.e., the responsibility of understanding.

As a consequence, diversity of discourses, eclecticism of forms of thought, a redefinition of practices vis-à-vis a type of reality that yields but continues to resist. It is the theoretically inexplicable encounter of two phenomena that ought in principle to spurn each other, namely, Mercantilism and Enlightenment. However, here they are together, articulated throughout the entire Pombaline period. It is at the level of the State where this articulation is processed, from which is supervened the 'modern,' learned image which characterizes the practice of Pombaline governing. (483)

Falcon's book suggests a desire to know, but to know qualitatively: to render phenomena intelligible. And to wait, convinced of what you say as an articulate awareness that claims to know well. Does it know well? Or could it be the outcome that one would expect of knowledge? This is the synecdochical duty of realism: the description of that property of understanding, providing meanings and emotions that function genetically as a reiterative point for their own reference.

To be truthful, what these images hide is the actual process of secularization, that passage from transcendence to immanence in which we place ourselves right at the start of our journey. It is the slow and difficult establishment of society finally free... of institutions and forms of thinking which no longer correspond to its actual movement. In this way individualism declared itself, while a new humanism and a modern rationalism conquered key positions at the level of ideologies. Seen through this perspective, with the most profound thoughts situated in this manner, the Pombaline period casts off its traditional Pombaline image—now, finally, a problem which no longer makes sense. (483)

This is justifiable. The author demonstrates a certain degree of impatience with the question that he had earlier considered. He escapes from historiographic premises without speculative fantasy. How can a responsible discourse narrate the responsibility of its own understanding? In other words, how to mold "historical organicities" by meanings that are interpreted and maintain the agreed intention of concepts? Thus, to expose the bases of a complex period is to absorb in writing the place of the shelves within the organization of some library. The writing is thus a place of formative reaction to everything that escapes the force of an organic narrative, so to speak.

> At the economic level, it may therefore be asked, what is the actual balance? Let us proceed step by step. First, we will focus on the relations between Mercantilism and commercial capital, both mercantilist dynamism and the capitalist weaknesses. An entire series of incentives were put into motion. (...) Second, the relations between Mercantilism and industrial capital are the focal point where certain opportunities of a conjectural kind are found, but where structural obstacles may persist… The proof of these assertions may be given by means of a third and final focus, namely, the relations between Mercantilism and the primitive accumulation of capital. (484)

The possibilities of change function in the synchronic description. It is all there, on a responsible basis. Evaluation makes reading the recognition of a text exactly as it is, aimed at producing a total presence, whose meaning is always the same. As history becomes an organic element of the logic of writing itself, so the act of returning to the past is made possible through the knowledge of the specialist. "Capital," "opportunities of a conjectural kind" and "structural obstacles" are clearly interrelated within the summarized network proposed by the historian.

Given the lack of anyone more determined than the author himself vis-à-vis his book, the origins of understanding turn the conclusion of the book into a synthesis. As such, it is no longer heritage viewed as a task, in which the authorial voice itself becomes capable of giving life to the responsibility of understanding.

> What is the conclusion at the political and ideological levels? Through various discourses that make up the 'enlightened discourse,' an entire rhetoric is revealed which is created from the repeated reference to those themes that can be identified as typical hypotheses and assumptions of the European enlightened discourse of that time… It is a desire to feel 'up-to-date,' without accepting different opinions. Is eclecticism also present in discourse? Perhaps. (487)

As the author is the owner of all his research acts, the truth requires that he forget the meandering, because without this act of forgetting one cannot achieve anything truly authorial. Thus, the author needs to be capable of demonstrating justice to inheritance, because he must not recognize any more than a single law of the craftsmanship itself: writing the book. Moreover, the only possible justice is the responsible act of understanding what justice is, which protects the present from the insoluble bygone idiosyncrasies that, in turn, poison all historical discourses. Discourse finds all it needs within itself, and allows itself to be seen. It is seen and remains tormented by the healthy disposition that it requires. Thus nothing should be neglected.

> There is, thus, clarity that is diffused, and obscurities that persist. The historian cannot fail to see in enlightened practice as a whole, an enormous variety of positive points, actual conquests, although the hesitations, the negative aspects are not lacking... A rejected piece of criticism and a restricted and restricting collaboration led, in the end, to a reality of the reforms that preserve. (488)

The organic support of contrasts provides the author with the self-confidence of writing, that is, organizing history through the very book: *A Época Pombalina*. Above all, authorship derives its consolation from having felt the need of victimizing contents. Once something is written, in a committed awareness of understanding, and a conscientious pairing of conflicts is presented in writing, it forms a single whole, a juxtaposition of ideas searching for balanced phrases and words.

> The xenophile is someone who has distanced himself, in mind and body, from his own society. Keeping a distance, he nevertheless tends to grow nearer, in the spirit of many reforms, to the followers of these reforms. There were 'xenophiles' within and beyond Portugal; therefore, the Enlightenment favored these xenophiles by justifying many of their cutting criticisms and reformist suggestions. However, at the same time, it harmed them even more in the eyes of those who considered themselves faithful to traditional values. (489-90)

It seems valid, if for no more than proverbial inconsequence, that certain final phrases of the few conclusions reached should propel the author beyond the limits of authorship. If the organic illusion of knowledge is to be maintained, it will be done so by rendering authorship as a systemic curse of the author. Falcon's authorial silence after having written his book is praiseworthy for its intellectual generosity. If his book prescribes the maxim of being obeyed, in order to understand his responsibility as a researcher, any later reading must necessarily recognize that the definitive author of *A Época Pombalina* will only achieve this authorship without the

MARCUS ALEXANDRE MOTTA

assumption of authority—for only he who does not claim authority is, in fact, a real authority.

Given that any work of authorship is an aggression against responsibility, a reading ought to mirror the author's individual perception. If the "xenophile" is someone who distances himself, in thought and body, from his own society, maintaining himself at a distance, then intellectual generosity requires the same act regarding something already written. This is something that is explained when the reading turns itself into an act of knowledge. And this is at the exact moment in which the author's generous mind acquires a wider dimension, becoming, in this way, an act of detaching oneself from praise. After all, he could have opted for no more than acclaim by the academic world. If ideas when written down, however, become public, then what is read is no longer only the author's shadow, even if authorship remains.

It is clear that this detachment has fallen into disuse. It is well known that academic authors feel the need to control the readings that may be made of their books. This is the basic function of seminars, conferences and contemporary collective publications. For an intellectual such as Francisco Falcon, the unbroken silence of production, stemming from misgivings regarding his own knowledge (his open generosity for differences of interpretation), is the best proof we have of his comprehensive responsibility. Indeed, *A Época Pombalina* is what we may call a classic. And, to plagiarize Harold Bloom, "it stands on its own feet," without the support of editorial marketing and without the "help" of graduate students.

If it is in this way that I reach the end of this essay, I do so because I have learned with Falcon that history does not bypass language; rather, it occurs within language itself. This lesson contrasts Falcon's works with that of other scholars. Whoever reads *A Época Pombalina* is amazed by the research involved and becomes aware of the range of the work and the depth of the author's commitment. That is why, at the very moment of writing, I can suggest that without authors such as Francisco Falcon we would not have the drive to devote time and study to those things which appear no longer to exist.

Notes

[1] A literal translation of the title is *The Pombaline Era*, which refers to the period in the eighteenth century when, in Portugal and in Brazil, the Marquis of Pombal was responsible for a series of economic, administrative and educational reforms. (Translator's note)

[2] Falcon's work was begun in 1967 and completed in 1975. It was presented as a thesis to the Instituto de Ciências Humanas e Filosofia of the Universidade Federal Fluminense as an academic prerequisite for the Chair in the Modern History division of the History Department.

Work Cited

Falcon, Francisco Calazans. *A Época Pombalina*. 1982. 2nd ed. São Paulo: Editora Ática, 1993.

MARCUS ALEXANDRE MOTTA

The Nation's Borders and the Construction of Plural Identities: *Carnivals, Rogues and Heroes,* or Roberto DaMatta and the In-between Place of Brazilian Culture

Valter Sinder

Translated by Shoshanna Lurie

Since the Second World War, fundamental changes have occurred in the world which social anthropology inhabits, changes which have affected the object, the ideological support and the organizational basis of social anthropology itself. And in noting these changes we remind ourselves that anthropology does not merely apprehend the world in which it is located, but that the world also determines how anthropology will apprehend it.

Talal Assad (12)

The 1979 publication of *Carnavais, Malandros e Heróis* can today be considered a milestone in the study of social thought in Brazil, regardless of the short amount of time that has since passed. In this work, now in its fifth Brazilian edition, Roberto DaMatta revived Brazil as a subject of anthropological reflection in a complex and original form.[1] As Mariza Peirano noted in her anthropological study of Brazilian anthropology, a doctoral dissertation presented two years after the publication of *Carnavais, Malandros e Heróis,* a shift in the focus of studies of Brazil can be identified after this moment. This transformation could be seen as a shift from a perspective that privileged territorial or class integration to a growing emphasis on cultural integration (Peirano 1981).

In addition, as Vilhena emphasizes when discussing Peirano's work, "if those authors [Roberto DaMatta and Antonio Candido] dealt with subjects that, according to them, defined Brazil as a nation (carnival and literature, respectively), they did it from a relativist and universalist perspective. Thus, they departed from the trend of Brazilian social science introduced by

Florestan Fernandes, in which the emphasis on Brazil as a nation in the form of an 'ultimate totality' to be interpreted led to a growing rejection of foreign theoretical influences" (Vilhena 62).

As DaMatta suggested in the introduction to *Carnavais*, his intention was to "know what makes brazil, Brazil," or, in other words, "to discuss the roads that make Brazilian society different and unique, although it is equally submitted to certain common social, political, and economic factors, as all other systems" (15). In works published since then, the discussion of these roads and their multiple paths has been DaMatta's main subject of reflection. "A Fábula das Três Raças" (published in *Relativizando*, 1981), *A Casa e a Rua* (1985), *Conta de Mentiroso* (1993), and *Águias, Burros e Borboletas* (1999), can be considered important moments in the development of a body of interpretive work that the author has been completing in his insightful construction of a sociology of the Brazilian dilemma, as he himself points out inspired in Gunnar Myrdal's classic study of race relations in the United States.

According to DaMatta himself, the understanding of Brazilian society through carnival, literature, music, *saudade*,[2] inflation, violence, and *jogo do bicho*[3] is the result of his "faithfulness to a certain style of social anthropology," compounded with an "obsession for Brazilian society" that he has been carefully crafting (*Conta de Mentiroso* 12). Keeping a clearly delineated interpretation of Brazil as a guide, we can follow the development of his work both as an attempt to completely distance itself from any substantive (essentialist) vision of a national identity or of a Brazilian character and as a proposal for understanding the construction of this identity as a process that is undergone by means of a story that Brazilians tell to themselves about themselves.

The reliance on this guide is due to a determination to understand Brazilian reality with the hypothesis that it is constructed through a paradox inherent in its social system. In general terms, this paradox is characterized by the Brazilian social system's reflection of modern values without "abandoning (or resolving) a series of traditional practices (and ideologies)… that continue to reproduce themselves and *relationally* and *hierarchically* govern social life" (*Conta de Mentiroso* 93, author's emphases). In this way, the enticing digression on the fable of the three races that appears in *Relativizando*, in which DaMatta presents his view of the emergence and construction of this paradox in Brazilian history, can be identified as a privileged example for the understanding of the author's thought. His new book, *Águias, Burros e Borboletas*, published in conjunction with Elena Soárez, should also be consulted. It focuses on the topic of the jogo do bicho, a lottery that emerges "at the dawn of the republican era, when the country finally embraces an intensely liberal economic policy" (*Águias* 32).

As DaMatta indicates, "it is as if the modern, individualist, and impersonal nation-state were completely unaware of its personal, relational and charismatic society. Or better said: it is as if the nation-state weren't in the least attuned to the prevailing social practices in society and culture" (*Conta de Mentiroso* 94). Or still yet: "it is as if modern universalism were demanded in public, but particularism continued to function on the personal and private planes" (*Conta de Mentiroso* 160).

This duality, which the author characterizes as the Brazilian dilemma, can be expressed as a group of conflicts that *structurally permeate* the development of national life. In *A Casa e a Rua* (1985), he explicitly posits the principal parameter for considering the literal meaning of this dilemma:

> I would say, then, that the secret to a correct interpretation of Brazil is rooted in the possibility of studying that which is located *between* things. It would be through the links and conjunctions that we could better see the oppositions, without unraveling, minimizing, or simply taking them as irreducible. Given that this is a basic teaching of the social anthropology that I practice, I assert that the Brazilian style is defined by an '&,' a thread that distinguishes two entities and simultaneously invents its own space. (21, author's emphasis)

A phenomenon common to all contemporary national societies, the oscillation between universalism and particularism, individualism and wholism, egalitarianism and hierarchy, sociologically expresses the Brazilian dilemma through the unique way it manifests itself in this society.

The consequences and evolution of this dilemma are the primary subject of analysis in the essays collected in *Conta de Mentiroso*. The matter is distilled into a condensed and engaging form in the essay "Da Matriz Cultural da Inflação: Notas sobre Inflação, Sociedade e Cidadania." DaMatta begins with the principle that "inflation cannot be lobotomized without first psychoanalyzing citizenship, or in other words, without first understanding ourselves, and above all, how we traditionally attempt to understand ourselves" (153). The Brazilian dilemma is then gradually revealed in

VALTER SINDER

practices of balanced coexistence between "bourgeois, egalitarian and individualist universalism," represented by the norms of the street, and the "relational system of personal relations that is its parallel and its opposite" (161), represented by the rules of the home. In a model organized in this way, "the social role of the citizen is the prevailing and official civic currency of the system, but we all know that this currency loses value when the number of citizens increases and citizenship becomes a universal right" (163). The devaluing/demoralizing of the civic currency, instead of overturning the regime, leads to the existence of "other currencies capable of diminishing, compensating for, and making financial losses formidably elastic" (171). As DaMatta notes, in an inflationary system of this kind, the most powerful are those who have the most *monies* and the widest access to all of the currencies. In this way, "it is confirmed that power lies very far from the common man, and very close to he who has the possibility of utilizing many codes and rules" (174).

As a backdrop to this gradual construction of what makes "brazil, Brazil," it is essential to stress the existence of a position that is sometimes present in an implicit and occasionally explicit way, namely questioning the very history of anthropology in Brazil. Constantly referring to his contemporaries ("his Brazilian colleagues" [*A Casa e a Rua* 10]), to his functional interlocutors (Gilberto Freyre, Sérgio Buarque de Holanda, and others), and to authors that contemplate the foundations and implications of a writing of (Brazilian?) culture, it could be said that DaMatta positions himself, in the sense of assuming new solutions, new dispositions, and new styles, in relation to the meta-anthropology that has been occurring primarily since the 1980s.

What is clear is that DaMatta, in spite of—and maybe even because of—his conscious conviction that he should or would like to do what he often has called *old-fashioned anthropology*, creates a dialogic text in which multiple voices are summoned to defend their individual ways and to position themselves in relation to the anthropological project. In this polyphony, we can see that the undeniable contemporary relevance of the questions raised in the texts is the fruit of the author's intentional effort to always stay attuned to anything that might *stir up* his positions. This so-called meta-anthropological production, when taken seriously, as DaMatta does, without reducing the authors and ideas to presumed movements, immediately produces a reaction. Its effect is a rethinking of anthropology in general, and of his anthropology in particular, though it also might be only a way of reaffirming his previous choices from new platforms.

VALTER SINDER

The author's healthy attitude means that we have in front of us a *writing of Brazilian society* that is the fruit of DaMatta's constant dialogue with anthropological production in general and with his own choices in particular. In this way, the already declared loyalty to a certain style of social anthropology is gradually manifested: "It is the category that leads to a sharp awareness of feeling, not to its opposite" (*Conta de Mentiroso* 21); or still, "the universal is not opposed to the particular, but complements and illuminates it. The contrary is equally true" (*Conta de Mentiroso* 27).

Much like his other works, this book can also be understood by the initial motivation to understand (Brazilian) society as a *totalized entity* (or through a totalizing analysis). The essay on anthropology and literature published in *Conta de Mentiroso*, clarifies much about the relationship between the *totalized entity* and DaMatta's work in a general way:

> To discover that a society can be invoked through many voices, perspectives, or texts does not mean that it can't have an integrated view of itself, and that, for this same reason, it hasn't established ways of speaking about itself that it considers the most adequate and correct. It is society that establishes the 'clearest' and most legitimate ways of speaking about itself! (37)

It is left to the analyst to identify these as well as understand them.

It seems that DaMatta accomplishes exactly this, seeking to reveal the dynamics of the constant and complex construction of Brazilian identity, either through literary texts taken as ethnographies or through the description, testing, and analysis of society as a text. Through death, women, citizenship, health, carnival music, the representation of nature, tradition, the cultural origins of inflation, discourses on violence and the *jogo do bicho*, all that might appear disjointed when seen with a dualistic logic—in which truth and lies are separate in an apparently neutral and unequivocal way—emerges in an integrated and at the same time, polysemic form: "the problem... is not 'to discover' that things are out of place, but to understand their place" (*Conta de Mentiroso* 134).

In the relationship that is established between the ethnographic task and the possibility of understanding that a totalizing analysis would enable, DaMatta directs us to respond as Nietzsche would:

> Hence, what is truth? A mobile battalion of metaphors, metonyms, anthropomorphisms, basically, a sum of human relations that have been poetically

and rhetorically emphasized, transposed, decorated, and that, after long use, now appear solid, canonical and obligatory to a people. Truths are illusions that have been forgotten as such, metaphors that were worn out and lost perceptible force, coins that lost their faces and are now only considered metal, and no longer coins. (56)

In the Brazilian case, this understanding requires a critique of the uses and abuses of dualistic readings of a social logic that, as DaMatta proposes, should be perceived as triadic, complementary, and hierarchical. This is the logic of the character-metaphor of Dona Flor, which DaMatta explores in *A Casa e a Rua*, the logic of feminine Brazil (108) and the logic that highlights the ambiguous and the intermediary in the creation of cultural borders and in-between spaces of the nation (a space of negotiation between identities and differences) and that, as DaMatta emphasizes, suggests another interpretive possibility that is "the key to sociologically understanding Brazil and, by extension, Latin America and the so-called 'Ibero-Latin tradition'" (*Conta de Mentiroso* 146-47).

To conclude these notes on the writing of an anthropology that DaMatta seems to propose, I reproduce a story told by Fernando Pessoa that appears as an epigraph in *Carnavais, Malandros e Heróis*:

Today on the street I encountered separately two friends of mine who had argued with each other. Each one told me the story of the reason they had gotten angry with each other. Each one told me the truth. Each one told me his reasons. They were both right. It was not that one of them saw one thing and the other, another thing, or that one saw one side of things and the other, another. No: each one saw things exactly as they had happened, each one with an identical criterion, but each one saw something different, and each one, therefore, was right. I was confused by this dual existence of truth.

Notes

[1] *Carnavais, Malandros e Heróis* was published in English as *Carnivals, Rogues, and Heroes: An Interpretation of the Brazilian Dilemma*.

[2] A type of longing that is considered typically Brazilian. When Brazilians miss someone or something, they have *saudade* for it. (Translator's note)

[3] An "illicit" type of lottery that is extensively played by Brazilians. (Translator's note)

Works Cited

Assad, Talal. Ed. *Anthropology and the Colonial Encounter.* London: Ithaca Press, 1973.

DaMatta, Roberto. *Carnavais, Malandros e Heróis. Por uma Sociologia do Dilema Brasileiro.* Rio de Janeiro: Zahar, 1979.

————. *Carnivals, Rogues, and Heroes: An Interpretation of the Brazilian Dilemma.* Trans. John Drury. Notre Dame: U of Notre Dame P, 1991.

————. *Relativizando; Uma Introdução à Antropologia Social.* Petrópolis: Vozes, 1981.

————. *A Casa e a Rua. Espaço, Cidadania, Mulher e Morte no Brasil.* São Paulo: Brasiliense, 1985.

————. *Conta de Mentiroso; Sete Ensaios de Antropologia Brasileira.* Rio de Janeiro: Rocco, 1993.

DaMatta, Roberto, and Elena Soárez. *Águias, Burros e Borboletas: um Estudo Antropológico do Jogo do Bicho.* Rio de Janeiro: Rocco, 1999.

Myrdal, Gunnar. *An American Dilemma: The Negro Problem and Modern Democracy.* 1944. New York: Pantheon Books, 1962.

Nietzsche, Friedrich. "Sobre a Verdade e a Mentira no Sentido Extra-moral." 1873. *Os Pensadores.* Trans. Rubens Rodrigues Torres Filho. São Paulo: Abril Cultural, 1974. 43-52.

Peirano, Mariza. *The Anthropology of Anthropology: The Brazilian Case.* Ph. D. Diss. U of Harvard. Cambridge, MA: U of Harvard, 1981.

Vilhena, L. R. *Projeto e Missão: o Movimento Folcórico Brasileiro (1947—1964).* Rio de Janeiro: Funarte, Fundação Getúlio Vargas, 1997.

VALTER SINDER

Cultural Intermediaries

Who Was Pero Vaz de Caminha?

Hans Ulrich Gumbrecht

Who would read *A Carta do Achamento do Brasil* today if we had not come to identify the adventure that its author describes as the first encounter with the land now called "Brazil"? This text is not one of those "classics" whose content and form fascinate us independently of the circumstances under which they were written. *A Carta do Achamento do Brasil* has the status of a historical document, which, in this specific case, means that its canonization is owed to a discovery of whose importance the protagonists involved could have been only half-aware at best. While it may be difficult to say why it is important to read such texts, it certainly feels good to have them—especially during years of historical commemoration. But the satisfaction that we draw from them (and the afterglow of a national pride that they still may produce here and there) should not be confused with a desire to react by interpreting them. Indeed there seem to be no interpretations of Pero Vaz de Caminha's *Carta* that one necessarily feels an urge to develop or to refute. So what, beyond having this text, should we do with it?

For those of us who know similar documents from the same historical context, a solution may come from the sympathy that a first reading of the *Carta* is likely to awaken. Its author comes across as more curious, as more capable of empathy for what is foreign to him, and as less greedy than other writers of early European colonialism. But could this reaction not simply be the projection of wishful thinking? Shall we really engage in celebrating the history of Portugal and Brazil as a mellow story of budding sympathies? Loving both these countries is certainly not an adequate intellectual reason to do so. This is all the more important to admit since, perhaps due to too many attempts at such national-colonial celebrations, it is not really clear to us what the standard was like—in curiosity, empathy, and greed—for such early colonial documents. Is it true that the *Logbooks* of Christopher Columbus were so much more permeated by the desire for conquest? Was Hernán Cortés as bad as his posthumous reputation? Is the emphatic monumentality in Luis de Camões' celebration of the Portuguese discovery, more than half a century after Pero Vaz de Caminha, the fulfillment or the opposite of what the *Carta* prefigures? I was about that far in my quest for an apt reaction to Pero Vaz de Caminha's text when I finally became aware of the extent to which that quest was an effect of the text's historical immediacy drawing my attention to it. For the ten days between April 22, 1500, and May 1, 1500, the *Carta* allows us to relive the experience of 500 years ago, the enthusiasm, the intellectual struggles, and the ambiguities of a man about whom, except for this text, we know next to nothing. He was probably born around 1450 in Porto. In 1496, he inherited the office of the *Mestre da Balança* from his father in what we think was his hometown. A year and a half later, he was chosen, among others, to write the *Capítulos* for the *Cortes* held by the Portuguese king on January 28, 1498. So we can assume that it was his writing competence that brought him on the expedition that, a year and four months later, was to "discover" Brazil. In 1501 Pero Vaz de Caminha died in India. These isolated, scarce bits of information are not enough to produce anything close to a biography—but such a void makes it all the more fascinating that, for ten days, we can be synchronized with Pero Vaz de Caminha's life. Out of a biographical emptiness, these ten days *come to life*, they straddle the half-millennium which separates us from the discovery of Brazil.

As with any other text from the past, however, the majority of the *Carta* is conventional enough to defer the immediacy of the author's experience during those ten days. By assuring, for example, the King, as the text's addressee, of his best intentions to serve as an objective observer, Pero Vaz de Caminha inscribes himself into an institutionalized discourse and thus into the standard culture of the larger historical context: "Queira porém Vossa Alteza tomar minha ignorância por boa vontade, e creia que certamente nada porei aqui, para embelezar nem para enfear, mais do que vi e me pareceu" (156).[1] The same is true, in principle, for the description of the discussion held among the participants in the expedition that became the origin of Caminha's *Carta*. After a few days in the new land that they believe to be on the way to Calcutta (cf. 184), they make a dual decision: first, to send an initial account of the new discovery to the King of Portugal and, second, to leave behind two members of their expedition that had been condemned to exile from Portugal, and whose assignment was to perform further exploration, rather than to assemble natives to bring the homeland: "não cuidássemos de tomar ninguém aqui à força, nem de fazer escândalos, mas sim, para que desta maneira fosse possível amansá-los e apaziguá-los, somente deixar os dois degredados quando daqui partíssemos" (168).

Appearance

If it is then plausible to imagine that Pero Vaz de Caminha started composing the text halfway through his stay in the newly discovered land, we may assume that its first part was written as a summarizing retrospective, whereas the second part ended up adopting the rhythm of a diary. Certain features of the *Carta* seem to confirm this thesis. It is only once, towards the end of the text, that the author, much in the style of a diary, informs his readers that, "on this day" there was nothing more that deserved to be mentioned: "E não houve mais nada nesse dia que merecesse ser contado" (177). Furthermore, only once, and again in the second part of the *Carta*, do we observe Pero Vaz de Caminha revise an opinion that he had—prematurely—formed. If at first he had become convinced that the dwellers in the unknown land did not build houses (172), he later includes in his report a detailed description of the "nine or ten" one-room houses, which other members of the expedition had discovered in the interim (174). With even more surprising immediacy, Caminha uses the noun "today" in reference to May 1, 1500, the last day of his stay in the new land: "E hoje, que é sexta-feira, primeiro dia de maio, saímos pela manhã em terra" (180). This is also the day on which the *Carta*, in its closing sentence, is officially dated, with formulaic ceremony: "Beijo as mãos de Vossa Alteza, deste Porto Seguro, de Vossa Ilha de Vera Cruz, hoje, sexta-feira, primeiro dia de maio de 1500" (184). We are indeed entitled to imagine that the final—not insubstantial—part of the text was written by Caminha immediately after he returned from his last visit to the newly discovered land, and only a few hours before his departure.

It is true that all the senses of immediacy that I have mentioned so far are, almost, without any content. They barely indicate the impression of freshness which the *Carta* conveys to its readers as authentic—but this does not even begin to answer the central question that motivates our conversations with the past: even if the extremely scarce information available to us gives us an impression of the social status and the profession of Pero Vaz de Caminha, we have not yet built an impression of who he was, or, in other words of what might have been his specific, individual interests, his fears, hopes, and obsessions during the days between April 22 and May 1, 1500. We only know that our desire to become more familiar with who Pero Vaz de Caminha was during those days—a desire, by the way, which has no general, political, or national relevance whatsoever—is no longer completely unfounded. And the best way, perhaps, to relive what Pero Vaz de Caminha lived, will be to revisit, in our imagination, the things and the situations with which he was most obsessed in the text.

The Gold and the Holy Cross

Not at all surprisingly, the first thing that we see occupying the minds of the Portuguese when they brought two of the natives to their ship, staging this occasion as if it was a reception at Court, was gold. Or was it that gold was one of the first things that Pero Vaz de Caminha felt should be mentioned in his report to the King of Portugal? The reference is prepared with unusual narrative care by the first sentence of the paragraph that describes the reception of the natives on one of the frigates: "Quando eles vieram a bordo, o Capitão estava sentado em uma cadeira, bem vestido, com um colar muito grande no pescoço, e tendo aos pés, por estrado, um tapete" (160). A few sentences later, the Captain's necklace becomes an object of fascination for one of the visitors to the ship, an object of fascination that triggers a complex act of signification: "Todavia, um deles fixou o olhar no colar do Capitão e começou a acenar para a terra e logo em seguida para o colar, como querendo dizer que ali havia ouro. Fixou igualmente um castiçal de prata e da mesma maneira acenava para a terra e logo em seguida para o colar, como querendo dizer que lá também houvesse prata" (161). How would the natives know that their hosts are longing for gold and for silver? And if they knew (or, if they could guess because they shared with the Portuguese the appreciation of these metals) why would they so eagerly give away the information that gold and silver could be found in their land? It seems as if we have caught Pero Vaz de Caminha in a lie here or, to say the least, as if we have caught him conveying a lie that somebody else fabricated, a lie, moreover, without which the legitimacy of the entire expedition would be threatened. A few days later, however, when our writer has already become interested in the many other things that the newly discovered land has to offer, his attitude regarding the availability of gold—or, more precisely, his attitude regarding the availability of information about gold—has become much more realistic. There is no way for this communication to take place without a shared language: "O velho falou enquanto o Capitão estava com ele, diante de todos nós: mas ninguém o entendia e nem ele a nós, por mais pergunta que lhe fizéssemos com respeito a ouro, porque desejávamos saber se o havia na terra" (170).

If the desire for gold, the one official obsession, is prominent on the first pages of the *Carta*, the other official obligation, namely to proselytize, seems to have preoccupied the Portuguese only during the last days of their visit to the shores of the new land. It is as if they had needed to come to terms with the material necessities of life before feeling safe enough to turn to spiritual things. Even then, the question of what the role of religion would be in this unknown world does not come up before two carpenters take the initiative of building a gigantic cross:

> Enquanto cortávamos lenha, dois carpinteiros faziam uma grande cruz de um pau que ontem se cortara especialmente para isso. Muitos deles vinham ali estar junto aos carpinteiros. E acredito que assim o faziam mais para verem a ferramenta de ferro com que os carpinteiros trabalhavam do que para verem a cruz, porque eles não têm coisas de ferro e cortam suas madeiras e paus com pedras. (175-76)

It appears that, at this point, the hope to find gold and silver in a land whose inhabitants did not use any metals was long gone. Thus it became all the more important for Pero Vaz de Caminha to keep up his addressees' hope of winning souls for the Christian faith. This issue becomes so important that, once again, we find the author fabricating one of those complicated and therefore very unlikely acts of signification. The following is what Caminha pretends happened after the Holy Mass that the Portuguese celebrated on May 1, 1500:

> Um deles, homem de cinqüenta ou cinqüenta e cinco anos, se conservou ali com aqueles que ficaram. Esse, enquanto assim estávamos, juntava aqueles que ali tinham ficado e ainda chamava outros. E andando assim entre eles, falando-lhes, acenou com o dedo para o altar, e depois mostrou com o dedo para o céu, como se lhes dissesse alguma coisa de bem; e nós assim o tomamos! (181)

Presents

A native whom the Portuguese interpret as the bearer of such divine inspiration will of course receive a present—and, invariably throughout Pero Vaz de Caminha's text, presents consist of apparel:

> E chegando ao fim disso—era já bem uma hora depois do meio-dia—viemos às naus a comer, tendo o Capitão trazido consigo aquele mesmo homem que fez aos outros aquele gesto para o altar e para o céu, e com ele um seu irmão. Aquele fez muita honra e deu-lhe uma camisa mourisca; ao outro, uma camisa d'estoutras. (182)

This scene takes place late in the game, when the Portuguese seem to feel safe enough to behave, inadvertently perhaps, as if they were the masters of the natives in some feudal relationship. Presents have turned into favors or rewards. Earlier on, presents were objects to be exchanged quite regularly, and it is this exchange that gives some structure and stability to the precariousness of the first encounters between the natives and the Portuguese. Their interactions indeed begin with an initially timid and improvised, but then almost unstoppable, exchange of headgear that Caminha, in his position as observer, seems to enjoy as a scene whose symmetry contains some carnivalesque flavor for him:

> Nessa ocasião não se pode haver deles fala nem entendimento que servisse, pelo grande estrondo das ondas que quebravam na praia. Nicolau Coelho somente lhes pode dar então um barrete vermelho e uma carapuça de linho que levava na cabeça e um sombreiro preto. E um deles lhe deu um sombreiro de penas de ave, compridas as penas, com uma copazinha pequena de penas vermelhas e pardas como de papagaios, e um outro deu-lhe um ramal grande de continhas brancas, miúdas, parecidas com as de aljòfer, peças essas que, creio, o Capitão está enviando a Vossa Alteza. (158)

Yet, in spite of Caminha's joyful glance at this scene, we also witness a breach of good faith of which he becomes a part. The presents which Nicolau Coelho receives are addressed to him—and only to him—as he stands face-to-face with the inhabitants of the new land. Pero Vaz de Caminha, however, points to the presents as transformed into objects which, sent to the King of Portugal, will authenticate the fact of the discovery. Seen from this angle, what looked like an exchange of presents turns into a trap, into a device that elicits a potential act of subjection.

Bodies

Clearly, Pero Vaz de Caminha is ambiguous about what he sees and hears. There are, on the one hand, multiple attempts at interpreting whatever is unknown according to the standard knowledge of the Christian world. But there is also, and increasingly so, a temptation to and a pleasure in letting loose, of allowing all these new things to seduce him into engaging with them. For example, the initial interest in the naked bodies that he writes about is exclusively an interest in male bodies—which, as he states with relief, are not circumcised: "Então deixaram-se na alcatifa, para dormir, sem nenhuma preocupação de cobrirem suas vergonhas, as quais não eram circuncisadas, e as cabeleiras delas estavam raspadas e feitas" (162). This observation certainly adds to Caminha's belief that these humans for whom he has no name must not have a religion (182), and will therefore be easily converted; he is happy to see it confirmed as often as possible: "Nenhum deles era circunciso, mas, ao contrário, todos eram assim como nós" (165). Sometimes, however, these bodies look very different from what Caminha is familiar with, and the fascination of such multiple otherness is quick to take over. An object of never ceasing wonder are the bones with which some of the natives pierce their lips:

… traziam o lábio de baixo furado e metido nele um osso branco e realmente osso, do comprimento de uma mão travessa, e da grossura de um fuso de algodão, agudo na ponta como um furador. Metem-no pela parte de dentro do lábio, e a parte que fica entre o lábio e os dentes é feita à roque-de-xadrez, ali encaixado de maneira a não prejudicar o falar, o comer e o beber. (160)

He enjoys the color with which the natives paint their bodies as much as the colors of the parrots (175, 176) that they are often carrying with them:

Alguns traziam uns ouriços verdes de árvores, que na cor pareciam de casta-nheiros, embora fossem muito menores. E eram igualmente cheios de uns grãos vermelhos pequenos que, quando esmagados entre os dedos, se desfaziam naquela tinta muito vermelha com que se apresentavam. E quanto mais se molhavam, mais vermelhos ficavam. Todos andavam rapados até por cima das orelhas, bem como as sobrancelhas e pestanas. Traziam todos as testas, de fonte a fonte, tintas de tintura preta, quase parecendo uma fita de largura de dois dedos. (174)

Caminha never doubts that these bodies want to be appealing, and he may well not be aware of how open he is to the beauty of the men: "Esse (. . .) andava por galanteria cheio de penas pegadas pelo corpo, de tal maneira que parecia um São Sebastião cheio de flechas" (164f). With female bodies however he is astonished that their nakedness does not produce any feelings of shame: "Ali andadavam... três ou quatro moças, muito novas e muito gentis, com cabelos muito pretos e compridos, caídos pelas espáduas, e suas vergonhas tão altas e tão cerradinhas e tão limpas das cabeleiras que, de as muito bem olharmos, não tínhamos nenhuma vergonha" (164). We will never know for sure exactly what Pero Vaz de Caminha intends to say by pointing to their lack of shame. He certainly underlines that shame did not overcome him, *even though* he thoroughly looked at these splendid young bodies. Was the lack of shame equal to his astonishment over a lack of desire? Or did he mean to say that, far from his own Christian world, he enjoyed desire without any threat of sin? That he compares—and very favorably compares—the bodies of the native women to those of the women back in Portugal seems to indicate that it was not the lack of desire that surprised Pero Vaz de Caminha: "era tão bem feita e tão redonda, e sua vergonha—que ela não tinha!—tão graciosa, que a muitas mulheres de nossa terra, vendo-lhes tais feições, provocaria vergonha, por não ter as suas como a dela" (165).

Food

Despite the bodies, there is nothing that interests him more than food. Pero Vaz de Caminha may not be completely aware of it, but he seems to consider food a medium of communication. And this is not just his individual obsession. When the Portuguese for the first time bring two inhabitants of the new lands to one of their ships, they quite systematically test their eating and drinking preferences:

> Mostraram-lhes um carneiro: não fizeram caso dela; uma galinha: quase tiveram medo dela—não lhe queriam tocar, para logo depois tomá-la, com grande espanto nos olhos. Deram-lhe de comer: pão e peixe cozido, confeitos, bolos, mel e figos passados. Não quiseram comer quase nada de tudo aquilo. E se provavam alguma coisa, logo a cuspiam com nojo. Trouxeram-lhes vinho numa taça, mas, apenas haviam provado o sabor, imediatamente demonstraram não gostar e não mais quiseram. Trouxeram-lhes água num jarro. Não beberam. Apenas bochechavam, lavando as bocas, e logo lançavam fora. (161)

Yet only a few days later, the natives and the Portuguese have in the meantime invented forms that allow them to be together without fear. Pero Vaz de Caminha, in a tone that is similar to parents speaking about their children, reports that two new guests to the ships have really been "eating well": "Os hóspedes sentaram-se cada um na própria cadeira; e de tudo que lhes deram comeram muito bem, especialmente presunto cozido frio e arroz" (177). Later during the same day, some of them even drink wine for the first time on the beach. The Portuguese, in contrast, although they harvest and eat the fruits of the new land (171), and although they know, in some detail, what the natives eat when they are among themselves (179), seem reluctant to have a meal with the natives. Were they afraid that, according to a logic similar to that of the Eucharist, they might become permeated by what they ate? Whatever the answer to this question may be, Caminha implies, quite naturally and quite consistently, that it was the Portuguese who wanted to know, who desired and who, therefore, shaped the encounters with the natives.

Dancing

As the encounters become increasingly happy encounters, Caminha is by no means surprised that one day, after the Portuguese have finished the service of the Holy Mass, the inhabitants of the new land begin to play music and finally start to dance: "E depois de acabada a missa, quando sentados nós escutávamos a pregação, muitos deles se levantaram e começaram a tocar corno ou buzina, saltando e dançando" (166). As with eating, dancing becomes one of the social forms in which the natives and the Portuguese have a chance to experience being at ease with each other. Unlike previous eating scenes, the natives provide the frame for the interaction—but, once again, it is only the Portuguese who decide to join in:

> E do outro lado do rio andavam muitos deles dançando e folgando, uns diante de outros, sem se tomarem pelas mãos. E faziam-no bem. Passou-se, então, além do rio. Diogo Dias, que fôra tesoureiro da Casa real em Sacavém, o qual é homem gracioso e de prazer; e levou consigo um gaiteiro nosso com sua gaita. Logo meteu-se com eles a dançar, tomando-os pelas mãos; e eles folgavam e riam, e o acompanhavam muito bem ao som da gaita. (171)

The Social

But Diogo Dias becomes too confident. Inspired by what he obviously interprets as their admiration for his dancing, he goes on to show them some acrobatic movements—and these end up scaring his spectators away: "Depois de dançarem, fez-lhe ali, andando no chão, muitas voltas ligeiras e o salto mortal, de que eles se espantavam muito e riam e folgavam. Como ele— Diogo Dias—com esses bailes muito os segurasse e os afagasse, logo se retraíram, como animais monteses, e se retiraram para cima do monte" (171). Apparently, Pero Vaz de Caminha is shocked—and saddened—by what he sees. He goes on to describe how the Portuguese, on their way back to the ships, killed a shark and brought it to the beach. But then, turning to his royal addressee, he decides to interpret the sudden withdrawal of the natives as a sign of their inferior cultural—if not cosmological—status: "Tudo isto bastará a Vossa Alteza para ver como eles passavam de uma confraternização a um retraimento, como pardais com medo do cevadoiro. Ninguém não lhes deve falar de rijo, porque então logo se esquivam; para bem os amansar é preciso que tudo se passe como eles querem" (172). But when he has finally pronounced the verdict that assigns the natives to the animal realm, another metaphor rekindles his admiration for them:

> Esses fatos me induzem a pensar que se trate de gente bestial e de pouco saber, e por isso mesmo tão esquiva. Mas, apesar de tudo isso, andam bem curados e muito limpos. E naquilo sempre mais me convenço que são como aves ou animais montesinhos, aos quais faz o ar melhor pena e melhor cabelo que aos mansos, porque os seus corpos são tão limpos, tão gordos e formosos, a não mais poder. (172)

Retrospectively, this episode, and Pero Vaz de Caminha's interpretation of it, will be no more than a brief intermission in the story that he wants to write—a story of increasing mutual familiarity and of increasing mutual interest. Almost obsessively, he gives account of the, almost, steadily growing numbers of natives who expect and who want to meet the Portuguese. When the new land first comes into sight, they find "seven or eight men" on the shore, "segundo disseram os navios pequenos que chegaram primeiro" (157). But a few moments later, there are already groups of naked men gathering: "acudiram pela praia homens em grupos de dois, três, de maneira que, ao chegar o batel à boca do rio, já ali estavam dezoito ou vinte homens" (158). The next day, he counts "sixty or seventy"

(159), and soon the number grows to "around two hundred" (162). The day after the dancing event and its sudden end, he sees "many of them but not as many as before" (173). Yet in the end the number reaches "close to three hundred" (177) and, finally, "four hundred or four hundred and fifty" (178). And Pero Vaz de Caminha is equally aware of an improvement in the quality of their interaction. With a sort of happy hyperbole, he complains about the intensity of their contact becoming an obstacle for the work that the Portuguese want to do: "A conversação deles conosco era já tanta, que quase nos estorvaram no nosso trabalho" (176); with a similar rhetorical move he seems to underline how the natives have definitely overcome the crisis of the dancing event: "estavam já mais mansos e seguros entre nós do que nós estávamos entre eles" (178). Caminha notices the one occasion on which the natives take the initiative of joining in with the Portuguese in a working activity and, above all, he understands well enough what it means to have some of them engage in a kind of a wrestling match—without this turning into an outburst of uncontrolled aggression: "e misturaram-se todos de maneira tal conosco, ao ponto de alguns nos ajudarem a acarretar lenha e a transportá-la para os batéis. E lutavam como os nossos, tomando nisto grande prazer" (175).

Vanishing

Only one of Pero Vaz de Caminha's hopes for the contact between the natives and the Portuguese remained unfulfilled. However hard the Portuguese tried, their hosts, the friendly masters of the new land, never allowed any of the newcomers to stay with them overnight: "Mandou o Capitão àquele degredado, Afonso Ribeiro, que se fosse outra vez com eles. Ele assim o fez e ficou por lá um bom pedaço, mas à tarde retornou, mandado por eles, que não o queriam por lá. E deram-lhe arcos e flechas; e de seu não lhe tomaram alguma coisa" (172). The scene repeated itself the next day: "E como já anoitecia, fizeram com que eles logo retornassem, pois não queriam que lá ficasse ninguém" (175). Nevertheless, when the ships left the new land on May 2, 1500, the commander of the expedition decided to leave behind the two exiled members of his crew to continue the exploration and to further develop the relationship with the natives. But no ship ever returned to discover their fate.[2] We know that Pero Vaz de Caminha lived for another year. But our closeness, our conversation with him ends on the day that separated the author of *A Carta do Achamento* from what would become Brazil.

Notes

[1] For reasons of readibility, I am quoting the "Transcriçao Atualizada da Carta."

[2] See Almeida Prado's "Apresentação" to the 1998 edition of *A Carta do Achamento do Brasil*, 103ff.

Works Cited

Caminha, Pero Vaz de. *A Carta do Achamento do Brasil*. "Apresentação" by J. F. de Almeida Prado. "Texto e Glossário" by Maria Beatriz Nizza da Silva. "Transcriçao Atualizada da Carta" de Silvio Castro. 5th ed. Rio de Janeiro: Agir Editora, 1998.

Prado, J. F. de Almeida. "Apresentação." Pero Vaz de Caminha. *A Carta do Achamento do Brasil*. 5th ed. Rio de Janeiro: Agir Editora, 1998. 11-122.

José de Anchieta:
Performing the History of Christianity in Brazil[1]

César Braga-Pinto

The Jesuit order played a central role in creating new strategies aimed at restoring Christian ideals. Indeed, early Portuguese colonial discourse reveals that the Portuguese assigned themselves a central role in the future of humanity and in the restoration of world Christianity. However, as the constant conflicts in India had already proved, and the encounter with the natives would later confirm, such a narrative of global restoration might have served to assimilate, to some degree, the novelty revealed by the New World into Christian mentality and history; but it did not convince non-Christian peoples of its "universal" validity. Representatives of Christian colonial powers soon realized that they had to create specific mechanisms of communication in order to convey this newly formulated history of the universe to peoples who, as they believed, "did not remember" their true Christian past. In order for communication to be established and the world to become One again, the foundation of a new discourse and a new pragmatics had to return from overseas, circulate within Europe and sail back to the new territories. The Jesuits created a global network of narratives and manuals whose purpose was to reform the ideals of universal Christianity and, at the same time, assimilate the New World, both symbolically and materially.

In this article I discuss some of the textual practices used by the Jesuits—particularly, by the Jesuit priest José de Anchieta (1534-1597)[2] in his longest and most important play, the *Auto de São Lourenço*—to replace both the native symbolic orders and the habits of "corrupted" Christians with a universal history aimed at restoring a hypothetical Christian past. The Jesuits' project of reforming Christianity within Europe, I argue, informed their strategies for introducing the Christian doctrine into the reality of the New World and resolving local conflicts. Loyola's (1491-1556)[3] guidelines for individual conversion strongly determined their strategies for the conversion of New World communities, which were often constituted by both European settlers and Natives. Ultimately, the goal of Anchieta's plays was to overcome ethnic differences by promoting the transformation of both Native and European cultures according to the structure of confession. The division inscribed by the reflection upon the past should efface contextual differences and unite communities around the promise of future reconciliation—a promise that should remain associated with the figure of the missionary. Furthermore, this division was intended to equate all individuals and construct them as childlike subjects who would be open to the expression of God's will and, consequently, ready to receive the institution of Christian doctrine. These plays thus gathered different peoples, in order to create, on Brazilian soil, the prototype of a community without divisions, and the figure of a new world in which ethnic diversity would be the very basis of prospective religious homogeneity.

Anchieta's plays illustrate how the Jesuits sought to create the image of a new (European) world by producing representations of an interminable dialogue within a diverse, but ultimately peaceful and fraternal community. Jesuit discourses and practices served not only to assimilate Brazilian Native cultures, but also to accommodate those elements in European history that were heterogeneous and difficult to reconcile. Whereas Anchieta's own mystical writings aim to produce the "I" as the result of what De Certeau has called the "*mutations de la parole*" [translated into English as "mutations of the spoken word" (*The Mystic Fable*, 15)], the work of the educator must engage in a different relationship with language: an assignable "you" (the learning subject) is required in order for any doctrine to be conveyed. Moreover, it is the "you" that has to be situated, defined and finally named. Unlike mystical speech, this new instance of Anchieta's discourse is no longer the divine entity that, as it is addressed, speaks, or rather promises to speak through an emptied "I." For the educator, language must become an instrument through which a supra-subjective "I" (Truth, God, etc.) conveys a meaning to an actual, finite "you" through an actual, human "I." This attempt at dialogue, which seeks to fix the locus of the listener, constitutes a fundamental aspect of Anchieta's several books of catechism and confession. With the purpose of better attaining this goal—of making his/God's word heard—Anchieta often wrote these texts in Tupi, the language of the Natives he wanted to address and thereby convert to Christianity. In order to ensure that the Natives could listen to and decipher his words he anticipated their answers—along with their identities—and situated them within a fictional dialogue that also could be employed by other missionaries:

P: Ereroyrōpe nde rekópuéra?
R: Aroyrō.
P: Ipoxype nde rekópuera endébe?
R: Ipoxy.
P: Ndererojebyrib´potáripe nde rekópuera?
R: Aáni. (*Doutrina Cristã* 132: bk.1)

[Q: *Do you hate your past habits?*
A: *I hate them.*
Q: *Do your past habits seem ugly to you?*
A: *They are ugly.*
Q: *Don't you want to go back to your past habits?*
A: *No, I don't*]

By thus anticipating, or rather prescribing his interlocutor's answers, the missionary strives to teach each aspect of the Christian Doctrine, while demanding that the listener deny, by means of the enactment of an already programmed confession, each aspect of his or her life which the missionary believes to contradict Christian doctrine. The missionary induces the Natives' self-effacement through the revision and condemnation of their habits. Furthermore, by introducing confession, Anchieta seems to believe that he cannot only change the Native's habits, but ultimately turn their words into the expression of God's will. Indeed, in one of his letters Anchieta writes that, according to a Native child, "the force of confession was so great that, after it, it seemed to them that they wanted to fly straight to heaven with great speed" (*Cartas*, 109). The work of the missionary is thus to educate and seduce, according to a specific pragmatics which produces the other's name (as a fictional entity) through the repetition of the addressee's position in the dialogue. This dialogue serves to construct the other's identity according to a relationship in which the disciple would seek to decipher the missionary's speech.

And yet, the Christian missionary seems not to master the alterity represented by his disciple. It was perhaps this sense that his/God's message could not be conveyed to the Native Brazilians, or even to the Portuguese settlers and local mestizos that made Anchieta look for additional strategies of catechism. Anchieta's plays, on the other hand, were not so much intended to convey a message or doctrine to his disciples as to induce them to experience a divided Christian subjectivity, by means of a practice that resembles the one proposed by Loyola's *Exercises*: "For just as taking a walk, traveling on foot, and running are physical exercises, so is the name of spiritual exercises given to any means of preparing and priming our soul to rid itself of all its disordered affections and then, after their removal, of seeking and finding God's will in the ordering of our life for the salvation of our soul" (97). The purpose of Anchieta's plays was to expose internal conflicts in order to resolve them by calling for mystical—and social— unification. Thus, the same elements that we find in Anchieta's mystical poetry and short dialogues are present in his plays: the performance of a division, the effacement of the self, the construction of a subjectivity that is defined by debt and one's incapacity to speak to the other, and the definition of identity through faith, or through the ritualistic pretense of restoration. But the goal of the performance, as we have seen, was to incite the participants and the audience to confession and communion. On the one hand, the play had to lead them to fix and narrativize the locus from which confession could be performed. On the other hand, the learning subjects had to address and assign power to the entity that gave them their own proper names: in this case, not just God, but the Jesuits who represented God's will.

Anchieta's *Auto de S. Lourenço* (c. 1587) reveals how the Jesuit missionary sought to transpose the construction of the individual Christian subject to the level of the community. Loyola's methods of contemplation, "colloquium" and prayer are turned into a heterogeneous discourse in which the dialogue is inscribed within the speech of a collective "I" who addresses a virtual, external "You." The play is structured as a progression from the representation of the individual, mystical subject to a stage of communal unification attained through the reiteration of the division between past habits and present reality. At the end, the play represents a unified voice that, while it expresses an infantile innocence, also remembers and condemns the history of the community in such a way that this duality ritualistically stages a future restoration. By assimilating elements of medieval theater as well as of Tupi rituals into a structure similar to Loyola's *Exercises*, Anchieta creates a hybrid performance that seeks to convey the foundations of Christian doctrine to an audience constituted by Europeans, Natives and mestizos.

Whereas the *Exercises* demanded that each disciple visualize the battle between Good and Evil, the dramatic sections of Anchieta's play seek to represent the actual image of that battle to a large audience gathered around the scene, in order for collective conversion to be attained. The audience should watch and ritualistically perform the conflict, just like Loyola's *Exercises* required one to stage comparisons in order for the "I" to be founded as the emanation of God's will. Anchieta's play resembles Loyola's "meditation on hell" (the fifth exercise of the first week), which directs the initiate to "see in their imagination the length, breadth, and depth of hell" and "ask for an interior sense of the pain suffered by the damned, so that if through [their] faults [they] should forget the *love* of the Eternal Lord, at least the *fear* of those pains will serve to keep [them] from falling into sin" (46, my emphases). The notion of "fear" is an essential stage in one's conversion, since it announces, by contrast, that which cannot be represented: the love of God. On the fourth day, the *Exercises* further direct one to "consider how Christ calls and desires all persons to come under his standard, and how in opposition Lucifer calls them under his," (65) and "summons innumerable devils, disperses some to one city and others to another, and thus throughout the whole world, without missing any provinces, places, states or individual persons" (66). Thus, in order to express God's will (or Love), the self has to become the scene of a confrontation, in such a way that one may consider the distance between "the standard of Satan" and "the standard of Christ." The tension between Good and Evil, or between fear and love should, according to the *Exercises*, lead to the rebirth of the "I" as an imitation and, moreover, as a direct manifestation of God's will. One would become such an impersonal "I" by first visualizing a picture of the world in which the Devil takes control of it and converts all peoples, and then by reversing that same scene and picturing how Christ can perform a similar, but final conversion: "Consider how the Lord of all the world chooses so many persons, apostles, disciples, and the like. He sends them throughout the whole world, to spread his doctrine among people of every state and condition" (66). Individual conversion in the *Exercises* can therefore be attained only after one has visualized Hell, almost as if one had to let oneself be converted by the Devil before being converted to Christianity. Moreover, the trace and memory of this first conversion must not disappear, but, on the contrary, must return as a threat that continuously provokes fear. Conversion is only attained through the visualization of the two stages of "universal" conversion, that is after one has pictured the world under Satan's sway, followed by the return, through a conversion by Jesus, to the original "standard." In other words, one must visualize Satan's rule or standard, the memory of which would enable one to visualize God's, and therefore understand the necessity and desirability of its expansion throughout the world. It is this temporal narrative of rupture and restoration that Anchieta attempts to translate to the Tupi symbolical order. Furthermore, he must construct an image that conveys the very essence of this division, and identify a single signifier that is both the expression of threat and reconciliation. It is the image of "fire" that performs this role of conveying a meaning that is always shifting between two opposites.

The image of "fire" is intended not only to overcome the distances between languages and between cultures, but also to underscore the unstable oppositions between literal and figural discourses, saying and meaning, past and future, destruction and restoration, death and rebirth. While it is possible that the Tupis associated Tupã with lightning and fire, the action of the play initially associates fire ("tatá") with destruction. Anchieta himself wrote elsewhere that the Native Tupi believed in a spirit called baetatá (the "fire thing"), which was something like a flying flame that presumably traveled and killed the Natives (Cartas, 128). Moreover, according to the legend, Guaixará, the Tamoio devil, was also associated with fire, and represented the threat of one being set on fire. In the play, Guaixará defines himself as "añangusú myxyra" (145), that is, "the great burned [or, literally, 'roasted'] añangá" (nocturnal traveling spirits). In addition, tatá is Anchieta's translation for "Hell," and the space to which the Native Tamoios, as well as all other Native enemies who were not converted by the Jesuits, had been sent after they were defeated in battles against the Portuguese.

The image of fire thus represents, at first, the locus of sheer destruction, but it is soon contrasted to the newly created Christian village ("taba"), where even former foreigners or enemies find protection and may live in harmony with the community. Thus, it expresses an ambivalent semantic field in which narratives of death and destruction must turn into a promise of salvation (or protection). This movement is staged according to a narrative that parallels the burning of Saint Lawrence represented in the first scene, at the same time that it displaces it. Whereas the burning of Saint Lawrence in the beginning of the play represents his sacrificial death, at the end of act 2 the Indians are burned as a form of punishment for their crimes and are held accountable for the death of Saint Lawrence. From the outset, Guaixará, the self-proclaimed "great roasted *añangá,*" compares Saint Lawrence's qualities to his own and to those of his two fellows: *"Akó Rore kae, jandé rapixá mixyra"* ("that burned Lawrence, roasted just like ourselves") (150). In addition, whereas Guaixará himself confesses to being the author of the death of "Bastião" ("Saint Sebastian") and "Roren" ("Saint Lawrence"), saying, *"ixé aé sapysaroéra / sekobé abé resy"* ("I am the one who burned him and roasted him alive") (150), Aimbirê reiterates the narrative according to which Saint Sebastian had set Guaixará's canoe on fire. The play thus stages the confrontation of two rival groups constituted of saints, on the one hand, and Native devils, on the other, each characterized by having burned and having been burned by the other. The roles are thus constantly reversed, until the Natives are finally condemned by Saint Lawrence to be burned on a bonfire.

By deploying the image of fire, in both the European and Indigenous languages, as an unstable signifier, Anchieta situates conversion in the space of linguistic ambivalence. Whereas act 2 deploys "fire" in order to translate Christian notions into the Tupi language according to a narrative of rupture and restoration, in act 3 "fire" appears as an image of both difference and identity which resolves internal conflicts and overcomes linguistic as well as cultural differences. Not only is this section of the play written in both Spanish and Tupi, but now both the Europeans and the Natives speak each other's languages. The purpose of the performance is no longer to constitute Christian subjectivities through notions of rupture and restoration, but to reunite Europeans and Natives in a single shared history—which is also a history of rupture and restoration.

The works of Jesuit missionaries sought to define the limits of such a subjectivity in the intersection between two external forces, derived from the potentially imminent repetition of past experiences, on the one hand, and the future achievement of a previously promised happiness, on the other. History was to be reiterated in the form of a collective memory that, in addition to narrativizing the past, was also aimed at shaping future actions. For this reason, it was important that the Natives learn, before anything, *how not to forget*: their own names, their past customs, their enemies, their own history, and the eschatological history that was not their own, but imposed on them through the interplay between promise and threat. In other words, only if the members of the newly constituted community remembered their (true or constructed) painful past, could they keep their own promises and, more importantly, desire that which had been promised to them. Rather than the actual past, it is the group's temporal projection of the promise into the future that constitutes *a common culture*, even though those narratives about the future emerge from the heterogeneous memory of past events.

The strategy of Anchieta's missionary plays included, in addition to rewriting Christian history, the eradication of conflicts which were internal and external to the Christian faith, represented by the remaining Indian customs, as well as the dangers represented by emerging Protestant "heresies." By transforming both images into mnemonic agents, his missionary works aimed to create a community whose divided speech—torn between painful memories and the promise of restored happiness—united its members toward a common future. What Anchieta's *Auto de S. Lourenço* aims to produce is a collective Christian subject capable to make promises. Furthermore, like Loyola's *Exercises*, it is intended to constitute the original place in which a dialogue or an exchange with God becomes possible. Anchieta ultimately seeks to convey in his play, as well as in his poetry, the space of a divided subjectivity that says nothing—and yet, expresses its desire to speak (to) God. Communication occurs only in the shared interval defined by the distance between God's divided message—for it is both a threat and a promise—and the sinners' double language of confession—characterized by fear and love. But for Anchieta, "fire" is not simply a metaphor for individual conversion. "Fire" represents the single locus of multiple gazes, as well as the gaze that creates the possibility of community. The world shows no opposition to the Christian faith insofar as this opposition is what defines it. The play seeks to convey nothing but the space from which the world, reunited by a shared division, can speak (to) God. And this shared division reconciles past histories as well as present realities within a single discourse whose meanings are always shifting between opposites, including between the literal and the figural. It is from this semantic movement that temporality is conveyed and with it, the promise of unification, or the stable meaning of God's will.

Anchieta sought to re-inscribe the Native Brazilians into the Christian lineage, which they had perhaps "forgotten." If their original innocence is no longer seen as undivided, they remain innocent insofar as they are now represented as Christian children who demonstrate no resistance to the institution of Christian doctrine. Moreover, they represent the common future of the community, regardless of the different ethnicities or past histories that constituted it. The colonial discourse of Christianity thus assimilates differences symbolically, at the same time that it seeks to efface them materially. Its universalistic discourse seeks to resolve contradictions, and yet it must not efface them completely. And if cultural manifestations are no longer associated with a history, not even with an ethnicity, they can always be displaced and appropriated. Anchieta's work thus prefigures a model of nationality that conciliates the antagonisms of a diverse community according to the discourse of a global, universal order that never presents itself. Rather, this order remains as a promise of development, articulated by a paternal figure who teaches the community its own identity.

Notes

[1] This article is a very shortened version of a chapter of my forthcoming book *Promises of History: Assimilation and Prophetic Discourses in Colonial Brazil (1500—1700)*. On the question of translation in Anchieta, see Braga-Pinto, 1996.

[2] José de Anchieta was born in the Canary Islands, the son of Spanish parents. At the age of 17 he entered the Society of Jesus. Two years later he was sent to Brazil as a member of the mission headed by Padre Luis da Grã; six months later he had already written his *Arte da Gramática da Língua Mais Usada na Costa do Brasil*, the first grammar of the Tupi language. The most often mentioned episode of his life tells the circumstances in which he and Padre Manuel da Nóbrega were held hostages by the Tamoio Indians near the beach of Iperoig, on whose sands Anchieta wrote the 4072 lines of his most famous Latin poem, *De Beata Virgini Dei Matre Maria*.

[3] Ignatius de Loyola (1491-1556) was the founder of the Society of Jesus. In Paris he became the inspiration for a group of seven students, including St. Francis Xavier. In 1540, Pope Paul II gave the final approval for the formation of the Society of Jesus. The Jesuits started as missionaries, but soon dedicated themselves to education in schools and universities in Europe and overseas. Loyola's *Spiritual Exercises* were published in 1548.

Works Cited

Anchieta, José de. *Arte Da Gramática da Língua Mais Usada na Costa do Brasil. Obras Completas*. Vol. 11. São Paulo: Ed. Loyola, 1990.

———. *Cartas, Informações Históricas e Sermões do Padre José de Anchieta*, S. J. São Paulo: Civilização Brasileira, 1933.

———. *Doutrina Cristã. Obras Completas*. Vol. 10. Ed. Pe. Armando Cardoso. São Paulo: Ed. Loyola, 1992/1993.

———. *Teatro de Anchieta. Obras Completas*. Vol. 3. Ed. Pe. Armando Cardoso. São Paulo: Ed. Loyola, 1977.

Braga-Pinto, César. "Translating, Meaning and the Community of Languages." *Studies in the Humanities* 22.1-2 (Summer 1996): 33-49.

De Certeau, Michel. *The Mystic Fable*, Vol. 1. Trans. Michael B. Smith. Chicago; London: U of Chicago P, 1992.

Loyola, Ignatius. *The Spiritual Exercises of Saint Ignatius*. Trans. George E. Ganss. Chicago: Loyola UP, 1992.

Guidelines for Reading Vieira

João Adolfo Hansen
Translated by David Shepherd and
Tania Shepherd
Revised by Mark Streeter

In the prophetic writings, sermons and correspondence of the Jesuit Antônio Vieira (b. Lisbon, 1608; d. Salvador, 1697), time conveys nature and history as factual figures or allegories of the divine. For Vieira, time is theologically categorized as deriving from God. This suggests, therefore, that the enlightened idea that God is dead and that history is no more than a human process, inherent to the *res publica*, are alien concepts for Vieira. These ideas, conceived in the second half of the eighteenth century, saw time quantitatively as a continuum of steps progressing towards the fulfillment of Reason in a utopian future. This concept of time does not entail, however, mythical or cyclical temporality; neither is it pantheism or a view of history as illusion or appearance. As a counter-reformed Jesuit, Vieira states that eternity is in all those periods that are part, as created periods, of the complete realization of the concept of God, a concept both totally indeterminate and totally identical to itself.

Therefore, two points must be borne in mind when reading Vieira's work. First of all, his interpretation of the events, which took place during the Portuguese Empire, asserts that all times are real and bear their own historicity. They are, thus, different because they are similar but not identical types of Time. The second point is that none of these times is repeated in Time, since the only Thing to be repeated in each and every moment is the Identity of the divine concept which guides them as First Cause and Final Cause. As an *example* or *shadow of things to come* (*umbra futurarum*), all times entail the eternal and the eternal is always the here-and-now, as both *Light* and *Prototype*. In their similitude, however, or rather, in their difference, times have not yet made Christ's Kingdom materialize. Completely present in God or in the identity of the concept of God, future is, and has always been, fulfilled by the eternal, but remains no more than virtual for humankind, who have used it or shared it only in an incomplete way. Christ has surely come once and Providence continues to charitably reveal to all men the efficacy of the New Alliance, by mysteriously foreshadowing the future of the Second Advent. Thus, according to Vieira, it is the will of all individuals, orders and institutions of the Portuguese Empire as the righteous will of the Good, as well as the freedom of all concerned as the straightforward choice for the Good already confirmed by Christ's sacrifice, that have to be sought to bring to pass the Kingdom of God on earth. The *recta ratio agibilium* and the *recta ratio factibilium*, that is, the straightforward reason behind all things to be undertaken and attained, is supported by God's innate Grace or His counsel, whose natural light *is* here-and-now, in the *synderesis* present in the human mind.

The past experiences of forefathers, prophets and heroes of Faith prefigure the fulfillment of the providential meaning of history. It is because of this that humankind and past events are re-focused by Vieira in the act of preaching, as *examples* to be imitated in the process of bettering the "mystical body" of the Portuguese State. In this case, a rhetoric of Aristotelian-Ciceronian nature proves to be entirely capable of persuading audiences of the providential meaning of history, thus illuminating their wills and their freedoms towards the coming of future generations. Vieira wrote the *História do Futuro* (*History of the Future*)—whose title has seemed paradoxical and imaginary since the eighteenth-century—with similar theological and political assumptions. However, the same title clearly becomes historically intelligible when both the contemporary foundations and the categories of its discursive logic as well as the material and institutional conditions of the time are reconstituted.

It is necessary to remember that nowadays we *read* Vieira's sermons by attributing to them an autonomy that dissociates them from their oral practice. In Vieira's day, they were *heard* rather than *read*. Catholic preaching presupposed both that the divine Light was within the Jesuit's mind, which was externalized in his voice, body and style by means of oratory *actio*, and that it would legitimize the Portuguese public institutions as the naturalness of the hierarchy. Delivered by an authorized voice, sermons worked as instruments of hierarchical subordination whenever they reinstated the divine presence that, in turn, authorized both power and its practices.

Sermons were orthodoxly polemical because they were papist, monarchist and anti-heretic. The decree of the Council of Trent on April 8, 1546, had already defined the voice of the Priest as the mediator of the truths of the faith. Vieira's preaching, therefore, combats the Lutheran theses and the practice of individual reading of the Bible, the *sola scriptura*, declared heretical by the Council. He also attacks the Machiavellian definition of political power as an artifice that is independent of Christian morals. His voice is entirely set on the earthly affairs of the Empire and thus establishes analogies between human beings and biblical events, as well as between human beings and the historical events of his homeland, i.e., Portugal.

As an agent of the Jesuit *devotio moderna*, Vieira never dissociates theory from practice. His actions and works were strategically opposed to the Inquisition, because he wished to retain the assets of those Jews persecuted in Portugal, who otherwise would take their assets and flee to Holland. In order to face the mercantile competition of the reformed European countries, mainly England and Holland, the Portuguese planned to use the Jewish money to found trading companies for India and Brazil. In exchange, the Inquisition would soften the "methods" used against new-Christians and Jews. The safekeeping of Jewish assets in Portugal was closely aligned with Vieira's prophetic style in relation to the Americas. Above all, his voice prophesied that Portugal's future as a universal instrument in favor of Catholicism would be outstanding, which proved to be an absolute mistake. In such a future, the role of Brazil and those of Maranhão and Grão Pará would be essential.

In the "Sermão da Epifania" ("Sermon of Epiphany"), which he delivered to the Portuguese court in 1662 after ten years of unsuccessful struggle to defend the Indigenous against enslaving colonizers in Maranhão and Grão Pará, Vieira states that the Portuguese discovery was a second, new creation of the world. The first time, God had created the world alone; this second time was an attempt to integrate "remote and alien peoples" to Christianity. God had made the Portuguese and Portugal His "second causes," or rather, the instruments of His Will:

> This is the end for which God chose, amongst all other nations, our own nation,
> which is considered pure in Faith and loved for her piety: these are the foreign and
> remote peoples, to whom God promised we would take His Holy name: this is
> His Empire, which He wanted to extend through us as well as to establish within

us; this is, was and will be the greatest and the highest glory of the Portuguese worth, zeal, religion and Christianity.[1] (2: 10)

In April, 1659, while at the Amazon Mission at Camutá, Vieira had written a letter to his friend, Father André Fernandes, later Bishop of Japan. The text, known as "Carta ao Bispo do Japão" ("Letter to the Bishop of Japan"), spelled out in detail his prophetic interpretation of the *Trovas* by Gonçalo Anes Bandarra, a sixteenth-century shoemaker. Castro has suggested that Vieira has transformed the *Trovas* into the "… foundation for a new concept of Sebastianism, according to which the return of the *Encoberto* ('a Portuguese king sent by Providence') would not bring King Sebastian back immediately, but indicated the advent of King John IV. This became the essential foundation of Vieira's belief in a Fifth Empire and in the inevitability of the King's resurrection" (125).[2]

The "Sermão dos Bons Anos" ("Sermon of the Good Years"), which Vieira delivered on January 1st, 1642, in the Royal Chapel of Lisbon, comments on one line from the Lord's Prayer, *adveniat Regnum tuum*, "thy Kingdom come." In this sermon, Vieira prophesied that King John IV, who was alive and present at the preaching of the sermon, would provide continuity for the dead King Sebastian, thus fulfilling God's promise to King Afonso made at the battle of Ourique. He claimed that the Kingdom that Portugal once was had come and that Portugal was still to be the future Kingdom, namely the Fifth Empire.[3] (The previous empires had been the Chaldean, the Persian, the Greek and the Roman.)

In 1647, in order to negotiate peace in Brazil and Africa, Vieira went to The Hague. During this time he was in contact with the Jews such as Menasseh-ben-Israel at the synagogue in Amsterdam. In 1640, the latter had written a prophetic text called *Esperança de Israel* (*Israel's Hope*), later imitated by Vieira in *Esperanças de Portugal* (*Portugal's Hopes*), the 1659 letter addressed to his friend André Fernandes. Vieira discussed the destiny of the lost tribes of Israel with his Jewish friend, as well as the recovery of Judea and the advent of the Messiah; these are also themes which were dealt with in Vieira's later letters and prophetic works in which he describes the providential role of the New World and of the Native Brazilians before the return of the Messiah. For him, armies of converted Native Brazilians would combat the Turks in Europe before the Second Advent. The biblical books of Daniel and Isaiah, the *Trovas* by Bandarra; the treatise *De Procuranda* written by the Peruvian Jesuit José de Acosta, among other works, provide the substance from which Vieira would later prophetically interpret the meaning of the Jesuits' teaching of the divine word to the Native Brazilians in the sixteenth century, beginning with the mission of Nóbrega and Anchieta.[4] For him, when the New World was included in the Christian fellowship of love, the Jesuit mission and the catechism of gentiles was a mystery of Providence that helped the Church in its spiritual redemption of humankind. It was precisely because Native Brazilians were savage, barbarian and "stupid and ignorant" that they had to be lovingly led to overcome their barbaric state. When colonizers enslaved the Natives, they also became responsible for their lack of faith, as well as for the loss of their souls to Satan. In this way, the Portuguese Crown was sanctified due to its apostolic work of sponsoring the Jesuit mission, which, in turn, bore witness to the existence of the innate Grace that brings about God's supernatural project in practice.

In the "Sermão XIV do Rosário," Vieira interprets African slavery in the same way, i.e., that it is by means of baptism that divine Providence frees the soul of the African gentiles from Hell, where they were destined to go had they remained in the natural freedom of their land of origin.[5] Almost 50 years afterwards, in 1691, Vieira was approached by the Council of Jesuit Missions regarding the measures which ought to be taken in relation to Palmares, the nation of runaway slaves led by Zumbi, and who were attacking the sugarcane mills of Pernambuco, in the Northeast of Brazil. Vieira provided five reasons in favor of the destruction of the *quilombos* (the runaway slave villages) and the extermination of its inhabitants. His first argument was that it might be possible to send African priests, originally from Angola, as ambassadors to *palmarinos*, the inhabitants of Palmares. Secondly, however, he suggested that these ambassadors might be regarded as spies of the Portuguese government and concluded that they would be slaughtered as a result of this. Vieira conceded that the *palmarinos*, might indeed stop all attacks against the settlers, but they would never stop sheltering runaway slaves. His fifth argument, the most decisive of all, stated that "... because they are rebels and slaves, they are and will continue to be in a state of sin, from which they cannot be freed, nor be given the Lord's grace, without going back to the service and obedience of the their masters, something which none of them shall willingly do" (D'Azevedo 372).[6]

Vieira was obviously not an adherent to the Enlightenment. As a counter-reformed Jesuit, he did not accept any doctrine that was dissociated from practical things, because he believed that these practical things were also endowed with the Lord's Presence. Slavery, the slaves' baptism, their salvation, as well as the extermination of rebel slaves, were all integral parts of his objective to achieve political-economic hegemony in the Southern Atlantic region. This hegemony would obviously be a Catholic hegemony, secured by a Portuguese monopoly in the trading of slaves and the African workforce. Therefore, when Vieira emphasized the slaves' duty of obedience, he presupposed that slavery was a subject that demanded deep meditation, a task, which had been assignèd to Portugal by divine Providence. As he often said, Brazil had its body in America but that its soul was in Africa.

The final aim of all of Vieira's actions and work was the orderly integration of individuals, public institutions and religious orders of the Portuguese Empire, ranging from the most humble slaves and "wild" Natives to court aristocrats and royal princes. His aim was their collective redemption in a single "mystical body" of guided wills and freedoms directed to bring to pass the Kingdom of God on earth, namely the return of the Messiah. Vieira made the Bragança dynasty sacred by establishing mysterious links between Catholic ritual, the canonical texts and absolute monarchy defined as an instrument of divinity. Therefore, in order to defend the universal destiny of his country, which included the catechism of the Indigenous, the enslaving of the Africans, the integration of the Jews and the New Christians, the founding of the trade companies, the disciplining of the nobles, the making sacred of the Braganças as chosen by God, among other aims, Vieira qualified the medium of language as something to be perceived as a form. The same theological concept of divine Identity grounded his rhetorical technique as the thinking of similitude or figural rationality. Here it is fundamental to discuss the question of form.

Inspired in the systemic approach developed by Niklas Luhmann, I may suggest that the Sun, the source of light, cannot be seen; rather, we see things in light. In the same way, we do not read letters, but rather, with the help of the alphabet, we read words. If we wish to read the alphabet itself, we must by necessity order it alphabetically. The coordination of elements produces form, but the means of support or coordination of form does not in itself usually attract attention. In Vieira's art, things are seen in light, yet Light itself is seen as well; we read words, signifiers, as well as the substance of both letters and sounds. Vieira's art is a device that "produces presence," a theological-political device for the production of divine Presence within the milieu of Portuguese institutions, both in the metropolis and in the colonies—I am referring to the concept of production of presence as proposed by Hans Ulrich Gumbrecht (1999). Vieira's doctrine of the sign is different, because his thought also encompasses a qualified metaphor for the divine. For Vieira, language is *never* instrumentally autonomous from form as an aesthetics. Rather, language itself, by nature made up of sounds in which a human set of signs resides, is the presence of the divine in the human mind and in the means by which social interaction takes place. In this way, the substance of both form and content, disdained in contemporary theories after Saussure, also takes part in the cohesive power of their metaphysical principle. The substantiation of language, therefore, also makes language visible as a medium.

Vieira's art multiplies what is One, mirroring it by means of attribution, proportion and proportionality in the similarity of sounds, letters, words, concepts, images and arguments. This is done in order to make both discourse and the act of discourse into an effective figure of the Presence, which makes the world be and wish for the Being. The substantiation of language is obviously a poetic and historical process that is outdated. It is not a trans-historical "(neo)baroque" structure. Nor is it an "aesthetic rupture" that can be made autonomous from its contemporary function of propaganda for an absolutist State. It is neither a literary nor an "original" manifestation of either "good" or "bad" taste. It is not a pre-enlightened irrationality damned by Hegelian-positivist retrospective accusations, which conceive the past as no more than a step towards the glories of a neo-liberal present.

The acuteness of styles is one of the main features of the metaphysical and logical analogy that articulates the complementary opposition of *finite/infinite* in seventeenth-century Luso-Brazilian practices. An inherent element of the historical form of absolutist rationality, acuteness teaches that representation is infinite. In its folds, folds that are not Deleuzean, it alludes to that which is unexpressed in its First Cause, that which appears unclear within the material medium of language as a tendentiously sublime void. The sublime effect of God's presence is similar to the effects produced by the impossibility of representation in our contemporary virtual reality. Such a comparison makes the counter-reformed metaphysics of the Jesuit's sermons and prophetic works intelligible. However, since the French Revolution, the metaphysical subordination of history to time, defined as divine presence, as well as the sublime effect of representations as concepts, have become ruins more than ruined. They are only interesting in as much as they can be seen as constituted by their irremediably extinct historical difference. One day, the present, acclaimed today as the global eternity of "post-utopia," will also ruin itself.

Notes

[1] "Este é o fim para que Deus entre todas as nações escolheu a nossa com o ilustre nome de pura na Fé, e amada na piedade: estas são as gentes estranhas e remotas, aonde nos prometeu que havíamos de levar seu Santíssimo Nome: este é o império seu, que por nós quis amplificar e em nós estabelecer; e esta é, foi, e será sempre a maior e a melhor glória do valor, do zelo, da religião e da cristandade portuguesa."

[2] "… fundamento de uma nova concepção de sebastianismo, segundo a qual o regresso do Encoberto não traria já D. Sebastião, mas significava o advento de D. João IV, e fazendo delas, por conseguinte, a base essencial da sua crença no Quinto Império e na inevitabilidade da ressurreição do Rei."

[3] See Vieira 1: 315-342.

[4] In a series of sermons focusing on Francis Xavier asleep and awake, Vieira established a homology between Xavier's work and that of other Jesuits in India and Japan and in the Brazilian Jesuit missions. He suggested that God attributed to the Portuguese monarchy the essential mission of universalizing Catholic faith by means of the Society of Jesus and thus prepare for the Advent of God's Kingdom.

[5] See Vieira 11: 301.

[6] "… sendo rebelados e cativos, estão e perseveram em pecado contínuo e atual, de que não podem ser absoltos, nem receber a graça de Deus, sem se restituírem ao serviço e obediência de seus senhores, o que de nenhum modo hão de fazer."

Works Cited

Castro, Aníbal Pinto. *Antônio Vieira. Uma Síntese do Barroco Luso-Brasileiro.* Lisboa: Clube do Colecionador dos Correios, 1997.

D'Azevedo, João Lúcio. *História de Antônio Vieira.* Vol. 2. Lisboa: Clássica, 1920.

Gumbrecht, Hans Ulrich. "Epiphany of Form: On the Beauty of Team Sports." *New Literary History* 30.2 (Spring 1999): 551-572.

Vieira, Antônio Padre. *Sermões.* 15 vols. Porto: Lello & Irmão, 1959.

The Image of Brazil in *Robinson Crusoe*

Marcus Vinicius de Freitas

Daniel Defoe's masterpiece, *Robinson Crusoe*, was originally published in 1719 and has been considered a landmark in the history of the novel, especially because of its powerful fusion of fact and fiction. By mixing these realms and exploiting links and gaps between them, Defoe, among other writers, helped to create the genre of the novel, which would come to be the written expression of the bourgeois world *par excellence*.

From the late fifteenth century on, with the discovery and conquest of the New World, reports from distant and exotic lands had already provoked a crisis of values within the literary world, since the borders between fact and imagination were now blurred by the influx of images from travel accounts and their literary impressions. In a society still dominated by the Bible as the paradigmatic book (which meant that all written words should embody the truth), the imagery coming from such accounts were a source of confusion, since their reality apparently relied only on the narrator's voice, which was the reader's best guarantee for understanding the meaning of these distant worlds. Some writers, such as Daniel Defoe—or Shakespeare in *The Tempest* as well as Fernão Mendes Pinto in his *Travels*, both early precursors to Defoe's *Robinson Crusoe*—soon became aware of the fictional and allegorical possibilities that such images of distant worlds opened and of the consequent disruption of the relationship between fact and narration. Those openings were developed in such a way that it is possible to say that they constitute one of the historical sources of the novel. Travel accounts, as one of the sources for the new genre, had their counterpart in trading activity, which was an equally central axis in the new bourgeois economic order, in which the aristocracy was no longer the only class capable of establishing economic and cultural forms (Fausett 20).

Robinson Crusoe embodies both the travel fiction and the trading issues of this historical moment. Hence we can see its importance in the later development of the novel as the chief expression of the bourgeois world. However, whether we read Robinson's wanderings as an economic or puritan parable, a political allegory, a realistic image of colonialism, or a framework for the discussion of religious matters, we should not forget their fictional status. Perhaps the most interesting standpoint from which to read *Robinson Crusoe*—as well as any other historical novel—is to try to understand how any context was introduced and reinvented by the novelist in the narrative, and, similarly, how that same narrative reconstructs our comprehension of the given context, always keeping in mind that text and context are played off against each other in a sort of continuous movement.

Brazil plays a unique role in Defoe's novel. Not only is the Portuguese colony from the mid-seventeenth century literally part of the novel's context, but the text itself also constructs for the reader a fictional image of that part of the world. Such an image, on the one hand, reinforces the widespread myth of Brazil as a paradise, a land of opportunity, a country of equitable social relations; on the other hand, it is a narrative device used by Defoe to develop his novel's plot and a portion of his political, economic and religious arguments.

After leaving his father's house to embrace a life of adventures at sea, Crusoe begins to work as a trader. In his first voyage he earns £300 by trading trinkets for ivory, gold and slaves on the Guinea coast. Leaving £200 for safekeeping with a friend's widow in London, he departs on a second voyage, but ends up being captured by Moors in Salee, Africa. Following an assortment of other events, he escapes in a boat. He has some provisions, tools and weapons, and a few small commodities. Finally, he is rescued by a Portuguese ship, which is carrying slaves from the coast of Guinea to Brazil. Arriving at Salvador around 1655, he sells all of his goods to the ship's captain and decides to start a new life in Brazil.

The Portuguese captain refers Crusoe to a *senhor de engenho* (a sugar plantation/mill owner). He lives on the planter's property for some time, learning how to plant and process sugar. Amazed by how a plantation owner could accumulate wealth, he decides to become one of them. Using his small stock of money, he buys as much land as possible and settles down as a farmer. For two years he plants only food. In the third year he plants some tobacco and prepares a plot of land for cultivating sugarcane. At this point he is in real need of more money to improve his plantation; without it, he would be forever no more than a provider of food and tobacco for the larger plantations. He thus arranges to have £100 remitted to him from England. The same Portuguese captain who saved his life at sea decides to bring the money from London, by investing it in English goods. Crusoe sells all of the goods for a large profit. Stocked with capital, Crusoe is now poised to turn himself into a powerful plantation owner.

Once established, Crusoe becomes acquainted with other landowners and with the merchants at the port in Salvador. During one of their conversations, Crusoe talks about his experience as a trader on the Guinea coast and explains how easy it was to go to Africa and trade directly with Africans. The local community then suggests that they should unite their resources and send a ship of their own to Africa, thus eliminating the middlemen and increasing the profitability of bringing slaves to Brazil. They offer him an equal share of the cargo without providing any part of the stock, and also offer to take care of his plantations while he is abroad. But it is during this voyage that he gets lost at sea and ends up spending 28 years on a remote island.

When he returns to England after this prolonged absence, he regains control of his property in Brazil, which was in the hands of the state and of a religious order. However, he decides to sell it, since he had become a self-taught Puritan who could not live among Catholics.

Having the character participate in the Brazilian sugarcane industry was Defoe's effective strategy to present a meditation on economics and society centered upon the idea of the self-made man. The Brazilian crop was one of the most profitable industries during Defoe's time and was also basically run by foreigners of low social extraction (Blackburn 173). In the late seventeenth century, 60% of the Brazilian planters were immigrants, a pattern that suggests a considerable level of mobility among them (Schwartz 89). Thus, Brazil functioned as a perfect setting for an economic parable of a middle-class, individualistic and mercantilist self-reliant man.

Since Karl Marx there is a tradition of reading Defoe's novel as an economic parable by focusing on Crusoe's settlement on the remote island and on his continuing labor, which leads to a sort of microcosmic reconstruction of civilization. However, as Michael Seidel points out, the island would not be suitable for an economic experience in the real sense of the expression, since it did not include relations between capital and labor; there were no problems of supply, demand, wages, monetary circulation, debts, loans or interest rates, all intricate parts of an economic system (Seidel 102). Ian Watt's characterization of Crusoe's life on the island as a case of *homo economicus* is thus viewed by Seidel as an overdetermined reading of the novel. Brazil, on the other hand, had all the necessary economic ingredients to bring about the rise of a middle-class adventurer. If Defoe uses the character to portray his own opinions about moral issues related to money and the free market, he does it by presenting Crusoe's Brazilian experience as the right, legal and moral way of trading, where everybody is reliable, and where everything falls into place. Even after 28 years on a desert island, Crusoe's investments are administered fairly by his trustees, and the capitalist relations stay as honest as any agreement among friends. This economic paradise is, in short, the parable constructed by Defoe.

On the one hand, a real social and economic environment, such as Brazil in 1655, grounds Defoe's imagined plot. In this respect, it is important to remember that Defoe was himself a merchant trader to Portugal and Spain during a period of his life and thus had some personal knowledge about Brazil. On the other hand, he reconstructs this social material in order to weave his story. The equitable Brazilian society is less a reflection of any real Iberian kindness than a criticism of English colonial policy (Seidel 103). In creating an utopian economic environment in Brazil, Defoe criticizes, by extension, his own countrymen. Despite his fictional intentions, Defoe builds a clear distinction between Iberian and British colonial policies. Defoe may thus be viewed as a sort of precursor to Gilberto Freyre's Luso-Tropicalism (Freyre 75-176). Indeed, it would be interesting to know to what extent Freyre was influenced by Defoe's conceptions of Iberian colonialism. Here we have the case of fiction creating reality. What was, for Defoe, merely a fictional mediation, a reconstruction of reality to produce a fictional effect and an economic parable, ended up being part of Freyre's theory on colonialism.

When Crusoe arrives in Brazil, the war against the Dutch in Pernambuco and Bahia had just finished. The war had disrupted the sugarcane industry, and it was time for reconstruction. However, Brazil was now facing serious competition with the French, British and Dutch colonies in the Caribbean, which had begun to cultivate sugar since the 1630s and in better growing conditions (Schwartz 97). The new producers integrated cultivation, processing and transportation, even financing and sales, into a single process (Blackburn 332). Modern capitalism replaced old mercantilism. In order to face the competition Brazil was in dire need of greater production at lower costs. New planters, like Crusoe, would have been very welcome in such a situation. Blackburn adds that, "… there were no shortage of lands, which could be acquired to grow foodstuffs and tobacco" (174).

Here we have exactly what Crusoe accomplishes. With the profit of his sale to the captain who had rescued him, he buys some land and starts planting foodstuffs and tobacco. By focusing on these subsidiary activities, Crusoe could foresee a better future, one in which he would have enough money to build his own sugar mill. The plot of a small planter growing rich, step by step, grounded in his own efforts, is the perfect parable of a self-reliant common man. Even Stuart Schwartz falls into this sublime allegory, when he designates such fundraising methods as "Robinson Crusoe" (Schwartz 93). But Schwartz fails to recognize that, based on his own data, it would be almost impossible for a small *manioc* and tobacco planter to become a sugar mill owner, since the investments necessary to build such a property were far greater than what a small planter could raise by means of his own labor. Other investment sources were needed. Crusoe himself notes this necessity when he states that he and his neighbor planter would need additional labor (Defoe 55).

It is at this point that he decides to retrieve some money from England. Although the step-by-step situation is tailored to create the economic parable, Crusoe only ascends when he receives the new money from London. The first thing he does with this money is to buy a black slave and a European servant (58). Thus, Defoe transforms his character into a real planter, since the possession of a larger labor force was what really distinguished a *senhor de engenho* from a mere *manioc* or tobacco farmer.

In relation to Crusoe's slavetrading activity, we can again find Defoe manipulating the same type of fictional devices. When Robinson talks with his fellow planters and merchants about the Guinean trading, they pay special attention to the part related to the buying of slaves,

> … which was a trade at that time not only far from entered into, but as far as it was, had been carried on by the *assientoes,* or permission of the kings of Spain and Portugal, and engrossed in the public, so that few negroes were brought, and those excessive dear. (59)

Here we have the perfect manipulation of real matters for fictional intentions. The trade was in fact in the hands of a few large contractors who purchased the right to import African slaves and then sold these licenses to actual traders (Blackburn 174). They were the middlemen whom Crusoe and his fellows were trying to bypass by going directly to the African coast. The price of a slave, in relation to the price of sugar, was also growing fast. In 1710, the price of a slave was about four times as much as it had been in 1608 (Schwartz 94). The plot is, thus, grounded on a very real situation. However, other elements in the same passage are clearly manipulated in order to create a fictional effect. During that time in Brazil, the slave trade was not small at all; consequently, the number of slaves who were brought to the colony was not small, as the novel suggests, but increasing. Between 1651 and 1675 the number of slaves who were taken from Africa doubled in relation to the second quarter of that same century (Blackburn 326). Nevertheless, Defoe's manipulation of these facts clearly serves the fictional purpose of training Crusoe as a leader, the one who provides the others with solutions to their problems. This narrative strategy also highlights, as far as the novel's fictional purposes are concerned, the character's entrepreneurial attitude.

The manner in which Crusoe describes the trade along the coast of Guinea is also a good example of such fictional manipulations of facts:

> I had frequently given them [the other planters] an account of my two voyages to the coast of Guinea, the manner of trading with the negroes there, and how easy it was to purchase upon the coast, for trifles, such as beads, toys, knives, scissors, hatchets, bits of glass, and the like, not only gold dust, Guinea grains, elephant teeth, etc, but negroes, for the service of the Brazil, in great numbers. (59)

The scene of a clever European exchanging trinkets for gold, ivory, silver, and other commodities has the power of a myth. It is perhaps the most Eurocentric and widespread image of the Conquest, in which American Natives, Africans and Asians are reduced to a bunch of idiots. Old and well-established trade communities in Africa, as well as in Asia, would not be impressed by such trifles. But the argument definitively has its fictional impact within the plot.

The real trade was quite different. Tobacco and rum were, without a doubt, very important commodities in those trading routes (Blackburn 174). But, overall, it is important to remember that the rapid growth of African slave exports from 1650 on was due not only to the explosion of growth of the plantation system in America, but also to the role played by the improved military technology brought to Africa by English and Dutch merchants. In other words, weapons and military technology played a large role in the slave trade after the second half of the seventeenth century (Thorton 116). When Defoe dismisses such facts, he is not unaware of them, but merely keeping in mind the effects produced in and by the narrative. We can obviously learn about mid-seventeenth century Brazil through Defoe's novel, as long as we discern the elements of fictional intention and do not take them as pure facts.

Defoe created a masterpiece. As a piece of art, the novel does not need to answer all of the historical and social questions of its time. Its role is not to fulfill our demand for facts, but to call our attention to various issues and lead us to meditate upon them. Colonial Brazil is one of these issues. Almost three hundred years after being published, the book still leads us through a superb historical vision and continues to be a complex and challenging document.

Works Cited

Blackburn, Robin. *The Making of New World Slavery: From the Baroque to the Modern, 1492—1800*. London: Verso, 1998.

Defoe, Daniel. *Robinson Crusoe*. 1719. Ed. and intro. Angus Ross. London: Penguin, 1985.

Fausett, David. *The Strange Surprising Sources of Robinson Crusoe*. Amsterdam: Rodopi, 1994.

Freyre, Gilberto. *Casa-Grande & Senzala*. 1933. Vol. I. Rio de Janeiro: José Olympio, 1943, 4th edition.

Schwartz, Stuart. "Plantations and Peripheries." *Colonial Brazil*. Ed. Leslie Bethel. Cambridge: Cambridge UP, 1987. 67-144.

Seidel, Michael. *Robinson Crusoe: Island Myths and the Novel*. Boston: Twayne, 1991.

Thornton, John. *Africa and Africans in the Making of the Atlantic World, 1400—1680*. Cambridge: Cambridge UP, 1992.

Watt, Ian. *The Rise of the Novel*. Berkeley: U of California P, 1957.

MARCUS VINICIUS DE FREITAS

Ferdinand Denis and Brazilian Literature:
A Successful Tutelary Relationship

Maria Helena Rouanet
Translated by Paulo Henriques Britto

Although in his own time, in France, he was no more than a reasonably well-known librarian, Ferdinand Denis (1798-1890) played a central role in the process of formation of a national literature in Brazil after Independence (1822)—at least, such is the opinion of the vast majority of those who have studied this issue, from the nineteenth century to the present.

Having lived in colonial Brazil for three years and—so it seems—learned the Portuguese language, Denis returned to France in 1818 as just another nineteenth-century European traveler who had made the journey to America. Soon, however, the Independence of the Portuguese colony provided him with an excellent opportunity to act as a privileged mediator between Brazil and Europe, in both the creation and the consumption of cultural products. At first he simply disseminated texts about Brazil, such as Pero Vaz de Caminha's *Letter*; nevertheless, he soon began to publish his own works, and in a few years he had consolidated his position as a specialist: he was an "Americanist," the term used at the time.

Denis' role in the history of Brazilian literature has always been emphasized, and he has been the object of many studies. Nevertheless, his work deserves further analysis, not so much with regards to the reasons why he was canonized, but rather in terms of the mechanism by means of which intercultural relations are able to create realities for the groups involved in the process, and how alterity operates in the constitution of cultural identity.

Much more noteworthy than his condition as a specialist, which made him the most suitable person to inform nineteenth-century Europe about Brazil, is Denis' project of establishing a "good" national literature, a goal that was to be reached through the incorporation of what he thought of as "tropical reality." This project, originally addressed to his fellow countrymen, later took on other proportions, probably as an effect of Sainte-Beuve's review of Denis' *Scènes de la Nature sous les Tropiques et de leur Influence sur la Poésie* (1824). In this article, Saint-Beuve, one of the most important names in French literary criticism of the day, not only pointed out the qualities of the young travel writer's work but also raised serious objections to the actualization of the proposal he had outlined in it. The critic warned Denis of "the danger... of talking to the nation about a nature of which it is ignorant, of alluding to memories that exist only for the writer himself, so that the average reader will be forced to refer to his Buffon or his Cuvier in order to understand a line of a poem" (*Scènes* 66).[1]

Two years later, Ferdinand Denis published his *Résumé de l'Histoire Littéraire du Portugal, Suivi du Résumé de l'Histoire Littéraire du Brésil*, this time with the Brazilian public in mind. It was the publication of this text that made the author a core around which an entire conception of Brazil and Brazilian culture took shape, in a process of retrospective reading that reached back to Caminha's *Carta do Achamento do Brasil*, a work that, not coincidentally, Denis translated and published in 1821.

The part of the work dedicated to Brazil is divided into eight sections of unequal length. The first is an introduction entitled "General Considerations on the Character that Poetry Ought to Assume in the New World." Then comes a "Summary Overview of Some Poets of the Seventeenth and Eighteenth Centuries," including references to works by Bento Teixeira Pinto, Botelho de Oliveira and the playwright Antônio José, among others. A longer section follows, exclusively concerned with "José de Santa Rita Durão, *Caramuru*, Epic Poem," containing Denis' own critical observations and more than ten stanzas of the poem. The fourth and fifth sections of the work are titled respectively, "Basílio da Gama, *O Uraguai*, Epic Poem; *Quitúbia*. Cardoso, *Trípoli*, Latin Poem" and "*Marília de Dirceu*, Elegiac Lyrics by Tomás Antônio Gonzaga—*Metamorfoses do Brasil*, by Diniz da Cruz; Caldas, Alvarenga, Poems by M. B., etc." The book closes with three sections of a more generic nature, concerning "Brazilians' Propensity to Music," "Brazilian Orators and Historians: Manuel de Morais, Rocha Pita, Azeredo" and "Geography, Travels, etc."

The first point that should be stressed is the massive presence, among the authors mentioned by Denis, of names later to be canonized in the history of

Brazilian literature under the label "Nativists" as the creators of the prehistory of Brazil's *national* literature. Even more important, however, is the fact that Denis' *Résumé* was the first work ever published to separate the literature produced in Brazil from that originating in Portugal. This was of such importance to Brazilians that, in many works, mention of Denis' book omits the first part of the title. One might say that with a mere comma and the adjective *suivi* Ferdinand Denis achieved, on the plane of literature, what Dom Pedro I had earlier in the sphere of politics: the proclamation of Brazilian Independence. Curiously, both proclamations were verbal events.

If the separate treatment of Brazilian literature is an important feature of the *Résumé*, the formulation proposed in the book's introduction is doubtless what made Denis such a major figure. When he stated that " *L'Amérique enfin doit être libre dans sa poésie comme dans son gouvernement*,"[2] Denis presented to Brazilians the possibility of an *effectively* Brazilian literature, "free" and "independent" for having freed itself from what was produced in Portugal.

It should be underscored, however, that "*doit*"—not only in this passage but throughout the book—takes on a clearly ethical connotation. To Ferdinand Denis, as he himself makes clear, political independence required that Brazilians be ever on the alert, an imperative that will be a constant presence in Brazilian thought from then on. Since the new nation, only recently freed from the colonial yoke, spoke the same language as its former mother country, some distinguishing factor should differentiate the cultural production of the two countries. According to Denis, this factor should be the inclusion, in every work produced in Brazil, of those elements seen as intrinsically Brazilian. In other words, the stamp of the tropics—and here we find once again the proposal he had made earlier in *Scènes de la Nature*—was the sole factor capable of setting off Brazil from Portugal, or, more generally, Brazil as an American nation separate from the European continent.

In another passage, Ferdinand Denis leaves no doubt about the didactic intention of his work. "Americans," he writes, "have not always made plain in their writings the influence of nature that has inspired them; before Independence they seemed to even forget their own land in order to borrow from Europe a share of its glory. *Now that they need to found their own literature, I repeat, it must have an original character*" (Résumé 47, emphasis added).

Another review of *Scènes*, published in France in the still Romantic climate of the 1820s, helps us to understand not only exactly what Denis

MARIA HELENA ROUANET

meant by "original character" but also the major opportunity his book offered to Brazilians of his time. In his *Mercure de France* article, Ader enthusiastically endorses Denis' proposal:

> ... the Guaycurú, the Maxakalí are Romantic... And this school [Romanticism], before it was established on the banks of the Seine, had flourished for centuries on those of the Mucuri. There one may hear, under the branches of the huge sapucaia trees, the plaintive notes of the *maracas*, which will perhaps someday replace Apollo's lyre. (66)

The history of literature has borne out Ader's prophecy: indeed, the *maraca* took the place of the classical lyre in so-called Indianism, the Romantic tendency that established the definite shape of a conception of Brazilian literature that survives to this day, even if it is no longer dominant. To depict Brazilian nature and treat Brazilian themes is still seen as the fundamental function of literature—and of art in general—by part of the wider public, though no longer by specialists. And this is not just Brazilians' view of their own country's cultural production, but also that of almost every foreign observer.

All of these issues have been studied in depth by a number of scholars. Although this panorama may be considered a historically proven "fact," it points to a highly questionable conception that has rarely been interrogated, perhaps precisely because it is seen as a fact. It involves a naturalization of perceptions that are themselves culturally shaped, and it consequently renders absolute a viewpoint that, however incongruous it may seem, makes Brazilians see themselves as *exotic*.

I have no intention of once again reopening the well-known and pointless discussion concerning the supposed nationality of Brazilian culture as opposed to the importation of more or less acclimated foreign ideas, a discussion that leads nowhere except to a hardening of polarities. The important point is that, in the sort of asymmetrical intercultural relations exemplified by the role of individuals like Ferdinand Denis, distortions are inevitable: the parameters dictated by a dominant culture are almost always assimilated by the dominated culture without any degree of critical reflection. Let us compare two apparently widely divergent texts in order to shed further light on this question.

In the "Preface to the First Edition" of his *Formação da Literatura Brasileira*, Antonio Candido proposes a differentiated treatment for the various literatures, arguing that some of them amount to such a major heritage that "a man need not go beyond their limits in order to cultivate himself and enrich his sensibility," while others require constant interchange so that they may reach the status of the former (9). According to him, Brazilian literature must be seen as belonging to the latter group, since it is "a secondary branch of Portuguese literature, itself a minor shrub in the garden of the Muses" (9).

Such a position, however, was roundly attacked 450 years ago by Joachim du Bellay in his *La Deffence et Illustration de la Langue Francoyse*, addressed to those scholars who believed that Greek and Latin were the only languages fit to be printed. To refute this contention, du Bellay, like Candido, develops his argument by means of botanical metaphors: languages, he writes, are not to be likened to "grasses, roots and trees," some of which are born "sickly and feeble," while others are "wholesome and robust" (12). And if in time some of them become "richer than others," such a "felicity" should be attributed exclusively to "the skill and industry of men" (13).

What the two authors have in common is the fact that both represent cultures considered "minor" in confrontation with "major" cultures; and though the positions they stand for are different, they are on opposite poles of the same axis. It is on the axis that we must focus: the naturalization of cultural phenomena—and the use of botanical imagery is exemplary here— makes it difficult to perceive them as products of "skill" and "industry" and disguises the relativity that is inherent to the very situation of confrontation.

It thus makes little difference whether one assumes the view of the dominant culture and sees a culture such as the Brazilian as "fated... to depend on the experience of other literatures" (Candido 10) or whether one accuses the dominant culture of "arrogance" for claiming the "privilege of legitimating... its nation and abasing the others," as du Bellay writes of the Greeks (17). The important thing is to realize that every culture is a *construct*, and that the attitude of valuing some at the expense of others is directly linked to the viewpoint one adopts in order to consider them.

Notes

[1]For further analysis of the specifics of this issue, see Chapter 4 of my *Eternamente em Berço Esplêndido*.

[2] I quote this passage—one of Denis' most widely quoted observations—in the original French, though others will be translated, because the many translations that have been proposed for it are widely divergent.

Works Cited

Ader, J. J. "Resenha," *Le Mercure de France* VII (1824): 529-538. Quoted in "As *Scènes de la Nature sous les Tropiques* e a Imprensa," an appendix to J. P. Bruyas, *Os Maxacalis,* critical edition. São Paulo: Conselho Estadual de Cultura, 1979. 61-67.

Bellay, Joachim du. *La Deffence et Illustration de la Langue Francoyse.* 1549. Facsimile critical edition. Paris: Didier, 1970.

Candido, Antonio. *Formação da Literatura Brasileira.* (*Momentos Decisivos*). 1959. 2 vols. 5th ed. Belo Horizonte; São Paulo: Ed. Itatiaia/Edusp, 1975.

Denis, Ferdinand. *Scènes de la Nature sous les Tropiques et de leur Influence sur la Poésie, Suivies de Camoëns et Jozé Indio.* Paris: Chez L. Janet, 1824.

———. *Résumé de l'Histoire Littéraire du Portugal, Suivi du Résumé de l'Histoire Littéraire du Brésil.* Paris: Chez Lecointe & Durey, 1826.

———. "Resumo da História Literária do Brasil." *Historiadores e Críticos do Romantismo, I. A Contribuição Européia: Crítica e História Literária,* Ed. and trans. Guilhermino César. São Paulo: Edusp, 1978. 35-82.

Rouanet, Maria Helena. *Eternamente em Berço Esplêndido.* São Paulo: Siciliano, 1991.

Sainte-Beuve, "Ferdinand Denis. *Scènes de la Nature...*" *Premiers Lundis. Œuvres,* vol. 1. Bibliothèque de la Pléiade. Originally published in the daily *Le Globe* in 1824. Paris: Gallimard, 1949. 65-71.

"Watercolors of Brazil": Jean Baptiste Debret's Work

Vera Beatriz Siqueira
Translated by Nöel de Souza
and Mark Streeter

The transfer of the Portuguese Court to Rio de Janeiro in 1808, and the consequent opening of the ports to friendly nations, transformed the old colonial city into a destination for several artistic, diplomatic and scientific missions. Among them was the French Artistic Mission,[1] bringing together men of letters, architects, sculptors, and landscape and historical painters with a twofold civilizing mission: to make the city worthy of being the new capital of the overseas Kingdom and to establish an Academy of Fine Arts. However, the transfer of Portuguese courtiers and French artists to Rio always seems to be marked by the negative sign of a reality that discourages such efforts designed to establish a civilization.

Being of a rigid neo-classical background—a pupil of Jacques Louis David, who was a historical painter commissioned by Napoleon—Jean Baptiste Debret finds in Brazil the promise of a solution to his personal and professional crisis (he had lost a son and had separated from his wife, finding himself without professional alternatives after the end of the Napoleonic period). As soon as his ship touches land in Rio de Janeiro, he realizes the distance between the ethical and aesthetic values of his artistic practice and the reality of the colonial city in which he was to settle down and teach the fine art of historical painting.

In a watercolor done in the year of his arrival in Brazil, *Debret na Pensão* (*Debret in the Pension*), the artist captures this dilemma. The irony comes across in the opposition between the figures of the painter seated at the table and of the slave carrying a tray in the background. The slave's presence is ambiguous. He is presented as the point of convergence for the lines that form the perspective of the inn's floor and roof. In hiding the vanishing point, he transforms the wall at his back into a more or less diffuse background and draws our gaze to the central scene: the artist seated at the table. Nevertheless, the structuring function of the slave's portrait can appear only in a doubtful manner, being obscured by the shadows of the watercolor.

The doubt concerning the slave's presence echoes the doubt concerning the artist's work itself. As with the *mise en abîme* in the works of the Dutch school, the shadowy presence of the slave necessitates a double vision, the adoption of another point of view from behind, as a counterpoint to our own frontal vision. It is as if the slave were looking both at the artist and at ourselves looking at the figure of Debret, making material the incongruity of the ethical discourse on the artistic work in a slavocrat society. At the same time, however, it is his presence that enables the functioning of the closed perspective of the inn.

The skepticism as to the real possibilities of an artist performing in that new world entails at the same time the necessary distance to exercise his work. If the traveler's narrative impulse finds its realization in its depiction of the particular data of that unknown universe, its foundation and consistency nevertheless elude him. The colonial city is not just uncultured, which would indeed be an asset for the French artists' missionary work, it is totally new; it doesn't even provide the material or social basis necessary to carry out the civilizing mission.

Only when he returns to France and publishes the narrative of his journey does Debret recover the heroic sense of the mission:

> Driven by the same zeal and the enthusiasm as the wise travellers who are no longer afraid of braving the vicissitudes of a long and oftentimes still dangerous voyage, we left France, our common homeland, to go and study a nature totally unknown to us and to leave, in that new world, the profound and useful mark, I hope, of the presence of French artists.[2]

To leave France to arrive in the New World, to return to one's homeland—in that trajectory, the travelling artist finds his *raison d'être*. In his Brazilian watercolors Debret takes up once again the counterpoint announced in that small space of his book between the *no longer*—"no longer afraid"—and the *still* —"a long and oftentimes still dangerous voyage." Debret's artistic novelty, that which makes him new on the European cultural scenery, is suddenly seen as being old in terms of the totally unheard-of natural and social situation of Brazil.

His watercolors speak to us of the impossibility of moving from the old to the new, of establishing a relationship of continuity between those different worlds and, consequently, of creating a lasting impression of that adverse reality. Hard to seize, Debret tries to convert Brazilian reality into particular elements, into partial views, into anonymous and ill-treated characters, in exotic and insignificant details. The artist himself, in his book *Viagem Pitoresca e Histórica ao Brasil,* presents his work as a "collection,"[3] whose end coincides with his return to France and the publication of his memoirs.

The result of years of study in a distant land, the warm welcome Debret received in Brazil emerges as the lone and fragile compensation for the sorrow of not re-encountering any of his old masters and colleagues whose "immortal works remain to be admired, a glorious but very melancholic consolation, if consolation there is for eternal separation."[4] In the work of the artist committed to documenting a strange reality, the attention paid to detail suggests his interest in the diversity of the world and, at the same time, his zeal in homogenizing it by means of a civilizing process.

During the years he spent in Brazil, Debret strives to record the old customs rapidly being modified by the vainglorious contact with the European courtiers' cosmopolitanism. His long stay enabled him to witness the change in clothes, footwear, daily habits, in building, and even in the political situation, with the shift in status from colony to independent Empire in 1822. Precisely that same year, Debret writes to his brother François about the decision to publish his travel memoirs after his return to Europe.

In the first watercolors displaying the city of Rio, generally done on a miniature scale, the emphasis falls on the descriptive details of the house, of the bedroom and the atelier in which the artist settles. Sent to his brother, these pictures present above all the new daily lifestyle of the Frenchman in the tropics. As of 1822, however, he begins to compose complete scenes, besides doing hundreds of studies that later on will help him prepare the lithographs for his travel album. It is then necessary to use one's memory to reconstitute habits that were lost or had fallen into disuse. In the famous representations of *Jantar Brasileiro* (*Brazilian Dinner*) and *Interior de uma Habitação de Ciganos* (*Interior of a Gypsies' Home*), or of the countless

VERA BEATRIZ SIQUEIRA

salespersons, there is more than the fear of the speed at which the denizens of the city took pains to adopt European habits and style. There is indeed the manifest desire for a narrative ordering of those mnemonic images.

The reminiscence, however, is not only fit for the revival of the Brazilian past. It is also useful in bringing him again closer to France, giving new meaning to his civilizing task. As the same city that shamelessly adheres to new fashions denies civic sense, it is seen as being impervious to urbanity itself. Unable to civilize Brazilians, Debret takes on the task of documenting his travels as well as his specific temporality: his travel is a kind of temporal hiatus, an interval between departing and returning, charged with collecting and recording data.

The watercolor of 1827, *Um Cientista em seu Gabinete* (*A Scientist in his Chamber*), reflects upon that question. Books, a globe, stuffed birds, notebooks, and glass shelves can scarcely erase the instability of the network that sustains the scientist in his bathrobe and slippers, with chairs and benches as a precarious support for recording his knowledge. It is worth noting that in this watercolor there are many of the characteristic elements of *Kunstkammer* or "Cabinet of Curiosities," which since the sixteenth century not only served as a model for collections, but also for scientific and artistic practice.

In the scientist's chamber there appears, meanwhile, a diverse order of the taxonomic strategy that presides over those collections of curiosities from the new world. After ten years of coexistence with a colonial society, Debret speaks about a non-ordering physical presence, an instability that defies reason itself. The proximity of the back of the room, the shut door, the dim light that comes in through the window on the left, lend form to that discomfort. The scientist is the intersection between the arrangement of the objects of his occupation and the chaotic dispersion of his annotations on the floor.

Differing from other travelers, who stay only for a few months or years in Brazil, Debret spends fifteen years in the tropics. In that span of time, the promise of a new life becomes a threat to his cultural values; yet that threat in turn becomes the promise of material to be converted into discourse— promise of recognition amongst peers, a melancholic comfort for staying away from one's homeland. In that movement, he needs to transform his study into remembrance, into a mnemonic calculation of times past, but also of the time that is lacking.

The images created by Debret, therefore, are not just meant to record a life gone by, but are also intended for the future, for the development of European art. In that regard, when structuring his memoirs, he places emphasis on duration as a phenomenon of memory, of that which since the very beginning is produced in the shape of what is absent, distant, disappeared. The very use of the watercolor—a technique that at the time was seen as preparatory—and the more or less peaceful acceptance of its fluidity and imprecision demonstrate that the artist conceived that set of works as something strange in his career. A strangeness that complements the difficulty of deciphering that New World and translates images into vestiges, fragments of an existence that abandons the empirical reality of the present in order to be transmuted into a memory of distance.

To write one's memoirs, to gather and select watercolors, to transpose them into lithographies, to order them according to topics, calls for the new direction embraced by the skepticism of the missionary artist. Medicine to Debret's disappointment with the actual civilizing possibilities, that special collection of images is not just the recording of Brazilian life at the start of the nineteenth century. It is, above all, the constitution of a specific narrativity, capable of turning the Brazilian characters, places and habits into something new and old at the same time, originary in its perennial need to be deciphered, but also dead as a memory.

Paradoxically, the absence of a discursive unity capable of merging those fragments does not imply the failure of Debret's classicist values, but rather reinforces them. For instead of endowing each part with autonomy so as to refer us to the whole—what Wölfflin understood as one of the fundamental characteristics of the linear style—, it summons its autonomous value through the lack of correspondence to any totality. Perhaps this has been the great legacy Debret has left to Brazilian art and culture—the understanding that it would not be possible to articulate old and new elements into a coherent whole, since these elements are of different sizes and shapes. The alternative would be to take each element as a whole, simultaneously departure and return, blessing and curse.

In one of his studies, Debret shows a black woman sitting on a step, her back to the wall. In tatters, barefoot, abandoned, she surrenders to the support of the wall. In this watercolor there is no past, no future; neither scene nor action. In the fullness of that instant, the black woman is still, resting. There is a certain degree of pathetic grandeur in that rest; there can

VERA BEATRIZ SIQUEIRA

even be noticed the vestiges of sensuality in the meeting of the woman with the stones and the ever-damp whitewash. Before and after there is pain, the brutality of a pro-slavery social order. It is there that the violence of abandonment and desolation lie, but also the postponement of pain, the present serenity, the only property of the slaves doomed to an existence whose actions are always devoid of freedom.

It is about that city deprived of a civic sense, whose beauty seems to emerge precisely from this absence, that Debret speaks to us. To snatch it from those scarce moments, from the intimacy of a private existence, calls for the artist's sensitive look and skeptical posture alike. In his watercolors, the existence of the beautiful comes from the weak, from the distance that memory can only bridge as a vestige. There is no—as some Brazilian scholars would like—enchantment with the gentle climate, the naturalness of habits, and the exuberant nature. There is indeed a renewed skepticism. From the objective standpoint, it perceives only the possibility of a superficial contact of the New World with European civilization, evident in the luxury of the vestments, in the brilliance of the honorary orders, and in the Emperor's particular interest in the development of the arts and sciences. From the subjective standpoint, it disallows any conversion to the New: it sustains the estrangement, the sensation of never having really arrived in Brazil at all.

Therefore, although most of the analyses on Jean Baptiste Debret's work tend to emphasize its documentary character and its relevance to the knowledge of daily life in Brazil at the beginning of the nineteenth century, in this essay I am proposing a different approach. Debret's work does not offer any set of empirical and verifiable data. It offers, rather, a collection of images, whose significance lies not in its capacity to decipher enigmas and to clarify experiences, but instead in its capacity to maintain the country as an enigma, something to be perpetually interrogated.

Notes

[1] Headed by the writer Joachim Lebreton, the French Artistic Mission arrived in Brazil on March 26, 1816. The artists that constituted it were Nicolas Antoine Taunay (landscape painter), Auguste Marie Taunay (sculptor), Auguste Henri Victor Grandjean de Montigny (architect), Charles Simon Pradier (recorder) and Jean Baptiste Debret (historical painter). Subsequently, the sculptor Marc Ferrez and the recorder and sculptor Zephirin Ferrez arrived.

[2] Debret 23.

[3] Debret repeatedly defines his work as a collection: "I had at my disposal all the documents on the customs and habits of the new country I inhabited and that constituted the starting

point of my collection;" "I had the opportunity to constantly maintain, through my students, direct relationships with the most interesting regions in Brazil, relationships that enabled me to obtain an abundance of documents necessary to complement my already incipient collection;" "Chance thus led me to start, at the heart of a civilized capital, that particular collection of savages;" "That remembrance is a collection of drawings especially on the vegetation and the character of the virgin forests of Brazil" (27, 347).

    4 Debret 347.

Works Cited

Debret, Jean Baptiste. "Introdução." *Viagem Pitoresca e Histórica ao Brasil.* Vol. I. São Paulo: EdUSP, 1978.

VERA BEATRIZ SIQUEIRA

Jean Baptiste Debret
A Scholar Working in His Library
1827
Watercolor
16.2x21.2cm
Arquivos dos Museus Castro Maya, Rio de Janeiro

Jean Baptiste Debret
My Studio
1827
Watercolor
16.2x21.2cm
Arquivos dos Museus Castro Maya, Rio de Janeiro

mon attelier de Catumbi à Rio-Janeiro. août 1816

Jean Baptiste Debret
A Brazilian Dinner
1827
Watercolor
16.2x21.2cm
Arquivos dos Museus Castro Maya, Rio de Janeiro

Stefan Zweig's *Brazil, Land of the Future:* A Topic of Debate

Cléia Schiavo Weyrauch
Translated by Cecília Pernambuco
Revised by Mark Streeter

Introduction

Stefan Zweig, a famous Austrian writer and defender of pacifist humanism, lived in Vienna among a privileged circle of intellectuals that included Arthur Schnitzler, Hugo von Hofmannsthal, Herman Hesse, Max Brod, Thomas and Heinrich Mann, Walter Rathenau and others. He studied in Paris and Berlin, and in 1934 left from Salzburg to escape Nazism and to live in London. In 1932 he had already begun corresponding with his Brazilian editor and in 1936 came to Brazil for the first time; during this trip he declared to a newspaperman that "he would like to write a book about Brazil" (Dines 40). In 1940 he moved to Brazil for good, where he continued with the research he had already started, which resulted in the book *Brasil, País do Futuro* (*Brazil, Land of the Future*), published in 1941.

Stefan Zweig's book was, undoubtedly, a book written by a self-exiled European under the influence of the American tropical experience and the failure of the liberal experience in Europe. Regarded by Afrânio Peixoto as one of the most well-known "portraits of Brazil," his poetic narration shortened the distances between the European and the American worlds, and the book revealed to Brazilians and foreigners alike the love this Austrian had for Brazil. His account expresses the pleasure of encountering nature in America, which he incessantly praised. He speaks with wonder of the social milieu, comparing the German and Brazilian experiences, and deciding upon Brazil as a new humanistic paradigm in view of the failure of the European political experiences. For the author of *Brasil, País do Futuro*, the positive features of Brazilian social life and the size of its territory predestined the country to become one of the most important in the future. Its level of humanity evidenced in the harmony among races comprised a patrimony that could be a corrective model for the authoritarian national projects that dominated the years 1930-1940 in Europe.[1]

In terms of daily life, the experience of the democratic dimension of Brazilian social life was contrary to Zweig's experience in Europe. In the book's introduction, we already observe the search for a new paradigm: "How will it be possible for human beings to live in the world peacefully together, regardless of all differences in race, class, skin pigmentation, religion and opinions?" (Zweig 14-15). The author believed that Brazil had solved this "complex" situation, and continued: "With the utmost awe we see all races (existing in Brazil) living in perfect harmony" (15). Zweig, certainly influenced by the Nazi brutality, could not see the limits of tolerance and the degree of social-political conflict occurring in Brazil among races, classes and nationalities. The magnitude of the violence of the German political process had made profound impressions on his personality and, as with other European humanists, Zweig had left Europe for political reasons. As opposed to Wilhelm Reich, Herbert Marcuse, Max Horkheimer, Berthold Brecht, and Thomas Mann, all of whom went to North America, Zweig chose to live in Brazil, as well as to commit suicide there in 1942. An ardent follower of Viennese culture, Zweig could not bear the abrupt interruption of democratic ideas in Europe and died, surely of "political pain," observing the Nazi ascendancy in his continent of origin. In respect to his death, other hypotheses have been formulated, but without the surety of the aforementioned one.

European Conjuncture

Although Austria's history had been marked by peculiarities in the cultural and political fields, Hitler used it to justify anti-Semitic actions.[2] Karl Lueger and Georg von Schonerer became, according to Carl Schorske, the Führer's inspiration and their ascension in the Austrian political scene marked the beginning of an era of obscurantism.

Stefan Zweig was a humanistic writer who lived in a post-Versailles Treaty Europe caught in the contrast between technical modernity and socio-political archaism, between the cultivated socio-cultural debate and the aggravation of themes such as national identity and xenophobia. Beyond these contrasts, he witnessed in Europe an unimaginable economic crisis with drastic social consequences for the continent and made possible by the great international crisis. The peace treaty of Versailles, known for its brutality towards Germany, provided the moderate and extreme right wings an opportunity to strengthen their perverse romantic ideas of people and nation. As expressed by the German spirit, both ideas held mystical connotations that demanded from their followers a fanatic loyalty such as that required by the national-socialists. (In Italy a similar regime had been installed in 1922, anchored in the remote history of Rome.) This ideology, marked by the defense of radical confrontations, foresaw the extinction of either a class, generation or race. The new German society would emerge from the ruins in the redemptive fight of an Aryan race threatened since 1918 by a presumed socialist, foreign and above all Jewish conspiracy. As opposed to the concept of *biophilia* defended by Erich Fromm, at the time the stakes were on *necrophilia*, regardless of the results that German and other European democrats had managed to achieve during the nineteenth and early twentieth centuries. The atmosphere that had sustained democracy assumed that, in a short period of time, all men would enter into total citizenship. Fiction or not, that idea, perhaps a limit-concept, fed the democratic project of modernity and moved legions of men who, through liberal and Marxist-Enlightenment programs, fought for the institutionalization of human rights. Themes such as social equality, tolerance, fighting despotism and moral and social improvement were commonly discussed by the society. In practice, the adepts of such ideas were in a hurry to exorcise the demons of despotism, racism and obscurantism.

However, after the 1920s, this utopic project began to show signs of fragility in view not only of nationalist-driven movements but also of ideologies of racial conflict. Nationality as opposed to universality, war as opposed to peace, fanaticism as opposed to human reason became dominant values.

With the ascent of Nazism, intransigence took over and from then on a radical and systematic policy of exclusion prevailed, one that considered the inclusive project of modernity a sign of decadence and the annihilation of authentic brotherhood. Justifying the defense of this brotherhood, Hitler stated, in *Mein Kampf* as well as in political speeches and in private conversations,[3] that it was necessary to reconnect the German people to their historical blood/soil, eliminating whenever necessary the enemies of this identity concept. For him, the reason for the "German society's lack of authority"[4] was its tolerance for democratic ideals as an enemy of the genuine German spirit. In practice, the culmination of this policy was directed against the Jews who were prevented from living as German citizens for political, ethnic, and simply individual reasons. The result is well known: almost six million Jews were exterminated in an unprecedented historical experience.

Similar to such figures as Mann, Brecht, Pollock, Horkheimer, and Marcuse, who perceived the failure of the democratic project in Austria and Germany, Zweig left Europe and tried to recreate a new human paradigm in exile. The urgency to construct the "thousand-year Reich" confirmed the conservative modernity of the Nazis whose objective was to establish a model of order that was irreconcilable with the victories that derived from political enlightenment. The concept of the future contained in Zweig's hopeful narration of Brazil included miscegenation that could not even be imagined in Nazi Germany. It clearly represents Zweig's reaction against Nazism.

The Place of the Capital City in the New Paradigm

In the book *Brasil, País do Futuro*, the proposed dialectic of complementarity and its emphasis on the socio-political universe is based on the essential convergence expressed in the relation between nature and culture. In the case of the city of Rio de Janeiro, the concepts of East and West are associated, allowing for the possibility of a city whose organization overcomes the models discussed by the European vanguard. For a European in the first half of the twentieth century, the modernity of a country was measured by the modern qualities of its capital and by the rationality and planning of its territory. In the case of Berlin, Hitler decided to make it even more cosmopolitan and monumental than Paris and Vienna; he considered it inadequate as only the capital of a Reich when it should be a model for the world. In conversations recorded by Albert Speer, Hitler said that "Berlin is no more than an irregular heap of buildings" (Speer 76). Therefore, it was necessary to make it above all symmetric.

For Stefan Zweig the city of Rio de Janeiro expressed the new civilizational paradigm through the range of supplementary contrasts accommodated by it. Besides emphasizing that Rio de Janeiro's social life tolerated all contrasts, he praised the city as not being prey to

> … a geometric delirium of straight avenues,… to the horrendous idea of excessive
> regularity of the modern large cities, which sacrifice to the symmetry of line and

to the monotony of forms, exactly that which is always incomparable in all cities: its surprises, its whims and angularity and above all its contrasts—those contrasts between old and new, city and nature, rich and poor,… contrasts found here in their incomparable harmony. (232)

His account of Rio de Janeiro refers to something new, built from an unheard-of dimension of history, and without the violence resulting from a purging dictated from above, such as that undertaken by the *Führer*. For Zweig, in the city of Rio de Janeiro the miscegenation brought together the new and the old, the ancient and the traditional. Perhaps being tired of the modern megaprojects, he found in the city of Rio de Janeiro the beauty of the necessary and ideal proximity between nature and culture, East and West so distant from the discussions of the European vanguard. "Everywhere nature is exuberant… *and it is within this nature that we find the same city*. And a forest of stone with its skyscrapers and small palaces, with its avenues and squares and *oriental-looking small streets*, with its Negro shacks, and gigantic ministries, with its bathing beaches and its casinos" (190, emphasis added).

In this account, Rio de Janeiro appears as the city that is inseparably enmeshed with nature, as a beautiful work of art attached to it. In reality, he saw it as a monument embedded in Guanabara Bay and in the forests surrounding it on all sides. Like the majority of Germans, he was influenced by the idea of union with nature, which he found realized in the tropics, either in the forest and environs, or in its intersections with the American civilized world. In Brazil, there was the possibility of a new, democratic society based on social-ethnic plurality, the starting point for the renewal of the concepts of culture and civilization understood until then as instrumental reason. As Zweig says: "We are no longer willing simply to make them conform to the idea of organization and comfort" (19), suggesting that only the degree of superiority of the human spirit would be able to neutralize hate between ethnic groups, classes, generations and nationalities.

Redeeming his initial prejudice described in the introduction of the book, Zweig thoroughly confesses: "I had the same pretentious idea of Brazil which the Europeans and North Americans have and now I find it difficult to go back to it" (2). Nevertheless, this "pretentious" Austrian was able to write a book that is still useful for the study of Brazil's future. In fact, Stefan Zweig already loved Brazil even before coming to know it. Back in Europe from his first trip to Brazil in 1936, he wrote "Short Trip to Brazil," which was published in several international newspapers. According to Alberto Dines, his major biographer in Brazil, Zweig stated at the time: "He who knows Brazil today, has gazed into the future" (Dines 78).

I leave as homage to Stefan Zweig the sentence he dedicated to Brazil and to the city of Rio de Janeiro in the last page of his book:

> Farewell.
>
> He who visits Brazil is loath to leave it. From wherever he is, he longs to return.
>
> Beauty is a rare thing and perfect beauty is almost a dream. Rio, this superb city, makes it real at even the saddest moments. There is no city more charming in the world. (302)

Notes

[1] Between Stefan Zweig's first, second, and final visits to Brazil, Vargas' dictatorship was implanted, a period called the *Estado Novo* ("New State"). During this period, some democratic guarantees were withheld, although most of the newspapers did not emphasize what the torture chambers were already recording.

[2] The Nationalist movements in Austria neutralized, from the middle of the twentieth century, the progress of Austrian liberal multinational ideas. Both Karl Lueger and Georg von Schonerer were important figures in the nationalist movements. Lueger, an anti-Semitic Christian, became mayor of Vienna at the beginning of the century. Schonerer, an industrialist, organized the radical nationalists in 1882 and implemented a drastic anti-Semitic policy.

[3] This information was taken from the book *Secret Conversations*, whose content defines, by the use of intimate documents, Adolf Hitler's conservative and radical ideas.

[4] In the second chapter of *Mein Kampf*, Hitler records his hostility towards social democracy and to socialism: "What kept me away from social democracy was its contrary position in relation to the movement for the preservation of the German spirit" (44). Later in the text, he identifies the French and Jews as responsible for the degradation of German souls.

Works Cited

Dines, Alberto. *Morte no Paraíso: A Tragédia de Stefan Zweig*. Rio de Janeiro: Nova Fronteira, 1981.

Fromm, Erich. *O Coração do Homem*. Rio de Janeiro: Zahar Editores, 1974.

Gay, Peter. *A Cultura de Weymar*. Rio de Janeiro: Paz e Terra, 1978.

Hitler, Adolf. *Minha Luta*. São Paulo: Mestre Jou, 1962.

———. *Secret Conversations: 1941—1944*. Trans. Norman Cameron and R. H. Stevens. New York: Octagon, 1972.

Kershaw, Ian. *Hitler, um Perfil do Poder*. Rio de Janeiro: Jorge Zahar Editor, 1993.

Lindholm, Charles. *Carisma*. Rio de Janeiro: Jorge Zahar Editor, 1942.

Loom, Hendrich Van. *Tolerância.* Rio de Janeiro: Companhia Editora Nacional, 1942.

Richard, Lionel. *A República de Weimar.* São Paulo: Companhia das Letras, 1988.

Scholem, Gerschom. *A Mística Judaica.* São Paulo: Perspectiva, 1972.

Schorske, Carl. *Vienna fin de siècle: Política e Cultura.* São Paulo: Companhia das Letras, 1988.

Shire, William. *The Rise and Fall of the III° Reich.* New York: Simon and Schuster, 1960.

Speer, Albert. *Por Dentro do III° Reich: Os Anos de Glória.* Rio de Janeiro: Artenova, 1971.

Zweig, Stefan. *Brasil, País do Futuro.* Rio de Janeiro: Guanabara, 1941.

———. *Brazil, Land of the Future.* Trans. Andrew St. James. New York: Viking, 1942.

———. *Brazil: A Land of the Future.* Trans. with an Afterword by Lowell A. Bangerter. Riverside, CA: Ariadne Press, 1999.

Elizabeth Bishop as Cultural Intermediary

Paulo Henriques Britto

Rien ne vous tue un homme comme d'être obligé de représenter un pays.
Jacques Vaché, letter to André Breton (qtd. in Julio Cortázar's *Rayuela*)

Elizabeth Bishop was an intensely private person. The public role of the poet as prophet or social critic—the sort of role that came naturally to her friend Robert Lowell—was not for her. The podium of the cultural critic or literary scholar was not for her either. As the Brazilian critic Luiz Costa Lima has observed, Bishop was an artist, not an intellectual (Lima 5); she was never comfortable with abstractions and generalizations and felt out of place among academics. As a poet, one of her major assets was her sight ("My eyes bulge and hurt. They are my one great beauty, even so," says the Giant Toad in "Rainy Season; Sub-Tropics," *Poems* 139), and most of the time what she cared to see were small, unimportant objects with a strictly personal meaning.

Yet the vagaries of circumstance—she met Lota de Macedo Soares in Brazil and they fell in love with each other—led her to spend the better part of two decades in a foreign country where she did not really feel at home, and whose language she never cared to learn properly. Necessarily, this made her a cultural intermediary of sorts, and in her abundant correspondence, her work in the Time-Life book *Brazil*, her translations of Helena Morley's diary, her anthology of modern Brazilian poetry (a project undertaken in collaboration with the late Emanuel Brasil) and, not least, her poems on Brazilian themes, she acted as an interpreter of Brazil for North Americans. On a smaller scale, among her associates in Petrópolis and Rio, she also played the role of an unofficial representative and interpreter of US culture—

and, particularly at the time of the 1964 military coup, of a defender of American foreign policy, including US support for the military dictatorship, roundly denounced at the time by the liberal press and intellectuals in the U.S. But the role of cultural ambassador suited her as little as that of interpreter of a foreign culture, and she always felt uneasy about her credentials for any such a position. As she worked on an introduction for an anthology of Brazilian poetry, Bishop wrote to Lowell in 1969: "It is awful to think I'll probably be regarded as some sort of authority on Brazil the rest of my life" (Millier 424).

When she first arrived in Brazil, Bishop knew little about the country. Like everyone else, however, she carried with her a number of stereotyped notions about the country, as soon became apparent. From the beginning she decided—to put it somewhat simplistically—that Brazil was basically "nature" whereas the U.S. stood for "culture." The early letters Bishop wrote in Brazil include enthusiastic descriptions of the natural beauties of the Petrópolis area;[1] and in some of the poems she began to work on at the time, most notably "Song for the Rainy Season," the physical environment around her—Lota's estate in Samambaia—is seen as protective, supportive, and life-assertive. For the rest of her life, Bishop was to extol Brazilian nature even as she decried Brazil's shortcomings as a country. In contrast, the U.S. seemed to her to be characterized by its "bright cleanness [, which] is what I always miss most at first" (OA 343); that is, it represented the values of material progress, civilization, culture. On the whole, Bishop saw herself as squarely on the side of culture—she made a point of saying that, even if she went on spending most of her time in Brazil, as she intended to do, she wanted to remain "a New Englander herring-choker bluenoser at the same time" (OA 384). But both nature and culture had good and bad points. Nature meant absence of culture, and therefore "underdevelopment" (to use the term current in the 1950s and 1960s), but it also implied spontaneity and warmth; and culture, for all its positive associations, meant artificiality and estrangement from basic human values, as we shall see.

Bishop's very first contact with Rio crystallized in a view of the city as a place inimical to work and civilization, an opinion that was never to change in the succeeding decades:

> ... it's such a mess—Mexico City and Miami combined is about the closest I can
> come to it; and men in bathing trunks kicking footballs all over the place. They

begin on the beach at 7 every morning—and keep it up apparently at their places of business all over town, all day long. (*OA* 226-27)

This passage, from the earliest of her published letters containing a description of her impressions of Brazil, sets the pattern for much that is to follow. Bishop traveled widely in the country, but she saw mostly what she already expected to see: a luxuriant natural environment and a population divided between the poor, who were "primitives" with all the attendant virtues and vices, and sophisticated aristocrats like Lota, who spoke several languages and traveled abroad frequently. There was no such thing as a middle class in Brazil, she wrote in one of her letters (*OA* 271). In fact, at the time there was a sizable Brazilian middle class already; but in the small world of Samambaia where Bishop lived the social structure was indeed starkly dichotomous: there was Lota's circle and there were Lota's servants. That Bishop could take this protected corner of Petrópolis as a reasonably representative sample of Brazil is typical of her inability to grasp larger realities; that from such a narrow perspective she was able to write a handful of sharply insightful poems about Brazil is the mark of her genius.

As the quotation in the previous paragraph indicates, one preconceived notion Bishop seems to have brought to Brazil as part of her intellectual baggage was that of Latin Americans' alleged aversion to work. In a letter to a friend in 1954, regarding the photographs of the Brazilian poet Manuel Bandeira writing in a hammock, she wrote that she believed the hammock aptly summarized "the Brazilian spirit in literature" (*OA* 289). A few days later, in another letter, she wrote: "I notice that literary people here often seem to have their pictures taken in [hammocks], and whether that's what wrong with Brazilian writing or not—perhaps I'll find out" (*OA* 291). This image was to reappear later in the Time-Life book *Brazil*: "A favorite way for Brazilian writers to have their pictures taken is pleasantly supine, in a fringed hammock. Too many genuine Brazilian talents seem to take to their beds too early—or to their hammocks" (Bishop, *Brazil* 104). Clearly, this passage reflects Bishop's opinion of Bandeira: in 1962 she wrote Robert Lowell that Bandeira seemed to her "very spoiled."[2] At the time, Bandeira was 75 and had published an impressive amount of poetry, journalism, and criticism; he also had taught literature, organized a multivolume anthology of Brazilian poetry and translated much poetry and drama from English, French, and German; he was already acknowledged as one of the greatest Brazilian poets of the century. But the forcefulness of the image of the indolent poet in his hammock, which reinforced her preconceptions about Brazil (or Latin America), outweighed whatever information Bishop may have had about Bandeira's career.

Lota's attitude toward her own country seems to have influenced Bishop's perceptions of Brazil and reinforced her prejudices. As Bishop wrote, "Lota refuses to have anything to do with anything Brazilian or 'primitives'" (*OA* 416). She was "extremely pro-English," and at the time Bishop first met her, in New York, professed her admiration for "'well-made,' 'well-finished'" things (OA 258), so different from the objects that surrounded one in Brazil. Thus Bishop's love for precisely the "primitive" aspects of Brazil was combined with condescension; even before coming to Brazil she had expressed this same sort of patronizing affection for the elements of Cuban culture she had found in Key West, most notably in her 1939 prose piece on a primitive painter, "Gregorio Valdes."[4] Lota's steadfast rejection of "backwardness" and her admiration for all things foreign must have dramatized Bishop's own perception of "how everything [in Brazil] is wretchedly made, unfinished" (*OA* 258). And so she saw herself—and Lota, who like most educated people of her class was thoroughly Europeanized— as committed to introducing civilized habits into Brazil.

A good example of this is Bishop's attitude about childrearing. Her correspondence is filled with expressions of concern with the way Lota's servants raised their children. She encouraged Lota to translate Dr. Spock's *Baby and Child Care*: "if she has a spark of patriotism in her bosom, she certainly should" (*OA* 343). When the cook in Samambaia had a baby, Bishop urged the parents to give her healthy food, such as spinach. "The diet here is unbelievable, for the rich as well as the poor, usually," she wrote (*OA* 307). When the child was 18 months old, Bishop commented:

> But she doesn't talk—just because her mother and young aunts are too stupid to talk *to* her, I think... Now I know why poor children cry more than rich ones. It isn't that they don't have enough to eat or anything like that; it's just because their parents are so dumb the way they treat them. (*OA* 321)

Primitivism is an important topic in her letters and poems, but it is always tempered by Bishop's precision of observation. In "Manuelzinho"—inspired by a real-life person, a "half squatter, half tenant" living on Lota's land—

Bishop presents the caricature of a Brazilian "primitive": Manuelzinho is a "helpless, foolish man," "the world's worst gardener since Cain" (*Poems* 96-99); he is ignorant, superstitious, and shamelessly abject. But the poem is "supposed to be Lota talking" (*OA* 315), and its effectiveness lies in the way it captures the exact mixture of helpless exasperation and condescending affection that characterizes the feelings of Brazilian patricians for their servants. And if, in "The Burglar of Babylon," primitivism and bumbling incompetence are traits shared by Micuçú and the policemen who finally manage to catch him, there is nothing reductionistic about this latter-day outlaw ballad: Micuçú, cruel but not devoid of affection, doomed but determined to survive as long as possible, is shown "in the round" and as a real person; he may be "primitive," but he is not stereotyped in the way Manuelzinho (as seen by Lota) is.

But the "dumb" primitivism of Brazilians also implied "naturalness." This was the quality that impressed Bishop so positively in her first few years in Samambaia, the idyllic period in her life that was immortalized by such splendid lyrics as "The Shampoo" and "Song for the Rainy Season." The letters she wrote in the early 1950s are full of passages like the following: "It is really a wonderful country in some ways. Where, when you arrive, the janitor and the porter and the cook all hug you tenderly and call you 'madame, my daughter'" (OA 244). Brazilians—particularly "in the small poor places"—were "so absolutely natural and so elegantly polite." They were "more realistic about, life, death, marriage, the sexes, etc."; and in their country "children are really loved more than anyplace else—except perhaps in Italy... With all its awfulness and stupidities—some of the Lost World hasn't quite been lost here yet" (*OA* 434). A year later, in Seattle, working as a teacher for the first time in her life, Bishop in her letters would often write nostalgically of Brazil, depicting it again as a place that preserved some of the simpler, basic human values that were necessarily lost as part of the price of civilization. Thus she observed about her students at the University of Washington:

> My 'students' are awfully nice, almost all of them—but I must say I am a bit concerned about American Youth. They are bright, almost all of them, but they don't seem to have much *fun*—so little *joie de vivre*, when I think of how much amusement Brazilian youths seem to get out of a guitar, or a dance, or just a cafézinho [sic] and some conversation... (*OA* 444)

PAULO HENRIQUES BRITTO

This early perception of Brazilian primitivism was to give way to a strikingly different view in the latter half of the 1960s, when Bishop's relationship with Lota began to go sour; it was exacerbated after Lota's suicide and in the period in the early 1970s when Bishop attempted to live with her new companion in Ouro Preto. While in the early fifties she had seen Brazilians as a loving, accepting, if primitive people, who had a more "natural" view of life, by the end of her stay in Brazil they seemed to her irrational, greedy and devoid of human solidarity. Of course, the two contrasting evaluations reflect directly her personal situation in the two periods of her life in Brazil and correspond to the two typical views of the "backward" Other—noble savage and barbarian. But they are not as contradictory as they may seem at first sight, if one takes into account Sérgio Buarque de Holanda's notion of "cordiality," that is, Brazilians' inability to relate to each other on any but the most personal basis, our failure to fashion a model of "civil man." According to Holanda, "cordiality" is opposed to "civility," "good manners" or "politeness". To Brazilians, the sort of interpersonal relations that are established in family life remain "the inescapable model" for all other relationships (106). For this reason, Brazilians are unable to develop the ritualistic polish of "politeness," a "disguise that allows... one to preserve intact one's sensibility and feelings" (107). Holanda goes on to observe: "Brazilians' ignorance of any form of coexistence not dictated by an emotionally-based ethics is an aspect of Brazilian life that few foreigners find easy to understand in depth" (109). Bishop's opposite perceptions are in fact two aspects of a single characteristic of Brazilians, and one that Bishop never really understood.

Since Brazil for Bishop was "nature," the idea of a Brazilian high culture seemed almost self-contradictory to her: it was among the poor that "real Brazilian culture" was to be found—that is, popular culture. Her admiration for Brazilian art is always colored by the notion that whatever is good about it must be primitive; thus she describes Aleijadinho's famous statues of the prophets in Congonhas do Campo as "crude, but powerful and dramatic" (*Brazil* 100)—though "crude" is the last adjective any unprejudiced observer would associate with the work of an artist as sophisticated as Aleijadinho. To Bishop, there was something inherently suspect in all Brazilian high art; in spite of her respect for Drummond, Cabral and other writers, the Brazilian works that really engaged her emotion were all marked by artlessness: Helena Morley's *Minha Vida de Menina*, an actual diary written by a teenage girl in the interior of Minas Gerais in the 1890s, which Bishop lovingly translated into English; the *cordel* poetry of Northeastern poet-singers; and Carnival songs, "some of the last folk poetry to be made in the world" (*OA* 382). The pristine quality of popular art was incompatible with the sophistication of high art, and any inroads made by the latter into the former could only be decried as impurity or inauthenticity. So Bishop tells Lowell that the lyrics to a samba for the Marcel Camus movie *Black Orpheus*, set in a Rio favela, are bad *because* they are "written by a *real* poet," Vinícius de Moraes: "they lack that surprise, the misused words, the big words, etc., that sambas always have" (*OA* 382).

Just as Bishop found it difficult to accept the idea of a Brazilian high culture, manifestations of primitive vigor in U.S. culture also made her uncomfortable. That is why she told "Brazilian intellectuals… that they really should read Edmund Wilson, say, instead of Henry Miller, to get an adequate idea of U.S. letters." She observed that authors like "Dreiser, Anderson, [and] Miller… correspond better to the mental picture [Brazilians] have of the USA" than a writer like Henry James. To her, it was James, the thoroughly Anglicized craftsman of polished prose and chronicler of a sophisticated transatlantic English-speaking society, that must represent the U.S. abroad, not the uncouth, barbaric Miller, who was "the new American Blake," or so Brazilians had been convinced by "some French mystic writers" (*OA* 336). This explains Bishop's mixed feelings about Whitman, whom in a 1938 letter she characterized as "dated and unpleasant" (*OA* 75), and about whom she had this to say in a 1970 interview:

> As to the greatest North American poet—I am reminded that once when Gide was asked who in his opinion was the greatest poet in the French language, he responded: 'Victor Hugo, alas!' I would say that, in my opinion, the greatest North American poet is Whitman, alas! (Monteiro 52)

While acknowledging Whitman's greatness, Bishop seems to have felt that his qualities were associated with precisely those aspects of American culture that were least refined and civilized, and from which she had been consciously trying to distance herself at least since she began to see herself as representing progressive American values in benighted Brazil.

But this role that she had taken on was sorely put to the test when, in 1964, a military coup overthrew President João Goulart and instituted a

PAULO HENRIQUES BRITTO

dictatorial regime. Bishop now found herself in the impossible position of having to stand for American liberalism in Brazil and at the same time defend an antidemocratic regime to her American friends. When the liberal U.S. press criticized the Brazilian military, she wrote: "I'm in a RAGE about what the U.S. papers are quoted as saying." She justified "the suspension of rights, dismissing lots of Congress, etc.", saying that it "had to be done—sinister as it may sound." She denied rumors of military violence, always carefully qualifying her statements with phrases like "as far as I know"; and at one point she confessed: "It will be a relief to get away. This constant pressure of violently opposed feelings does not suit the 'artistic temperament' (all I lay claim to)."[5] Since at no point in the letter does she express any misgivings about the new military government itself, the "violently opposed feelings" Bishop alludes to here seem to be her approval of a dictatorial regime and her lifelong liberal tendencies.

The years immediately before and after 1964 were the period in which Bishop was most obviously miscast as a cultural intermediary. But the entire period of her direct or indirect involvement with Brazil, as an American expatriate in Rio de Janeiro and Minas Gerais or, in her final years, as a would-be "authority on Brazil," must be seen, on the whole, as a succession of misunderstandings large and small. Unable or unwilling to learn Portuguese properly, and incapable of seeing the forest for the trees, Elizabeth Bishop was a most ineffective (and reluctant) cultural intermediary; in fact, all she asked of Brazil was a home—a place where she would be loved and understood and where she could write in peace. This is indeed what she got, for about ten years; but in the turbulent period that began in the early 1960s—turbulent for Brazil in general and for Bishop in particular—her position became increasingly equivocal, and ultimately unbearable. It seems fitting, then, that in her late masterpiece "Crusoe in England" she should have identified with a solitary castaway on a tropical island with only one other inhabitant. For Bishop, the things that truly mattered in the country where she lived for almost twenty years were her lover and the magnificent natural environment around her. When, back in Massachusetts towards the end of her life, she felt *saudade do Brasil,* what she really missed was Lota and the magical, protected world of Samambaia, where for a time she found the home that had eluded her for so long.

PAULO HENRIQUES BRITTO

Notes

[1] Here is a fairly typical example, from a 1953 letter: "It is the season of those pale blue butterflies... They are drifting along all over the place, sometimes in clusters of four or five, and when they come close or come *in*, they are semi-transparent. The 'Lent' trees... are purple all over the mountains, mixed with pink and yellow acacias." (Bishop, *One Art* [henceforward abbreviated *OA*] 255).

[2] This letter remains unpublished in English, but has appeared in the Brazilian edition of *OA*. See Bishop, *Uma Arte* 718.

[3] For a discussion of Lota's feelings about Brazilianness and modernity, see Jaguaribe.

[4] Included in Bishop, *Collected Prose*.

[5] Unpublished letter; translation included in *Uma Arte*, 741-5.

Works Cited

Bishop, Elizabeth. *The Collected Prose*. New York: Noonday-Farrar, 1984.

———. *The Complete Poems, 1927-1979*. New York: Noonday-Farrar, 1991.

———. *One Art*. New York: Farrar, 1994.

———. *Uma Arte*. Trans. Paulo Henriques Britto. São Paulo: Companhia das Letras, 1995.

Bishop, Elizabeth, and the eds. of *LIFE*. *Brazil*. New York: Time World Library, 1962.

Holanda, Sérgio Buarque de. *Raízes do Brasil*. 1936. Rio de Janeiro: José Olympio, 1982.

Jaguaribe, Beatriz. "Diamantes e Feijão Preto: Elizabeth Bishop e o Brasil." *Fins de Século: Cidade e Cultura no Rio de Janeiro*. Rio de Janeiro: Rocco, 1998. 77-118.

Lima, Luiz Costa. "Bishop: A Arte da Perda." *Idéias, Jornal do Brasil* 3 Feb. 1996. 5.

Millier, Brett C. *Elizabeth Bishop: Life and the Memory of It*. Berkeley: U of California P, 1993.

Monteiro, George, ed. *Conversations with Elizabeth Bishop*. Jackson: UP of Mississippi, 1996.

Roger Bastide and Brazil: At the Crossroads Between Viewpoints

Fernanda Peixoto
Translated by Shoshanna Lurie

The centrality of Brazil in the work of Roger Bastide (1898-1974) is unquestionable. Brazil is an exceptional example of the interpenetration of civilizations for the interpreter to observe and, at the same time, soil upon which distinct intellectual traditions cross paths. It is also a producer of original theories of which Bastide would take advantage not only to understand the specificities of the country, but also to forge his own particular point of view. In Brazil, at the crossroads between disparate viewpoints, the sociologist polished his analytical perspective. This essay deals with Bastide's discussions of Brazil.[1]

When he arrived in Brazil in 1938, Roger Bastide brought with him an *aggregation* degree in philosophy, experience teaching in different French lyceums, some political experience, an interrupted literary project, two books, and a series of published articles.[2] In his earlier work, a number of persevering themes can be identified, including religion, the sacred, literature, mystic life, dreams, the imaginary, and memory. An intellectual attitude that would always be exercised and that implied a combination of different approaches—sociological, anthropological, psychological, and historical—can also be found in his work.

Although the contact between civilizations, which would become the thematic axis of all of Bastide's later work, had still not been explored at this point, it was not completely absent in his earlier work. In his 1935 text, *Éléments de Sociologie Religieuse*, in his discussion of religious systems and their transformation, Bastide refers to the mixtures that are produced between different systems and demonstrates that these intersections and mixtures can give birth to the transformation of a religious system into a magical system, such as what occurred with Afro-Brazilians in Bahia.[3]

A series of questions posed during this formational period allow us to trace the threads between Bastide's earlier and later works, though the theoretical framework changes significantly over time. In order to understand Brazilian religious syncretism, one of the principal themes in his work from this point forward, Bastide would retrieve the primary theses of Durkheim-grounded French sociology. He had been critically debating them since his earliest work,[4] and would incorporate Marcel Griaule's and Michel Leiris' formulations of French Africanism into his work during the 1950s. Another theoretical influence that was decisive in the elaboration of the notion of the interpenetration of civilizations was Georges Gurvitch, with whom he would intensify his relations toward the end of the 1940s.[5] The dialogue established with North American sociology and anthropology (mainly with the work of M. Herskovits and with authors linked to the Chicago School), with which Bastide became familiar during his Brazilian period, was also central in the definition of the concept of syncretism.[6]

In Brazil, new theoretical affinities were established—redefinitions that were formulated through Bastide's fieldwork observations, through the (re)discoveries of French and North American traditions, and above all through his engagement with Brazilian literary and sociological production. During his sixteen years in Brazil as a sociology professor at the recently founded Universidade de São Paulo (1938-1954),[7] Bastide elaborated a personal, essentially hybrid perspective, constructed by crossing different approaches.[8]

Bastide thought and wrote about Brazil as he grew more and more familiar with the country. In newspaper reviews,[9] university classes, *candomblé* houses, art galleries, readings, discussions, and on trips, he continuously developed and reformulated analytical perspectives. His vast and varied work on Brazil grew out of his daily contact with others, through disagreements and debates. In his dialogue with national production, Bastide focused on Brazilian culture's broadest issue—its genesis and formation—not limiting himself to any exclusive aspect of cultural phenomena, which, with few exceptions, was the approach chosen by foreigners in the country.

Bastide took his first steps in Brazil with the help of critics and writers linked to Modernism. Following in the tracks of these intellectuals, he grew to know the country, its arts, literature, and folklore. He reviewed Mário de

Andrade's readings on the baroque and Aleijadinho,[10] and fundamentally agreed with the Modernist leader's conceptualizations of the "authenticity" of Brazilian culture. It is also through these discussions about the "genuinely national" that Bastide questioned his own place as a foreign interpreter seeking to grasp authentic Brazilian culture.

The interpreter faced the issue of determining the origins of Brazilian culture and of syncretism in his dialogue with the literary tradition and in his education on Brazil and Africa.[11] Bastide, since his arrival in the country and as a reader of the modernists, was aware that the originality of Brazilian culture resided in its hybridity—in the unique mixture resulting from the intersection of distinct civilizations. As Mário de Andrade and the modernists showed him, this authenticity was not to be mistaken for purity.

Bastide claimed that the modernists were seeking Afro-Brazilian themes, "exoticism in the heart of an exotic land" (*Poetas* 49). In other words, they went in search of differences within their own country, capable of creating a sensation of *dépaysement*. This differentiated element within Brazil was precisely Africa (*Poetas* 50). The foreign sociologist, determined to overcome an artificial vision of the country, would have to address an even higher degree of exoticism, since for him Brazil was the quintessential synonym of exotic. In this sense, his position supposes a radicalization of the Modernist quest. For Bastide, the search for Africa in Brazil was in fact the search for "the exotic's exotic," or "the other's other."

In Bastide's case, an analytical perspective was elaborated with the aid of a sort of specular game, permanently dislocating the observing subject. The Frenchman viewed Africa from Brazil and, vice-versa, Brazil from Africa. Consequently, this is his field of Brazilian observation: the Africa, Europe and Brazil triangle, with the last country defined as the bargaining table between the African and European symbolic systems. The choice of effective methodological tools and adequate thematic refining allowed for an understanding of the successive arrangements that operate within the triangle.

Folklore, the baroque, and literature allow Bastide to view the country through a syncretic lens dominated by European tones. Religion too would offer the interpreter a new angle of observation. His analysis of Afro-Brazilian worship functioned as a key for illuminating the presence of African resistance in Brazil. In this way, it made the sifting of Africa through *mestiço* composition possible for the interpreter.

FERNANDA PEIXOTO

Research on African religions in Brazil obligated the analyst to re-configure the discussion of syncretism and also brought other speakers onto the national scene. The formation of Brazilian society and culture were on the agenda due to the debate over a specific sociological approach, namely that of Gilberto Freyre. This time, however, the African presence in Brazil's formation had attained prominence in the discussion. The *sui generis* profile of Bastide-Africanist emerged from this debate, simultaneously engaged with an ethnography of the African cultural islands within Brazil and with developing a sociology of cultural contact between Brazil and Africa.[12] But not only this. From Freyre's "amphibious and hybrid sociology" (Bastide, "Passeio"), Bastide learned about the links between micro and macro levels of analysis, about the combination of sociological and anthropological perspectives, and how to master sociological narrative with literary value.

Gilberto Freyre is present, both explicitly and implicity, throughout the entire first volume of *As Religiões Africanas no Brasil* (1960). Bastide unfolded his explanation by way of a close reading of Freyre's *Casa-Grande & Senzala* (1933) and *Sobrados e Mucambos* (1936), generally endorsing the broad panorama of Brazilian society sketched by Freyre. According to Bastide, the distance between the two was due to the choice of different perspectives on the approach to cultural contact.[13]

It can be claimed that the idea of *formation* is present both in Freyre's above-mentioned works as well as in *As Religiões Africanas no Brasil.* In Freyre's case, it is the formation of the patriarchal family, while in Bastide's case, of African civilization. In both authors, the formation of a new civilization occurs with eclectic materials from diverse sources. In Freyre's as well as in many others' interpretive models, Brazilian civilization originates from the mixture of Portuguese, Indigenous, and African inheritances. In Bastide's terms, African civilization is recreated in Brazil through (and in spite of) the encounter between these three civilizations. Thus, the Brazilian Africa is not a copy of the original model, but a re-elaborated, hybrid product.

In these authors, the discussion of formative processes was based on tracing the historical conditions of the formation of the patriarchal family (in Freyre's case) and of the implantation of Africa in Brazil (in Bastide's). Freyre described a dually-structured society—master's house and slave quarters, master and slave, blacks and whites, mansions and shanties—whose dualism did not compromise the survival of the whole. On the contrary, the totality was nourished precisely by the "balance of antagonisms."[14] The characterization of the Brazilian formative process as grounded in a principle of balanced antagonisms, emblematic of Freyre's work, was generally corroborated by Bastide in his 1960 text, in his earlier work *Brasil, Terra de Contrastes* (1957), and later in *As Américas Negras* (1967). However, the dual structure was complicated by the French scholar. For Bastide, the contrasts that sever the Brazilian social fabric are multiple; therefore, integration or balance are always problematic.

As I have tried to demonstrate, Bastide was a careful reader of schools of thought already consolidated in Brazil; however, his role as a creator of new traditions in the country cannot be forgotten. Through his activities at the Universidade de São Paulo as a professor and research advisor, he was responsible for the initiation of a new approach to sociological studies in Brazil. For instance, Florestan Fernandes was one of his direct heirs. Along with Bastide, Fernandes began his sociological research investigating folklore in the city of São Paulo. During the 1950s, professor and student joined to coordinate São Paulo's contribution to the broad research project on race relations in Brazil sponsored by Unesco.[15]

Not only sociological studies benefited from Bastide's presence at the Universidade de São Paulo. Along with Jean Maugué and Lévi-Strauss, he was also responsible for the formation of well-prepared and productive critics—Antonio Candido, Gilda de Mello e Souza, Décio de Almeida Prado, Paulo Emílio Salles Gomes, among others, these Brazilian students with their French teachers have "learned how to study" and to be interested in Brazilian topics. Ruy Coelho's words exemplify this: "Bastide, like all French professors, directed us to Brazil."[16]

Notes

[1] This argument is further developed in my book, *Diálogos Brasileiros*.

[2] An intellectual biography of Roger Bastide can be found in Ravelet, "Bio-Bibliographie de R. Bastide." On the literary ambitions of the author, see Ravelet, "Roger Bastide et la Poesie," and Morin.

[3] *Éléments* 143. Bastide probably became aware of the example of black Bahians as a result of Mauss' reference to the work of Nina Rodrigues, "O Animismo Fetichista dos Negros Baianos," published in *Année Sociologique* 5 (1900-1). Reuter suggests that a desire to research Bahia was the decisive factor in Bastide's coming to Brazil.

[4] It is curious that Bastide returned to the work of Durkheim during his Brazilian period, especially through Mauss' and Lévy-Bruhl's interpretations, and abandoned Gaston Richard, who was a fundamental reference in Bastide's earlier work. The sociologist's education came through its link to Richard, a specialist in legal sociology and his professor in Bordeaux, and to

the group of Protestant intellectuals gathered around the *Revue Internationale de Sociologie*, home of opponents of the Durkheimian school. On the group led by Richard in the context of French sociology of the 1920s, see Pickering.

[5] All information suggests that the relationship between Bastide and Gurvitch began before the (re)encounter in Brazil, where the Russian-born sociologist (1894-1965) was also working as a Professor of Sociology. See Morin, 38-39. Among Gurvitch's sociological works are those published after 1950, especially *La Vocation Actuelle de la Sociologie*, that would more directly impact Bastide's conceptions regarding the contact of civilizations.

[6] Though he was said to prefer the notion of "interpenetration of civilizations" over syncretism, Bastide used both indistinctively.

[7] On the founding of the Universidade de São Paulo in 1934, see Cardoso and Limongi.

[8] The essays of Queiroz and Simon call attention to this point.

[9] By regularly writing reviews in newspapers, Bastide followed Brazilian visual arts and literature. For this reason, it's not unusual that his name is remembered as one of the active critics during the 1930s and 1940s, along with Sérgio Milliet. It should also be mentioned that in additon to his activity on the domestic scene, he remained tied to the French press in Brazil (*Boletim da Aliança Francesa*) and also to French agencies, such as the magazine *Mercure de France*, with which he collaborated between 1948-1965. On this production, see Amaral.

10 Bastide's reflections on the Brazilian baroque can be found in *Psicanálise do Cafuné* and his account of his trip to the Northeast in *Imagens do Nordeste Místico*.

11 See "A Poesia Afro-Brasileira" and "A Incorporação da Poesia Africana à Poesia Brasileira" in *Poetas do Brasil*.

12 See *O Candomblé* and *As Religiões*.

13 In his words: "Gilberto Freyre estudou bem em *Casa-Grande & Senzala* esses diversos fenômenos (do sincretismo) mas estudou-os do ponto de vista da civilização brasileira, e não do ponto de vista que aqui nos preocupa: o das civilizações africanas. Precisamos, pois, retomar à questão, examinando-a, se nos permite a expressão, pelo outra extremidade da luneta" (*As Religiões* 103).

14 For an analysis of the centrality of the notion of the "balance of antagonisms" in Freyre's work of the 1930s, see Araújo.

15 See Maio. The results of the research project in São Paulo were published in Bastide and Fernandes, *Brancos e Negros em São Paulo*.

16 Ruy Coelho, statement for the magazine *Língua e Literatura* (São Paulo) 10-13 (1981-4): 129. On the French professors at the Universidade de São Paulo, see Peixoto [Massi], "Franceses e Norte-Americanos" and "Lévi-Strauss no Brasil." On this generation of critics, see Pontes.

Works Cited

Amaral, Glória C. "Roger Bastide au Mercure de France." *Bastidiana* (Université de Caen) 10-11 (1995): 23-34.

Araujo, Ricardo Benzaquen de. *Guerra e Paz:* Casa-Grande & Senzala *e a Obra de Gilberto Feyre nos Anos 30*. Rio de Janeiro: Editora 34, 1994.

Bastide, Roger. *O Candomblé da Bahia: Rito Nagô*. São Paulo: Editora Nacional, 1958.

———. *Éléments de Sociologie Religieuse*. Paris: Armind Colin, 1935.

———. *Imagens do Nordeste Místico em Branco e Preto*. Rio de Janeiro: O Cruzeiro, 1945.

————. "Passeio Sociológico (A Propósito da 'Sociologia' de Gilberto Freyre)." *Diário de São Paulo*, 7 Dec. 1945.

————. "A Poesia Afro-Brasileira." 1941. *Estudos Afro-Brasileiros*. São Paulo: Perspectiva, 1973.

————. *Poetas do Brasil*. 1946. São Paulo: EdUSP; Duas Cidades, 1996.

————. *Psicanálise do Cafuné*. Curitiba: Guaíra, 1941.

————. *As Religiões Africanas no Brasil*. 1960. 2 vols. São Paulo: Edusp; Pioneira, 1971.

Bastide, Roger, and Florestan Fernandes. *Relações entre Negros e Brancos em São Paulo*. São Paulo: Anhembi, 1955. (Reprinted in 1958 by Cia. Editora Nacional as *Brancos e Negros em São Paulo*.)

Cardoso, Irene. *A Universidade da Comunhão Paulista*. São Paulo: Cortez, 1982.

Coelho, Ruy. "Declaração." *Língua e Literatura* (São Paulo) 10-13 (1981-4): 129.

Limongi, Fernando. "Mentores e Clientela da Universidade de São Paulo." *História das Ciências Sociais no Brasil*. Vol. 1. Ed. Sérgio Miceli. São Paulo: Idesp; Sumaré, 1989. 111-187.

Maio, Marcos Chor. *História do Projeto Unesco: Estudos Raciais e Ciências Sociais no Brasil*. Diss. Instituto Universitário de Pesquisas do Rio de Janeiro, 1997.

Morin, Françoise. "Les Inédits et la Correspondance de Roger Bastide." *Roger Bastide ou le Réjouissement de l'Abîme*. Ed. P. Laburthe-Tolra. Paris: L'Harmattan, 1994. 21-42.

Peixoto, Fernanda. "Franceses e Norte-Americanos nas Ciências Sociais Brasileiras (1930-1960)." *História das Ciências Sociais no Brasil*. Vol. 1. Ed. Sérgio Miceli. São Paulo: Idesp; Sumaré, 1989. 410-460.

————. "Lévi-Strauss no Brasil: A Formação do Etnólogo." *MANA-Estudos de Antropologia Social* (Rio de Janeiro) 4.1 (1998): 79-108.

————. *Diálogos Brasileiros: Uma Análise da Obra de Roger Bastide*. São Paulo: EdUSP/FAPESP, 2001.

Pickering, William S.F. "Gaston Richard: Collaborateur et Adversaire." *Revue Française de Sociologie* XX (1979): 163-182.

Pontes, Heloisa. *Destinos Mistos: Os Críticos do Grupo Clima em São Paulo*. São Paulo: Cia. das Letras, 1998.

Queiroz, Maria Isaura P. "Nostalgia do Outro e do Alhures: A Obra Sociológica de Roger Bastide." *Roger Bastide*. Ed. Maria Isaura P. Queiroz. São Paulo: Ática, 1983. 7-75.

Ravelet, Claude. "Bio-bibliographie de Roger Bastide." *Bastidiana* 1 (1993): 39-48.

————. "Roger Bastide et la Poésie." *Bastidiana* 10-11 (1995): 7-22.

Reuter, Astrid. *Entre les Civilisations. Roger Bastide (1898-1974) et les Religions Africaines au Brésil*. Paris: Diplôme d'Études Approfondis de l'EHESS, 1987.

Simon, Jean-Pierre. "Roger Bastide et l'Histoire de la Sociologie." *Roger Bastide ou le Réjouissement de l'Abîme*. Ed. P. Laburthe-Tolra. Paris: L'Harmattan, 1994. 55-68.

FERNANDA PEIXOTO

The Logic of the Backward and the Boomerang Effect: The Case of Ziembinski

Victor Hugo Adler Pereira

Translated by Ross G. Forman

Different masks of the foreigner cover the career and personal history of the director and actor Zbigniew Ziembinski from the time he arrived in Rio de Janeiro as a war refugee in 1941, at the age of 33, to his death in 1978. Finding it impossible to continue with the journey on to New York, the actor and director—like many other immigrants of the period—was forced to seek work in a country where he had no friends and did not even speak the language. Nevertheless, within two years, he had transformed himself into a crucial figure for the revival of Brazilian theater. Already having overcome the image of the poor immigrant, in its place he fashioned an image for himself as the mouthpiece of European culture among a circle of influential intellectuals and the high society of Rio de Janeiro, at the time the Republic's capital.

In this milieu, the prevailing interpretation of the local problem was that Brazil was a backward-looking country, in comparison with Europe and North America. Such an interpretation meant assuming the perspective of the colonized, which in practice entailed conceding prestige and decision-making powers to representatives of "more civilized" centers. Ziembinski's role as an outsider therefore made it easier for him to begin demonstrating his abilities as a director and actor. The innovative form of his early efforts in Brazil were much more creative than his previous work in Poland, which—according to Yan Michalski in his detailed and well-documented biography of Ziembinski—had been "primarily commercial and conventional" (35). Brazil thus inspired Ziembinski to new uses of the considerable technical skill he had acquired in Poland. This image of him certainly offers a generalizing and idealized representation of the "advanced stage" of European art, which then serves as a creative catalyst when transplanted to Brazil.

Ziembinski's association with the amateur group "Os Comediantes" led to his first season of productions, which consisted of Robert C. Sherriff's *Journey's End*, Maurice Maeterlinck's *Pelléas et Mélisande*, and the groundbreaking premiere of Nelson Rodrigues' *Vestido de Noiva* on December 28, 1943. The staging of *Vestido de Noiva* featured a new use of scenic space, involving not only a type of lighting never before seen in Brazil, but also hundreds of changes in the lighting that accompanied the action. The production also featured a set by the talented sculptor Santa Rosa. Another aspect of the production's success was that it evidenced Ziembinski's deep understanding of Nelson Rodrigues' work. The premiere of *Vestido de Noiva* transformed the two of them into well-known figures in Brazilian cultural life, and from that point on they collaborated on a variety of successful or controversial productions until the end of their lives. Ziembinski directed the first productions of two of Nelson Rodrigues' "unpleasant theater" plays, *Anjo Negro* (1949) and *Dorotéia* (1950). He also was the first to direct two of his "Rio tragedies," *Boca de Ouro* (1960) and *Toda Nudez será Castigada* (1965). Chance may have brought the two close together in theater, but over the course of their artistic careers, both shared a similar fate in the reception of their efforts. Critics swung between extremes when evaluating their work, which at times was seen as representative of the avant-garde and at other times was viewed as subservient to market conditions. This sort of contradiction was symptomatic of the instability of criteria and positions in the field of cultural production during the period of their careers. To commemorate the tenth anniversary of Ziembinski's presence in Brazil, for instance, the critic Décio de Almeida Prado characterized the director's collaboration with "Os Comediantes" as a significant development in the history of Brazilian theater:

> In practice, this very experimental director presided over a theatrical revolution: new writers, new scenarios, new techniques, and above all, a new mode of representation, a new conception of theater as spectacle. At last modern theater had arrived in Brazil, noisily, triumphantly, and more than fifty years too late. (qtd. in Michalski 202-03)

Almeida Prado's comments make it clear that, on the one hand, Ziembinski's successful first season had superseded the backwardness of the country's theater; on the other hand, it indicated that local preconditions, such as the presence of talented professionals and daring perspectives, had facilitated Ziembinski's work as a director. The connection that this critic makes between this particular work and a larger project for a national theater and culture (even when that project represents a break with local traditions) suggests a parallel with the "engagement" that Antonio Candido argues was imposed on writers involved in the construction of Brazilian literature (Candido 26). In other words, as Mariângela Alves de Lima has noted, in the scenic arts, groups or individuals similarly felt compelled to engage in a national cultural project in their efforts to construct or reform Brazilian theater (Arrabal and Lima 98).

The prominence of internationalism or the appeal to universal values evident in some of the initiatives in which Ziembinski was involved does not negate this obligation to participate in a determined project to build a national culture. In this case, modernization or cosmopolitanism was incorporated into the project without considering the larger ideological questions this raised. Ziembinski's work was framed by the cultural project of a group of intellectuals and reflected their contradictions.

Indigenous Complexes

In keeping with the authoritarian modernization promoted in the 1930s by the Vargas regime and consolidated after 1937 in the *Estado Novo*, a group of intellectuals connected to public offices controlled theater and promoted the staging of spectacles based on international patterns. As I have tried to show in my earlier work, *A Musa Carrancuda*, these intellectuals and dramaturges grouped themselves around a particular discourse structuring some general viewpoint on Brazilian culture and social relations, which supported a project of organization of the cultural field in Brazil. This project was characterized by the implementation of practical methods that stimulated or supported theatrical troupes representing an alternative to what they saw as the "uncultured" forms that dominated Brazilian theater, such as *chanchada*, revue theater and the Trianon comedies. Their impoverished pattern of artistic expression was measured against the vigor of theater being produced in the great centers of Europe and North America. As Lima and Arrabal note, the groups with which Ziembinski was involved embraced a desire that cut across Brazilian theater since the days of the Empire, namely that of "being as good as . . . ." The proclamation "I am not an Indigenous" humorously

VICTOR HUGO ADLER PEREIRA

characterized this desire. "Behind this lay the ideal of universal communication attached to a pattern of perfect form" (Arrabal and Lima 98). Ziembinski's method of executing this project resembles the process of cultural mimicry described by Homi Bhabha (85-92). In carrying out this process over a number of years and in different projects, Ziembinski exercised a key role, thanks to the authority given him by the mask of foreigner; a mask that he gladly accepted. While spreading and implanting new techniques, his work functioned as a fetish or emblem that upheld a notion of European cultural superiority. (He was a renowned master of lighting, and he imposed a unity on the spectacles he directed, despite using actor-oriented staging techniques and despite the sometimes dubious results he achieved.) As Bhabha points out, the logic of mimicry is based on an imperfect process of adaptation, on the disjunction between model and copy (86). Ziembinski's career seems to open up a gap between his efforts to give the country a model of what, as a foreigner, he judged representative and the pressure of dynamic, local forms of cultural expression. Therein lies the breach between these two spheres. The succession of masks and roles that the character of Ziembinski filled in the realms of theater and culture shows in a rather sad way how these disjunctions forced him to move from company to company. It also shows the changes going on in the symbolic position he occupied within the intellectual field.

From 1951 onward, Ziembinski served as a director and actor with the "Teatro Brasileiro de Comédia" (TBC) founded by Franco Zampari; in this capacity he played a decisive role in maintaining the company's image as a leading force behind the introduction of European patterns of quality to Brazil. TBC's owner developed a strong infrastructure for the company, which included a carpentry and costume-making shop and a special rehearsal room next to the theater on "Major Diogo" Road in São Paulo. These efforts at modernization went together with a rejection of any traces of Indigenous traditions of staging and audience. This starting from scratch even included a refusal to hire Brazilian professionals of long standing (Arrabal and Lima 100). Zampari hired a cast of amateurs, who were overseen by foreign (mostly Italian) directors, such as Adolfo Celi, Ruggero Jacobbi, Luciano Salce, Flamínio Bollini and Gianni Ratto.

Through "Os Comediantes" and the TBC, the two principal laboratories for Ziembinski's work, the actor developed his style and revealed his talents. His work served as a contrast to the intuitive or native training in different ideas of artistic interpretation then prevalent among Brazilian professionals. Many of his roles were seen as groundbreaking, particularly when he did not direct his own acting. Such was the case with the role of the pilgrim Luka in Maxim Gorky's *The Lower Depths*. (This production was an exception to the usual repertoire of the TBC, which under Zampari kept away from disturbing themes that might upset an audience drawn from the wealthier residents of São Paulo.) Michalski sees this role as one of the most brilliant of Ziembinski's career, recalling that the play was directed by the young Flamínio Bollini, an apt pupil of the Stanislavski method (Michalski 199-200).

As a director, Ziembinski faced allegations about the ways in which he sought to instill an imitation of his personal version of European culture; his techniques were particularly questioned during the 1960s. For example, he was accused of having adapted the Stanislavski method in such a way that instead of allowing actors to create their roles, he subjected them to a method of interpretation so personal that the actors were forced to imitate even his mispronunciation of Portuguese. The excessive slowness of his style as actor and director was also seen as a defect, one that was attributed to his cultural background. Michalski bolsters this argument by stating that Central and Eastern Europe lacked the "dynamism and agility that make up a part of our national profile" (384). Thus the mask of the foreigner, which opened many doors for him at the start of his career, later proved to hinder him or render him incapable of cultural understanding. However, this same critic adds that this difference in rhythm also came from "the secular literary tradition of European theater, in which the audience enjoys listening to an intelligently interpreted text delivered by actors with well-trained voices, even when the scenic translation of the text is realized in a static and sluggish manner" (384). This argument might explain why Ziembinski's involvement in staging Tennessee Williams' *A Streetcar Named Desire*, Eugene O'Neill's *Desire under the Elms*, and Nelson Rodrigues' work—all of which privilege the role of the word—received such a positive reception.

One of Ziembinski's productions, that of Jules Renard's *Pinga-fogo*, made theater history because of his collaboration as actor and director with the actress Cacilda Becker. This work's great success among critics and audiences was seen to stem from the director's efficient way of acting with Becker, which showed the range of his professional abilities. They continued their work together in 1958 and 1959 in the actress' theater company "Teatro

VICTOR HUGO ADLER PEREIRA

Cacilda Becker." In this and other prestigious companies formed following the success of the commercial model of the TBC, Ziembinski's participation appears to have been decisive for the formation of a professional ethic. At a time when Brazil's "star system" was in crisis, and when a director-centered model of staging was spreading across the country, Ziembinski's strict control over rehearsals became legendary. At the same time, certain conceptions of staging had to be introduced in order to create a repertory in tune with the prevailing taste in the major centers. Thus Fernanda Montenegro states that Ziembinski "goes down in the history of Brazilian theater as being the man who taught us how to do characters; he also taught us for the first time what unity of spectacle is" (Michalski 366).

Revolutions and Boomerangs

The historical transformations that influenced cultural production in Brazil during the 1960s created the conditions for the reception of Ziembinski's works, which were radically different from the Brazilian theatrical scenery previous to his arrival. The level of industrialization achieved, the tightening of relations with the United States, the participation in a pattern of cultural dissemination different from that of Europe, and above all the expansion of audiences with a higher degree of education all contributed to setting the stage for this reception. In addition, a new realization of the functions fulfilled by theater—intimately related to the politicization of the middle classes and of student culture—as well as the base of experiments offered by groups like the Teatro de Arena, provided the tools for critical interest in the kind of contributions being made by Ziembinski and the TBC. The notion of quality—formerly grounded in ideas of technical development and through a repertory of the so-called universal classics or works catering to middlebrow European taste—no longer corresponded to audience demands, which were not governed solely by comparison with European models. In the larger newspapers, some more informed critics followed this desire for renewal. The copy seemed to have gained sufficient autonomy from the model to escape its control, throwing the model itself out of balance.

Ziembinski's sad return to Poland in 1963, at a time when he had lost favor with Brazil's public and critics, proves that even there he was unable to find an adequate place for himself. For many Polish, he had become a stranger in his own country. They found his methods of directing and the repertory he presented during a season at several important theatrical venues to be strange. The specter of backwardness in style and staging methods came back to haunt Ziembinski himself.

By 1971, Ziembinski recognized an impasse in projects to save national theater, which questioned the validity of the mission itself. Ignoring the difficulties and contradictions inherent in the country's theatrical traditions, Ziembinski developed a belief in the extremely radical potential of theater in Brazilian cultural life that deserves to be remembered today. At an important moment in the following interview, he declared:

> What's happening is that the country is still searching for the right idea of what constitutes theatrical spectacle, although perhaps we should not call it theatrical spectacle any more, but the way in which a country conceives of itself through concepts like those of theater and adapts them to its temperament, its blood, its landscape, and its sense of harmony. The path, of course, is a long one, yet it's also a seductive one because a fantastic revolution can come from it. This revolution will create a theater that might no longer have a structure, or at least not a structure that has anything to do with the theatrical edifice, perhaps a meeting on the grass by the beach or a sort of pagan festival. Therefore we won't need to write 'Let's go to the theater' [the title of a government campaign to promote theater-going] because people will go spontaneously. (Michalski 344)

The old Ziembinski found a way out of his personal and professional impasse by dedicating himself as an actor and director to television, where he won public fame through his roles in various soap operas. Nevertheless, as was the case in theater, he himself sadly realized that the Brazilian public saw him as detached from the day-to-day concerns that occupied them.

There are still some questions about the so-called model of quality in the type of television drama that Ziembinski helped consolidate, which has been hailed as television's highest triumph. Is this model merely a reinstallation of a version of modernism adapted to a mid-level international taste that part of Brazilian theater has been rejecting since the 1960s (Costa 130)? Or is there some originality to it? At the heart of the debate at the end of the 1960s was a resurgence of interest in theatrical forms previously labeled as "backward" and culturally inferior, in contrast to the good-taste TBC model that was representative of a wave of reforms in the 1940s (Pereira 163-180).[1] The avant-garde during the 1960s demanded a radical revision of the terms of the 1940s theatrical reform. On another, more current level, the lessons in

VICTOR HUGO ADLER PEREIRA

technical dramaturgy and the predominance of middle-class models of taste (implanted in Brazil by the active participation of Italians and a Polish artist) remain visible in the form of the soap opera—a form that dominates the country's television screens, influences the local aesthetics of theater, and increasingly markets its products to European television networks. Is this the revenge of the Indigenous wielding a boomerang?

Ziembinski clearly had a part in setting off this chain of reactions, many of which rebounded on him, setting before him the contradictions of the various roles he played in Brazilian cultural life. As became clear from his reception during a brief return to his native Poland, his trajectory led him to the point at which it becomes possible to say that the foreigner himself became an Indigenous.

Notes

[1] In this context, it is necessary to recall José Celso Martinez Correa's memorable staging of Oswald de Andrade's *O Rei da Vela* in 1967 by the Grupo Oficina.

Works Cited

Arrabal, José and Mariângela Alves de Lima. *O Nacional e o Popular na Cultura Brasileira.* São Paulo: Brasiliense, 1983.

Bhabha, Homi. *The Location of Culture.* London: Routledge, 1994.

Candido, Antonio. *Formação da Literatura Brasileira: Momentos Decisivos.* 1959. Belo Horizonte: Ed. Itatiaia, 1975.

Costa, Iná Camargo. *A Hora do Teatro Épico no Brasil.* Rio de Janeiro: Graal, 1996.

Michalski, Yan. *Ziembinski e o Teatro Brasileiro.* São Paulo: HUCITEC; Rio de Janeiro: Ministério da Cultura/FUNARTE, 1995.

Pereira, Victor Hugo Adler. *A Musa Carrancuda: Teatro e Poder no Estado Novo.* Rio de Janeiro: Editora da Fundação Getúlio Vargas, 1998.

———. "O Rei e as Revoluções Possíveis." *Oswald Plural.* Ed. Gilberto Mendonça Telles et al. Rio de Janeiro: EdUERJ, 1995. 163-180.

Otto Maria Carpeaux

Olavo de Carvalho
Translated by David Shepherd and
Tania Shepherd
Revised by Mark Streeter

Knowledge begins with the unexpected, and the unexpected comes from an awareness of problems. A problem, as Ortega y Gasset would say, is the awareness of a contradiction. Insensitivity to problems, which derives from relying on conventional certainties without even being disturbed by the most glaring contradictions, is a sure sign of intellectual decadence, either of individuals, groups or nations. Anyone who wishes to evaluate the low level of Brazilian intellectual life today, be it in terms of sociological curiosity, or in its attraction to bottomless pits, may obtain a significant proof of the phenomena in the unanimous reaction on the part of the Brazilian cultural press to the recent publication of *Ensaios Reunidos* (1999) by Otto Maria Carpeaux. These reactions have repeated the praises made at the writer's funeral in 1978, without a single mention of the interpretative problems associated with his life and work.[1] Let me provide a selection of these problems.

1.

Otto Maria Carpeaux arrived in Brazil in 1939. As soon as he began his career in journalism, with a number of literary essays published in the newspaper *Correio da Manhã*, he became the target of a violent slander campaign stirred up by Brazilian communists. When he died, in 1978, Carpeaux had become the idol of Brazilian communist intellectuals. This later idolatry may be due to his violent opposition to the right-wing military regime that took power in 1964. However, if this explanation were valid, it would also have been applicable to the novelist Carlos Heitor Cony,

Carpeaux's fellow fighter in this heroic and unequal battle, who still is disliked by Brazilian communists. Carpeaux's transfiguration from *bête noire* to canonized saint therefore, remains, a problem, even more so because Carpeaux, the critic and historian, never became a Marxist. It is well-known in Brazil that financial contributions to the Communist party, strongly hegemonic both in the press and in editorial circles, would be enough to absolve a writer from any ideological sin. This is true of writer José Geraldo Vieira, for example, who became a sworn communist, but who, in his books, continued to be the conservative Christian which he had always been. (If the American reader cannot understand these intrigues, then it may help to know that no one understands them in Brazil either; nevertheless, they admit their existence.) Carpeaux, however, was never rich.

2.

Carpeaux, or rather Otto Karpsen, a Jew born in Vienna in 1900, converted to Catholicism when he was thirty-years old, and in the following decade became one of the leading theoreticians of the Catholic right that governed Austria under the leadership of Engelbert Dolfuss. After the demise of the regime due to the Nazi invasion, Carpeaux found shelter in Brazil, thanks to the intervention of the Vatican. In Avram Milgren's remarkable study *Os Judeus do Vaticano*, Carpeaux's misspelled name is mentioned as being on the list of Jews who had received false baptism certificates in order to escape the persecution (49). This is a misconception because Carpeaux was not only a Catholic long before the war, but when the Nazis entered Vienna he was already well-known as an intellectual of the Austro-Catholic regime due to his 1936 book *Österreichs Europäische Sendung* (*Austria's European Mission*). In addition, his feelings are quite evident in the correspondence he exchanged with Álvaro Lins after his arrival in Brazil. It is surprising therefore that this Catholic should have been buried without religious rites, as being, or so his widow claimed to the press, a "man without religion" (Houaiss 148). Even if the hypothesis of a senile apostasy after a late conversion may be somewhat extravagant, it might have been accepted save for two pieces of additional information. According to Carlos Heitor Cony, the writer's closest friend, Carpeaux prayed regularly, up until the end of his life.[2] According to the words of philologist Antonio Houaiss, who is equally trustworthy, Carpeaux was afraid of touching upon religious matters in the highly materialist Brazilian intellectual circles. This is a complex problem for a biographer. In order to suggest a better understanding of this issue, I have put forward the hypothesis that, because he was in exile and tired of suffering, he would disguise his opinion in order not to displease his Brazilian hosts, almost all atheists. This is, however, only a hypothesis, and one that is full of flaws. How is it that a man who is so outspoken against his enemies can be so weak among his friends? Furthermore, how can one claim that the writer's careful attitudes would "seduce" his wife to the point that she would allow him to take the disguise beyond the grave. No, my hypothesis explains nothing.

3.

Carpeaux wrote the most valuable part of his work, his important essays and his monumental *História da Literatura Ocidental* (*History of Western Literature*), which comprises almost 5000 pages, within less than six years, between 1941 and 1947. Apart from this, his production continued to be vast, but the quality decreased, as is evident in the somewhat conventional praise garnered by his biography of Alceu Amoroso Lima, his last work. In 1968, Carpeaux announced the end of his literary career, promising to devote the rest of his days to political struggle. He thus diverted his talents to polemics against the military regime, and, although his writings had startling repercussions, they are nowadays regarded as no more than historical documents. The fact is that he had already been losing impetus for twenty years, so much so that his abdication in favor of political writing seemed to have been the final crystallization of a long process of depressive self-denial, which cannot be interpreted solely in terms of political motivation. This is also no more than speculation, despite the fact that it has been confirmed by another close friend of Carpeaux's, the Pernambuco-born writer Edson Nery da Fonseca.[3]

These examples should already suffice to show that Otto Maria Carpeaux is as unknown in Brazil as he is celebrated. The careless manner in which, for twenty years, his vast circle of admirers and friends refrained from collecting his scattered journalistic writings into a book seems to signal that that they were more interested in creating a cult around a stereotype than increasing an awareness of his work. The reason is clear. Carpeaux was, at the beginning, rejected by the Brazilian left-wing intelligentsia and was only accepted by a select group of privileged minds, a politically diverse group which included the communist Graciliano Ramos as well as the conservatives Manuel Bandeira and Augusto Frederico Schmidt. In the end, he became a leader of the left-wingers, thanks to a series of political articles published from 1964 onwards in *Correio da Manhã* that gave him the reputation of being the country's leading opponent of the military regime. The regime never really persecuted Carpeaux seriously, but limited itself to starting a legal suit against him; the writer was politely interrogated for a few hours, and the suit was subsequently dropped by the prosecution. Carpeaux's image was consolidated by the press into one of a communist militant who helped this political faction by means of prodigiously erudite writing, and whose literary style may be defined as "delightful," at the very least. However, the publication of his complete literary essays would dissolve this simplistic image, revealing a mystical and religious Carpeaux, an admirer of Léon Bloy, an elitist concerned with the ascent of the ignorant masses at the head of a cultural machine, in the same fashion as Ortega y Gasset. It is not surprising, therefore, that left-wing intellectuals foresaw these difficulties and postponed confronting such contradictions, just as after the publication of *Ensaios Reunidos* they opted to pretend that they had not seen the contradictions.

There is no posthumous homage that can do justice to a writer, if the praise in the homage is not combined with serious reflection. Therefore, the praise that followed Carpeaux's death, and which has now followed the publication of *Ensaios* as well, seems to have paradoxically diminished the writer, by highlighting his less important merits as an erudite spokesperson without focusing on the original and valuable elements of his work. This is because the value and the originality of his work reside precisely in its contradictions.

First of all, the *História da Literatura Ocidental* is an attempt to meet in a synthetic and simultaneous manner concerns that are hardly compatible: a sociological understanding of literary periods and the stylistic individualization of writers; the understanding of a civilization's historical unity and the judicious evaluation of singular works. Carpeaux seeks to be both a historian and a critic, by relying not only on the methods learned from Burckhardt, Dilthey, Weber and Max Dvorak but also inspired by the Crocean sense of the irreducible individuality of poetic work. If he eventually fails by exaggerating his judgment of individual works in order to harmonize with the patterns of a specific period, he succeeds on the whole. Carpeaux composes a unique work in the tradition of literary history, akin to what Francesco de Sanctis has done for Italian literature. In the opinion of the critic Mauro Gama, *História da Literatura Ocidental* is simply "the most important work of its genre published in any language and in any setting" (n. p.).

Secondly, Carpeaux's way of thinking emphasizes problems rather than solutions, which may make it appear inconclusive. With a soul shaken by fearful doubts and contradictions, he uses his own interior perplexity as a survey instrument for works and periods. As an outcome he proposes questions with no answers. For many readers, the shock produced by these contradictions is an equally disturbing experience, as they do not perceive that this is the writer's *forma mentis* that allows him to follow the intimate drama of ideas underlying literary manifestations, without resorting to simplistic contrived solutions.

Carpeaux's literary style reflects the paradoxical character of his view of the world. At times, page after page, he takes the point of view of the writer under analysis, defending his ideas as if they were his own; yet, soon afterwards he either rejects them brutally or relativizes them by mentioning a number of contradictory facts. Readers who demand final certainties are driven to despair; for those who delight in viewing reality as it is, the reading of Carpeaux is a rare spiritual experience. On the whole, the *História da Literatura Ocidental* remains as one of the most solid works of the genre, much superior to a similar one written by Arnold Hauser and published in Brazil at the same time, and which is still regarded as reliable and prestigious.[4]

In this way, it is not right to claim, as Franklin de Oliveira did, that Carpeaux's greatest merit is to have introduced Dilthey's *Geisteswissenschaften* in Brazil. The *História da Literatura Ocidental* may have been produced according to these methods, yet it is more than a propagation of the same. It is, in fact, an achievement which goes beyond any of the applications which the original creators may have devised, thanks to its amplitude and perfection. In this sense, it is not a contribution from Dilthey's school to Brazilian culture, but rather a Brazilian contribution to Dilthey's school.

It is for this reason that elsewhere I have already proposed a sifting of the mass of works that reflect Brazilian thought and a list of the quintessential achievements that are to remain when everything else has faded.[5] The criterion I adopted was straightforward. I considered works that are intrinsically capable of retaining their validity, not those that "represented Brazil," since there are no guarantees of what future generations will want to know of Brazil; rather, I chose those works that would enable anyone, in any country, to extract something that would help them understand the meaning of life in general and the meaning of one's own life in particular. That which is classical, by definition, does not focus on itself, on its own time, or on its country of origin. It focuses on each one of us. Side by side with the writings of Gilberto Freyre, Miguel Reale and Mário Ferreira dos Santos, I have placed the historiographic works and essays of Otto Maria Carpeaux. A body of historical works, prepared, supported and completed by a multitude of essays, which succeeds in showing that the internal unity of Western literary development, from Homer to Valéry, is in itself a microcosm of the human soul. It thus deserves to be approached not with the awe of the devout, but with an awareness of the Latin dictum: *De te fabula narratur*.

Notes

[1] For a more complete discussion of these issues, see my Foreword to Carpeaux, *Ensaios Reunidos*.

[2] Statement by Carlos Heitor Cony to the author.

[3] Statement by Edson Nery da Fonseca to the author.

[4] I am referring to the well-known *Sozialgeschichte der Kunst und Literatur*, made popular as *The Social History of Art*, in the translation by Stanley Godman, made in collaboration with the author (New York: Knopf, 1952).

[5] See my *O Futuro do Pensamento Brasileiro*.

Works Cited

Carpeaux, Otto Maria. *Österreichs Europäische Sendung*. 1936. Wien: Reinhold Verlag, 1935.

———. *História da Literatura Ocidental*. 2nd ed. Rio de Janeiro: Alhambra, 1978.

———. *Ensaios Reunidos*. Organização, introdução e notas de Olavo de Carvalho. Vol. 1. Rio de Janeiro: Topbooks, 1999.

Carvalho, Olavo de. *O Futuro do Pensamento Brasileiro*. Rio de Janeiro: Faculdade da Cidade Editora, 1998.

———. "Introdução a um Exame de Consciência." Otto Maria Carpeaux. *Ensaios Reunidos*. Vol. 1. Rio de Janeiro: Topbooks, 1999. 15-70.

Gama, Mauro. "Apresentação." *História da Literatura Ocidental*. 2nd ed. Rio de Janeiro: Alhambra, 1978.

Houaiss, Antônio. "Depoimento." Otto Maria Carpeaux. *Alceu Amoroso Lima*. Rio de Janeiro: Graal, 1977.

Milgren, Avram. *Os Judeus do Vaticano*. Rio de Janeiro: Imago, 1996.

The Foreigner

Gustavo Bernardo

The foreigner (and the foreign) is the one who affirms his own being in the world that surrounds him. Thus, he makes sense of the world, and in a certain way he dominates the world. But he dominates it tragically: he does not integrate into the world. The cedar tree is foreign in my park. I am foreign in France. Man is foreign in the world. (*Natural: Mente* 47)

When Vilém Flusser wrote these words, (*Natural: Mente* 47) he was living in France, after having lived for thirty years in Brazil. His life and work were really built between two continents. He was Jewish and born Czech in 1920. In 1939 he escaped from the Nazis and came to Brazil with his girlfriend, Edith Barth—at the time, all of his family was dead. He lived in São Paulo until 1971, when he moved to Robion, France. In 1991, he returned to Prague, the city of his birth, for a conference, where he died in a traffic accident.

Better known as a media philosopher, Flusser wrote in four languages—Portuguese, English, French and German—, translating his texts himself into those languages. To translate for him was both a political and an existential gesture: to translate is to go through the experience of death and, paradoxically, to go through the experience of the Other. He always tried to maintain the point of view of the immigrant, that is to say, the point of view of the foreigner.

He wrote many books, most of them published in German. He does not have many Brazilian readers, but his importance to us is greater than we usually acknowledge. His *Fenomenologia do Brasileiro*, published in German in 1994 and in Portuguese in 1998, is a provocative and very interesting study of Brazilian character and culture. His thought brings together Husserl's phenomenology and Wittgenstein's logic, always trying to take the phenomenon by surprise in the moment immediately before symbolization takes place, in the moment immediately before the words freeze it.

Naturally, such an attempt cannot be achieved. We can call it a horizon, or a Kantian regulatory idea. But this attempt reminds literary theorists of Coleridge's "willing suspension of disbelief." According to Coleridge, all poetry and fiction readers must suspend their disbelief in order to allow themselves to dive into the text they read. However, this willing suspension of disbelief is, in fact, impossible, or possible only as a fiction. As theorists and teachers, however, we develop a sort of "suspension of the suspension of disbelief" in order to understand the process that allows and provokes that "suspension of disbelief." What Vilém Flusser proposes in his philosophy is something similar, but a step further. Perhaps we can call it a "suspension of belief"—a suspension of belief in *maps*, since maps include all theories, philosophies and sciences. This exercise of "suspension of belief" would be indispensable in order to learn to discern and to make choices.

In philosophical jargon, the suspension of belief is better known by the Greek term *epokhé*. For the Greeks, it was a state of mental rest, in which we neither assert nor deny. This state very often leads us to stillness, and leaves us open to all the perspectives of *phenomena*. Husserl revives the concept, turning it into the axis of his "phenomenological reduction." *Epokhé*, then, corresponds to the momentary suspension of judgment, so that one can try to "see" the phenomenon from a new perspective. In absolute terms, it is but an intellectual device. Thought, which necessarily merges itself with judgment, and thus with belief, has no condition of suspending itself. As a consequence, thought needs "to be deceived" to open new roads to another truth. Thought needs "to suspend itself," or to try to do so, even though the task seems impossible.

The whole of Flusser's life lies in this experience. He recognizes two basic possibilities for the appreciation of a literary work: it can function either as an answer or as a question. In the first case, literary work is regarded as an answer to the historical context where it appeared. In the second case, the literary work is regarded as a question to a particular reader at a given moment. If we try to understand the literary work as an answer, we need to analyze its relationships to the context from which it emerged. The realm of this attempt is that of criticism. If we try to face the literary work as a question, as a provocation, we are obliged to converse with it. The realm of the second attempt is that of speculation. Without undermining criticism, Flusser opts for speculation, that is to say, he opts for taking his place in the "general conversation" implied in literature. But Flusser doesn't suspend belief only to read fiction or poetry, but also to "read" culture as well as human beings. His movement of suspending judgment works by implication, resisting the reification of *phenomena*, thinking "ahead." Indeed, he tries to think ahead of philosophy itself.

To do so, he brings religious practice close to literature as well as myth to culture. In an article published in 1965, Flusser recalls *Exodus* 20.4: "Thou shalt not make unto thee any graven image, or any likeness *of any thing* that *is* in heaven above, or that *is* in the earth beneath, or that *is* in the water under the earth." This commandment can be synthesized in four words: "Thou shalt not imagine." We can explain the prohibition as a result of the horror of the Bible towards paganism and the adoration of images. Images would be horrible because they are not the "thing," that is, because they are fake. The Western form of monotheism relies on the fight against the falsehood of images. The monotheistic God is unimaginable, because He cannot and should not be imagined. If we understand God as the foundation of reality, and visual images as the models of reality, what our monotheism purports is that models of reality cannot exhaust reality itself and that they are therefore false. Paganism, as a consequence, is the belief that all models represent reality; idolatry would then be the explanation of reality through models. Models are false gods "against whom we address the hatred and nausea of the prophets" (Flusser, "Não Imaginarás"). Therefore, according to the Decalogue, the construction of models is considered a sin.

This context suggests that the prohibition of images should be regarded as an ethical commandment. Out of context, the prohibition can even present itself as an aesthetic norm—it could be prohibiting figurative art, allowing only abstract art. Under more careful consideration, a theory of knowledge is also revealed when it is said that images bring us false knowledge. To Vilém Flusser, nevertheless, the three aspects of the commandment are inseparable. "Theory" is nothing but the imagination of reality by means of the construction of models, models which take the place of reality. For instance, Newton handed down to us a model that makes the movement of bodies imaginable; Darwin a model that makes the development of life imaginable; Freud a model that makes the operation of the *psyche* imaginable; Marx a model that makes the behavior of society imaginable. But, if the models take the place of reality, other models can take the place of previous models. The theory of relativity prevails over Newton's model, but it did so in a problematic way: the theory of relativity does not make the movement of bodies imaginable; on the contrary, it makes the terms "movement" and "body" themselves unimaginable. In physics, we would find ourselves in a situation similar to that of the Israelites before the Golden Calf. Reality appears from behind Newton's model as an instructive demonstration—one of how inadequate the human imagination is.

Immersed with Flusser in the atmosphere of the Old Testament, we are trying to understand why the prophets feel disgust and horror before false gods, while people are attracted to them. We are trying to understand why the commandment "thou shalt not imagine" is far from being followed, since images and models of the surrounding reality and of God Himself do not cease to multiply, in people's homes as well as in churches. Idolatry can be readily understood: models make reality imaginable, and with it life becomes meaningful. In some way, "man builds models to protect himself against reality and to prevent its rays from reaching him" ("Não Imaginarás"). Reality—the deity—blinds man. Models are our sunglasses, so to speak. If we recall the models in fashion magazines, half-naked on billboards and in the centerfolds of male publications, we will see that these models depicted in two-dimensional photographs represent beauty and allow us to imagine and desire the women. However, at the same time, these models protect us from the real, three-dimensional women.

Biblical exegeses try to contextualize the commandment historically so that it becomes innocuous and inoperative, presupposing that its object was simply and solely the cult of Ichtar and not the cult of Freud. Flusser, however, distances himself from biblical exegeses and acknowledges, on both the existential and the aesthetic levels, the current validity of the commandment "thou shalt not imagine." The sight of a model, in fact, can cause disgust and horror, once it hides from us what we inwardly conceive of as being the reality or the beauty of life. Due to the omnipresence of the media, we try to deny this inner feeling even to ourselves, but the truth is that models (and female models) are dangerously close to disgust and despair. This means that Flusser doesn't make a liberating and glorious defense of imagination. The defense of the imagination *per se* does not combine with phenomenology.

GUSTAVO BERNARDO

Intimately, we feel that any model—Darwinism, Psychoanalysis, Marxism, Constructivism, Deconstructionism—is a self-enclosed model which explains too well everything that it approaches. And this proves, without any doubt, its intrinsic falsehood. In other words, its condition is that of a model that pretends that it is not a model, but rather reality itself. Noticing this does not imply denying the need for models, but it forces us to critically reflect upon the reification of models. We now return to the starting point: the philosophical need not only for the suspension of disbelief, but, mainly, the suspension of belief and judgment. This is so because phenomenology is, according to Flusser, the attempt to adopt before any phenomenon a certain attitude in accordance with the commandment. Phenomenology avoids the models in order to ensure that the phenomenon is itself revealed existentially.

Flusser says in "Não Imaginarás" that our civilization is the synthesis of two great inheritances: the Greek and the Jewish. In the fields of morals and ethics, the Jewish inheritance prevails, in its Christian variant. In the fields of aesthetics and knowledge, the Greek inheritance prevails. Our art, science and philosophy owe much more to the Greeks than to the Jews. In these fields, in terms of the meaning of the commandment, we would still be pagans devoted to the construction of models. However, at present the Jewish inheritance seems to be felt in these fields as well, forcing us to experience our models as the expressions of false gods. The so-called postmodern theories, on the one hand, and Heisenberg's "uncertainty principle," on the other, steer toward the fear of belief. As a consequence, we would be starting to exist inside an unimaginable world, which brings about a sense of disorientation and the loss of what we thought we possessed: the sense of reality. The world would gradually become more and more absurd. This means that, for the first time in the history of the Western civilization the Jewish experience of the world is articulated in science, art and philosophy through phenomenology and existentialism. The Jewish philosopher Vilém Flusser, however, does not celebrate that circumstance. He understands that this would be a dangerous moment for the development of our thought, because it can result in anti-intellectualism as well as in the articulation of a new religiosity. The two results are probably compatible, in spite of their inner contradictions.

The resurgence of the commandment "thou shalt not imagine" brings to the surface an inheritance that had been submerged. We must view the event not only from an aesthetic angle, but also from ethical and epistemological perspectives. The commandment "thou shalt not imagine" forbids one to imagine God in our own image and likeness. The commandment can thus be updated in the following way: "the world rhymes with itself." It implies that we cannot imagine ourselves as the measure of the world, which certainly represents a more demanding imperative than the Kantian categorical imperative. We understand the extension of this demand when we admit, along with Flusser, that language in fact creates reality, which does not mean that language has it under control, but rather the opposite. Just like Sisyphus, language articulates the foundation of the world, in other words, that which cannot be articulated. Language follows a direction that is opposite to the one the commandment establishes. "Thou shalt not imagine" means: "Thou shalt not mirror thyself," or: "Thou shalt not multiply thyself." The verb "multiply" in turn serves another command, in truth a curse, at the expulsion from Eden (*Genesis* 3:16): "Unto the woman He said, I will greatly multiply thy sorrow and thy conception." Due to that existential contradiction, language becomes less than a means of communication, but rather an inexhaustible source of multiple misunderstandings.

Consequently, to undo the enigma is a sin. To search for the truth, to make it a tool, is a sin. The last chapter of Vilém Flusser's last book, *Gesten (Gestures)*, begins precisely with the gesture of searching. It maintains that our present crisis is in reality a crisis of science: a crisis of our gesture of searching. The gesture of searching, or of researching, would be the paradigm of all our current gestures, just as the religious gesture informed all other gestures in the Middle Ages. However, Flusser contends that the gesture of searching *should not* be a model for other gestures, because it does not search for anything that has been lost. It searches with indifference; it does not set goals, does not ascribe values. The place taken by scientific investigation in our society would be, therefore, in contradiction with the very meaning of investigation. The scientific investigation escapes from the problems that interest men and is devoted to unimportant objects. Because those objects stay at a distance, they are "simply" objects, and man can become their subject, knowing them in an "objective" way. In relation to such things as rocks and stars, man puts himself in the place of god, establishing coordinates and formulas. In relation to such things as illnesses and wars, man puts himself in the place of a victim, defending himself with vaccines and short-term agreements. When his interest is vital, scientific interest is paradoxically hidden. When there is no vital interest, then science is interested. However, the gesture of searching for objective and exact knowledge

GUSTAVO BERNARDO

is about to be converted into something impossible. Contemporary physicists (with extreme seriousness) search for the ultimate theory, the one that can integrate the infinitely small into the infinitely large. They search for—in this manner and *hybris*—God, or rather, they want to make God their object. We find ourselves, therefore, on the edge of the abyss.

This forces the emergence of new perspectives. One discovers the search with desire and suffering, that is, with values. Knowledge is, among other things, passion, and passion is in its turn a type of knowledge. All this happens in the fullness of the human life. The gesture of a "pure" attitude, ethically neutral, is a concealed gesture. It is an inhuman gesture, alienation, madness. When it comes to know inanimate objects, this alienation is exclusively epistemological, and in this case it is simply a mistake. But when other things come into play, such as illnesses, wars, injustices, alienation turns into a criminal gesture. The social scientist, who approaches society as if it were an anthill, and the technocrat, who manipulates the economy as if it were a chess game—these two characters are criminals.

They are as criminal as, for example, the brilliant engineer mentioned in *Territorio Comanche*, the novel by Arturo Pérez-Reverte. He invents a bullet that zigzags inside the enemy's body, names it *Bala Louise* and goes with his family to Disneyland to celebrate. Doctor Frankenstein and Oppenheimer shake hands. The researcher transforms *phenomena* into objects: from the song of a bird he makes an acoustic vibration, from human pain, a dysfunction of the organism. He disconnects from his conscience the fact that he is paid by someone to research, he does not consider whether the invention he might devise (or the research paper he delivers) is good or bad for society. He is solely concerned with publishing (or perishing).

Vilém Flusser formulates a proposal to confront the apparatus, technicism and "developmentism"—to confront sin. Flusser's proposal, as usual, lies in the text and in the philosopher's style. His proposal consists of attributing value. Only in this way does the gesture of researching, as well as the other gestures, turn into a gesture that searches for the other—for the one whom we simply cannot and should not turn into an object. He saw, in his relationship with the other, the road that begins in religious revelation and ends in a moral imperative, which helps us to understand the road traveled by Flusser from prayer to literature.

Just as art was made from religion, literature can be made from prayer. Literature, then, can be seen as a privileged realization of ethics, since it allows for the perspectivization of truth. Questions make sense only when they have no answers. Questions engender a sweet, heavy and mysterious fruit, commonly known as "fiction." This fruit is a prayer directed towards authenticity.

Works Cited

The Bible. Authorized King James Version. 1611. Intro. and notes by Robert Carrol and Stephen Prickett. Oxford: Oxford UP, 1997.

Flusser, Vilém. *Língua e Realidade.* São Paulo: Herder, 1963.

———. "Não Imaginarás." *O Estado de São Paulo* 9 Oct. 1965.

———. *Da Religiosidade.* São Paulo: Comissão Estadual de Cultura, 1967.

———. *Natural:Mente.* São Paulo: Duas Cidades, 1978.

———. *Für eine Philosophie der Fotografie.* Göttingen: European Photography, 1983.

———. *Filosofia da Caixa Preta.* São Paulo: Hucitec, 1985

———. *Gesten: Versuch einer Phänomenologie.* Düsseldorf: Bollmann, 1991.

———. *Von der Freiheit des Migranten: Einspräche gegen den Nationalismus.* Bernsheim: Bollmann, 1994.

———. *Brasilien oder die Suche nach dem neuen Menschen: Für eine Phänomenologie der Unterentwicklung.* Bensheim: Bolmann, 1994.

———. *Fenomenologia do Brasileiro: Em Busca de um Novo Homem.* Ed. Gustavo Bernardo. Rio de Janeiro: EdUERJ, 1998.

———. *Ficções Filosóficas.* São Paulo: EdUSP, 1998.

———. *Kommunikologie.* Frankfurt: Fischer, 1998.

Rapsch, Volker, ed. *Überflusser: Die Fest-Schrift zum 70, von Vilém Flusser.* Düsseldorf: Bollmann Verlag, 1990.

Back to the *Tristes Tropiques*:
Notes on Lévi-Strauss and Brazil

Roberto DaMatta
Translated by Nöel de Souza
Revised by Mark Streeter

I can't really say how Claude Lévi-Strauss' work is viewed in Brazil. This would take more than a few pages; nor do I have that enviable propensity of some colleagues, whose careers are entirely dedicated to cutting, snipping and putting together what they call the "intellectual field." I'm not cut out to be a tailor of values, just as I'm not too keen on the topography or archeology of mental life. I am indeed intuitive and am aware that in general Lévi-Strauss' work enjoys great prestige in the Brazilian intellectual world. But there does exist, the structuralists know, a revealing and obvious relationship between his work and the tropics. It so happens that social prestige and the ritualization of his ideas are inversely proportional to the critical reading of his work. Thus, his work is seen through a prism of untouchability, like the gods on Olympus: that region situated somewhat between "Rue des Écoles" and "Boulevard Saint Michel," that magic area where the true "mythologiques" happen. It is there that, in the minds of many Brazilian intellectuals, the gods reside. But it is here, between the beach full of bodies tanned by the sun of our cheerful tropical summer and the constant and stern drizzle of the "avenida Paulista," that these gods are welcomed by their idolaters, discussed by their oracles and symbolically sacrificed by their enemies.

In the universe of the *tristes tropiques*, even today we have this endless ritual of succession of god-intellectuals who, emerging one after another, recreate in native lands, and through their exclusive representatives, the academic dynamics of the sacred places. And all of this happens in spaces as suspicious as a bar in "Baixo Leblon"— in Rio de Janeiro—, an unknown restaurant in Niterói or a fashionable tavern in São Paulo. It is actually, as Lévi-Strauss himself pointed out (in a famous passage for the inhabitants of the *tristes tropiques*), a universe fascinated by hierarchy, by ideas that cannot be fully understood and, especially, by a vague commitment to the authors being discussed. This commitment, as I'll explain later on, has nothing to do with the application or professional and concrete use of their ideas but is closely related to the waves of prestige that such ideas carry. Besides, this truly symbolic kinship is yet to be duly studied. It is a kinship built with books, essays and articles coming to us from Paris in the shape of newfound ideas; and its parentage makes the brilliant thesis, the happy discourse, the victory of the new and suddenly soaring flight of a new star in the literary and social firmament all possible.

In the *tristes tropiques*, the ideas that come from within are like undesired emotions—a chest pain that hopefully will soon disappear and about which one does not need to bother much. But when the ideas come from without, everything changes. They immediately lull us to sleep and keep us safe, like a canopy under which, henceforth, such and such a problem is definitively presented or merely resolved. And these ideas obviously obtain immediate success, although one never really knows what the author is talking about. I only realized this a few years ago when I did a *structural analysis of the quotations* in the dissertations and books written in Brazil and tried to situate foreign colleagues vis-à-vis national ones. The foreigner was always a sort of "ancestor," whereas the Brazilian was viewed with ambivalence and opposition. Foreign bibliographic reference replaces national bibliography. The result is a perfect mythological series, thanks to the general inability to discuss the genealogy of any major problematic in the field of human sciences.

We are, then, left with an embarrassing alternative: either the foreigners made it all up or the Brazilians copied everything. And nobody has ever succeeded in establishing any intelligent middle ground. The immediate concrete fact is that in Brazil a quotation is used like a totem, something that at once grants legitimacy and, with it, intellectual identity. Therefore, the reversal of an author's work takes place in the tropics. It so happens that it always begins at the end. Just like a film running backwards, you see the last images and only after a great deal of time—and, sometimes never—do you discover and read the early works of the author. As with Lévi-Strauss in Brazil, for instance, it is worth stressing that the translation of *Structural Anthropology* dates back to 1967, whereas that of the *Elementary Structures of*

Kinship, Lévi-Strauss' second book, dates from only 1976. By the same token, even today no thought is given to publishing his early ethnographic essays on the Bororo and the Nambikwara. In this case, we've got the film rewound halfway, since there is no more talk about publishing the *Mythologiques*, which clearly mark a critical stage of the author's thinking, especially since they form a kind of concrete application of his perspective to a complex and heterogeneous collection of ethnographic data. And this undoubtedly explains the nonsense we may read in some anthologies of structuralist texts published in Brazil, where, in the course of the work matrilinear is mistaken for matrilateral and parallel with cross-cousins!

All of this, however, does have a name, which typifies the arrival of any original and deeply innovative work—as is the case with Claude Lévi-Strauss' anthropology—in the *tristes tropiques*. It so happens that the works turn up without flesh. Divorced right away from the concrete human beings that have created them, coming as distant echoes of an academic milieu whose rules, values, mediocrity and daily life are unknown, the ideas hit us as truth's revelation: words without mouth or face, texts divinized by the most utter and complete lack of contextualization. Thus, it is odd to see that we have to leave the West in order to be able to speak of *mana orenda* and witchcraft, when in actual fact we know so well this charm, this glamour, and this *charisma* which come along with the text that is (reportedly) revolutionizing Paris and becoming a must (nothing more truly magical than this noun) for a "civilized" intellectual life. This is where the myth of the *mythologiques* lies!

This is then the overall picture of the tropics. But with Lévi-Strauss and Brazil things are complicated. He became known to Brazilians far before he became the Lévi-Strauss of the theories of kinship and of the savage mind; before he became the producer of a work that succeeded brilliantly at synthesizing the best of Anglo-Saxon social anthropology (such as the most original productions of North American Boasian culturalism), and the best of Roman Jakobson's linguistics with the great revolutionary roots of Durkheim and Mauss; an intellectual who had the intuition and courage to take the thinking of tribal groups that he studied seriously, seeing them as being on the same level as some of our most sophisticated literary and philosophical works.

It may be said that there are two moments in the presence of Lévi-Strauss in Brazil. In the first, he is one of us, working as a teacher at the newly

ROBERTO DAMATTA

founded Universidade de São Paulo, discovering with fascination a Brazilian land teeming with social, political, urban and cultural facts likely to spin the head of any observer keen on capitalizing on the social experience as critical data for any intellectual experience—an innovative attitude which only Boas' and Malinowski's social anthropology had, at that time, succeeded in developing. Here again it was Lévi-Strauss who coordinated a large expedition to Central Brazil. It was a trip that earned him a varied bureaucratic and sociological experience as well as an association with the National Museum. And in this institution, he met Luiz de Castro Faria.[1] I don't need to say that this phase has been described in *Tristes Tropiques*— which makes this anthropological exercise of combining the practical with the intellect, form with content, simply fascinating and courageous. Of this early moment there still remains a photograph, which Castro Faria so generously let me have.[2] In it one can see the patio of the Museu Nacional do Rio de Janeiro in March 1939, a young Lévi-Strauss in the company of American (Charles Wagley and Ruth Landis) and Brazilian colleagues. It was in that photograph that I saw, for the very first time in my life, an embodied Claude Lévi-Strauss. This very same picture also conveys the great metaphor of the intellectual life of our *tristes tropiques*. Allow me then to study it "structurally" to show the encounter between the Lévi-Strauss of the second phase in Brazil with that of the first. The photograph tells us more about this meeting than the merely intellectual specification of Lévi-Strauss' second moment in Brazil.

What do we find? First, the cast of characters. All foreigners are to the right of the Museum's Director, Dona Heloísa Alberto Torres, the only person wearing black, with a long necklace and carrying a briefcase in her right hand—the hand of justice, rule and control. Her white hair and broad, open smile likewise provide a stunning contrast with the seriousness of the foreigners, as opposed to the apparently happier faces of the Brazilians Luiz de Castro Faria, Raimundo Lopes and Édison Carneiro, all standing to the left of Dona Heloísa. Yet another striking detail is that the Museum's Director, like the institution she runs itself, stands in the middle—a mediator between the foreign and national researchers, who often find themselves in different and opposing camps. In this regard, it is worth stressing the positions of Lévi-Strauss and Édison Carneiro in the picture. Both are most formally dressed. Charles Wagley wears something rather sporty and American, while the Brazilian colleagues of the Museum (Castro Faria and

Raimundo Lopes) have on their white aprons typical of "naturalist anthropologists," showing that, after all, they work in a museum—that place dedicated to studies of natural history, "natural populations" in that old sense that Lévi-Strauss' work has so helped to demolish. Today, thanks to structuralism, we know that there are no "natural peoples" studied by naturalists or "civilized peoples" studied by historians.

Furthermore, one of the impacts in Brazil of Lévi-Strauss' work (or of the Lévi-Strauss in his second phase in Brazil) was the upheaval his ideas caused in the reified concept of time as history and of history as the single scientific measure of the study of man. Rather, Lévi-Strauss defended the idea—especially in *Totemism Today* and in *The Savage Mind*—that there can be as many histories as we wish, and that it is impossible to have a total "history," since it is necessary to be both oblivious and reminiscent of events in order for history to exist. This has caused serious problems in an intellectual environment dominated by the evolutionist linearity of a bureaucratized and almost always crass Marxism.

Likewise, it was Lévi-Strauss' work that made the development of a new approach to "Indigenous peoples" possible when he introduced another type of measurement between them and us. Prior to structuralism, tribal studies were the fruit of cultural contact and acculturation. It was within the context of a research project developed at the Museu Nacional by Harvard University, with David Maybury-Lewis at Harvard and Roberto Cardoso de Oliveira in Brazil, that various books emerged on the Gê language groups of Central Brazil, among them the Kayapó, the Krahó, the Krikati, the Apinayé and also the Bororo. According to this new perspective, we were able to study the tribal societies as structures that transformed in space, without falling prey to a comfortable, demagogic and repetitive evolutionism such as that of Leslie Whyte, which is typical of Darcy Ribero's studies. But that's not all....

It so happens that Édison Carneiro and Lévi-Strauss also contrast in terms of skin color in the photograph. The most European is located in spatial opposition to the most Brazilian. It is also impressive to note that this spatial difference emerges in the work of both of them. In that of Édison Carneiro, who became one of the most important scholars of Brazilian folklore, a certain theoretical ingenuity comes across and so does an enormous care lavished on the mass of data described and discovered during his research work. His work takes us within Brazil. With Claude Lévi-Strauss, however, it's what one already knows. The particular gains universal stature when the facts are placed in relational equations that link them in a chain with a theory that is inevitably all-encompassing and vertiginous. But wouldn't this be what is revealed by the positions of the subjects in this picture? Also, the closer one is to one's "center," the more one is concerned with the Brazilian society, as is reflected in Castro Faria, Ruth Landis or Charles Wagley. The "margins," predominantly more eclectic, are more radical than the center. And lastly, it remains to be suggested that in this photograph, Lévi-Strauss gives the impression of wanting to leave, as he did later on in his work and in his "savage thinking," which revealed a new way of looking at the *tristes tropiques*. Furthermore, there is nothing more visible in the photograph than the great Levistraussian dichotomy between *nature* and *nurture*, since the characters are almost absorbed by the trees that form the entire background of the photograph. But between *nature* and *nurture*, what is it that exists? A look at the portraits affords a glimpse of yet another image quite consistent with Lévi-Strauss's concepts. I'm thinking of that wrought-iron grille that so clearly stands between the people and the trees and, in so doing, suggests how they would survive in and where they would pose for posterity.

Today we can say that this photograph, so "revealing," gives hopes for a greater integration between "foreign" and "Brazilian" anthropologists, as well as for a Claude Lévi-Strauss who is the human remembrance of the Lévi-Strauss of the *mythologiques* and the masks. Wouldn't this definitive dissolution of all possible oppositions then be the true message of structuralism?

Notes

[1] See Luiz de Castro Faria, "A Antropologia no Brasil." In this major essay, Faria recalls and recovers that phase. Part of that experience is also recalled by Prof. Egon Schaden's essay in the same *Anuário Antropológico*.

[2] See the photograph on page 537.

Works Cited

Faria, Luiz de Castro. "A Antropologia no Brasil. Depoimento sem Compromissos de um Militante em Recesso." *Anuário Antropológico*. Fortaleza & Rio de Janeiro: Edições Universidade Federal do Ceará / Tempo Brasileiro, 1982. 228-250.

Lévi-Strauss, Claude. *Structural Anthropology*. Trans. Claire Jacobson and Brooke Grundfest Schoepf. New York: Basic Books, 1963.

———. *Totemism*. Trans. Rodney Needham. Boston: Beacon Press, 1963.

————. *The Savage Mind.* London: Weidenfeld & Nicolson, 1966.

————. *The Elementary Structures of Kinship.* Trans. James Harle Bell, John Richard von Sturmer, and Rodney Needham. Boston: Beacon Press, 1969.

————. *Tristes Tropiques.* Trans. John and Doreen Weightman. New York: Modern Library, 1997.

Shaden, Egon. "Os Primeiros Tempos da Antropologia em São Paulo." *Anuário Antropológico.* Fortaleza & Rio de Janeiro: Edições Universidade Federal do Ceará / Tempo Brasileiro, 1982. 251-258.

Claude Lévi-Strauss, Ruth Landis, Charles Wagley, Heloisa Alberto Torres, Luiz de Castro Faria, Raimundo Lopes and Edison Carneiro.
March 1939
Photograph
Museu Nacional (Rio de Janeiro)

Literary History and Literary Criticism

Brazilian Literary Historiography: Its Beginnings[1]

Roberto Acízelo de Souza

We can say that the establishment of Brazilian literary history as a discipline takes place in the period situated between 1805 and 1888. The former date corresponds to the publication of the fourth volume of the work *Geschichte der Poesie und Beredsamkeit seit dem Ende des 13*, entitled *Geschichte der Portugiesischen Poesie und Beredsamkeit*, by Friedrich Bouterwek, in which the presence of Brazil—then still a Portuguese colony—is restricted to the mention of two writers born in the country, Antônio José da Silva and Cláudio Manuel da Costa. The latter date corresponds to the publication of *História da Literatura Brasileira* by Sílvio Romero, a work whose extension and conceptual grounds attest to the consolidation of the discipline. Between these widely separated dates, several contributions took place, varying in importance and nature, and produced by both Brazilian and foreign authors. We will present here a generic description of these contributions, beginning with those made by foreign authors. For practical purposes, we will classify them in five categories.

First of all, we have works that mention authors born in Brazil in historiographic studies about Portuguese literature. Besides the above-mentioned work by the German Friedrich Bouterwek (1766-1828), we might include in this category *De la Littérature du Midi de l'Europe* (1813), by the Swiss Simonde de Sismondi (1773-1842) and "História Abreviada da Língua e Poesia Portuguesa"—later published under the title of "Bosquejo da História da Poesia e Língua Portuguesa"—an introduction to *Parnaso Lusitano* (1826), by the Portuguese João Batista Leitão de Almeida Garrett (1799-1854). In this category we can also include the *Dicionário Bibliográfico*

Português, which stands out for its dimensions and the fact that it grants equal space to both Portuguese and Brazilian authors. Subtitled *Estudos Aplicáveis a Portugal e ao Brasil*, the publication of its twenty-two volumes began in 1858 and ended in 1923, under the algis of Inocêncio Francisco da Silva (1810-1876), succeeded by Brito Aranha, Gomes de Brito and Álvaro Neves.[2]

In a second category, the history of Brazilian literature becomes the object of a more extensive and autonomous treatment, although it still remains an addendum to Portuguese literary history. This category is represented by a book written in French by Ferdinand Denis (1798-1890), entitled *Résumé de l'Histoire Littéraire du Portugal, Suivi du Résumé de l'Histoire Littéraire du Brésil* (1826).

In a third category, only Brazilian authors are studied. The essay that represents this group—"De la Poesía Brasileña" (1855)—was written by the Spaniard Juan Valera (1824-1905). Originally it was published in *Revista Espanhola de Ambos os Mundos*, and it deals only with poetry, as indicated in its title.

A fourth category contains essays whose content is more critical than historiographic, such as a chapter of the book *Rio de Janeiro wie es ist* (1829), by German C. Schlichthorst, and work by two Portuguese authors, José da Gama e Castro—who wrote an answer to a reader, published in the *Jornal do Comércio* (Rio de Janeiro, 1842)—and Alexandre Herculano de Carvalho e Araújo (1810-1877), who wrote "Futuro Literário de Portugal e do Brasil," an article included in the *Revista Universal Lisbonense* (1847-1848).

Finally, a fifth category is represented by the work *Le Brésil Littéraire— Histoire de la Littérature Brésilienne* (1862), written by the Austrian Ferdinad Wolf (1796-1866), the first book completely dedicated to Brazilian literary history.

Some of these foreign contributions stand out, namely those of Ferdinand Denis and Ferdinand Wolf. Denis exerted a great influence on Brazil's Romantic authors, with exhortations to literary nationalism, and by recommending, with the authority of an European writer, severing ties with the Old World. Denis' *Résumé* presents several passages such as the following: "America, fiery with youth, must sport new and strong thoughts just like her own essence; our literary glory cannot enlighten her forever as a focus that weakens on crossing the seas, being bound to extinguish itself thoroughly when faced with the primitive aspirations of a nation full of strength... America must be free in its poetry as well as in its government" (36). Wolf, in his turn, besides having also influenced the Brazilian literary scene with his encouragement to adopt a nationalistic view both in the production and appreciation of literary works, became an important didactic reference, because his work—originally written in German, afterwards translated into French and published in Berlin under the patronage of the Emperor Pedro II—was among the textbooks adopted in Brazilian schools in the nineteenth century.

Now let's proceed to the examination of the works produced by Brazilian authors, starting by establishing a division of this corpus into its various modalities. First of all, we have poetry anthologies, then called *parnasos* or *florilégios*, preceded by prologues that sometimes reach the size of historiographic syntheses. There are also essays that constitute statements of principles concerning the idea of Brazilian literature, implying reconstitutions and evaluations of the past as well as projects for the productions both of the present and of the future. Another modality is composed of studies about the lives of the writers, constituting the so-called *galerias*, collections of biographies of *varões ilustres* ("eminent men") or *brasileiras célebres* ("renowned Brazilian women"). There are also critical editions of texts with biographical information about their authors and explanatory notes. A fourth specific category, consisting of a bibliographical dictionary, can also be distinguished. Last, we have literary histories *stricto sensu*, that is to say, books aimed at establishing literary periods and historiographic syntheses, concerned with presenting the panorama of successive epochs rather than with covering individual authors, books which were then called *cursos* ("courses") or *resumos* ("summaries"). Let's proceed to the examination of some outstanding works in each modality.

Among the anthologies, *Parnaso Brasileiro* (1829-1832), by Januário da Cunha Barbosa (1780-1846), is the earliest work in this genre. It has two brief introductory texts of little importance in terms of historiographic information. Afterwards, other anthologies appeared, better organized and endowed with more extensive and informative prologues: a second *Parnaso Brasileiro* (1843-1848), by João Manuel Pereira da Silva (1817-1898); the *Florilégio da Poesia Brasileira* (1850-1853), by Francisco Adolfo de Varnhagen (1816-1878); the *Mosaico Poético* (1844), by Joaquim Norberto de Sousa Silva (1820-1891) and Emílio Adet (1818-1867). The list of anthologies also includes the following works: *Meandro Poético* (1864), by Joaquim Caetano

ROBERTO ACÍZELO DE SOUZA

Fernandes Pinheiro (1825-1876), without a prologue of historiographic content, but presenting information about selected authors; *Curso de Literatura Brasileira* (1870)—an anthology, despite its title—and *Parnaso Brasileiro* (1885), by Alexandre José de Melo Morais Filho (1844-1919), both poor in historiographic content.

Among the texts that it is possible to include in the category we have termed "statements of principles," there are true Romantic manifestos, concerned both with evaluating the country's literary past according to nationalistic premises by stressing the growing identification of our production with the specific character of Brazilian nature and history, as well as with projecting a future in which the last signs of colonial submission to Europe would have been definitively overcome. The paradigm for this kind of work is the "Ensaio sobre a História da Literatura do Brasil" (1836), whose title afterwards would have its first word changed to "Discurso," by Domingos José Gonçalves de Magalhães (1811-1882), a writer considered by his contemporaries as the "leader of the Romantic school." This work, an essay originally published in the first number of the periodical *Niterói*, was published in Paris in 1836 aimed at promoting Romanticism in Brazil.

Although the usual tone of these essays is characterized by a nationalistic boastfulness, it is important to point out two works that are dissonant. One of them was written by José Inácio de Abreu e Lima (1794-1869), an interesting revolutionary and intellectual, who joined Simon Bolivar's army and reached the rank of general. The chapter "Conclusão: Nosso Estado Intelectual," from the book *Bosquejo Histórico, Político e Literário do Brasil* (1835), in which the author reveals an extremely disillusioned viewpoint about the possibilities of a Brazilian literature, constitutes an example of his conclusions, expressed in a direct and rough language that contrasts with the cheerful euphoria of other Romantic historians: ... as we are descendants of the Portuguese, we find ourselves in a much more underdeveloped position as to knowledge than our neighbours, and because of this we are *the most ignorant people of the American continent...*" (74). The other essay that escapes the prevailing paradigm of the epoch is "Literatura e Civilização em Portugal," by Manuel Antônio Álvares de Azevedo (1831-1852), one of the main representatives of the second Romantic generation. Written about 1850, and therefore during a period dominated by nationalistic ideals, the essay conveys the poet's disdain for nationalism as a criterion for the definition of literature. Thus, the author expresses his conviction that

Portuguese and Brazilian poets, as members of the same linguistic community, are part of the same literature: "... I ignore whoever would profit ... from refusing to pour our hands full of jewels into this native literature's abundant coffer; because of Durão, can't we call Camões ours?" (340).

In the modality of *galerias*, the following works stand out: *Plutarco Brasileiro* (1847), by the previously mentioned author João Manuel Pereira da Silva, a book re-published subsequently in substantially altered versions under the title *Varões Ilustres do Brasil Durante os Tempos Coloniais* (1856 e 1868); *Biografias de Alguns Poetas e Homens Ilustres da Província de Pernambuco* (1856-1858), by Antônio Joaquim de Melo (1794-1873); *Brasileiras Célebres* (1862), by Joaquim Norberto de Sousa Silva (1873-1875); and *Panteon Maranhense* (1873-1875), by Antônio Henriques Leal (1828-1885).

Among the critical editions, there are the works of two authors already mentioned, Joaquim Norberto de Sousa Silva and Francisco Adolfo de Varnhagen. The former is responsible for several editions of poets of his century and of the eighteenth century: Gonzaga (1862), Silva Alvarenga (1864), Alvarenga Peixoto (1865), Gonçalves Dias (1870), Álvares de Azevedo (1873), Laurindo Rabelo (1876), and Casimiro de Abreu (1877). Varnhagen produced editions of poems from the eighteenth century by José Basílio da Gama (*O Uraguai*) and José de Santa Rita Durão (*Caramuru*), collected in the book *Épicos Brasileiros*, as well as texts from the colonial period by the poet Bento Teixeira and by the prose writers Vicente do Salvador, Ambrósio Fernandes Brandão, and Gabriel Soares de Sousa. One must also mention the edition of the first volume of the works of Gregório de Matos—until then a poet published only in anthologies—that was published in 1882 under the direction of Alfredo do Vale Cabral (1851-1896).

The category of bibliographical dictionaries is represented by the *Dicionário Bibliográfico Brasileiro*, by Augusto Vitorino Alves Sacramento Blake (1827-1903), a work in seven volumes, published between 1883 and 1902.

At last, with the most extensive narratives of the literary process, the literary histories *stricto sensu*, which were conceived with a didactic purpose explicit in their titles, we find the works by Joaquim Caetano Fernandes Pinheiro (1825-1876) and Francisco Sotero dos Reis (1800-1871).

Fernandes Pinheiro is the author of *Curso Elementar de Literatura Nacional* (1862), which, in spite of its title, does not deal solely with Brazilian literature but with Portuguese literary works as well, to which the largest portion of the book is devoted. In effect, according to Pinheiro's viewpoint, Brazilian literature would be distinct from Portuguese literature only after the country's Independence and after the Romantic movement, because, until then, although "… certain specific features… characterized American poets and… distinguished them from their overseas brothers, these differences, proceeding from the influence of climate and customs,… were not sufficient to constitute an independent literature" (493). Pinheiro is also the author of *Resumo de História Literária* (1872), in which he remains faithful to the thesis expressed in the *Curso* concerning the late dissociation between Portuguese and Brazilian literatures. The book has the pretension, due to its Romantic historicism that today seems so ingenuous, of comprising the literature of all epochs and countries. So its first volume, besides the usual prolegomena, presents chapters dedicated to Eastern, Hebraic, Greek, Latin, Italian, French, English (completed by an appendix dedicated to what Pinheiro calls "Anglo-American literature"), German and Spanish literatures (with an appendix dedicated to "Hispanic-American literature"). The second volume covers literatures in Portuguese and is divided into two parts: Portuguese literature and Portuguese-Brazilian literature.

Francisco Sotero dos Reis is the author of *Curso de Literatura Portuguesa e Brasileira* (1866-1873). Contents related to Brazilian literature are found in chapters of the fourth and the fifth volumes, and the author begins his narrative and analyses with poets from the eighteenth century, considered by him as "forerunners." Thus, according to him, only the writers of the post-independence period fit in what he calls "Brazilian literature in a proper sense."

Among the works concerned with establishing periodization and tracing general panoramas of the literary process, we must still mention the *História da Literatura Brasileira*, whose project was conceived by an author noted above, Joaquim Norberto de Sousa Silva. Unlike other similar works mentioned previously, this one has no didactic purpose, constituting rather an impassioned defense of Romantic ideas about the concept of Brazilian literature. Thus, it exalts the magnificent and Edenic Brazilian nature as well as the primitive inhabitants of the country—the Native Brazilians—, considering nature and the natives as favorable elements for the development of an original and authentically Brazilian literature. Published between 1859 and 1862, in chapters in successive numbers of a Romantic periodical from

Rio de Janeiro—the *Revista Popular*—the work was never actually concluded, and failed to become the book that the author had intended to organize afterwards.

We can add still another type to the five modalities of historiographic production that we have tried to distinguish—anthologies, statements of principle, biography collections, critical editions, and literary histories *stricto sensu*—essays not properly historiographic, but of a critical nature, linked with literary history by the circumstance of dealing with the *leitmotif* of nationalism as a reference for an analysis that involves a judgment of value. In this kind of essay, Antônio Joaquim de Macedo Soares (1838-1905) excels. We can also include in this type the extensive and important contribution of José Martiniano de Alencar (1829-1877)—the most eminent Brazilian Romantic novelist—, which consists mainly of a reflection about the meaning of his own works in the collective effort to construct a genuinely national literary expression.

In conclusion, it is convenient to mention the new directions that critical and historiographic studies began to take from the end of the 1860s, but which were better defined in the 1870s and 1880s. By then the Romantic perspective had been gradually surpassed, and its declamatory and informal style replaced by a more analytic language that tried to support its objectivity in the great philosophical systems that simultaneously derived from Romanticism and promoted its contestation, such as Positivism, Evolutionism, Determinism, and Transformism. From the authors of this post-Romantic period, we will briefly present the most important.

First there is with Joaquim Maria Machado de Assis (1839-1908), considered by many critics to be the best Brazilian writer. His critical thought, besides other contributions, did not adhere to the anti-Romantic attitudes mentioned above, but tried to reconsider the Romantic principle of "local color," arguing that the national character of literary manifestations does not define itself through exterior evidence, such as, for instance, the representation of typical landscapes, but through inner properties endowed with a universal scope. Machado de Assis synthesized these properties with the word *instinct*, which reaches an outstanding position in the title of a famous essay: "Notícia da Atual Literatura Brasileira: Instinto de Nacionalidade" (1873). Besides Machado de Assis, we must still mention: João Capistrano de Abreu (1853-1927), Tristão de Alencar Araripe Júnior (1848-1911), Sílvio Vasconcelos da Silveira Ramos Romero (1851-1914) and

ROBERTO ACÍZELO DE SOUZA

José Veríssimo Dias de Matos (1857-1916). Capistrano de Abreu abandoned literary studies in favor of history early in his career; Araripe, Sílvio e Veríssimo, in their turn, became the principal Brazilian references in the field of literary studies in the passage from the nineteenth to the twentieth century. We shall point out, at last, that Sílvio and Veríssimo—the former in 1888 and the latter in 1916—, in publishing their respective *Histórias da Literatura Brasileira*, offered decisive contributions to the process of consolidation of the discipline.

Notes

[1] My special thanks to Prof. Peonia Vianna Guedes for a thorough revision of the first English version of this text.

[2] If we want to take into account the origins of seventeenth-century Brazilian literary historiography, we must mention another dictionary, entitled *Biblioteca Lusitana* (1741-1759), by Diogo Barbosa Machado (1682-1772), which also includes Brazilian authors.

Works Cited

Azevedo, Álvares de. *Obras Completas.* Vol. 2. São Paulo: Cia. Ed. Nacional, 1942.

Candido, Antonio. *Formação da Literatura Brasileira.* (*Momentos Decisivos*). 1959. 2 vols. São Paulo: Martins, 1971.

César, Guilhermino. *Historiadores e Críticos do Romantismo.* Vol. 1. *A Contribuição Européia: Crítica e História Literária.* São Paulo: Edusp; Rio de Janeiro: Livros Técnicos e Científicos, 1978.

Coutinho, Afrânio. *A Tradição Afortunada: O Espírito de Nacionalidade na Crítica Brasileira.* Rio de Janeiro: José Olympio, 1968.

———, ed. *Caminhos do Pensamento Crítico.* 2 vols. Rio de Janeiro: Pallas; Brasília: INL, 1980.

Denis, Ferdinand. *Resumo de História Literária do Brasil.* César, Guilhermino. *Historiadores e Críticos do Romantismo.* 35-82.

Lima, José Inácio de Abreu e. *Bosquejo Histórico, Político e Literário do Brasil.* Niterói: Tipografia Niterói do Rego, 1835.

Nunes, Benedito. "Historiografia Literária do Brasil." *Crivo de Papel.* Rio de Janeiro: Fundação Biblioteca Nacional; Mogi das Cruzes (SP): Universidade de Mogi das Cruze; São Paulo: Ática, 1988. 205-246.

Pinheiro, Joaquim Caetano Fernandes. *Curso Elementar de Literatura Nacional.* 3rd ed. Rio de Janeiro: Cátedra, 1972.

Zilberman, Regina and Maria Eunice Moreira, eds. *Crítica Literária Romântica no Brasil: Primeiras Manifestações. Cadernos do Centro de Pesquisas Literárias da PUC/RS.* 5.2. Porto Alegre: Pontifícia Universidade Católica/Rio Grande do Sul, (Aug 1999).

———, eds. *História da Literatura e Literatura Brasileira. Cadernos do Centro de Pesquisas Literárias da PUC/RS.* 1.2. Porto Alegre: Pontifícia Universidade Católica/Rio Grande do Sul, (June 1995).

Between Two Histories: From Sílvio Romero to José Veríssimo

Regina Zilberman

Translated by David Shepherd

and Tania Shepherd

Sílvio Romero (1851-1914) has often been given the title of forefather in the history of Brazilian literature. From the title of the 1888 publication, *História da Literatura Brasileira*, that presented his literary history, Romero proposed to narrate a trajectory of literary production in Brazil, from its beginnings to the contemporary world of the author. José Veríssimo (1857-1916) arrived in Rio some years later and worked as a member of the capital city press from 1891 onwards. Veríssimo's *História da Literatura Brasileira* appeared in 1916, after his death. These two intellectuals were contemporaries, and yet the 25 years that separated their most important works mark an important, though not always sufficiently well-known, era of Brazilian literary life.

The circumstances that brought them together appear fortuitous. They were both born far from Rio de Janeiro and migrated to the capital, where they engaged in similar activities. Each wrote a history of Brazilian literature and died around 1915. However, it is their disagreements that are most noteworthy, since they argued for opposing and irreconcilable points of view. These differences reached a head when, in 1910, Romero published his *Zeveríssimações Ineptas da Crítica*, thus deliberately offending his opponent. The era in which they were active—if bracketed by the dates of their respective "Histories," namely from 1888 to 1916—is one of the most fertile of Brazilian literature. Paradoxically, however, it has been undervalued either as "society's smile"[1] by Lúcia Miguel-Pereira (253), or as "Pre-Modernism" by Alceu Amoroso Lima and Alfredo Bosi—indeed, an inadequate label that incorporates a wide range of diverse and sometimes incompatible factors. An examination of the works written by Romero and Veríssimo may help to understand the reasons for the lack of prestige that characterizes the era of which they were part.

The first historian of Brazilian literature, the title given to Sílvio Romero, took the rough trail opened up by the Brazilian Romantics: Gonçalves de Magalhães, Pereira da Silva, Joaquim Norberto, and Varnhagen. They had indeed gathered the fundamental data needed to systematize the past, not only setting in order knowledge already established, but also creating facts through the discovery of unknown authors and their works. Without this preparatory work, which Romero recognized, albeit unenthusiastically, his historical efforts could not have been successful. Nevertheless, his aim was both to verify his intuitions by using collected material and to evaluate the evolution of these according to the theoretical scientific principles developed at his time.

Romero's concern to create a history of Brazilian literature was already clear in his 1880 publication, *A Literatura Brasileira e a Crítica Moderna*. Based on Taine's notions of race, setting and time, he attempted "a systematic formulation of his critical theory" (Candido xv). In *Introdução à História da Literatura Brasileira*, published in 1881, he developed deterministic principles, proposing that racial elements had been predominant in the formation of Brazilian culture and emphasizing the role of the process of miscegenation.

In stressing race as a formative factor, Romero agrees with relevant aspects of Taine's methodology. However, this was only partially the case, for Romero also had in mind the distinct ethnic origins that played a part in the construction of Brazilian nationality: the African, the Amerindian, and the Caucasian. In contrast, the French scholar touched upon no more than European artistic expressions, which he distinguished according to nations, then also known as races. In addition, Taine, probably following Mme. de Staël, emphasized the setting as the preeminent factor. Romero refused to accept this idea. It had been a central concern to the romantic generation, for which Brazilian literature was exemplary, once poets and intellectuals had ceased to resist the influence of the fertile nature of the Americas, which was translated into texts full of "local color"—a key concept in Romanticism. To replace the role of setting, Romero proposed "race" as the decisive factor. In this methodological and ideological innovation, he underlined the contribution of the "Africans," thus positioning himself in open opposition against the *partido indianista* ("Native Party"), which had been the most influential and fashionable movement. In emphasizing "miscegenation," he developed the concept of "a national history from the standpoint of the fight and fusion of races" (Ventura 90).

The publication of *História da Literatura Brasileira* began in 1888 and was completed in 1902; this is the edition referred to in this essay. However, there is a contemporary edition of five volumes, the result of a praiseworthy compilation carried out by Nelson Romero; it incorporates, along with the original text, a variety of diverse materials from different eras.[2] The prologue of the first edition makes explicit allusions to the precise moment when the book was published, namely, after the emancipation of the slaves in Brazil (1888), but before the founding of the Republic, a movement which counted on the support of the author. Dated ostensibly on the 18th and 19th of May, 1888, Romero declares his politics as being in agreement with "*autonomous and popular emancipation*" and states that he is a "sectarian of a single, free, autonomous republic, compatible with a thorough and wide administrative and economic decentralization, and also compatible with the political, spiritual and ethnic unity of the country" (xviii-xx). The production of *História da Literatura Brasileira* was integrated within these principles by avoiding the dissociation of politics from literary criticism: "The idea of an autonomous Brazil, independent in politics and even more so in literature has always inspired me. This is the initial thought underlining all my forays into the field of letters" (xxiv).

This affirmation exemplifies his actions as literary critic, literary historian and active party member. His fusion of literary history with a political framework made his work controversial, a result that he not only aimed for but achieved. The interpretations he offers are not always acceptable, the choices of certain authors reveal questionable taste, the rebuffs seem rather offensive. All of this, however, is a result of the original purpose of the publication itself, written as it was with the passion described in the prologue and which contaminates each chapter of the book. It was destined to force Brazilian intellectuals to reflect on the past and the present of Brazilian literature and culture.

Book I, focusing on the "Factors of Brazilian Literature," is devoted to theoretical and methodological questions. He expounds the fundamental hypothesis that guides his interpretation of Brazilian national life and miscegenation: "Every Brazilian is a mestizo, if not in the blood, then in his ideas" (4). The mestizo creates the "genuine Brazilian historic development"

(54), for the mestizo is "a physiological product, ethnically and historically within Brazil; this is the new form of our national differentiation" (75). It is miscegenation that is the distinguishing factor privileged by Romero, a choice that contradicted the traditional selection of nature as the most specific manifestation of being Brazilian. However, Romero included certain race-oriented concepts, in that he considered racial fusion to be a kind of degradation that should be overcome through a process of natural selection in which the strongest race, namely the whites of European descent, would prove to be the fittest.

The originality of the differentiating factor adopted by Romero did not exempt it from incorporating ethnic prejudices that were common at the end of the nineteenth century. Nor did those of his contemporaries, including Euclides da Cunha, who interpreted the massacre at Canudos as a victory of white, European civilization over "sertanejo" barbarism, since the latter consisted of inferior beings, the result of intercourse between different biological groups that had affected the genetic development of the population. However, Romero introduced new data, including the racial and mestizo factors, in his interpretation of Brazilian national life. Scholars of Brazilian culture were slow to absorb these ideas—they had to wait until the modernist explosion of the 1920s before accepting miscegenation as a positive force.

Based on positivist sociology, Romero included in "Book I" a chapter describing economic relations, in which he analyzed the political and social institutions of Brazil as a colony and as an empire. For Romero, the "state of wealth or poverty of a nation has a direct influence on the development of its literature" (94). This certainly was the case for Brazil, whose economy was characterized by foreign domination and a powerful land-owning class. Thus, in his view, the literary movements throughout the first four hundred years of Brazilian history could be reduced to Bahia's school of the seventeenth century, led by Gregório de Matos, the school of Minas Gerais of the eighteenth century, dominated by the authors Gonzaga and Durão, and the "Fluminense" School from Rio in the first half of the nineteenth century, in which Gonçalves de Magalhães and Gonçalves Dias were prominent. According to Romero "all these isolated movements, from one or another province, were examples of a great national upheaval... a torrent still scarcely defined, defending all sorts of projects, but having a single aim, i.e., social change" (12).

His portrait of the present is melancholic, given the "complete indifference for what is a Brazilian intellectual product" (97). Romero concludes from this that "the widespread poverty of the popular classes, the lack of education, and all the abuses of a problematic civil and social system, should be included among the stumbling blocks of the development of our literature" (98). But his edicts are no less energetic. He considered that "every national writer of the present day is burdened by the overwhelming duty to tell the whole truth to our nation, even if its harshness displeases most" (99). He also proposes that "We must take up all the duties that the centuries have bequeathed us and make sure to meet them" (100).

Romero subsequently examines the four eras of Brazilian letters: the founding moment (1500 to 1750), the autonomous development (1750 to 1830), the romantic transformation (1830 to 1870) and the critical reaction (after 1870). In the 1888 edition, Romero focuses on the first two periods; Romanticism was analyzed in the 1902 edition. The final period of "critical reaction," in which he played a role, was never written. From the 1890s on, Romero was involved in politics and distanced himself from the systematic study of literary history. His subsequent work appears in *Evolução da Literatura Brasileira* and in *Evolução do Lirismo Brasileiro* (1905); in *Compêndio da Literatura Brasileira* (1906), with João Ribeiro; and in *Quadro Sintético da Evolução dos Gêneros da Literatura Brasileira* (1909). None of these works diverge from the panorama offered by História da Literatura Brasileira; however, they are more didactic and less controversial. The voice of Sílvio Romero, *par excellence* the vehement polarizing force, is found in the 1902 publication, whose sociological methodology, when purged of its racist and dysphonic components, remains valid in Brazilian literary studies.

In common with Romero, José Veríssimo wrote *História da Literatura Brasileira* after he had served as a literary critic and teacher. In the city of Rio de Janeiro, to which he migrated during the first years of the Republic, he worked mainly for newspapers. He also edited *Revista Brasileira,* a culturally oriented periodical, published from 1895 to 1899. Preceded by six volumes of the *Estudos de Literatura Brasileira,* which were published between 1901 and 1907, his *História* was released in 1916, after his death, as the crowning glory of his career. Thus, while Romero's *História da Literatura Brasileira* was an extension of his theoretical and methodological concerns, Veríssimo's *História* is an outcome of his previous work as a literary critic, his full-time occupation. The book represents the arrival point of a journey that began with the study of contemporary literature; it led the author to understand both the origins and the course that, from an evolutionary perspective, finally and coherently led to the present from which he began, and served also the most complete moment of representation for the entire grouping.

His introduction, dated 4 December 1912, illustrates the notion that the *História da Literatura Brasileira* functions as the final touch to his critical itinerary, complementing it. It also reveals the author's main conceptions regarding Brazilian literature—both its historical trajectory and the contemporary situation. In this sense, it occupies the same role as that of the prologue of Romero's *História*. In other words, it is the platform from which Veríssimo clarifies the hypotheses which ground the book. In the introduction, Veríssimo provides his stance concerning the question of cultural emancipation. He affirms that literature "written in Brazil" is "already the expression of a thought and feeling which should no longer be confused with that of the Portuguese"(3). He thus immediately eliminates the theme of dependence which had tormented the romantics, who had fought to guarantee the autonomy of national poetry in relation to Portuguese literature.

His belief in the self-sufficiency of Brazilian literature resulted in an approach via historical cycles. Veríssimo recognized only two periods: the colonial and the national, as equivalent to the divisions "of our history as a nation" (6). He refuted the hypothesis that subdivided the colonial era, arguing that the production achieved during this period is "entirely and strictly linked to that of Portugal" (6). This is a perspective which also placed him in conflict with Romanticism. The Romantic historians had attempted to find evidence of nativism during the colonial period, improbable given the political and cultural constraints of the time, but that they thought possible because of the influence of nature. Veríssimo is straightforward as far as this is concerned, and concludes that it is "meaningless," the result of contrived efforts "to discern examples of autonomous literary feeling" (6) in the literary expressions of the seventeenth and eighteenth centuries. The "national period," in turn, is born with Romanticism, which continued until 1870, when the exhaustion of romantic poetry led him to a discussion of contemporary elements, lingering on scientism, which he did not admire. Although his approach was radically different from Romero's, he was equally disenchanted with what he observed in the Brazilian art and culture of his own time.

A third hypothesis proposed by Veríssimo may be summed up in the following statement: "literature is literary art" (12). This view informed the main outline of his work, which was "to systematically exclude from the history of Brazilian literature what, in this light, ought not to be considered literature" (12). This concept—similar to the aestheticism developed since the eighteenth century and which, in the twentieth century, has guaranteed literature a specific theoretical field—contradicted the dominant approaches of Veríssimo's lifetime. Romantics collected each and every possible literary fact from the past in order to incorporate them within the Brazilian artistic tradition. Romero, on the contrary, analyzed certain paths and evaluated various tendencies, as he saw literature as a means or instrument for contemplating culture. Veríssimo operated with cuts and incisions, isolating literature because, on the one hand, he considered it sufficiently independent not to be seen as a branch of Portuguese literature; on the other, he believed that it was capable of sustaining itself without the crutches of social studies.

The chosen tripartite foundation—the autonomy of Brazilian literature following political independence, the historical division between colonial and national literature, and the concept of literature as an expression of nationalism—determines the historical route inaugurated by Bento Teixeira. From that onwards, isolated and to a certain degree discontinuous manifestations are followed, represented either by individual efforts, such as that of Gregório de Matos, or by small groups, such as that of Minas Gerais. Above all, Veríssimo is interested in national literature, which he mapped out carefully, despite the fact that he gave special emphasis to those groups that were active in the city of Rio de Janeiro. He rarely distanced himself from the perspective of the Federal Capital, the site of the previous Court, which had centralized Brazilian cultural life and in which he found his place. Perhaps because regional artistic expression had no real impact on the heart of Brazil, Veríssimo adhered to the principle of reading put forward in his introduction: "a literature... exists in so far as there are living works, books of a positive and permanent, rather than momentary and contingent value" (14). In addition, perhaps because he was more interested in quickly reaching the climax, he opens the chapter devoted to Machado de Assis in an exalted fashion: "We have now come to a writer who is the highest expression of our literary genius, the most eminent figure of our literature, Joaquim Maria Machado de Assis" (304).

The end of his *História* coincides with the arrival at the peak of a trajectory identifiable by the oscillations between aesthetic autonomy and the expression of nationalism, between poetic modernization and the indiscriminate imitation of fashionable foreigners. The latter accusation is made by Veríssimo above all of his contemporaries, whom he considered duped by their own "intellectual petulance," "improvisation and falsehood, the thoughtless acceptance of contradictory inspirations and the ease of rash enthusiasms for new aesthetics, philosophies or literatures" (12). Machado de Assis is the opposite of these inclinations, an expression of excellence, but also, consequently, a singular and isolated figure.

Veríssimo's *História* ends in a paradoxical manner. On the one hand, it presents the work of the greatest Brazilian writer, suggesting that the course of history coincides with an ascending path that leads to the present day, setting it above all the other previous periods, thanks to the appearance of the greatest exponent of national art. On the other hand, Machado de Assis refuses the collective tendencies of the time. It is here that the critic sides with the novelist. The majority of Brazilian intellectuals have taken one path, whereas Machado de Assis and Veríssimo took another, leading to the isolation of both, especially Veríssimo, after Machado's death in 1908.

For various, even contradictory, reasons Romero and Veríssimo were disenchanted with their own time, between 1888 and 1916. One denounced the backwardness and ignorance of the day; the other expressed his disillusion. Thus, they contradicted a cliché of literary historiography, later restored by the modernists of the 1920s, namely, that the account should culminate at the present day, praised as the pinnacle of a process, both the effect and the synthesis. The two historians saw ruin and failure in the contemporary period, even though they—especially Romero—were a product of their time, which included these evolutionary ideas. Future literary history would eventually absorb the two diagnoses: one that narrates a chronological trajectory, the other that judges the present period as decadent. Modern historiography would also blend the prescribed medicine with the identified symptom, perceiving itself and its era as salvational. The historiography of Brazilian literature produced after Modernism salvaged the natural inclination of the genre to describe the present as the culminating historical moment, the outcome of a continuing evolutionary progress. For their part, Romero and Veríssimo remained imprisoned by the diagnosis that they had formulated, and that had enveloped and fixed them in the past—a silent snapshot of an era in need of revitalization.

Notes

1 The expression "society's smile" was first used by Peixoto, *Panorama da Literatura Brasileira* 5.

2 In the third edition of volume I, Nelson Romero has added "New Contributions for the Study of Brazilian Folklore," composed of three parts: 1. "Social Brazil and the Elements from which It Was Molded;" 2. "General Conclusions," (taken from the *Compêndio de Literatura Brasileira* [2nd edition, 1909]) and containing "I. The Setting; II. The Race; III. The Foreign Influx; IV. The Theoretical Paths of Brazilian Literature; V. The Evolutionary Phases of Brazilian Literature;" 3. "On Criticism and its Precise Definition." Nelson Romero begins volume II in this way: 1. "The Third Era or Period of Romantic Transformation—Theater and Novel," which consists of, "Martins Pena," "Macedo," "Alencar, Agrário, Manuel de Almeida, Pinheiro Guimarães, Franklin Távora, Taunay," "Machado de Assis;" 2. "Various Manifestations in Prose—History," consisting of a study of Martius and the "Historians;" 3. "Various Manifestations in Prose—Public Speakers and Orators;" 4. "A Literary Retrospective" (consisting of "A Literary Retrospective," 1888, and "Confrontation in Retrospect," 1904); 5. "Anti-Romantic Reactions in Poetry—Evolution of Lyricism;" 6. "Diverse Articles" on João Ribeiro, Lopes Trovão, Tito Lívio de Castro, José do Patrocínio, Barão do Rio Branco, Joaquim Nabuco, Farias Brito, Nestor Vítor and Euclides da Cunha; and 6. "Synthesis of the Evolution of Genres in Brazilian Literature," which incorporates the book with the same title of 1909.

Works Cited

Candido, Antonio. Introdução. *Sílvio Romero: Teoria, Crítica e História Literária*. Selection and Introduction by Antonio Candido. Rio de Janeiro: Livros Técnicos e Científicos; São Paulo: EDUSP, 1978.

Miguel-Pereira, Lúcia. *Prosa de Ficção—de 1870 a 1920*. 3rd ed. Brasília: Instituto Nacional do Livro; Rio de Janeiro: José Olympio, 1973.

Peixoto, Afrânio. *Panorama da Literatura Brasileira*. São Paulo: Companhia Editora Nacional, 1940.

Romero, Sílvio. *História da Literatura Brasileira*. Rio de Janeiro: Garnier, 1888.

Romero, Sílvio and João Ribeiro. *Compêndio de História da Literatura Brasileira*. 2nd ed. Rio de Janeiro: Francisco Alves, 1909.

Ventura, Roberto. *Estilo Tropical: História Cultural e Polêmicas Literárias no Brasil*. São Paulo: Companhia das Letras, 1991.

Veríssimo, José. *História da Literatura Brasileira. De Bento Teixeira (1601) a Machado de Assis (1908)*. 1916. 4th ed. Brasília: Ed. da Universidade de Brasília, 1963.

"The Abstract Brazilian": Antonio Candido's *Malandro* as National Persona

K. David Jackson

The representation of the social world in Brazilian prose fiction continues a long-standing practice of chronicling and caricaturing national life, which has been recognized as one of the special features of Brazilian arts. The presence of a broad social world is an essential frame of reference in the novel, although its presence may not be readily apparent or emphasized by the author. The Rio de Janeiro of Machado de Assis, for example, is identifiable only by the names of some streets, districts, or edifices. Some of the most celebrated novels in Brazilian literature—*Memórias Póstumas de Brás Cubas* [*Posthumous Memoirs of Brás Cubas*], by Machado de Assis, *Macunaíma*, by Mário de Andrade, and *Memórias Sentimentais de João Miramar* [*Sentimental Memoirs of John Seaborne*], by Oswald de Andrade—are drawn against an unobtrusive yet expansive canvas of national personae. In prose fiction, the relationship between a chronicler narrator-hero and caricatures of the social world is a dialectical construct, established in the mid-nineteenth century, which lies at the heart of questions of national identity and social organization in Brazilian literature.

In an influential essay, "Dialectics of Malandroism" (1970), or "Dialectics of the Rogue," leading critic and scholar Antonio Candido called attention to the first novel of manners set in Rio de Janeiro, the *Memoirs of a Militia Sargent* (1854-55) by Manuel Antônio de Almeida—recently retranslated to English—, which mirrored the social hierarchy of the Empire. The *Memoirs* chronicles a period of national life on the colonial model, taken from the merchant class. Its sketches are considered reminiscent of a series of well-known drawings depicting Brazilian daily life and culture in the first decades of the nineteenth century by Jean Baptiste Debret, published in three volumes in 1834 as *Voyage Pittoresque et Historique au Brésil.* Drawing on physical description and outward appearance, the novel creates a self-image, a "veritable self-portrait" of national personae. At the same time, in recording daily life from the streets, it dissolves individuals into the social categories of the Empire or frames them as caricatures of semi-folkloric figures.

> (They are) designated only by profession or their position in a group that, on the one hand, dissolves them into typical social categories, but on the other approximates them to legendary paradigms and the indeterminacy of the fable... (Candido 84)

One explanation of the origin of these two currents speaks of "two very different European prose traditions: semi-picaresque, satirical English novels of the eighteenth century, like those of Fielding and Smollett, which Almeida and other Brazilians read in French translation; and the early romantic costumbrismo of Spain and Portugal—generally sympathetic, even nostalgic, descriptions of local customs and traditions imperiled by modernization" (Haberly 140-41). While recognizing picaresque features in Almeida's *Memoirs,* Brazilian critics prefer to draw our attention, however, to comic and satiric antecedents in the Regency (1831-1840) and Second Empire (1840-1889).

The depiction of "lower middle class, Gypsies, mobsters, and grenadiers"—the phrase is from an introduction by Mário de Andrade—is foreshadowed by verbal and pictorial satire published by newspapers. The *crônica*—a short semi-fictional episode, a popular genre found in the Brazilian press since the 1830s—often functioned as a laboratory in which writers prepared themselves for the novel (Arrigucci 58). The chronicler-hero, pervasive in modern prose, gives voice to a perennial current of national self-consciousness in Brazilian thought (Daniel 157), often explored through characters or personae. The chronicle may be responsible for the mixing of historical figures and fictional characters created to reflect them. Such is the case in the *Memoirs* of Major Vidigal, the capricious head of Rio's *Guarda Real de Polícia,* who as a fictional character acts as "an ogre, a devourer of happy people..." (Candido 84). Embodying the dual nature of authority, Vidigal may be considered a predecessor of the rapacious Italian industrialist Pietro Pietra in *Macunaíma,* a figure who itself caricatures an actual historical captain of São Paulo's industry, Matarazzo. Pietro Pietra appears in the guise of an urban cannibal, also associated with a mythical giant, Piaiman, "Eater of Men."

Caricature began to take hold in this period in variety supplements, influencing the process of character construction with its comic resources. Journalism also seems to have given rise to a practice of self-satire, noticeable in the characterization of main personages by physical descriptions and outward appearance:

> [C]onsidering the heterogeneous material itself and the need to review the issues of the week, as well as the need to be brief and to record daily life and particular forces in the fictional sense, it is not surprising that chroniclers and novelists working alongside each other might find themselves forced to create a self-image, that they might experiment with self-satire in the midst of their obligatory changes. (Süssekind 177)

Cartoons in the press helped to set the satirical tone of this writing, while the reproduction of popular speech set the colloquial tone of Brazilian language. Eschewing both slaves and elite, the social portrait restricted its field of vision to "the free lower classes, existing on the margins of the power hierarchy and occupying interstices of the social structure..." (Holloway xii). The author imitated the caricaturist, whose candid depictions of personages in the press ranged from "not exactly flattering" to "devastating" (Süssekind 178). Use of satire in chronicles and pictorial caricatures helped to transform mere depiction of a social world into the complexity of a novel, employing a narrow and superficial cast of characters to construct incisive social critiques.

Leonardo, the adventurous and picaresque hero of the *Memoirs*, sets a pattern for the satirical hero and articulates a particular form of social criticism that remains characteristic of a line of satirical fiction:

> The narrative voice is perhaps Almeida's most significant contribution to prose fiction, ... the narrative voice serves as the sole guarantor of the authenticity and truthfulness of the text [and] controls his readers reactions ... (Haberly 140-41)

Candido's essay traces some of the enduring characteristics of this kind of hero and his function in the social world. Leonardo does not represent the viewpoints or values of the elite, being but one character among many; neither is he a symbol of class or popular interests, per se. His point of view,

K. DAVID JACKSON

rather, cuts across a flexible, moveable social fabric and is motivated by an instinct of survival often evident in a picaresque hero, "a kind of irreverent common sense, which is pre-critical, but which… becomes in the end more demystifying" (100). His special position floating between social levels also produces a certain type of objectivity, marked by cynical reflections but absent of moral judgments. It seems that, as Candido writes, the hero purposefully "concludes nothing and learns nothing" (81), for at heart he remains optimistic and cheerfully accepts the given state of society. This is his special formula as a modern hero, "cynicism plus good nature" (91). Deviating from picaresque norms, Leonardo plays more the "clever adventurer," while he doubtless embodies the very Portuguese category of *"menino da sua mãe"* ("his mother's son") in its patriarchal form.

In the essay, Candido suggests forms of symbolic interpretation of social functions in the novel, without claiming that his reading amounts to a general theory of the function of Brazilian social reality. His literary analysis nevertheless contains observations that have proved to be central to the contemporary debate on the nature and function of Brazil as a national entity. First, in Brazilian society of that time he sees a dialectics between order and disorder, which are capriciously balanced in the system of human relationships. There is a relative equivalence between the worlds symbolizing order and those of disorder, resulting in a morally neutral world, inhabited by a society without guilt, sin, remorse, repression, or sanction, where actions are evaluated only on the basis of their practical result:

> [T]he dialectic game of order and disorder [functioned] as a correlative of what existed in Brazilian society at that time. Order imposed and maintained with difficulty, surrounded on every side by a lively disorder, which opposed twenty situations of concubinage to every marriage and a thousand chance unions to every situation of concubinage. (Candido 95)

If disorder is the unruly expression of a vigorous young society, order stands for its attempt to refine itself in the molds of the old colonial cultures that were its models.

The second observation of importance here is that the narrator-hero mediates between the dialectical categories, which are porous positions in the social world. The hybrid composition of the social hierarchy allowed for such a space in-between:

In its more intimate structure and its latent vision of things, this book expresses the vast general accommodation that dissolves the extremes, confuses the meaning of law and order, manifests the reciprocal penetration of groups, of ideas, of the most disparate attitudes, creating a kind of moral no-man's-land, where transgression is only a nuance in the spectrum that runs from norm to crime. (Candido 100)

Candido perceives a rhythm in the social construct created by the passage between institutions or types, on one side, and the demystifying, irreverent satire of realist popular expression on the other:

[T]he tension of the two lines that constitute the author's vision, and those lines are translated in two narrative directions, dynamically interrelated. On the one hand, the stamp of the popular introduces archetypal elements, which bring with them the presence of what is most universal in cultures, pulling it toward the legendary and the unreal, without recognizing the particular historical situation. On the other hand, the perception of the social rhythm pulls it toward the representations of a concrete, historically delimited society... (Candido 96)

The rogue or *malandro* comes to represent the spontaneous forms of social life in the novel. A third essential observation in the essay concerns the hero's act of renunciation. In the social dialectic of the *malandro*, Candido detects a particular form of "corrosive tolerance" (101) at the root of culture, desiring legitimacy while attacking the rigidity of any norm or law. By attempting to participate in the discipline and order of conventional or legitimate culture, the hero was required to repress or renounce his street personality in favor of what Candido termed an alienated or mutilated, automatic self. The rogue or *malandro*, however, possesses an almost "magical liberty" (99) because he identifies with the spontaneous forms of the free lower classes, serving as a mediator in the social dialectic. Finally, Candido observes that an amoral world of picaresque irreverence governed only by free agency and impunity evokes archetypes of legendary chivalric heroes. Their lives and memoirs constitute a chain of fabulous events germane for the Brazilian satirical novel to follow, in which events proceed from a hero's birth to economic failure, and to the absurdity of social relations. The dialectical drama ends in a form of *opera buffa* (93, 95) wherein the exchangeability of social order and disorder is accepted and celebrated in a positive comic spirit.

By displaying the primacy of imagination and improvisation over portraiture or historical reconstitution in the *Memoirs*, Candido's essay founds a Brazilian comic tradition that expresses the humorous irreverence and amorality of oral and folk narratives. This line of satirical fiction, according to Candido, reaches its apex in the experimental fiction of modernism, Mário de Andrade's *Macunaíma* and Oswald de Andrade's *Miramar* and its sequel, *Seraphim Grosse Pointe*. The "Dialectics of Malandroism" presents the *Memoirs of a Militia Sargent* as "a representative novel," whose irreverent humor only comes to be recognized fully in those great modernist novels that raise the *malandro* to a national symbol. The essay neither claims a line of originality or authenticity in its interpretation of national society nor does it analyze any succeeding work in the lineage of the modern satirical novel, which remains a tantalizing suggestion. The present study carries the dialectic of the *malandro* into the modern novel, where the pertinence of Candido's major observations can be assessed. At the same time, by placing the "Dialectic of Malandroism" in the light of recent symbolic and structural interpretations of Brazilian society, the full authenticity and originality of the satirical tradition in Brazilian fiction becomes clearer.

Brazil as a System

In *Carnivals, Rogues, and Heroes* (1978), anthropologist Roberto DaMatta attempts to interpret Brazil as a system, proposing conceptual categories almost identical to Candido's observations in the "Dialectic of Malandroism." As does the literary analyst, the anthropologist also searches for the origins of Brazilian specificity or individuality in universal human forces or systems. DaMatta discusses the ritualization of Brazilian social organization as a dichotomy or dialectic, dominated by a similar opposition between order and disorder and led by its principal character types, the rogues and heroes:

> It is obvious that we have a continuum ranging from order to disorder, from tightly closed routine to total liminal openness, with each marked point corresponding to stereotyped social positions that are familiar to all sectors of Brazilian society. (DaMatta 208)

Spheres of order and disorder are the recognized stereotypes of daily life, in which the drama of Brazilian society is enacted. DaMatta's study juxtaposes carnival and the national holiday; costumes and uniforms; people and the authorities; the house and the street; the free individual and the juridical person. In each case, the first element of the equation represents the rights, conscience, and rules of equal individuals, while the second is governed by the juridical definition of the social totality.

DaMatta's second observation, recapitulating Candido's analysis, is that the categories are changeable, eliding one another as a result of their own instability. Transit from one category to another, for example, allows for an exchange of identity between *malandro* and hero: "We know, for example, that the heroes of Carnival, the figures who reveal that moment as 'carnivalesque,' are representations (or *fantasias*) of marginal people..." (208). The world of the *malandro* is usually one of misplaced or out of place figures:

> Either because they are situated at the boundaries or limits of historical time, like the Greeks... or because they may be situated at the extremes of our geographical frontiers, like the Hawaiians, the Chinese, and the legionnaires; or because they may be hidden by our prisons or the police [or by our ingenuousness]... we know that they are all to be classified as *malandros*. (208-9)

The role of mediator played by the *malandro*, who is allergic to work and insinuates himself into the individual spaces of the social hierarchy, such as those of carnival, is considered to be "much more creative and free" than that of his opposite, a figure in military uniform who marches in processions symbolizing order.

There are two additional points of comparison with Candido's essay. In the neutral, hesitant space opened between order and disorder in DaMatta's analysis, the hero becomes a renouncer. His rejection of society is of a higher degree than the *malandro*'s, making him comparable to messianic or revolutionary figures. The renouncing hero is an archetype in Brazilian social history, and DaMatta identifies the figure in history and literature, whether he be "Augusto Matraga" of João Guimarães Rosa, Antônio Conselheiro of *Os Sertões* [*Rebellion in the Backlands*] by Euclides da Cunha, or the folk heroes Lampião or Padre Cícero in the Northeastern oral tradition. Likewise, the *malandros* are amply represented by the archetypes of traditional popular tales, such as folk hero Pedro Malasartes, to whom DaMatta dedicates an extended analysis. Once again, the flexibility of the dialectical social order leads to the exchangeability of roles. Just as the *malandro* runs the risk of taking on a completely marginal existence, DaMatta reminds us, the renouncer may cross the line into banditry and revenge. Thus, the rituals of the Brazilian drama constitute a social theatre comparable to Candido's *opera buffa*, a "dialectical drama governed by indecision…and paradoxes" (DaMatta 1). It expresses an essentially comic spirit, in which "a bandit can enter a carnival salon or a futurist-cannibal become a revolutionary on the beach" (1).

The Narrator-Chroniclers

In the seventy years after Leonardo and his *Memoirs of a Militia Sargent*, two major narrator-chroniclers continued development of the satirical novel, Machado de Assis' Brás Cubas, who writes posthumous memoirs, and Oswald de Andrade's João Miramar, who composes sentimental memoirs. Both are examples of unreliable narration by a character at a distance from society. An examination of the dynamic of the *malandro* and society in these two satirical novels using Candido's categories should illuminate the persistence and pertinence of the genre in the modern novel. In a recent essay, Samira Mesquita indeed mixes the two novels in the clever title, "Posthumous Memoirs of João Miramar/Sentimental Memoirs of Brás Cubas."

Brás Cubas embodies the voice of disorder since he is a deceased narrator, recounting his life from beyond the grave, and aware of the freedom that this privileged position allows. He has, apparently, nothing to gain from anything but a frank appraisal; yet the question remains whether the narrator is fully aware that he has lived or, indeed, has sought a life of disorder outside of the social body. His ancestors, we learn, have fabricated a genealogy for the Cubas family with false claims to nobility. Congruently, the main themes of his life occur on the margins of society and in spaces of prohibition, symbolizing his failures, the estranged intrusions of a deceased narrator. His affair with the society wife Virgília, a central theme of the memoirs, represents his potential marriage that failed to occur when Brás hesitated, remaining too long in his exile or mourning and alienation in Petrópolis, upon which Virgília chose a rising political figure. Their revived passion is an undercurrent, a social antithesis enacted in a vice world of the suburbs, and Brás' political relationship with the husband, Lobo Neves, is based on the deception of a kind of false kinship. When Brás does become a deputy, at the height of his own political fortunes, he can only dedicate his inaugural speech to a critique of the style of hat worn by the militia, in what is perhaps a comic homage to Leonardo's *Memoirs*. The depths of his dedication to "disorder" is manifested in the style of the novel, with its short chapters that truncate description, full of allusion and suggestion, and at times consisting only of punctuation marks or semiotic symbols.

Brás' mediation between levels of the social universe is a central yet veiled clue to his social function. He creates for Virgília a prohibited world, while using the servant D. Plácida, who owes him her rescue from economic destitution, to lend respectability to their rendezvous. He inverts the serious, exterior social roles represented by the husband, Lobo Neves. Finally, by becoming the disciple of the mad philosopher, Quincas Borba, Brás demonstrates that intellectually he has "concluded nothing and learned nothing" from his own memoirs, being unable to distinguish between the coherent and the mad or deviant in society.

Always the *malandro*, Brás opens the novel with the dedication to "the worm that first gnawed the cold flesh of my corpse," and intensifies his satire stylistically when he bids adieu to the reader in the preface with a "snap of the finger." The numbered chapters of his impossible "posthumous autobiography" carry ironic titles of self-portraiture and satire. As a mere youth at a society soirée, Brás unwittingly denounces a kiss exchanged in the garden between Dr. Vilaça and D. Eusébia, surprising and delighting the gossipy society. This moment subtly returns to his autobiography in the character of their beautiful but lame daughter Eugênia, whose sincere love Brás rejects because of her physical defect, and which foreshadows his own path of illicit fortunes and insincerity. His picaresque youth in Brazil comes to an abrupt end when his father packs him off to Europe, in order to tear him away from the avaricious Marcela, who extorts lavish presents that are depleting his fortune and exercising his powers of deception. As a student in Coimbra, he continues his festive life while waiting to receive a worthless degree.

"How I Didn't Become a Minister of State," the clever title of an almost empty chapter, indicates his path of renunciation of self and society in the memoirs. Brás has renounced Eugênia, avoided marriage with Virgília, delayed entrance into political life; it is no surprise that his political ambitions are truncated, since his objectives are fraudulent, being those of a parasite or a copy on the margins of actual institutions. The question is suggested whether Brás, consciously or not, is carefully constructing the universally marginal, negative life of a *malandro*, for whom satire also becomes a form of renunciation. The narrator, after all, is aware of "defects in composition" of the memoirs, an idea to which he dedicates a chapter:

> But the book is tedious, it has the smell of the grave about it; it has a certain cadaveric contraction about it, a serious fault, insignificant to boot because the main defect of this book is you, reader. You're in a hurry to grow old and the book moves slowly. (111)

The apparent lack of meaningful sequence, chronology, and conclusion—whether in life or memoirs—is the clue to the inverse, negative function of Brás' satire. In the final chapter, he utters a frequently quoted line, understood to express his philosophical pessimism: "I had a small balance, which is the final negative in this chapter of negatives—I had no children, I haven't transmitted the legacy of our misery to any creature." Yet even here a double purpose and occult message is hidden. Brás is alluding to the chapter "The Secret Cause," in which Virgília mysteriously reveals her pregnancy to him, which for a moment gives Brás the hope of a place in the outer world of order. Virgília's miscarriage, revealed in the following chapter by her husband, is the devastating condemnation to marginality and subliminality that he has constantly desired and sought, but that now can be justified and even lamented as a blow of fate. The declaration of his "small gain" in having had no children, rather than bitter pessimism, can be read as a disguised confirmation of the total coherence of his life as a *malandro*, which has successfully achieved and avoided what life both could and could not give him.

In the sentimental memoirs, João Miramar ("John Seaborne"), who is both a narrator and character, takes advantage of retrospective narration to reconstruct a satirical view of the Brazilian world. The novel is written not by a deceased narrator but by one aged thirty-five, the symbolic halfway point of life, taken from Dante. The novel constructs a second exterior point of view based on the narrator's voyage to Europe as a youth and his return to Brazil with different perspectives. The chapters, which are small fragments written in Cubist style with clever ironic titles, are written in a deceptive present time, resembling snapshots of formative moments in Miramar's life, but colored by ironic overlays both by the mature narrator-chronicler and by the returned traveler. Much like Joyce's *A Portrait of the Artist as a Young Man*, Miramar's memoirs begin with infantile language and the ingenuous self-portrait of an innocent youth's apprenticeship in the national social world, hackneyed and superficial.

Miramar speaks from the perspective of disorder on several counts: his alienation from family and society, his childhood discovery of the forbidden fruits of Eros and carnival—a teacher's Pantheism, a circus performance— and his confusion of ritual with sexuality in his religious education:

> Lord with thee, blessed art thou amongst women, women don't have any legs, they're just mama's manikin even down there. Why should women have legs, amen. (114)

Upon his return to Brazil from Europe, after witnessing the vast "slope of the world," the exiled Miramar finds that he is also an orphan, thus doubly alienated from the social and family worlds. His attempted reintegration into the Brazilian world leads to satire of social types, including João Miramar, the good-natured, cynical hero. In *Miramar*, satire begins with the family circle and friends, whom he has always found "abominable": the hero's loquacious and vacuous cousins Nair and Cotita, the ingenuous aunt Gabriela, the picaresque, scheming "Count" José Chelinini, and his future trivial wife "Célia." In the professional world, each name satirizes a type: the acid critic Dr. Wilde Lemmon, the slippery Dr. Joe Rubber, the great moral guide Dr. Pontius Pilate. The semi-folkloric dimensions of a national family of personages is illustrated by the danseuse Catherine Drip-Fire, the femme fatal Madame Rollingboule, and several rustic letters from unlettered relatives on the *fazenda* "New Lombardy."

As Brás Cubas, João Miramar is a renouncer. In terms of style, the ironic distance between the titles of his fragmentary chapters and their content represents his digressive, antithetical, and non-logical relationship toward the language of a culture with which he now feels out of step. In "The Great Divorced" and "Last Movie," João's failures at marriage and business symbolize his failure at reintegration into the Brazilian world. He compares his life to an irregular verb—"*crackar*"—in "The Verb to Bust," an anglicism that will later be applied to Wall Street. In the final chapter, "Interview/Interviewed," João suspends his memoirs, faced with pressure to conform to the conservative literary standards of the day. His final "meditative pause" marks the depth of his alienation and ends the memoirs with an open form.

Finally, João Miramar—a pseudonym standing for the young Brazilian writer as a modernist—is classified in the novel as an archetype by the conservative pillars of critical opinion who counsel him about his work. Machado Penumbra ("Nathaniel Webster Darkling"), who in his preface accepts syntactical simultaneity but draws the line at errors of punctuation, asks "Can this be the Brazilian of the twenty-first century?" And Pontius Pilate, who reads João's memoirs before a voyage to Europe, pronounces them "reminiscent of Virgil, just a bit more nervous in style." Thus with the consecration of conservative nationalism, Miramar reenacts the voyage of Ulysses in the ironic mode, sailing out of Brazil in order to form the modern social conscience of his race.

Modernist Self-Portraits

In their portrayal of society, major works of modernist fiction do not break new ground, as they do in matters of structure and style by following innovations of the European avant-garde movements. Following the modern art movement of 1922, some novels identified themselves as chronicles of the city of São Paulo in their subtitles. On this point, they may be considered extensions of nineteenth-century novels of manners, in which the chronicle and the caricature continue to dominate social portraits. The reason for this apparent anachronism lies in the difference between the modernists' view of art and social progress and the actual urban reality of São Paulo, as outlined in an essay by Jorge de Sena:

> [T]he demolition of everything that was considered sacred and respectable would be directed, in Brazil, not only against the established intellectual, but also against the abyss that existed between real life and contemporary times, in which there was only the external appearance of progress. (Sena 100)

Daily life was the sphere in which the modernist writers sought authenticity, since it corresponded with their own experience of a Brazil tied to its own past:

> [T]hey encountered authenticity... in daily life that, like their own past, was profoundly inlaid with extremely patriarchal social structures and patterns, tremendously conservative, and dramatically bringing to mind everything that kept Brazil in a state of semi-colonial and semi-feudal slavery. (Sena 100)

K. DAVID JACKSON

Monica Schpun confirmed the state of social relationships in São Paulo of the 1920s in *Les Années Folles a S. Paulo* (1997), in which she classifies as chronicles ["Chroniques"] contemporary essays by Ercília N. Cobra and Maria Lacerda de Moura denouncing the repression of women. Nicolau Sevcenko chronicles the interrelationship of modernist society and culture and the urbanization of São Paulo in *Orfeu Extático na Metrópole* (1992).

Oswald de Andrade in 1918 appears in the satirical press in a series of caricatures, featuring his rotund profile. In the scandalous "O Parafuso," his photo in a white suit is captioned "Mr. Oswald de Andrade, seducer of minors," while in the aestheticist *fin de siècle* fashion journal *Papel e Tinta* he is identified as "Marquis d'Olz." The name alludes to "D'Olzani," maiden name of the spirited young woman he met in the *garçonnière*, whom he married on her deathbed in 1919. Early in his youth, Oswald had taken the name "João Miramar" to represent his poetic persona, a signature and identity he assumes, which reaches its culmination in Miramar's sentimental memoirs of 1924.

Oswald kept a collective diary-scrapbook in the São Paulo *garçonnière* in 1918-19, in which the artist's studio is invaded by the rhythms of downtown streets:

> This collective diary written in Oswald's *garçonnière* in 1918 is not that of a writer in his *fin de siècle* studio, but rather a text that is composed consonant with the rhythms of the street... The relation between writing the diary and the city is presumed: references to the city are not as important as the shape of the text (its rhythm, its structure) in which the *urbe* is a tacit presence... Outside is not a familiar place to the comfortable members of the *garçonnière* (many belong to traditional families of São Paulo), but a strange place dominated by the multitude and fortuitous encounters. The experience of a city that becomes distant finds consolation in the close community of signatures and annotations contained in the diary, once one crosses the door of the *garçonnière*, located in the center of the city. (Aguilar 185)

Oswald de Andrade collects satirical sketches of the members of the city's modernist circles in the style of the lightning portraits, amounting to caricatures of social personae. These impressions are drawn with incisive wit, playing on the identity of the person in question, as in the sketch of Mário de Andrade, "Macunaíma de Conservatório" ("Macunaíma in the Conservatory of Music"). This satiric collection of caricatures was kept in a notebook and selectively published in 1990 as *Dicionário de Bolso* (*Pocket Dictionary*). Mário de Andrade caricatured Law School graduates in a satirical sketch in *Macunaíma*, when in his flight through the jungle the hero ran upon a *bacharel*:

> Running like mad, they came to a house a league and a half farther on where the bachelor of Cananéia lived. This old coot was sitting in the doorway reading some obscure manuscript. Macunaíma said to him, "How do you do, bachelor?"
> —Not too bad, unknown traveler.
> —Taking a little fresh air, are you?
> —*C'est vrai*, as they say in French.
> —Well, so long, bachelor. I'm super in a hurry. (26)

Given the reference to Cananéia, the probable object of Mário's satire was the diplomat Graça Aranha, author of *Canaã* [*Canaan*], whom Oswald also privately called an "old beast."

In *Macunaíma*, Mário de Andrade brought his modernist circle into a scene of macumba festivities:

> Macunaíma and his fellow celebrants of the macumba, including Jaime Ovalle, Dodô, Manu Bandeira, Blaise Cendrars, Ascenso Ferreira, Raul Bopp and Antônio Bento, all went out into the dawn. (59)

He also named several regional artisans of handicrafts, blending the national and actual with mythical lore:

> They sent to São Paulo for the famous woolen booties knitted by Dona Ana Francisca de Almeida Leite Morais; to Pernambuco for lace in traditional designs such as 'Alpine Rose,' 'Myrtle Flower,' and 'I long for thee' woven by the hands of Joaquina Leitão, better known as Quinquina Cacunda. From the best tamarind cordial made by the Sisters Loura Vieira of Óbidos they prepared a refreshing drink... (20)

His satires of the social world of São Paulo invoke types and categories, such as the city's ladies, as described by Macunaíma in his famous letter to the Amazon women. The jungle emperor parodies urban elite women:

[E]nchanted monsters who amuse themselves only with 'showers of filthy lucre, ostentatious fountains of champagne… They are greatly preoccupied with themselves, [obtaining] from all parts of the globe everything that is most refined and elegant…[that] they think adds to their attractions—for example, tiny feet from Japan, rubies from India, insolence from North America, and many other international treasures and delights.' (69-72)

The letter can be compared with an assessment of socially acceptable roles normally open to Brazilian women, described by Michelle Perrot:

Aux femmes, la maison, la direction d'une nombreuse domesticité, une maternité revalorisée, les rencontres de l'intérieur, des apparitions publiques ritualisées, de plus en plus obsédées par le devoir de cette beauté que les femmes se doivent d'offrir en spectacle aux hommes. (Schpun ii)

In urban fiction of this period, many of the characters were recognizable portraits or caricatures of the city's modernists. Not only was the city life and landscape considered a source of the modernist aesthetic, rather they were all the readers of their mutual works. With the passage of time, few are left who can identify specific allusions to personalities in São Paulo in the modernist novels, except by extrapolating from references or from an author's biography.

The social world in *Miramar*, the experimental cubist novel of Oswald de Andrade, confirms the kinship of this modern novel with a superficial and caricatured social world. Social organization can be described in terms similar to the two universalizing strata established by Candido for the 1855 *Memoirs of a Militia Sargent*, one illustrating a "wide circle of culture" involving archetypal situations and characters, and the other Brazilian. Representing the first stratum, and illustrating the author's general cultural and education, is a cast of characters, both historical and fictional, that dots each modernist novel, drawn from the universal world of political culture, humanities, and arts. In *Miramar*, the gallery of names includes the classical world (Alexander the Great, Aspasia, Cleopatra, Cupid, Icarus, Petronius, Plutarch, Telemachus), political culture (Lloyd George, the Kaiser, Lenin, Catarina de Médici, Mussolini, Napoleon, Kemal Pacha, Poincaré, Woodrow Wilson), writers (Lord Byron, Cocteau, Musset, Rimbaud, Virgil), film stars (Sarah Bernhardt, Baby Daniels, Mae Murray), music and dance (Chopin, Isadora Duncan, Mozart, Puccini, Salomé, Satie, Schubert, Tosca), and painting (the

Gioconda, Picasso, Rafael). Brazilian names figure on the universal list in the cases of widely known or representative figures: the statesman Rui Barbosa; writers Olavo Bilac and Basílio da Gama; political figures José Bonifácio, Dom Pedro I and II, Tiradentes; and aviator Santos Dumont. If these novels convince us, it is not through the pastiche and caricature of social types, but through a satirical vision of the whole or universal social construct. The narrator-chronicler-heroes themselves act as the rogues and heroes of their own satirical histories, following DaMatta's analysis of the Brazilian social dilemma.

The Abstract Brazilians: The *Malandros*

In the essay "Brazilian Culture: Nationalism by Elimination," critic Roberto Schwarz considers the problem of imitative literature and culture in Brazil, plagued historically by copying of models imported from other metropolitan sources. The suggestion, originating in the colonial background, is that Brazil has been the subject of "cultural expropriation" and is still in search of genuine national roots. The troublesome paradigm of source and copy gives rise to an historical divide that Schwarz observes in the Brazilian social world and that is inevitably reminiscent of Candido's dialectic, order and disorder. Noting that colonial institutions such as slavery, *latifundia*, and clientelism constituted a set of relations with their own rules and impervious to outside influences (disorder), these conflicted with provisions for equality under the Law, set down in the nineteenth century (order). Schwarz concludes that this dialectical background of the personal and the legal gives rise to a society that displays elements both of originality (disorder) and lack of originality (order), yet without entirely solving its dilemma.

Referring to the modernist attempt to define an authentic national character, Schwarz coins the term "abstract Brazilian" to refer to a modernist hero who is a synthesis of national characteristics, represented by the polymorphous Macunaíma, for example. For Schwarz this is a negative category, since it is not class specific. If the synthetic hero is viewed as a mediator among the levels of a dialectical social system, however, and moreover if he writes from an exterior point of view such as the posthumous Cubas or voyaging Miramar, then the abstract Brazilian fits Candido's positive description of a cathartic, satirical hero. Our reading of the satirical novel in the Brazilian tradition proposes that the synthetic or abstract Brazilian is also a national *malandro*, whether he be Malasartes, Macunaíma, or Miramar, a figure who makes possible an outside, miscegenated reading of

Brazil's absurd cultural configuration through his role as narrator-chronicler, mediator, and renouncer. The chronicling of popular society plus the caricature of comic social institutions is a novel, authentic expression of the Brazilian system of carnivals, rogues, and heroes. Embodying popular irreverence and mocking hierarchy and institutions, the malandro—as the writer of retrospective, satirical and unreliable memoirs—develops a special quality that Schwarz finds in the novels of Machado de Assis: the ability to perceive a "particular mode of ideological functioning" (13) in a society of copy and exception. The set of satirical memoirs whose heroes—Leonardo, Brás, and João—are at odds with the social system argues that carnivalization and ritualization of the social world, as described by Candido and DaMatta, defuse the stigma of imitation and copy of European cultural models. The abstract Brazilian, capable of crossing social barriers and mocking rigid hierarchies, evokes the fabulous events of his national autobiography and self-portrait and founds a current of originality and authenticity in Brazilian arts, uniting humor and popular culture in the chronicling of Brazil's flexible, hybrid social world.

K. DAVID JACKSON

Works Cited

Aguilar, Gonzalo. *Poesía Concreta Brasileña: Las Vanguardias en la Encrucijada Modernista.* Tesis de doctorado. Universidad de Buenos Aires: Facultad de Filosofía y Letras, 2000.

Almeida, Manuel Antônio de. *Memoirs of a Militia Sargent.* Trans. Ronald W. Sousa. Oxford: Oxford UP, 1999; trans. L. L. Barrett. Washington, D.C.: Pan American Union, 1959; *Memórias de um Sargento de Milícias.* Rio de Janeiro: Tipografia Brasiliense, 1854.

Andrade, Mário de. *Macunaíma.* Trans. E. A. Goodland. New York: Random House, 1984; *Macunaíma.* São Paulo: E. Cupolo, 1928.

Andrade, Oswald de. *Sentimental Memoirs of John Seaborne.* Trans. Ralph Niebuhr and Albert Bork. Texas Quarterly 15.4 (Winter 1972): 112-160; *Memórias Sentimentais de João Miramar.* São Paulo: Independência, 1924.

———. *Seraphim Grosse Pointe.* Trans. K. David Jackson and Albert G. Bork. Austin: New Latin Quarter, 1979; *Serafim Ponte Grande.* Rio de Janeiro: Ariel, 1933.

Arrigucci, Jr., Davi. "Fragmentos sobre a Crônica." *Enigma e Comentário.* São Paulo: Companhia das Letras, 1987. 51-66.

Assis, Joaquim Maria Machado de. *The Posthumous Memoirs of Brás Cubas.* Trans. Gregory Rabassa. New York: Oxford UP, 1997; *Epitaph of a Small Winner.* Trans. W. L. Grossman. New York: Noonday, 1952; *Memórias Póstumas de Brás Cubas.* Rio de Janeiro: Tipografia Nacional, 1881.

Candido, Antonio. "Dialectic of Malandroism." *On Literature and Society.* Trans., ed., and intro. Howard S. Becker. Princeton: Princeton UP, 1995. 79-103; "Dialética da Malandragem." *Revista do Instituto de Estudos Brasileiros,* 8 (1970): 67-89; reprinted in *O Discurso e a Cidade.* São Paulo: Duas Cidades, 1993. 48-49.

———. "Literature and Underdevelopment." *On Literature and Society*. Trans., ed., and intro. Howard S. Becker. Princeton: Princeton U P, 1995. 119-41.

DaMatta, Roberto. *Carnivals, Rogues, and Heroes: An Interpretation of the Brazilian Dilemma*. Trans. John Drury. Notre Dame: U of Notre Dame P, 1991; *Carnavais, Malandros e Heróis: Para uma Sociologia do Dilema Brasileiro*. Rio de Janeiro: Zahar, 1979.

Daniel, Mary L. "Brazilian Fiction from 1900 to 1945." *The Cambridge History of Latin American Literature*. Eds. Roberto González Echevarría and Enrique Pupo-Walker. Cambridge: Cambridge UP, 1996. 157-187.

Debret, Jean Baptiste. *Voyage Pittoresque et Historique au Brésil*. 3 vols. Paris: Didot Freres, 1834.

Ferreira, Antonio Celso. *Um Eldorado Errante: São Paulo na Ficção Histórica de Oswald de Andrade*. Sao Paulo: Editora UNESP, 1996.

Haberly, David T. "The Brazilian Novel from 1850 to 1900." *The Cambridge History of Latin American Literature*. Eds. Roberto González Echevarría and Enrique Pupo-Walker. Cambridge: Cambridge UP, 1996. 137-156.

Holloway, Thomas H. "Historical Context and Social Topography of *Memoirs of a Militia Sergeant*." In Manuel Antônio de Almeida, *Memoirs of a Militia Sergeant*. Trans. Ronald W. Sousa. Oxford: Oxford UP, 1999. xi-xxii.

Mesquita, Samira Nahid. "Memórias Póstumas de João Miramar/Memórias Sentimentais de Brás Cubas." *Oswald Plural*. Ed. Gilberto Mendonça Telles et al. Rio de Janeiro: EdUERJ, 1995. 147-158; repub. in Gilda Santos, Jorge Fernandes da Silveira e Teresa Cristina Cerdeira da Silva, eds. *Cleonice: Clara em sua Geração*. Rio de Janeiro: Editora da Universidade Federal do Rio de Janeiro, 1999. 609-21.

Schpun, Monica Raisa. *Les Années Folles a São Paulo: Hommes et Femmes au Temps de l'Explosion Urbaine (1920—1929)*. Paris: L'Harmattan, 1997.

Schwarz, Roberto. "Brazilian Culture: Nationalism by Elimination." *Misplaced Ideas*. Trans., ed. John Gledson. London: Verso, 1992. 1-18.

Sena, Jorge de. "Modernismo Brasileiro: 1922 e hoje." In K. David Jackson, *A Vanguarda Literária no Brasil: Bibliografia e Antologia Crítica*. Frankfurt: Vervuert, 1998. 97-110.

Sevcenko, Nicolau. *Orfeu Extático na Metrópole: São Paulo, Sociedade e Cultura nos Frementes Anos 20*. São Paulo: Companhia das Letras, 1992.

Süssekind, Flora. "The Novel and the *Crônica*." In Manuel Antônio de Almeida, *Memoirs of a Militia Sergeant*. Ronald W. Sousa, trans. Oxford: Oxford U P, 1999. 171-84.

Roberto Schwarz' Dialectical Criticism

Regina Lúcia de Faria

Translated by Paulo Henriques Britto

To understand Brazil was to understand these dislocations, which were experienced and practiced by everyone as a sort of inescapable fate that had no name, for the improper use of names was precisely their nature.

Roberto Schwarz, *Ao Vencedor as Batatas*[1]

I

Within the limits imposed by the very nature of this essay, I shall attempt to outline Roberto Schwarz' objectives as a critic by examining his studies of the novels of Machado de Assis. Such studies are mostly contained in his books *Ao Vencedor as Batatas* (1977), an examination of Machado's early novels;[2] *Um Mestre na Periferia do Capitalismo: Machado de Assis* (1990), an analysis of *Memórias Póstumas de Brás Cubas*;[3] and *Duas Meninas* (1997), on *Dom Casmurro*,[4] but also including a comparative study of Capitu, the book's female protagonist, and Helena, the narrator of Helena Morley's *Minha Vida de Menina*.[5] My aim is to evidence the importance of Schwarz' work in the context of Brazilian academic criticism in the last three decades.

II

Roberto Schwarz belongs to the second generation of university-trained Brazilian literary critics, who systematized the methods of literary analysis and renovated the debate on cultural dependence and Brazilian culture in general. The theoretical reflections of these intellectuals, active both as professors and as authors of books and essays published in newspapers or periodicals, acquired unquestionable importance in the academic world in the latter half of the 1960s, when they began publishing,[6] and even more in the 1970s, when their work became required reading for undergraduate and graduate students in literature programs across the country. Schwarz studied at the Universidade de São Paulo, and like Davi Arrigucci Jr., João Luiz Lafetá, Walnice Nogueira Galvão, João Alexandre Barbosa and others, he is associated with the critical-dialectical tradition of literary analysis adopted by Antonio Candido.

Silviano Santiago, another member of this generation, but one of the critic-scholars who have pursued their careers in Rio de Janeiro universities, has written that perhaps the best approach to Schwarz' work is "to trace it to the most significant works of his teachers at the Universidade de São Paulo," namely Caio Prado Jr. and Antonio Candido (Santiago 217). Caio Prado, who identified in nineteenth-century Brazilian society the presence of a segment of the population until then neglected by historians—freemen—offered Schwarz the interpretive key to the analysis of the shifts in meaning undergone by liberal ideas as they were adapted to the Brazilian environment. Antonio Candido, by excluding the so-called "first" Machado de Assis—that is, the author of works that preceded the 1881 publication of *The Posthumous Memoirs of Brás Cubas*—from his *Formação da Literatura Brasileira*, opened the way for Schwarz to build "an original field of studies of his own" concerning Brazil's greatest nineteenth-century writer (Santiago 217). This undertaking began with the publication of *Ao Vencedor as Batatas*.

III

The point of departure of Schwarz' "As Idéias Fora do Lugar," ("Misplaced Ideas"), the opening essay in *Ao Vencedor as Batatas*, is the discrepancy between Brazilian cultural and quotidian life in the nineteenth century and its original European model. According to Schwarz, this discrepancy—which might be broadly summarized as the disparity between the Brazilian Empire's liberal façade, based on various French, English and US liberal ideas, and the predominance of slave labor—"was in fact a constant, pervasive presence that unbalanced the ideological life of the Second Empire down to the smallest details," as attested by the Brazilian fiction of the period (14). Slave labor—inimical to the effectiveness so highly valued by rationalism but still profitable to a certain degree, "founded on violence and on military discipline" and relying on authority—was incompatible with liberalism. However, Schwarz observes, slavery was not the only sign of the incongruity of liberal ideals in Brazil; nor was it the effective nexus of Brazilian ideological life in the nineteenth century. The relations between the members of the propertied class and "freemen"—the "multitude of third parties… who were neither proprietors nor proletarians, whose access to social life and to their own property depend[ed] materially on the indirect or direct favor of a grandee"—insidiously contributed to the distortion of the liberal ideal, by displacing it at the moment of its absorption (16-19).

The process of colonization based on the monopoly of land, Schwarz argues, generated three classes: "the landowner, the slave and the 'freeman,' who was in fact a dependent." While the relation between landowners and slaves was clear-cut and guaranteed by force, that between landowners and freemen was regulated by the mechanism of favor. A disguised form of the violence that was the rule in the sphere of production, favor "assured the two parties, particularly the weaker one, that neither was in the condition of slavery" (18). This mechanism, made into "our nearly universal mediation," affected and governed all kinds of activities, "such as government, politics, industry, trade, city life, the Court, and so on," and even "professions, such as medicine, and occupations, such as printing, that in Europe owed nothing to favor." In this way, the practice of favor dislocated the ideals of bourgeois society, such as "the autonomy of the individual, the universality of the law, disinterested cultured, objective remuneration, the work ethic, and so on" that in the European context were seen as breaking both with feudal privilege and with the class prerogatives of the *Ancien Régime* (16). Brazil never experienced feudalism, directly or indirectly, since the process of colonization resulted from the mercantilistic spirit; but Brazilians were fundamentally followers of European tendencies and adopted, on the plane of ideas, the arguments that the European bourgeoisie had developed in order to oppose arbitrary power and slavery, while in actual practice they accepted the fact of favor, unceasingly reaffirming "the sentiments and notions" inherent in it (17).

The slave system and the practice of favor resulted in an unprecedented acclimatization of modern thought in Brazilian society: it acquired a rather original stamp, with unique practical and ideological-moral characteristics. Brazil provided a curious context for the adoption of the modern spirit:

> … *once European ideas and reasons were accepted, they could and often did serve as a nominally 'objective' justification for the arbitrariness that is the natural corollary of favor.* With no detriment to its existence, the antagonism vanished into thin air

REGINA LÚCIA DE FARIA

and the incompatible terms were reconciled. This harmonization was of capital importance. It had a number of effects, and its impact on our literature was profound. From the ideology it had originally been—that is, an involuntary deception, well-founded on appearances—liberalism turned into what can only be called an intentional token of various kinds of prestige that in fact had nothing to do with it. The favored party, as he legitimated arbitrariness by dint of some 'rational' reason, consciously aggrandized himself and his benefactor, who in turn did not see why he should contradict him, living as he did in an era dominated by reasons. (17, author's emphasis)

This dislocation in the meaning of liberal ideas thus became a problem for and a topic of nineteenth-century Brazilian literature, even when writers were unaware of the fact. The task of Brazilian writers became to trace the process of acclimatization of liberal ideas in Brazil, re-creating it as fiction, lest the inevitable difference should appear as an involuntary defect, formally identified as "naiveté, garrulousness, narrowness, servility, crudeness, and so on" (24). This formal discrepancy was a consequence of the fact that local writers were forced to treat themes of universal history and contemporary European issues—which were invariably present in the French and English novels that served as a model for them—and of the introduction of a localism, itself derived from European Romanticism, that clashed with the "grand plots that were characteristic of a Realism tinged with Romanticism" (32). To discern, in the subtlest way possible, how the real form—that is, social relations in Brazil placed in a practical configuration—is transformed into literary form—that is, a principle of construction of an imaginary world—is Roberto Schwarz' task in his seminal study of Machado de Assis' work.

Form, understood as a mediating principle that organizes in depth the elements of fiction and reality and that operates on both planes simultaneously, is the nexus between the novel and society. Therefore, even before it is captured by the novelist's intuition and objectified by him, form is a product of the social process. In agreement with Marxist theory—in particular with the brand of Marxism associated with the German tradition and the influence of Lukács—the notion of social form may be understood as the product of material constraints on the reproduction of society in different areas of social life. Hence the forms found in works "are the repetition or the transformation, as a variable result, of preexisting artistic or extra-artistic forms" ("Originalidade" 36) How profitably can the study of form be applied to literary studies?

Being "a practical schema, with its own logic, programmed in accordance with the historical conditions that it responds to and that simultaneously historicize it," form retains and reproduces in a certain way the contingent set of historical conditions under which it is born. These conditions, in turn, become "its literary effect, its reality effect, the world they signify," reappearing, "with the same logic, on the plane of fiction and as a formal result" ("Originalidade" 35; *Ao Vencedor* 38-39). As Schwarz emphasizes, "every form always articulates a heterogeneous compact of sociohistorical relations," and "makes historicity, to be deciphered by criticism, the very substance of the works" ("Originalidade" 36). In this sense, literary representation configures, in a dynamic way, the socioeconomic organization that is contemporary to it, taking society and the structural relations represented in it as an active inner element. Thus a literary work comes to be a privileged source of knowledge about the historical reality configured in it.

Formally, the aesthetic result of José de Alencar's work is a compound fracture. This is explained by the fact that the author addresses topics (for instance, "the power of money" in *Senhora*) whose symbolical force has to do with a "demythologized" and "mystified" society resulting from bourgeois rationality, to directly reflect a social universe organized by the logic of paternalistic relations. On the other hand, this fracture expresses, even if only involuntarily, the cultural and ideological discrepancy that characterizes Brazilian life.

While Alencar represents the "involuntary reflection" of a Brazilian cultural discrepancy, in Machado the "incongruence of ideas" is elevated to the category of "artistic truth"—that is, the discrepancy appears as the result of a "reflective elaboration" to the extent that it is formally assimilated. This process, tentatively achieved in *Iaiá Garcia*, is first accomplished with mastery in *Memórias Póstumas de Brás Cubas*, according to Roberto Schwarz' thesis in *Ao Vencedor as Batatas* and its companion volumes.

In his early novels, which reflect the subaltern status of those who are not sufficiently independent to criticize, Machado relegates to the background any references to the liberal ideals, to the new civilization centered on capital, to the libertarian ideologies of Romantic individualism; instead he focuses on the sphere of the family and paternalistic relations—present only secondarily in Alencar's novels—to whose authority all conflict submits. Social injustice is mentioned, but there is not even a hint of revolt about the underprivileged characters, who conform to the demands of the logic of favor. This solution gave the novels greater verisimilitude in terms of local themes, but also made them seem "stale," "stifling," "mawkish"; worse still, by severing all connections with the contemporary world, it had the effect of heightening Brazilian provincialism (*Ao Vencedor* 65-66). Machado overcomes this formal shortcoming, beginning with *Memórias Póstumas de Brás Cubas*, by having the narrator of the novel adopt, "in a poisoned way," the viewpoint of the ruling class. This device allows the author to take on European social assumptions and adapt them to Brazilian local conditions, thus transforming "the disproportion between bourgeois ideas and the swings of favor into a specific diction, a sardonic and familiar music" (*Ao Vencedor* 50). The formal adjustment obtained by extending the cultural maladjustment into the structure of the novel also pioneers a path that can be followed by the literature of a dependent country.

IV

In his essay "A Originalidade da Crítica de Antonio Candido," Roberto Schwarz emphasizes that formal study makes it possible "to speak of the work and reality, one in terms of the other" through the articulation of their structures. Hence the originality of the method and its evident relevance to literary discussions (45). Elsewhere, also referring to the method of analysis developed by his former teacher, Schwarz states that "for the first time the dialectics of literary form and social process was more than an empty word" (*Que Horas* 154). As Silviano Santiago has observed, the same could be said about Schwarz' studies of Machado de Assis (Santiago 219).

The critic's strategy is to seek the testimony of form and the logic that organize the novel, if he is to avoid the simplistic view of a literary work as a mere illustration of society, even when it adopts a critical tone. What makes Machado's fiction refreshingly new, Schwarz says, is the fact that it places the narrator in a social situation. That is: since the narrator is placed in a field of antagonisms, his logic requires the mediation of the social types that are complementary in relation to him and through which he is specified—for instance, "the poor young woman, the rich and elegant lady, the agregado."[7] Imitating Machado's own writing, Schwarz captures and describes, through the dialectical presentation of opposites, the relations in which Machado's narrators are involved. As one of Schwarz' commentators, Davi Arrigucci Jr., has observed, it is as if they were moral and social filigrees, unveiling, naming and formalizing aspects of Brazilian life as they are experienced and practiced, but never before named (78).

Notes

[1] Schwarz, *Ao Vencedor as Batatas* 21.

[2] In addition to José de Alencar's *Senhora* (1875), in this book Schwarz analyzes in detail three novels by Machado: *A Mão e a Luva* (1874), *Helena* (1876) and *Iaiá Garcia* (1878).

[3] English translation: *The Posthumous Memoirs of Bras Cubas*. Trans. Gregory Rabassa (Oxford: Oxford UP, 1997). (Translator's note)

[4] English translation: *Dom Casmurro*. Trans. Robert L. Scott-Buccleuch (New York: Viking, 1995). (Translator's note)

[5] English translation: *The Diary of "Helena Morley."* Trans. Elizabeth Bishop (New York: Farrar, 1957). (Translator's note)

[6] Schwarz' first book, *A Sereia e o Desconfiado: Ensaios Críticos*, was published in 1965. Luiz Costa Lima, an intellectual associated with the Rio de Janeiro group (though in fact he was educated in Recife) published *Por Que Literatura?* in 1966.

[7] The term *agregado* refers to a person who lives with a family without actually belonging to it, whose status is somewhat inferior to that of an actual member but higher than that of a servant, even if the *agregado* performs some sort of useful service for the family, such as odd jobs, babysitting, etc. (Translator's note)

Works Cited

Arrigucci Jr., Davi, et al. "Machado de Assis: Um Debate. Conversa com Roberto Schwarz." *Novos Estudos CEBRAP* 29 (March 1991): 59-84.

Candido, Antonio. "Dialética da Malandragem." *Memórias de um Sargento de Milícias* by Manuel Antônio de Almeida. Critical edition. Ed. Célia Lara. Rio de Janeiro: Livros Técnicos e Científicos, 1978. 317-342.

Machado de Assis. *Obra Completa*. Vol. I. 5th ed. Rio de Janeiro: Nova Aguilar, 1985.

Santiago, Silviano. *Nas Malhas da Letra: Ensaios*. São Paulo: Companhia das Letras, 1989.

Schwarz, Roberto. *Ao Vencedor as Batatas: Forma Literária e Processo Social nos Inícios do Romance Brasileiro*. São Paulo: Duas Cidades, 1977.

———. *Que Horas São? Ensaios*. São Paulo: Companhia das Letras, 1987.

———. *Um Mestre na Periferia do Capitalismo: Machado de Assis*. São Paulo: Duas Cidades, 1990.

———. "A Originalidade da Crítica de Antonio Candido." *Novos Estudos CEBRAP*, 32 (Mar 1992), 31-46.

———. *Duas Meninas*. São Paulo: Companhias das Letras, 1997.

Süssekind, Flora. *Papéis Colados: Ensaios*. Rio de Janeiro: Editora UFRJ, 1993.

Hybrid Criticism and Historical Form

Raúl Antelo
Translated by Nöel de Souza and
Mark Streeter

La déconstruction n'a jamais eu de sens et d'intérêt, à mes yeux du moins, que comme une radicalisation, c'est-à-dire aussi *dans la tradition* d'un certain marxisme, dans un certain *esprit de marxisme.*
Jacques Derrida, *Spectres de Marx*

"The national literary system appears to be a repository of forces in the process of breaking down" (Schwarz 58). This is Roberto Schwarz' paradigmatic diagnosis as set out in his most recent book assessing the current state of the crucial contribution by Antonio Candido to literary and cultural studies in Brazil, to the extent that this contribution may be perceived in the present. Describing the situation of a peripheral country in a runaway globalization process, Schwarz understands that the system, outlined by Candido as the outcome of a peculiar historical and cultural formation, is now beginning, or may shortly begin, to operate as the real, insofar as this is one of the spaces where it is possible to sense that which is in the process of crumbling. The brief description maintains something of the *Unheimlich* in its reference to the disintegrating and abject transformation of the system (not only an organization but also a hierarchy). In a nutshell, the critic tells us that the nation—this Brazil that the previous generation beheld in the process of forming and that today is sliding into abject abandon—is the real thing, that which cannot be symbolized, the opposite of desire or, as Lacan put it, "ce qui ne cesse pas de ne pas s'écrire" (*Séminaire* 20, *Scilicet* 17).

The real of the present situation (the impossibility of this very present, its unbearable presence but also its reprehensible presentation) introduces an unequivocal deformation and an unyielding distance vis-à-vis its own image. It is a point at which the framework of the present takes shape in the recesses of the very material content of representation. It thus spills over into a radical dissymmetry between glance and vision, that which transforms all communication—just as the one that is presupposed in the initial pages of the *Formação da Literatura Brasileira* by Antonio Candido—into a fruitful error. Consequently, the argument by Haroldo de Campos that censures Candido's debt to the Jakobsonian linguistic functions is limited (it would be more trustworthy, perhaps, to evoke Bühler's communicative triangulation), because, in addition to the functionalistic mark unequivocally present in the model of formation, the very idea of communication and the existence of a community is presented as something that, in order to be introduced, requires something "real." In other words, for this community to come into being and for intersubjective communication to work satisfactorily, a response of the real finally becomes imperative. We are, however, obviously aware of the non-existence of symbolic communication; that is, there is no community in formation without a correlative *Unheimlich* dimension of its own experience. It is this that ultimately defines the real.

It is not the observer then who sees the nation but it is it, the Thing, that sees us, just as Brazilian literature itself, at its heights of modernity, was able to make clear.[1] This concept of the real cannot, however, introduce elements that energize the apparently quite stereotyped debate about the idea of formation and its yield in the critical tradition that goes back to Antonio Candido. We should then recall that there exists, at least for Freud, two ways of rejecting the real. The first is based on sublimation or, as Mário de Andrade preferred to translate the Freudian term *Verdrängung*, "sequestration." There is however another way, deriving or stemming from refusal. That which is sequestered can return in the pre-conscience in a symbolized way, since that which is rejected can also return, nonetheless, in the shape of a new and delirious reality. Following this line of reasoning, we could then say that within Candido's idea of formation, the Baroque is, in fact, sequestered, as Haroldo de Campos desires, with the proviso, however, that it can come back and, in fact, does return, since Góngora is, in Roberto Schwarz' words, "an explicit presupposition of the *Formation*, where it forms a defining contrast with a neo-classical type of image" (Schwarz 51). This proves that we should correct the disjunctive presented by Schwarz—"the historical cycles either exist or they don't"—to the form of a historical trilemma: the historical cycles exist and do not exist because it is typical of the event (and the Baroque unquestionably comprises this peculiarity) to exasperate the ur-history and the post-history when confronted with the present. Or, in other words, in Benjamin's terms, it actually falls to the present to define where and how the ur-historical aspects (the ghastly colonial administration, for example) and the post-historical ones (the contemporary acephalicness) mutually diverge and intensify each other in order to better evaluate the event and to circumscribe its core (Benjamin 494).

Let us then once again look at the prospects outlined by Roberto Schwarz in exhaustively identifying the idea of formation in the face of the emergence of the real.

> One perspective is that it (the formation) is also an ideal that has lost its meaning, disqualified by the course of history. The nation is not going to be formed, it is going to fall apart, the 'advanced' sectors of the Brazilian society have already become part of the most modern dynamics of the international order and will let the rest go to pot. Finally, given that the nation will not join in, the very process of formation will have been a mirage, which for the sake of being realistic, might as well be abandoned. There is an enormous gap between what was promised and what was fulfilled.

> Another possible perspective: let us suppose that the economy ceased to push towards national integration and the formation of a relatively self-regulated and self-sufficient whole (actually, it is pushing in the opposite direction). If this were the nature of the pressure, then the only entity that continues to state that it is a whole, and that it needs to have a future, is the cultural unit that for better or for worse was formed historically, and which was completed in literature. Along these lines, the formed culture, which attained a certain degree of organicity, works as an antidote to the economy's tendency towards dissociation. Nevertheless, one will not fail to note the idealism behind this defensive position. Every person with some materialistic fiber in their being knows that the economy is in the driver's seat and that the cultural sphere only follows along. However, it must be acknowledged that our more or less accomplished cultural atmosphere is indeed an element of anti-barbarism, insofar as it is said that here it formed a whole, and that this whole exists and is part and parcel of all of us that are concerned with this issue, and also many others who are not concerned with it.

> Another hypothesis: divorced from a national economic project, which ceased to exist in the strong sense of the term, the very desire towards formation is emptied and loses any inner dynamic. However, it is not only because of this that it ceases to exist, as it is an element that can be used in the market of cultural differences,

and even in tourism. The national formation may have ceased to be a perspective of substantive accomplishment, based on a certain political and economic autonomy, but may not have ceased to exist as a historical feature and to be perhaps a commercial triumph all along, in the context of the international commercialization of culture. Finally, by being disconnected from the process of social and economic self-realization of the country, which included important tasks for the sake of humankind, such as historically surmounting colonial inequalities, formation does not cease to be merchandise. And it can, in the present moment, have a great future on that level. (57-58)

Having enumerated these hypothetical scenerios, Schwarz, as we can see, relegates to the background the aesthetic argument according to which the formative framework no longer makes any sense since literary models come from all times and places. Schwarz, however, argues that "if instead of the literary influences, which in fact are as if hand-picked, we think of the language we use, infused—on the verge of becoming pasteurized—with the social fabric of experience, we will see that the globalized mobility of the writer can be illusory. The new world order produces its own scissions and even qualifies the aspirations of intellectuals" (58). Now, it is Antonio Candido's own critical sensitivity, no less divided and qualified than our own, that problematizes this observation, which is accurate in general, but not in all aspects.

In his analysis of *O Cortiço*, which aims at isolating the point of view of the free Brazilian in the slavocratic order, i.e., in the national and autonomous focus that structures the work, Candido analyzes the subject of enunciation of a popular saying, seemingly secondary or subaltern: "para português, negro e burro, três pês: pão para comer, pano para vestir, pau para trabalhar" ("for the Portuguese, the black man and the ass, three f's: food to eat, fabric to dress, ferrule/stick to work"). The critic notices in this saying something real, i.e., its vacuous gratuity. It is built in the style of the peremptory judgments of the poetry of Gregório de Matos—such as "Neste mundo é mais rico o que mais rapa" ("In this world he who steals gets to be the richest") or "De dois ff se compõe / esta cidade a meu ver/ un furtar, outro foder" ("Of two f's is made up / this city in my view / one filching, the other fucking")—which can still be heard on the lips of a mulatto known as Macunaíma. He, in his turn, in an open parody of Gregório's fifth epigram, avers the evils of the colonial land, the ethical axiom predicated upon the line "pão-pano-pau" ("food-fabric-ferrule"), which exposes not only aspects of social life, but also pre-formed figurative representations of identity or of dominant values. It further exposes the very structure of the literary series, its energy released with the intention of formation, and, in the final analysis, confronts us with the relevance that, in its Baroque poetic style and in its modernist repetition, the paronomasia maintains. The attentiveness of Antonio Candido—according to which the paronomastic series goes beyond the form, and that its truth lies in the density of an ideological form—cannot be justified within a formalist theory alien to the critic's own sensitivity. It is in fact he himself who points to the substitution of the metaphor by the paronomasia as one of the defining lines of modern literature. He explains:

> We had a literature predominated by image, by analogy—'you are as beautiful as a rose'—and now we have a literature dominated more and more by paronomasia, that is to say, by that figure of speech that brings together words sounding similar but of a different meaning. (Candido 184)

Against the approach based on analogy and reference presupposed by metaphor the critic observes the allegorical dominance of the simulacrum and the ready-made, in which "the discourse takes the world as an arsenal of comparisons… creating a parallel world, an autonomous world, which is a type of duplication of the natural world." (Candido 187)

Thanks to this device as well as to his critical acuity, Candido proposes a reciprocal determination or a specific overdetermination between the social and the aesthetic in which none of the levels obscures or diminishes the other. Rather, on the contrary, they mutually determine and reciprocally energize each other. Furthermore, we could derive from the notion of paronomasia, in the wake of Michel Serres' well-known *Le Parasite*, a deconstructive theory of self-sufficiency in the parasite's economy.

Parodistic, parasitic, paronomastic, there's nothing irrelevant in these symptoms. After all, for instance, Paul Valéry would use this paronomastic movement as the definition of the poetic, ever oscillating between *son* and *sens*. It may further be observed that to formulate it the poet was forced to give up precisely the very resource he wanted to define, making this tautological theory the fictional meeting place of the subject of what was uttered with that of the utterance itself.

Nevertheless, not even Valéry's definition authorizes overlooking this autonomous way of forming statements. On the contrary, the oscillation between *sens* and *son* resonates beyond the metaphor/metonym tension in other critical binomials that are equally enlightening: representation/stereoscopy; identity/becoming; formation/dissemination; *beginnings* (Edward Said) / *becomings* (Andrew Benjamin). In the final analysis, we may say that while metaphor rallies behind the limits, the teleological marks that guide the entire formation—paronomasia—signals the threshold that, being always the penultimate, does not cease to re-open the signifying chain. And in so doing, it persuades us that every completion comes from the order of the imaginary.

The center of this debate revolves, as you can see, around the concept of *formation*. In order to better assess this, Roberto Schwarz attempts to formulate an archaeology of the concept, recalling that, upon being published, Candido's book joined with other works that also used the concept of formation.

> In the progressive field, the most important related works known are those by Caio Prado Jr., Sérgio Buarque de Holanda and Celso Furtado. A comparative study of these works is still in its infancy, awaiting works of synthesis. I'd like to suggest very briefly some differences between them. For Caio Prado Jr., the Brazilian formation would be completed at the moment in which our heritage of social inorganicity was overcome—the opposite of interconnecting with internal goals brought from the Colony. This high moment would be, or was, in the future. If we look at Sérgio Buarque de Holanda, we find something similar. The country will be modern and will be formed when it overcomes its Portuguese, rural and authoritarian heritage, and we would then have a democratic country. Here again the point of arrival is farther forward, dependent upon the decisions of the present. Celso Furtado, for that matter, will say that the nation is not complete while the tools of command, mainly the economic ones, are not in the country. That is to say, while the basic decisions that concern us are made abroad, the nation continues to be incomplete. Just as with the other two, the conclusion of the process lies in the future, which seemed close to the author's generation, and now seems remote, as suggested by the title of one of his latest books: *Brasil: A Construção Interrompida* (1992). (Schwarz 54-55)

Candido's concept of formation, far from adhering to a linear and prospective sense or to an unequivocal inscription like the other works mentioned by Schwarz, is equipped with the benefit of hindsight, in relation to an apex located in the past, around 1870, prior to the abolition of slavery.

Such a development results in a structural ambiguity in the system, or rather, in an ambivalent evaluation of the very process of Brazilian modernization that simultaneously exists and does not. It has a defined profile and a ghostly consistency. It so happens that if we accept Candido's lacunal premise—that all evaluation, besides being fragmentary, is radically ambivalent—we are compelled to suspend until further notice our unflinching trust in the existence of a "progressive field." It becomes necessary, therefore, to re-equip the genealogy of the concept with a much more wide-ranging and broader vision. After all, it is not the glance that constitutes the object; rather, on the contrary, it is the vision that overdetermines the subject.

I thus find in Silviano Santiago the matrix of the counter-modernist genealogy that can snatch us from the illusions of completion. In "Atração do Mundo (Políticas de Identidade e de Globalização na Moderna Cultura Brasileira)," Santiago undertakes a re-reading of the concept of formation. But surprisingly enough, it is not based on the essays of national interpretation, which attempt to return structural homogeneity and systematic balance to national formations hit by the crisis of capitalism. On the contrary, it is a fragment of *Minha Formação*, a hybrid, memorialistic and speculative text by Joaquim Nabuco that traces the indispensable scene for the constellation he proposes. This constellation is the critic's attitude as the observer of a performance (the theatrical metaphor soon becomes necessary) and the globalizing mediation of technology, when applied to actions restricted to the local level (the telegraph for Nabuco, computer networks for us).

This analysis of the constellations of the concept of formation and its very cultural spectrality give rise then to an enlightening reading, which may not be materialistic, and yet is not dualistic.

The models of analysis, inspired respectively by the 1920s and 1930s, have a clear universalistic posture in common, [concludes Santiago], but they do distance themselves from one another just as they lay the foundations for one another as disciplines (culture *versus* economy, and vice versa) and in the way they conceive of the historical process (pluralism *versus* one-way, and vice versa). It is through these differences that there is a distinction both in the weight given to the national thing [and perhaps it would be timely to say to the national Thing], and in terms of how to assess it as part of the quest for *moral* progress for Brazilians; the differences are still distinguished in the concept of the socio-political development of humankind.[2] (Santiago, "Atração" 50)

Silviano Santiago's reading explicitly refers to the unilaterality and narrowness of rationalistic and universalistic positions that, according to their urban and cosmopolitan character, repress that which goes back to the amorphous condition of human drives. Implicitly, however, in his recourse to Nabuco's formation (an author admittedly admired by Fernando Henrique Cardoso), Santiago reveals that the hypermoral character of this dominant liberalism paradoxically nurtures the simplistic, acritical and regressive irrationalism of an irreversible globalization. Santiago, however, seems to recycle his own concept of the "in-between-place" ("*o entre--lugar*"), and position himself *between* the sterility of criticism and the return of nationalism, *between* theory and fiction, in other words, *between* Enlightenment and narrative.

This between should not be seen as ethical abstraction or abstinence, but rather as a specific genre of theoretical fiction: that which is common to the two.[3] To affirm and to deny, to appreciate and to depreciate thus create a surpassing of the formative model of structural tensions; they move in the direction of an active becoming, that of transgression and of reactive forces, and in the direction of a reactive becoming, that of the will to nothing and of the active forces.

We can thus return to Roberto Schwarz' initial diagnosis, where he lamented the diminishment of the civilizing effort of Antonio Candido's formation, reduced, in the present, to "a repository of forces in the process of breaking down." Now, in my view, it is in that in-between-place of contradictory forces, of integration and resistance, that the dynamic and fictional ambivalence of the work of the hybrid lies. This being the case, in his criticism of the Romanesque model of formation, it is not at all surprising that Santiago should return to the disseminating proliferation of his *Em Liberdade* (a counter-formative fiction of the modern). Santiago's in-between-place is therefore defined according to a twofold assessment, in history and without, in name (*onomastic*) and beyond it (*paronomastic*), affirmative in its becoming-active and, at the same time, nihilistic in its becoming-reactive. This in-between-place symptomatically is similar to the position taken recently by Derrida: that of being a Marrano, like Spinoza and like Marx as well, "a sort of clandestine immigrant, the Hispano-Portuguese disguised as a German Jew who, we will assume, pretended to have converted to Protestantism." As a supreme paradox of this paronomastic fantasy (Marx-Marrano-Evil), the Marrano's condition of being out of place does not simply end there, but would be applied to his descendants as well, Marx's children, those who "had forgotten the fact that they were Marranos, repressed it, denied it, disavowed it. It is well known that this sometimes happens to 'real' Marranos as well, to those who, despite really, presently, currently, effectively, *ontologically* being Marranos, no longer even know it themselves" (Derrida, *Spectres de Marx* 261-2).

Notes

[1] I am thinking of the aphorisms of *O Discípulo de Emaús* (1945) by Murilo Mendes, which problematized the active character of reading and the original dimension of the parasite, as well as Clarice Lispector's fictions, notably, *Água Viva* (1973).

[2] The world concept (still impregnated with post-utopian connotations when not with Resnais' and Borges' acephalic bio-politics) appears in another essay in which Silviano Santiago asks himself questions about the consistency of the narrative experience and opposes the narrator of Machado de Assis, a contemporary of Nabuco, with the post-modern narrator. See "Toda a Memória do Mundo."

[3] In *L'Autre Cap*, Jacques Derrida insists on this preliminary position of a law that incessantly unfolds itself. Refuting the perennial universalistic ambition of French culture, he feels compelled

> (...) de rappeler ce qui s'est promis sous le nom de l'Europe, de réidentifier l'Europe, c'est un devoir qui dicte aussi d'ouvrir l'Europe, depuis le cap qui se divise parce qu'il est aussi un rivage: l'ouvrir sur ce qui n'est pas, n'a jamais été et ne sera jamais l'Europe. Le *même devoir* dicte non seulement d'accueillir l'étranger pour l'intégrer, mais aussi pour reconnaître et accepter son altérité. Le *même devoir* dicte de critiquer un dogmatisme totalitaire qui, sous prétexte de mettre fin au capital, a détruit la démocratie et 1'héritage européen, mais, aussi de critiquer une religion du capital qui installe son dogmatisme sous de nouveaux visages que nous devons apprendre à identifier. Le *même devoir* dicte d'assumer l'héritage européen d'une idée de la démocratie, mais aussi de reconnaître que celle-ci n'est jamais donnée; ce n'est même pas une idée régulatrice au sens kantien, plutôt quelque chose qui reste à penser et à venir: non pas qui arrivera demain, mais qui a la structure de la promesse et donc porte l'avenir ici maintenant. Le *même devoir* dicte de respecter la différence, l'idiome, la minorité, la singularité, mais aussi l'universalité du droit formel, le désir de traduction, l'accord et 1'univocité, la loi de la majorité, l'opposition au racisme, au nationalisme, à la xénophobie. Le *même devoir* commande de tolérer et de respecter tout ce qui ne se place pas sous 1'autorité de la raison.
>
> Il peut s'agir de la foi, des différentes formes de foi. Il peut s'agir aussi de questions ou d'affirmations qui, pour penser l'histoire de la raison, excèdent son ordre, sans devenir pour autant irrationnelles, encore moins irrationalistes; elles peuvent même rester assez fidèles à l'idéal des Lumières, 1'*Aufklärung* ou de l'*Illuminismo*, tout en reconnaissant ses limites, pour travailler aux Lumières d'aujourd'hui. Ce *même devoir* appelle certes la responsabilité de penser, de parler et d'agir conformément à un impératif qui paraît contradictoire.

For Derrida, in short, to take a concept seriously is to take it in inverted commas, in its paronomastic dissemination, which occurs recurrently as le *même devoir*. See *L'Autre Cap*.

Works Cited

Benjamin, Walter. *Paris Capitale du XIX Siècle: Le Livre des Passages.* Trans. Jean Lacoste. Paris: Cerf, 1993.

Candido, Antonio. "Intervenção no Ciclo de Debates do Teatro Casa Grande." Rio de Janeiro: Inúbia, 1976.

Derrida, Jacques. *L'Autre Cap; Suivi de la Democratie Ajourneé.* Paris: Editions de Minuit, 1991.

———. *The Other Heading: Reflections on Today's Europe.* Trans. Pascale-Anne Brault and Michael B. Naas; Afterword Michael B. Naas. Bloomington: Indiana University Press, 1992.

———. *Spectres de Marx: L'Etat de la Dette, le Travail du Deuil et la Nouvelle Internationale.* Paris: Galilee, 1993.

———. *Specters of Marx: The State of the Debt, the Work of Mourning, and the New International.* Trans. Peggy Kamuf; Afterword Bernd Magnus and Stephen Cullenberg. New York: Routledge, 1994.

———. "Marx and Sons." *Ghostly Demarcations: The Symposium on Jacques Derrida's Spectres de Marx.* Ed. Michael Sprinker. London: Verso, 1999.

Lacan, Jacques. *Séminaire.* Paris: Seuil, 1975.

———. *Scilicet.* Paris: Seuil.

Santiago, Silviano. "Atração do Mundo. Políticas de Identidade e de Globalização na Moderna Cultura Brasileira." *Gragoatá* 1 (1996): 31-54.

———. "Toda a Memória do Mundo." *Folha de São Paulo,* 13 Aug. 1988.

Schwarz, Roberto. "Os Sete Fôlegos de um Livro." *Sequências Brasileiras. Ensaios.* São Paulo: Companhia das Letras, 1999. 46-58.

The Itinerary of a Problem: Luiz Costa Lima and the "Control of the Imaginary"

Sérgio Alcides
Translated by Nöel de Souza
and Mark Streeter

Only recently have Brazilian scholars begun to acknowledge the efforts of Luiz Costa Lima in proposing a new way of thinking about the relationship between reason and imagination, which Costa Lima based on his analysis of the concept of mimesis. Sixteen years have already passed since the publication of *O Controle do Imaginário* (*Control of the Imaginary*), the first volume of the trilogy completed by *Sociedade e Discurso Ficcional* and *O Fingidor e o Censor*. The initial volume was re-edited in 1989 and other books have followed without any significant reaction in Brazilian departments of Literature, let alone in those of History, with the exception of the universitary circles in Rio de Janeiro with which the author is immediately connected. It is an interesting case in which the written word fails to broaden the reach that the spoken word has already established in face-to-face communication, in the classroom, in colloquia or in conversation.

This late and certainly embarrassed reception contrasts with the readiness with which those works were welcomed at leading centers in Europe and the United States. The American translation of the first volume appeared in 1988, just four years after the publication of the original. In 1990 the German version was released. Two years later the remaining books of the trilogy appeared in English in a single volume.[1] A casual reader might suppose that the publication of those books in languages more accessible to foreign scholars than Portuguese would reflect the growing international interest in so-called "emerging literatures" or in post-colonial studies. That impression, however, quickly fades when one considers the books' tables of contents, where themes of much older academic substance prevail, in particular those linked to European literature and the history of ideas. In fact, the trilogy of the *Control of the Imaginary* has been read and discussed as a set of theoretical and epistemological inquiries pertinent to Western culture, in the broadest possible sense.

The insight that drove the entire series is relatively simple. It is the assumption that modern reason, as it developed from the Italian Renaissance on, found in the imagination a potentially disruptive faculty that should be kept under constant suspicion and control, framed within specific spaces and social activities and according to very strict criteria. Literature would thus be an object of that control, especially in regard to the status and the autonomy granted to fiction, hierarchically dependent on a principle of reality conceived as a given essence, always identical to itself, immutable and exterior to its eventual observers' subjectivities.

This assumption already demonstrates that the author is working within theoretical perspectives that have increasingly challenged the meta-historical concept of literature since the late 1960s. According to the traditional point of view, literature was to be "a type of product that man (at least in the West) would naturally secrete" ("Pós-escrito" 271). Nevertheless, the problematization of the control of the imaginary enables us to grasp the historical construction of the dominant concept of literature that came into effect in the transition from the eighteenth to the nineteenth century. At the same time, we see how its three main institutional supports, regarded as "natural" and prior to history itself, were built: the nation with its specificities, the self-centered individual and the privilege given to "fact" as undeniable truth. The ensuing "secretion" would be the literary work, requiring an interpretation always marked by these three essential referents.

The three books that make up the series examine this assumption from different angles, without following any chronological or thematic order. The trilogy was "imposed" upon the author: "When I began to put together *Control of the Imaginary*, I didn't foresee the volumes that followed," he wrote in the postscript to the second edition of the initial volume (266). Seen as a whole, the books give the impression of a work in progress, in the process of being perfected, moving back and forth, as though stemming from a thought that wants to scrutinize itself endlessly. The chapters follow in a seemingly disorderly fashion, skipping from the Renaissance to German Romanticism, to the clever gimmicks of Machado de Assis, to digressions on the discourse of History, to Enlightenment fiction, to the occupation of the New World, to culture and society in the Old Regime, to the reception of the work of Jorge Luis Borges and so on. The only thread is the initial assumption that unfolds in a series of pictures in the gallery of the *Control of the Imaginary*. With the conclusion of the third volume the author realized that the materials of the chapters seemed to be dispersed, so much so that in the postscript he presented "a kind of map" which could serve as a guide for the exposition, splitting his work into three subsets or three general approaches to the same collection. Each one of these is composed of chapters spread across the three volumes of the series.

Costa Lima begins with an analysis of Renaissance theoretical texts on poetry and their attempt to tame the wildness of poetical imagination by establishing the primacy of truth over verisimilitude. As Costa Lima points out, the concept of verisimilitude was then deprived of the Aristotelian notion of *enérgeia*, originally directed not at what is already existent but at what is possible at large. A parallel consideration of French classicism enabled the author to identify an initially religious justification to the control of the imaginary, which would thus help strengthen the bases of legitimacy of the Old Regime and its colonial presence in the Americas. These themes constitute the first subset of the collection.

The second subset already refers to another type of control, that of the Enlightenment, which replaced religion with science as the controlling principle of the productions of human imagination. In this context, Costa Lima tackles the resistance of German romanticism to restrictions raised by the controlling reason. This theme was to become one of the areas of the author's mastery, in subsequent books such as *Limites da voz* (*The Limits of the Voice*) and *Vida e Mímesis*. Finally, the "map" indicates a third "subset": the trilogy questions the situation of the control of the imaginary in contemporary times. In this it confronts a possible reversal, in which the systematic criticism of the idea of truth threatens to turn fiction from a controlled product into a controlling factor.

The "map," drawn *a posteriori*, reveals, however, the internal coherence of the various threads. These were begun more from the need to increase and expand rather than through prior planning. It was not for want of competent architecture, but rather due to the very fecundity of the assumption proposed, which slowly revealed to the author its great capacity and versatility. In a statement so simple that it can be reduced to eight words— the control of the imaginary by modern reason—Luiz Costa Lima was able to discover much more than an empirical opening for his reflections on *mimesis* in modernity. His reflections lay the foundation for an entire theory of culture, far broader than the one encompassing the phenomena that can be historically demarcated as literary. One gets the impression that the succession of the "pictures" in the trilogy could be indefinitely extended and could apply to other areas that are subject to the incidence of the imaginary as well, such as the culture industry, behavior, politics and even ethics. It is up to other scholars to accept such a challenge, necessarily within an interdisciplinary context.

The trigger to the insight into control, however, was activated by a range of material that initially seemed connected to literature, especially in terms of the concern to better define the status of fiction—that is to say, of the product of an activity far too human, viz., *mimesis*. The whole reflection of *Control of the Imaginary* would be impossible without Luiz Costa Lima having first worked out a brilliant deconstruction, in its broadest sense, of a tradition that linked the concepts of *mimesis* and *imitatio*. It was in *Mímesis e Modernidade* (1980) that the author separated those terms by demonstrating that mimesis cannot be taken as a representation by reflection or imitation of an already given real; on the contrary, its specificity is the production of difference. In other words, the mimetic activity does not reproduce what is similar, but rather engenders something different from it.

That argument, here roughly summarized, was the first result of Luiz Costa Lima's contact with the theoretical perspectives of the aesthetics of reception begun by Hans Robert Jauss in Germany in 1967. The Brazilian scholar made his first contacts with that current in the mid-1970s, at a time when he might have already reached the limits of the structuralist approach he had until then adopted. The focus on reception produced a reversal in the literary field by introducing the role of the reader, as an agent who creates meaning, as central. Any fictional product is aesthetically fulfilled only according to the references of experience and expectation that historically demarcate the social activity of reading. Fiction, therefore, arouses the imagination of the recipient. Thus, the actual result of *mimesis* is variable in time and in space. For someone who had reached a dead end in his long reflection on the operation of *mimesis*, this was a promising opportunity for approaching it no longer from its point of departure, but rather from its arrival as a process in the reader. It is only then possible to catch a glimpse of what *mimesis* produces in its reception: not likeness, but otherness, that which is not represented in the thing itself, but instead what the reader calls for from literature.

This formulation—*mimesis* as the production of difference—was just a step towards the insight into reason's control. In modern times, a series of historical shifts has broken open the security of the Christian cosmology that for centuries had been underpinned by medieval order. A new rationality then began to become obvious, with the tacit acknowledgment of the inadequacy of the revelation. It was now necessary to reconcile the assumption of a univocal real with the new human responsibility of describing it, interpreting it and, finally, inhabiting it. For that reason, if the product of *mimesis* is difference, then this is where its danger lies. It was, therefore, a matter of establishing a control that could inscribe this activity in specific areas of social experience and thus limit its impact on the very univocality presupposed in the real. As a result of that imperative came the slow process of the historical construction of what at the beginning of the nineteenth century already was seen as a meta-historical human property: literature, as the concept has been understood since.

The first chapter of *Control of the Imaginary* seeks to reconstruct "the itinerary of a problem," incorporating the major contributions of historians, critics and theoreticians of literature, who are all concerned with the fictional, such as Paul Zumthor, Howard Bloch, Jacqueline Cerquiglini, and Hans Ulrich Gumbrecht among others. In this manner, Costa Lima takes a dynamic approach to the crucial moments in the trajectory of control in modern times, that is, from the poetics of the Renaissance to the outbreak of early Romanticism and its subsequent decline. As the author points out in his beautiful "Sketch of an Intellectual Autobiography," if the *mimesis*-difference was the outcome of an abstract, theoretical reflection, now "the observation of control was being performed at the empirical level" ("Esboço" 48). It is through this intimate contact with the empirical that something is constructed that otherwise would be difficult to consolidate through speculation alone, namely, the connection of control to the emergence of an individual subjectivity dependent on the primacy of a substantially conceived Truth. The latter, in turn, encouraged special attention to another "indivisible" being (here, analogous to the "individual"): the *fact*, from which the truth draws its legitimacy and becomes generalized by means of law.

Another important connection concerns the political circumstances that have presided over this *démarche*. The metahistorical concept of literature is formed in conjunction with the processes of the individual's becoming autonomous as intention and will, of the institutionalization of fact as a unit of truth and of the construction of politically sovereign national identities within the borders of the nation-state. This explains the importance taken in Costa Lima's subsequent work by the formation of the discourse of History as a true narration of related facts and, therefore, as a counterpoint to the discourse of fiction. By being situated in the sights of the control of the imaginary, the author could echo in our times the distrust expressed by Nietzsche in his second "untimely meditation" against the "admiration of the event" and of the "idolatry of the factual," which for the German philosopher tended to foster acquiescence to any kind of power, be it of the government, of public opinion or of the numerical majority (Nietzsche 147).

These are the beacons that guided the opening of the arguments of Costa Lima's trilogy. As the work progressed, they became clear in terms of the initial hypothesis. What in the first volume was described as the "itinerary of a problem" can at the end of the third be characterized only as a question that has many pathways—so many in fact that the author himself is forced to admit his inability to travel them alone. Since the second edition of *Control of the Imaginary* (1989), Costa Lima, when referring to his work, mentions with a certain melancholy his feeling of impotence in the face of the vastness of the continent where he himself "moored his ship." For example, in his postscript: "The price paid for trusting the hypothesis of control was the outrageous certainty that, no matter how much I tried, I would never get even close to exhausting the theme. The possible joy of having found a new and viable pathway turned into the sensation of an inescapable failure" ("Pós-escrito" 268). He made it clear shortly afterwards that this failure should not be mistaken as a fault, since he recognized the value of its contribution.

The same complaint reappears in a memorial text written six years later, accompanied by the same proviso. This time, however, a new element surfaces:

> Failure meant the recognition of one's limits in the face of the magnitude involved in the idea of control. That recognition would have had other dimensions had the author belonged to a firmly established culture, but since he did not belong to a metropolitan culture, he lacked efficient exchange, and was hampered by the suspicion of peripheral scholars of their own ability to say anything new, as well as by an intellectual pettiness for which anything goes. All this lent a melancholic overtone to the recognition of failure. ("Esboço" 50-1)

The contrast between "metropolitan culture" and the "periphery" brings out the irony of the paradox mentioned at the outset and which marked the reception given to Costa Lima's trilogy. The "place" of its construction can be best understood only by other agents, who also bring to bear their own seal of place. For the latter, however, examining and scrutinizing the familiar terrain seems more risky than continuing to contemplate the firmament from afar.

As for that paradox, Costa Lima's work can be tested with some of his own tools. To begin with a relatively simple statement, it may be said that to glimpse the control of the imaginary is already the beginning of escape. As a theoretician and historian of literature, the author allows his own activity to be subject to a curious analogy with the vitality of the *mimesis*-difference and its transforming potential. Like *mimesis*, the trilogy of the control of the imaginary also manifests the place where one produces and thinks about culture. Thus, Costa Lima's previous essay on the *antiphysis* in Jorge Luis Borges is also useful for the critic himself. To understand fully *Control of the Imaginary*, it is necessary to question the role that the place of South America played in fashioning the singularity of such a work. While this task does not fit within the limited scope of a summary such as this, several points can be outlined.

The importance of the "place" did not escape the shrewdness of Hans Ulrich Gumbrecht in his afterword to the second edition of *Control*, in which the German theoretician and historian describes this "twofold perspective." "Luiz Costa Lima locates the origin of this thinking from both a Latin American and a Western point of view, or given a more political emphasis, from both a post-colonial dependent and a hegemonic point of view" ("Posfácio" 265). The term "place" does not refer to a fixed reality, fully independent of who and what in fact occupies it, nor can it be thought of as a source of immanence that projects its reflections on everything that is a local product. Only by avoiding a theory of reflection can we realize that the mechanism of the control of the imaginary could not have been uncovered so accurately by any intellectual belonging to a "metropolitan culture," since in his milieu the mechanism operates with an efficiency that resists such uncovering. Furthermore, in the peripheral "place," the precarious operation of the mechanism of control does not allow the periphery a perfect identification with the metropolis as a model. Therefore, the leaks in the mechanism of control are all the more evident. On one side of the coin, it is melancholy, on the other, an opportunity for escape: only those who live far from fashionable areas know the city well.

The coordinates of *Control of the Imaginary* would not be complete without also taking into consideration, besides the peripheral "place," the occurrence of this line of thinking at a particular "time" that can also be characterized as at the periphery of Western modernity, where it encounters the prefix "post." Perhaps it is this common point between the First and Third worlds that makes Costa Lima's work intelligible as much in Bochum as in Berlin, Minneapolis and Stanford. It is no accident then that the equation literature/individual/nation/fact should receive its formulation more clearly at the very instant in which those four terms find themselves so profoundly destabilized. The "humanist illusion" of their metahistoricity, we may agree, no longer deceives any who are at least minimally informed and still attentive.

Thus, it was exactly from an unfavorable "place" that one could open a breach in the same scene that from a theater box would appear to be nature itself on display. The initial disadvantage remains, however, even though the original observer has taken advantage of it. One way or the other, the melancholy of failure does indeed occur. If I am not mistaken, this is the deadlock described by Costa Lima himself in a recent and still scarcely discussed text, "O Pai e o *Trickster.* Indivíduo e Cultura nos Campos Metropolitano e Marginal." There the author seems to reflect in a veiled fashion on the sensation about which he himself complained in the postscript to *Controle* in 1989 and in the "Sketch of an Intellectual Autobiography" in 1994. To an intellectual belonging to a metropolitan culture, defined here in terms of stability, there are not many opportunities for a glimpse that would reach all the way to the very foundations that underpin his world. He is confined to exploring the themes already delineated within pre-existing limits. The system itself protects him from the shadow of a melancholy caused by the failure of his professional efforts. Whereas for his foreign colleague, belonging to a marginal field defined by instability, mere exploration within limits is impossible, for that would be false, and at most would result in cheap imitation. The only alternative he is left with is the "explosion of limits," which can offer a stronger and more fecund insight, albeit at the terrible price of insecurity and discontinuity.

In the passage from the autobiographical "Sketch" mentioned above, Costa Lima said that the recognition of failure (though not of any fault) would have other dimensions if he "belonged to a firmly established culture." A few years later in "O Pai e o *Trickster*" he writes:

The stable agent can talk about a 'zero degree' because, unconsciously, he feels he is setting off from a firm place. The sensation mentioned does not spread to the creative agent of the unstable area. (...) *To explode the limits means not only the sensation of starting from a no man's land, but also achieving a limited conquest.* That characterization weighs upon a quite positive possibility: the freedom of movement rises with the fall in effectiveness. (270-1; author's emphasis)

Two mythical images are then associated with these distant colleagues. The "explorer within limits" (of the metropolitan field) is compared to the hieratic, opaque Father, full of authority and surrounded by the stability of the best of traditions. The "detonator of limits" is associated with the brilliant figure of the *trickster*, the man of the seven keys, who is not to be mistaken for a simple improviser since he has in fact become a master in the art of evading the law established by the other. "The *trickster...* is one whose success depends on the cunning of dodging the rules of a game that are stacked against him. For the *trickster*, the father is one whose power must be destroyed. His victory will be one of cunning over internalized law" (271). The success of the trick, however, is always doomed to the provisional: "the explosion of limits after all proves to be a victory of that particular situation alone" (273). The only other possibility lies in the chance that the field to which the *trickster* belongs finally attains some stability. According to Costa Lima, there is no escaping from one point: "The field we belong to marks us. It is our navel" (274).

And it is through that navel that we come back to *Control of the Imaginary.* In the first volume, the final chapter on Machado de Assis' fiction provides an interesting quotation from Freud's *Interpretation of Dreams*, in which the, let us say, Father of psychoanalysis mentions the portion of onirical material unable to contribute to the clarification of the meaning of a particular dream: "This is the dream's navel, the spot where it reaches down into the unknown [*Dies ist dann der Nabel des Traums, die Stelle, an der er dem Unerkannten aufsitzt*]" (Freud 530). Costa Lima then suggests a possible flaw in Freud's assumption: "... the navel can be seen as the limit point of a semantically motivated interpretation. The navel would, then, set the scene for the imaginary, i. e., for that which has no redeemable semantic basis of its own" (246, note 1). The imaginary is the unknown upon which the dream rests. As a troubling presence, the imaginary does not allow the interpretation of meanings presumed as already given. It can only be attained through the reconstruction of its movements in its interactions with otherness. "In this sense," explains Costa Lima in his preface, "the analytic construction is also the construction of the analyst subject, yet a construction that sets off from a navel, which always remains the same" (8). It is around that mark, then, that a personal region can be demarcated, from which to trade with the world and the others, whether as a hieratic "explorer within limits" or a trickster "detonator of limits".

These contacts are indeed what move the imaginary and its transforming potential. I believe that this consideration can be added to the extra variable of a "peripheral time," so that, together, they put into perspective the fatalism that Costa Lima attributes to our insecure condition as intellectuals of the "marginal field," the navel upon which we rest and dream. How far today does the real stability of the opposite field go? On the other hand, if the navel is less a center than a frame to which we belong and which marks us definitively, this does not eliminate its analogy with the imaginary, not only in its lack of an interpretable matrix and semantic substance, but also as a signifier of singularity and difference in action.

Notes

[1] *Sociedade e Discurso Ficcional* and *O Fingidor e o Censor* were published in a single volume entitled *The Dark Side of Reason*. For a full bibliographical reference of the translation of Costa Lima's books, see "Works Cited" below.

Works Cited

Freud, Sigmund. *Die Traumdeutung.* 1900. *Gesammelte Werke.* Vols. 2/3. Frankfurt am Main: Fischer Verlag, 1975.

Gumbrecht, Hans Ulrich. "Posfácio. A Inquietude de Luiz Costa Lima." Luiz Costa Lima. *O Controle do Imaginário. Razão e Imaginação nos Tempos Modernos.* 1984. 2nd edition. Rio de Janeiro: Forense, 1989. 263-266.

Lima, Luiz Costa. "O Leitor Demanda (d)a Literatura." *A Literatura e o Leitor. Textos de Estética da Recepção.* Ed. Luiz Costa Lima. São Paulo: Paz e Terra, 1979. 9-39.

———. *Mímesis e Modernidade (Formas das Sombras).* Rio de Janeiro: Graal, 1980.

———. *O Controle do Imaginário. Razão e Imaginação nos Tempos Modernos.* 1984. 2nd edition. Rio de Janeiro: Forense, 1989.

———. *Control of the Imaginary: Reason and Imagination in Modern Times.* Trans. and Foreword Ronald Sousa; Afterword Jochen Schulte-Sasse. Minneapolis: U of Minnesota P, 1988.

———. *Die Kontrolle des Imaginären. Vernunft und Imagination in der Moderne.* Trans. Armin Biermann; Nachwort Karl Ludwig Pfeiffer. Frankfurt: Suhrkamp, 1990.

————. *Sociedade e Discurso Ficcional.* Rio de Janeiro: Guanabara, 1986.

————. *O Fingidor e o Censor. No Ancien Régime, no Iluminismo e Hoje.* Rio de Janeiro: Forense, 1988.

————. *The Dark Side of Reason: Fictionality and Power.* Trans. Paulo Henriques Britto; Afterword Hans Ulrich Gumbrecht. Stanford: Stanford UP, 1992.

————. "Pós-escrito à Segunda Edição." 1989. *O Controle do Imaginário.* 267-277.

————. *Limites da Voz (Montaigne, Schlegel, Kafka).* Rio de Janeiro: Rocco, 1993.

————. *The Limits of Voice: Montaigne, Schlegel, Kafka.* Trans. Paulo Henriques Britto. Stanford: Stanford UP, 1996.

————. "Esboço de uma Autobiografia Intelectual." 1994. *Vida e Mímesis.* Rio de Janeiro: 34, 1995. 15-57.

————. "O Pai e o *Trickster.* Indivíduo e Cultura nos Campos Metropolitano e Marginal." *Terra Ignota. A Construção de* Os Sertões. Rio de Janeiro: Civilização Brasileira, 1997. 239-274.

Nietzsche, Friedrich. "De l'Utilité et des Inconvénients de l'Histoire pour la Vie." 1874. *Considérations Inactuelles I et II.* Trans. Pierre Rusch. *Œuvres Complètes.* Vol. 2. Paris: Gallimard, 1990. 91-169.

SÉRGIO ALCIDES

Comparative Literature in Brazil in the 1990s

Eduardo Coutinho

There have been studies in Comparative Literature in Brazil since the mid-twentieth century, when even a handbook in the style of Van Tieghem or Guyard was published by Tasso da Silveira (1964). Comparativism also was already present in the critical and theoretical reflections upon literature since nineteenth-century Romanticism. Nevertheless, the discipline's boom has occurred only since the 1970s, thus coinciding with the transformation that the discipline has undergone internationally, following the long hegemony of the Formalist perspective. At this moment, in which the discipline evolved from a cohesive and unanimous discourse to one that is more pluralistic, decentered and historically defined, it flourished with great vigor in Brazil and came to hold a special position within the scope of the discourses on literature. Since then, comparativism has continued conquering more space in the Brazilian academic milieu and has yielded important fruit. However, before we discuss the role that Comparative Literature has been playing in this context, we will proceed to a few comments upon the transformations that the discipline has experienced on the international level.

Initially marked by a historicist perspective based on scientific-causalist principles stemming from the historical moment and context in which it was formed, and subsequently by a predominantly formalist outlook (which, however, coexisted with dissonant voices of significant relevance), Comparative Literature celebrated its first century of existence amid intense debate, albeit sustained by certain pillars of distinctly ethnocentric coloring. Among these pillars, which remained almost unshaken until the 1970s, it is impossible not to recognize a claim to universality for which the cosmopolitanism of comparative studies was often mistaken, and the apolitical discourse preached above all others by the so-called "American School," which dominated the field in the middle of the twentieth century.

Although these two types of discourse present superficial variations, they contain a strong common denominator—the hegemonic character of their construction—and it was upon this fundamental fact that a good deal of criticism toward traditional comparativism was based. In the name of a pseudo-democracy of letters, which proposed a general history of literature or a universal poetics aimed at developing a common instrument with which to approach the literary phenomenon regardless of specific circumstances, what comparativists (of predominantly Euro-North American origin) did was to extend to other literatures those parameters instituted from reflections on the European literary canon. The inevitable result of all this was the overestimation of a given system and the identification of this system—the European—as universal. Similarly, the idea that literature ought to be approached from an apolitical perspective, a notion we currently understand to be impossible, only served to camouflage the reaffirmation of one system's supremacy.

The challenge to this universalizing posture and the demythification of the proposal of apoliticization, which became a keynote of Comparative Literature during the 1970s, had different effects both on the hegemonic centers and on the focal points of comparative studies that might be considered peripheral. But a similar phenomenon could be verified in both contexts: the increasingly greater approximation of comparativism to issues of national and cultural identity. On the Western European/North American axis, the essential concerns were displaced onto ethnic or sexual minority groups, whose voices were heard with increasing strength, seeking public discussion for alternative forms of expression. Elsewhere in the world there were claims for a displacement of the gaze, so that one might focus upon literary questions from one's own *locus*. Preoccupation with literary historiography, theory and criticism remained relevant in both of the aforementioned contexts, but it came to be directly associated with everyday political praxis. Theoretical discussions about the search for universals ceased to have meaning and were replaced by localized questions that began to dominate the subject's agenda: problems such as the relationships between local and imported traditions, the political implications of cultural influence, and the need for a revision of both the literary canon and the criteria for periodization.

This decentering that took place within the scope of comparative studies, now much more attuned to contextualized issues, greatly expanded the international and interdisciplinary character of Comparative Literature, which came to embrace a complex network of cultural relationships. The literary work or series could no longer be approached from an exclusively aesthetic perspective; as cultural products, it was necessary to take into account their relationship with other fields of knowledge. Besides, elements which until then had functioned as safe references in comparative studies, such as the concepts of nation and language, had been dethroned, and the traditionally established dichotomy between National and Comparative Literature was seriously upset. The linear perspective of historicism gave way to a multiple, mobile vision, able to account for specific differences, and it became imperative that literary series or sets be seen from a plural perspective that would consider such aspects.

The shift of gaze that occurred at the core of comparativism, which resulted from an awareness of the ethnocentric character that had dominated it in its previous phases, bestowed new life upon the subject. The result was a great effervescence in precisely those places that were situated in the periphery and that had now become fundamental sites in the international debate. In these places, including Brazil, where there is no sense of incompatibility between National Literatures and Comparative Literature, the other, dominant Eurocentric model has been increasingly questioned, and traditional paradigms have given way to rich and flexible alternative constructions, whose main preoccupation resides in articulating the perception of local cultural products in relation to the products of other cultures, especially those with which the former had maintained ties of subordination. When critics such as Edward Said and Homi Bhabha challenge the systematic process of "inventing" other cultures, the repercussions are enormous and give rise to claims for the constitution of a literary history based on local tradition, the recovery of which became indispensable in places such as India, Africa and Latin America. The political element of comparativism is now not only consciously assumed, but even emphasized, and an imperative need arises for a review of the literary canon.

Central to Comparative Literature's current situation, the "question of the canon," as it has been designated, constitutes one of the most vital instances of the struggle against Eurocentrism currently being fought in the academic milieu. To discuss the canon amounts to little more than an attempt to curb a value system instituted by the ruling groups that have legitimized individual opinions with a globalizing discourse. Courses on the "great books," for example, so frequently offered in Comparative Literature, have almost always been restricted to the canon of Western tradition (in reality, to the tradition of a few powerful European countries that maintain cultural politics of a hegemonic stamp), and have always been based on premises that either completely ignore all production outside of a certain restricted geographical radius, or touch only tangentially upon such production by including a symbolic number of its manifestations as a sort of concession. Reactions to this stance have arisen in many forms depending upon their origins. In countries at the "center," it is obviously the so-called "minority groups" who once again ask the main questions while, in peripheral contexts, the question of the canon has become a constant one, sometimes situated on the front lines of the process of cultural decolonization.

Large, complex and varied, the question of the literary canon exceeds the objectives of the present paper, as it could not be treated with the necessary care. But it should be mentioned that the question extends from the exclusion of the vigorous literary production of minority groups in the hegemonic centers and the stifling of a significant literary tradition in recently colonized countries such as India, all the way to problems of the specificity or non-specificity of the literary element, standards for an aesthetic evaluation, and the establishment of frontiers between constructs such as National Literatures and Comparative Literature. With the deconstruction of the pillars upon which traditional literary studies once stood and the lack of definition that established itself between referential limits, the traditional canon or canons no longer possess a foundational base, thus affecting the entire structure of literary historiography, theory and criticism. How to construct canons, whether on a national or international level, that account for differences voiced by each group or nation, and how to attribute to these new constructs a sufficiently flexible character that would allow them constant reformulations, are questions being raised today about such rapidly shifting ground.

Comparativism would appear to leave such questions nearly always unanswered, especially after the development of so-called Postcolonial and Cultural Studies, which attacked the field's ethnocentrism with a vehemence hitherto unseen. Criticism of this element, expressed by means of a supposedly liberal discourse that at bottom concealed its authoritarian and totalizing content, had already started during the time of Wellek and Etiemble and, if we observe the spectrum of Comparative Literature, we shall see that during its evolution it always flourished with great variety. In most cases, however, this criticism manifested itself by means of a binary opposition, which paradoxically continued to hold the European element as its point of reference. Aware of the fact that it is no longer a question of a simple inversion of models nor of the substitution of what had been considered central by its peripheral antithesis, current comparativists who question the hegemony of the colonizing cultures abandon the dichotomistic paradigm and engage in an exploration of the multiple paths that have been opened up as a result of the contact between colonizer and colonized. Consequently, they see themselves before a hermetic, albeit useful, labyrinth generated by the de-hierarchization of those elements involved in the comparative process, and their greatest task lies precisely within this open construction, this voyage of discovery devoid of definite markers.

Profoundly marked by a process of colonization, which is still alive today from both a cultural and an economic standpoint, literary studies in Brazil were always undertaken following the European models, and a brief glance at questions such as the ones that have been considered here shall suffice as evidence of this. The practice of comparing authors, works or literary movements had long existed in the country, albeit from a traditional viewpoint, based on the French school's celebrated studies of sources and influences, which, beyond this, were carried out quite unilaterally. It consisted of a distinctly hierarchizing system, according to which a source or primary text, taken as a reference in the comparison, was wrapped in an aura of superiority, while the other term in the procedure, in its restricted condition as debtor, was regarded at an obvious disadvantage and relegated to secondary status. Since every time this method was employed in the study of Brazilian literature the source text was a European (or, more recently, North American) work, the situation of inequality resulting from the procedure immediately became explicit. The inevitable result was an accentuation of dependence and the incontestable ratification of the still dominant state of cultural colonialism.

This type of comparativism found in Brazil a soil that stimulated its flowering, having already been sown by powerful allies in the fields of history and literary theory, to wit: an alien and inadequate historiography, as well as a method that might be designated as the application of presumably universal theoretical models. In the first case, one needs only recall the issue of the establishment of literary periods, which was always based on movements or schools of European origins, and which regarded local manifestations as their extensions, reduced to a sort of pale reflection of foreign models. And in the second case, the dogmatic application, as much in criticism as in the teaching of literature, of postulates of European literary currents to any literary work, without taking into consideration the specificities that characterized it and the differences between its historical-cultural context and the one from which such postulates sprang. Such formulations, incidentally, had emerged for the most part from serious and profound reflections made in reference to the Western European literary corpus, yet in becoming generalized they worked to legitimize the identification, so dear to Europeans, of their culture with the universal.

Encouraged by Deconstruction, with its emphasis on the notion of difference and the re-evaluation of historical perspective, which once more called attention to the importance of context, this practice, which achieved its zenith during the golden years of French Structuralism, began to be questioned in Brazil at the end of the seventies. The questioning of such crystallized notions as authorship, copy, influence and originality undertaken by French post-structuralist philosophers had a useful effect on the Brazilian academic milieu, leading comparatists to restructure many of the concepts and categories that supported the discipline, including those of sources and influences. As a result, the second text in a comparison was now no longer merely the "debtor" but also the one responsible for revitalizing the first text. Rather than being unidirectional, the relationship between the two texts acquired a sense of reciprocity, consequently becoming richer and more dynamic. What soon prevailed in a comparativist reading was no longer the issue of similarity or continuity, always disadvantageous to the second text, but instead the element of differentiation that the second introduced in the intertextual dialogue established with the first.

Although the change in outlook that took place in the heart of comparativism originated once again in the European milieu, it came at exactly the right moment in studies of Comparative Literature in Brazil. What had once characterized itself as an imperfect copy of the model established by the culture of the "center" came to be regarded as a creative response, while the deviation from the norm became valued for the desecration that it performed upon the artistic object. What had been until that time indispensable criteria of originality and antecedence were overthrown and the value of the Brazilian contribution came to exist precisely in the manner by which it appropriated European literary forms, transforming and conferring new vigor upon them. The terms of the preceding hierarchic system were evidently merely inverted in the process, with the text of the dominant culture still ending up as the richer of the two.

The other tendency of contemporary thought that contributed to the questioning of a Eurocentric world vision—the revalorization of the historical perspective—also found fertile ground in the field of Brazilian literary studies. While Marxism and Historicism always had great prevalence, and issues such as economic dependence could always be found at the heart of any cultural or political debate, the idea that literary manifestations constitute networks of relations and may only be sufficiently understood if approached from a global perspective that accounts for these relationships both rekindled the flame of ancient disputes that had been dampened by the reign of Structuralism and opened up ample and fruitful possibilities for a new type of comparativism. Accordingly, it was not enough to insist upon the importance of Brazilian differences: it also became necessary to study the relationship between them and the system of which they are part—the literature of the country in its various registers—and investigate the meaning they acquire in the general panorama of the Western literary tradition.

It is by means of the study of the differences resulting from the process of appropriation of foreign forms and of their relationship to the Brazilian literary and cultural system as a whole that comparativism acquires meaning in Brazil, evolving from a mechanical and unilateral study of sources and influences to a discipline dedicated to the examination of literary phenomena and capable of unleashing a true dialogue between cultures. As Claudio Guillén once said, comparativism is "a resolutely historical discipline" (Guillén 27); since Brazilian literature, by virtue of the very historical circumstances that engendered it, carries the dialectic between the local and the universal as a sort of mark, it is in this plurality, in this non-disjunctive syntagm, that it should be understood. No doubt Brazilian literature is strongly influenced by European literatures and assimilates a series of aspects from them as well as from other literatures. But it substantially modifies these aspects at the moment of appropriation. This, for example, was what took place with Brazilian Modernism, which originated, on the one hand, from the transculturation of the many European avant-gardes and, on the other hand, from a critical rereading of the literary tradition of the country, especially of the historical period designated as Romantic.

In response to its own colonial condition, Brazil had already developed during this time a strong tradition based on the search for identity. However, as much in literature as in essay writing, comparativism in Brazil generally remained tied to the French model of sources and influences or the North American formalist perspective, both of which gave it a sterile quality and solidified its situation as dependent. However, with the changes made from the 1970s to the present date, it appears to have been reborn from the ashes, and is today one of the centers of greatest activity in Brazilian studies. Associating itself with the search for identity, no longer seen from an ontological perspective, but rather as a construction open to questioning and renewal, Comparative Literature in Brazil seems to have taken seriously the need to focus on literary production from its own perspective, and has been seeking true dialogue on an international level. Thus, questions such as those of the canon and literary history have acquired a new countenance and theoretical and critical models have been relativized, giving way to a more effective reflection.

All of these topics, which examine Brazilian differences, reveal the inadequacy of transferring paradigms from one culture into another. The very idea of a "national literature," conceived within the European academic environment and based on notions of unity and homogeneity, cannot be applied without problems to the hybrid reality of a country like Brazil. Any monolithic conception of Brazilian culture is currently being questioned and frequently substituted by alternative proposals that seek to account for its hybrid nature. Such proposals, diversified and subject to constant critical scrutiny, indicate the many directions being taken by comparativism in Brazil, in perfect consonance with the general tendencies observable in other regions that were also previously considered peripheral. Comparative Literature today, especially in these places, is a wide and mobile field, with countless possibilities for exploration. It has gone beyond the totalizing hopes of its earlier stages, and is on the rise as a transcultural dialogue based on the acceptance of differences.

Works Cited

Guillén, Claudio. *Lo Uno y lo Diverso: Introducción a la Literatura Comparada*. Barcelona: Ed. Crítica, 1985.

Silveira, Tasso da. *Literatura Comparada*. Rio de Janeiro: Edições GRD, 1964.

Audiovisual

The Role of Radio in Everyday Brazilian Society (1923—1960)

Lia Calabre
Translated by Shoshanna Lurie

As the lights dim on the twentieth century, we can conclude that this has been the revolutionary era in forms of long-distance communication. Many will say that it is a time of acceleration of technical discoveries in all sectors of human knowledge. They are, without a doubt, correct. However, without rapid means of communication, only small groups of people would have access to these discoveries. The immediacy of events is directly proportional to their distribution throughout the world.

The story of rapid communication originated with the emergence of radio broadcasting. In Brazil, the first radio station began activity in 1923. Over the course of its more than seventy-year history, Brazilian radio has played many roles, responded to various interests, and adapted to changing times. Today, Brazilian radio reaches more than 115 million listeners, in comparison with 85 million television spectators and no more than 8 million readers of newspapers and magazines. Regardless of its broad participation in the construction of a modern mass society in Brazil, radio has not been viewed as a promising field of study and its importance has largely been eclipsed by a more powerful competitor: television.

Television transmission in Brazil began in 1950, only reaching a significant number of televisions during the 1960s. In other words, between the 1920s and the 1960s radio was the principal vehicle of mass communication in Brazil. This article will analyze some of the primary aspects of Brazilian radio and its role during this period. Similar to the dynamic which established itself in the majority of Western countries, these years reflected profound changes in social, cultural, economic and political structures in Brazilian society. Radio at times played secondary and often fundamental roles in these transformations.

Radio made its first public and official appearance in Brazil in 1922 at the National Exposition prepared for the celebration of the Centennial of Brazilian Independence.[1] The President of the Republic, Epitácio Pessoa, gave a speech in one of the Fair's pavilions as part of the solemnity of the inauguration. After the presidential address, Carlos Gomes' opera, *The Guarany*, was broadcast directly from the Municipal Theater. The following year, the success of the first radio transmissions in the contemporary press resulted in the establishment of the first Brazilian radio broadcasting station, the "Radio Society of Rio de Janeiro."

Radio's growth during its first decade of existence in Brazil was slow. Brazilian law did not permit the transmission of commercials, which made the financial survival of the Radio Societies difficult. However, although the broadcasters were not producing commercial segments, their programs were sponsored by specific advertisers whose products were recommended to the audience throughout the program. During the early years, radio's reach was small, since the price of radio receivers was high, making them inaccessible to a large portion of the population.

By the beginning of the 1930s, the situation had changed and radio had become a more popular vehicle of communication. In São Paulo (which offered the country's highest salaries), a radio cost approximately one sixth of the average working family's monthly salary.[2] In March of 1932, in Decree #21,111, the government legalized and regulated the broadcasting of commercial advertising over radio, reiterating that it considered radio broadcasting to be a sector of national interest with educational purposes.[3]

In May of 1932, radio began to show signs of its potential for political mobilization. A movement to oust the current president, Getúlio Vargas, was initiated in São Paulo. São Paulo's radio stations, particularly "Record Radio," were transformed into powerful arms against the president. The armed rebellion known as the Constitutional Revolution, which demanded not only the removal of the president, but also the call for elections to form a Constitutional Assembly, began in July. The country was in need of a new constitution. Citizens of São Paulo were called to participate in the movement over the radio. When federal forces surrounded the city of São Paulo, only the radio stations could communicate events to other parts of the country. In October, the revolutionaries were defeated, but radio emerged reinvigorated. During the course of the conflict, radio stations were used as advanced combat posts. Some radio announcers, such as César Ladeira, became nationally known through their roles at the microphone during the revolt.

Over the course of the 1930s, radio became a promising advertising medium. The 1932 law offered solutions to the problem of radio station survival, and simultaneously guaranteed the State one hour per day of programming throughout the entire country for the transmission of the government's official program. The *Programa Nacional*, which was foreseen in the 1932 legislation, only reached its objectives in 1939 with the creation of the *Hora do Brasil*. Through this program, the government attempted to personalize the political relationship with each citizen[4] without being required to establish its own system of radio stations. To attract the listening audience, the Department of Press and Propaganda (*DIP*—Departamento de Imprensa e Propaganda) invited famous celebrities to appear on the program, which was composed of news stories of a general nature, entertainment and political news.

In 1936 the "National Radio of Rio de Janeiro" was founded, and this event was considered a historic development in the history of Brazilian radio. After its first four years, the National Radio grew enough to compete for first place in audience share.[5] In 1940, the group of companies to which the National Radio belonged was incorporated into the government patrimony and control of the station was assumed by the State. Unlike the treatment given to other state stations, the National Radio continued to be run like a private company, receiving financial support from resources accumulated through the sale of advertising time. Between 1940 and 1946 the National Radio became an audience champion as well as a collector of huge advertising investments. Similar to the case of the entrance of Coca-Cola into the Brazilian market, the company invested an amount significant enough to place *A Million Melodies*, a program created exclusively for launching a product, on the air.

During the 1940s, multinational companies gained an ally in their bid to enter the Brazilian market, similar to developments in other countries in the Americas. In 1941 the first radio soap opera, *Em Busca da Felicidade* (*In Search of Happiness*), premiered on National Radio. According to Brazilian sociologist Renato Ortiz, radio soap operas were used in some Latin American countries and in the United States as a strategy to increase sales of cleaning and personal hygiene products.[6] *Em Busca da Felicidade* was originally created by the Cuban Leandro Blanco, then adapted by Gilberto

Martins of "Standart Advertising Company." "Standart Advertising" not only sponsored the show, but also chose the morning time-slot for its premiere. The project seemed risky since the time chosen was one of low audience listening. However, the sponsor created a strategy to evaluate receptiveness to the new genre by offering a free gift to each listener who mailed in a Colgate toothpaste label. Over 48,000 labels were returned in the first month of the offer alone, demonstrating the commercial effectiveness of the new programming. As a result of the success of the genre, many more radio soap operas emerged throughout the entire day. The National Radio became a veritable fantasy factory; its soaps marked eras, forged habits and attitudes, raised debates, and were highly successful with the listening public.[7]

In 1942, the National Radio inaugurated the first short-wave station in the country, transmitting its programs throughout the entire country and making the station yet more attractive to sponsors. Technical quality and the hiring of highly qualified professionals guaranteed high audience rates and transformed the National Radio into a model to be emulated. Two sectors clinched the station's success throughout the country: the soap operas and music programs.

The so-called "golden age of Brazilian radio" spans the period between 1945 through the end of the 1950s. It is important to stress that the expression "golden" is related to a series of characteristics of the era and does not mean that radio during this period attracted more listeners than it does today. This would be statistically impossible because the current Brazilian population is numerically much larger and the number of radios produced continues to multiply rapidly (primarily through the phenomenon of portable personal-use radios). During the 1940s and 1950s, radio possessed a certain glamour and was considered a type of Brazilian Hollywood. Being an actor or singer on a large Rio or São Paulo station was enough for an artist to attain success throughout the entire country, to obtain prominence in the written press, and to frequent political circles (as an invited guest or even as a candidate for a political office). These artists' national tours were usually highly popular; their admirers in all parts of the country wanted to see and, perhaps, even touch their stars. This almost magical aura that surrounded the National Radio artists prompted many young people to dream of becoming a radio celebrity.[8]

With the end of the Second World War, consumer goods industries renewed their growth and some of the products already available in the United States and Europe since the beginning of the century began to arrive

LIA CALABRE

in Brazil. Between 1945 and 1950, a process of accelerated growth in the radio sector occurred. New stations emerged, equipment was perfected (sometimes by legal mandate), and the number of short-wave stations multiplied.

This new panorama, which took shape at the beginning of the 1950s, created a situation of favoritism to sponsors who already possessed a range of domestic activities. For a better conceptualization of the process, see the growth statistics of the Brazilian stations:

Founding Year	Number
1923 to 1930	013
1931 to 1940	056
1941 to 1950	223
1951 to 1956	180
Unspecified	009
Total	481

IBGE (Brazilian Geographical and Statistical Institute)—*Annual Statistical Publication*, 1958

The table indicates that radio stations multiplied rapidly between 1940 and 1950. For a better understanding of radio's reach throughout the Brazilian population, it is important to remember that at the end of the 1950s the country had a 53.16% illiteracy rate, and 61.98% of those who couldn't read were inhabitants of rural areas. In other words, radio was the source of information, modernization, and contact with the rest of society for more than half of the population.

The 1960 census provides more data regarding the primary characteristics of private households, revealing information on the supply of electricity and the ownership of home appliances such as radios, refrigerators and televisions.

	Total households		Urban households		Rural households	
	number	%	number	%	number	%
Totals	13,497,823		6,350,126		7,147,697	
Electricity	5,201,521	38.54	4,604,057	72.50	597,464	8.36
Radio	4,776,300	35.38	3,912,238	61.61	864,062	12.09
Refrigerator	1,570,924	11.09	1,479,299	15.82	91,625	1.29
Television	621,919	4.3	601,552	9.47	20,367	0.28

IBGE—Seventh General Census, 1960

The table points to a link between rates of electric service and the existence of radios in the households visited—38.54% of the total population with electricity and 35.38% of the population with radios. Only a small portion of the population had access to television sets—4.6% of the total—and of the rural households, virtually none had televisions. The correspondence between electrical rates and radios demonstrates that a process of popularization of radio had occurred, turning it into an almost obligatory presence in Brazilian homes, or a type of indispensable utensil. Radios of the 1940s and the 1950s were relatively large, especially if compared to current sizes, and needed electricity or generators in order to operate. Transistor radios only invaded the consumer market toward the end of the 1960s. The mere physical characteristics of radios meant that they were primarily for collective listening, permitting an exchange of impressions among those united around them. Attention should be called to the fact that Brazilian families had the habit of congregating for meals, listening to the radio, and discussing daily news.

Another indication of the popularization, and even the trivialization of the presence of radios in large urban centers, is a 1960 IBOPE (Brazilian Institute of Public Opinion) study on the effective potential of the Rio and São Paulo markets for household goods.[9] The study examined the presence of televisions, mattresses, washing machines, refrigerators, blenders, and floor polishers, but did not seek information on whether households possessed radios. In other words, radio had become so popular that it no longer served as an indication of income. Still in 1960, the IBOPE conducted a study of the ways that residents of Belo Horizonte became familiar with the store *Ducal*, and 73% of those interviewed had learned of it through radio, 18% through newspapers, and 12% through television.

By the end of the 1950s and the early 1960s, Brazilian radio had consolidated its position as a medium of mass communication and as a fundamental component in the formation of Brazilian society's habits. Between the 1930s and the 1960s, radio was the medium through which technological innovations, cultural trends, political changes, news and entertainment simultaneously reached the most distant parts of the country, promoting the encounter between tradition and modernity. Radio helped to create new cultural and consumer practices throughout all of Brazilian society.

Notes

LIA CALABRE

[1] On the Centennial, see Motta.

[2] Tota 87.

[3] On the State/radio relationship, see Calabre, "O Estado na Onda".

[4] Lenharo, *Sacralização* 42.

[5] On National Radio, see Saroldi and Moreira, *Rádio Nacional.*

[6] Ortiz 44-45.

[7] On National Radio soap operas, see Calabre, "Na Sintonia do Tempo".

[8] On radio singers, see Lenharo *Cantores do Rádio*; and Miriam Goldfeder, *Por trás das Ondas da Rádio Nacional.*

[9] IBOPE, Pesquisas Especiais 1-31, 1960.

Works Cited

Calabre, Lia. "O Estado na Onda: Reflexões sobre o Rádio e o Poder nas Décadas de 30 e 40," *Cadernos de Memória Cultural* 1.2. (Rio de Janeiro: Museu da República, 1996): 61-67.

———. *Na Sintonia do Tempo: Um Leitura do Cotidiano Através da Produção Ficcional Radiofônica,* diss., Universidade Federal Fluminense, 1996.

Goldfeder, Miriam. *Por trás das Ondas da Rádio Nacional.* Rio de Janeiro: Paz e Terra, 1980.

Motta, Marly S. *A Nação Fez Cem Anos: A Questão Nacional no Centenário da Independência.* Rio de Janeiro: Fundação Getúlio Vargas, 1992.

Lenharo, Alcir. *Sacralização da Política.* Campinas: Papirus, 1986.

———. *Cantores do Rádio.* Campinas: Ed. da UNICAMP, 1995.

Ortiz, Renato. *A Moderna Tradição Brasileira—Cultura Brasileira e Indústria Cultural.* São Paulo: Brasiliense, 1988.

Saroldi, Luiz Carlos and Sônia Virgínia Moreira. *Rádio Nacional: O Brasil em Sintonia.* Rio de Janeiro: FUNARTE, 1984.

Tota, Antônio Pedro. *A Locomotiva no Ar: Rádio e Modernidade em São Paulo, 1924—1934.* São Paulo: Secretaria de Estado e Cultura/PW, 1990.

The Orphan Brotherland[1]: Rap's Civilizing Effort on the Periphery of São Paulo

Maria Rita Kehl

Translated by Shoshanna Lurie

In addition to a fascination with the poetic effect that the lyrics produce in me, my interest in the work of the Racionais MC's, one of the most important Brazilian rap groups, relates to what I consider this group's civilizing effort in relation to living conditions and a call for pleasure among poor youth in São Paulo's periphery. This civilizing effort is characteristic of rap in general, and more specifically of that produced in the context of urban poverty in Brazil. The origin of rap, as is well-known, lies in the young residents of ghettoes typical of the social and racial segregation of North American society. In my opinion, the Racionais are the most expressive of the many groups that have proliferated in Brazil for the last ten years.

In order to understand this civilizing effort of still uncertain outcome, we will examine how the Racionais present themselves before their immense audience, largely composed of poor black youth from the urban peripheries of Brazil. The four young people who form the group—Mano Brown, Ice Blue, KL Jay and Edy Rock—refuse any identification as pop stars, despite the one million copies sold of their last CD, *Sobrevivendo no Inferno* (*Surviving in Hell*). To them, the issue of recognition and inclusion is not resolved through the ascension offered by the logic of the market, according to which two or three exceptional individuals are tolerated for their talent and can even rise above their miserable origins, narcissistically endowed by the star system. These individuals then offer themselves as objects of adoration, identification, and consolation for the great masses of fans, who individually dream of one day themselves becoming the exception.

The members of the Racionais address the multitude of peripheral youth from another location: the place of the similar. For this reason, they necessarily plays little stake in and concede little to the media. "We are not a commodity, we are artists," says KL Jay in an interview with *Jornal da Tarde* (8/5/98), explaining that this is why they refuse to appear on Globo Network (a station that supported the military dictatorship and "makes the population continuously more ignorant") and on SBT Network ("how can I go to 'Gugu' if his program only shows naked girls shaking their hips or exploring the bizarre?"). Even the label of artist is questioned, in a rejection of any type of "domestication:" "I am not an artist. Artists make art. I make weapons. I'm a terrorist" (Mano Brown).

The name *mano* ("brother") is not gratuitous. It indicates an attempt at equality, a feeling of fraternity, a *horizontal* field of identification as opposed to a mode of vertical identification/domination of the mass audience in relation to the leader or idol. The lyrics are appeals to similar individuals, to brothers: join us, increase our force. Stay aware, stay conscious—don't do what they expect of you, don't be the "limited black" (the title of one of Brown's songs) that the system wants, don't justify the "racist suckers'" prejudice (the title of another song). Rap groups' force does not come from their ability to exclude, to place themselves above the masses and produce fascination and jealousy. It comes from their power of inclusion, from the insistence on equality between artists and audience, all black, all poor, all victims of the same discrimination and scarcity of opportunity. Rappers do not want to exclude any young person who is similar to them. "I am merely a Latin-American guy / supported by more than fifty thousand *manos* / collateral effect that your system created," Mano Brown, leader of the Racionais, sings in "Capítulo 4, Versículo 3" ("Chapter 4, Verse 3"). Unlike hard rock bands, they do not offer their audience the masochistic pleasure of being insulted by a millionaire pop-star masquerading as an outsider. The designation *mano* makes sense: they seek to expand the great brotherland of the excluded, transforming "consciousness" into a weapon capable of turning the tables of marginalization. "We are the most dangerous blacks in the country and we are going to change a lot of things around here. Until recently we weren't aware of this" (KL Jay).

To what danger is Jay referring? Judging from some statements to the press and the great majority of the tracks on the Racionais' CDs, there is a change in attitude, originating from the rappers and seeking to transform the self-image and behavior of all poor blacks in Brazil: the end of humility and of the feeling of inferiority that pleases the elite, accustomed to benefiting from docility. In other words, to benefit from the fear of our "good people of color."

> —Interviewer from the magazine, *Raça*: "When you speak with a guy, what do you expect to happen afterwards?"
> —Brown: "That he lift up his head, lose his fear, and face it. If he gets punched, that he returns it."
> —*Raça*: "And what would happen if all blacks from the periphery acted this way?"
> —Brown: "Brazil would be a more just country."

The Racionais' messages for those who listen to and buy their CDs are the following: "I would like them to place value upon themselves and to like themselves" (Mano Brown). "Ideology and self-valorization" (KL Jay). "Dignity should be their motto" (Ice Blue). "That they listen to the Racionais, of course. And peace!" (Edy Rock) (interview with *DJ Sound* 15, 1991).

The Racionais call for the consciousness of each individual, for changes in attitude that can only result from individual choices; yet the self-valorization and dignity of each black person, of each rap listener, depends on the production of a discourse in which blacks' place is different from that indicated by the Brazilian tradition. Here emerges the difference between the Racionais and another young and very charismatic black musician, our other Brown, this one Bahian. "Some people say that São Paulo rap is sad (*Raça's* reporter). Carlinhos Brown said that this means not knowing how to prevail over misery." —Mano Brown: "In Bahia, they have to hide misery in order for the tourists to come, to bring money to the guys there, including Carlinhos Brown. São Paulo is not a tourist destination. And the comment on prevailing over misery, you can't accept misery. But I do think that what he does for his community is valid."

It seems that the Racionais aren't interested either in prevailing over misery (and what would this be? a more seductive form of domination?) nor in hiding misery *para inglês ver*.[2] Their targeted audience is not the tourist, but rather poor blacks like them. No, they do not exclude their peers, nor do they consider themselves superior to the anonymous groups of the periphery. If they exclude anyone, it is me, it is you, middle-class consumer—"boy," "bourgeois," "dope," "racist sucker,"—he who enjoys the Racionais' sound on the CD player of an imported car "and who feels like he's part of the

banditry" (KL Jay). In other words: they are not selling a slice of marginal life
—*malandragem*—to alleviate middle-class youth's tedium.

Thus, it is difficult to like them if you are not one of them. Even more
difficult to discuss them. They do not authorize us to, they do not open the
doors to us. "We" are from the other side. On the side of those who have
everything that they do not have. On the side of those they envy, almost
admittedly, and of those they also hate, openly. But above all, on the side of
those they disdain. On this point, the limit of the rappers' civilizing effort is
placed in question: the emancipation they propose to the *manos* runs the
serious risk of colliding with the segregation that they themselves produce by
closing themselves off to everything and everyone that differs from them. I
will deal with this question at the end of this essay.

How does one like this music that allows for no happiness, no exaltation?
How does one listen to the intimidating, accusatory, and frequently
authoritarian lyrics, wrapped up in a rhythm that suggests a forced labor
camp or a prisoners' march around a courtyard, to which young people dance
with heads down, faces almost hidden by the hoods of sweatshirts and dark
glasses, hunched over, as if they still had the shackles of slavery around their
feet? Where is the identification that breaks the barrier of segregation and
crosses an abyss of differences produced, making rich adolescents listen in
order to (and why not?) understand what the Racionais are denouncing?
What makes a middle-class adult woman like myself take rap's violent slap in
the face not as an insult but as a shared relief, not as an affront *pour épater*,
but as a denunciation that immediately binds me to them?

If they do not authorize me, I will have to make a forced entrance.
Identification facilitates things for me; I gamble on the virtual, symbolic and
potentially inexhaustive space of the brotherland and I pass over to the side
of the *manos*, without forgetting (nor could I) my difference. It is from
another place, from "my" place, that I listen to and can speak of the Racionais
MC's. It is because they directly address the discomfort that I feel living in a
country that daily reproduces, with the speed of an industrial assembly line,
the violent exclusion of thousands of young people and children who
encounter no opportunities to escape the marginalized state in which they
find themselves, despite current neo-liberal discourses that emphasize
individual competence and effort. It is the ability to symbolize the experience
of abandonment of these millions of urban periphery residents, to insist that
their faces be definitively included in the current portrait of the country (a

portrait that still passes for well-behaved, polite, miscegenated). It is the ability to produce a significant and new language on exclusion, that makes the Racionais MC's the most important mass musical phenomenon in the Brazil of the 1990s.

The orphan brotherland

60% of youth from the periphery with no police record have suffered police violence / For every 4 people killed by the police, three are black / Only 2% of students in Brazilian universities are black / Every four hours a black youth is killed violently in São Paulo / Speaking here is Cousin Black, yet another survivor. ("Chapter 4, Verse 3").[3]

The listener who pays attention to the extensive lyrics of rap will probably feel uncomfortable with the tone with which these discourses are pronounced. It is a tone that could be called authoritarian, a mixture of warning and accusation. The voice of the singer/narrator directly addresses itself to the listener, sometimes assuming him to be another *mano* and advising, warning, trying to "raise consciousness," sometimes assuming he is an enemy and, in this case, accusing him unambiguously. Faced with such a threatening voice, with a discourse that invites us to "exchange ideas" yet does not exchange anything, does not negotiate its point of view and its position (an always moral, but not always moralizing position, as we will see), it is left to the listener to ask: but how does he authorize himself? Who does he think he is?

Brazil is a country that traditionally considers itself to be orphaned of a father. We do not honor our Portuguese ancestors; we do not respect a governing elite that does not even respect the law, society, or itself; we have no great heroes among the founders of our current society, capable of providing symbols for our self-esteem or identifying ideas for the masses. Our "national heroes" are not historical figures linked to some foundational myth of our society, but characters emerging from the world of sports and popular music. These figures are much closer, then, to the position of more talented or astute brothers than to that of an exemplary (totemic) father linked to a myth of origins.

Our passage from "state of nature" (which is how Indigenous cultures are mistakenly symbolized) to "state of culture" was not accomplished through the arrival of a group of Puritans carrying the project of founding a religious community, as in the United States, but through the emptying out of a band of exiles by the Portuguese Crown onto the land which is now Brazil. They came not to civilize, but to benefit, and, primarily, to usurp. This is how the arrival of the Portuguese to Brazil is popularly interpreted at least, with a large dose of irony.[4] Thus, we have the myth of the "pátria-mãe-gentil" ("kind motherland") that Caetano Veloso correctly called "mátria," followed by a request: "quero fratria!" ("I want a brotherland!"), which authorizes everything, tolerates everything and in which everything is possible.

It is obvious that the myth of facile abundance led to exploitation, to a concentration of wealth that places us first in the ranking of "world shame" and misery. It is obvious that symbolic orphanhood led not to an absence of paternal figures but to an excess of *real*, abusive, arbitrary and brutal fathers like the father of the primitive horde of the Freudian myth. What is lacking in Brazilian society is not another bossy and pseudo-protective godfather (such as Antônio Carlos Magalhães and Getúlio Vargas, for example), but a strong *brotherland* that believes in itself and is capable of supplanting the power of the father of the horde and of instating a symbolic father, in the form of a just law that considers the needs of all and not the voracity of a few. It is brothers who realize the paternal function, voluntarily renouncing the pleasures that were once the privilege of the father at the cost of the servitude of all his sons.

In a country also accustomed to authoritarian paternalism for fraternal formations in their function of creating signifiers and citizenship, a question is raised: how to avoid a new usurper, in the figure of a hero, from being produced from the act of *collective* courage that eliminates the age-old domination of the omnipotent father and institutes a new civilizing pact? On the other hand, how can a consistent discourse supporting and legitimating social formations produced in the horizontality of democratic relations be maintained in the absence of the concentrated hero of collective speech (think of Roland Barthes: "myth is stolen speech" in *Mitologias*)? How can the "orphan letter," in Jacques Rancière's expression for the new forms of language produced through horizontal exchanges that attempt to communicate experiences that make sense between like individuals, produce value and suggest a "minimum program"(9) of necessary renunciations in order to sustain an ethic of shared living?

In the two texts in which he relates collective formations to the assassination of the primitive father,[5] Freud suggests that the hero who constructs himself as the only author of a collective act is the epic poet himself. It is he who creates the myth of the assassination of the tyrannical father, placing himself at the center of his own narrative. "Myth constitutes the step with which the individual separates from collective psychology" (2605). Thus, the poet is someone who simultaneously maintains the unity of the brotherland around the memory of a (fictitious) act of origins while psychologically detaching himself from the collective.

The Racionais' speech oscillates between the communal place of the *manos* and the place of the exemplary poet/hero, slipping from here to the place of authority, speaking in the name of a "father" who knows more, who can counsel, judge, advise. Why "Racionais?," a *Raça* reporter asked. Edy Rock replied, "It comes from reasoning, right? A name that relates to the lyrics, that has to do with us. *You think in order to speak.*" Brown: "At that time rap was really silly. Rap to mislead, understand, *mano*? It didn't make you think." Later, responding to the question of why rap is political, Brown answered:

> You were already born black, descendant of slaves that suffered, son of a slave that suffered, you keep taking the police's abuse, you keep living among drugs, drug-traffic, alcoholism, with all the crap that other people brought in here. It was them who brought it here to us. So it's not a matter of choice, just like the air one breathes. So rap talks about that, about why life is like that.

I will address one of the many examples from their lyrics that illustrates this double insertion of the subject, who on the one hand "thinks in order to speak"—produces his own speech differentiated from the discourses of the Other—but who on the other hand could not speak of any other thing "because life is like that." In other words, the subject's thinking and critical autonomy is not confused with an arbitrariness of references, like the delirium of self-sufficiency typical of the subjective alienation of consumer societies. The distancing necessary to think before speaking comes from immersion in one's own history (we are "descendants of slaves who suffered") and from an active and non-acquiescent acceptance of one's condition. It also emerges from belonging to a place and a collectivity that both strengthens enunciation and delimits the field from which the subject can speak, making an escape into fantasies of adherence to imaginary formulas of seduction or of consolation difficult.

I don't know if they / are or aren't authorized / to decide what is right or wrong / innocent or guilty spoken portrait / does justice no longer exist or am I mistaken? / If I were to cite the names of all who are now gone / I would have no time to say anything else... / and I will remember that it remained at that / and then what security is possible in this situation / how many will have to suffer for steps to be taken / or are they just going to sit around and watch what happens / and surely ignore the provenance / Sensationalism is the greatest to them / they love to get rid of the delinquents / as long as its not a relative, of course / or their own children are next... Ei Brown, what's your attitude going to be? / Change will be in our consciousness / practicing our activities coherently / and the consequence will be the end of fear itself / since who likes us is we ourselves / like, why won't anyone take care of you / don't get involved without thinking / don't provide a motive to die / honesty will never be too much / your morale is not won, it's made / we are not masters of the truth / this is why we don't lie / we feel the need for improvement / our philosophy is to always communicate / reality as it is / Racionais MC's. ("Panic in the South Zone")[6]

In the last lines of "Júri Racional" ("Rational Jury"), the group condemns a black *otário* ("sucker") who "passed over to the other side," refusing to identify with the *manos* in exchange for acceptance from the *playboys* ("rich kids").

What I want is to recover our value, that the other race stole / That is my point of view. I'm not racist, understand? / And though many of our people have warned you / but you, unfortunately / don't even show interest in freeing yourself / That is the question, self-valorization / that is the title of our revolution. / Chapter 1: / The real black has to be able / to row against the current, against any sacrifice. / But in your case it's difficult: you only think of your own benefit / Since the beginning, you showed me signs / that your skills are unoriginal vices / artificial, too whitened / White sheep of the race, traitor! You sold your sold your soul to the enemy, denied your color; / Refrain: But our jury is rational, it makes no errors / Why? we are no fans of scoundrels!; Conclusion: by unanimous vote / the jury of this court declares the following sentence / and considers the defendent guilty / of ignoring the struggle of black ancestors / of scorning ancient black culture / of humiliating and demeaning the other brothers / as a voluntary pawn of the racist enemy / Case closed.[7]

The authoritarian bent of these verses, which utilize the image of a court as a form of upholding the law that demands the renunciation of pleasure ("but in your case it's difficult: you only think of your own benefit"), has at least three determinants. First, the certainty that a collective cause is at stake: that of stopping the flow of blood from many generations of black people, of impeding discrimination without denying the marker of race. No more lowering one's head, acting like a "black with a white soul" that the elite have always valued. Also, no more attempting, for example through the rapid ascension made possible by drug-traffic, to cross over "to the other side." It is a matter of creating an improvement in life on the periphery. In order to do this, however—and here the second reason emerges—it is necessary to communicate "reality as it is." This is because the greatest threat does not come necessarily from police violence nor from the indifference of the "boys." Rather, it emerges from the hoax produced by the appeal of advertising and by the confusion between consumer and citizen established in neo-liberal Brazil, making peripheral youth, fascinated by the signs of bourgeois power, abandon their own culture and devalue their peers and their origins. This despite the fact that it is frequently the very ostentation of these signs of economic power that guarantees some respect, recognition, and citizenship in Brazil. It is for precisely this reason, Brown's lyrics indicate, that the individual is misguided.

Here the third determination emerges, making it clear that the predominantly moral discourse of the Racionais should not be confused with moralizing, since it does not speak in the name of any universal value beyond the preservation of life itself. The lyric's authoritarian tone warns the *manos*: where the "law of the jungle" reigns, the death sentence has already been handed down without prior judgement. Faced with a life constantly in danger, one cannot take any wrong steps.

Terror, not power, provides the exasperated tone of these lyrics. Crime and drugs are an enormous temptation, further exacerbated by the lack of alternatives. Clearly, rap does not offer any material escape from misery; it also does not wager on transgression as a means of self-affirmation, as is common among middle-class youth (an example of this is the success of the group Planet Hemp). Much less does it bet on direct confrontation with what is according to rap the primary source of threat to youth's lives, the police themselves. Acquiescence or wisdom? Most likely a little of both—that is if the *manos'* cynicism in regards to the possibility of facing police institutions in Brazil can be considered acquiescence.

The threat of the police is not the only reason that the Racionais speak out against the consumption of drugs. Drugs are seen as destructive, not only to the body but also to self-esteem, and also deliver the addict into the hands of the worst type of savage capitalist—the drug-dealer. Drugs represent the epitome of individualism, with their appeal to solitary and immediate pleasure, and the kings of the drug-traffic are not differentiated from the violent police or from the great capitalist speculators. They exploit children and youths, addicts and petty drug-dealers. They do not suffer the living conditions of the periphery, but rather take advantage of them.

On the other hand, the straight side of consumer society, the fetish for merchandise, also produces alienation and can lead to crime. Rap seeks to promote individual attitudes founded on a collective reference.

> If I were that guy who humiliates himself at the stoplight / for less than a real, my chances would be few / but if I were that kid wearing a mask / who cocks and thrusts a gun barrel into your mouth / all of a sudden, you and your girl, naked / one, two, didn't even see me! I already disappeared into the fog / But no! I'm still alive, I follow the mystique / 27 years *contradicting statistics* / Your TV commercial doesn't fool me / I don't need status, nor fame / Your car and your money don't seduce me / nor your blue-eyed whore / I'm merely a Latin-American guy / *supported by fifty thousand manos* / collateral effect that your system produced. ("Chapter 4, Verse 3," my emphasis")[8]

The call seems simple: to stay alive "contradicting statistics," following an unexplained "mystique," yet also suggests the need to adhere to values shared by "more than fifty thousand *manos*." Producing a lifestyle, a style of speech, a location from which to speak, without reproducing advertising clichés. This is not a simple task when one is destined, by the Other, to be the "collateral effect that [its] system produced."

Father's functions, *manos'* inventions

The fifty thousand *manos* create support—but where's a father? What is the signifier that is capable of subsuming a law, a prohibition of pleasure, when the only compensation is the right to continue "contradicting statistics," fighting for survival? Surprisingly, Mano Brown "uses" God for this function. Although at no time does he speak of any particular church, God is mentioned—but for what reason?

> Brother, the devil fucks up everything around you / on the radio, newspaper, magazine, and outdoors / He offers you money, calmly converses / contaminates

your character, steals your soul / then he throws you into the shit alone / he turns a "preto tipo A" into a *neguinho* / My word sooths your pain / lights up my soul, blessed be my Father / who doesn't allow the *mano* here to go down the wrong path / ah, not even lay a finger on any scoundrel / But no son of a bitch ignores my law. ("Chapter 4, Verse 3")[9]

God is mentioned as a reference that "doesn't let the *mano* go down the wrong path," since all other references ("radio, newspaper, magazine, and outdoor") are there to "turn a *'preto tipo A'* into a *neguinho*." God is mentioned as the father whose desire indicates to the son what it means to be a man, a *preto tipo A;* since it is necessary that the Other loves one in order for one to love oneself. The Other must point to a place of dignity (which cannot be known, though culture never stops producing trails for it to be imagined), so that the subject feels worthy of occupying some place.

I will not venture an interpretation of the personal, intimate religiosity of the members of the group. But I do suggest that the Father who appears in some of these raps (along with the Orixás: see "A Fórmula Mágica da Paz" ("Magical Formula for Peace") in which Mano Brown says: "I thank God and the Orixás / I stopped in the middle of the trip and looked back"), in addition to symbolizing the Law, has the function of conferring meaning upon life, which for a common *mano* "is worth less than his cellular phone and his computer" (Brown/Jocenir, a prisoner in the São Paulo penitentiary, "Diário de um detento".) As far as the law of men, these youths indeed are already excluded, even from the minimum program of the "Declaration of the Rights of Man." The imminent modern symbolic alternative to God would be "society," this being an abstract, over-arching entity that should symbolize common interest among men, insisting that you be a "good" person, and offering in exchange protection, opportunities, and even some alternatives for pleasure.

But according to rap lyrics, society does not seem willing to alter its system of privilege to include and consider their rights. Society does not enforce the law for everyone—the portion of the renunciation necessary to sustain the social bond is always demanded from the *other*. The return to God (from a philosophical point of view) makes sense within the context of extreme social injustice, considering that the alternative is a return to barbarism. It is worth mentioning—am I being optimistic?—that Brown's God does not produce acquiescence, faith in a magical salvation, or the devalorization of this life in the name of any eternal happiness. God is present as a symbolic reference, to keep the lives of these rebellious young men, who speak of a revolution here on earth and who always remind us that the one "who likes us is we ourselves" ("Panic in the South Zone"), "from going down the wrong path" ("God is with me, but the revolver also accompanies me"— Ice Blue to *Jornal da Tarde*).

However, do not confuse this "liking ourselves" with an assertion of self-sufficiency, of an individualism that only sustains itself (hypothetically!) in cases in which it is possible to carry out the conditions imposed by consumer society, such as the acquisition of goods whose function is to fill the gaps in the "narcissistic fortress" of the self, the alienation of the "master's" position, which does not allow him to discover his own dependence on "slave's" work, and the presence of money as a fetish capable of obscuring from the subject a consciousness of his own destitution. The Racionais' command "like yourself" could not be an encouragement of individualism even if it wanted to, since these conditions are very far from being attainable given the situation of permanent destitution and concrete lack that characterizes life on the periphery, with the exception of the barbaric face of drug-trafficking and consumption, of course.

In Brown's and Edy Rock's lyrics, the trafficker represents the barbaric face of bourgeois individualism: the guy who could not care less about anyone else, who only defends what is his, who has no scruples about addicting young people and exposing children to danger by having them carry out the delivery of drugs. The other face is that of the sucker, the "limited black," who has no attitude and who deceives himself into thinking that he can distinguish himself from his peers by denying his race, etc.: "I don't want to be the most correct / but rather the most astute *mano*," Brown responds to the "limited black." Yet again, a moral posture grounds itself in the extreme threat of extermination. The "astute *mano*" knows that the choice of alienation—which on the periphery can only be sustained through drugs— is subject to a death sentence, to the Brazilian police's law of the jungle or that of the savage capitalists who own and operate the drug-traffic:

> The second choice is the fastest path / it's easy, death travels the same road, yes /
> inevitable / they plan our restriction, that is the title / of our revolution, according
> to verse / read, study, realize yourself, remember / before uniformed racist suckers
> with atrophied minds / blow your brains out and everything is over / Careful / the

Bulletin of Incidents with your name in some book / in any archive, in any district / case closed, no more than this. ("Limited Black")[10]

The insignificance of life, of the emptiness that our passage through the world of the living will leave after our death—we who always bet on leaving the mark of our presence with a work, a word, an immortal memory—that which psychoanalysis identifies as the precariousness of the human condition and that for which a middle-class neurotic so needs work in order to support, is provided in the day-to-day concrete living in the "peripheral hell" (Edy Rock) from which they come. Thus, the possibility of a narcissistic-individualist delirium is excluded unless one faces the consequences of opting for crime.

I wasn't even paying attention, nor taking anything seriously / I admired the older thieves and rogues / but wake up, look around you, and say / after all that, who was left, I don't know / a lot of funerals between then and now / who's the next mother to cry / it took a while but today I can understand / *that true roguery is living* / I thank God and the Orixás / I stopped half-way down the road and looked back… (Brown "Magical Formula for Peace," my emphasis)[11]

The other option—the first according to the lyrics of "Limited Black"— is the appeal to the other as a partner in the construction of other references, in the invention of symbolic spaces that allow for some independence from the seduction of the crime-consumerism-extermination circuit. Thus, the edict "like yourself" does not sound as an isolated command or as a closing in on oneself as an answer to all problems. Conversely, the sentence sounds as an *appeal* to the other to recognize and value the traits that mark the similarities between them.

I do not ignore that, in its extreme form, the attempt to adhere to a collectivity in order to escape from solitary confrontation with one's own desire can produce a blind obedience to the group, fanaticism, extreme forms of alienation, the fruit of what Contardo Calligaris called the "passion of instrumentality" (1991). The question remains as to what is the mark of difference between the two modes in which the fraternal reference operates: the first that strengthens the subject in his difference in relation to the desire of the Other; the second that produces the shared illusion of an "Other's Other" whose desire is exposed and who the subject blindly obeys, taking pleasure in the imaginary possibility of causing the Other pleasure. The always present possibility of passage from one mode of operating to the other attests to the fragility of fraternal formations, but does not authorize us to dismiss their importance in the production and renewal of social ties.

It is important to stress that the brotherland is not summoned to operate only in the absence of the father. But when no one in that life embodies the civilizing father and the will typical of the "father of the primitive horde" prevails, when it is necessary to appeal to the "Father" in order to imagine that "someone" (in the vertical axis of subject formation) loves you and keeps you from being abused, the recognition among brothers becomes essential. Even simply to sustain the existence of this God who, if he weren't the signifier of a symbolic (therefore collective) formation, would otherwise be the central element in a psychotic delirium. In addition, in the absence of the recognition of a father, it is the libidinal circulation between the members of the brotherland that produces the place from which the subject views himself, seen through the gaze of the other(s). Proof of this is the great importance that the creation of nicknames acquires in adolescent groups as indicators of a "second baptism," for example, from other identificatory fields in which the subjects can move, broadening the narrow limitations rooted in the unitary aspect of identification with the paternal ideal. Horizontal identification may permit the passage from the illusion of an "identity" (in which the subject believes himself to be identical to himself, fixed to his own name given him by his father) to the precariousness of secondary identifications, made from other locations the subject occupies in relation to his peers, and that the nickname given him by the group may reveal. Horizontal identification allows the subject to travel from the imaginary prison of an "identity" (which supposes an impossible subjective agreement of the subject with himself and produces, as a result of repression, the haunting ghost of the other in the form of the *double*) to more mobile possibilities of circulation through a field of identifications.

At this point, it is worth asking: when the Racionais call for the *manos* to identify with the cause of blacks, are they proposing a field of identification—with its diversity of singular manifestations—or the production of an identity, with its subjective straitjacket?

> I like Nelson Mandela, I admire Spike Lee / Zumbi, a great hero, Brazil's greatest /
> They are important to me, but you laugh and turn your back / so I think I know
> what kind of shit you like: / dressing like a *playboy*, going to discos / pleasing the

rogues, watching soap-operas every day / what shit / If that's your ideal / it's a shame / its probable that you screw yourself often / that you destroy yourself and want to include us in it / but, I don't want to, I won't go / I'm black, I won't adopt it / What are expensive clothes worth, if you have no attitude? / and what is negritude worth, if you don't put it into practice? / The principal tactic, heritage of our Mother Africa / the only thing that they couldn't steal! / if they knew the value that our race has / they would dye the palm of their hands to be black also! (Brown "Rational Jury").[12]

The issue is complex. Once questioned about his identification with Judaism, Freud responded that if anti-Semitism didn't exist, he wouldn't bother to circumcise his own sons; however, faced with prejudice, he had no other choice but to assert himself as a Jew. Perhaps the Racionais' call for an "attitude" supporting self-love among blacks in opposition to the feeling of inferiority produced by discrimination can be interpreted in this way. The "attitude" is directed through the affirmation of race—this dubious signifier that produces discrimination as it points to difference.

Who knows, however, if this imaginary limitation can be surpassed, this physical support—skin color—that simultaneously produces identification and racial discrimination? Who knows if the multitude of rap groups' admirers aren't trying to say, like the Parisian students in May of 1968 when the government tried to remove Daniel Cohn-Bendit with the allegation that he was not French— "we are all German Jews!"—and explode the barriers of race and segregation through identifications with cultural formations: are we all black *manos* from the periphery? If the assertion of identificatory fields (I am intentionally rejecting the term *identity*) does not produce social bonds, elective affinities that include the similar within difference (making traits of race, or sex, for example, obsolete), it will always lead to isolation between groups, and in some way or another, discrimination. That peripheral black youths' self-esteem and dignity do not depend on acceptance from the white elite does not mean that they do not produce other ties, other forms of communication, including those with groups more or less marginal to this same elite. In this case, identification, originally based on skin color, is broadened to include other meanings: exclusion, indignation, repudiation of violence and of injustice. It also entails the identification with a style—music, dance, rhythm-and-poetry— as well as with the "attitude" the rappers proclaim. It produces aesthetic effects that affect the social reality. We are not "all" poor blacks from the periphery, but we are much more than they supposed when they began to speak.[13]

Notes

1 "Brotherland" is my translation of *fratria* in an attempt to capture the sense of fraternity between brothers within a social formation taking the place of a "fatherland" and dialoguing with this term. (Translator's note)

2 A common expression among Brazilians, used to describe a behavior, which consists in officially holding a position that is never truly accomplished. (Translator's note)

3 60% dos jovens de periferia sem antecedentes criminais já sofreram violência policial. A cada 4 pessoas mortas pela polícia, 3 são negras. Nas universidades brasileiras, apenas 3% dos alunos são negros. A cada 4 horas, um jovem negro morre violentamente em São Paulo. Aqui quem fala é Primo Preto, mais um sobrevivente. ("Cap. 4, Versículo 3")

4 See the article by Contardo Calligaris, "Este País não Presta," introduction to *Hello Brasil!* (São Paulo: Ed. Escuta, 1991).

5 *Totem e Tabu* (1912) and *Psicologia das Massas e Análise do Eu* (1920/21).

6 Eu não sei se eles / estão ou não autorizados / a decidir o que é certo ou errado / inocente ou culpado retrato falado / não existe mais justiça ou estou enganado? Se eu fosse citar o nome de todos os que se foram / o meu tempo não daria para falar mais... / e eu vou lembrar que ficou por isso mesmo / e então que segurança se tem em tal situação / quantos terão que sofrer pra se tomar providência / ou vão dar mais um tempo e assistir a seqüência / e com certeza ignorar a procedência / O sensacionalismo pra eles é o máximo / acabar com delinquentes eles acham ótimo / desde que nenhum parente ou então é lógico / seus próprios filhos sejam os próximos (...) Ei Brown, qual será a nossa atitude? / A mudança estará em nossa consciência / praticando nossos atos com coerência / e a conseqüência será o fim do próprio medo / pois quem gosta de nós somos nós mesmos / tipo, porque ninguém cuidará de você / não entre nessa à toa / não dê motivo pra morrer / honestidade nunca será demais / sua moral não se ganha, se faz / não somos donos da verdade / por isso não mentimos / sentimos a necessidade de uma melhoria / nossa filosofia é sempre transmitir / a realidade em si / Racionais MC's. ("Pânico na Zona Sul")

7 Eu quero é devolver nosso valor, que a outra raça tirou / Esse é meu ponto de vista. Não sou racista, morou? / E se avisaram sua mente, muitos de nossa gente / mas você, infelizmente / sequer demonstra interesse em se libertar. / Essa é a questão, auto-valorização / esse é o título da nossa revolução/. Capítulo 1: / O verdadeiro negro tem que ser capaz / de remar contra a maré, contra qualquer sacrifício. / Mas no seu caso é difícil: você só pensa no próprio benefício. / Desde o início, me mostrou indícios / que seus artifícios são vícios pouco originais / artificiais, embranquiçados demais. / Ovelha branca da raça, traidor! Vendeu a alma ao inimigo, renegou sua cor; / Refrão: Mas nosso júri é racional / não falha / por que? não somos fãs de canalha!; Conclusão: Por unanimidade / o júri deste tribunal declara a ação procedente / e considera o réu culpado/por ignorar a luta dos antepassados negros / por menosprezar a cultura negra milenar/por humilhar e ridicularizar os demais irmãos / sendo instrumento voluntário do inimigo racista / Caso encerrado.

8 Se eu fosse aquele cara que se humilha no sinal / por menos de um real, minha chance era pouca / mas se eu fosse aquele moleque de touca / que engatilha e enfia o cano dentro de sua boca / de quebrada, sem roupa, você e sua mina / um, dois, nem me viu! já sumi na neblina/. Mas não! permaneço vivo, eu sigo a mística / 27 anos contrariando a estatística. / Seu comercial de TV não me engana / eu não preciso de status, nem fama. / Seu carro e sua grana já não me seduz / e nem a sua puta de olhos azuis. / Eu sou apenas um rapaz latino-americano / apoiado por mais de cinqüenta mil manos / efeito colateral que seu sistema produz. ("Capitulo 4, Versículo 3")

9 Irmão, o demônio fode tudo ao seu redor / pelo rádio, jornal, revista e outdoor / Te oferece dinheiro, conversa com calma/contamina seu caráter, rouba sua alma / depois te joga na merda sozinho, / transforma um preto tipo A num neguinho. / Minha palavra alivia sua dor, / ilumina minha alma, louvado seja o meu Senhor / que não deixa o mano aqui desandar, / ah,

nem sentar o dedo em nenhum pilantra. / Mas que nenhum filho da puta ignore a minha lei. ("Capítulo 4, Versículo 3")

[10] A segunda opção é o caminho mais rápido / e fácil, a morte percorre a mesma estrada, é / inevitável. / planejam nossa restrição, esse é o título / da nossa revolução, segundo versículo / leia, se forme, se atualize, decore / antes que racistas otários fardados de cérebro atrofiado/os seus miolos estourem e estará tudo acabado. / Cuidado! / O Boletim de Ocorrência com seu nome em algum livro / em qualquer arquivo, em qualquer distrito / caso encerrado, nada mais que isso. ("Negro Limitado")

[11] Não tava nem aí, nem levava nada a sério/admirava os ladrão e os malandro mais velho / mas se liga, olhe ao redor e diga / o que melhorou da função, quem sobrou, sei lá / muito velório rolou de lá pra cá / qual a próxima mãe a chorar / já demorou mas hoje eu posso compreender / que malandragem de verdade é viver (grifo meu) / Agradeço a Deus e aos Orixás / parei no meio do caminho e olhei para trás. (...) (Brown "Fórmula Mágica da Paz").

[12] Gosto de Nelson Mandela, admiro Spike Lee, / Zumbi, um grande herói, o maior daqui. / São importantes pra mim, mas você ri e dá as costas / então acho que sei de que porra você gosta: / se vestir como playboy, freqüentar danceterias / agradar os vagabundos, ver novela todo dia, / que merda! / Se esse é seu ideal, é lamentável / é bem provável que você se foda muito / você se autodestrói e também quer nos incluir / porém, não quero, não vou / sou negro, não vou admitir! / De que valem roupas caras, se não tem atitude? / e o que vale a negritude, se não pô-la em prática? / A principal tática, herança da nossa mãe África / a única coisa que não puderam roubar! / se soubessem o valor que a nossa raça tem / tingiam a palma da mão pra ser escura também! (Brown "Júri racional")

[13] A longer version of this essay was published as "A Fratria Órfã." I have worked with the concept of "função fraterna" in the introduction of *Função Fraterna*.

Works Cited and Suggestions for Further Reading

Assoun, P.L. *Frères et Soeurs I. (Le Lien Inconscient)*. Paris: Anthropos, 1998.

Barthes, Roland. "O Mito como Linguagem Roubada." *Mitologias*. São Paulo: Difel, 1975. 152-58.

Calligaris, Castardo. "Função Paterna." *Hello Brasil*. São Paulo: Escuta, 1991. 59-81.

Dör, J. *O Pai e sua Função em Psicanálise*. Rio de Janeiro: Zahar, 1985.

Freud, Sigmund. *Totem y Tabu. Obras Completas*. Vol. II. Madrid: Biblioteca Nueva, 1973.

———. *Psicologia das Massas e Análise do Eu. Obras Completas*. Vol. III. Madrid: Biblioteca Nueva, 1973.

Kehl, Maria Rita. "Introdução: Existe uma Função Fraterna?" *Função Fraterna*. Ed. Maria Rita Kehl. Rio de Janeiro: Relume Dumará, 2000. 31-47.

———. "A Fratria Órfã." *Op. cit.* 209-244.

KL Jay. Entrevista. *Jornal da Tarde* 5 Aug. 1998.

Racionais MC's. *Sobrevivendo no Inferno*. Zambia, 1997.

Rancière, Jacques. "Prefácio". *Políticas da Escrita*. Rio de Janeiro: Ed. 34, 1999. 7-24.

Renault, A. *O Indivíduo*. São Paulo: Difel, 1998.

MARIA RITA KEHL

Funk and Hip-Hop Transculture: Cultural Conciliation and Racial Identification in the "Divided City"

Shoshanna Lurie

This article introduces funk and hip-hop culture in urban Brazil and discusses changing racial and spatial identifications rooted in the globalization of US black cultural forms and their accompanying ideologies. In my fieldwork in Rio de Janeiro over the last three years, I have found that the globalization of culture is challenging traditional forms of hegemony and marginalization, making new forms of democratization of culture possible, as well as precipitating new forms of exploitation and disenfranchisement. Globalization should be seen neither as purely a matter of transnational domination and uniformity nor as a source of the liberation of local culture from hegemonic state and national forms. Developments in global communication have opened the market and facilitated contact with transnational cultural production, enabling international group identification on the basis of parameters such as race, youth, and gender. For example, Spike Lee films widely shown in Brazil have increased consciousness of both racial polarization and social disparities based on race while creating a parallel between poor, largely black and *mulato* communities in Brazil and US ghettoes.

These new "ethnic" identifications compete with those founded on the prioritization of "Brazilian" identity, privileged by cultural nationalism and traditionally seen as paramount to combating the cultural imperialism resulting from colonial and post-colonial domination and exploitation. However, they complement and add complexity to nationalistic discourses and symbols among the popular sectors of Brazilian society rather than simply supplanting previous modes of identity formation.[1] Funk and hip-hop in Rio de Janeiro can be located among black diasporic cultures which relate simultaneously to local systems of class and race relations and global phenomena, and can be seen both as a tool and a reflection of the construction of a simultaneously local and deterritorialized cultural citizenship. They demand a recognition of the localized populace's dynamism and hybridity in relation to transnational culture, and suggest a type of "modernization from below." They are popular urban cultural phenomena which respond to and collaborate with both the positive and violent forces of globalization and suggest changing cultural, social and economic dynamics at both the local and national levels.

My approach to Brazilian funk and hip-hop places theories of globalization of culture into dialogue with a specific history of consensus-building through culture in Brazil and with lyrical, dance, journalistic, media, and interview material, attempting to equally value and engage these diverse sources. Funk and hip-hop are placed in historical perspective within the context of other black and popular cultural forms in Brazil such as *samba, candomblé,* and *capoeira,* which have each functioned to bring people of different races and socio-economic backgrounds together for delimited times and within controlled spaces. The predominance of the notion of "anthropophagy" in Brazilian intellectual thought has often ignored transnational influences on Brazilian popular culture and, as Roberto Schwarz has noted, masked the social relationship between the elite and the popular sectors within Brazil. In order to begin to understand the meaning that funk and hip-hop have for this population, it is useful to address the concept of "division" of urban space and the ideological mapping of social relationships which accompanies conceptions of physical space in the city in terms of the ways culture, and particularly popular music, has functioned as a social glue in this so-called "divided city." Funk and hip-hop comprise a diversity of expressions reflecting both conciliatory and oppositional aesthetics between the popular and privileged sectors and spaces, both resisting and conciliatory to dominant culture.

My discussion of the conciliatory function of popular culture is intimately linked to a history of race and racial ideologies in Brazil. Many cultural critics attack US critical approaches to race in Brazil which seem to categorize a reality according to standards germane to an alien social system. Though it is important to avoid this theoretical pitfall, a review of some basic statistics and concepts can help to illuminate the serious disparities tied to race which have long been occluded by a privileging of class difference, among other tropes, in Brazil. Brazil is a country that is at least 50% black, and where 90% of black Brazilians live below the poverty line, as opposed to 50% of non-Blacks. One-third of black Brazilians receive less than one *salário mínimo* (minimum wage) and no more than 3% of university students are black. The notion of "racial democracy" has been the dominant racial ideology in Brazil since the 1930s, operating in close conjunction with the myths of social harmony and cultural democracy. This concept was developed partially in response to earlier notions of whitening as the ideal path for Brazil to follow as a nation entering into modernity; however, what was arguably originally an attempt to place value upon miscegenation and the mixed-race Brazilian majority and on Brazilian cultural exceptionalism turned into a hegemonic tool for controlling social and racial opposition. Numerous studies have confirmed that differential opportunity and treatment correspond to skin-color, so that lighter blacks are generally better off, and racial hierarchy is very present in Brazil. There has been no broad-based civil rights movement as in the US and the black movement has been very limited in scope, nor would most poor black Brazilians identify with it. The excessive culturalism and focus on cultural revalorization of the black movement has also often de-emphasized socio-economic injustice (see Hanchard, Hasenbalg). Links between cultural valorization and the struggle for socio-economic justice characterize much Brazilian funk and hip-hop.

Funk

Brazilian funk and hip-hop are very different, though they share physical and social proximity in Rio. Brazilian funk began in the 1970s when DJs went to New York to actively seek out the latest funk being produced there and to bring it back to Rio. Funk culture was briefly linked to a somewhat superficial black-consciousness movement called "Black Rio," which was deeply influenced by 1970s soul music such as that of James Brown and stressed the aesthetics more than the politics of black identity. Funk then passed through a process of hybridization and is now sung mostly in Portuguese while incorporating some Brazilian rhythms such as *samba* and *pagode*. During the 1980s funk lost most of its component of racial consciousness and came to be seen as a de-politicized cultural phenomenon. Though current funk differs dramatically from the overt political militancy of much rap, funk is anything but apolitical, registering its politics on the level of form as well as content.

Hundreds of dances of up to 10,000 young people each are held each weekend in Rio suburbs and *favelas* and are attended by as many as a million young people who have few other options for leisure in the areas in which they live. A relatively independent industry has been built around funk that includes the production of CDs, magazines, newspapers, radio and television programs, creating jobs for many people. However, funk producers arguably practice exploitation in ways comparable to multinational record labels and it is important not to glorify this industry uncritically but rather to address all aspects of its related production, distribution, and consumption.

Many funk lyrics, such as the "Rap do Brasileiro" by MC Flávio and MC Magrão (*Jet Black*, 1995), subtly function to build consensus in the city by brushing over social differences.[2]

I am a humble guy and I have no money
But I am proud to be Brazilian

Foreigners have imported cars
While Brazilians have junkers
A lot of people are living under bridges
While others have a ton of houses

I ask you all, let's all join hands
Let's end the people's misery
There are people suffering, there are people dying
In our Brazil, everything is happening

Stop, stop fighting
We are Brazilians, let's stop and think
Stop, stop fighting
We are Brazilians and our place doesn't matter

Now I'm going to say the names of all the places
That all *cariocas** would like to live
Copacabana, Leblon, and Ipanema,
Barra da Tijuca** and don't forget Saquarema
Rocinha, Vidigal, Borel, Andaraí, Chácara do
Céu and Morro do Tuiti***[3]

This song reflects the valorization of poverty, humility, and pride in being Brazilian common until recently in the majority of portraits of the popular classes (and particularly characteristic of populism). It invites all Brazilians to join together to overcome the misery in the country. It also reproduces the expected vilification of foreign capital and sees all Brazilians as disadvantaged. Though these lyrics reflect the reaffirmation of identity through home/space, by constructing a lyrical parity between opposite sides of the city, rich and poor, black and white, they also avoid engaging the class/race opposition intimately linked to these spaces, instead placing it between Brazil and foreign capital.

Songs frequently pay homage to the MCs' communities of origin, and this rootedness in a specific place, communal history and collective memory, combined with the *galera*-based organization of funk dances, complicates interpretations based on theories of the deterritorialization of culture (Canclini), of a diffused global culture as disconnected from the past (Smith), as well as those of a new urban tribalism (Maffesoli). In fact, funk acts more like a battery which recharges a sense of community, demonstrating that the local and the global clearly do not work in simple opposition to one another. Numerous funk songs, such as "Rap da Felicidade," by MCs Kátia, Cidinho and Doca (*Carnarap*, 1995), which became one of the largest funk successes with a mass audience and was made into a *samba*, reproduce this double-edged re-valorization of marginalized and de-valued urban space. Depending upon their audience and reading, they can function to justify continued segregation:

All I want is to be happy
To walk peacefully in the *favela* where I was born
And to be able to be proud
And know that the poor have their place.[4]

In the context of the historical appropriation of black popular culture by the Brazilian nation without the accompaniment of any improvement in the socioeconomic situation of the black population,[5] it is interesting that young black people would choose to identify with transnational black culture instead of the traditionally "Brazilian."[6] It is difficult to imagine funk and rap becoming national symbols as *samba* did, because they are undeniably transcultural forms. However, most of the *funkeiros* and rappers interviewed for this study never expressed a consciousness of this choice, and some even denied that this had anything to do with their decisions to listen to funk or rap. Hypotheses such as this one must be continuously engaged with *funkeiros*, and rappers' testimonies regarding the issues, and the dialogue produced is the most important component of this type of research. Another interesting phenomenon in funk and hip-hop is the popularization of these forms with cross-class and cross-race audiences and their entrance into the mainstream.

The challenge to consensus

For the most part, funk has not been a race-conscious movement since the 1970s. Recently however, physical and social proximity to rap and the globalization of US valorization of difference has instigated a transformation. During the early 1990s, a number of violent incidents seemed to bring social opposition to the fore and cause a crisis in the Brazilian national myth of social harmony and racial democracy. For this discussion, the most important of these was the *arrastões* ("rioting") of 1992 and 1993, which was attributed largely to *funkeiros* and contributed to an increased consciousness of the division and difference in Rio associated with black people and black music. My argument, however, is that the *arrastões* were more a symptom than a cause—a reflection of the local integration and interpretation of US-based conceptualizations of race, difference, and social opposition resulting from what Arjun Appadurai calls "global ideological flows," specifically from the globalization of media forces and of black US music and its accompanying ideologies.

Funk songs such as "Rap da Benedita" by MC Dandara and MC Baiano (*Jet Black*, 1995), present race-and-class-conscious messages which challenge the smooth operation of consensus culture. MC Dandara, whose name pays homage to Dandara, the queen of the seventeenth-century maroon slave community of Palmares, praises Benedita da Silva, the first black woman in the Brazilian Congress and critic of the Brazilian myth of racial democracy. The song criticizes lies being circulated about Benedita in the mainstream media and encourages *funkeiros* to disregard them and choose alternative sources of information. The song then explains how MC Dandara sees pursuing her dream to be a star as following in Benedita da Silva's footsteps:

> Just be smart and act consciously
> I am proud of myself and I speak to all them [funk's critics]

My mother always spoke and guided me with words
See if you can forget about funk, since you won't get ahead
One day she nervously made me choose
Between funk and *a real** and I had a hard time
But I never abandoned my dream, I followed my *flashback***
And now I'm trying to be a star and shine on *Jet Black****
Bene, Benedita, senator of progress
As your miniature, I will, I will be successful...[7]

Funk has changed significantly since its origins in the 1970s, and violence
has become a greater part of much funk culture. Simultaneously, funk has
been vilified in the mass media and associated with urban violence, a
characterization which is not always merited. The media fails to acknowledge
the immense diversity within funk, ranging from violent club dances to
entirely pacific community-based dances. It is important to engage the
interpretations that *funkeiros* themselves make of their participation in this
often violent activity. Interestingly, much of the discourse that emerges from
the funk movement reflects statements made by academics attempting to
vindicate it and compensate for its negative media image. These individuals
have mostly failed to recognize the true violence involved in funk and have
erred on the side of apology. Two of the major funk producers in Rio were
recently arrested for promoting violence and covering up deaths and injuries
at funk dances. Nevertheless, funk organizations also frequently display a
public discourse of promoting peace, fighting violence, and placing value
upon a culture which is marginalized and repressed by dominant society.
They also organize blood and food drives and other humanitarian efforts,
reflecting the deep contradictions within the funk movement and the
difficulty of portraying any kind of unified vision or interpretation.

Hip-Hop

As in the US, Brazilian hip-hop culture comprises the musical expression of
rap, visual graffiti, and break dance. Rap is very different from funk in Brazil,
and in fact they are sometimes defined partially in opposition to one another.
Whereas funk reflects primarily an "aesthetics of affirmation," rap more
frequently asserts an aggressive and oppositional "aesthetics of dispossession."
Rap grew largely in São Paulo, but has a rapidly expanding contingent in Rio.
Since its origins in the mid-1980s, it has been much more overtly political,

militant, and racially identified than funk. It has also received much more acceptance as an aesthetically valid cultural form than funk. Brazilian rap consciously uses a US aesthetic to address a very local reality, though frequently Brazilian musical influences appear in rap as well. Brazilian rappers look primarily to earlier US message rap by groups like Public Enemy and harshly criticize gangsta rap and the commercial nature of the majority of current hip-hop culture. Rio and São Paulo rappers' stated role models often include people such as Martin Luther King, Jr. and Malcolm X. Recently, a greater diversity of middle-class and non-community based rap has been growing in Brazil, represented by rappers such as Marcelo D2. Thus, as with funk, it is important to recognize that rap cannot be rigidly defined.

During the 1990s, the most influential and successful current in Brazilian rap was led by the São Paulo group, the Racionais MC's. Their last CD, *Sobrevivendo no Inferno* (*Surviving in Hell*) (1997), has sold over a million copies and is called "The Bible" by many fans. Their philosophy includes staying in the neighborhood, giving back to the community, keeping their own record label, and refusing interviews with Globo, the dominant media network. They now appear regularly on MTV, won best Brazilian video at the MTV video music awards in 1998, and their DJ KL Jay is the host of *Yo! MTV Raps Brasil*. Though many would question the ramifications of this success, the Racionais have continued to be very militant, which makes sense since they are selling records this way. Marginality has become very commercially marketable in Brazil during the last few years, a phenomenon I believe is linked to a new type of valorization of difference.

The video for their song "Diário de um Detento" ("Prisoner's Journal") from the CD *Sobrevivendo no Inferno* (1997) is an angry portrait of the uprising and massacre at Carandiru Penitentiary in 1992, in which at least one hundred and eleven prisoners were killed by the military police. An aggressive aesthetics of dispossession is reflected in the words of the narrator of the song, a prisoner disappropriated of his civil rights, his right to speech and a fair trial, who asks at the end of his story of the massacre: "but who will believe my statement?" The video achieves its impact partially through visual imagery: it was filmed in part at Carandiru Penitentiary and includes photos of real prisoners, real news footage from the day of the massacre, and images of real prisoner's bodies in boxes. It is cut with footage from the Holocaust, linking racism in Brazil to genocide and, similar to many of their songs, includes a great deal of religious imagery.

This was the opportunity the system wanted
Notify the IML*, the big day has arrived
It all depends on the whims of the big man
who prefers to be neutral on the telephone

Ratatatá caviar and champagne
Fleury went to have lunch, fuck my mother
assassin dogs, tear gas...
[the officer] who kills more thieves wins a medal

The human being is disposable in Brazil
like a used maxi- or scouring pad
Prison? Certainly the system didn't want it
hides what the soap opera doesn't reveal...

cadavers in the pit, in the interior courtyard
Adolph Hitler smiles in hell
the government's Robocop is cold, feels nothing
only hate, and he laughs like a hyena

Ratatatá, Fleury and his gang
they're gonna swim in a pool of blood
but who will believe my statement
October 3, diary of a prisoner.[8]

Changing ideologies of race

The introduction to the Racionais' song "Capítulo 4, Versículo 3" (*Sobrevivendo no Inferno*, 1997), which is spoken almost as an alternative news report, is an aggressive condemnation of racial inequalities in Brazil. Depending on the listener, it is either a slap in the face to the dominant audience or a call for identification with a group of dispossessed black people:

60% of youth from the periphery with no police record have suffered police violence
For every 4 people killed by the police, three are black
Only 2% of students in Brazilian universities are black
Every four hours a black youth is killed violently in São Paulo
Speaking here is Cousin Black, yet another survivor.[9]

The Racionais and other "conscious rappers" use the term *preto* instead of *negro*, insisting on a term historically used more pejoratively by non-blacks and also further articulating their disidentification with the *Movimento Negro*, which they believe is elitist and unable to reach the majority of the black population. Rio DJ TR, ("Racial Test"),[10] a biracial person who opts to identify himself as black, takes advantage of the discussions of race and whitening that his name evokes to raise consciousness among his interlocutors. Many rappers point to the need for a binary black/white definition of race as a necessary step toward creating the racial unity required for change in Brazil. By asserting a discourse of racial equality and citizenship and by accessing US sources of racial tension and conceptions of civil rights in their own public discourse, Brazilian rappers are challenging to the urban consensus. They strike at the core of hegemonic conceptions of "Brazilian" identity by aggressively critiquing racial inequality. By embracing US ideas of racial consciousness (as they interpret them) and of race as biologically determined, they dispute the notion of the harmonious Brazilian racial continuum. Assuming and respecting blackness is a common theme in Brazilian rap songs and is represented in graffiti in Rio's cohabitational facility (project) *Cidade de Deus* which reads "Negralize já" ("Blacken now").

US black music and hip-hop style, made more accessible in Brazil by the globalization of media and commerce, has served as a medium for the transmission of racial consciousness and as a motivation to further question issues such as racial identification. MC Bill described his first introduction to rap, which was after seeing the movie *Colors*:

> In 1988, I heard the soundtrack to the film *Colors*, directed by Dennis Hopper, which included a lot of rap. I had a magazine that told the history of the film and talking about the rap artists and what they discussed in their lyrics. This was when I became interested. Only in 1990, after researching a lot, reading about people mentioned in the lyrics like Martin Luther King and Malcolm X and understanding the reasons for talking about those issues, did I write my first lyrics. (Personal Interview)

Though many critics would argue that following a US path to decreased racism and discrimination is at best a mixed-bag, my point here is not to address the relative merit of US or Brazilian forms of racism and anti-racism nor to argue that Brazilian rappers' interpretations of the US situation is even accurate. Rather, I attempt to trace how these appropriations play out in Brazilian society and I believe the key to these groups' influence is in the locating and adaptation of these US-originated discourses in and to specific places in urban Brazil.

In the Racionais MC's video for "Mágico de Oz" (*Sobrevivendo no Inferno*, 1997), the hope for change is associated with the US civil rights movement, accomplished by invoking images of Malcolm X, the KKK, the Rodney King beating, lynching, and chain gangs. A T-shirt panned-in on at the end of the video reads "Nothing changed. Let's change it," thus appealing for the cooperation of the viewer in a movement for racial justice. The song and the video together perform an almost ritualistic naming and extensive showing of poor, largely black, suburban, peripheral areas of São Paulo, similar to what occurs in much funk:

> Jardim Filhos da Terra e Tal, Jardim Leblon, Jaçana and Jova Rural*,
> Piqueri, Mazzei, Nova Galvão, Jardim Curisco, Fontales and then.
> Campo Limpo, Guarulhos, Jardim Peri, JB , Edu Chaves and Tucuruvi.
> Alô Doze, Mimosa, São Raphael, Zaki Narchi all have a place in heaven.[11]

The significance of this placing of peripheral and marginal spaces and of active figures from these spaces on the map and in the public sphere, viewed by millions of largely young Brazilians on MTV, cannot be overestimated. The creation of an alternative public sphere upon which this broader visibility depends is extremely significant. These developments will necessarily have repercussions on both poor and affluent, black and white members of this generation and on their conceptions of race and the urban spaces associated with it. The MTV model (which is international and not bound by the particular conciliatory forces of the dominant Brazilian media that originated with and are intimately tied to the authoritarian military dictatorship) has given marginalized groups a mass forum to get their oppositional messages out.[12] Second, and perhaps even more importantly, media like MTV and other transmitters of US black music and style have given people the idea that expressing and disseminating their ideas in this way is worthwhile and necessary.

This article has attempted to introduce Brazilian funk and hip-hop to the US audience as well as demonstrate some of the ways that funk, like many popular cultural forms, has played a conciliatory role in Brazilian society. It has argued that the emergence of a growing social and racial oppositional consciousness in both funk and hip-hop can be partially attributed to flows tied to cultural globalization. Rather than view the crisis of hegemonic ideologies of cultural, social, and racial consensus and harmony as rooted in the increased violence in contemporary urban society, this article places culture at the center of a challenge to these reified national myths. Confrontations and transformations are occurring through the media of popular music largely as a result of poor black Brazilians' identification with and local adaptation of an aesthetics and politics of "global" black culture.

Notes

[1] Mike Featherstone stresses that it is misleading to conceive global culture as necessarily entailing a weakening of the sovereignty of nation-states and an eventual global cultural homogeneity and integration. Ulf Hannerz suggests that global culture is marked more by an organization of diversity than by a replication of uniformity (237), or what Arjun Appadurai calls the "repatriation of difference" (307).

[2] This theoretical approach is indebted to George Yúdice's analysis of funk. However, whereas Yúdice saw funk as a reflection of a waning national identity, I demonstrate that funk is both invested in and contestatory of national symbols.

[3] Eu sou um cara humilde e não tenho dinheiro
Mas eu me orgulho de ser um brasileiro

Os estrangeiros têm carro importado
Enquanto os brasileiros só tem carro esculachado
Tem muita gente morando embaixo da ponte
Enquanto que tem outras que de casa têm um monte

Eu peço pra vocês, vamos todos dar as mãos
Vamos acabar com a miséria do povão
Tem gente sofrendo, tem gente morrendo
No nosso Brasil tudo está acontecendo

Pare, pare de brigar
Nós somos brasileiros, vamos parar pra pensar
Pare, pare de brigar
Nós somos brasileiros e não importa o lugar

Agora vou falar os nomes dos lugares
Que todos cariocas* gostariam de morar

Copacabana, Leblon, Ipanema
Barra da Tijuca** e não esqueça Saquarema
Rocinha, Vidigal, Borel, Andaraí, Chácara do
Céu e o Morro do Tuiti***

*cariocas: people from Rio
**affluent neighborhoods
***favelas

4 Eu só quero é ser feliz
Andar tranqüilamente na favela onde eu nasci
E poder me orgulhar
E ter a consciência que o pobre tem seu lugar

5 A process I acknowledge is much more complex than I am able to portray here and which I also don't argue has been entirely negative.

6 George Yúdice sees allegiance to funk as an "opting out" of other musics associated with nationalism. Young people interviewed for this research who listen to funk most frequently also listen to *samba*, *pagode*, rap and other types of Brazilian music, so the impact is one of complementation more than substitution.

7 Basta ser esperto e agir consciente
Tenho orgulho de mim e falo pra essa gente:
Minha mãe sempre falou e com palavras me guiou
Vê se esquece essa de funk, que você não vai pra frente
Um dia ela nervosa, mandou eu resolver
Entre a real* e o funk sem saber o que escolher
Jamais deixei meu sonho, segui meu flashback**
Hoje tento ser estrela e brilhar na Jet Black***
Bene, Benedita, senadora de progresso
Sendo sua miniatura, faço, faço sucesso....

*a real: reality
**flashback: a style of funk music which samples 1970s and 1980s music
***Jet Black: a funk CD collection.

8 Era o brecha que o sistema queria
Avise o IML*, chegou o grande dia
Depende do sim ou do não de um só homem
que prefere ser neutro no telefone

Ratatatá caviar e champagne
Fleury foi almoçar que se foda a minha mãe
cachorros assassinos, gás lacrimogêneo...
quem mata mais ladrão ganha medalha de prêmio

O ser humano é descartável no Brasil
como módes usado ou Bombril
Cadeia? Claro que o sistema não quis
esconde o que a novela não diz...

cadáveres no poço, no pátio interno
Adolph Hitler sorri no inferno
O Robocop do governo é frio, não sente pena
só ódio e ri como a hiena

Ratatatá, Fleury e sua gangue
vão nadar numa piscina de sangue
Mas quem vai acreditar no meu depoimento?
Dia três de outubro, diário de um detento.

*Legal Medical Institute (the agency that removes cadavers for autopsy)

[9] 60% dos jovens de periferia sem antecendências criminais já sofreram violência policial
a cada 4 pessoas morta pela polícia três são negros
nas universidades brasileiras apenas 2% dos alunos são negros
a cada 4 horas um jovem negro morre violentamente em SP
aqui quem fala é Primo Preto, mais um sobrevivente.

[10] My thanks to Jennifer Roth Gordon for introducing me to DJ TR.

[11] Jardim Filhos da Terra e Tal, Jardim Leblon, Jaçana e Jova Rural*,
Piqueri, Mazzei, Nova Galvão, Jardim Curisco, Fontales e então,
Campo Limpo, Guarulhos, Jardim Peri, JB , Edu Chaves e Tucuruvi.
Alô Doze, Mimosa, São Raphael, Zaki Narchi tem um lugar no céu.

*peripheral neighborhoods of São Paulo

[12] Though global media have also made poor young people even more conscious of their relative deprivation and have forced them to make all kinds of sacrifices to possess US consumer goods, a trend deeply criticized by "conscious" rappers.

Works Cited

Appadurai, Argun. "Disjuncture and Difference in Global Cultural Economy." *Global Culture: Nationalism, Globalization and Modernity.* Ed. Mike Featherstone. London: Sage, 1990. 295-310.

Carnarap: O Grande Carnaval do Rap. Som Livre, 1995.

Featherstone, Mike. "Global Culture: An Introduction." *Global Culture: Nationalism, Globalization and Modernity.* Ed. Mike Featherstone. London: Sage, 1990. 1-14.

García Canclini, Néstor. *Hybrid Cultures: Strategies for Entering and Leaving Modernity.* Minneapolis and London: U of Minnesota P, 1995.

Hanchard, Michael George. *Orpheus and Power: The Movimento Negro of Rio de Janeiro and São Paulo, 1945—1988.* Princeton: Princeton UP, 1994.

Hannerz, Ulf. "Cosmopolitans and Locals in World Culture." *Global Culture: Nationalism, Globalization and Modernity.* Ed. Mike Featherstone. London: Sage, 1990. 237-53.

Hasenbalg, Carlos. "Relações Raciais no Contexto Nacional e Internacional." *Racismo: Perspectivas para um Estudo Contextualizado da Sociedade Brasileira.* Niterói, RJ: Editora da Universidade Federal Fluminense, 1998. 9-41.

Jet Black. Vol. 7. Afegan Produções Artísticas, 1995.

Maffesoli, Michel. *The Time of the Tribes: The Decline of the Individual in Mass Society.* London: Sage, 1996.

MC Bill. Personal Interview with Shoshanna Lurie. *Cidade de Deus* (August 28, 1999).

Racionais MC's. *Sobrevivendo no Inferno.* Zambia, 1997.

Schwarz, Roberto. *Misplaced Ideas: Essays on Brazilian Culture.* Trans. and intro. John Gledson. London: Verso, 1992.

Smith, Anthony D. "Towards a Global Culture." *Global Culture: Nationalism, Globalization and Modernity.* Ed. Mike Featherstone. London: Sage, 1990. 171-91.

Ventura, Zuenir. *Cidade Partida.* São Paulo: Companhia das Letras, 1994.

Yúdice, George. "The Funkification of Rio." *Microphone Fiends: Youth Music, Youth Culture.* Eds. Andrew Ross and Tricia Rose. New York: Routledge, 1994. 193-217.

SHOSHANNA LURIE

Politics and Aesthetics of Myth in *Black God, White Devil*

Ivana Bentes

Translated by Bonnie Wasserman

Revised by Vladimir Freire

Deus e o Diabo na Terra do Sol is a synthesis-film that poses central questions of Glauber Rocha's thinking. It is also a key film in the context of the first phase of the Brazilian "Cinema Novo" (from 1962 to 1965), a cinema that rediscovers and gives visibility to the social and human landscape of the Brazilian Northeast. The Northeastern *sertão* ("backlands") is rife with social conflicts and becomes a symbol of another nationality, a paradoxical one, on the margin of traditional representations.

This rural Brazil became the backdrop for important works of the early Cinema Novo, such as the classics *Vidas Secas* (*Barren Lives*) by Nelson Pereira dos Santos (1963), *Os Fuzis* (*The Guns*) by Ruy Guerra (1963), as well as *Deus e o Diabo na Terra do Sol* (*Black God, White Devil*) by Glauber Rocha (1964). These are films that thematize the *sertão* as a territory of social borders and fractures (misery, injustice, abandonment) but also, as in the case of Rocha's film, as a mythical territory, full of symbols and signs of a culture of resistance full of possibilities.

The Northeastern *sertão* was always the "other" of the modern and positive Brazil: a place of misery, of mysticism, of the disinherited, a non-place, and simultaneously a type of perverted postcard, with its reserves of typicality where tradition and invention are extracted from adversity. The *sertão* is an important figure in the construction of the idea of the nation and of "Brazilianness," which surfaces with different meanings in the literature of Euclides da Cunha, Graciliano Ramos, and Guimarães Rosa. The mythic and imagined *sertão*, literary and cinematic, is a territory of utopias linked to the nation, to religion, and to *cangaço*, or "banditry."

In *Deus e o Diabo na Terra do Sol,* Rocha is able to synthesize and combine, in an exceptional and paradigmatic way, different angles from modern Brazilian literature (again, Euclides da Cunha, Graciliano Ramos, Guimarães Rosa) with the cinema. He sifts through realism and documentaries and selects the mythic and allegorical, which achieve in this film a monumental and operatic form. The film also makes a real contribution to studies of the relations between myth, politics, religion, and popular culture, recreating and politicizing popular myths from historical and living myths.

The narrative of *Deus e o Diabo na Terra do Sol* has as its context three important cycles of Northeastern life juxtaposed: the popular messianic movements (*"beatismo"*), the cycle of banditry (*"cangaço"*) and the power of the local political bosses (*"coronelismo"*). These are three distinct forms of parallel power, combining crime and belief and challenging laws and customs. In choosing the characters—the cowboy Manuel, the pious Sebastião, the bandit Corisco and Antonio das Mortes, the killer for hire— Rocha creates synthetic types that concentrate in their actions and their pathos entire moments of modern Northeastern history. The characters bear the features of historical figures who are easily identifiable, yet who at the same time attain the stature of legendary and mythical figures, characters from popular backlands fables, such as in the "literatura de cordel."[1] History, myth and fable combine in a hybrid narrative.

Rocha samples from history and from realism, but transcends them by transforming the backlands into a mythical and metaphysical territory. As in the literature of Guimarães Rosa, in Rocha "the *sertão* is the world," a place of possible utopias and of radical transformations, a place distant in time and yet also crossed by the wars of the present.

It is this articulation between myth, politics and real life, between a narrative that is at the same time pathetic—in the Eisensteinian sense—and critical, epic and didactic. It makes the film an exceptional work, capable of rivaling a sociological study, without abandoning the concerns of an expressive and aesthetic order.

The film is structured from the story of the cowboy Manuel and his wife Rosa, two common characters who pass through three rites of initiation. These rites provide three very well delineated phases through which the narrative synthesizes the fundamental historical cycles in the Northeast, historical elements that are deconstructed and re-elaborated in the construction of a new mythology.

The film is set in a territory that is both actual and atemporal. In the beginning, it describes a Northeast that is perfectly contemporaneous, marked by the domination of local political bosses (*"coronelismo"*), and where the cowboy Manuel kills a landlord after being cheated and humiliated by him. For revenge, his house is invaded and his mother is killed. The unequal labor relations, the subsistence economy of the *sertanejo* ("peasant"), and the small commerce of the fairs are all presented to the viewer in a synthetic form. This is done in a raw narrative with short cuts, where the story is at the same time told and sung by the character of the blind singer who "witnesses" the story and circulates the myth.

The film's first rupture and inversion takes place in a scene of immobility, in which actions and habits are repeated. The first gesture of Manuel's revolt has as its outcome the crime, that is, justice performed by his own hands. The theme of personal exile after an act of individual rebellion is of course a hallmark of the American Western movies. The difference is that Rocha provides a political rationale for this revolt, whose horizon in the film is a radical transformation: a collective revolt in the making. Contrary to the Western genre, the violence is not "natural" or a "given" but a symptom of a larger change, which Rocha tries to approach and explicate in his manifesto "Eztetyka da Fome."

Everything in the first sequences recalls the hardness and cruelty of life on the *sertão*, in a kind of explicated prologue that describes the land, the scenery of immemorial and actual fights, and the man who survives in that hell. The images elongate in a movement of repetition and exasperation, descriptive images like those in the initial sequence that present the vastness of the land burnt by the sun, constituting a natural theater that will be transformed by Rocha into a Brechtian platform. In contrast to the vast landscape, the foreground shows the head of a dead steer and the solitary cowboy mounting his horse.

Already in these initial sequences, Rocha punctuates the realist and almost documentary aesthetic—marked by the monotonous sound and repetition of the process of making flour and by the grandiose and indifferent face of Rosa carrying out the chores—with a playful vision, that of a group of *beatos* who sing and pray following Saint Sebastião, grasping flags in the desolate landscape like a magical apparition.

The camera oscillates between indifferent description and the subjective expression of a vision of the cowboy Manuel who patrols the group of *beatos*.

Fascinated he says to Rosa upon arriving at home: "I saw!" All of the initial sequence is given in a "silent monologue"—so to speak—in which Manuel talks to himself and comes up with a better future for the couple after the vision of the saint: "A miracle might happen!"

The conversation is punctuated by the skeptic, indifferent and exhausted face of Rosa. In this introduction, Rocha comments on and narrates the story through the voice of a singer, in the style of the popular singers of the Northeast and the *cordel* literature. The song advances the narrative, anticipating and commenting on the story, as in the ballads of the Westerns. It also functions as the place of the construction of the myth. The music precedes and triggers comments on the action.

The second movement of the film arrives with the transformation of the cowboy into a *beato* or pious man, who searches for an expiation for the crime he has committed. "It was the hand of God calling me through the path of disgrace. Now there is no other way besides asking for help from the *beato* Sebastião. Let's go quickly, there is nothing for us to carry except our destiny."[2]

Rocha pulls away from the initial realism to create a grandiose vision of a mystic trance. Inspired by the Euclides da Cunha's descriptions in *Os Sertões* (*Rebellion in the Backlands*) of the religious community of Canudos founded by Antonio Conselheiro and exterminated by the Brazilian army, the director recreates, in an original format, the genesis of the popular religious leaders who construct powerful religious communities, threatening the hegemony of the Church and the established powers. "Imagined communities"—as Benedict Anderson[3] has called them—that rival the nation and the state that have abandoned them, ushering in a new "reign" of justice and abundance.

From the personal revolt that leads him to the crime, Manuel arrives on the other side of misery: from the mysticism that turns him from a cowboy into a *beato*. Throughout the second movement, the film immerses itself in a trance, in messianism, religious utopia and the technologies of mastering the body and spirit. Humiliation, martyrdom, the exaltation of pain and suffering, penitence and redemptive expiation lead the way to the Promised Land, described by the *beato* Sebastião as a kind of exuberant *sertão*:

> On the other side of the sacred mountain there exists a land where everything is green, the horses eat the flowers and the children drink milk in the waters of the river... There is water and food, there is abundance from the heavens and every

day when the sun rises Jesus Christ and the Virgin Mary appear, Saint Jorge and my Saint Sebastião filled with arrows in his chest.[4]

The ascension and initiation of Manuel takes place on the way to the sacred mountain, in a painful climb on a trail of penitents, which becomes a type of natural and monumental "Via Sacra," and which today is still undertaken by the faithful of the Northeastern *sertão*.

The film builds through music, the monumental and playful space of the hills and mountains, from the sound of the wind to the voice of Saint Sebastião—a climate of growing exaltation that arrives at hysteria, at commotion and exasperation. "I hand over my power to my saint to liberate my people!" cries Manuel. In a few sequences, the songs of praise mix with the sound of bullets. Weapons and rosaries, crosses and rifles, transform the *beatos* into the armed guard of the Saint: "Jesus ordered that a warrior angle with his lance to cut off the head of his enemies."[5]

Religion is depicted as a place of pacification, conformism, humiliation, but also as a theater of violence, of exaltation and of ecstasy. In these sequences the montage breaks with the realism for a final effect of violence and pathos. Visual and audio violence created by the movement of an unstable camera that watches, pursues, and surrounds the characters. Violence is treated in different forms that both oppose and complete the film, creating a rhythm of dissension and exasperation. Violence is experienced through the extension and exhaustion of time, as in the sequence of Manuel's penance as he slowly carries an immense rock on his head while he is flogged by a *beato*'s whip.

Violence is represented in a ritualistic and hieratic form, recorded with natural sound, like the sequence in which the Saint sacrifices a child offered by Manuel. The camera remains motionless, impotently contemplating the scene, in a narrative indifference that contrasts with the explosion of hatred and revolt in Rosa, who ends up stabbing and killing Saint Sebastião. With this second liberating crime Manuel and Rosa free themselves from the Saint's influence.

The other form of violence that defines the film is the trance of the handheld camera rotating between the characters. Rocha turns the trance into the most remarkable feature of his camera in sequences such as those of the mystic exaltation of the people of the "Monte Santo" listening to the prophecies of the *beato*, of the delirium and pain of Rosa's character as she tries to free her husband Manuel from the influence of Saint Sebastião, and finally of the massacre and horror of this very people, decimated by Antonio das Mortes.

The production of a trance or a crisis is the most prominent figure of Rocha's thought and cinema. The trance is the transition, the passage, duty, and possession. In order to enter into a crisis or into a trance one has to be possessed by the "Other." The characters' trance is presented and experienced by means of the handheld camera and the rhythmic montage.

Rocha makes the trance a form of experience and understanding. To enter into a trance is to be in tune with an object or situation; it is to know from within. And it is this crisis and trance of the land, of man and of the social formations that we follow in *Deus e o Diabo na Terra do Sol*, in which the images do not represent the trance, but enter into a trance, or in tune, with the characters, the scenes and objects, as well as with the spectator, forming, in many sequences, one sole flux.

The trance and the possession also mark the character of Corisco, the "two-headed bandit," who has one head to kill and one to think. This marks the third moment of the film: the conversion of the cowboy and subsequent *beato* Manuel into banditry. "Órfão do Deus Negro," Saint Sebastião, whose faithful are decimated by Antonio das Mortes, sees in Diabo Louro, Corisco, a new force of leadership and command, a new myth that makes sense to the exploited life of the peasant. The Saint as well as Corisco appear in the cinema of Rocha as primitive rebels, in a revolt that also marks the character of the killer for hire, Antonio das Mortes.

The Saint, the bandit and the killer are in *Deus e o Diabo* our primitive rebels, carriers of a diffuse revolutionary hatred, emissaries of a hatred of the earth and of man. Rocha uses the imagination of Euclides da Cunha in *Os Sertões*, where the violence, the ferocity, the hunger and the revolt are attributes or conditions of man and the earth, and proceeds to transmute them in such a way that all of the violence of the earth, whether from the environment, religion, banditry, the massacred people, or from rebellion (both crime and mysticism) becomes an embryonic form of revolutionary ire. Rocha tries to give political, ethical, and aesthetic meaning to this rebellion.

This was Galuber Rocha way of transforming *beatos*, cowboys and killers-for-hire into potential agents of the revolution. For Rocha, "only through violence and horror, can the colonizer understand the power of culture that he exploits," he writes in "A Eztetyka da Fome" (31-32). The violence is not just a simple symptom, it is a desire for transformation, "the most noble cultural manifestation of hunger," he writes (31). Rocha's Marxism has something sadistic and hysterical about it. A revolution has to be preceded by a crime or massacre.

The *beato* Sebastião inflicts penitences and punishments on the faithful; the bandit Corisco kills with his the rifle "so that the poor won't be left to die of hunger." Antonio das Mortes kills *beatos* and bandits in the name of the revolution that will come: "a war larger than this *sertão*, an enormous war, without the blindness of God nor the Devil"—he says to justify why he indifferently kills the religious mystics and bandits, saints and demons. Figures of a past that must disappear forever, just like himself, Antonio das Mortes. Saint, bandit, killer are these primitive rebels, destabilizing forces in their blindness, prophets and announcers of a "great war" that will come.

Rocha subverts the Christian Gospel, combining Christianity, messianism, Sebastianism and Marxism, in an incredible political twist that appropriates immemorial symbols and myths in the construction of a pre-revolutionary mythology. The character of Corisco, beautiful, violent, amoral and anarchic, a destabilizing force that comes to "mess up the ordered," functions as a character who synthesizes of this revolutionary process. When Manuel sees Corisco, he falls to his knees, in ecstasy with the figure of the bandit: "This is my Saint Jorge"—the Christian warrior saint. Corisco takes and baptizes Manuel, giving him a new name: "Satan." Religion and banditry get along with the same forces of belonging that give meaning to the group, the reign, the band or nation.

Corisco is a character who is a mystic himself, but it is a hybrid and syncretic mysticism that mixes the practices of different religions: baptism, exorcism, possession, and "closing of the body" (*"fechamento do corpo"*), namely, getting a strong spiritual as well as physical protection to one's body. Christianity, *beatismo* and *candomblé* form a part of his religious experience, but Corisco also proclaims the power of arms, rifles, and of force, as instruments of transformation in the place of prayers and of rosaries.

The entrance of Manuel and Rosa into Corisco's band constitutes a new rite of initiation, where the idea of rebellion and anarchy brings with it a sexuality devoid of taboos and prohibition that involves and unites Corisco, Dadá, Manuel and Rosa. In three sequences this free sexuality is expressed: in the encounter of Rosa and Dadá, expressing a sensuality and admiration in which women desire and touch one another. There is also the scene in which

Rosa gives herself to Corisco, succumbing to the charm of the Diabo Louro. A third example is when Corisco's band invades a farm and sets up a theater of orgy and cruelty, in which they kill and rape.

Almost symmetrical to the sufferings imposed by Saint Sebastião, Manuel, after doubting the bloody methods of the bandit, is also humiliated and whipped by Corisco until he "converts" to banditry. Manuel, guided by Corisco's hand, commits a new crime, affiliating himself with the bandits through the blood and the sacrifice of an innocent, just as he became affiliated with Saint Sebastião through the sacrifice of a child. Mysticism and banditry are equated and propose a world with its own ethics and rules, beyond good or evil, a world that makes sense to the life of the disinherited and outlaws.

The scenes in the presentation of Corisco's band are marked by an extraordinary use of sequential shots and the movement of actors who displace the natural stage: the white and infinite *sertão*, an almost abstract scene that valorizes the gestures and dislocations of the space. The handheld camera delineates long plain sequences, accompanying the coming and going of the characters: moments of hesitation, of oscillation, of uneasiness, which characterize all of the "theater" surrounding Corisco.

The anti-naturalism of the interpretation, the almost operatic character of Corisco, who spins, jumps, rotates, in an admirable and dazed way, links him to the effect of the Brechtian interpretation of Othon Bastos and the Eisensteinian montage of Rocha, which confers to the character an epic and monumental character. An example is the scene in which Corisco incorporates Lampião and engages in a dialogue with him, alternating the voices and gestures of one then the other, transforming himself into the bandit with two heads in the same body. Ownership and possession resuscitate the dead: "Virgulino [Lampião] died in the flesh but his spirit is alive here in me," says Corisco. Possession is achieved through the effect of montage and impressive interpretations.

The cycle of mysticism and banditry are brought together in the hands of the same agent: Antonio das Mortes, presented in the song that describes the man without god and without law: "praying in ten churches, without a patron saint, Antonio das Mortes, killer of the bandit." The character of Antonio das Mortes is constructed as a paradoxical figure, at the same time critical and conscious of his acts to serve the church and the local political bosses in the extermination of the religious fanatics and bandits who upset the good business of the priests and landlords. Antonio das Mortes kills out of the belief that mysticism and banditry are forces of the past that should disappear, like himself, in the name of a radical transformation. Mixing the figures of a solitary horseman, mercenary, righteous person, bodyguard, Zorro, the black cape, hat and rifle in hand he is completely in the realm of legend. He is a character from a Western and at the same time a type of politicized killer, who kills the fanatics of the Saint and at the end, Corisco himself in a stylized duel that ends with the cry of the bandit urging on the fight: "Strongest are the powers of the people."

Removing himself from conciliatory or paternalistic solutions in the representation of the relationship between the Church, the landlords, the bandits, the mystics and the poor people, Glauber Rocha proposes a pedagogy of violence and of revolt in a pure state. In *Deus e o Diabo*, there is no intellectual character who serves as a legitimate representative of or mediator for the people, nor is there a discourse of praise or victimization of this people, as was common in the 1960s.

In the film the people are whipped, humiliated, flogged, massacred on different levels. Contrary to morally condemning the violence and exploitation of these people, Rocha represents violence with such radicalness and force that it becomes intolerable to the viewer. Rocha also points to new agents and intermediaries in this process of change (the bandit, the *beato*, the mercenary), who deprive the intellectual of his privileged position as an agent of change.

After so many trials and humiliations, Manuel and Rosa, free from Deus and the Diabo, of mysticism and the banditry, assume the place of a people to come, a people who invent themselves, a mythic couple, who run in a desperate chase across the *sertão*, in a long and magnificent sequence of shots that end in the finale of the film, realizing cinematographically the prophecy of Saint Sebastião that "the *sertão* will become the sea and the sea will become the *sertão*." The film adopts a messianic or mythic version, juxtaposing, at the end of the sequence in which Rosa and Manuel run aimlessly, the image of the *sertão* to the image of an immense sea, which covers everything.

A cinematographic utopia of transformation, with the voice of the blind narrator who chants: "My story is told, truth and imagination. I hope that you have learned a lesson. This is how the barely divided world goes wrong, that the land belongs to man, not God or the Devil."[6] The film changes its register abruptly and passes from the popular to the erudite, invading the sertão of the cordel with the sea and the symphony, ending with the music of Villa Lobos.

With *Deus e o Diabo*, Rocha constructs a narrative that expresses his infinite belief in transformation and in destabilizing forces, whether impure, ambiguous or fragile (the mystic, the bandit, the poor, the killer). He also brings a new understanding of movements such as mysticism and banditry, viewed not as "obscurantism" or "alienation," but as expressions of discontentment, rebellion capable of constituting powerful communities. The film emphasizes this force of the unification of religion, such as in the violent destabilization of banditry, a violence that could serve any ideology, including the revolution. Rocha pursues this rebellion in its pure state, a type of intolerable from which a real revolution could arise.

In this way he tries to build a new national mythology "on the margins of a nation" and to promote radical change, calling attention to the different forms of identity and belonging created by the mystic experience, by communities, by groups of disinherited and exiles of the nation. In this construction of different "imagined communities," Rocha believes that the cinema itself, or "a group of films in evolution could give, in the end, to the public, the conscience of its very existence" (33).

Notes

[1] Sebastião, the pious man, was inspired by Antonio Conselheiro, the religious leader of the Canudos community, destroyed in 1897 by the Brazilian army, as well as by other "saints" such as Lourenço do Caldeirão and Padre Cícero, both considered performers of miracles

[2] Quoted from original film dialogue.

[3] Anderson's *Imagined Communities* was translated into Portuguese as *Nação e Consciência Nacional*.

[4] Quoted from original film dialogue.

[5] Quoted from original film dialogue.

[6] Quoted from original film dialogue.

Glossary

Beatismo: a recurrent phenomenon in the Northeastern *sertão* or backlands in which priests and devotees appear, declaring themselves to be saints or prophets, and are considered as messianic saviors by the people. The Northeastern *beatos* become important political and religious leaders, capable of bringing together great multitudes and communities around themselves. Some examples of beatos who even today are cult figures in the Northeast, are Antonio Conselheiro of Canudos, São Lourenço of Caldeirão and Padre Cícero.

Beato: an excessively devoted man or a fanatic that follows a "saint."

Cangaço: Northeastern Brazilian social banditry that flourished in the *sertão* between 1870 and 1940.

Cangaceiros: the bandits of the *sertão*. Those who belonged to the *cangaço* were heavily armed, living off raids on farms and settlements. Bandits such as Lampião and Corisco became symbols of a way out from the misery and of the freedom for the poor backlanders.

Coronelismo: a system of land concentration in the hands of few owners that became a political and economic force parallel to the government.

Coronel: a landowner, influential political leader or owner of lands in the Northeast.

Sertão (plural: *Sertões*): hinterland, in opposition to the coast. In Northeastern Brazil, the *sertão* is a semi-arid region, subject to periodic droughts, and where there is an impoverished population as well as large landowners.

Sertanejo: an inhabitant of the *sertão*, a peasant.

Works Cited

Anderson, Benedict. *Nação e Consciência Nacional*. Trans. Lólio Lourenço de Oliveira. São Paulo: Ática, 1989.

Deleuze, Gilles. *Cinema 2—A Imagem-Tempo*. Trans. Stella Senra. São Paulo: Brasiliense, 1989.

Bentes, Ivana, ed. *Cartas ao Mundo. Glauber Rocha*. São Paulo: Companhia das Letras. 1997.

———. *Teoria e Biografia na Obra de Glauber Rocha*. Diss. Escola de Comunicação da Universidade Federal do Rio de Janeiro, 1997.

Bernadet, Jean-Claude. *Brasil em Tempo de Cinema*. Rio de Janeiro: Civilização Brasileira, 1967.

Rocha, Glauber. "A Eztetyka da Fome." *A Revolução do Cinema Novo*. Rio de Janeiro: Alhambra/Embrafilme, 1981. 28-33.

———. *Revisão Crítica do Cinema Brasileiro*. Rio de Janeiro: Civilização Brasileira, 1963.

———. *Roteiros do Terceyro Mundo*. Ed. Orlando Senna. Rio de Janeiro: Embrafilme/Alhambra, 1985.

Rocha, Glauber, et al. *Deus e o Diabo na Terra do Sol*. Rio de Janeiro: Civilização Brasileira, 1965.

Xavier, Ismail. *Sertão Mar: Glauber Rocha e a Estética da Fome*. São Paulo: Brasiliense, 1983.

Redemption Through the Excess of Sin

José Carlos Avellar
Translated by Ross G. Forman

At the back of the frame, the dead husband on the bed—his body, already prepared for burial, overshadowed by the son who stoops, crying over his father's face. In the foreground, the widow cackles with pleasure, her almost toothless mouth widening in a loud peal of laughter. At the back, the dead old man and, at his side, the son busy shooing away the flies that swarm around the dead man's face, trying to push their way into his half-opened mouth. In front, the widow, her empty mouth heavily made up, wearing brightly colored clothes, pleased because the old man died before she did, leaving her free to enjoy herself.

In the foreground of the frame, a small flight of stairs that leads to the front door of a house, with a mangy dog sprawled on the last step. At the back of the frame, a stretch of road and a man walking with slow steps in the direction of the house. All of this in slow motion: the dog is so shrunken that it seems to be part of the steps, while the man, Nelsinho, walks so slowly that he seems to be standing still. Suddenly, rapid movement; after climbing the stairs step by slow step to the last one, just before entering the house, the man gives the dog a violent kick.

These two images—the old woman Amália's laughter and Nelsinho's attack on the dog—comment on the political violence of the moment in which Joaquim Pedro's *Guerra Conjugal* was made, when the military dictatorship that had installed itself in 1964 became increasingly strict after December 1968, with the passage of Institutional Act Number 5. Yet the images also refer to a certain characteristic of Brazilian society, a certain way of covering violence under a veneer of politeness. Amália laughs distractedly, showing a toothless mouth that could at any moment hang open for an instant, in intimacy, in secret, openly chuckling to herself, anticipating a kind of happiness that has not yet arrived. Nelsinho kicks indifferently, without anger, in an almost mechanical way, like someone trying to push away with their foot some rubbish in the street. These are brief and interior gestures. They are not meant for anyone to see; they are not even to be seen in a mirror. The son, busy flicking the flies from around his father's face, does not see his mother's frank laugh; in the empty street, no one sees Nelsinho kick the dog. These are acts of aggression aimed at nothing in particular, or rather they are aimed at everything, at life in a more general sense. Amália is not upset with Joãozinho. The old woman laughs indifferently; she laughs because she has already stopped feeling the anger she felt towards him when he was alive. She no longer needs to think about how disgusted she used to be when, at the table, he guzzled his soup as if he were eating the last meal of his life. She no longer needs to listen to Joãozinho whispering his last wish to his son, pointing at his wife and saying, "when I die, at my funeral, don't let her kiss me." Nelsinho does not see the dog as a dog; it's just something on the step. He kicks the animal merely to move his foot—gymnastics, stretching, exercise, sport, football with a dog in the absence of a ball. Inside, his girlfriend tries to please him with a tender kiss, and Nelsinho gruffly complains about it: "You're still sucking those mints like crazy." He finds the clothes she is wearing hideous, but when she offers to change, he complains again: "Don't bother, I don't care." This is not violence, but indifference. Or better yet, it is indifference that amounts to violence.

The torture of political prisoners seemed to be diminishing at the time when *Guerra Conjugal* was released. State brutality was taming itself. And the film shows exactly that, violence being incorporated into day-to-day life: simple, everyday gestures thus shrunken to a show of good manners, to a polite discussion that everyone understands. We no longer put up with angry words and a fist in the face. In place of the blow, an interrupted kiss: the mouth pulls back in disgust in the middle of the embrace. *Guerra Conjugal* shows how life was lived at the time through a new kind of intervention. It shows not what, but why things happen. It depicts what happens from its apparent place in a particular space and at a particular time in order to understand what is going on as an integral part of a tradition, a cannibal tradition. It picks up Macunaíma's cry when he arrives in the big city with his brothers Jiguê and Maanape: "now, everyone for himself and God against us

JOSÉ CARLOS AVELLAR

all." This cry is portrayed through images with "a concentration exaggerated to emphasize certain points, surpassing realist convention to arrive at a fundamental form of expression, revealing the essence of things" (*Jornal do Brasil*, 5/6/1974, 2). These words, which Joaquim Pedro used to introduce *Macunaíma* in 1969, could be applied equally to *Guerra Conjugal* in 1974. Through a process of cannibalism, Brazil consumes the Brazilians:

> In fact, in our society men just eat each other. All consumption [can be] reduced in the final analysis to cannibalism. Labor relationships, like those between people, social, political, and economic relationships, all are basically anthropophagus. In the end, those who can eat others do, either through intermediaries or directly, as in sexual relations. Cannibalism institutionalizes and disguises itself. Based on indigenous legend, *Macunaíma* is the story of a Brazilian consumed by Brazil. The legends hold a certain truth, for Pietro Pietra, the biggest man-eater, to give an example, is the typical Brazilian industrialist. Yet, nonetheless, Brazil consumes plenty of Brazilians. (qtd. Holanda, 114)

Brazil was celebrating 150 years of independence in 1972 when Joaquim Pedro filmed the story of the "Inconfidência Mineira" (an early Brazilian movement to free the country from the Portuguese yoke). The film struck viewers as an expression that says in a bitter tone the same things that have been said in *Macunaíma*, anticipating the explosion to follow in *Guerra Conjugal*. Let me give an example: a cut that switches the action from Tiradentes's time to the present day. We are at the end of *Os Inconfidentes*. Tiradentes is about to be hanged in Ouro Preto. At the exact moment when his body is lifted into the air, with the camera at the height of the scaffold, the film cuts to a group of students in the same city of Ouro Preto, in the present—the present in which the film was made, the present of the audience—who celebrate the rebellion of 1779 for its role in Brazil's overall struggle for independence. The connection between the two images is effected by a neat and simple cut. We see Tiradentes at the gallows, and in the next shot the students clap. What is special about the juxtaposition of these two shots is that the viewer (led by the camera from one position to the next) experiences at the same time the point of view of the condemned man (the camera films the students from above, as if it were swinging from the gallows in the square) and the point of view of today's schoolchildren, who applaud the hanging of Tiradentes. We go from the past to the present, from a staged moment to news footage, from the violence of history to a celebration. The design of the image makes the irony of this immediately apparent, accentuated by sound effects, by clapping, and then by music. The song is "Aquarela do Brasil" by Ari Barroso, in a new arrangement by Tom Jobim that has nothing whatsoever in common with the aggrandizing tone of the national anthem of earlier recordings, but, on the contrary, soars in a playful and carnivalesque manner. *Os Inconfidentes* thus presents itself to the viewer as an investigation, to be read on two levels. It treats a failed attempt to liberate the country (at the exact moment in which a repressive government is commemorating 150 years of independence) in order to ask whether history is repeating itself, to ask whether all of those who dream of living in a free country are not still stuck in jail.

To celebrate 150 years of independence, Joaquim Pedro gives us a film in which nearly all the action takes place in a prison cell, a film about a Brazilian consumed by Brazil: Tiradentes. "The entire history of the conspiracy is seen from the moment of imprisonment," he stated at the time of the film's release,

> ... because we have only the point of view of the documents that exist about the *Inconfidência*. It was only from that point that we begin to be interested in the conspiracy that never happened... action, that remains only in meetings, conversations, discussions. The results of the investigation we made into the documents led us to... the conclusion that Tiradentes really oversaw the others. We were convinced, Eduardo Escorel and I, from examining all the material, that Tiradentes knew what he was doing and tried to use the others. He was the only one who had common sense and who really wanted to start a revolution. The others were more interested in speculating about what might happen. They liked to talk about how things would be, but always at the instigation of Tiradentes, who was more visionary. (*Jornal do Brasil*, 4/15/1972, 4)

Here is another scene to serve as an example: Tiradentes and Maciel are walking slowly, and the camera moves with them. They are filmed in profile, their whole bodies shown on the screen. As they amble, they talk about the natural bounty of the country. Slowly, the camera approaches them until all that can be seen is a close-up of Tiradentes' face, still in profile. Tiradentes stops, lowers his head, takes off his hat, and turning his face to the camera, says: "The Governors are not at all interested in the development of Brazil.

On the contrary, what they want is to keep the people poor and ignorant because that way they can rob them more easily."

When Tiradentes is almost finished uttering this sentence, the camera pans to show Maciel, who is walking behind him and who replies as Tiradentes watches him: "What's surprising is that we Brazilians put up with all this without the least complaint. Wherever I went in Europe, people praised Brazil for not yet having followed the example of the United States and sent Portugal packing, as they did to England."

A cut puts us in front of Tiradentes once more. He is looking straight at the camera again, but this time he is staring deeper, right at the viewer. His voice is different, too, whispering. He talks like someone hiding something, someone telling a secret, as if he were thinking out loud: "That's when it occurred to me that Brazil could be independent, and I started to desire that. It was only later that I began to think how it could happen."

This scene from *Os Inconfidentes*—in which the characters talk to each other and, almost at the same time, talk directly to the audience with another tone of voice and another dramatic register—provides a good example of the overall narrative structure of the film. And, we could also say, here is yet another displaced image portraying the Brazil of the 1970s, the Brazil of the military dictatorship (when there was a repression of a popular dream just like that which motivated Tiradentes' eighteenth-century rebellion) through an image of the country nearly two hundred years before. With dialogues drawn from the "Autos da Devassa"—the official records of the interrogatory of the "inconfidentes"—and from the poetry of the "inconfidentes" Cláudio Manuel da Costa, Tomás Antônio Gonzaga, and Alvarenga Peixoto (as well as from poems by Cecília Meireles), the film is grounded in language. It tries to screen the text with a freedom equal to that which filmic images have to link up with each other and to screen the images with a freedom equal to that with which words in a poem flow. In this way, in a single take, without a cut to separate the two bits of dialogue, Tiradentes and Maciel first appear in the time and space of the "Inconfidência," in the reality/alterity of the film; shortly after Tiradentes appears in another, intermediate dimension, partly in the scene, partly in fictional space, partly away from it all, as if he had jumped from the film into the auditorium to talk with the viewer face-to-face.

The image as text, the text as image. Let me offer another example: an interrogation room. Alvarenga, while being questioned, describes a meeting with Colonel Francisco de Paula. The frame is shot to make it seem that the audience is right next to the inquisitor. Alvarenga's face occupies half of the screen. In the other half, far removed from the front, at the back of the frame, we see Colonel Francisco de Paula, smiling and in the uniform he wore before being arrested. Alvarenga speaks without moving his face, without looking behind him, with his eyes trained on his interrogator (or on the viewer or on posterity). He is simultaneously describing his meeting with Colonel Fransico de Paula to the interrogator and talking to the colonel. It is as if all the comments made by the colonel during the meeting that Alvarenga is now confessing to, are being spoken by the colonel himself, who is there, in the scene, behind him—memory turned into the present and brought to life, the visible past that speaks in the present. As the colonel talks, he moves from the back of the frame towards a close up.

The bringing together of these two actions (which occur in different places and times) in the same shot is a good example of the way in which the film uses images to support its dialogue. In the same frame the viewer gets a picture of Alvarenga in prison and a picture of Francisco de Paula before the jailing of the *inconfidentes* group. Two different stretches of time, two different scenarios are collapsed into a single shot. In one part of the frame, in the foreground, we see Alvarenga, imprisoned and cowed, with his disheveled hair, wrinkled brow, and dirty clothes. In another part of the frame, in the background, we see Colonel Francisco de Paula as he was before their arrest: well dressed, self-satisfied, arrogant, and optimistic. And the imprisoned character in the interrogation room of the present is talking to the free one in the past. All this enriches our reading of the scene: we are not simply watching a man answer an interrogator, nor are we simply watching two characters talk before being arrested; the two actions are presented concurrently. One qualifies the other. Thus viewers are not informed by a single point of view, be it that of Alvarenga or of Colonel Francisco de Paula or of the interrogator. They follow the scene with greater perspective: they see things that happened at different times combined as if in a perpetual present. They see better than the three characters on scene.

To describe an independence movement that was more a dream than a reality, the film focuses on images almost without action. The characters barely move on the sets. They stay put, constrained by the tight space of the cell. It is the camera that actually moves, free and unencumbered, an invisible character observing the interrogation. The camera acts as it wishes; it acts as we all do when we are in an auditorium in front of a film. In the theater, the audience watches and hears everything half inside the scene and half outside of it. The audience sees the images as if from a bridge perched between the reality of the film and the reality/otherness in which they themselves live. And they stay there, on this bridge, because on screen what matters most is that invisible character, the camera—which sees and analyzes, which hears and asks—and not the travails of the visible characters.

When Tiradentes is beaten in prison and turns a face covered with blood to the camera, the audience (particularly those who saw the film when it was first exhibited, but not just them) without neglecting the historical context of the film, can return to their own period. They can retreat, in other words, to the things which, behind the murmured phrases and the reading between the lines, were going on under the dictatorship. The audience experiences the scene, the violence of the action, as if it were real, and they experience it, above all, as spectators, the violence of representation. The image grabs and forces open the viewer's eyes because Joaquim Pedro has created a real image, not a reconstitution of the past or an allegory for the present. The scene cannot be reduced to a utilitarian function, nor does it address itself only to the viewer who lived through the period in which the film was made. It provides *an image*, a dramatic scene, an open and independent reality, alternative or not, equal to ours, but produced in reference to it: *a critical image*, more reflexive than reflex. What actually is projected on the screen is not the appearance but the structure of things. Or, in the words of the filmmaker, what appears on screen is "an exaggerated focus to pull apart its elements, surpassing realist conventions and arriving at fundamental expression."

> The principle of composition in all three films, *Macunaíma, Os Inconfidentes*, and *Guerra Conjugal* is the use of excess to recover the human: domestic service, the rotten kiss, warts, the open door, arteriosclerosis, the burp, the erotics of the kitchen, senile lust, slaps in the belly, the delirium of ripe flesh, the spiked bed, necrophilic voyeurism, interior decorating, hesitant sex, the asthmatic's cough, and even the final triumph of prostitution over aging indicate, above all, the possibility of redemption through an excess of sinning. (*Jornal do Brasil*, 5/6/1974, 2).

This is a principle of composition that is developed in *O Padre e a Moça* and which, after *Guerra Conjugal*, is continued in *O Homem do Pau-Brasil* and especially—perhaps even most of all—in Pedro's *Vereda Tropical*, an "educational

JOSÉ CARLOS AVELLAR

and mind-opening" story of the absolute impossibility of human contact, translated into a relationship of sex and passion between a man and a melon. The basis of the film is one of those images which—no sooner is it mentioned than the question jumps in front of us—need not even be seen to be imagined, whether through the picture it conjures up or through its means of stimulating the mind. The image is more conceptual than real. What matters is more the absurdity of the situation, of a man who has sexual relations with watermelons, than a direct vision of the situation—more what is suggested than what is seen. It is more about what lies in the shadows, with what is glimpsed and imagined in outline, than it is about something concrete. The film plays with this absurd conceit, this imprecise and disturbing vision, treating the tale with simplicity and an almost neo-realist style. There is nothing fantastic; everything is very simple, with a few overfamiliar details that punctuate this rather unfamiliar story. A young teacher arrives home on a bicycle, dejected, stressed, his face twitching. His mouth is moving as if he were trying to say something, but nothing comes out. He takes the watermelon he has bought at the market and runs with it to the shower, and after washing, takes it to bed. We see a sexual encounter, marked by the man's words as he whispers his feelings, his face pressed against the robe of his lover. We try to guess her feelings as she lays silent, round, green, and covered in talcum and perfume. This is a sexual encounter marked by the snuffling voice of the man and the ironically tender gaze of the camera, which prudishly takes in the scene in the same way tasteful films usually take in love scenes—by trying politely to lower eyes when good breeding demands it. It all starts off very simply, all within the scope of the normal. The teacher washes the watermelon that he has brought from the market. But then he does something quite absurd. He makes a little cut at one end of the melon, nervously gets out of the shower, almost letting the melon fall to the ground, and goes to the bedroom to devour it, sexually, in bed.

Later, we see the teacher talking to a friend. He confesses to her his passion for watermelons while they are traveling by boat (books and notebooks under their arms) between Rio de Janeiro and the island of Paquetá, where he lives. Then we see them riding bicycles around Paquetá ("a beautiful spot to make love," according to the song "The Moonlight of Paquetá," which Carlos Galhardo sings at the film's end). We see the man and his friend walking around the market. She is already convinced of the sexual virtues of fruits and vegetables, and starts examining the possibilities of each one, in search of perfect love. "Educational and mind-opening," Joaquim

Pedro called the film. *Vereda Tropical* is one of four parts of the feature-length *Contos Eróticos*, which was made in 1977 but banned for two years:

> The chronicle of a noble flaw, a lyrical encounter along the escapist footpaths of an imagined Paquetá, a verbalization and shamelessly lewd display of erotic fantasies, *Vereda Tropical* involves the declaration of the genital function of vegetables, the intelligence of flowering maidens, a taste of life, and the poetic finale of Carlos Galhardo. It was great to make, just as I hope it's great to watch: educational and mind-expanding. (*Vereda Tropical*, Press Book)

It is a short film, a little nothing, an extension of the universe of *Guerra Conjugal.* The country starts to open up politically, and, in a rather romantic retreat to the tropical state (clearly present when it gave rise at a certain moment in the nineteenth century to the love story of *A Moreninha*, a classic of Brazilian romantic literature, by Joaquim Manuel de Macedo), a young teacher opens his heart to a friend and confesses, in a muffled voice and with his eyes staring from behind his thick glasses, that as far as he is concerned, the only woman for him is a watermelon. It is the response to a question posed by the French newspaper *Liberation* at a meeting of filmmakers in May 1985: "Pourquoi filmez-vous?" In all seriousness, to produce a text that functions as an image, as a piece of film, Joaquim Pedro always splices this kind of text into his films, concise and demanding, something that although not inserted between images on the screen, is a part of the projection, functioning as an image that prepares all the others and that is structurally linked to them. What Joaquim Pedro said to the French newspaper at the time (four years before his death) has become an image as inseparable from his cinema as any other:

> To annoy the imbeciles. To not get applause after scenes that hit the top of the scale. To live on the edge of the abyss. To run the risk of being exposed before the entire public. So that friends and strangers can really enjoy it. So that the just and the good make money, especially me. Because otherwise life's just not worth it. To see and show what's never been seen before, the good and the bad, the ugly and the beautiful. Because I saw [Buñuel's] *Simón del Desierto*. To insult the arrogant and powerful when they act like 'dogs in the water' in the darkness of the theater. To have my copyright screwed up. (*Liberation*, May 1985)

The feature films of Joaquim Pedro de Andrade are: *Garrincha Alegria do Povo* (1963), *O Padre e a Moça* (1966), *Macunaíma* (1969), *Os Inconfidentes* (1972),

JOSÉ CARLOS AVELLAR

Guerra Conjugal (1974) and *O Homem do Pau-Brasil* (1981). His eight shorts are: *O Mestre de Apipucos* (1959), *O Poeta do Castelo* (1959), *Couro de Gato* (1961), *Cinema Novo/Improvisiert und Zielbewusst* (1967), *Brasília: Contradições de uma Cidade Nova* (1967), *A Linguagem da Persuasão* (1970), *Vereda Tropical* (1977) and *O Aleijadinho* (1978). He also wrote many scripts that were never filmed, among them *Casa-Grande & Senzala* and *O Imponderável Bento Contra o Crioulo Voador*, texts as deliciously full of images as the films he directed. Images so inventive and critical that they leave us with the sensation that otherwise film just is not worth it.

Works Cited and Suggestions for Further Reading

Amaral, Sérgio Botelho do. "*Guerra Conjugal*: Uma Batalha de Joaquim Pedro." *Cinema Brasileiro. Três Olhares de Sérgio Botelho do Amaral, Marcos da Silva Graça e Sônia Goulart.* Niterói: Ed. Universidade Federal Fluminense, 1997. 127-177.

Andrade, Joaquim Pedro de. Interview with José Carlos Avellar. *Jornal do Brasil,* 15 Apr. 1972.

———. Interview with José Carlos Avellar. *Jornal do Brasil,* 6 May 1974.

———. "Pourquoi filmez-vous?" *Liberation,* May 1985.

———. *O Imponderável Bento contra o Crioulo Voador.* São Paulo: Ed. Marco Zero, 1990.

Avellar, José Carlos. "O Grito Desumano." *O Cinema Dilacerado.* Rio de Janeiro: Ed. Alhambra, 1987. 143-157.

———. *O Chão da Palavra, Cinema e Literatura no Brasil.* São Paulo: Prêmio Editorial, 1994.

Bentes, Ivana. *Joaquim Pedro de Andrade, a Revolução Intimista.* Rio de Janeiro: Ed. Relume Dumará, 1996.

Holanda, Heloísa Buarque de. Macunaíma, *da Literatura ao Cinema.* Rio de Janeiro: Livraria José Olympio Ed., 1978.

"Joaquim Pedro de Andrade, Intimidade com as Coisas do Brasil." Catálogo da Retrospectiva organizada pelo Festival de Brasília de Cinema Brasileiro, 1998.

Johnson, Randal. "Joaquim Pedro: The Poet of Satire." *Cinema Novo x 5 Masters of Contemporary Brazilian Film.* Austin: U Texas P, 1984. 13-51.

Monteiro, Ronald F. "O Filme de Nossa Gente." *O Eureka das Artes Puras. Cadernos de Cinema e Crítica* 3 (Sept. 1993): Edição da Associação de Críticos de Cinema do Rio de Janeiro e Universidade do Estado do Rio de Janeiro. 34-47.

Pierre, Sylvie. "O Cinema Novo e o Modernismo." *Cinemais* 6 (1997): 87-109.

———. "Joaquim, le Majeur et les Autres." *Cahiers du Cinema* (May 1984).

Stam, Robert. *O Espetáculo Interrompido: Literatura e Cinema de Desmistificação.* Rio de Janeiro: Ed. Paz e Terra, 1981.

Viany, Alex. *O Processo de Cinema Novo.* Rio de Janeiro: Ed. Aeroplano, 1999. 157-172; 257-270.

Xavier, Ismail. "*Macunaíma*: As Ilusões da Eterna Infância." *Alegorias do Subdesenvolvimento.* São Paulo: Ed. Brasiliense, 1993. 139-158.

Brazil 2001 and Walter Salles:
Cinema for the Global Village?

Jorge Ruffinelli

Alex: "You have no idea where you are, do you? This is the tip of Europe. (Opening her arms) This is the end." (*Terra Estrangeira*)[1]

Civil Servant: Ma'am, this is the end of the world... (*Central do Brasil*)[2]

The feeling is romantic; the image, symbolic. At two different moments, in two different films by the same author, two characters find themselves at "the end of the world." It is more a feeling than a geographical certainty; it is more a myth than a real border. In the first case, the character has traveled from São Paulo to a beach in Portugal. In the second, from Rio de Janeiro to the "heart" of the most miserable Brazil: the *sertão* or hinterland. The trip does not matter. It does not matter that the traveler goes to the heart of Brazil or to his Portuguese "origin," because in both cases he gets to "the end of the world." And what does he find beyond that? The void.

Walter Salles, the author of these two films, was referring to the period of crisis that Brazilians experienced under the government of Fernando Collor de Mello.[3] What took place then was a disoriented migration that could only take travelers to "the end of the world." Salles found the best metaphor for the economic stagnation and individual desolation of the period in the image of the ship run aground not far from the coast, as well as in the image of stateless "orphans" embracing in the solitude of the landscape.[4]

There is another epiphany in *Central do Brasil* (*Central Station*). When Dora and Josué, already in the Northeast, look for the boy's father they find a multitude of pilgrims who, had they lived in the last century, would probably have been faithful followers of Antonio Conselheiro. *Central Station* registers them and certifies their existence. But the problem is that the multitude is going toward some place in the desert, they are not leaving Brazil. They are going to worship images at a shrine located in the arid "no man's land" of the Northeast, and they are aiming for a point that contains the entire universe, the *aleph*.

A few years ago, I asked Gabriel García Márquez: "Why do you think moviemakers keep filming in Latin America, when production conditions make that activity an almost futile effort, full of risks and absurdity, without noticeable economic benefits or imponderable artistic celebrity?" García Márquez pulverized my sinuous question with a simple and irrefutable phrase: "Because they would die if they did not." Walter Salles answered a question by Carlos Alberto Mattos in a similar fashion: "I find that the filmmaker has to tell a story as a visceral matter, because he can never stop 'not telling' a story."[5] Brazilian cinema, which had been destroyed by Collor de Mello, was reborn. Instead of dying, filmmakers showed that they were still being consumed by the passion for a young art capable of rejuvenating them even more, by an activity for visionaries, magicians and marvelous inventors of reality.

In the 1990s, Brazilian cinema could not ignore Indigenous ethnicities, but, on the other hand, it could revert its gaze ironically and see *how cinema had looked* at those "objects of study." It was the equivalent of what the black filmmaker Manthia Diawara had done with Jean Rouch: an ethnographic documentary about the ethnographer (*Rouch in Reverse*, 1995). Also in 1995, the tireless Sylvio Back presented *Yndio do Brasil*, documenting how movies had seen Natives since the origins of the medium.

The *sertão*—which Glauber Rocha had portrayed with energy and originality in the sixties (*Deus e o Diabo na Terra do Sol* [1964]; *O Dragão da Maldade contra o Santo Guerreiro* [1969])—could also not be left out, although naturally the aesthetic in the 1990s was different. Thus Sergio Rezende returned to the *sertão* with an epic gaze in *Guerra de Canudos* (1998), while Paulo Caldas and Lírio Ferreira danced in the excellent *Baile Perfumado* (1996).

At the same time, Sandra Werneck explored love affairs in *Pequeno Diciónario Amoroso* (1996). Domingos de Oliveira did the same from a male perspective in *Amores* (1998).

Murilo Salles turned his eye toward marginalized people in *Como Nascem os Anjos* (1996), as did José Joffily in *Quem Matou Pixote?* (1996) and Tizuka

Yamasaki in *Fica Comigo* (1996). In 1994, farce and parody were applied to Brazil's colonial history in *Carlota Joaquina, Princesa do Brasil* (Carla Camurati), while contemporary history, including the guerrilla, appeared in Sergio Rezende (*Lamarca* [1994]), and Bruno Barreto (*Que é isso, Companheiro?* [1997]). Nevertheless, very few of these films, which are only examples, reached huge international audiences. On the other hand, Walter Salles' *Central Station* far exceeded box office expectations, and it is thus worth examining why.

One tends to confuse the roads toward international cinema with the search for a widening public and market. Both can coincide, but not necessarily. These roads, we know, intersect, are sinuous and can cross one another. Many seem to arrive at the same point, but they go to different places. Thus the difficult distinction between *popular* cinema and *populist* cinema. The search for an audience is legitimate. What is not legitimate, we also know, is sacrificing the artistic integrity of a work for the sake of obtaining a box office hit. A popular cinema is sometimes confused with a populist cinema, and the test that differentiates between them is the author's intention.

If these questions are posed from a theoretical standpoint, there would be others made from concrete data. For example, how can one understand that in an important United States festival a director as "national" as Francis Ford Coppola would choose *Deus e o Diabo na Terra do Sol* (*Black God, White Devil*) from among 4000 films from the whole world,[6] or that Martin Scorsese would write with profound admiration about *O Dragão da Maldade contra o Santo Guerreiro* (*Antonio das Mortes*)?[7] When did Glauber's "universalization" come about?

Was it through the previous inverse operation that Glauber Rocha transculturated the films of John Ford and Orson Welles in order to create his own? This hypothesis is seductive. As Ángel Rama observed, referring to literature in his seminal *Transculturación Narrativa en América Latina* (1983), the concept of *transculturation* is the dialectical process whereby peripheral cultures appropriate, actively and selectively, elements of a central culture. Rama thus substituted the traditional—and simplistic—notion of the theory of influence. In this sense, Coppola's and Scorsese's "acknowledgment" of Rocha could be a return road, a *re-acknowledgment* of active elements in their own culture which have been transformed by the Latin American élan.

Brazilian cinema of the nineties did not stop being *national*, nor did it stop speaking to its natural audience, which could understand its historical, social, political and everyday codes. *Quem Matou Pixote?* would be incomprehensible for an audience foreign to the real facts recounted by journalism, or unaware of Hector Babenco's movie that had made the character and actor famous, all within the social context of underage delinquents in the streets of Rio de Janeiro and São Paulo. By the same token, *Que é isso, Companheiro?* would be incomprehensible to an audience alien to the experiences of the period of military dictatorship to which the movie refers.

Yet, not everything depends on the historical context. Some parameters are related to the superstructure of "genres," which allows one to move beyond local and national "frontiers," since it deals with particular elements of narrative functions. When traditional interest in problems and thematics is displaced by structural and narrative elements, "genre" comes across like an ideal form of transnational reception. National characteristics then stop being obstacles and begin to function like foreign "accents" in the same language. Thus, in a successful genre like the police thriller, national variants (like the French *cine noir*, the Italian political variant, the superaction films from Hong Kong, the British whodunit, and the American street cinema) are accepted without the genre's losing any of its identity.

Precisely due to the complex relation between public and melodrama, and also because of his use of and recourse to the police thriller, Walter Salles' films are an interesting source of debate. The discussion of the audience seems not only pertinent but fascinating when a film stands out because of its having overcome its "nationalism" and having conquered audiences beyond its national borders. This pertinence and interest emerged in a conversation among various Brazilian critics (Ivana Bentes, Carlos Alberto Mattos, José Carlos Avellar) with Walter Salles, regarding *Central Station* and its conquest of non-Brazilian audiences (in addition to its notable critical and box office success in Brazil). A first problem considered in the dialogue entails distinguishing what is spontaneously popular from "populism."

Salles defends himself from any implication of populism, from deliberately looking for an audience. In the following response he denies any sign of *calculation* or *deliberation:*

> I find that he [the director] cannot think about the public. All hypotheses that include a calculated point of departure seem suicidal to me, because that calculation will be implanted in the film, do you see? To do something with a

specific end is really a suicidal act. I find that telling a story is a visceral issue, because you can never stop 'not telling' a story.

His interviewers insist, and so does Salles: "If you were to ask me: 'did you depart with that emotional voltage to make that film?' I would answer: 'No. I did not know that I would get to that result.'"

Later:

Really, behind your questions there is one that might be simpler or less articulated: why are people moved by the film? The answer might be: because I was moved making the film. I was not afraid anymore and did not seek the distancing that I imposed on myself in the first film. I tried to approach and like those characters, and a moment arrived in which the characters would do things and I would try to serve them.

In any case, the remarkable reception that *Central Station* received with different audiences allowed Salles to make a sharp analysis of the stimuli that conquer audiences. It was not a matter of national *cinema* but of national and specific *publics*. Mattos asked if the reception of *Central Station* in the United States corresponded to "a certain image that is expected abroad from Brazilian cinema, from Brazil." Salles responded:

I find the question very interesting because I myself was not hoping for the kind of reception that the film had. Now, I find that that happened in the United States due to a clear fact, an exhaustion of the theme of violence, an exhaustion of all the possible inflections of the Tarantino's universe in which the issue of cynicism is essential and elemental. Strangely the film fit within what American newspapers called 'the new humanism,' which was the theme for this year's Sundance. Before getting there, I noticed that the film went against the current, and that it was actually in a synchronic flux. Well, that on one hand. On the other, I find that there is a pluralization and diversification in what gets to United States' cinemas today. Films that a few years ago would not have been distributed there are starting to appear... That denotes a change, a reaction to the issue of transnational image. Every time there is an imposition of a mass image, there is a counterflow, which also explains the space conquered by Iranian cinema, [or by] a Chinese fifth generation.

Salles has worked in documentaries, thrillers and melodramas. His are various paths that, without his "taking into account" *a priori* a potential or real public, brought him closer or distanced him from different publics.

His first feature film was the most obviously international or "transnational." Spoken in English, with Americans as main actors, its result was mixed. Nevertheless, that road was not new. Other Latin American filmmakers (Luis Puenzo, Héctor Olivera, Christine Lucas, Carlos Sorin, Luis Mandoki, Luis Llosa) had followed that same path, almost always with disappointing results. Salles' film, released in 1991, was based on a novel by Rubem Fonseca and was titled *A Grande Arte / Exposure*. Well done from a technical point of view, at no moment did it convince anyone that its director had felt comfortable with that hybrid enterprise.

In *A Grande Arte / Exposure*, Peter Mandrake is an American photographer who lives in Rio de Janeiro. He is writing a book on the poverty and violent lives of young people, while at the same time a serial killer murders women, leaving a knife scar on their faces. For a while, *A Grande Arte* seems to link the violence of those killings (filmed in interiors) with the miserable street life. But this is not a social film but rather a violent thriller, respectful of the genre's norms and more akin to the action films of American television.

That is why Rio de Janeiro generates little interest as the scenery of the story. Bolivia generates more attention, as do the great dusty plains of the frontier, in a sequence that is among the best in the film. Mandrake's profession links him to a young prostitute, and when she is murdered after she confesses to him that she has been threatened, it also links him to the world of guns and drugs. When the young woman dies, her killers think that she gave Mandrake a diskette with information about their operations, and he becomes a new target to eliminate. As soon as she gets to Rio de Janeiro, the beautiful Marie, Mandrake's young archaeologist girlfriend, also becomes a victim. One night two killers rob them, stab Mandrake and rape Marie.

Mandrake recovers from the wounds and decides to learn how to fight with a knife and avenge the death of the prostitute, as well as Marie's rape and the aggression he suffered. He looks for Hermes, an expert in handling knives, so that the latter will pay him an old debt with his training. Hermes does train him, but Mandrake does not know that his trainer also works for the head of the drug dealers, the elegant Lima Prada, who among other things is the prostitute's killer.

The film gets its characters from the surroundings in which they exist. But the secondary characters seem to have come out of a circus. These include Zakkai, a midget who is the owner of a whorehouse; Chink, a giant Bolivian gangster; and Rafael, a sadistic exterminator. Although everyday life is presented as "documented" in Mandrake's photographs (the connection to the cartoon hero "Mandrake the Magician" should not be lost), the film does without that life and takes all capacity for illusion out of that environment. It is as if drug dealing and weapons were an international institution that is neutral and similar everywhere, oblivious to specific social circumstances. The film chooses to concentrate on the American character, with the stereotyped story of his ritual preparation as a "hero." As was to be expected, Mandrake finally confronts (and overcomes) the major Enemy, the knife Master, and the brains of the criminal gang. The artistic failure of *A Grande Arte* was not determined by the genre itself but rather by its use of an abstract and neutral quality.

The second path taken by Walter Salles, *Terra Estrangeira* (with Daniela Thomas as co-director), insisted on the thriller genre, but this time it was placed culturally at the heart of the political circumstances of Brazil and Portugal in the nineties. That was his initial seal of legitimacy, which began by allowing him to find a public that belonged to the same horizon of experience as the author, that is, a *generational* public. In this sense, a particular and original stylistic inflection, with a visual and musical lyricism that emerged from culture itself, was linked to a more "authentic" thematics. Salles and Thomas appealed on a double level: it was the same linguistic and historical culture (Portuguese) and, at the same time, two different countries and national cultures were put together, Brazil and Portugal. The film's locations were circumscribed even more to that of just two cities: São Paulo and Lisbon. Regarding photography, the directors opted for the "unpopular" use of black and white. In music, they made accurate use of the Portuguese *fado*, whose melancholy charge as a musical genre was perfectly in tune, as it were, to the story. The camera was released of its support and became agile and fluid, always at the service of the story. The aestheticism turned out to be well received and *Terra Estrangeira* brilliantly told a story of emotion, thrills, and melancholy.

The precise date at which the story of *Terra Estrangeira* begins in the two countries and cities mentioned is important because it indirectly declares, from the beginning, that this is not a conventional thriller but rather an original meditation on Brazil, its origins, identity, and history. By linking two distant places synchronically, Salles and Thomas allowed their story to alternate the "parallel lives" of the main characters in two lines, until their meeting in Lisbon. Thus, in São Paulo, where Manuela and her son Paco live, the events of March 1990 were a historical date: the moment when the new government of Collor de Mello initiated the economic downfall of the country, with the freezing of savings accounts, money controls and other measures that threw Brazil into chaos and generated a palpable emigration due to economic conditions. The humble seamstress of Basque origin, who had gathered her life's savings to return to her parents' land, cannot take the fatal news she hears on television, and dies. In disaster the only thing left to Paco—who is twenty-one, has a theatrical vocation, and reads *Faust*—is solitude.

At the same time in Lisbon, Alex, twenty-eight years old, makes a living as a restaurant waitress and is unhappy with her companion Miguel, an unemployed musician who verbally mistreats her and steals her money to buy drugs. Actually Miguel is an indicator of the European "crisis." A bar musician without a job, he is one of the Europeans "without a future," surviving a bohemian life of drugs and smuggling. (Another of the indicators of the European "situation" is the group of Africans crammed in a building whom Paco meets on his trip to Lisbon).

Paco meets Igor at a bar during his despairing wake for his mother. Igor, an expansive antiquarian, later invites Paco to see his business, and shows him the most dissimilar and oldest objects he owns, assuring Paco that they contain Brazil's complete history from the time of the conquerors. National history has been reduced to that: a bunch of objects in an antique store. Igor hires Paco to take a Stradivarius to Lisbon, since it is convenient for the young man who is on his way to his mother's little town, San Sebastian, in Spain. But Paco does not know that he would also be smuggling hidden diamonds. It is then that an unforeseeable and tragic adventure begins, because his contact in Lisbon is Miguel, who betrays his own contacts, who kill him before Paco's arrival in Lisbon. That mix-up nevertheless causes the meeting between Paco and Alex after the deception, a trip to the coast, the loss of the diamonds, the chasing of the youths by the French delinquents and even Igor himself, and at the same time the unexpected affective relationship between Alex and Paco. It is a love story lived by losers, immigrants and persecuted.

On the road to the border with Spain and San Sebastian, Alex and Paco stop at an inn, where Igor and an accomplice reach them. In the surprise meeting, Igor is badly wounded and his accomplice dies. Alex leaves in her car for San Sebastian, with Paco dying next to her due to a bullet in his stomach. The moving final sequence—when Alex begs Paco not to sleep (that is, not to die), desperately promises to take him "home," and clumsily and sweetly sings a *fado* by Gal Costa that they had heard together—fuses individual and collective histories, intimate vision (within the car) with exterior vision (the aerial sequence of the road and the car), and the song that Alex sings with Gal Costa's voice (suddenly, the actress' voice is replaced by the singer's in the soundtrack, in a subtle and poetic symbolic transition).

The beach (the film's initial image) is the final point of the world, as Alex explains in the phrase I quoted as an epigraph. Departing from that metaphor-allegory this movie can be understood as a story of borders, of migrations and exiles toward a *u-topica*. Even more, some Angolan immigrants live next to the Lisbon hotel where Igor had told Paco to wait for his contact. Although they are on the periphery of the story, they are part of that universe of constant changes in the world, in search of better economic opportunities. But even though they have gone from Africa to Europe (or to Portugal, at least), the Angolans live huddled in a boarding house: there is no future for them either. Loli, the Angolan whom Paco quickly befriends, asks him what he was looking for in Lisbon, and the dialogue immediately turns allegorical: "I came here… at least to discover something. Wasn't it from here that people left to discover the whole world?" Nevertheless, Lisbon is "the ideal place to lose someone or to lose oneself," as Loli answers. The captivating motive of the movie is finding something in the wrong time. Utopia, the place without a place, the "ideal place," makes Paco find a twinkle of love, of sexual happiness and passion. The return "home" (either to the maternal San Sebastian, or to Lisbon, from where the elder left "to discover the world") turns out to be impossible. But the movie bets its high melancholic charge on the Faustian desire for the absolute, and on the intuition of having touched it at least for an instant.

Terra Estrangeira was the path toward a more open and secure cinema, which allowed its authors to easily overcome the conventional limitations of the genre. At the same time, they employed the photographic texture of black and white as a tribute to the best French and American *film noir*. After *Terra Estrangeira*, it was possible to speak of the poetry of the image, which Salles started to control and manage with captivating emotion and beauty.

A third path took Walter Salles even farther into the heart of Brazil, with a moving story of endless searches: *Central Station*. In some aspects, this movie could be related to *Terra Estrangeira*: they are both *road movies*, and in both the characters are persecuted. They also differ. *Central Station* opens up to a hope that the "closed" story (due to the limitations of the "lyrical" police genre and even due to the historical circumstances of the period represented) had prevented *Terra Estrangeira* from achieving.

Based on the theme of a search for a father by the child who never knew him, Salles builds a simple story, yet one that is full of nuances and resonances. Although in its second half the movie centers on the trip undertaken by Dora and Josué to the *sertão* (a "mythical" space in Brazilian cinematic culture), it is not by chance that *Central Station* starts with a powerful collective image: the impressive human mass coming out of the trains in Rio de Janeiro's Central Station, as if they were leaving jail, or were in a horse race toward an unpredictable end. It is also not random that that general take is continued in close-ups of humble characters who verbalize their desire to communicate to a letter writer, Dora. She is a former grammar school teacher whose job is to use her knowledge to edit on paper the oral letters that the illiterate dictate to her. But Dora is no Good Samaritan at all. She plays a cynical and sinister game. When she returns home, tired from her journey, she meets with her neighbor Irene, and together they read and "select" the letters, most of which wind up in the garbage or in a drawer that Irene calls "Purgatory." Thus, most of the anxieties and humble dreams of the people never unfold.

In his third feature, Water Salles wanted to tell, through cinematic images, a story that came from a single idea: *a letter that does not arrive at its destination*. The letter is the one that Ana, Josué's mother, writes to the child's father (who disappeared nine years before), telling him that his child is anxious to see him. Ana dies in a traffic accident at the doors of the Station. Like many other kids, Josué becomes an orphan, thrown to the voracity of the streets, to robbery, to a quick death (execution) by the "parapolice," or possibly to become an involuntary donor of vital organs in an illegal and sinister international market. In that context, Dora, far from being the best mother substitute, is the child's main antagonist. Yet, the story of *Central Station* is also that of her redemption, and in this sense the movie has been understood as a humanist film.

It is interesting to notice how Salles rereads one of his favorite directors, John Cassavettes, for example. When the repentant Dora rescues Josué after selling him to Pedrão for a thousand dollars, and flees with the child to protect him from the assassin, she is recreating the character Gloria from John Cassavettes' *Gloria* (1980). The viewer can find the same type of verbal antagonism between the mature woman and the child, who argue at every minute and reproach one another mutually, exactly like in *Gloria*. And in both cases the initial relationship is transformed: for Josué, the meeting with a friend, grandmother or substitute mother; for Dora, the redemption through which she recovers her generous and affective fibers in a world that does not have many of those values left.

The film becomes a road movie from the time the two characters leave Rio de Janeiro. Time and again, with different vicissitudes, Dora and Josué go on to Bom Jesus do Norte, and at the end of that road they meet with believers, fanatics and pilgrims (all of which are in abundance in the hinterland), until they are submerged in a great liturgy, in a human mass that goes toward a vestry wallpapered by hundreds of photographs and personal objects. The scene is almost out of the fantastic, and the film uses it as a framework of thousands of wishes, hopes, and collective utopias in which Dora and Josué seem to get lost, at least for a few hours. They re-emerge nevertheless in an image of beatitude, especially when at dawn of the next day Dora wakes up from her faint in the child's arms in a sort of inverted *Pietà*.

The story does not conclude with Josué's meeting the father he sought, but with the discovery that he has two half-brothers. The final sequence contains another cinematic re-reading by Salles. When Dora leaves the following morning, without saying goodbye, she writes that "goodbye" in the form of a letter (the first she is to send without being an intermediary). At the same time Josué, after awakening and noticing Dora's absence, runs uselessly to try to catch her, like the child (Joey) behind Shane, in George Stevens' *Shane* (1953). All they have left is a duplicated photograph, which both look at the same time, as a memory fetish or a defense to combat the necessary forgetfulness.

Paradoxically, the route taken by *Central Station*, the route that made it an example of a humanist movie, includes another road. That road, if not secret, is at least lesser known, which explains the need for redemption implied at the end of the film. Although that road is autonomous in itself, it has another story behind it, the story of a discovery. And that story has to do with a Polish émigré and with a woman in prison. They are Franz Krajcberg and Socorro Nobre. Without them, *Central Station* would probably not exist.

In 1995, Salles discovered Franz Krajcberg, or at least "discovered" him for moviegoers, with his documentary *Franz Krajcberg: O Poeta dos Vestígios* (*Franz Krajcberg: The Poet of Vestiges*). Krajcberg, born in Poland, lived and suffered through the European war, during which his mother died. Emigrating to Brazil around 1948, Krajcberg decided to isolate himself from the world of men little by little, due to his deep disappointment with human destructiveness. The problem is that he found that destructiveness again in Brazil, with the exploitation of natural resources, the *queimadas* (literally atavistic "burnings" of great and lasting effect in the forest) and deforestation, frequently caused by what Krajcberg himself calls "headless progress."

Then, Salles filmed a short documentary, *Socorro Nobre.* This excellent film was the origin for Salles' 1997 fictive feature *Central Station.* Just as *Central Station* arose from the idea of a letter not reaching its destination, *Socorro Nobre* bases itself on a letter that did get to its recipient, but that could just as well have not. In one way or another, the letter meant a change in destiny. That is why *Central Station* begins by registering the circumstances of the letter's recipient, the sculptor Franz Krajcberg, to whose extraordinary work Salles devoted the five-segment television documentary, *Franz Krajcberg: O Poeta dos Vestígios.* His story is the same, but we find a more optimistic view of it in *Socorro Nobre.* Krajcberg's experience is unique, despite having come from the collective suffering of the Second World War. As he briefly tells it in the documentary, he was born in Poland, lived in a ghetto, and lost all his family in 1940. In the ghetto, he suffered deprivation and daily contact with death.

Once the war ended he fled from a people devoted to demonstrating the "superiority of its race," isolated himself from humans, thought about suicide, and finally found in Brazil the peace that he could not find in Europe. "There is another side to my life" he warns, because in the nature of the Amazon and the Matto Grosso, and later in Bahia, he jubilantly discovers the "forms" that inspired his sculpture: "I was so happy I wanted to dance when I found those marvelous plants." His sculptures are thus based on a return to humanity through nature, and also because of his sudden conversion into an ecological crusader. Just as he found the model for all possible forms and colors, he again found the destruction of what is natural in the brutal *queimadas* with which men continue to destroy nature in Brazil. As a result, and as a manifestation of rebellious and radical art, Krajcberg devoted himself brilliantly to make art from the "vestiges" of arson. What remains of the destroyed nature can give an idea of what is lost every day.

Krajcberg adds that he received hundreds of letters because of his ecological and artistic activities. But one that impressed him deeply arrived from the women's prison in Salvador. It was from a woman called Socorro Nobre who had been sent to jail for twenty-one years. This prisoner had read a report on Franz Krajcberg published in the weekly magazine *Veja*, and she wrote to the artist explaining her own need for redemption, having an example in his own redemption after the European horror. This had inspired her in the same way; she wanted to change and had started to do so, with the dream of finding her lost liberty some day.

After starting with images of Krajcberg enjoying the beautiful liberty that nature gives him (he runs and plays with his dog at the seashore, sinks his hands into the waves) the film moves to the prison. A brief transition fuses the sound with the visual image: while images of Krajcberg are shown, the soundtrack lets us hear the voice of Socorro Nobre reading the initial letter she had sent to him. From that moment on, the documentary alternates the open and renewed world of Franz Krajcberg with Socorro Nobre's prison world. The documentary turns the voice over to the woman, who speaks and expresses ideas and thoughts in brief flashes, amidst a series of "punctuations" or visual pauses. Instead of a conventional "report," Salles cuts the filmed interview and replaces what could have been the use of jump cuts or fade ins and fade outs with instants of silence and a black screen. This mechanism allows him to "isolate" fragments of Socorro Nobre's story, and even to emphasize ideas: "One has to dream, once in a while." At the same time, with remarkable photographic work, the documentary "discovers" forms in the rain, in washed clothing hung out to dry, in the faces of women. This is seen even (since we are speaking about film images) in the extraordinary use of silence with which the camera briefly halts on the static expressions of women, reflecting the silent wait for time that jail is.

The letter to Krajcberg was instrumental for Socorro Nobre's own existential transformation, and eventually for her parole. As the documentary notes in a final caption, at the start of 1995 Socorro Nobre was paroled and "lives with her three sons in the interior of Bahia." The documentary ends with brief shots of a meeting between Nobre and Krajcberg. Nevertheless, the almost magical "story" of the letter that had a good end is continued in *Central Station.* At the start of this movie, Socorro Nobre "acts" like the first person that sits in front of Dora's table to dictate a letter to her. It is a moving self-referential game, and a scene that captures or exemplifies once again the philosophy of cinematic creation that Walter Salles has had the fortune to put into practice. It is the philosophy of a cinema that influences lives, a cinema that starts becoming an *event*, a *reality*, even before getting to the screen and moving its viewers. As shown by the lives of Krajcberg and Nobre, it is not in vain that *Central Station* is a story of redemption.

In 1998, Walter Salles made still another film, but the international path was already established, and others had to travel it to get to him. *O Primeiro Dia* (1998) was made for an international series in which directors from different countries would imagine in one hour the moment of transition from the twentieth century and the millennium. For this reason the story arrives at the final minute of December 31, the end of the twentieth century. Once again there are two parallel stories and two characters that will meet. The woman is a teacher of sign language; the man is a convict in jail. Ironically, the film soon makes clear that there is no communication between the woman, whose job is in the field of communication, and her partner. One day he decides to leave her, and does it by leaving her a goodbye note. She goes into a crisis, cannot stand the loneliness and change, and decides to commit suicide.

In the meantime, the convict manages to escape with the help of his jailers, by means of an assassination contract that he must complete. He actually gets his freedom in exchange for killing a best friend, which he does. He immediately flees upon noticing that he has been merely the executioner and that his liberators have decided to eliminate him. He escapes and finds refuge on the roof of a building. A meeting place. The last minutes of the year are approaching and the citizens of Rio de Janeiro are getting ready to end it with fireworks. The man then sees a woman who is approaching the parapet to kill herself. He prevents her from doing so, while fireworks go off as if in a "spectacle." Beings in a borderline situation, fleeing from imaginary and real ghosts, they end up celebrating the moment, the meeting, and the possibility of sexual pleasure, which seemed to be a closed road in their lives. The following morning, the beach awaits them. She bathes while he waits for her seated in the sand. His pursuers find him, and when she emerges from the sea he is dead. Some lives are saved, others are lost.

O Primeiro Dia is a brief and yet a perfect film. It does not leave any room for melodrama. Everything happens unexpectedly and fleetingly. Very few times has Brazilian cinema been able, as in this case, to show with so much brilliance the precariousness as well as the force of life. Like Josué, with *Central Station* and with *O Primeiro Dia*, Walter Salles himself "returned home." Georg Lukács used to say that the universal can only be achieved through the particular. That is the best lesson learned by Walter Salles in his short career, and the best lesson he can give to Brazilian cinema in order that it can be authentically international without ceasing to be national. May it become a cinema for the global village of the second millennium.

JORGE RUFFINELLI

Notes

[1] Alex: "Você não tem nem idéia de onde você está, né? Isso aqui é a ponta da Europa. (Abrindo os braços) Isso aqui é o fim!"

Daniela Thomas, Marcos Bernstein, and Walter Salles 67.

[2] "Funcionário: Isso aqui é o fim do mundo, dona…"

João Emanuel Carneiro, Marcos Bernstein, and Walter Salles 90.

[3] See Walter Salles, "Terra à Vista," *Terra Estrangeira* 5.

[4] "How does a film come about? In the case of *Terra Estrangeira*, at the beginning, there was only an image: of a couple adrift, stuck on a deserted beach like a ship stuck in the sand. A little later, the image materialized in the cover of a book by Jean Pierre Favreau. Oddly, it was at that moment that we were sure that the film would also exist" (*Terra Estrangeira* 5, my translation).

[5] Carlos Alberto Mattos, Ivana Bentes, José Carlos Avellar 7ss.

[6] In 1997, the San Francisco International Film Festival asked some famous filmmakers for their personal selection of films among the four thousand that the film festival had shown throughout four decades. The only Latin American movies chosen were two by Glauber Rocha. Lourdes Portillo chose *Antonio das Mortes* and Francis Ford Coppola chose *Black God, White Devil* (*Deus e o Diabo na Terra do Sol*). An example of the French reception: Salles is the only Latin American director consulted in a survey on "1990-2000, Une Décennie en Question" by *Cahiers du Cinema* 452 (Jan. 2000).

[7] See Scorsese.

Walter Salles' Filmography

Several documentaries on popular music and musicians: *Chico no País da Delicadeza; Visão do Paraíso; Caetano Cinqüenta Anos,* etc.

A Grande Arte / Exposure. Alberto Flaksman (Paulo Carlos de Brito Production), 1991.

Franz Krajcberg: O Poeta dos Vestígios. Rede Manchete-Vídeofilmes, 1995.

Socorro Nobre. Vídeofilmes Mini Kerti, 1995.

Terra Estrangeira. Co-dir. Daniela Thomas. Produced by Movi Art, Secretaria para o Desenvolvimento do Audiovisual, Riofilme (Flavio Tambellini, Brazil; Antonio da Cunha Telles and Maria João Mayer, Portugal), 1995.

Central do Brasil. Vídeo Filmes (Brazil), co-prod. Arthur Cohn Production—MACT Productions (Paris) and Rio Filme (Rio de Janeiro), 1997.

O Primeiro Dia. Co-dir. Daniela Thomas. Hart & Court, 1998.

Le Premier Jour. (A longer version of *O Primeiro Dia*, 80 minutes.)

Works Cited

Carneiro, João Emanuel, Marcos Bernstein and Walter Salles. *Central do Brasil.* Rio de Janeiro: Objetiva, 1998.

Mattos, Carlos Alberto, Ivana Bentes, José Carlos Avellar. "Conversa com Walter Salles: O Documental como Socorro Nobre da Ficção." *Cinemais* 9 (Jan./Feb.): 7-40.

Scorsese, Martin. "Three Portraits in the Form of an Homage-Ida Lupino, John Cassavettes, Glauber Rocha." *Projections* 7 (London: Faber and Faber, 1997): 87-92.

Thomas, Daniela, Marcos Bernstein and Walter Salles. *Terra Estrangeira.* Rio de Janeiro: Rocco, 1996.

Praying in the Sand: Paula Rego and Visual Representations of The First Mass in Brazil

Memory Holloway

On May 1, 1550, Pero Vaz de Caminha wrote a letter to the king of Portugal in which he described in great detail the First Mass in Brazil, celebrated on April 26.[1] In his letter, the writer, an educated government official, described how he and others who had disembarked had set up a cross on the southern bank of a river so that it might be seen to the best advantage. "There," he writes, describing the scene, "the admiral marked the place for a pit to be made in which to plant the cross."[2] Once the site was ready, friars, priests, and the rest of the arriving party carried the cross in procession, a ceremony observed by a large gathering of local inhabitants.

After the cross was planted and an altar set up by its side, Friar Henrique de Coimbra preached the gospel of the day, which was Pascoela, the Sunday after Easter. The passages included the resurrection of Christ, the disciples' strange sightings of Him, and the doubting Thomas, all stories that seemed appropriate to the discovery of this new land. To the place where they landed, the Portuguese had given the name of Porto Seguro, as if to sum up their impression of this reef sheltering port.

Along with the Portuguese, Caminha reports that fifty or sixty "people of the place," as he calls them, were also on their knees. When the Gospel was shown, they followed the Portuguese and arose and lifted their hands; when the Portuguese sat, the local people sat. When the Portuguese knelt, they knelt. And when the priest gave those who remained after the Mass a tin crucifix, each man kissed it as it was hung around his neck. All this led Caminha to observe that these people were ready to accept Christianity. They lack nothing, he says, to become completely Christian, except understanding our language, for they accepted all they saw us do.

Caminha's letter, based on the acutely observed details recorded in his diary, has been acknowledged as the founding narrative of the discovery of Brazil, and its representation in paintings and engravings constitutes a parallel history that illustrates and celebrates Portuguese expansion and conquest. Yet both text and image place in sharp relief the use of conventions, of travel narratives and letters as well as the visual conventions of representing exotic peoples.[3]

Caminha already had half a century of the genre of discovery narrative behind him, although his rare gifts as an observer and narrator distinguish him from earlier writers.[4] Unlike some of them, who described the imagined indigenous population as monsters (people born with tails, one-eyed men, people with their eyes on their shoulders),[5] Caminha carefully observed what he saw and described it with accuracy. It was, in fact, his highly visual account of the landing of the explorers and their subsequent celebration of the first Mass that prompted artists to represent this scene in painting and engraving.

Among those representations is Paula Rego's *First Mass in Brazil* (1993),[6] which refers to a painting of the First Mass by Victor Meirelles,[7] which also refers to a painting by Horace Vernet. Rather than seeing the link between the two pictures as one in which the earlier artist "influenced" the later, we might view it instead as a way in which Rego reconfigured what was handed down. To see Rego's picture is to take into account the ways in which earlier images of the First Mass are fully mediated by her own idiosyncratic and personal readings in terms of the colonization of dual territories: land and the female body.

Although Meirelles' painting *The First Mass in Brazil* remained in Rio de Janeiro, the engravings based on it were commonly seen in homes across Portugal in the 1950s under the Salazar regime. Historically, the engraving or reproduction of a painting circulates more widely than the original painting. Engravings are portable, made with relative ease and, because comparatively inexpensive, can be widely owned, a development that led Walter Benjamin to observe that even the most perfect reproduction is stripped of its unique existence in time and space. The mechanically reproduced object no longer has the same history to which it was subject throughout the time of its existence, he writes. More importantly, technical reproduction can put the copy of the original into situations that would be out of reach for the original itself.[8] This was precisely the case with the engraving of the First Mass which Paula Rego saw as a child. Its popularity depended on the fact that its meanings were multiple and could be read according to various points of view. On one level, the engraving worked as a reminder of the success of Portuguese exploration and discovery, and of a physical and linguistic empire. It also functioned as a reminder of the power of Catholicism as a mechanism of control of the local people. Caminha was well aware of this possibility when he wrote that "any stamp we wish may be easily printed on them, for the Lord has given them good bodies and good faces, like good men."[9] Further, it worked to suggest an originary moment of colonizing and civilizing the local people, and of bestowing European culture on a populace seen as primitive. Yet on a darker level, and one less acknowledged, it worked as a reminder of loss: loss of the colony, loss of wealth, loss of control. Finally, it worked as a reminder of immigration, of familial ties and of links to Brazil.

As a result, the engraving of the First Mass in Brazil was a success because all of these meanings co-existed at the same time. In this sense it might be compared to the same kinds of operation on a mythical level that similar paintings and engravings have for North Americans. One thinks of Emanuel Leutze's *George Washington Crossing the Delaware* or Grant Wood's *Midnight Ride of Paul Revere*.[10] All of these narrate significant historical moments of the nation in what Homi Bhabha has described as a "language of national belonging," even when these narratives might be those of genocide, death, failure and control as well as those celebrating heroic deeds.[11] These narratives work on the level of what Barthes called myth or depoliticized speech, things that just "are," things that have no territory of contestation. As for the engraving, it presents things as they "really" were, and we are asked to witness what happened in this First Mass, and to agree to its configuration as a "natural" development of events. Moreover, the engraving is already one step removed from the original painting, since the very process of making an engraving results in a reversal of the original image on which it is based.[12]

In her painting *The First Mass in Brazil,* done in 1993, Rego called the engraving into service to support a surprising range of additional meanings. For one, it had hung in her old nanny Luzia's house in Ericeira, north of Estoril, near the villa of her paternal grandparents where she spent summers; thus, in including it in the painting, she summoned a figure who had featured as a significant source of love in her childhood. But even more, in compositional terms, the engraving cuts fiercely across the painting in a way that divides it into two parts, both of which deal with the same topic, that of the colonizing forces of *pátria* and patriarchy.

In the top part, that of the engraving, the land and its people are claimed in the name of God and King, with the cross of Sagres as a metonymy linking the two. Below, in the lower half of the picture, is the colonized body of woman, marked by her pregnancy, reclining on a garment of scarlet, with a blue vestment with the outlines of an anchor and a ship from the voyage. In one sense, we can read the engraving as though it were a real, though distant event viewed through a window, a tactic familiar to modernist painting (one thinks of Matisse), where its use leads us to ask whether we should regard painting as a window onto reality, or as the flat surface of a wall made up of abstract marks on a surface. For Paula Rego, the engraving with all of these multiple meanings acts sharply on the figure below.

How are we to read this reclining figure? As a woman abandoned for another shore? As a woman who is a victim of her own desire? As a woman sacrificed? Or can we see these two parts of the picture as a commentary on power and control? Furthermore, there is no continuity of time in this narrative; rather, time is assigned a fluidity that surges between present fact (Paula has said that her daughter Victoria was pregnant at the time), an originary history (the discovery of Brazil in 1500), and models of pictorial history of the nineteenth century, that moment when the exotic female Other comes into play.

On one level, the picture is about sacrifice. There is religious sacrifice enacted by the priest on the shores of Brazil who raises the chalice at that moment in the Eucharist when Christ the Lamb of God is sacrificed for the salvation of the world, his blood now wine. There is the sacrifice of the turkey for human consumption, with Luzia, the nanny in a blood-stained apron. And there is the enigma of the girl who ponders her unwanted pregnancy.[13] Yet there is far more that we can bring to the picture, including intertextuality that links the positions of the body in this picture to many others. Rather than seeing this as a painting about sacrifice, I will argue that Paula Rego uncovers the operations of colonizing the Other and the overarching practice of control that extends both to the so-called exotic figures of the people of Brazil, as well as to the female body. To do this, she uncovers the ways in which the very positioning of the body itself carries meanings.

To see how this body positioning works, and the differing meanings of a face up, face down or lateral position, we have only to turn to two well-known examples from the nineteenth century, those of Manet and Gauguin. In his letters from Tahiti in the 1890s, Paul Gauguin expressed doubts that what he had been doing was sufficient to confirm him as the leading avant-garde painter of his time. Specifically, he was provoked by Manet's *Olympia*,[14] which lay behind a painting that he began in 1892, a work that has been judged the most significant and controversial of his career. Gauguin called his painting *Manao Tupapau*, which translated from the Tahitian is known as *The Spirit of the Dead Keeping Watch*, or *The Specter Watches over Her*. In it, Gauguin attempted to record the superstitious fears of the local people, in particular their notion of the spirits of the dead. The scene shows a young girl stretched out on a large couch in an interior hut at night. Behind her is the ghostly figure located at the bottom of the bed, one that either watches her, in which case her apparent fear is explained, or watches over her, in which case the reason for her need for protection is made clear.

In one sense, Gauguin appears to take an anthropological interest in the beliefs of the Indigenous culture. But the placement of the body suggests a more sinister explanation. She is seen from behind, and the unsettling position of her head and the way that it turns towards the viewer, who in the first instance is Gauguin, suggests that is it not the ghostly figure in the background who menaces her, but the artist himself whom she fears.[15] Both the body position and the averted gaze, suggest the counterpart against which Gauguin was working, Manet's *Olympia*, whose visual address moves in the opposite direction, towards self-confidence and a visual challenge to the viewer. Gauguin's Tahitian model lies face down; Manet's model, configured as the prostitute Olympia, lies face up, directly challenging the conventional portrayal of the odalisque. Marked as modern and a threat, Olympia stared back.

In all of these paintings, Rego's included, love, simple affection, physical desire and their consequences circulate in varying degrees. Olympia and the Tahitian girl were seemingly polar opposites. If Olympia touched on the desire for illicit sex, the Tahitian girl touched on the fantasy of the woman-child and passivity and it was surely this upon which Gauguin had seized in his painting that set an "exotic savage" in place. By contrast, Rego's painting sums up the *effects* of desire and assigns the burden to the woman who bears its physical traces.[16]

What we have seen so far is the way that particular poses carry hermeneutic weight and I want now to return to the young woman on the bed in Paula Rego's picture. I mentioned earlier the detail revealed by Paula

Rego that her daughter Victoria had been pregnant at the time. Among Rego's studies for the painting is a drawing of her daughter in which she lies in a deep sleep on a ticking mattress, her body swollen in the late stages of pregnancy. Underneath the bed are old-fashioned suitcases with brass brackets and leather handles, of the kind popular in the 1950s, exactly the time when Paula remembers seeing the engraving of Meirelles' *The First Mass* in her nanny's house. She lies on her side, a position that we associate primarily with odalisques, such as those by Velázquez or Titian. But in Rego's study we have the very image of maternity, of deep, undisturbed and untroubled sleep, unusual in the sense of secure calm that it suggests. When women are shown sleeping in painting they are frequently menaced by nightmares and by figures who come to prey, attack or control them through fear. Instead, Rego's drawing presents pregnancy as a state of assured self-containment.

What I am proposing is that only when the artist put together the woman in black on the bed, under the heavy weight of the meaning carried by the engraving, did there emerge a reading in direct contradiction to the fullness and health and plenitude of the drawing on the theme of pregnancy. That meaning, seen in the context of the colonization of Brazil, is the colonization of the body, marked by biology and institutions: the Church and the State. We can see this body as the expression of fecundity and possibility, or more plausibly in the context of the engraving as a physical expression of the forces of colonial and patriarchal power, identified by Gayatri Spivak as the two prongs of the post-colonial debate.

There is one other aspect of *The First Mass in Brazil* that merits attention, for it opens onto the work that has followed over the past five years. That is the aspect of horizontality and the ways in which it is made to carry particular meaning, in both the pose and the format of the picture. That meaning is subjugation and carnality: Nature rather than Culture, the primitive rather than the civilized, female rather than male.

By contrast, the vertical axis predominates in our culture as the axis of beauty. It reproduces the upright body of the viewer, what gestalt psychologists refer to as the fronto-parallel position. The vertical axis represents the moment in evolution when humans stood up and looked forward, from which point the carnal instinct was sublimated.[17]

Now to return to Paula Rego's picture, and to the *Dog Woman Series* (1994) that followed, is to find there a horizontality, in which woman as dog reveals a powerful physicality, an inner animal force. "To be a dog woman," the artist claims, "is not necessarily to be downtrodden, but powerful, utterly believable. It emphasizes the physical side of her being."[18] The dog woman, the ur-image of female horizontality, required of the artist the courage to invest in areas previously left open: humiliation, love, loyalty and complicity, a certain female machismo.[19] Seen in these terms, the pregnant woman of *The First Mass* gains new strength in her horizontality as resistance to the colonizing forces of patriarchy. It may be fairly observed, then, that Rego's *The First Mass in Brazil* calls into play all of the above, and marks out a territory in which the horizontality of the body and all that it evokes—nature, control, physicality—is a forceful match for the heightened verticality effected in that very instant when the Host is raised in the name of King and Country. If we read this picture as an allegory, the moment of subjugation is indeed the very moment when resistance and independence begins.

Notes

[1] The description of the Mass transcribed into modern Portuguese by Jaime Cortesão reads as follows: "Ao domingo de Pascoela pela manhã, determinou o Capitão de ir ouvir missa e pregação naquele ilhéu. Mandou a todos os capitães que se aprestassem no batéis e fossem com ele. E assim foi feito. Mandou naquele ilhéu armar um esperável, e dentro dele um altar mui bem corregido. E ali com todos nos outros fez dizer missa, a qual foi dita pela padre Frei Henrique, em voz entoada, e oficiada com aquela mesma voz pelos outros padres e sacerdotes, que todos eram ali. A qual missa, segundo meu parecer, foi ouvida por todos com muito prazer e devoção. F.5/Domingo, 26 de Abril" *A Carta de Pero Vaz de Caminha*, in Cortesão 233-234.

[2] Caminha 26.

[3] For a further discussion of the conventions of representing exotic peoples and in particular the representation of the female "other," see Harriet Guest, "Figures of the Exotic William Hodges's Work." In Isobel Armstrong's *New Feminist Discourses: Critical Essays on Theories and Texts*. New York: Routledge, 1992. 283-96.

[4] Cortesão 18-22.

[5] Both Columbus and later Sir Walter Raleigh were so impressed with the unexpected scenery that reports of strange humans were presented as fact. "I have seen things as fantastic and prodigious as any of those," wrote Raleigh in reference to these humanoid monsters (qtd. in Greenblatt 21-22.)

[6] Paula Rego, *The First Mass in Brazil*.

[7] Victor Meirelles, *A Primeira Missa no Brasil* [*The First Mass in Brazil*]. Meirelles' painting is one of the most widely reproduced images of a painting in Brazil, and has appeared in scholarly publications, in art books, catalogues and journals, and on stamps and money. There have been other contemporary responses to the painting, namely that of Nelson Leirner's *Terra à Vista* [*A Primeira Vista*], 1983/2000, which views the First Mass from a Brazilian point of view. Figures including miniature cars, planes, dwarfs and Snow Whites encircle a big paper pineapple while other figures emerge from the circle in a straight procession. The second to last row is of Indians and the last figure that of a large Christ. This is the First Mass, modern Brazilian style. I would like to thank Ruth Rosengarten for bringing this piece to my attention.

[8] Walter Benjamin, "The Work of Art in the Age of Mechanical Reproduction." *Illuminations*. New York: Schocken, 1985. 179.

[9] Caminha, in Cortesão 25.

[10] Emanuel Leutze, *George Washington Crossing the Delaware*; Grant Wood, *The Midnight Ride of Paul Revere*.

[11] See Bhabha 176.

[12] An engraving is drawn onto a metal plate and when printed, appears in reverse. This explains the reversed image in Rego's painting, based as it was on an observation of the engraving and not the original oil painting by Meirelles.

[13] This sacrificial aspect is seen as the meaning of the picture by McEwen 207.

[14] Édouard Manet, *Olympia*.

[15] For a further discussion of this painting, see Sweetman 326-7.

[16] Considering how easily these poses of women can be summoned for particular purposes, we might remark on how few examples there are of the male body at rest rather that in a state of action. One of these is the Barberini Faun (200 BC), in which the openly erotic effect of a nude male laying on his back is modified by the realization that the subject is a satyr who has fallen into a deep and drunken sleep, making it a provocative study in homoerotic voyeurism. Illustrated in Boardman 206.

[17] This argument is fully developed in Rosalind E. Krauss, "Cindy Sherman: Untitled" *Bachelors*. New York: The MIT Press, 1999. 130.

[18] McEwen 215-16.

[19] Macedo 12-13.

Works Cited

Benjamin, Walter. "The Work of Art in the Age of Mechanical Reproduction." *Illuminations*. Ed. and intro. Hannah Arendt; trans. Harry Zohn. New York: Schocken Books, 1968.

Bhabha, Homi. "Dissemination. Time, Narrative, and the Margins of the Modern Nation," *The Post-Colonial Studies Reader*. Eds. Bill Ashcroft, Gareth Griffiths, and Helen Tiffin. London: Routledge, 1995.

Boardman, John. *The Oxford History of Classical Art*. Oxford: Oxford UP, 1993.

Caminha, Pero Vaz de. *A Carta do Achamento do Brasil*. In *A Documentary History of Brazil*. Ed. E. Bradford Burns. New York: Knopf, 1966.

Cortesão, Jaime. *A Carta de Pero Vaz de Caminha*. *Obras Completas*, vol. 7. Lisboa: Portugália Editora, 1967.

Greenblatt, Stephen *Marvelous Possessions: The Wonder of the New World*. Chicago: U of Chicago P, 1991.

Guest, Harriet. "Figures of the Exotic in William Hodges's Work." Ed. Isabel Armstrong. *New Feminist Discourses: Critical Essays on Theories and Texts*. New York: Routledge, 1992.

Leirner, Nelson. *Terra à Vista [A Primeira Vista]*, 1983/2000.

Krauss, Rosalind E. "Cindy Sherman: Untitled." *Bachelors*. New York: MIT Press, 1999.

Leutze, Emanuel. *George Washington Crossing the Delaware*, 1851, Metropolitan Museum of New York.

Macedo, Ana Gabriela. "Paula Rego: Pintura Como Denúncia." *Jornal de Letras* 747 (19 May-

1 June 1999): 12-13.

Manet, Édouard. *Olympia*, 1863, Musée d'Orsay.

McEwen, John. *Paula Rego*. London: Phaidon, 1993.

Meirelles, Victor. *A Primeira Missa no Brasil*, 1861. Oil on canvas. Museu Nacional de Belas Artes, Rio de Janeiro.

Rego, Paula. *A Primeira Missa no Brasil*, 1993. Acrylic on paper laid on canvas.

Sweetman, David. *Paul Gauguin: A Life*. New York: Simon and Schuster, 1995.

Wood, Grant. *The Midnight Ride of Paul Revere*, 1931, Metropolitan Museum of New York.

Paula Rego
First Mass in Brazil
1993
Acrylic on canvas
130x180cm
Private Collection

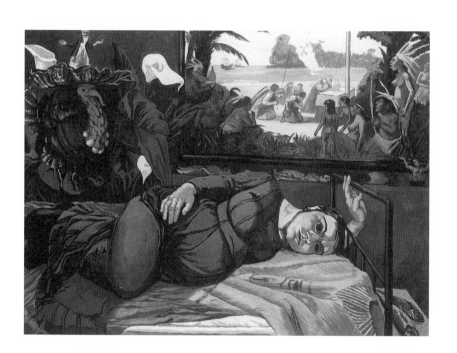

Paula Rego
First Mass in Brazil, detail

The Media: The Past and the Years to Come

Eduardo Neiva

On May 20, 1653, when Brazil was no more than a draft in the Portuguese empire, Padre Antônio Vieira writes to D. João IV, then ruler of Portugal. The relationship between the king and the greatest classical prose writer in the Portuguese language is close enough to qualify Vieira as the preeminent advisor in matters concerning Brazil and its inhabitants. In many ways, Vieira's attitude to the Native Brazilians is similar to any other priest of the new colony: his goal is to save the souls of the unChristian people. In his letter, Vieira's majestic and glittering prose bristles against the Portuguese landowners living in Brazil. The barbaric violence of the colonizers horrifies him and, worse, sends the natives running away to inaccessible regions. Then how could he convert them? Vieira asks D. João to stop the enslavement of the Natives. No one should be forced to work like that. No one should be allowed to use them to labor the tobacco plantations.[1]

Vieira's requests were not fulfilled. D. João died and Vieira's dreams, not only of fair treatment of the Natives, but also of a European Catholic revival led by a Portuguese monarch, never came true. Vieira would endure banishment from the Portuguese court, exile, and the charge of unorthodox beliefs by the Inquisition. In 1691, near the end of his life, then living in Bahia, Brazil, Vieira was still writing to another Portuguese king, D. Pedro II, complaining of abuses of the natives by a Portuguese sergeant major. Nothing had really changed.

It is quite true that, since the colonial days, there have been radical transformations in Brazilian life; however, it is also true that, in dealing with many of the issues of today, Brazil sticks to archaic mechanisms that were at the core of its colonial past. To solve the pressing questions of social life, Brazilians still look for solutions that come from the top, not so very distinct from Vieira writing to a monarch with whom he was personally acquainted and who would listen to him. What should be impersonal and common to all social actors is in fact personalized. The law may be hard, but one can soften it through personal ties, if one has relations with the rulers, or else with anyone in authority (Barbosa). The result is a widespread value given to informal relationships,[2] though at an enormous social price: social justice, and with it a general sense of legitimacy, is torn apart. Society becomes a stage for selfish means for empowering individuals who feel uncommitted to other individuals.

Ever since the Portuguese colonial experience, Brazilians have been used to regarding some modes of accumulating private property as a governmental donation, as the outcome of personal influence and liaisons. This is how the colonizers split the country in 1532. The monarch selected well-born and well-connected individuals to receive the *capitanias hereditárias*. The donation was made on a perpetual basis, as it was supposed to be a privilege extended to the families of the *donatários*. There would be no other law of the land than the will and the discretion of such favored individuals. In spite of his powerful acumen and courage in many issues, Antônio Vieira did not notice that the logic of such donations easily entailed the use of a slave labor force. The country was divided into strata: one privileged, existing side by side with another lacking rights. Discipline and respect ought to be imposed with all due brutality. By the same token, a group of individuals hovers above all and their members can dismiss and disregard what is imposed as norms to the rest.

The law of the land in Brazil can easily suffer from the actions of predatory individualism. Rules have not been established as the clear interplay of rights and duties reciprocally shared by all individuals of the group. Rules are made into tools of dominance, instruments of oppression, and are used to discriminate if not to humiliate. It is not as though equally distributed rights for all of the community could create autonomy and respect for all. The individual whims of the happy few determine the social frame. Brazil seems to oscillate between the fearful implementation of order and rampant anarchy. The country is neither rigidly authoritarian nor anarchically fluid. It foments rituals emphasizing order, like the military parades mandatory on the holiday reserved for celebrating national independence from Portugal, as well as the orgiastic and unruly partying of carnival (DaMatta). Order and its inversion are the extremes around which one lives the Brazilian experience.

In this social environment, the promiscuity of individual interests and governmental action is appalling. Since its beginning, the Brazilian press has been essentially an extension, because a concession, of the central government (Sodré 23). In his analysis of our press, Nelson Werneck Sodré notes that, as early as the nineteenth century, the dominant issues in a publication such as *A Gazeta do Rio de Janeiro* are either official notes, or else praise and adulation of the Portuguese Court and European nobility. Recent research (Sá and Neiva, Neiva) shows that the Federal Government is the main subject of television coverage. The trends of early colonial times are still present today. The main advertiser, and therefore sponsor, of the Brazilian press has been for a long time the government (Mattos).

The implementation of modern Brazilian media was not the result of the actions of private entrepreneurs. A federal agency, the "Empresa Brasileira de Telecomunicações" (EMBRATEL), put together the satellite system that was then used by a small band of private companies. Furthermore, the technological infrastructure that enabled color broadcasting were implemented by the military administrations after the coup of 1964 (Mattos 218).

The partnership of governments and entrepreneurs must not be considered an exclusive phenomenon of Brazil, and can be found in many moments of world history. In England, for example, at the dawn of the Industrial Revolution, the production of textiles could find markets beyond English boundaries thanks to the tentacles of colonial bureaucracy spreading themselves throughout the British Empire. But, when one compares England in early industrial times with the expansion of the media in Brazil during the two decades of military dictatorship, one sees that, contrary to what happened in the Brazilian case, the English industrial revolution followed the upheaval in the property system of its pre-industrial economy. Facing a shortage of laborers to work in their unfragmented properties, the English landowners had to drop their prior economic model, based on the dominance of masters over serfs renting the property of the aristocrats and bound to the dominant class by ideas of obligation and ideological submission. The landowners began to pay wages to their laborers, thus creating an incipient market of consumers. The transformation of the rural class system in England eventually created the conditions for an internal market that would expand, and therefore stimulate the growth of the industry during the Industrial Revolution (Brenner 51). A revolution in technology was matched by a transformation in social structure.

Nothing of the sort could occur in the impressive expansion of the media during the 1960s in Brazil. The military coup d'état, which orchestrated the development of Brazilian mass communication, was a joint operation with the business elite to keep labour unrest and social demands at bay (Dreifuss). If the point of the coup was an alliance with the military to take over the governmental apparatus, the class system of the country had to remain unscathed. Subsidies and fiscal policies were implemented with the purpose of promoting wealth for those who either articulated or supported the coup. In fact, the conservative nature of what could have been a major social revolution is nowhere more clear than in the legal definition of ownership of the electromagnetic spectrum through which broadcasting ventures would be transmitted. The spectrum was dictatorially kept in the hands of the Brazilian federal government, which could then control its licensing.

How can it be a surprise that the creation of broadcasting ventures was mainly the result of political influence and bargaining? The media market has been split in a manner not altogether different from the ancient *capitanias hereditárias*. If in the United States, for example, the role of media legislation is to restrict the power of individuals or economic groups in specific market areas, in Brazil, up to today, all attempts to legislate and reshape the control and the management of the media have failed miserably (Festa 17). Without control from the bottom, without legitimate democratic representation, the outcome of any media expansion in Brazil leads to social distortion. Between 1985 and 1988, during the tenure of President José Sarney, there was an expansion of 62% in the number of new television stations. However, at the time of the expansion, José Sarney was negotiating, with the Brazilian Congress, an extension of the presidential mandate that would make him the direct beneficiary of the constitutional change. Everything was just political plundering and the granting of economic benefits.[3]

Political minuets of this kind may not be obvious to the common Brazilian viewer. Yet, when the public sphere is so brashly assaulted by personal interests, with utter disregard for democratic participation, the media tends to be hopelessly conformist. In any case, as was so patent in the intentions of the military governments, if politics exclude democratic participation, one has an anemic media incapable of incorporating the vitality of social life. Criticism is muffled. The images on the screens are reduced to promoting a dreamlike social Eden, detached from the conflicts and the contradictions of civil society.

Over the future lies the burden of our past. Is that a reason for complete despair? I am not sure how to answer this question. I would like to believe that things will be different. In the age of internet networks, individuals are more empowered than ever. The action of central governments over media interaction could be drastically reduced to mere regulatory oversight. In fact, what we now see is a set of individuals communicating as free agents without any decisive restraint. But what will happen to the masses of individual Brazilians that have been systematically kept at the margins of social progress? Will we have still a Brazil divided into privileged haves and absolutely deprived have-nots? The task of bridging this gap is big enough to give anyone facing it dizzy spells. My optimism tells me that sooner or later the country will have to wake up to it. A docile, cheap, conformist labor force is not very attractive in the post-industrial world. In the years to come, sheepish and uncreative social actors will be less and less valued as economic agents. The post-industrial revolution in the productive sphere will demand critical, autonomous, and creative social participants. The pressure may be such that Brazil will have to deal seriously with the challenges and the demands opened in the new millennium.

Notes

[1] See Vieira 84-90.

[2] A recent article by Jair Ferreira dos Santos (1999) analyzes this trend with great insight.

[3] The Brazilian weekly *Isto É* of July 31, 1991, reported that the Fernando Collor's administration handed out cable TV licenses as political payoffs. A year later, Mr. Collor de Mello was impeached under the generalized accusation of corruption. The law remains the same, as does the monopolistic trend of the Brazilian media.

Works Cited

Barbosa, Lívia. *O Jeitinho Brasileiro: Ou a Arte de Ser Mais Igual que os Outros*. Rio de Janeiro: Campus, 1992.

Brenner, Robert. "Agrarian Class Structure and Economic Development in Pre-Industrial Europe." *The Brenner Debate*. Ed. T. H. Aston & C. E. H. Philpin. Cambridge: Cambridge UP. 10-63.

DaMatta, Roberto. *Carnavais, Malandros e Heróis. Por uma Sociologia do Dilema Brasileiro*. Rio de Janeiro: Zahar, 1979.

———. *Carnivals, Rogues, and Heroes: An Interpretation of the Brazilian Dilema.* South Bend, IN: Notre Dame UP, 1991.

Dreifuss, René Armand. *1964, A Conquista do Estado: Ação Política, Poder, e Golpe de Estado.* 5th ed. Petrópolis: Vozes, 1987.

Festa, Regina. "A TV na América Latina: Um Pouco Menos de Euforia." *Políticas Governamentais* 7.1 (1991): 16-20.

Mattos, Sérgio. "Advertising and Government: The Case of Brazilian Television." *Communication Research* 11.2 (1984): 203-20.

———. *The Impact of the 1964 Revolution on Brazilian Television.* San Antonio: Klingensmith, 1982.

Neiva, Eduardo. "Brasil: El Arraigo de la Corrupción y la Superficialidad de los Medios." *Chasqui* 45 (1993): 79-84.

Sá, Fernando and Eduardo Neiva. "O Espelho Mágico." *Políticas Governamentais* 7.8 (1992): 17-20.

Santos, Jair Ferreira dos. "A Estrutura do Oba-Oba." *Folha de Londrina. Caderno Retrospectiva, O País* 2. Dec. 31, 1999.

Vieira, Antônio. *Cartas.* Rio de Janeiro: W. W. Jackson, 1948.

Abstracts / Resumos

Gilberto Freyre: 100 Years

A Sea Full of Waves: Ambiguity and Modernity in Brazilian Culture

Ricardo Benzaquen de Araujo

This article's contention is that Gilberto Freyre's work is directly related to a critical view of the process of modernization that has dominated Brazil from the nineteenth century. Freyre would have opposed such modernity, grounded on positivism, through the valorization of ambiguity. It is within this opposition that Freyre envisages the Portuguese as a colonizer willing to interact and to adapt himself—and not simply to impose his worldview.

The Road to *Casa-Grande*. Itineraries by Gilberto Freyre

Enrique Rodríguez Larreta

This article presents the principal stages of the intellectual formation of Gilberto Freyre from his college years in Recife to his cosmopolitan experiences at Columbia and Stanford Universities. The paper introduces new facts about his contacts with Franz Boas, a controversial issue in Brazilian research on Gilberto Freyre.

The UNESCO Project: Social Sciences and Race Studies in Brazil in the 1950s

Marcos Chor Maio

This article focuses on the relationship between race studies and the social sciences in Brazil, taking the UNESCO Project as a case study on Brazilian race relations. The essay argues that the UNESCO project successfully determined the agenda for Brazilian social sciences in the last years of the 1940s. There was a confluence of the pragmatic tradition of Brazilian social sciences with the aims of the UNESCO project.

The Mansions and the Shanties: "The Flesh and the Stone" in Nineteenth-Century Brazil

Mary Del Priore

This article discusses Gilberto Freyre's book *Sobrados e Mucambos*, published for the first time in 1936. The title refers to the constructions that characterized the cities of Brazil during the nineteenth century. Furthermore, it is a crucial analysis of the traditions and the customs of the population. The article explores the interdisciplinary framework adopted by Freyre.

The Origins and Errors of Brazilian Cordiality

João Cezar de Castro Rocha

This article deals with one of the most intriguing misreadings in the tradition of Brazilian culture, namely, the interpretation of the concept of "cordial man," proposed by Sérgio Buarque de Holanda in *Raízes do Brasil*. This concept has been interpreted through an approach based on Gilberto Freyre's understanding of Brazilian culture. It is argued that such a misreading was made possible because Freyre, in *Sobrados e Mucambos*, resorted to a particular understanding of Buarque de Holanda's concept of "cordial man."

Literature

Theater of the Impressed: the Brazilian Stage in the Nineteenth Century

Ross G. Forman

This essay offers a re-evaluation of nineteenth-century Brazilian theater as "mediocre" by considering its role in projects of nation building and its function within elite society as a means to examine and debate a variety of social, economic, and political problems facing the country at the time.

Gonçalves Dias

José Luís Jobim

Gonçalves Dias (1823-1864) belonged to a generation of writers that was responsible for creating a national literature in Brazil. Although his work encompasses many other aspects, this essay focuses on his effort to articulate the experiences, feelings and aspirations of Brazil, seen as an "imagined community."

Memoirs of a Militia Sergeant: A Singular Novel

Marcus Vinicius Nogueira Soares

This article is an analysis of the critical readings of *Memórias de um Sargento de Milícias*, and discusses the anachronism of certain critical approaches to the novel. It highlights Antonio Candido's reading as an attempt at understanding the novel within its historical context.

Iracema: The Tupinization of Portuguese

Ivo Barbieri

This essay focuses on the mixture between elements of the Tupi-Guarani language spoken by the indigenous peoples of coastal Brazil at the time of colonization and the Portuguese language poetically re-elaborated by the novelist. This theme finds its double in the hybridity between the customs and religious rituals of the civilized white man and the Native Brazilians. The article shows that modernist authors such as Mário de Andrade and Guimarães Rosa were influenced by *Iracema*.

Machado de Assis and The Posthumous Memoirs of Brás Cubas

Bluma Waddington Vilar

This article discusses the novel *Memórias Póstumas de Brás Cubas* (1881), considered a turning point in Machado de Assis' work. It reviews a number of critical readings of Machado's writings and of *The Posthumous Memoirs*;

the objective is to highlight certain aspects of these readings and the complementarity between them, and to assert that the incorporation of different analytical perspectives can broaden the understanding of a work as sophisticated as Machado's.

Rebellion in the Backlands: Landscape with Figures
Walnice Nogueira Galvão

This article addresses the Brazilian historical context, as well as Euclides da Cunha's background, in the avant-gardist "Escola Militar" of Rio de Janeiro in the nineteenth century, both of which inform the writing of *Os Sertões*. This book, a chronicle of a war, illustrates an encyclopedic attempt at incorporating the scientific knowledge of the time, an ambition expressed in two trends: polyphonism and intertextuality.

The Patriot: The Exclusion of the Hero Full of Character
Beatriz Resende

Triste Fim de Policarpo Quaresma is the most important novel written by Lima Barreto (1881-1922). Barreto was a poor, mulatto writer who lived on the outskirts of Rio de Janeiro. In spite of his sophisticated intellectual formation, he gave voice to the socially "excluded," criticizing the power of the elite. The nationalist dream of Policarpo Quaresma, the main character of the novel, does not achieve victory over totalitarianism, nor has the author himself found the recognition he deserves.

Plantation Boy: The Memory of Loss
Heloisa Toller Gomes

This essay discusses the importance of *Menino de Engenho* in Brazilian Modernism and argues that there is a paradoxical aspect to Lins do Rego's first novel, concealed under its incantatory writing. The book exposes, but never questions, the harsh realities of the Brazilian *sertão*. The predominant patriarchal order orients the narrative voice, and inevitable tension arises in this attempt to neutralize social disorders in the (utopic) elaboration of a harmonious textual *continuum*.

Monteiro Lobato Today—Semicolon

Silviano Santiago

This essay was written as part of the celebrations on the occasion of the 50th anniversary of Monteiro Lobato's death. It proposes a critical evaluation of Lobato's work for "grownups," since he is better known for his juvenile and children's literature. The themes of death, "dead cities" and the destruction of nature are intertwined. Finally, the major critical intervention of Lobato is studied through the connections between his character Jeca Tatu and the work of Manoel Bomfim.

Contemporary Brazilian Women's Autobiography and the Forgotten Case of Adalgisa Nery

Sabrina Karpa-Wilson

Brazil has produced a plethora of autobiographies since the 1930s, but there have been relatively few female autobiographies published. Women have apparently preferred to write about the self in *crônicas* or autobiographical novels. Adalgisa Nery uses novelistic structures to undermine traditional notions of autobiography and autobiographical authority.

Devil to Pay in the Backlands and João Guimarães Rosa's Quest of Universality

Kathrin H. Rosenfield

This essay shows the double framework of Rosa's *Grande Sertão: Veredas*. On the one hand, the novel gives epic form to the myths and beliefs, the language and customs of the remotest part of the country (*sertão*). On the other hand, it follows up Euclides da Cunha's effort to locate a place for a typically Brazilian story within universal literary and philosophical structures.

Archives and Memories in Pedro Nava
Eneida Maria de Souza

This essay has the purpose of introducing the memoir writing of Pedro Nava, considering both his place in the history of Brazilian literature as well as his writing process based on detailed and rigorous research. Since it is a text of memoirs, the different stages of the construction of the writing are described through an analysis of the manuscripts of his works.

The Hour of the Star or Clarice Lispector's Trash Hour
Italo Moriconi

Published in 1977, the year of its author's death, *A Hora da Estrela* is part of a group of texts by Clarice Lispector that stage the end, depicting it as dissolution. End of a life, of a career, of an oeuvre. In *The Hour of the Star*, the narrative act makes few concessions to anything that is not sarcastic or grotesque.

The Case of Fonseca—The Search for Reality
Karl Erik Schøllhammer

Since the 1960s Rubem Fonseca has defined the emergence of an urban literature characterized by its obsessive interest in marginal milieus dominated by prostitution, violence and crime. This essay suggests a reading of Fonseca's *brutalist* realism as the author's literary search for renewed expressiveness.

João Cabral in Perspective
Antonio Carlos Secchin

This essay focuses on the originality of João Cabral's poetry by elucidating its multidimensionality—from the sound and the word to the overall work. Step by step, from word to verse, to strophe, to the complete poem itself, this analysis traces the conception of João Cabral's poetic craft.

ABSTRACTS/RESUMOS

Two Poetics, Two Moments

Heloísa Buarque de Hollanda

This article is an analysis of the responses made by an emergent poetry to two moments of crisis and change in the Brazilian cultural scene. On the one hand, the *marginal poetry* articulates a discourse based on a vitalistic resistance to the post-1964 military regime. On the other hand, an *aesthetics of rigor* rearticulates the modernist values and canon within the scenery of globalization and redemocratization in the 1990s in Brazil.

Brazilian Fiction Today: A Point of Departure

Therezinha Barbieri

This essay seeks to understand Brazilian literary production of the 1980s and 1990s through the dialogue between languages that make the visual image their axis of articulation and development. However, although the essay concentrates on the moment when image and text come together, it is important not to lose sight of the context of simultaneity in which this encounter occurs.

A Brief Introduction to Contemporary Afro-Brazilian Women's Literature

Maria Aparecida Ferreira de Andrade Salgueiro

This article aims at introducing contemporary Afro-Brazilian women's literature. The article provides an overview of this literature through the presentation of its most distinguished writers and compares its features with African-American women's literature.

Down with Tordesilhas!

Jorge Schwartz

This essay calls the reader's attention to the traditional gap that has excluded Brazil from the so-called Latin American critical and cultural discourse. It also tracks Brazilians who study Panamericanist discourse, in which Spanish America and Brazil do have a common dialogue: José Veríssimo, Mário de

Andrade, Manuel Bandeira, and Brito Broca, among others. The essay also mentions several initiatives today—by both institutions and intellectuals—that are trying to bridge this gap.

Culture

Politics as History and Literature

Valdei Lopes Araujo

The main purpose of this paper is to present the book *Um Estadista do Império* by Joaquim Nabuco (1849-1910), a Brazilian writer and diplomat. The essay also focuses on the intellectual formation of Nabuco and his unique interpretation of Brazilian society in the nineteenth century.

Manoel Bomfim: The State and Elites Seen as Parasites of the People-Nation

Roberto Ventura

Manoel Bomfim (1868-1932) was a politician, historian and educator, and one of Brazil's most original thinkers. His essay, *A América Latina*, published in 1905, presents a provocative reflection on the defects of the origins of the countries of South America. He discussed the exploitation of the colonies by the metropolis, and the exploitation of the slaves and workers by plantation owners, by resorting to a concept derived from biology, namely, parasitism.

D. João VI no Brasil

Luiz Costa Lima

Oliveira Lima (1865-1928) is one of the most important Brazilian historians, but also the most unknown. His masterwork, *D. Joao VI no Brasil*, originally published in 1908, analyses the period of 1808-1821, in which the prince—crowned in 1818—lived in Rio de Janeiro, first fleeing from Napoleon's troops, and later resisting the pressure to return to Lisbon. This was a decisive period for the future of the Portuguese colony.

ABSTRACTS/RESUMOS

Citizenship in Rui Barbosa: "A Questão Social e Política no Brasil"
Tarcisio Costa

This article addresses the lecture Rui Barbosa gave at Rio de Janeiro's Teatro Lírico during the 1919 presidential campaign, in which he introduced the theme of social rights in Brazilian liberal discourse and recommended the establishment of social citizenship together with the modernization of political institutions.

"A Portrait of Brazil" in the Postmodern Context
Tereza Virginia de Almeida

First published in 1928, *Retrato do Brasil* is a reconstruction of Brazilian history in which the seductive appeal of sensual pleasure and the land's material resources determine the characteristic features of the racially mixed population that emerged from the encounter of the white Portuguese colonizers with the Native and African peoples. This essay sees the book within the frame of contemporary Brazilian culture in its relation to its own major modernist artifacts.

The USA and Brazil: Capitalism and Pre-Capitalism According to Oliveira Vianna
Ângela de Castro Gomes

This article studies the last unfinished book by Oliveira Vianna, one of the most important thinkers and interpreters of Brazilian society. It stresses Vianna's interpretation of the social traits of the Brazilian economy, which is, according to Vianna, a pre-capitalist economy. In order to sustain this viewpoint, he compares Brazil and the United States, remarking upon the differences between the two countries.

Raymundo Faoro's Roundabout Voyage in *Os Donos do Poder*
Marcelo Jasmin

The article intends to expose the main arguments of Raymundo Faoro's *Os Donos do Poder*, showing how his understanding of Brazilian history reinterprets Weberian concepts from the sociology of traditional domination—patrimonialism, status group, etc.—with the notion of a civilization incapable of liberal development.

America, Joy of Man's Desiring: A Comparison of *Visão do Paraíso* with *Wilderness and Paradise in Christian Thought*
Robert Wegner

This article presents the central argument of the book *Visão do Paraíso* by Sérgio Buarque de Holanda, published in 1959. It also compares *Visão do Paraíso* with *Wilderness and Paradise in Christian Thought* by George Williams. Thus, through a reading of these books, this article designs three types of mentalities presented in the discovery and colonization of America: the Portuguese, the Spanish and the Anglo-Saxon.

Florestan Fernandes: Memory and Utopia
Carlos Guilherme Mota

Florestan Fernandes was a multi-faceted intellectual, whose exemplary and conscious trajectory reflects and at the same time dialectizes in an eclectic fashion the politico-cultural history of São Paulo, Brazil and Latin America. This article proposes that no other social scientist or writer has reflected so much and so compulsively on their own institutional and political role, and on the significance of their discipline.

Discovering "Brazil's Soul": A Reading of Luís da Câmara Cascudo
Margarida de Souza Neves

Luís da Câmara Cascudo, a writer from Brazil's Northeast, is known in the academic milieu above all for his monumental *Dicionário do Folclore Brasileiro*. This article suggests that Cascudo might be regarded as one of the "modern discoverers of Brazil." At the same time, the essay uncovers some routes of his peculiar "discovery."

The Theater of Politics: The King as Character in the Imperial Brazilian State—A Reading of *A Construção da Ordem: A Elite Política Imperial* and *Teatro de Sombras: A Política Imperial*

Lilia K. Moritz Schwarcz

This article analyzes the work of the historian José Murilo de Carvalho, taking his book *Teatro de Sombras: A Política Imperial* as a guide. The essay shows how it is possible to analyze the structure of the Brazilian empire and, at the same time, to remark its contradictions and ambiguities as well as the singular role played by the Emperor who occupied the core of the local scene.

References, Responsibilities and Reading: *A Época Pombalina*

Marcus Alexandre Motta

This article establishes a critical dialogue with the already classic work of the Brazilian historian Francisco José Calazans Falcon, *A Época Pombalina*. The task of understanding its significance for Luso-Brazilian historiography implies not only the contextualization of the book at the moment of its appearance, but above all supposes the questioning of its relevance for contemporary issues.

The Nation's Borders and the Construction of Plural Identities: *Carnival, Rogues and Heroes* or Roberto DaMatta and the In-Between Place of Brazilian Culture

Valter Sinder

The publication, in 1979, of *Carnavais, Malandros e Heróis* meant the return of "Brazil" as an object of anthropological reflection. In this work, Roberto DaMatta proposes an interpretation of the Brazilian dilemma detached of any essentialistic understanding of national identity. Therefore, DaMatta sees the construction of Brazilian identity as stressing the ambiguous and the intermediary in the production of the in-between cultural places of the nation.

Cultural Intermediaries

Who Was Pero Vaz de Caminha?
Hans Ulrich Gumbrecht

Are there any specific features that set Pero Vaz de Caminha's *Carta do Achamento do Brasil* apart from most of the other early historical documents of Western colonialism? This essay suggests that there is a surprising degree of "immediacy" in his descriptions, a specific effect of "presence" which this text is capable of producing. It seems to provide the reader with access to an episode of lived experience that took place five hundred years ago, whose subject has been otherwise completely annulled by the black hole of history.

José de Anchieta: Performing the History of Christianity in Brazil
César Braga-Pinto

This article discusses the intersections of historical and prophetic discourses in the works of the Jesuit missionary José de Anchieta. Anchieta's multi-lingual plays were aimed at teaching Christian religion to a heterogeneous society constituted by both Native and European subjects. By creating the notion of a shared interrupted past, Anchieta aims to inscribe both communities within a single Christian lineage.

Guidelines for Reading Vieira
João Adolfo Hansen

This text is a reconstruction of some of the rhetorical and theological political categories of Vieira's work in Portugal and Brazil in the seventeenth century.

The Image of Brazil in *Robinson Crusoe*

Marcus Vinicius de Freitas

This paper aims at analyzing the image of Brazil in Daniel Defoe's *Robinson Crusoe*, and discusses the author's contributions to the myth of Brazil as a tropical paradise. The paper also focuses on Defoe's use of historical background for fictional purposes.

Ferdinand Denis and Brazilian Literature: A Successful Tutelary Relationship

Maria Helena Rouanet

This article analyzes Ferdinand Denis' role in the institutionalization of a body of cultural production in Brazil. It is argued here that the French scholar became a successful "tutor" because he met Brazilians' expectations of finding legitimacy through the approval of an external source of authority. The article also addresses the problem of the naturalization of cultural practices.

"Watercolors of Brazil": Jean Baptiste Debret's Work

Vera Beatriz Siqueira

From a rigid neo-classical background—he was a pupil of Jacques Louis David, an historical painter requisitioned by Napoleon—Debret finds in Brazil the promise of a solution to his personal and professional crisis. This article suggests that the skepticism with regard to the real possibilities of the artist performing in the New World functions as a guarantee of the distance necessary to exercise his work.

Stefan Zweig's *Brazil, Land of the Future*: A Topic of Debate

Cléia Weyrauch Schiavo

The book *Brasil, País do Futuro*, by the Austrian writer Stefan Zweig, is studied in this essay by taking into account its relations to the sociocultural context of Europe in the first half of the twentieth century. Grounded on the difference between an old world in crisis and a tropical future, Zweig imagined a new civilizational paradigm whose model was the city of Rio de Janeiro, celebrated for its mediation of conflicts and contrasts.

Elizabeth Bishop as Cultural Intermediary
Paulo Henriques Britto

A brief examination of Elizabeth Bishop's attempt to act as a kind of translator of Brazilian culture for a US audience and as a defender of US culture and policy in Brazil, despite her reluctance to play a public role and her insufficient command of Portuguese.

Roger Bastide and Brazil: At the Crossroads Between Viewpoints
Fernanda Peixoto

Brazil takes a central place in Roger Bastide's work because of its thought-provoking examples of syncretism. Brazil also offers native models fundamental to the author's original analytical perspective. The purpose of this paper is to outline the framework of Bastide's social thought, built at the crossroads between distinct intellectual traditions.

The Logic of the Backward and the Boomerang Effect: The Case of Ziembinski
Victor Hugo Adler Pereira

Fleeing from World War II to Brazil in 1941, Zbigniew Ziembinski—Polish actor and director—was soon engaged in the most prominent experiments to modernize Brazilian theater. Two decades later he became a symbol of the reaction against avant-garde theater and decided to dedicate himself to television. In this article, the analysis of these artistic controversies leads to a discussion of cultural mimicry in Brazil.

Otto Maria Carpeaux
Olavo de Carvalho

The Austrian writer Otto Maria Carpeaux (Karpfen) fled from Nazi persecution to Latin America and became one of Brazil's outstanding literary critics from 1946 until his death in 1978. Much more than a mere first-class cultural journalist, he was a real historian, and the author of one of the best overall surveys of Western literature ever written.

The Foreigner
Gustavo Bernardo

This article is a brief presentation of Vilém Flusser's life and work. It discusses the idea of translation as an experience of death; the suspension of disbelief to the suspension of belief—the "epoché"; literature as an answer and literature as a question; science, religion and fiction as models; phenomenology and irony; and Brazilian civilization as a synthesis of Greek and Jewish inheritances.

Back to the *Tristes Tropiques*: Notes on Lévi-Strauss and Brazil
Roberto DaMatta

This essay deals with a crucial problem of Brazilian intellectual life: foreign, especially French authors, receive an axiomatic prestige while their local colleagues remain unquoted and buried in oblivion. Using the extraordinary importance and success of Lévi-Strauss' work, the essay reveals how true this is of the French anthropology master. The essay provides a "structural analysis" of an old picture taken at the National Museum in 1938, when Lévi-Strauss was returning from the fieldwork.

Literary History and Literary Criticism

Brazilian Literary Historiography: Its Beginnings
Roberto Acízelo de Sousa

The establishment of Brazilian literature as a discipline takes place in the period between 1805 and 1888, during which several significant contributions were published. Works written by Brazilian authors, as well as those produced by foreigners, can be classified into five categories: anthologies, statements of principles concerning the notion of Brazilian literature, biography collections, critical editions, and literary histories *stricto sensu*. These contributions represented the beginning of a tradition.

Between Two Histories: From Sílvio Romero to José Veríssimo
Regina Zilberman

Sílvio Romero wrote in 1888 the first complete *História da Literatura Brasileira*; in 1916, another *História da Literatura Brasileira* was published, this time by José Veríssimo, and just as complete as Sílvio Romero's. The two works, which are still used today, are radically different and propose diametrically opposed ways of understanding and explaining Brazilian literature.

"The Abstract Brazilian": Antonio Candido's *Malandro* as National Persona
K. David Jackson

This article interprets Antonio Candido's construct of the novelistic hero and the social world in his celebrated essay "Dialética da Malandragem" as a prototype for an authentic national persona. Candido's analysis is compared to Roberto DaMatta's study of Brazil as a system and applied to novelistic memoirs by Machado de Assis and Oswald de Andrade.

Roberto Schwarz' Dialectical Criticism

Regina Lúcia de Faria

Drawing mainly on his studies of Machado de Assis, this essay tries to analyze Roberto Schwarz' seminal theoretical reflections on Brazilian literature, showing that his criticism is associated with the critical-dialectical tradition of literary analysis developed by Antonio Candido.

Hybrid Criticism and Historical Form

Raul Antelo

Cultural heterogeneity is still a Modernist and transculturative premise operating within a notion of diversity between cultures, i.e., a diversity that is controlled by disciplinary limits that are still unequivocal. Cultural hybridism, however, works in the wake of the notion of difference. While heterogeneity is a tributary of comparatist universalism, hybridism derives from globalized culturalism. Both positions are relevant for debating Roberto Schwarz' theses in *Seqüências Brasileiras* (1999).

The Itinerary of a Problem: Luiz Costa Lima and the "Control of the Imaginary"

Sérgio Alcides

The hypothesis of the control of the imaginary by modern reason, as it was developed by Luiz Costa Lima, reaches far beyond its original goals within the theory of literature. This article aims at indicating the theoretical pathways that led the author to his insight into the relations between *mimesis* and modernity. It intends also to emphasize the non-metropolitan setting of Costa Lima's thought.

Comparative Literature in Brazil in the 1990s

Eduardo Coutinho

This article is a study of the function and role played by Comparative Literature in Brazil in the age of multiculturalism. It addresses the issues of criticism by both the historicist and the formalist methods, based on an ethnocentric perspective, and the approximation of comparativism to issues of national and cultural identity. It also engages the debates surrounding the canon, the influence of Postcolonial and Cultural Studies, and Brazilians' response to traditional comparativism: a critical appropriation and deconstruction of hegemonic discourse.

Audiovisual

The Role of Radio in Everyday Brazilian Society (1923-1960)
Lia Calabre

This article focuses on the history of radio in Brazil, stressing its impact on everyday life. From the 1920s to the 1960s, the radio was instrumental in the formation of cultural practices since it was the primary mass medium of the time. For the same reason, radio was also heavily used for political purposes. This article introduces its history, remarking on the importance of "Rádio Nacional," which was inaugurated in 1936.

The Orphan Brotherland: Rap's Civilizing Effort on the Periphery of São Paulo
Maria Rita Kehl

The Racionais MC's are the most outstanding rap group in Brazil. Coming from the outskirts of the city of São Paulo, they are much more than a new phenomenon in the market of pop music; they represent a kind of front for struggle against racism and drugs, warning the impoverished youth of large Brazilian cities against the temptations of the consumer society and their reverse: crime and addiction.

Funk and Hip-Hop Transculture: Cultural Conciliation and Racial Identification in the "Divided City"
Shoshanna Lurie

An introduction to funk and hip-hop culture in urban Brazil, highlighting issues of race, the globalization of culture, and local, national, post-national,

ABSTRACTS/RESUMOS

and black diasporic identity formation. This article addresses the processes through which the globalization of black cultural forms is involved in shifting forms of racial and spatial identification in Rio de Janeiro.

Politics and the Aesthetics of Myth in *Black God, White Devil*
Ivana Bentes

The main theme of this study is the relationship between myth and politics in the film *Deus e o Diabo na Terra do Sol* (1964), by Glauber Rocha. The article analyzes the concepts of trance, belief and people in Glauber's work, as well as his project of construction of a new Brazilian mythology able to appropriate languages and mythologies already existent (the American Western, folklore from Brazil's Northeast, Brechtian theater, opera) in the building of an experimental and political cinema.

Redemption Through the Excess of Sin
José Carlos Avellar

There is a common principle of composition in Joaquim Pedro's major films, *Macunaíma, Os Inconfidentes* and *Guerra Conjugal,* a principle that started in the first feature film he made, *O Padre e a Moça:* the use of excess to recover the human. This principle is continued especially in a delicious and very provocative short film, *Vereda Tropical,* a story of the absolute impossibility of human contact translated into a passionate sexual relationship between a man and a melon.

Brazil 2001 and Walter Salles: Cinema for the Global Village?
Jorge Ruffinelli

This essay examines three different international/transnational paths taken by the Brazilian filmmaker Walter Salles during his well-known career, including both his internationally acclaimed film *Central Station* and his latest film, *O Primeiro Dia.* Throughout Salles' career there is underlined a subtle thread which links each one of his films, and that is the sense of a humanist "redemption" in both a classic and new fashion. This essay tries to illuminate every stance (or path), evaluating Salles' failures and accomplishments.

Praying in the Sand: Paula Rego and Visual Representations of the First Mass in Brazil
Memory Holloway

Pero Vaz de Caminha's letter describing the First Mass in Brazil has been identified as the founding narrative of the discovery of Brazil, and its representation in paintings and engravings constitutes a parallel history that illustrates, celebrates and critiques Portuguese expansion and conquest. Among those representations is Paula Rego's *First Mass in Brazil* (1993), which refers to an engraving based on a painting of the First Mass by Victor Meirelles (1861). The essay argues that Paula Rego uncovers the operations of colonizing the Other and the overarching practice of control that extends both to the indigenous people of Brazil, as well as to the female body.

The Media: The Past and the Years to Come
Eduardo Neiva

The constitution and development of the media in Brazil have followed archaic mechanisms that come from the country's colonial past. The ownership of the media is concentrated in the hands of the very few favored by those in power. The result is a passive and uncritical media with serious consequences for the future of the country.

Contributors/Colaboradores

Sérgio Alcides holds a master's degree in Social History of Culture at Pontifícia Universidade Católica/RJ with a thesis on the Luso-American poet Cláudio Manuel da Costa. He is a doctoral candidate in Social History at the Universidade de São Paulo, researching the relations between the modern State, melancholy and poetry during the sixteenth century in Portugal. Also a poet, he published *Nada a Ver com a Lua* (1996) and *O Ar das Cidades* (2001). He is co-translator of Joan Brossa's *Poemas Civis* (1998).
E-mail: sergioalc@hotmail.com

Tereza Virginia de Almeida is a Professor of Brazilian Literature at the Universidade Federal de Santa Catarina and the author of *A Ausência Lilás da Semana de Arte Moderna: O Olhar Pós-Moderno* (1998). She is currently working on a collection of essays entitled *Por uma Crítica da Razão Canibal: Tecnologia e Barbárie*, the result of recently developed research within the Department of Comparative Literature at Stanford University.
E-mail: virginiaalmeida@hotmail.com

Raúl Antelo is the Chair of Brazilian Literature at the Universidade Federal de Santa Catarina, Brazil. He has been a visiting professor at American and European universities. He is the author of several books and the editor of *Obra Completa* by Oliverio Girondo (UNESCO, 1999). Currently he is working on Latin American acefalism, i.e., on the tradition of Bataille's thinking in the contemporary cultural debate, and points to a rereading of the Situanionist International.
E-mail: antelo@correio.iaccess.com.br

Ricardo Benzaquen de Araujo is Professor of History at the Pontifícia Universidade Católica/RJ. His research and teaching focus on the area of social thought in Brazil, and his chief publications are related to this topic: *Totalitarismo e Revolução: o Integralismo de Plínio Salgado* (1988) and *Guerra e Paz:* Casa-Grande & Senzala *e a Obra de Gilberto Freyre nos Anos 30* (1994). He is now initiating a research project on Freyre's thought between the end of World War II and his death in 1987.
E-mail: smiceli@ax.apc.org

Valdei Lopes Araujo was a substitute professor of Historiography at the Universidade do Estado do Rio de Janeiro. He is currently working on a doctoral thesis for the Department of History at the Pontifícia Universidade Católica/RJ on the relationship between history and literature in the nineteenth century. He has published in several specialized journals.
E-mail: valdei32@ig.com.br

José Carlos Avellar is a film critic. He is the author of six books on Brazilian and Latin American cinema, among them: *A Ponte Clandestina* (1995), essays on Latin American film theory, and *A Linha Reta, O Melaço de Cana e o Retrato do Artista quando Jovem* (1997), an essay on Glauber Rocha's *Deus e o Diabo na Terra do Sol.* He is now the Director of Riofilme.
E-mail: avellar@ism.com.br

Ivo Barbieri is the Chair of Brazilian Literature at the Universidade do Estado do Rio de Janeiro. His research interests include themes of modernity. His books *Oficina da Palavra* (1981) and *Geometria da Composição* (1997) are studies of contemporary poetry. He is researching the presence of nineteenth century psychiatry and psychology in the works of Machado de Assis, and their impact on the great Brazilian novelist. His most recent essays address this topic.
E-mail: eduerj@uerj.br

Therezinha Barbieri is a Professor of Brazilian Literature at the Universidade do Estado do Rio de Janeiro. She received her Ph.D. from the Pontifícia Universidade Católica/RJ. She did post-graduate work at the Universities of Pennsylvania, Maryland, Florida and Clarion State College. Her latest publications include "Colonização a Ferro e Fogo," "Percurso

Desbussolado" (preface to João Gilberto Noll's *Hotel Atlântico*), and "De Olho no Leitor."
E-mail: eduerj@uerj.br

Ivana Bentes is a researcher of cinema and Professor of Graduate Studies in the School of Communication at Universidade Federal do Rio de Janeiro. She holds a Ph.D. in Communication and is the author of *Joaquim Pedro de Andrade: A Revolução Intimista* (1996) and *Cartas ao Mundo* (1997). She is the co-editor of *Cinemais*, a journal devoted to cinema and audiovisual questions. Currently, she researches representations of the popular in Brazilian contemporary cinema.
E-mail: ivana@ax.apc.org

Gustavo Bernardo is a Professor of Literary Theory at the Universidade do Estado do Rio de Janeiro. He has published the essays *Quem Pode Julgar a Primeira Pedra?* (1993), and *Educação pelo Argumento* (2000). He has also written the novels *Pedro Pedra* (1982), *Me Nina* (1989), *A Alma do Urso* (1999) and *Lúcia* (1999). His current research is on Vilém Flusser's work, especially on the relationship between literature and prayer.
E-mail: gustavobernardo@msm.com.br

César Braga-Pinto is an Assistant Professor of Portuguese, Latin American Studies and African Studies at Rutgers, the State University of New Jersey, New Brunswick. He has published articles on colonial Brazil as well as on Brazilian popular music and culture. He is currently revising a manuscript entitled *Promises of History: Assimilation and Prophetic Discourses in Colonial Brazil.*
E-mail: cbpinto@rci.rutgers.edu

Paulo Henriques Britto is a translator and Professor of Translation at Pontifícia Universidade Católica/RJ. He has published three books of poetry: *Liturgia da Matéria* (1982), *Mínima Lírica* (1989) and *Trovar Claro* (1997). Among his most recent translations are Thomas Pynchon's *Gravity's Rainbow* (1998), Don de Lillo's *Underworld* (1999), Ted Hughes' *Birthday Letters* (1999) and an anthology of Elizabeth Bishop's "Brazilian" poems, *Poemas do Brasil* (1999).
E-mail: phbritto@alfalink.com.br

Lia Calabre is a doctoral candidate in the Department of Social History of Ideas at the Universidade Federal Fluminense, where she has focused her research on the history of Brazilian radio. She has published in specialized journals and has contributed to the production of a CD-ROM on the history of Rio de Janeiro. E-mail: lcalabre@uol.com.br

Olavo de Carvalho is a Brazilian writer and philosopher, presently in charge of the Seminar of Philosophy at the UniverCidade, Rio de Janeiro. Among his several books are *O Jardim das Aflições: Ensaio sobre o Materialismo e a Religião Civil* (1995) and *Aristóteles em Nova Perspectiva* (1997). He also writes on cultural topics for several newspapers and magazines in Brazil. E-mail: lumen@openlink.com.br

Tarcisio Costa is a career diplomat and a political theorist. He received his Ph.D. degree in Political Theory from Cambridge University. After a two-year term as Visiting Scholar at Stanford University he joined the post-doctorate program of the Institute of Advanced Studies of the Universidade de São Paulo, where he is currently doing research on the history of political ideas in Brazil previous to the early twentieth century. He is a senior associate researcher of the Foreign Affairs Department at the Universidade de Brasília. E-mail: tcosta@planalto.gov.br

Eduardo Coutinho is a Professor of Comparative Literature at the Universidade Federal do Rio de Janeiro. His main field of interest is Latin American Literature and Culture. He has published several essays in specialized journals and periodicals. Some of his books are: *Guimarães Rosa: A Unidade Diversa; The 'Synthesis' Novel in Latin America; Em Busca da Terceira Margem* and *Literatura Comparada: Textos Fundadores* (with Tania Carvalhal). E-mail: coutinho@diamante.imagelink.com.br

Roberto DaMatta is the Reverend Edmund P. Joyce c. sc. Professor of Anthropology at the University of Notre Dame, Indiana. He has been a visiting Professor at the University of Wisconsin, the University of California, Cambridge University and he has also been "Directeur d'Études" at the Maison des Sciences de l'Homme. He is the author of, among other books, *Carnavais, Malandros e Heróis* (1979) (translated into French and English); *A Casa & A Rua* (1985); and *Conta de Mentiroso* (1993). E-mail: roberto.a.damatta.1@nd.edu

Regina Lúcia de Faria is an Associate Professor of Literature and Portuguese Language at the UniverCidade in Rio de Janeiro, and a Lecturer in Portuguese/Brazilian and Latin American Studies at the Romansk Institut, Aarhus University, Denmark (1999-2001). She holds a doctorate degree in Portuguese-language Literatures from Pontifícia Universidade Católica/RJ. She has published in specialized journals.
E-mail: romfaria@mail.hum.au.dk

Marcus Vinicius de Freitas is an Assistant Professor of Portuguese Literature at the Universidade Federal de Minas Gerais, Belo Horizonte. He has a master's degree in Brazilian Literature from the same institution, with a thesis on Portuguese travel accounts during the sixteenth century in Brazil. He holds a Ph.D. in Portuguese and Brazilian Studies from Brown University, with a dissertation on the life and work of Charles Frederick Hartt. The author has published several articles in specialized journals.
E-mail: marcus_freitas@brown.edu

Ross G. Forman is a Research Fellow at Kingston University in the United Kingdom. A specialist in nineteenth-century British "informal" imperialism in Latin America and China, he received his Ph.D. from the Department of Comparative Literature at Stanford University in 1998. Recent work includes "When Britons Brave Brazil: British Imperialism and the Adventure Tale in Latin America, 1850-1918" (*Victorian Studies*, Spring 2000).
E-mail: Rossforman@aol.com

Walnice Nogueira Galvão is a Professor of Literary Theory and Comparative Literature at the Universidade de São Paulo. She is a specialist on the works of Guimarães Rosa and Euclides da Cunha, as well as on literary criticism and cultural critique. Among her several books are *Correspondência de Euclides da Cunha* (1997); *Desconversa* (1998); *A Donzela-Guerreira* (1998); *Le Carnaval de Rio* (2000); and *Guimarães Rosa* (2000). She is also researching carnival and popular music.
E-mail: wngalvao@uol.com.br

Ângela de Castro Gomes is a Professor in the Department of History at the Universidade Federal Fluminense, and works at the Center of Research and Documentation of Contemporary History, at Fundação Getúlio Vargas.

CONTRIBUTORS/COLABORADORES

Author of *A Invenção do Trabalhismo* (1994); *História e Historiadores* (1996); and *Essa Gente do Rio… Modernismo e Nacionalismo* (1999).
E-mail: acastro@fgv.br

Heloisa Toller Gomes holds a Ph.D. in Comparative Literature from the Pontifícia Universidade Católica/RJ and did post-doctorate studies at Yale University. Among her publications are *O Negro e o Romantismo Brasileiro* (1988) and *As Marcas da Escravidão* (1994). She has also translated and prepared a critical edition in Brazil of Du Bois's *The Souls of Black Folk* (1999). She currently teaches and conducts research on Afro-Brazilian and Afro-American culture at PROAFRO/UERJ.
E-mail: htoller@inx.com.br

Hans Ulrich Gumbrecht is the Albert Gérard Professor of Literature at Stanford University and Professeur Associé in the Départment de Littérature Comparée at the Université de Montréal. He has worked on the histories of French and Spanish culture and, recently, on Brazilian literature. He is a Fellow of the American Academy of Arts and Literature, and a regular contributor to *Frankfurter Allgemeine Zeitung, Neue Zürcher Zeitung, Die Zeit,* and *Der Merkur*. His next book will be *The Non-Hermeneutic and the Present* (2001). At present, he is also working on a book on "The Beauty of American Football."
E-mail: sepp@stanford.edu

João Adolfo Hansen is a Professor of Brazilian Literature at the Universidade de São Paulo. He researches Luso-Brazilian practices of representation in the seventeenth and eighteenth centuries. Among his books are *A Sátira e o Engenho: Gregório de Matos e a Bahia do Século XVII* (1989); *Carlos Bracher* (1997) and *o O. A Ficção da Literatura em* Grande Sertão: Veredas (2000). He has published several articles in specialized journals.
E-mail: jhansen@uol.com.br

Heloísa Buarque de Hollanda is the Chair of Critical Theory at the Universidade Federal do Rio de Janeiro. She is the Head of the Programa Avançado de Cultura Contemporânea (PACC). She is the editor-in-chief of the Aeroplano Publishing House. She has published widely in specialized journals. Among her several books are *Impressões de Viagem* (1979); *Cultura e Participação nos Anos 60* (1982); *Pós-Modernismo e Política* (1991); *O*

CONTRIBUTORS/COLABORADORES

Feminismo Como Crítica da Cultura (1994); *Esses Poetas* (1998) and *Cultura em Trânsito* (2000).
E-mail: hollanda@centroin.com.br

Memory Holloway is a Professor of twentieth-century Art History at the University of Massachusetts Dartmouth. Her catalogue, *Paula Rego: Open Secrets*, was prepared for an exhibition of the artist's work that appeared in Fall 1999 at both the University of Massachusetts and in Paris at the Calouste Gulbenkian Foundation. She is currently at work on a book of essays on twentieth-century Portuguese art.
E-mail: mholloway@umassd.edu

K. David Jackson is a Professor of Portuguese and Brazilian literatures and cultures at Yale University and Acting Chair of the Council on Latin American & Iberian Studies of the Yale Center for International and Area Studies. Author of *A Vanguarda Literária no Brasil*, his research interests include, among others, Portuguese *cafrinha* and *baila* music of Sri Lanka.
E-mail: k.david@yale.edu

Marcelo Jasmin is a Professor and Director of the Department of History at Pontifícia Universidade Católica/RJ and a Professor in the Political Science graduate program at Instituto Universitário de Pesquisa do Rio de Janeiro (IUPERJ). He is the author of *Alexis de Tocqueville: A Historiografia como Ciência da Política* (1997) and *Princípios Racionais e História na Teoria Política* (1998).
E-mail: jasmin@ax.apc.org

José Luís Jobim is a Professor of Brazilian and Comparative Literature at the Universidade do Estado do Rio de Janeiro and Universidade Federal Fluminense. He is the author of several books, including *Palavras da Crítica* (1992); *A Poética do Fundamento* (1996); *Introdução ao Romantismo* (1999); *Literatura e Identidades* (1999) and *A Biblioteca de Machado de Assis* (2001).
E-mail: joseluisjobim@aol.com

Sabrina Karpa-Wilson is an Assistant Professor and Director of Portuguese Studies at Indiana University, Bloomington. She is currently working on a history of Brazilian autobiography in the twentieth century and the diverse

political meanings conveyed through the textual mapping of personal memory.
E-mail: skarpawi@indiana.edu

Maria Rita Kehl is a psychoanalyst and essayist. She holds a Ph.D. in Psychoanalysis from the Pontifícia Universidade Católica/SP. She is presently doing post-doctoral research on "The Literary Determining of the Modern Subject." She is the author of *A Mínima Diferença* (1996) and *Deslocamentos do Feminino* (1998), and is the editor of *A Função Fraterna* (2000). Also a poet, she has published *Processos Primários* (1996).
E-mail: ritak@zip.net

Enrique Rodríguez Larreta is a Social Anthropologist. He is the Executive Director of the Institute of Cultural Pluralism at the Universidade Candido Mendes. Recently he edited *Représentation et Complexité* (1997); *Ethics of the Future* (1998); *Media and Social Perception* (1999) and *Time in the Making and Possible Futures* (2000).
E-mail: larreta@candidomendes.br

Luiz Costa Lima is the Chair of Comparative Literature at the Universidade do Estado do Rio de Janeiro and at Pontifícia Universidade Católica/RJ. He has three books translated into English, among them *The Limits of the Voice* (1997). In 1992 he received the "Humboldt Award" for his work on the "control of the imaginary."
E-mail: costalim@visualnet.com.br

Shoshanna Lurie is a doctoral candidate in the Department of Spanish and Portuguese at Stanford University, where she has concentrated on Mexican and Brazilian Literature and Cultural Studies, and has taught both Spanish and Portuguese. She is currently a Geballe Dissertation Fellow at the Stanford Humanities Center and is completing her dissertation, "Funk and Hip-Hop Transculture: Urban Aesthetics in the 'Divided City.'"
E-mail: slurie@usc.edu

Marcos Chor Maio is a Senior Researcher at the Casa de Oswaldo Cruz, Oswaldo Cruz Foundation, in Rio de Janeiro, and holds a Ph.D. in Political Science from the Instituto Universitário de Pesquisas do Rio de Janeiro (IUPERJ). He is the author of *Nem Rotschild, Nem Trotsky: O Pensamento*

Anti-Semita de Gustavo Barroso (1992). He is the co-editor with R. V. Santos of *Raça, Ciência e Sociedade* (1996). Currently, he is studying the construction of networks of international scientists after the Second World War based on research sponsored by UNESCO.
E-mail: maio@ax.apc.org

Italo Moriconi is the author of *A Provocação Pós-Moderna* (1994); *Ana Cristina Cesar: O Sangue de uma Poeta* (1996) and the editor of *Os Cem Melhores Contos Brasileiros do Século* (2000). He is the editor of the forthcoming *Os Cem Melhores Poemas do Século* (2001). He is developing post-doctoral research for a book on the Brazilian intellectual and literary scene over the last two decades. As a poet he has published the following books: *Léu* (1988), *A Cidade e as Ruas* (1992), and *Quase Sertão* (1996).
E-mail: italomori@ax.apc.org

Carlos Guilherme Mota is the Chair of Contemporary History at the Universidade de São Paulo and a Professor in the Graduate Program in Education at Universidade Mackenzie. He was Director of the "Instituto de Estudos Avançados" of the Universidade de São Paulo. He was the creator of the Chair Jaime Cortesão. Among his several books are *A Ideologia da Cultura Brasileira* (1977); *Nordeste 1817* (1972). He has also edited several books, among them *Brasil em Perspectiva* (1968); *A Viagem Incompleta 1500-2000* (2000).
E-mail: cgmota@mailmac.macbbs.com.br

Marcus Alexandre Motta is a Professor and holds a Ph.D. in History at the Universidade Federal do Rio de Janeiro. He is also a researcher with the project "A Questão do Moderno na Historiografia da Cultura Brasileira" at the Pontifícia Universidade Católica/RJ. He has published several articles in specialized journals. He is the author of *Anchieta: Dívida de Papel* (2000).
E-mail: mam123@net.sapo.pt

Eduardo Neiva is a Full Professor in the Department of Communication Studies at the University of Alabama at Birmingham. His two latest books are *Mythologies of Vision: Image, Culture, and Visuality* (1999) and *O Racionalismo Crítico de Popper* (1999). He is presently writing a series of articles on the biological aspects of communication.
E-mail: neiva@uab.edu

Margarida de Souza Neves is a Professor in the Department of History of the Pontifícia Universidade Católica/RJ. Her recent publications deal with topics related to the question of social memory. Currently, with the support of CNPq/PRONEX (PUC/Rio), she is developing the project "The Modern Discoverers of Brazil," in which she researches authors such as Mário de Andrade, Cecília Meirelles and Luis da Câmara Cascudo. She has published in several specialized journals.
E-mail: guida@openlink.com.br

Fernanda Peixoto is a Professor of Anthropology at the Universidade do Estado de São Paulo/Araraquara. Her areas of research revolve around Brazilian social thought and the history of social science in Brazil, on which she has published various articles. She is a co-author, with Heloisa Pontes, of the *Guia Biobibliográfico dos Brasilianistas: 1930-1988* (1989); and she is the author of *Dialogos Brasileiros: Uma Análise da Obra de Roger Bastide* (2001).
E-mail: fpeixoto@uol.com.br

Victor Hugo Adler Pereira is a Professor of Theory of Literature at the Universidade do Estado do Rio de Janeiro. He researches modern and contemporary Brazilian theatre. Among his latest publications are the books *Nelson Rodrigues e a Obs-cena* Contemporânea (1999); *A Musa Carrancuda: Teatro e Poder no Estado Novo* (1998), and the article "Endemias e Vanguardas: Teatro Brasileiro no Fim do Milênio" (Luso-Brazilian Review, Winter 1998).
E-mail: vhap@uol.com.br

Mary Del Priore is a Professor of History at the Universidade de São Paulo (USP) and a Lecturer in History at the Pontifícia Universidade Católica/RJ. Her 15 books include *Ao Sul do Corpo: Condição Feminina e Mentalidades na Colônia; A História das Mulheres no Brasil; Festas e Utopias no Brasil Colonial; Esquecidos por Deus: Monstros no Ocidente Cristão*. She has won several literary prizes. Her current interests include the history of cities during the colonial period.
E-mail: mdpriore@highway.com.br

Beatriz Resende is a Professor of Comparative Literature and Literary Theory at the Universidade Federal do Rio de Janeiro (UFRJ). She holds a Ph.D. in Comparative Literature and is a researcher at the Centro Nacional

de Pesquisa (CNPq), coordinating the Integrated Project "Exclusions in the Literary History of Brazilian Modernism." Among her several books are *Cronistas do Rio* (1995) and *Lima Barreto e o Rio de Janeiro em Fragmentos* (1993). She is the editor of the electronic journal *Z* (www.cfch.ufrj/pacc/z).
E-mail: bresende@centroin.com.br

João Cezar de Castro Rocha is a Professor of Comparative Literature at the Universidade do Estado do Rio de Janeiro. He is the author of *Literatura e Cordialidade: O Público e o Privado na Cultura Brasileira.* The book received the Biblioteca Nacional's "Mário de Andrade" award for best literary essay published in Brazil in 1998. He has edited several books and special issues of academic journals. He is a researcher with CNPq/PRONEX at the Department of History of Pontifícia Universidade Católica/RJ.
E-mail: jccr@uerj.br

Kathrin H. Rosenfield is a Professor in the Department of Philosophy and in the Graduate Program of Comparative Literature of the Universidade Federal do Rio Grande do Sul. She has published books on French medieval literature, on Brazilian literature (in particular on João Guimarães Rosa: *Os Descaminhos do Demo* and *Grande Sertão: Veredas. Roteiro de Leitura*), on German Romanticism, on T. S. Eliot, and on Greek tragedy (*Hölderlin's Sophocles*). A new book on João Guimarães Rosa's work is forthcoming.
E-mail: delros@zaz.com.br

Maria Helena Rouanet holds a Ph.D. in Portuguese-language and Literatures and teaches Brazilian and French literatures. She published *Eternamente em Berço Esplêndido: A Fundação da Literatura Nacional* (1991), in which she analyzes the institutionalization of a body of cultural production in Brazil through Ferdinand Denis' participation in the process. She has published in several specialized journals.
E-mail: jsenna@montreal.com.br

Jorge Ruffinelli has been a Professor at the Universidad de Buenos Aires and Universidad Veracruzana. Since 1986 he has been a Professor in Latin American Literature and Film at Stanford University. Among his many books are *Crítica en Marcha*, *El Lugar de Rulfo* and *Poesía y Descolonización*. He is preparing an *Encyclopedia of Latin American Film*. His book on Chilean film

documentarist Patricio Guzman is forthcoming. He is editor-in-chief of *Nuevo Texto Crítico*.
E-mail: jorge321@aol.com

Maria Aparecida Ferreira de Andrade Salgueiro is a Professor of North American Literature and Culture at the Universidade do Estado do Rio de Janeiro. She holds a Ph. D. in Comparative Literature at the Universidade Federal Fluminense. Her dissertation, entitled "Gender, Ethnicity and Literary Prose", analyzes contemporary issues in Afro-Brazilian and African-American literatures. She is also a researcher and member of the Technical Advisory Board of PROAFRO/Universidade do Estado do Rio de Janeiro.
E-mail: cidasal@uerj.br

Silviano Santiago is a Professor of Brazilian Literature and Literary Theory at the Universidade Federal Fluminense. He has published widely in specialized journals. A literary critic as well as a novelist, he is the author of several books. Among them, are *Stella Manhattan* (1985); *Keith Jarret no Blue Note* (1996); and *Uma Literatura nos Trópicos* (1978). He has organized, introduced and coordinated the anthology in three volumes *Intérpretes do Brasil* (2000).
E-mail: silviano@ax.apc.org

Karl Erik Schøllhammer holds a Ph.D. (1991) in Semiotics from the University of Aarhus, Denmark. Currently he is an Associate Professor in Brazilian Literature and Literary Theory in the Literature Department at Pontifícia Universidade Católica/RJ. His recent research is on contemporary literature and arts in Latin America. He has published several essays on this subject and is preparing a book entitled *Constellations Between Arts and Literature in Latin America*.
E-mail: karlerik@let.puc-rio.br

Lilia K. Moritz Schwarcz is a Professor in the Department of Anthropology in the Universidade de São Paulo. Among her several books are *Portrait in Black and White: Slaves, Newspapers and Citizens in São Paulo* (1987); *Spectacle of Races: Scientists, Institutions and Racial Theories in Brazil at the End of the NIneteenth Century* (1993); published in the US by Farrar, Straus and Giroux in 1999); and *The Emperor's Beard: D. Pedro II, a Tropical King* (1998);

forthcoming in the US from Farrar, Straus and Giroux). She has also edited several books.
E-mail: lilia@mtecnetsp.com.br

Jorge Schwartz is the Chair of Latin American Literature at the Universidade de São Paulo. Among his books are *Murilo Rubião: A Poética do Uroboro* (1981), *Vanguarda e Cosmopolitismo na Década de Vinte* (1993); Associação Paulista de Críticos de Arte Award), and *Vanguardias Latinoamericanas* (1995). He is the editor of *Oswald de Andrade: Obra Incompleta* (forthcoming) and of Jorge Luis Borges' *Obras Completas* (1999), which won the Prêmio Jabuti (National Translation Award). He is the editor-in-chief of *Cuadernos de Recienvenidos* and has received several visiting professorships, including Tinker Professor at the University of Texas, Austin.
E-mail: jschwart@usp.br

Antonio Carlos Secchin is the Chair of Brazilian Literature at the Universidade Federal do Rio de Janeiro. He holds a Ph.D. in Literature. As an essayist and a poet he has published seven books, among them *João Cabral: A Poesia do Menos* (2nd ed., 1999), which received an award in the "Concurso Nacional de Ensaios Literários do Ministério da Educação e Cultura." *Escritos Sobre Poesia & Alguma Ficção* is forthcoming and mainly deals with Brazilian contemporary poetry.
E-mail: asecchin@ism.com.br

Valter Sinder is a Professor of Anthropology at the Universidade do Estado do Rio de Janeiro and at Pontifícia Universidade Católica/RJ. Currently his research focuses on the theory of culture and on social thought in Brazil. He has published several essays in specialized journals.
E-mail: vsinder@hotmail.com.br

Vera Beatriz Siqueira is an art historian and a Professor at the Universidade do Estado do Rio de Janeiro. She is a researcher with PRONEX at the Department of History of Pontifícia Universidade Católica/RJ. She has worked as the curator for several exhibitions and has published in several specialized journals.
E-mail: siqueira@rio.com.br

Marcus Vinicius Nogueira Soares holds a Ph.D. in Comparative Literature from the Universidade do Estado do Rio de Janeiro, where he currently teaches Brazilian literature. His research focuses on the relationship between the production of Brazilian novels and the process of their dissemination in newspapers during the nineteenth century. Thanks to a grant from CAPES, he served as a visiting student at Stanford University in 1998.
E-mail: soaresmarcus@hotmail.com

Roberto Acízelo de Sousa is a Professor of Literary Theory at the Universidade Federal Fluminense and the Chair of Brazilian Literature at the Universidade do Estado do Rio de Janeiro. He holds a Ph.D. in Literary Theory from the Universidade Federal do Rio de Janeiro, and currently is researching on the founding fathers of literary historiography in Brazil. His published works include *Teoria da Literatura* (1986); *Formação da Teoria da Literatura* (1987) and *O Império da Eloqüência* (1999).
E-mail: leticia@cyberwal.com.br

Eneida Maria de Souza is the Chair of Literary Theory at the Universidade Federal de Minas Gerais. She holds a doctorate in Comparative Literature from the Université de Paris VII and was the President of the Brazilian Association for Comparative Literature (1988-1990). Among her books are *A Pedra Mágica do Discurso* (1988, 1999); *Traço Crítico* (1993); *Autran Dourado* (1996); *Modernidades Tardias* (1998) and *O Século de Borges* (1999). She is the co-author of *Mário de Andrade–Carta aos Mineiros* (1997) with Paulo Schmidt.
E-mail: eneidas@race.prime.com.br

Roberto Ventura is a Professor of Literary Theory and Comparative Literature at the Universidade de São Paulo. He is the co-author with Flora Süssekind of *História e Dependência: Cultura e Sociedade em Manoel Bomfim* (1984), and the author of *Escritores, Escravos e Mestiços em um País Tropical* (1987); *Estilo Tropical: História Cultural e Polêmicas Literárias no Brasil* (1991); and *Casa-Grand & Senzala* (2000). He is currently writing a biography of Euclides da Cunha.
E-mail: robvent@terra.com.br

Bluma Waddington Vilar is a doctoral candidate in the Department of Comparative Literature at the Universidade do Estado do Rio de Janeiro. She

researches on intertextuality, especially in the work of Machado de Assis, Jorge Luis Borges and Murilo Mendes. She has taught Brazilian literature at Universidade do Estado do Rio de Janeiro and also works as a translator. She has published in specialized journals. As a poet she published *Album* (1996). She is the author of *Diário de um Menino Cismado*, which received the "João de Barro Award" for children's book (2000).
E-mail: bwv@terra.com.br

Robert Wegner holds a Ph.D. in Sociology from the Instituto Universitário de Pesquisas do Rio de Janeiro (IUPERJ). He is a guest researcher at Casa de Oswaldo Cruz, and is an associate researcher in the History Department of the Pontifícia Universidade Católica/RJ. He is the author of *A Conquista do Oeste: A Fronteira na Obra de Sérgio Buarque de Holanda* (2000).
E-mail: rwegner@pobox.com

Cléia Schiavo Weyrauch holds a Ph.D. in Communication from the Universidade Federal do Rio de Janeiro and is currently a Professor of Sociology at the Universidade do Estado do Rio de Janeiro. Among her several books are *Memória, Cidade e Cultura* (1998) and *Pioneiros Alemães de Nova Filadélfia* (1998). She was the President of the "Comissão UERJ: Brasil 500 Anos."
E-mail: cultural@uerj.br

Regina Zilberman is a Professor of Theory of Literature and Brazilian Literature at the Catholic University of Rio Grande do Sul. She holds a Ph.D. in Romanistics from the University of Heidelberg, Germany. She has been a visiting scholar at the University of London and at Brown University. Among her several books are *Estética da Recepção e História da Literatura; A Terra em que Nasceste: Imagens do Brasil na Literatura; A Formação da Leitura no Brasil,* and *O Berço do Cânone.*
E-mail: reginaz@portoweb.com.br

Translators / Tradutores

Paulo Henriques Britto is a translator and a Professor of Translation at Pontifícia Universidade Católica/RJ. Among his most recent translations are Thomas Pynchon's *Gravity's Rainbow* (1998), Ted Hughes's *Birthday Letters* (1999) and an anthology of Elizabeth Bishop's "Brazilian" poems, *Poemas do Brasil* (1999).
E-mail: phbritto@alfalink.com.br

Ross G. Forman is a Research Fellow at Kingston University in the United Kingdom. A specialist in nineteenth-century British "informal" imperialism in Latin America and China, he received his Ph.D. from the Department of Comparative Literature at Stanford University in 1998.
E-mail: Rossforman@aol.com

Shoshanna Lurie is a doctoral candidate in the Department of Spanish and Portuguese at Stanford University, where she has concentrated on Mexican and Brazilian Literature and Cultural Studies and has taught both Spanish and Portuguese.
E-mail: slurie@usc.edu

David Shepherd is the Coordinator of the M. A. Program in Applied Linguistics at the Universidade Federal Fluminense. His Ph.D. (University of Durham, UK) included work on the contrastive analysis of English and Portuguese genres.
E-mail: dshepherd@uol.com.br

Tania M. G. Shepherd is Associate Professor in English at the Universidade do Estado do Rio de Janeiro. Her Ph.D. (University of Birmingham, UK) was on aspects of repetition and intertextuality in narrative discourse. Her present research interests include patterns of lexis in translated texts.
E-mail: shepherd@uninet.com.br

Nöel de Sousa is a freelance translator and conference interpreter (AIIC, Geneva). E-mail: noeldesouza@pobox.com

Dana Stevens is a doctoral candidate in Comparative Literature at the University of California, Berkeley and is currently teaching at Columbia University in New York. She has translated Brazilian and Portuguese poetry, including that of Fernando Pessoa, Orides Fontela and Herberto Helder.
E-mail: ds956@columbia.edu

Mark Streeter is a doctoral candidate in Comparative Literature at the University of Wisconsin-Madison. He is the Assistant to the Editors for the *Luso-Brazilian Review* and also has served as Assistant to the Editors for *Portuguese Literary & Cultural Studies 4-5: Brazil 2001: A Revisionary History of Brazilian Literature and Culture.*
E-mail: mstreete@students.wisc.edu

Bonnie Wasserman teaches Portuguese and coordinates foreign language examinations at New York University. Her current research interests include historical drama and Lusophone-African literature.
E-mail: bonwass@yahoo.com

Issues of *Portuguese Literary & Cultural Studies*

Portuguese Literary & Cultural Studies 1. Fall 1998.
Fronteiras/Borders.

Portuguese Literary & Cultural Studies 2. Spring 1999.
Lídia Jorge in other words / por outras palavras.
Guest Editor: Cláudia Pazos Alonso, Oxford University

Portuguese Literary & Cultural Studies 3. Fall 1999.
Pessoa's Alberto Caeiro.

Portuguese Literary & Cultural Studies 4/5. Spring/Fall 2000.
Brazil 2001. A Revisionary History of Brazilian Literature and Culture.
Guest Editor: João Cezar de Castro Rocha, Universidade do Estado do Rio
de Janeiro

Forthcoming
Portuguese Literary & Cultural Studies 6. Spring 2001.
On José Saramago, including an essay by Harold Bloom.
Guest Editor: Anna Klobucka, University of Georgia

Portuguese Literary & Cultural Studies 7. Fall 2001.
Portuguese Poetry Since 1961.

Portuguese Literary & Cultural Studies 8. Spring 2002.
On Cape Verdean Literature and Culture.
Guest Editor: Ana Mafalda Leite, Universidade de Lisboa

Volumes of *Portuguese Literary & Cultural Studies Book Series*

Forthcoming
Eduardo Lourenço. *Selected Essays.*
Edited by Carlos Veloso, New York University

Garrett's Travels & Its Descendants.
Edited by Victor J. Mendes

The Last Eça Revisited.
Edited by Frank F. Sousa

Eça de Queirós, *The Relic.* Trans. Aubrey Bell.
Preface by Harold Bloom

Portuguese Language Textbooks
Francisco Cota Fagundes. *Mais Um Passo No Português Moderno: Gramática Avançada, Leituras, Composição e Vocabulário.*

The Portuguese in the Americas
Who are the Portuguese? The New Evidence—Five Studies on the Portuguese-American Community of Southeastern Massachusetts
Coordination by Clyde Barrow, Center for Policy Analysis, University of Massachusetts Dartmouth

University of Massachusetts Dartmouth
Center for Portuguese Studies and Culture

Founded in 1996, the University of Massachusetts Dartmouth Center for Portuguese Studies and Culture is designed as a forum for the interdisciplinary study of the language, literatures, and cultures of the Portuguese-speaking world. The Center aims to serve as a liaison between the University of Massachusetts Dartmouth and other institutions involved in Portuguese Studies in the United States and abroad.

The Center proposes to develop pedagogical materials to aid in the teaching and learning of the Portuguese language at all levels of instruction through its *Portuguese Language Textbook Series*. The Center will publish an advanced grammar textbook in 2001 written by Prof. Francisco C. Fagundes, entitled *Um Passo Mais no Português Moderno: Leituras, Gramática Avançada e Composição*. In addition, a first-year textbook (*Encontros*), for the teaching of both Brazilian and European Portuguese at the college level is currently in preparation.

The Center fosters the development and dissemination of knowledge about the Portuguese-speaking communities of the United States through the *Portuguese in the Americas Series*. The first volume, *Who Are the Portuguese? The New Evidence – Five Studies on the Portuguese-American Community of Southeastern Massachusetts*, will be published this year. This initial publication is undertaken collaboratively with the University of Massachusetts Dartmouth Center for Policy Analysis.

The agreement between the University of Masschusetts Dartmouth and RádioTelevisãoPortuguesa (RTP) in 1999 established RTPi's North American television studio on the UMD campus. Locally produced programming will be transmitted internationally to more than 20 million homes, including 1.1 million in the United States. In turn, the University has received a complete RTP Video Collection that will soon be available at the University Library.

Accentuating its commitment to the intellectual preparation of students at all levels of higher education, the University of Massachusetts Dartmouth recently created the Department of Portuguese, which will begin full operation in Fall 2001. The new Department is in the proces of creating an Endowed Chair in Portuguese Studies and a graduate program in Portuguese. In this context, the semiannual publication of the scholarly journal, *Portuguese Literary & Cultural Studies*, underscores both the Center's and the Department's research goals in the field of Portuguese Studies. Further, the Summer Program in Portuguese, founded in 1994, will hold its 8th annual program this year (June 25-July 27), offering seven different courses, from beginning language to a seminar on Portuguese Women's Literature in Translation and a production of a classic Gil Vicente play. The Center will once again organize the Summer Program in Portuguese for Children to run concurrently with the regular Summer Program in Portuguese.

The Center also promotes exchanges of students and faculty with universities in the Portuguese-speaking world, as exemplified by the University's agreement with the University of the Azores, signed in 1998. In addition, the Center is developing a Study Abroad Program that will make UMD the conduit for any American student who wishes to study in Portugal.

The Center also promotes international colloquia on topics and authors related to the Portuguese-speaking world. Conferences include "25 Years of Portuguese Democracy" (October 2, 1999), "Garrett's *Travels* and Its Descendants" (October 22-23, 1999), "The *Later Eça* Revisited" (November 3-4, 2000), and the forthcoming "Race, Culture, Nation: Arguments across the Portuguese-Speaking World" (April 6-8, 2001). On April 30, 2001, the Center will cosponsor a colloquium at the Library of Congress entitled "Brazil 2001: A Revisionary History of Brazilian Literature and Culture."

Other activities, such as lecture, concert, and dance series and art exhibitions, emphasize the Center's commitment to the University community and local region. In Fall 1999 the University Art Gallery hosted an exhibition on the drawings and etchings by Paula Rego. Another exhibition is being planned for 2002. The Center also supports a Visiting Distinguished Scholar program, and in Fall 2000 Prof. John Russell-Wood of Johns Hopkins University taught a course on the Portuguese Discoveries. In addition, the Center takes active part in recommending candidates for honorary degrees. Largely through the efforts of the Center for Portuguese Studies and Culture, in October 1999 the University of Massachusetts Dartmouth awarded a Doctorate *Honoris Causa* in Humane Letters to the Nobel Laureate for Literature, José Saramago. And acting on the Center's recommendation, the University will award an honorary doctorate to world-renowned literary scholar Harold Bloom, on September 14, 2001, with participation by José Saramago. In connection with this occasion, the Department of Portuguese and the New York Public Library will cosponsor an evening with José Saramago and Harold Bloom in New York City, on September 17, 2001.

The Center's objectives and endeavors are made possible by the generous support of the following individuals and institutions: Chancellor Jean F. MacCormack and Provost Thomas J. Curry, University of Massachusetts Dartmouth; the Luso-American Foundation, the Foreign Ministry of the Government of Portugal, the Embassy of Portugal in the United States, the Camões Institute, and the Calouste Gulbenkian Foundation. In addition, the Center gratefully acknowledges the financial support of individuals and institutions in Massachusetts and Rhode Island, such as Lawrence Fish, President of Citizens Financial Group; Anthony Andrade, former President of Universal Press; Manuel Fernando Neto, President of Neto Insurance Group; and Frank B. Sousa, President of Colonial Wholesale Beverage Corp. In particular, the Center wishes to thank Representative Robert Correia and the other Portuguese-American members of the State House and Senate of the Commonwealth of Massachusetts, for their tireless efforts in the development and funding of the Center for Portuguese Studies and Culture.